The Sovereignty of Children in Law

The Sovereignty of Children in Law

Edited by

Farhad Malekian and Kerstin Nordlöf

CAMBRIDGE SCHOLARS

PUBLISHING

The Sovereignty of Children in Law,
Edited by Farhad Malekian and Kerstin Nordlöf

This book first published 2012

Cambridge Scholars Publishing

12 Back Chapman Street, Newcastle upon Tyne, NE6 2XX, UK

British Library Cataloguing in Publication Data
A catalogue record for this book is available from the British Library

Cover illustration:
Escaping Criticism by Pere Borrell del Caso (1874)
Permission obtained from the
Collection of the Bank of Spain, Madrid, Spain

ISBN (10): 1-4438-3635-4, ISBN (13): 978-1-4438-3635-7

To our four children, whose names have been selected from nature

Alvan: *the sovereignty of colour in nature*
Paliz: *the kingdom of a garden of flowers*
Cariz: *the spring of water in a natural environment*
Afrang: *the power of the sun, the galaxy and the universe*

TABLE OF CONTENTS

Chapter Five: Legal Procedure

Chapter Six: Jurisdiction of Criminal Courts

ABSTRACT

The system of the United Nations, as well as many international and regional bodies, imposes various duties on states that consequently have obligations towards the rights of their individuals. This is particularly significant in the case of children who are not only considered one of the most valuable subjects of international regulations, but are also an integral part of the legislation of domestic laws. Despite the fact that laws concerning the rights of children are well settled in the international sphere, and are recognized under the *jus cogens* norms, national laws about children, or national laws having an effect on children, are still not completely adequate. Many legislative and cultural practices expose the fact that children are not recognized as the holders of rights. National legal authorities should not, in accordance with the existing international legislations, plead provisions of their own laws or deficiencies of those laws in response to a request against them for alleged violations of children's rights that have occurred under their jurisdiction. In fact, the absence of appropriate legislation within national legal systems and the reluctance of legal authorities to seriously take children's rights into consideration, have been two of the key reasons for the contraventions of children's rights in national or international conflicts. This book examines many different areas within the law which deal with the specific rights of children such as the philosophy of law, civil law, health law, social law, tax law, criminal law, procedural law, international law, human rights law and the humanitarian law of armed conflict. The intention is to show that there are many rules, provisions, norms, and principles within various areas of the law that relate to the rights of children. The extent of these rights implies the existence of certain regions of law which have to be acknowledged and respected by national authorities. However, the acknowledgement of rights is also a matter of intention, and may be implied or expressed by the practice of authorities. The question of the child constituting a self-ruling subject of justice and its legal ability to create an independent individual legal personality for the protection of its rights, but not necessarily for the exercise of those rights, are the central issues of this book.

CONTRIBUTORS

Editors

Distinguished Visiting Professor **Farhad Malekian** is the founder and director of the Institute of International Criminal Law, Uppsala, Sweden. He was one of the leading academics in The World Conference on the Establishment of an International Criminal Court to Enforce International Criminal Law and Human Rights, Associated with the United Nations, International Institute of Higher Studies in Criminal Sciences, Syracuse, Italy (1992 and 1995). Malekian was nominated in Who is Who in 1996. He was listed among the "distinguished leaders in the field" of international criminal law in the twentieth century by L'Association Internationale de Droit Pénal. In 2005, he introduced the Principle of International Tribunality of Jurisdiction at the Cornell Law School. Malekian's views are analysed internationally and within doctoral dissertations. He is the author of outstanding "selected major treatises" as well as a considerable number of books and articles which have been an integral part of reading literature in different universities such as Europa-universität Viadrina in Frankfurt, Germany; Faculty of Law, University of New South Wales, Sydney, Australia; School of International Studies, University of Trento, Italy; Institute of Hartford Seminary, United States; Mid Sweden University and Stockholm University, Sweden; International Summer University Ohrid, Macedonia; Faculty of Law, University of Canterbury, New Zealand; Kent Law School, University of Kent, Canterbury, United Kingdom.

Malekian's works are referred to in many languages e.g. English, Arabic, Chinese, Finish, Danish, Serbian, Russian, German, Norwegian, Latvian, French, Swedish, Turkish and Spanish. To mention just a few, his works include International Criminal Law: The Legal and Critical Analysis of International Crimes (2 volumes, 1991); The Monopolization of International Criminal Law in the United Nations, A Jurisprudential Approach (2nd ed., 1995); Documents on the Principles of International Human Rights (2007); Emasculating the Philosophy of International Criminal Justice in the Iraqi Special Tribunal, Cornell International Law Journal (2005); The Homogeneity of International Criminal Court with the

Islamic Jurisprudence, International Criminal Law Review (2009); Principles of Islamic International Criminal Law, A Comparative Search (2nd ed., 2011), Principles of International Criminal Justice (forthcoming 2011), and invitation to contribute two articles to the most comprehensive reference work -Encyclopaedia of Criminology & Criminal Justice - to be published by Wiley-Blackwell (5 volumes 2012). Malekian also is known for his "dynamic presentations". F.Malekian.In.Crim.L@telia.com

Professor and Dr of Laws **Kerstin Nordlöf** joined the Örebro University Department of Law in December 2008. In addition to her responsibilities as a professor of law and teaching Penal Law, Criminal Procedural Law, Social Law, International Law, European Union Law, she also lectures on Juvenile Criminal Law. Her basic research interests include Penal Law, Criminal Procedural Law and Evidence, International Law and Social law, with a particular focus on children's rights before the criminal justice system. She is also engaged in questions of trafficking in women and children. Nordlöf also has a particular research interest in the implementation of the rights of children at an international level.

Before joining the Örebro University in Sweden, Nordlöf was an adjunct judge in the Court of Appeal in Stockholm in 2007-2008. For several years she was associate professor of law in Mid Sweden University and head of the Department of Law at the same university. She was also a visiting professor of law in 2005. Nordlöf has also taught for several years in Stockholm where she obtained her degree Doctor of Laws. She has written extensively in the fields of criminal procedure law and criminal law, and delivered international lectures. Some of her articles deal with The Legal Philosophy of Protecting a Suspect Child (2006), International Principles and Rights of Children in Criminal Cases (2007), and Economic Raison d'être of Trafficking in Children (2012). Her forthcoming books are the Prohibition of *Sex Trafficking Constituting Obligatio Erga Omnes, the International Rules of Law for the Protection of Children: Analysis and Documents* (2012) as well as in Swedish the Criminal Law Procedure for Juveniles (2012). She is also contributing an article to an indispensable source - the Encyclopaedia of Criminology & Criminal Justice - to be published by Wiley-Blackwell (5 volumes 2012). Kerstin.Nordlof@oru.se

Contributors

Batohi, Shamila is a special adviser to the Office of the Prosecutor of the ICC. Shamila.Batohi@icc-cpi.int

Burns, Angela, Solicitor, Freelance Author, formerly Senior Lecturer, Programme Director LL.M in Professional Legal Practice, and Deputy Programme Director Legal Practice Course, City Law School, City University, London. angelajburns@hotmail.com

Chapagai, Raju Prasad was an adjunct Professor of law at Kathmandu School of Law, 2004-2007. He is mainly educated in constitutional law (LL.M). He has worked as Legal Adviser to the UN Office of the High Commissioner for Human Rights in Nepal (OHCHR-Nepal). He has also worked in various capacities including a private/defense lawyer in civil and criminal law cases, National Legal Officer and Thematic Adviser on Transitional Justice and Rule of Law, and as a Public Interest Lawyer in the Supreme Court of Nepal on a wide range of human rights issues. He was a former editor of Nepal Bar Council Law Journal (2007 Issue). RChapagai@ohchr.org

Enquist, Hjördis Flodström is a lecturer in the Faculty of Health and Occupational Studies Department of Social Work and Psychology University of Gävle, Sweden. She works extensively with law questions. Hjordis.Flodstrom.Enquist@hig.se

Ervo, Laura is professor of law and a researcher at the Örebro University, School of Law, Psychology and Social Work, Sweden. Dr. Ervo is also an adjunct professor at the Universities of Turku, Helsinki and Eastern Finland. Her main field of research is procedural law, especially human rights in proceedings and the law of evidence. Laura.Ervo@oru.se

Ghazanfari, Hengameh is a Ph.D. candidate in International Law, Member of Law Faculty, Azad University, Khorramabad Branch, Iran. She also teaches law. ghazanfari_h50@yahoo.com

Hamzei, Helen LL.M. is Ph.D. Fellow and Lecturer at the Grotius Center for International Legal Studies, Faculty of Law, Leiden University, the Netherlands. h.beckmann-hamzei@law.leidenuniv.nl

Kristoffersson, Eleonor is professor of law and a lecturer, as well as a researcher at Örebro University in Sweden. She holds a Ph.D. from Jönköping International Business School. She worked at Uppsala University until 2009. She became a professor in tax law at the same university in 2009. She has also been a partner of the Tax Consultancy Firm Svalner Skatt & Transaction in Stockholm, and a member of the Board of advanced rulings (*Skatterättsnämnden*). She is also the head of the Institute for Value-Added Tax research at Stockholm University. Eleonor.Kristoffersson@oru.se

Köhler-Olsen, Julia has a Master of Law degree from the University of Oslo (2003), Norway. Since 2006 she has been a Ph.D. student at the Department for Public and International Law, Law Faculty, University of Oslo. Her Ph.D. project is on the child's right to self-determination in relation to religious norms. j.f.kohler-olsen@jus.uio.no

Mattsson, Titti, B.A.1988 (Washington D.C.), LL.M. 1991, J.D. 2002 (Lund), is Associate Professor in Public Law at the Faculty of Law at Lund University, Sweden. The main area of her research is on child protection and legal security for children and youth, with a focus on human rights and ethical issues. She has been widely published in monographs, anthologies and in international journals. She is an expert in child law for the Ombudsman for Children in Sweden and member of the Nordic Committee on Bioethics. Titti.Mattsson@jur.lu.se

Peleg, Noam is a Ph.D. candidate at University College London, Faculty of Laws, United Kingdom. He has worked as a lawyer with different human rights NGOs in Israel, after a career in journalism. As a practitioner, Noam litigated in cases concerning children's rights, humanitarian law, education law and family. He also worked for the National Committee on the Rights of the Child in Israel.
n.peleg@ucl.ac.uk

Persson, Annina is a Professor of law. She was educated in law at the University of Stockholm and obtained her PhD in 1998 at the same university. Her thesis was on 'Retention of Title Clauses. A study of the present and future position of a security interest', a comparative study of the legal treatment on retention of title clauses in seven countries. In 2000, she was appointed Associate Professor at the Faculty of Law, Stockholm University. In 2008, she was appointed professor at the School of Law, Psychology and Social work, Örebro University, Sweden, where she lectures Swedish Commercial Law, Comparative Law and International Trade and Insolvency Law. She has also been guest professor at the Centre for Banking and Finance at Royal Institute of Technology in Stockholm. Annina.persson@oru.se

Prucnal, Marta, Doctor of Laws, Jagiellonian University, Cracow, Poland; Visiting Researcher, Max Planck Institute for Comparative Public Law and International Law, Heidelberg, Germany.
martpru@googlemail.com

Ragnesten, Lisa, LL.M., Örebro University, is now working as a Notary at Jönköping District Court, Sweden. She has also lectured in law in the Department of Law in Örebro University. lisa.ragnesten@gmail.com

Reid, James is a Senior Lecturer in Childhood Studies in the School of Education and Professional Development at the University of Huddersfield, the United Kingdom. His academic interests include practice with families, particularly with fathers. He is a registered social worker, with experience in practice with children and their families. Prior to his current position, Reid lectured on social work at the University of Teesside and worked with UNICEF in Central Asia. Reid is a Fellow of the Higher Education Academy in the UK. J.Reid@hud.ac.uk

Sandberg, Kirsten is Professor of Law at the Department of Public and International Law in University of Oslo. She lectures on child law, welfare law and public administration law. She was recently elected as a member of the UN Committee on the Rights of the child, 2011-2015. She is a co-editor of a book on the CRC and its implementation in Norway, and has written articles on children's right to be heard, the discrimination against children, and the rights of asylum-seeking children, etc. Sandberg is currently heading a research project on children's rights in Norway. She has also temporarily worked as judge in the Supreme Court of Norway in 2010-2011. kirsten.sandberg@jus.uio.no

Sasan, Navdeep Kour is assistant Professor in Law at the Law School, University of Jammu, Jammu, India, and has lectured for several years in advance courses in the same university. Kour also has a Ph.D. in law, and is actively involved in the publication of legal articles, individually and collectively. ndksasan.law@gmail.com

Sveri, Knut received his law degree and PhD in Oslo. He is the first well-known distinguished professor of criminology in Sweden. Emeritus Professor Dr. Sveri was the head of the Scandinavian Research Council for Criminology between 1974 -1978. He has long debated the nature of law, its formulation, adoption and miss-implementation in Sweden and other Scandinavian countries. Professor Sveri has published extensively on different areas of law and criminology. KNUT.SVERI@SPRAY.SE

Takata, Kiyoe is Associate Professor of Social Security Law and Social Service Law, Faculty of Law and Letters, University of the Ryukyus, Japan. She has lectured extensively in law and worked on questions of comparative and social law. In particular, she has a wide range of knowledge regarding the legal system in Scandinavia countries. Takata has also been a visiting scholar in a number of universities. ktakata@ll.u-ryukyu.ac.jp

Tolonen, Hannele, LL.M. (University of Helsinki), Trained on the Bench, B.Sc. Econ. & Bus. Adm. (Helsinki School of Economics) is a doctoral student at the University of Helsinki, Finland. Tolonen is writing her dissertation on custody and child care proceedings, her research interests being in the fields of procedural and family law. She is currently working as an assistant at the University of Helsinki, Unit for Legal Studies in Vaasa. Before taking up doctoral studies, she worked as a legal aid counsel. hannele.tolonen@helsinki.fi

Wang, Lydia Yu-yeh obtained her degrees from National Taiwan University (LL.B.), University of Washington (LL.M.) and Washington University (J.D.) and is currently an Associate Research Follow at the Institute of European and American Studies, Academia Sinica (Taipei, Taiwan). Wang was a visiting scholar at the Harvard Law School, University of Leuven and Örebro University. She has written widely on American legal history, American civil rights, European human rights, and European Union law. She is now an associate Research Fellow at the Institute of European and American Studies, Academia Sinica. The majority of her publications and research work can be found at http://www.ea.sinica.edu.tw. yywang@sinica.edu.tw

Wergens, Anna is a lawyer specialising in issues related to crime victims. She has been working at the Crime Victim Compensation and Support Authority (Brottsoffermyndigheten) in Sweden. She has primarily worked with issues connected to crime victims at an international level. She has led several EU-funded projects on crime victims and published three books on crime victims in the European Union. During 2005-2007 she was the secretary of a governmental committee directed at putting forward proposals on legislation dealing with the counsel for injured persons in Sweden. At present she is connected with International Victimology Institute at Tilburg University and works on her doctoral studies on international standards on victims' rights.
anna.wergens@brottsoffermyndigheten.se

Öztürk, Fatih, is assistant Professor of International Law in the Faculty of Law, Melikşah University, Kayseri, Turkey. He is the director of International Affairs Office, Lecturer of Administrative and Comparative Law. He obtained an LL.B. from Istanbul University, Turkey, an LL.M. from California Western School of Law, San Diego, USA, an LL.M. from Queen's University, Kingston, Canada, and a Ph.D. from Istanbul University, Turkey. attorney33@hotmail.com

INTRODUCTION

By analogy with the rules which exist to provide legal, social and economic aid to the victims of national or international crimes, it may be possible to suggest that there is also an established legal duty for all states to provide access to resources which can, under reasonable criteria, protect children from the improper conducts of individuals, organisations, and the administration of justice. However, what constitutes the definition of the child is a very intricate question. In accordance with the Convention on the Rights of the Child, a child is a person under 18. It is, not however, easy to describe the precise acceptance or rejection of this age within the national systems of different states. Some states have adhered to this age limit under the Convention, some have accepted it with reservations, and still others have rejected it entirely. Nevertheless, the real issue does not actually relate to recognizing the age limits of childhood or adulthood, but rather the way in which we deal with different matters concerning children under our legal systems. Their rights have not only been given insufficient attention under the jurisdiction of states, but have also been seriously violated by transnational or international criminal actions. The ignoring of children's rights under the jurisdiction of a state covers legislative, judicial, and administrative measures and practices.

It is far from easy to state the current legal position of children in terms of the conventional, customary, general principles of law and case law, although many international treaties dealing directly or indirectly with the rights of children have been ratified. Modern writers therefore assert that there is a trend within the legal machinery of states towards encouraging the doctrine of the protection of children under a particular realm of law called the sovereignty of children. Yet the practice of different legal systems is far from consistent, and there is a persistent divergence between legislation supporting the theory of the recognition of the rights, self-protection, various securities, or autonomous personality of children, and that of the restrictive personality of children under the complete supervision of parents or guardians.

The increased complexity in estimating the effect of ignoring the rights of children under national practices, and the irreversible harm to children which has been caused by the provisions of different legislations and legal authorities, has resulted in conscious efforts in national and international legal and political communities for the establishment, improvement and protection of the rights of children. This effort has been especially strengthened as a result of the physical and psychological vulnerability of children confronting national, regional, and international problems, for example: the 1989 Convention on the Rights of the Child; the 2000 Optional Protocols on the Involvement of Children in Armed Conflict and on the Sale of Children, Child Prostitution and Child Pornography; the 1980 Hague Convention on the Civil Aspects of International Child Abduction; the 1993 Hague Convention on Protection of Children and Cooperation in respect of Inter-Country, as well as the 1980 European Convention on Recognition and Enforcement of Decisions concerning Custody of Children and on Restoration of Custody of Children. The frameworks of these conventions must be regarded as integral parts of the *jus cogens* system. This is because their provisions are crucial to the protection of the rights of children as a whole, and are therefore obligatory upon all states.

This book examines many different areas of the law, dealing with the rights of children like the philosophy of law, civil law, health law, social law, tax law, criminal law, procedural law, international law, human rights law and humanitarian law of armed conflict. The intention is to show that there are many rules, provisions, norms, and principles within various areas of the law that relate to the rights of children. The anthology of these rights undoubtedly implies the existence of certain regions of law which have to be acknowledged and respected by the national authorities. However, acknowledgement of rights is also a matter of intention, and may be implied or expressed by the practice of the authorities. The question of the child constituting a self-ruling subject of justice and its legal ability to create an independent individual legal personality for the protection of its rights, but not necessarily for the exercise of those rights, are central issues of this book.

The book is the result of a number of different scholars dealing in different ways with the questions of children's issues. These specialist writers, from different parts of the world, examine the impact of regulations and practices relating to children in different legal areas. The intention of these articles is to scrutinize different legal systems in Africa, Asia, Europe and the United States. The editing of the book has therefore been a challenge, owing to the fact that regulations and practices in different societies diverge to some extent from one another. By presenting them simultaneously, our purpose has been to struggle against the defects of the law and the serious ignorance of legal authorities concerning the issues of children. The themes and the conclusions of different articles demand the modifications, amendments, draft or strengthening of regulations applicable to the rights of children.

It is axiomatic that as long as children are considered inferior human beings and not one of the significant subjects of national law, violations of their rights by different means will, critically, not be recognized as violations. The problems of children, whether cultural, social, economic, educational, medical, criminal, procedural or otherwise, may not be resolved merely by formulating children's terms into national, regional or international legislation. The legal body of law, and the legal practice including the cultural attitudes of various nations have to adapt themselves to the new conditions of the protection of children by exposing and then shifting from traditional methods such as ignorance, threat or force. The fundamental mechanisms of our societies, such as economy, culture and religion, must take into account that the protection of children cannot be carried out by physical force or the unsuccessful words of parents, guardians, teachers, social workers, lawyers, judges or rehabilitation teams.

We have to learn that the integrity of our children cannot solely be guaranteed by the expression of the word love, but by full respect of their position and rights. Strange as it may seem, when we do not respect the rights of others, it might be considered a civil violation or a crime. But when the rights of children are violated it has, on many occasions, been dismissed as custom or argued that they gave their express consent. For example, in the nineties, when a child of 11 was raped in Sweden, the judgment concluded that there was an implicit consent. Similarly, when a child of 7 was raped by an Iranian priest in a Mosque, it was judged as the victim receiving spiritual enlightenment. It is, in principle, true that literally millions of people believe that children are their property or that a child has no rights of his or her own, and thus the conduct of parents, guardians, representatives of organisations, and the administration of justice relating to children are permitted as a matter of law or nature. This basic misunderstanding has to be rectified and the general attitudes of many nations which basically have a culture which decides on children must be promoted by laws. As the United Nations Millennium Declaration of 2000 points out, as leaders we therefore have a serious responsibility to the entire world, "especially the most vulnerable and, in particular, the children of the world, to whom the future belongs".

Farhad Malekian
Chief Editor
Carolina Rediviva Library
Uppsala, January 2012

CHAPTER ONE:

DIMENSIONS OF THE BEST INTERESTS OF THE CHILD

THE CHILD AS AN AUTONOMOUS SUBJECT OF JUSTICE

FARHAD MALEKIAN

Abstract

Justice is certainly not based on self-satisfaction. Nor it is the giving or receiving of pain. If these were the case, justice could be achieved simply by everyone fighting everyone else. Nor is justice the concrete knowledge of empirical laws, legislative frameworks or a collection of particular norms. In each social case, it has its own way of reasoning, approach, understanding, theory, philosophy and conclusion. But the common presumption is that justice should have one supreme aim. This is the protection of the personality of individuals. Thus, justice should have its own sovereignty, its own legal territory and its own autonomy of self-independence. This also includes the way in which we treat the *integrity* of the child. Whatever we are and whatever we want, it is axiomatic that our vision should not be blinded or affected by other, superficial, matters surrounding our social life. The sovereignty of justice should be so strong that no principles of its strength can be associated with other subjective aspirations. Here our intention is, as far as possible, to find a feasible *modus operandi* for the effective recognition and implementation of the rights of the child. The intention is not to convince the state's authorities about those rights, but to realize the *de facto* existence of the rights of the child. This article challenges the theory of justice for children and the understanding of its nature, philosophy, principles, norms, and particularly the interpretation of its *de jure* sources. The question of the child constituting the self-ruling subject of justice and its legal ability in creating an independent individual legal personality for the protection of its rights but not necessarily for the exercise or emancipation of those rights by the child, are the focus of attention of this article.

Key words: justice, child, protection

1. Introduction

The position of the child as a separate subject of law is a relatively new innovation;[1] there are probably not many legislative bodies around the world that have given the child the recognition of full legal personality as compared to adults. That recognition does not necessarily mean the personal capacity to use the rights, but the capacity to be, and be accepted, in his or her personal capacity as a child. Some movement has, however, been made to that end, but with no particular admission within the domestic practice of states. The criteria of mental ability, wisdom perception, physical power, and personal skill have, as a whole, been some of the most recognized reasons for the prevention of their identification as a full legal person. But, unfortunately, "l'enfant est traité comme une marchandise."[2]

---

[1] For example consult Jane Fortin, Children's Rights and the Developing Law (2009); Elaine E Sutherland., Children Rights in Scotland (2009); Martin Guggenheim., What's wrong with children's rights? (2005); Elaine E Sutherland, Child and Family Law (2008); Marie Parker-Jenkins, Sparing the Rod: schools discipline and children's rights (1999); Priscilla Alderson, Young Children's Rights: Exploring Beliefs, Attitudes, Principles and Practice (2000); Michael D. A. Freeman, The moral status of children: essays on the Rights of the Child (1997); Mary John, Children's Rights and Power: Charging up for a New Century (2003); Philip E. Veerman, The Rights of the Child and the Changing Image of Childhood (1992); Michael D. A. Freeman, Philip E. Veerman, The Ideologies of Children's Rights (1992); Eugeen Verhellen, Monitoring children's rights (1996); David Archard, Children: Rights and Childhood (1993); Geraldine Van Bueren, The International Law on the Rights of the Child (1998); James R. Himes, Implementing the Convention on the Rights of the Child: resource mobilization in low-income countries (1995); Sharon Detrick, Paul Vlaardingerbroek, Globalization of child Law: the role of the Hague Conventions (1999); Sharon Detrick, Jaap Doek, Nigel Cantwell, The United Nations Convention on the Rights of the Child: a Guide to the "Travaux Préparatoires" (1992); Lawrence J. LeBlanc, The Convention on the Rights of the Child: United Nations Lawmaking on Human Rights (1995); Alfred Glenn Mower, The Convention on the Rights of the Child: International Support for Chidren (1997); Eugeen Verhellen, Convention on the Rights of the Child: background, motivation, strategies, main themes (2000); Geraldine Van Bueren., International Dokuments on Children (1998); and Sharon Detrick, A commentary on the United Nations Convention on the Rights of the Child (1999).

[2] Jean Zermatten., La convention des droits de l'enfant 20 ans, déjà! www.swiss-paediatrics.org/sites/default/files/29-32.pdf.

Compared with earlier rules of traditional international law, the rights of the child within our society may be likened to the position of a state controlled by suzerain power. In international law, these rules mean that a state or nation is juridically and politically controlled by another state regarding its external relations with other states. The state in question is, however, permitted to deal with its internal affairs. This is precisely the position of most children in contemporary international society: they are solely accepted as children but are heavily ignored in their external relations. These may include social, educational, economic and other potential activities. The position does not necessarily mean that they do not have regulated rights within various legal systems, but that the rights stipulated within those legal instruments, are mostly integrated into other regulations within our social unity. This gap between rights, to have rights, but not to be given sufficient rights to recognize and use those rights, appropriately is a fact that can be seen within most branches of the legal system such as criminal law, criminal procedures, family law, labour law and also financial regulations.

The aim of this article is not to list different rights of children or analyse them according to the principles of custody or care within civil and common law systems. Such a task has, in effect, been carried out by many of the other writers in this collection on the Sovereignty of Children in Law. The purpose here is, as far as possible, to find a feasible apparatus which may be useful in the effective recognition and implementation of the rights of the child. By "effective recognition and implementation", we do not mean the acknowledgement of the rights by different legal systems and their implementations. Rather, we simply mean the correct way, with accurate measures, to establish the nature of the legal personality of the child. The purpose is not to convince the social or legal authorities about the existence of those rights, but to realize the existence of the child as a consolidated subject of our legal mechanism. This work therefore challenges the theory of justice and understanding its nature, philosophy, principles, norms and particularly its interpretation in order to reach a definition of justice in connection with the philosophy of the protection of children. The question of the child constituting the self-ruling subject of justice and its legal ability to create an independent, individual legal personality for the protection of its rights but not necessarily for the exercise of those rights by the child, is therefore the main thrust of this article.

2. The Concept of Protection

2.1. Uniformity of Protection

Sooner or later, the protection of the rights of children will have to become one of the most remarkable tasks of our living society.[3] This is based on the fact that children are one of the most frequently referred to subjects of law whether in connection with domestic or international law. In particular, the protection of children has become one of the main aims of international entities such as the various United Nations bodies, the permanent International Criminal Court, Amnesty International, or Human Rights Watch. Speaking personally, what is uppermost in my mind is always, do I provide those necessary pre-conditional shelters for the safety of my four children? Of course, reference to my own children does not necessarily mean that in order to understand the position of children one needs to be a parent, or to be responsible for the care of a child. But the reference is only to provide a hortatory and practical example in the discussion relating to the philosophy of child protection. I nevertheless believe that the protection of my children is necessary, and the granting of such protection should not violate the rights of other minors or adults. Similarly, I ask myself: should the protection of the rights of my children take priority over my own personal protection, ability, and security? In other words, how far should I go without various natural, normal, or legal protections when I estimate the importance of the protection of my children? Does the concept of protection have natural and legal limits, or is it permanent in whatever situation?[4]

My mind is not necessarily occupied by the rule of law and its pressure upon me, but, by the rule of moral law, my personal responsibilities, duties, tasks and the very outer limits of my brain's capacity to understand the fundamental rights of my children in connection with universal values in a world where breaches of law are the most widely reported national or international news stories. I therefore seek for the truth, the ethics of conscience, bliss and harmony between what I understand from the moral

---

[3] See The New Handbook Of Children's Rights: Comparative Policy And Practice (Bob Franklin, ed., 1991); Children, Rights, And The Law (Philip Alston, Stephen Parker, John Seymour editors, 1992). Martin Guggenheim, What's Wrong With Children's Rights? (2005).

[4] The history of rights of children, for example, in the United States demonstrates that children were legally subordinate to adults and also subject to adult authority. Martin Guggenheim, ibid, p 9.

law or natural law with a slight combination with positive law.[5] The reason is, I feel, that the first cornerstone of the understanding of the nature of the protection of my children is not law, but the way in which I treat their personal or *natural integrity*. This includes the integrity when I shared their creation in the womb, their birth, their infancy, babyhood and childhood, and so on. To these, I may also add the requirements of certain laws that have been discussed and accepted within our social structure. When I talk about "certain laws", I intentionally draw a line between a good law and a bad law, between a conservative law and a radical law, between a dictatorial law and a democratic law, as well as between the philosophies of one law and another. Thus, one may speak of a just law and an unjust law.[6] Law may give order for the protection of certain subjects due to its own requirements, but the substance of protection, because of its very sensitive perception, cannot be exclusively based on an order and the law itself. This means that sacrificing our own protection may not still be enough for the protection of children, based on the fact that the question of protection is purely conceptual, hypothetical, and personal. Nevertheless, the protection of children should be combined with *faith, trust, belief, worship*, and *love*.

2.2. Realm of Protection

What the source or sources of natural integrity are is not as complicated as in the case of positive law.[7] This is because positive law may not only be heavily subjected to interpretation by philosophers of law or legal authorities of administration of justice, but also by the ordinary layman who does not know about the legal provisions but has his own way of understanding the provisions of social orders.[8] For him, the protection of the rights of children may solely mean having a home, food, drinks,

---

[5] For a discussion on the nature of morality and its effects on our judgments see Bernard Gert, Common Morality: Deciding What to Do (2004).

[6] The concepts of just and unjust law are two interrelated concepts that have usually been analyzed side-by-side facing each other's arguments. The concepts have been deeply rooted in the traditional philosophy of law and also extended within contemporary national or international law. For many, an unjust law is not law, but the circumstances of power and force. A just law is a law which has *inter alia* the character of human rights norms and respects the personal integrity of minors or adults.

[7] Farhad Malekian, *The Miserable Wedding of Naturalism into Positivism,* ID EST Journal, (2009), pp.139-143.

[8] Ibid, pp.145-146.

clothes, schooling and his/her way of presenting happiness. Here, our intention is not to draw a line between natural law and positive law and assert that one is better than another, or that one is superior to the theory of the other.[9] The purpose, rather, is to become aware that in order to realize the boundaries of positive law one needs to understand the boundaries of natural law.[10] But the contrary may scarcely be the truth. This is as long as our motivation does not coincide with the provisions of positive law.[11] It means that the protection of our children according to the rules of law is not a gift, but that one has to ask or fight for it. This protection may not only be asked for from the administration of justice and legislation authorities, but also from all types of social services.

As we have mentioned above, to understand the purpose of the enhancement of positive law for the protection of the rights of children, an understanding of the natural law may to some extent be a corollary condition. The reason is that the jurisprudence of law rests not only on legal theories, legal philosophers, legal reasoning and the historical theories of law, but also on the elementary principles of natural law, civil law and the law of nations.[12] This can easily be seen within the provisions of the Universal Declaration of Human Rights which fundamentally integrate the principles of natural law into positive law.[13] Although the whole theory of the Declaration is based on a resolution of the General Assembly, and does not therefore have the binding effect of law making treaties, it is considered an integral part of *jus cogens* law because of the safeguarding of some of the most fundamental principles of human civilization.[14] This is the law, the provisions of which are peremptory, and it should not be ignored in the national or international relations of states. Consequently, even though we may have different schools of thought regarding how those significant norms of human rights are to be faced, the philosophy of human rights not only speaks about moral law, but also about positive law. Together, these create a combination of legal protection for all subjects of law and its categories.

---

[9] Ibid.,pp.147-149.
[10] Ibid., pp.145.
[11] Ibid., pp.145-149.
[12] Ibid.,p.146.
[13] Ibid.,p.144.
[14] See *infera* section on *Jus Cogens.*

2.3. Strength of Adaptability

In the above, I am not trying to put the functions of laws or the real facet of laws alongside one line and habitually present them. My chief intention is to find the way in which I meet the requirements of my children, and which may suit the character of natural or positive law. The reason is that the creation of particular protection for children does not necessarily arrive by email or legislative measures, but how one interprets as well as understands the ethical or practical legislation of social relations. The fact is that I have to understand my children as they wish so that I can realise their interests. This means that I need to be corrected, and if necessary, to be modified so that the personal integrity of my children is not harmed and we will most probably reach the most central points in our minds. Understanding this logic is not so difficult, because if we are all animals by nature, we have to be protected and in a way that, our reasoning will not harm our natural equality, human morality and freedom of expressions as a whole.[15] Protection and expression are thus an integral part of one another and should not be separated from one another, even regarding our children who are minors.

Despite the known or unknown fact that we are, or are not, animals, we have intelligence, and understand that we should not damage each other's integrity.[16] The term "animal" is thus a term of art, but not a term of battle with nature and the reason for our existence.[17] Whatever we are, and whatever we want, it is obviously clear that our vision should not be clouded or be monopolized or affected by other superficial matters surrounding our social life. These might include such things as intellectual pursuits, socializing with colleagues or friends, taking delight in material possessions, sex, taking pleasure in our families and basking in the reflected glory of any of their successes, the environment, and so on.

It is axiomatic that there is nothing wrong with being self-confident or overconfident, which increases our ability reach to achieve various goals. But these feelings or attitudes must unquestionably not conflict with the rights of others, which also includes minors. For us, then, this overconfident ability should be orientated to recognizing the social rights of all persons, old or young. In one sense, it may take legislation to

---

[15] For an analysis of moral law see Catherine Wilson, Moral Animals: Ideals And Constraints In Moral Theory (2004).

[16] Ibid., at 2.

[17] Ibid., at 2-3.

demonstrate, limit or organize the social protection of whatever kind that may be necessary for the safety or protection of different persons, both theoretically and practically. But, obviously, legislative measures are not always clear and require interpretation, reference to cases, modification, and even sometimes, 'candid appraisal' as to whether the rights of children and their interests are being served.[18] We have to reconcile, devote and face these eventualities of our social life with others that are the reasons for the confirmation of our social existence. The social position is like an apple tree laden with apples offering themselves to one and all, and although the tree seems to be independent, this is merely superficial. The tree naturally has the strength to adapt to the conditions of social order. Thus, we have to see ourselves in the mirror of justice, not selfishness, and not use children's rights for our own purposes.[19] What the mirror of justice is, and what its principles, norms or rules are, are some of the most elementary questions in evaluating the system of the protection of children.

2.4. The Epitomization of Justice

Justice is definitely not self-satisfaction. If this were the case, justice could be achieved simply by everyone fighting everyone else. Nor is justice the giving or receiving of sadness, otherwise the philosophy of justice would always be in danger, not only from accused persons, but also from the victims. It is not easy to define the term "justice". In general, "justice" is a term of art. It is neither designed to create happiness nor to generate sadness. Its function is to find the truth. In other words, everyone is, in reality, subject to justice, but the reverse is not true. Justice cannot and should not be subject to anything—this includes a material object, a physical person, an entity or a state. The notion of justice, if it is bound by these substances or concepts loses its moral and judicial validity. Justice should thus have its own sovereignty, its own legal territory and its own autonomy. In fact, the moral or legal values of justice are based on its self-governing status. This means that the sovereignty of justice should be so strong that no monopolization of its strength can occur. In addition, justice is not the concrete knowledge of empirical laws, legislative frameworks or a collection of particular norms. In each social case, it has its own way of reasoning, approach, understanding, theory, philosophy and conclusion. In

[18] Martin Guggenheim, What's Wrong With Children's Rights? (2005), xiii.
[19] Ibid., x-xii.

all these issues of presumptions, justice should have, and should present, one aim. This is what we call protection of its subjects.

Protection appears to be the first philosophy of justice. Based on this philosophy, justice may achieve a convincing result. In civil, criminal or procedural matters, the first primary function of justice is also to ensure protection. This may include protection for victims, accused persons and witnesses. The second function of justice is the acquisition of a protective judgment. This means justice has to be very cautious in delivering a decision. The reason is that the decision has to be formulated within a specially articulated policy that should not harm any of the subjects of justice i.e. accused, victim and witness. Yet, the function of justice as a means of protection does not end with the delivery of the decision; justice has to be alert to any misunderstanding of its own function, philosophy and misinterpretation. When new evidence becomes available, the previous judgement may be changed and the previous evidence becomes invalid. This is because the principles of accurate justice require the appropriate application of the *status quo*.

Justice cannot be right when its policy has been proven to harm its subjects. In other words, in a well-organized society the principles of justice are publicly known and are understandable to the layman, because those principles have evolved out of the social attitudes of that society. Even so, those principles cannot be modified by the will of the legislature. There must be a certain code of conduct within the social structure of the given society that demonstrates the need for the modification or complete change of the principles of justice. This may result in a different understanding of the core principles of justice, and a comparative examination of the issue may demonstrate that the principles of justice differ from one society to another. Nonetheless, an inquiry into the laws of various civilizations proves that the differences between the principles of justice do not prevent the application of the theory of fair and objective justice.

Justice has to guarantee protection for all its subjects, and this protection should not be affected by variations within its principles. Thus, while individual laws may be wrong or unjust, it does not necessarily mean that the administration of justice as a whole is wrong or unjust. Dealing with the principles of justice requires access to the spirit of justice or the strength of a rational mind. Thus, the principles of justice may be slightly different from one another, but the spirit of justice may not, but only if the authority to judge is not misused or misunderstood by the judges. The subjects of justice should not be harmed by different principles of justice; and the integrity of justice, as well as judgments must always be respected by human morality and not just legality. Thus, appropriate justice has to be the cornerstone of the protection of social institution and its evolution.

2.5. Harmony of Justice

Even in a dictatorship, justice should not be devalued by a judge yielding to pressure from politicians or religious groups, etc. Justice should always be impartial, and the provisions of legal order should be interpreted in such a way that a judgment reflects the content or the intention of justice. This means that protecting the subjects of justice should be given priority and the dictatorial rules interpreted in such a way that justice is not devalued by rules which are unreasonable, irrational, illogical and unfounded within the general theory and policy of justice. That is why the institution of justice should not violate the mirror of justice or purity. This is the mirror which is colour blind, although different rules of law have been used for its construction.

The theory of justice in fact has a very complex structure, consisting of principles, norms, rules and provisions. They may have an independent characterization, or may be dependent, although this legal personality of justice does not necessarily have anything to do with its intention and inspiration. The common understanding of the theory of justice demonstrates that there must be reasonable or logical harmonies between parts of its body for the purpose of protecting its subjects; this means that such harmonies should not devalue the subjects of justice. They have to be used or interpreted in the ethical or legal personality of a person. Justice should remember that each person has his/her own social equality compared with others, and is not subject to the imposition of power, because, as a general rule accepted by most civilizations, the possession of the power of justice is not encouraged within the theory of the pure inspiration of justice. In other words, the institution of justice may be in danger, and infringe the theory of the protection of different subjects of justice if the power of justice is used in contrast to the motivation of justice. The security and immunity of the theory of justice and its principles concerning understanding the rights of its subjects should be guarded within all institutional services of law. This may be more necessary in the case of those who are weak, minor or dependent.

Most significantly, justice must be based on goodwill, good interests and good results. By "good" we do not necessarily mean the requirements of a good test, or good as opposed to bad. It is meant to present certain highly qualified values that bring trust and enlightenment to the machinery of justice, for the administration of equality and for the consolidation of the rights of individuals including minors. In fact, looking at the concept of justice and its theory of existence, the ideal end would be to achieve a just and fair society in which all individuals are respected and recognized as full subjects of law, with no age discrimination. The role of justice is thus to create a balance between what we want, and what justice sees as essential for our nature. In other words, justice should not depart from its subjects, old or young, healthy or sick, alive or dead. It should not ignore their personalities, characters or natures. This is because the theory of justice recognizes that its subjects are not always equal in terms of reasoning, age or ability. These differences should not be essential for justice and should not make one better than another. Obviously, all human subjects of justice have a type of legal personality and it is the complex body of this legal personality that should be realized, identified and respected including children.[20]

2.6. Legal Personality

A legal person in law is mostly referred to as a legal body that has officially obtained a status as a juristic person. This means that natural persons may, by way of legal application, ask the legal authorities for admission of their activities as a legal person. Thus, a legal person is not a human but has received, to a certain extent, the legal characterization of a natural person. Although a legal personality is not a human, its activities are usually carried out by several human beings. Normally, legal personality may only be granted if certain conditions are fulfilled. These conditions are fixed, and if a legal body changes the conditions upon which it has received its legal personality, it may lose that personality. A legal personality creates rights, duties, privileges and liabilities for the legal person and a capacity to engage in different activities.

The theory of legal personality speaks, in general, about the power of law and how law can be used and empowered by certain persons to achieve the

---

[20] As it is rightly asserted rights without recognition are meaningless. See the introduction on The Children's Rights Movement: Overcoming The Oppression Of Young People (Beatrice Gross & Ronald Gross eds., 1977).

intention of their legal body. The philosophy of legal personality does not exclusively belong to common law or civil law countries. It can be found within most legal systems, but at different levels.

One of the essential reasons for granting a body or entity legal personality is to increase its legal validity within society and the law, and to simultaneously confirm its existence. Thus, the concept of legal personality has always been important for the recognition of positive or negative activities. The maintenance of legal personality also increases the legal duties of the authorities to respect the legal status of the legal personality. In addition, the legal personality establishes accountability for the legal body and for its future conducts. Although it is commonly accepted that the term "legal personality" is used in the case of entities or a juridical person, the term is also employed in the case of natural persons in order to emphasis their legal rights. Some of the rights of a juridical person or a natural person are *a)* the right to integrity, *b)* the right to express its/his/her views, *c)* the right to be a party to an agreement, *d)* the right to be respected in all legal procedures, e*)* the right to self-governing activities, *f)* the right to property, ownership and *g)* the right to be treated as a person in his/her own right. However, one must underline that there may be different types of legal personality depending on the borderline of juridical permission.

In juridical terms, the concept of legal personality opens the window to the recognition of the rights, self-protection, various securities, and autonomous personality. Due to the merits surrounding legal personality, a child may receive a recognized status which has to be faced by all persons and entities. This means that the legal personality creates legal integrity and an obvious juridical respect. The question is always to what extent the recognition of the legal personality of the child helps in the issues governing the protection of their integrity and their rights within national and international society. The question of the integrity of the child always faces certain problems of interpretation. This depends on several factors such as certain cultural definitions of the term "child", the legal definition of the term, and the general practice prevailing within the decisions of legal authorities. The intention of the recognition of the legal personality of the child is to identify him/her as a complete person compared with his/her mother, father, guardian or sponsor. The purpose is also to emphasise that children's rights are not an integral part of parent's rights.[21]

2.7. Wisdom

The recognition of the legal personality of the child does not necessarily imply his/her awareness. This is because the legal personality is a statute which is recognized by law and is acknowledged in practice, but does not intend, in all circumstances, to demonstrate the knowledge of the understanding of the personality. Therefore, the term "legal personality of the child" is the acknowledgement of the child's rights in a complete context. It refers to the fact that the child has certain established rights which are integrated into one framework that may be called the charter for the protection of rights, and simultaneously the development of the recognition of the rights of the child. The term is also the identification of a particular *status quo* for the child. On the one hand, the term accepts that certain collected rights belong to the position of the child and are not separable from his/her personal or legal nature. On the other hand, these rights are not automatically permitted to be used by the child without the evaluation of his/her custodian, guardian, protector or parents. This may, however, depend on the age of the child. It may, at first glance, sound somewhat unwise to grant a legal personality to the child, and at the same time restrict its use to the control of a particular person. The theoretical notion is nevertheless different.

Wisdom is understanding and realizing the means for the existence of certain rights, and cannot be granted by law, but solely by personal development. However, the word wisdom is itself subject to debate and may have different levels and degrees. This means that wisdom is a person's ability to understand, initially, what is good or not good for that person, although there are no criteria for measuring good or bad. All these also depend, to a great extent, on a person's ability to distinguish between good and bad, between beneficial and non-beneficial, and between valuable and invaluable matters. It must nevertheless be understood that wisdom presents the stage of understanding of a person's capacity to deal with certain important matters: at the same time, accepting legal rights means, for a natural person, that his personal existence is already accepted by law. Thus, it may not be incorrect to say that rights not only imply the

---

[21] Peter Edelman, *The Children's Rights Movement in* The Children's Rights Movement: Overcoming The Oppression Of Young People, ibid, at 204-05.

existence of objective or subjective ownership, but also the way to recognise a person' physical or intellectual priorities. This includes all categories including minors. Once we have accepted that the existence of rights is *a priori* a form of perception, the question remains what exactly we mean by the rights of minors. If these rights naturally or juridically belong to minors, why should we doubt the cognitive sense of minors? Although we are aware that the cognition of children is commonly develops with age, this should not hinder the acceptance of legal personality of the child as a protected subject of our social order. Naturally, we should not limit our judgments concerning the legal personality of children and protection, on their age, but on the qualified position of the rights governing the child as a person.

The natural or positive law surely makes no particular distinction between the rights of adults and of minors. The difference is surely minor rather than exploitive. The distinction between the variety of rights for adults and variety of rights for minors is therefore surely synthetic rather than substantive. There is hence sufficient evidence in law for the acknowledgement of the legal personality of each age, i.e. adult as well as minor, and also *a priori* for possible cognition. This is the ability to acquire, by the use of obvious reasoning, perception and awareness, the knowledge that both subjects have wisdom, although they may have different capacities. These are what we will call the sovereignty of adults and sovereignty of minors.

3. The Principle of Sovereignty of Children

3.1. The Sovereignty of Minors

The term "sovereignty of minors" or "sovereignty of children" is an innovative term that has not apparently been previously used. The term implies that certain different rights of children have been recognized by the sources of law. These are such things as general principles of law, customary law, conventional law, court decisions, national legislation, and so forth.[22] By customary, law we mean all those rights that have been recognized as the consequence of the existence of certain customary rules accepted within different social relations such as the right to food, clothes, inheritance, and any other principal needs. By conventional law, we mean those rights of children that have been acknowledged by the provisions of

[22] See the section on the sources of law, below.

written law. These may include such rights as the right to schooling, medical services, assistance in different juridical matters and the right to be sheltered during armed conflicts. Thus, when we speak of the sovereignty of children we mean that there are certain recognized sources of law that are particularly accepted or regulated to acknowledge the rights that belong to children. More clearly, in conventional law, we mean not only the rights of children which have been formulated into various national or international agreements, but also all types of legislative or constitutional rules, measures, provisions, principles, norms and methods which deal with the rights of children. In addition, we also mean all other regional conventions, treaties, agreements, and protocols. Yet, one may also add to this category, the declarations, recommendations or resolutions of the General Assembly and the Security Council which do not have the character of law-making treaties, but are the manifestation of the rapid development of certain rules that cannot, for one reason or another, be formulated into international treaties but are significant in for the protecting children's rights.

With reference to the above, by "sovereignty of children" we mean a juridical territory in which the child is supposed to be saved from all types of intrigues. These include internal humiliation such as ignorance of his/her integrity in procedural matters or external monopolization such as trafficking.[23] Whilst the term "sovereignty of children" is not similar to the term "sovereignty of states", it is used to emphasise the potentiality of the respect of the rights of the child and the strength of legitimate childhood duration.[24]

"Sovereignty of children" creates some type of legal strength for the child against strong rules of national society, offices or authorities who have ignored the rights of the weaker parties in the process of social justice. Here the word "sovereignty" is an essential component in the maintenance of their rights and integrities. In other words, the concept of the sovereignty of children creates the concept of inviolability of their rights

---

[23] It is rightly asserted that "P*olitically* children's rights have become contested territory for mainstream political parties." Bob Franklin, *Children's rights: An introduction* in The New Handbook Of Children's Rights: Comparative Policy And Practice (Bob Franklin, ed., 1991) p.3.

[24] However, it is to be stated that we do not speak here about absolute sovereignty that has been challenged by many international lawyers in the case of legitimate rights of states. The term, neither in the case of states, nor in the case of children, matches such issues.

in a national or international context. This is based on the fact that in recent decades the boundaries of the rights of children have been increasingly debated and a considerable number of national, regional or international documents dealing with the specific rights of children and their authenticity have been written. As a result, the perspectives on the role of the sovereignty of children over the past decades have, for the most part, been developed rapidly and significantly. Some of the reasons for the recognition of the sovereignty of children in law are:

i) To give sufficient strength to the recognized age of the child
ii) To understand their wisdom, weakness, and their incontrovertible rights to protection
iii) To acknowledge the juridical dimensions of the rights of the child
iv) A clear identification of children's rights in a national, regional and international context
v) To give effect to *de lege lata*
vi) To recognize the rights of children and their violations
vii) To recognize the child as an independent subject of law
viii) To emphasise on the legal personality of the child
ix) To distinguish between the rights of adults and the rights of child
x) A clear acknowledgment of the natural and positive rights of children within constitutional provisions
xi) To recognize the rights of all children to food, a home, clothes and primary education
xii) To provide a full guarantee for the use of social services for all children on an equal footing.
xiii) To accentuate the equality of all children concerning legal, religious, cultural, language, race, ethnic, or any other matters
xiv) To secure the scope and significance of the rights of children in different regions of jurisprudence
xv) To secure the implementation of the rights of the child in civil procedures
xvi) To guarantee the legal identity of children in criminal procedures
xvii) To reduce, as much as possible, the infringement of the integrity of the child in internal relations
xviii) To prohibit infanticide
xix) To minimize national crimes against children
xx) To minimize transnational crimes against children
xxi) To minimize international crimes against children
xxii) To emphasize the criminality of armed attacks on children's shelters

xxiii) To underline the prohibition of employment of children in armed conflicts

3.2. The Purpose of the Sovereignty of Children

Sovereignty of children implies the legal recognition, juridical reverence, and practical equality of children before different legal bodies. The concept of the sovereignty of children encompasses all matters concerning children's rights, and their inviolability by national, regional and international authorities. The concept also aims to construct a clear framework of the rights of children, and to emphasize the importance of the protection of those rights in all civil and criminal procedures. The concept also underlines that legal violations of the right to grow up with parents, the right to be saved from various conflicts between partners, and not to be used for various types of exploitations including different forms of labour, and various ideas of slavery such as sexual and experimental, are not permitted. In other words, the child has, according to a large number of regional and international conventions, the right to be saved from all types of intrusion which may harm his/her integrity. This means that the legal rights of children are perpetual and should not be ignored in the procedure of justice.

Similarly, the concept of the sovereignty of children not only protects the integrity of children, but also the inalienable rights of female children from unlawful exploitation, rape and other sexual abuses.[25] Because of this, the recognition of the sovereignty of children will create an adequate power for children to act over their inalienable rights to the exclusion of other persons from their own legal territories and their violations. The significant value of the recognition of a circle which encompasses all children's rights is particularly necessary when one considers that respecting those rights are fundamentally essential for the protection of children from unlawful measures of dictatorial or one-party government. From a comparative aspect, the value of the power of sovereignty can be seen in the words of the International Court of Justice, which states that "between independent States, respect for territorial sovereignty is an essential foundation of international relations".[26] This recognition by the Court was restated almost three decades later, when it observed that it is

[25] See David S. Mitchell, *The Prohibition of Rape in International Humanitarian Law as a Norm of Jus Cogens: Clarifying Doctrine*15 Duke Journal of Comparative and International Law, 219-258 (2005).
[26] ICJ Reports, 1949, p. 4.

"the fundamental principle of state sovereignty on which the whole of international law rests".[27] The analogy between the sovereignty of children and states shows that granting sovereignty to children's rights, even in the form of a concept and not necessarily a law, creates *a custom of respect,* not only in our daily relationships, for the rights of the child, but also, under the pressure of the rules of law.

Although we are aware that the theory of the sovereignty of states is becoming weaker, and certain changes are rapidly taking place within the traditional concept of state sovereignty, this does not weaken the concept of the "sovereignty of children", because "sovereignty of children" is quite different from the use of the term "state sovereignty". The former does not talk about territorial independence, territorial power, political strength, or military forces, but about the value of the protection of the rights of the child before national, regional and international bodies and authorities. The latter is, in fact, a strong traditional and conventional power of state under the provisions of the United Nations, while the former solely means the use of the word *sovereignty* in order to orientate, adjust, and familiarize the rights of children in a juridical compact.

4. Applicable Sources of Law

A source of law within the traditional concept is the will of the sovereign of a state. This is what is known as a dictatorial system, monarchy regulation, a democratic approach, and a republic rule. All these imply the power of the relevant sovereign. All these laws come through a person or persons who have the right to express their will in the form of law to the whole relevant society under certain parliamentary or non-parliamentary procedures. The relevant society is thus responsible for reparation. This is also true within the democratic system where the overwhelming majority, in different combinations, have authority to pass laws. Similarly, in the system of international law, rules and provisions are regulated by the will of the states parties, and their communities are therefore under obligation to enforce a given law. What is of interest here is the principle of *pacta sunt servanda*, which is based on good faith, pertaining to the moral or mental state of reliability. The principle of *pacta sunt servanda* requires all parties to give sufficient attention to the will of the law, the sources of which are the party states. The principle concerns the legal duties of states within treaty law. According to the principle, the states in question have an

[27] ICJ Reports, 1986, para. 263.

international responsibility to carry out their legal obligations, which are formulated within the provisions of a treaty. The principle is, in fact, a legal guarantee of the words which have assumed the force of law. This means the accepted duties, obligations, responsibilities, and liabilities of the ratifying parties. The principle of *pacta sunt servanda* is also significant with regard to national rules and obligations. The word *pacta* refers to the provisions of an agreement concluded between two or more groups, to carry out or fulfil certain acts as have been seen necessary for the sake of their societies. *Pacta sunt servanda* refers to the obligations of those people or groups to maintain their stated promises. These promises can be of different natures and kinds: they can be national or international promises regulating, for instance, the rights of certain subjects such as the application of human rights, the respect of foreigners' rights, refuge issues, and children.

The rights of children are combinations of different categories of laws including, but not excluding, constitutional law, civil law, family law, taxation law, financial or economic law, criminal law, procedural law, school law, social service law, administrative law, gift and inheritance law, medical law, human rights law, refugee law, asylum law, children law, humanitarian law, and military law. All these laws have, more or less, some implicit or explicit provisions about children's rights, and have been formulated by legal authorities in order to minimize, as far as is reasonable, any possible conflict between different subjects or sections of laws regarding children's rights. *Thus, it will not be incorrect to assert that the sources of the rights of children within our laws are our own way of expressing of duties and these rights or laws have to be gathered within one single union under the term the "sovereignty of children in law"*. The second source of law governing the rights of children emanates from the circumstances of natural law. These are rules that are fundamental to the protection of the rights of children. Furthermore, the concept of the social integration of human beings and its close proximity with one another requires the understanding that the source of law on children is not necessarily based on positive law, but also on those principal factors that cannot be separated from human nature by law or other manipulations. This foundation of law in natural law contains certain principles that any individual in society is born with, without any regard to the existence of positive law. Natural law has thus self-habitual, self-conducting, self-policing, and self-protecting norms. Natural law does not therefore discriminate between the subjects of its law. These subjects are individual beings, including children. It is on these criteria that the term the "sovereignty of children in law" also benefits from the standard of natural law of children.

4.1. Sovereignty within Positive Law

Whilst the scope of the term "sovereignty of children" might seem narrow, the purposes, aims, intentions and spirit of most relevant international conventions cover this area of law. This may be simply examined within the words of many international conventions which directly or indirectly deal with the rights of the child. Direct international conventions are those international agreements the subject matters of which deal exclusively with the rights of children. Indirect international agreements are those international agreements which do not necessarily deal with the rights of children and their protection but have, by one means or another, dealt with the questions relating to the rights of children.[28] A glance at the historical evolution of the right of children demonstrates this.[29] One of the cornerstones of these international instruments is the 1948 Universal Declaration of Human Rights. The Declaration reads that "Motherhood and childhood are entitled to special care and assistance. All children, whether born in or out of wedlock, shall enjoy the same social protection".[30] The words of the Declaration surely refer to the sovereignty of children, the realm of their rights and where they can receive sufficient protection. This means that the Declaration has a clear tendency to specify

---

[28] Universal Declaration of Human Rights, 1948; Proclamation of Tehran, 1968; Declaration on Social Progress and Development, 1969; Universal Declaration on the Eradication of Hunger and Malnutrition, 1974; Declaration on the Human Rights of Individuals Who are not Nationals of the Country in which They Live, 198; Declaration on the Protection of all Persons from Enforced Disappearance, 1992.

[29] For instance, the 1924 Geneva Declaration of the Rights of the Child is one of the illustrative examples of these international conventions. The words of the declaration are worth stating here. It reads that "1. The child must be given the means requisite for its normal development, both materially and spiritually. 2. The child that is hungry must be fed, the child that is sick must be helped, the child that is backward must be helped, the delinquent child must be reclaimed, and the orphan and the waif must be sheltered and succoured. 3. The child must be the first to receive relief in times of distress. 4. The child must be put in a position to earn a livelihood, and must be protected against every form of exploitation. 5. The child must be brought up in the consciousness that its talents must be devoted to the service of its fellow men."

[30] Article 25 (2). Article 26 (3) of the same Declaration reads that: "Parents have a prior right to choose the kind of education that shall be given to their children."

the rights of the child in a legal context. Although we accept that the Declaration is not a law-making treaty, and does not therefore have the binding effect of international conventions, it is recognized as an integral part of international law of *jus cogens*.[31] Moreover, most of its principles, such as political rights, women rights, children's rights, and cultural rights, have been formulated into many separate international conventions and are therefore considered an integral part of positive international law. Other instruments indirectly referring to the sovereignty of children in law are the 1924 Geneva Declaration of the Rights of the Child, the 1959 Declaration of the Rights of the Child, the 1966 International Covenant on Civil and Political Rights, articles 23 and 24, and the 1966 International Covenant on Economic, Social and Cultural Rights, Article 10.

It must, however, be stated here that with positive law, and the concept of the sovereignty of children, we do not exclusively emphasise the provisions of international conventional law. Certain legislation of states which deal with the rights of children is also the manifestation of the regulation of those rights under a particular realm of law. This creates a recognized region for the rights of children. A clear example is the provisions of the constitutional legislation of Belgium, which clearly contains the wording of the International Convention on the Rights of the Child.[32] In other words, the constitution has confirmed the provisions of the convention on the Rights of the Child concerning the best interest of the child and its power of judgment in different cases.

Obviously, the Convention on the Rights of the Child is one of the most authoritative instruments applicable to the rights of the child within positive international law.[33] The Convention lists a considerable number of rights that are formulated to create direct recognition of the rights of the child in a legal context.[34] The Convention has therefore prescribed the way

---

[31] On *jus cogens* see the relevant section.

[32] See Article 22 bis of the Convention of the Belgium, 2008. It reads that "Chaque enfant a le droit de s'exprimer sur toute question qui le concerne; son opinion est prise en considération, eu égard à son âge et à son discernement. Chaque enfant a le droit de bénéficier des mesures et services qui concourent à son développement. Dans toute décision qui le concerne, l'intérêt de l'enfant est pris en considération de manière primordiale. La loi, le décret ou la règle visée à l'article 134 garantissent ces droits de l'enfant. »

[33] See generally Lawrence J. Leblanc, The Convention On The Rights Of The Child: United Nations Lawmaking On Human Rights (1995).

[34] Examine ibid, pp.65-184.

in which national authorities should deal with the rights of the child and their protection.[35] One may strongly assert that the Convention has a vivid policy for the protection of the rights of the child, and for that reason is one of the most recognized instruments tackling the concept of sovereignty of children in law.[36] This means that the Convention sees all rights as an integral part of one stem.[37] In other words, the provisions of the Convention cannot be read in isolation from one another and are consequently to be seen in conjunction with their main purpose.[38]

Terminologically, the Convention on the Rights of the Child does not refer to the expression of the sovereignty of children or the sovereignty of the child, but it does, however, cover the concept of sovereignty using other terminology. A close examination of its content illustrates this. In its preamble the Convention states that "childhood is entitled to special care and assistance". The parties to the Convention are convinced that "the family, as the fundamental group of society and the natural environment for the growth and well-being of all its members and particularly children, should be afforded the necessary protection and assistance so that it can fully assume its responsibilities within the community". The preamble of the Convention also stresses the recognition of the legal personality of the child, which means in other words a particular realm for its development.[39] It goes further and declares that "the child should be fully prepared to live an individual life in society, and be brought up in the spirit of the ideals proclaimed in the Charter of the United Nations, and in particular in the spirit of peace, dignity, tolerance, freedom, equality and solidarity". The Convention has particularly emphasized "special safeguards and care, including the appropriate legal protection, before as well as after the birth" of the child. What is meant by special safeguards and appropriate protection is not solely and obviously the presentation of the rights of the child, but, creating, recognizing or keeping an exceptional region of law

---

[35] Ibid., at 1-3.

[36] "The Convention is structured in a manner that promotes its use as an instrument in domestic as well as international law and politics." Gary B. *Melton,* Foreword in Implementing The U.N. Convention On The Rights Of The Child: A Standard Of Living Adequate For Development (Arlene Bowers Andrews, Natalie Hevener Kaufman, des., 1999), at vii.

[37] Ibid.

[38] Ibid.

[39] The preamble reads that "Recognizing that the child, for the full and harmonious development of his or her personality, should grow up in a family environment, in an atmosphere of happiness, love and understanding."

for the appropriate safeguarding or development of the rights of the child.[40] "These rights support each human's preparation to live as an individual in society *while a child.* All rights apply regardless of age, although methods to assure the rights vary by the child's age and competence".[41] This is what we have repeatedly called the legal personality of the child or sovereignty of children in law.

One of the most remarkable provisions of the Convention on the Rights of the Child is the limit of the age for the recognition of a person as child. According to it, a child is a person under 18.[42] This means the Convention makes it clear that its provisions are applicable to all those who are under 18 and those persons will be covered by the framework of all children's legislation. Although we do not deny that the provisions of the Convention governing the limit of the age of children have been criticized, the general impression is that the relevant provisions of the Convention put sufficient value on the recognition of the sovereignty of children in law. With the above age, the Convention has therefore emphasized the physical or mental immaturity of a person as an adult and the necessity of a collaborative effort between the contracting parties and the legislations of their homeland as a whole. Undoubtedly, the purpose of the Convention is to provide the necessary support for the protection of a person's legal rights. This is what we call the legal protection of the child in a conventional context. In addition, it is on the basis of the provisions of the convention that the child likewise has the right to live a fully individual life. "Fully" and "an individual life", in the formulations of the Convention, are surely a comparison between childhood adulthood, and their parallel resemblances. The Convention has, at least, recognized two identical periods of life: those who are under eighteen, and all those above it. This means a legitimated key for the presentation of the sovereignty of the law in national and international contexts.

---

[40] For example, Article 27 of the Convention provides attainment of adequate living condition for the development and protection of the rights of children. Arlene Bowers Andrews, *Securing Adequate Living Conditions for Each Child's Development* in IMPLEMENTING THE U.N. CONVENTION ON THE RIGHTS OF THE CHILD: A STANDARD OF LIVING ADEQUATE FOR DEVELOPMENT, at 7.

[41] Ibid., at 4-5.

[42] Article 1.

4.2. The Specific Sources of Law

Since the establishment of the International Court of Justice (ICJ), the provisions of Article 38 of the Statute of the ICJ as the way in which to identify the sources of law in a national, regional or international context have become very familiar.[43] More significantly, the Statute of the ICJ is considered an integral part of the Charter of the United Nations Organization, and is also annexed to it. Modification of the provisions of the Statute can only be carried out under the supervision of the General Assembly, and by a two-thirds majority vote in the Assembly, including ratification by two-thirds of the member states.[44] Since Article 38 of the Statute has not hitherto been modified, and since its provisions have been referred to in various connections as well as in a wider perspective, it could be argued that they have become an integral part of customary law. As a whole Article 38 of the ICJ provides:

a. international conventions, whether general or particular, establishing rules expressly recognized by the contesting states;
b. international custom, as evidence of a general practice accepted as law;
c. the general principles of law recognized by civilized nations;
d. subject to the provisions of Article 59, judicial decisions and the teachings of the most highly qualified publicists of the various nations, as subsidiary means for the determination of rules of law.

Subparagraphs (*a*) and (*b*) (above) refer to conventional and customary law. The function of subparagraph (*c*), as is evident, concerns the general principles of law. But subparagraph *(d)* has several functions regarding the sources of law. It may be divided into judicial decisions, which in its own terms can be divided into national, regional and international decisions and the teachings of the most highly qualified publicists of the various nations. The subparagraph refers to these sources as subsidiary sources of law. It must be stated here that reference to the provisions of Article 38 should not prevent references to other materials as secondary sources of law if certain criteria are integrated into the materials. . Examples of secondary sources are the primary works of legislators, highly significant records of international meetings, and certain resolutions of the Security Council or General Assembly of the United Nations. The value and functions of most of these sources are very briefly studied below.

---

[43] See Ian Brownlie, Principles of Public International Law, 3 (1979).
[44] Article 69.

4.3. Treaties

Treaties are one of the principle sources in positive law for the recognition of the rights of children in law. They simultaneously constitute the most acknowledged legal sources. This is because treaties create clear rights and obligations for the contracting parties. Normally, a treaty's subject matter is developed according to the wishes of the contracting parties, and formulated after a series of negotiations. The binding effect of a treaty is based on *pacta sunt servanda.*[45] This means that the provisions of treaties which have directly or indirectly dealt with the rights of children in law created obligations for the contracting parties; their provisions should not therefore be denied by the states parties.

Treaties relating to the rights of children may be presented under such different names as conventions, agreements, declarations, pacts, protocols or arrangements, though the name of a treaty has nothing to do with its legal validity. Good examples are the 1924 Geneva Declaration of the Rights of the Child, the 1985 United Nations Standard Minimum Rules for the Administration of Juvenile Justice, the 1989 Convention on the Rights of the Child, the 2000 Optional Protocol to the Convention on the Rights of the Child on the Sale of Children, Child Prostitution and Child Pornography, and the 1990 African Charter on the Rights and Welfare of the Child. All these address the special region of law concerning the rights of the child; this is what we call the legal territory of children, or the power of sovereignty of law for children.

The function of treaties is very significant in the system of the sovereignty of children in law because they demonstrate specific rules of conduct that cannot be denied by the contracting parties.[46] However, the provisions of a treaty on the rights of children may also be misinterpreted, and be given another definition: that is one of the general problems of the Convention on the Rights of the Child. It is for this, and many other reasons, that the complementary Optional Protocols to the Convention on the Rights of the Child were added to the main convention in 2000, and these treaties are considered as an integral part of *jus cogens* norms.

---

[45] See above sections.

[46] For instance, the provisions of Article 27 of the Fourth Geneva Convention state that "women shall be especially protected against any attack on their honour, in particular against rape, enforced prostitution, or any form of indecent assault". This means that the provisions of the Article clearly speak about the protection of female children and the criminal nature of violations of their protective rights.

A treaty that has been referred to as an integral part of the international law of *jus cogens* should not be denied by any state, and also be respected by those states that have not ratified the treaty.[47] This is because their maintenance is essential for the safeguarding of human beings and the fundamental recognition of the principles of civilization. One could argue that the provisions of the Convention on the Rights of the Child are regarded as an integral part of the *jus cogens* law, and therefore binding upon all states. A similar conclusion may be reached in the case of other international treaties governing the rights of the child. However, given the present state of the world, there is no authoritative power to list which treaties are considered as an integral part of the *jus cogens* law. The opinions of writers vary considerably, and may depend on the political nature of the question as a whole. Nevertheless, it is clear that certain rules regarding children cannot be rejected, and cannot be neutralized by contrary provisions. Examples are rules governing the prohibition of the use of children in armed conflict, rules regarding the abolition of child slavery, principles concerning the protection of children from unlawful sexual or pornographic exploitations, guarantees dealing with educational rights, provisions regarding criminal or procedural protections within the machinery of justice, the non-application of the death penalty regarding children, the standard of rules regarding institutional treatment and the reintegration of juvenile criminality, prohibition regarding upholding juvenile criminality in adults prisons and jails, and also the prohibition regarding corporal punishment in the juvenile justice system.[48] The above lists, and many other similar rules are an integral part of customary and conventional law and should also, under *jus cogens* norms, be respected by all states.

4.4. Customs

Custom is the second source of law dealing with the concept of the legal protection of children. A customary rule comes from the repetition, duration, and systematic respect of certain acts that seem necessary for the maintenance of national or international relations. It is also possible that a

---

[47] See also section below on *jus cogens*.

[48] See also *Guidelines for the Prevention of Juvenile Delinquency (The Riyadh Guidelines).* G.A. res. 45/112, annex, 45 U.N. GAOR Supp. (No. 49A) at 201, U.N. Doc. A/45/49 (1990); *Rules for the Protection of Juveniles Deprived of their Liberty.* G.A. res. 45/113, annex, 45 U.N. GAOR Supp. (No. 49A) at 205, U.N. Doc. A/45/49 (1990); *Report of the Committee on the Rights of the Child.* U.N. GAOR, 57th Sess., Supp. No. 41, U.N. Doc. A/57/41 (2002).

customary rule governing the protection of children becomes an integral part of conventional law, or a conventional rule, because of its significant value, becomes an integral part of customary law. In the case of the former, the provisions of customary law are formulated into the provisions of a treaty, and are binding on the parties. This is sometimes done with the purpose of preventing any misinterpretation of a customary rule of international law. Good examples are the provisions of customary international law regarding the protection of children in times of armed conflict, which were incorporated in the provisions of the 1948 Geneva Convention, and later conventions.

The provisions of a treaty regarding the protection of children may achieve the status of customary law and be binding over those states which are not parties to the treaty.[49] However, there are certain conditions for accepting that the provisions of a treaty have the effect of customary law. These are for instance: *a)* the significant function of the treaty for the safeguarding of children as a whole; *b)* the moral requirements of the treaty for the perpetuation of equality between children; *c)* the exercise of certain provisions of the treaty within the practice of overwhelming majority of states; *d)* the widespread and systematic repetition of the relevant provisions of the treaty for the purpose of the protection of children; *e)* the judicial value of the provisions for the safe-guarding of children; *f)* the incorporation of those provisions in other mutual or multilateral treaties in the relations of states; *g)* the adoption and formulation of those provisions within the constitution of states, in particular those which are not parties to the treaty; *i)* the entrance of those provisions within different legislations of states; *h)* reference to the provisions of the treaty as the evidence of the existence of customary law, *j)* reference to the provisions of the treaty within *jus cogens* law.

The above list contains some of the conditions for the recognition of treaty provisions as an integral part of customary law. However, it is important to emphasise that not all the above conditions are essential for the recognition of the provisions of a treaty as customary provisions. Still, certain provisions of a treaty on children's rights may reach the standard of admissibility to customary law without fulfilling any of the above conditions—this is when the treaty is ratified by an overwhelming majority of states with the sole purpose of defending children. In addition

[49] For the effect of customary law examine *North Sea Continental Shelf,* I.C.J. 42, 44 (1969). *See* also *Case Concerning the Continental Shelf,* I.C.J. 29 (1985), para.27.

such provisions may be entered into the various provisions of United Nations resolutions, and thus gradually become a part of customary international law. This means that customary law can be developed by various means depending on the requirements of the international community as a whole. Nonetheless, many provisions of customary law can be found within other sources of law for the protection of children. They may be seen within conventional law, general principles of law, resolutions of the United Nations, decisions of Courts, and also within certain norms of the *jus cogens* law. Therefore, separating a customary rule from a conventional rule may be very difficult, depending on their legal values and historical strength.

4.5. General Principles of Law

General principles of law are also one of the authoritative sources for recognizing the rights of children and their protection under the term "sovereignty of children in law". General principles of law refer to those rules and provisions that are generally practiced under different national legal systems for protecting children under such provisions of law as family law, criminal law, procedural law, and marriage or divorce law. Socially, general principles of law are those accepted and settled rules between civilizations of mankind concerning the protection of children, which we can expect to find in the legislation of most states, and contribute to the development of international provisions for the protection of children. This means that for the effective protection and prevention of violations of children's rights, general principles of law may be formulated into the provisions of international treaties. The separation of general principles of law, customary law and conventional law may thus be very difficult, and overlap one another in substance.[50]

---

[50] For instance, regarding sexual intercourse, it is stated that "Sexual violence affects a nexus of rights under international protection. The right to life, to physical and psychological integrity, to security, to personal liberty, and to dignity and honour form part of the essential principles of human rights or the so-called core rights, which should be respected by states. These rights are part of the conventional law of human rights and form part of customary international law". Statement by the Commission for the Historical Clarification of Human Rights Violations and Acts of Violence concerning the suffering to the Population of Guatemala. *Report from the United Nations Commission of the Secretary-General* (1994). http://shr.aaas.org/guatemala/ceh/mds/spanish/toc.html (Spanish), *Cited* and *Quoted* in Ana Elena Obado, the International Criminal Court: An Opportunity

The usefulness of general principles of law is that they may encourage the comparative aspects of law regarding the protection of children. These may include conflicts of law governing the juvenile criminal justice system, *ne bis in idem,* the problems of interpretation, application and implementation of certain laws concerning the protection of those children who have been the subjects of the abuse of rights within two different legal systems, and the cooperation and assistance between different legal systems for solving certain penal matters.

One of the most serious problems with the general principles of law as a source of protection of the rights of children is that they may lack the unanimous agreement of states with respect to a particular term or definition strengthening the protection of the rights of children. That is why the general principles of law require common compliance between the legislation of different states in order to place them under the absolute principles regarding the protection of the rights of children in a juridical context. In any event, one has to be very cautious regarding the choice of those principles which are commonly accepted between various nations as general principles of law for the protection of children. This is because the recognition of the general principles of law may not be easy, and may require different cultural attitudes to be taken into consideration. For instance, although the prohibition regarding corporal punishment of children or juveniles is considered one of the core elements of customary, conventional and general principles of law, interpretations of what constitutes corporal punishment may vary according to culture.[51] For example, punitive interference with the daily food, sleep and living conditions of juvenile criminals might not be regarded as corporal punishment by all nations,[52] but they should be, as a general rule of the protection of the rights of children:[53] This is implicit in the intentions of positive law regarding the protection of children.[54] Similar conclusions may be drawn with regard to humiliation, personal injury, mental abuse,

---

for Women (2004) www.whrnet.org/docs/issue-international_court.html - 69k (last visited Oct.27, 2006).

[51] But for more study see *also* Readings in Juvenile Justice Administration (Feld, Barry C., Ed, 1999). International Handbook On Juvenile Justice (Shoemaker, Donald, ed. 1996).

[52] Consult also United Nations 1985 *Standard Minimum Rules for the Administration of Juvenile Justice (The Beijing Rules).* G.A. Res. 40/33, 40U.N. GAOR Supp. No. 53 at 207, U.N. Doc. A/40/53.

[53] Ibid.

[54] Ibid.

and harassment.[55] All these may come under the Bill of Rights for Young Offenders which was suggested at the United Nations, but which was finally named the Standard Minimum Rules for the Administration of Juvenile Justice.[56] Consequently, the Standard Minimum Rules speak about the respect of legal personality of juveniles.[57]

4.6. Resolutions

The resolutions of certain international bodies are a good source for the recognition of the rights of children in the national, regional and international arenas. Thus, the national authorities of a state may be under certain obligations to respect the provisions of a resolution of the Security Council, the General Assembly, the International Labour Organization, and the European Union. Although all the resolutions of those international bodies are not authoritative and do not create legislative power, they may nevertheless have significance for the recognition of children's rights of or create *soft law*. For example, although the UDHR, adopted by the General Assembly, is not a treaty, and does not therefore impose any legal obligations on states, its provisions are certainly important with regard to children and the sovereignty of children in law, and are considered an integral part of customary law and *jus cogens* norms.

It is possible that a resolution of the General Assembly, which is accepted by the vote of the majority of member states, creates rights for the protection of children and therefore duties and obligations for member states. Resolutions may therefore contribute to the development of customary or conventional law. They may also have a '*quasi legislative*

---

[55] Ibid.

[56] Ibid.

[57] "Many of the United Nations rules concerning juveniles under arrest or awaiting trial reiterate provisions found in global and regional human rights treaties. The main thrust of the Rules in this area is that pre-trial detention should only be used after considering alternative measures such as close supervision, placement with a family or in an educational setting or home. However, once in detention, juveniles should be kept in a separate institution from adults or in a separate part of an institution also holding adults and only for the shortest possible period. While in custody juveniles should receive all social, educational, vocational, psychological, medical and physical care taking into account their age, gender and personality". Geraldine Van Bueren and Anne-Marie Tootell., *United Nations Standard Minimum Rules for the Administration of Juvenile Justice: Beijing Rules, child-abuse.com/childhouse/...rights/dci_be29.html, visited on 2010-11-09.*

force', and for that reason be considered as *'soft laws'* creating obligations for all states. This is particularly imperative in the case of resolutions of the General Assembly which aim to safeguard certain principal rights of children such as the prohibition of death penalty, prohibition of corporal punishment, rules regarding the prohibition of the use of children in armed conflicts, and the promotion of social justice. Many resolutions may also reemphasize the rights of children which have already been formulated within other internationally recognized human rights law instruments. The General Assembly of the United Nations has especially been active in the area of children's right.[58] And that is more or less the same in the case of resolutions of the Security Council,[59] which has, for instance, expressed "deep concern about the growing number of attacks or threats of attacks in contravention of applicable international law against schools and educational facilities, and teachers and pupils, in particular the specific targeting of girls and in this regard calls upon all parties to armed conflict to cease immediately these violations of international humanitarian law".[60] The Council is here emphasizing the importance of the maintenance of humanitarian law in the case of children.

---

[58] For instance see resolutions of the General Assembly A/RES/64/146 3 Mar 2010 Rights of the Child; A/RES/63/24113 Mar 2009 Rights of the child; A/Res/62/14122 Feb 2008 Rights of the Child; A/Res/61/146 9 Nov 2006 Rights of the Child; A/RES/60/231 9 Dec 2005 Rights of the Child; A/RES/59/261 24 Feb 2005 Rights of the Child; A/RES/58/157 9 Mar 2004 Rights of the Child; A/RES/57/190 19 Feb 2003 The Rights of the Child; A/RES/56/138 19 Dec 2001 The rights of the child; A/RES/55/79 4 Dec 2000 The rights of the child; A/RES/54/263 25 May 2000 Optional protocols to the Convention on the Rights of the Child; A/RES/54/149 17 Dec 1999 The rights of the child; A/RES/53/128 9 Dec 1998 The rights of the child: A/RES/51/77 20 Feb 1997 Rights of the Child.

[59] For instance see resolutions of the Security Council S/PRST/2010/10 16 Jun 2010 Statement by the President of the Security Council; S/RES/1882 (2009) 4 Aug 2009 Resolution 1882 (2009); S/PRST/2009/9 29 Apr 2009 Statement by the President of the Security Council; S/PRST/2008/28 17 Jul 2008 Statement by the President of the Security Council; S/PRST/2008/6 12 Feb 2008 Statement by the President of the Security Council; S/PRST/2006/48 28 Nov 2006 Statement by the President of the Security Council; S/RES/1612 (2005) 25 Jul 2005 Resolution 1612 (2005); S/RES/1539 (2004) 22 Apr 2004 Resolution 1539 (2004); S/RES/1460 (2003) 30 Jan 2003 Resolution 1460 (2003); S/RES/1379 (2001) 20 Nov 2001 Resolution 1379 (2001); S/RES/1314 (2000) 11 Aug 2000 Resolution 1314 (2000); S/RES/1261 (1999) 25 Aug 1999 Resolution 1261 (1999).

[60] Resolution of the Security Council S/PRST/2010/10 16 Jun 2010, Statement by the President of the Security Council. The resolution further "underscores the importance of training in child rights and child protection for all personnel involved in United Nations peacekeeping, peace building and political missions."

One or more of the following conditions are essential for a resolution of the General Assembly to be identified as law-creating rights for the protection of the child:[61]

i) A resolution of the General Assembly may pertain to an already existing treaty, agreement, convention, protocol or declarations concerning certain rights of children.[62]

ii) A resolution may refer to the duties of states concerning the full respect of a definite international convention.[63]

iii) A resolution may refer to the already existing practice of states concerning the existence of certain rights regarding the safeguarding of children.[64]

---

[61] For the examination of the resolutions of the Security Council or the General Assembly see Farhad Malekian., The Monopolization of International Criminal Law in the United Nations, a Jurisprudential Approach (1993), and (1995).

[62] For example see Resolution 64/293, 12 August 2010 of the General Assembly which refers to the valuable function of the following instruments: United Nations Convention against Transnational Organized Crime and the Protocol to Prevent, Suppress and Punish Trafficking in Persons, Especially Women and Children, supplementing the United Nations Convention against Transnational Organized Crime, the Forced Labour Convention, 1930 (No. 29), the Worst Forms of Child Labour Convention, 1999 (No. 182) of the International Labour Organization, the Supplementary Convention on the Abolition of Slavery, the Slave Trade, and Institutions and Practices Similar to Slavery, the Convention on the Rights of the Child and the Optional Protocols thereto on the sale of children, child prostitution and child pornography and on the involvement of children in armed conflict, and the Convention on the Elimination of All Forms of Discrimination against Women. See *also* Resolution 60/147, 21 March 2006 relating to Basic Principles and Guidelines on the Right to a Remedy and Reparation for Victims of Gross Violations of International Human Rights Law and Serious Violations of International Humanitarian Law which refers to article 39 of the Convention on the Rights of the Child. See also Resolution 60/1, 24 October 2005 concerning to World Summit Outcome. The resolution reemphasizes the importance of the provisions of the International Labour Organization Convention No. 182.

[63] *Ibid.*

[64] Such is G.A. Resolution 61/295 of 2 October 2007 regarding the United Nations Declaration on the Rights of Indigenous Peoples which states that "Indigenous peoples have the collective right to live in freedom, peace and security as distinct peoples and shall not be subjected to any act of genocide or any other act of violence, including forcibly removing children of the group to another group... Indigenous individuals, particularly children, have the right to all levels and forms of education of the State without discrimination".

iv) The content of a resolution may refer to the existence of a norm of customary law governing the security of children.[65]

v) A resolution which aims to promote those fundamental social relations which are a necessary condition for the protection of children.[66]

vi) A resolution which intends to eliminate a particular disease against children.[67]

vii) A resolution which is voted with the ambition of preventing a wrongful act against children.[68]

viii) The content of a resolution which recognizes certain acts as crimes against children.[69]

ix) A resolution which reaffirms the abolition of slavery, prohibition of domestic child labour, condemnation of prostitution, sexual exploitation and pornography of children.[70]

---

[65] For instance see G.A. Resolution 63/1, 8 October 2008 governing the Political declaration on Africa's development needs. It states that "We note with concern that violence against women and children everywhere continues and often increases, and resolve to ensure the strict universal adherence to international norms regarding violence against women and girls".

[66] For instance see G.A. Resolution 60/1, 24 October 2005 concerning the World Summit Outcome. It reads that "We reaffirm our commitment to support developing country efforts to ensure that all children have access to and complete free and compulsory primary education of good quality, to eliminate gender inequality and imbalance and to renew efforts to improve girls' education".

[67] See G.A. Resolution S-26/2, 2 August 2001 setting out the Declaration of Commitment on HIV/AIDS. The resolution deals with different rights of children concerning their health conditions. It has, in particular, pointed out that Children orphaned and affected by HIV/AIDS need special assistance. See G.A. Resolution 60/1, 24 October 2005 concerning to World Summit Outcome. The resolution mobilizes *inter alia* members of the General Assembly for the prevention of HIV/AIDS, malaria, tuberculosis, reducing child mortality and other health issues. It concerns in particular orphaned and vulnerable children.

[68] Examine different provisions of G.A. Resolution 60/1, 24 October 2005 concerning to World Summit Outcome.

[69] See G.A. Resolution 60/1, 24 October 2005. Due to the content of the resolution, states have to eliminate "all forms of discrimination and violence against women and the girl child, including by ending impunity and by ensuring the protection of civilians, in particular women and the girl child, during and after armed conflicts in accordance with the obligations of States under international humanitarian law and international human rights law".

[70] Such as G.A. Resolution 64/293**.** The resolution *inter alia* reaffirms the work of different bodies of the UN. For instance, it refers to the works of the "Commission on Human Rights decision 2004/110 of 19 April 2004, by which the Commission

x) A resolution which emphasizes the prevention of a particular sanction against children.[71]

xi) The subject of a resolution which is intended to recognize the legal sovereignty of children in order to safeguard their rights.[72]

xii) When certain provisions of a resolution re-emphasize the importance of the maintenance of the guarantees for the rights of the child in times of armed conflict.[73]

xiii) When a resolution promotes effective recognition of the rights of the child.[74]

---

appointed the Special Rapporteur on trafficking in persons, especially women and children, to highlight the importance of a victim-centred, rights-based approach to combating trafficking in persons, especially women and children, Human Rights Council resolution 6/14 of28 September 2007, by which the Council appointed the Special Rapporteur on contemporary forms of slavery, including its causes and consequences, Commission on Human Rights resolution 1990/68 of 7 March 1990, by which the Commission appointed the Special Rapporteur on the sale of children, child prostitution and child pornography, and the General Assembly resolution 62/141 of 18 December 2007, in which the Assembly requested the Secretary-General to appoint a Special Representative on violence against children, and noting the appointment of the Special Representative of the Secretary-General on sexual violence in conflict".

[71] See G.A. Resolution 27/2, 11 October 2002 concerning "A world fit for children". The resolution encourages the states members of the UN to "Assess and monitor regularly the impact of sanctions on children and take urgent and effective measures in accordance with international law with a view to alleviating the negative impact of economic sanctions on women and children".

[72] See G.A. Resolution 4/185, 3 Dec. 1986 concerning the Declaration on Social and Legal Principles relating to the Protection and Welfare of Children, with Special Reference to Foster Placement and Adoption Nationally and Internationally. For instance see G.A. Resolution 60/1, 24 October 2005 concerning the World Summit Outcome has under the title "Protecting children in situations of armed conflict" dealt with many rights of children and acts which constitute crimes against children.

[73] For instance see G.A. Resolution 60/1, 24 October 2005 concerning the World Summit Outcome has under the title "Protecting children in situations of armed conflict" dealt with many rights of children and acts which constitute crimes against children.

[74] G.A. Resolution 60/1, 24 October 2005 referring to the World Summit Outcome emphasizes the effective protection of the rights of the child. It reads that "Children's rights: 141. We express dismay at the increasing number of children involved in and affected by armed conflict, as well as all other forms of violence, including domestic violence, sexual abuse and exploitation and trafficking. We support cooperation policies aimed at strengthening national capacities to improve the situation of those children and to assist in their rehabilitation and reintegration

xiv) A resolution of the United Nations which mobilizes economic help for the safety of children who are victims of social poverty, discrimination, epidemic, or natural catastrophes.[75]

xv) The content of a resolution which is mobilized against certain cultural practices that violate obviously natural or positive rights of children.[76]

xvi) A resolution which strengthens juvenile criminal justice for the purpose of their protection.[77]

xvii) A resolution which encourages cooperation and assistance between states for the sake of protection of the rights of the child.[78]

---

into society. 142. We commit ourselves to respecting and ensuring the rights of each child without discrimination of any kind, irrespective of the race, colour, sex, language, religion, political or other opinion, national, ethnic or social origin, property, disability, birth or other status of the child or his or her parent(s) or legal guardian(s). We call upon States to consider as a priority becoming a party to the Convention on the Rights of the Child".

[75] Examine the content of G.A. Resolution 27/2, 11 October 2002 concerning "A world fit for children". The resolution states, for instance, that "Discrimination gives rise to a self-perpetuating cycle of social and economic exclusion and undermines children's ability to develop to the fullest. We will make every effort to eliminate discrimination against children, whether rooted in the child's or his or her parent's or legal guardian's race, colour, sex, language, religion, political or other opinion, national, ethnic or social origin, property, disability, birth or other status".

[76] See G.A. Resolution 48/104, 20 Dec. 1993 concerning Declaration on the Elimination of Violence against Women.

[77] See G.A. Resolution 55/59, 17 January 2001 containing the Vienna Declaration on Crime and Justice: Meeting the Challenges of the Twenty-first Century. The resolution aims to "recognize with great concern that juveniles in difficult circumstances are often at risk of becoming delinquent or easy candidates for recruitment by criminal groups, including groups involved in transnational organized crime, and we commit ourselves to undertaking countermeasures to prevent this growing phenomenon and to including, where necessary, provisions for juvenile justice in national development plans and international development strategies and to including the administration of juvenile justice in our funding policies for development cooperation". See *also* G.A. Resolution 52/86, 12 December 199. The annexed to the resolution deals with Model Strategies and Practical Measures on the Elimination of Violence against Women in the Field of Crime Prevention and Criminal Justice.

[78] See G.A. Resolution S-26/2, 2 August 2001 setting out the Declaration of Commitment on HIV/AIDS. Study *also* the content of G.A. Resolution 27/2, 11 October 2002 concerning "A world fit for children".

4.7. Court Decisions

The courts' decisions are also another source of the recognition of the rights of children: they help to clarify certain rules, provisions, norms, or principles that are unclear, or where there has been serious controversy about their nature and use. These decisions are therefore key to the successive national, regional or international implementation of children's rights. However, it must be stressed that court decisions do not have the same character as a treaty law, because a decision expresses the final opinion of judges regarding the evidence given in a specific case and may not be used in other cases. Article 38 of the Statute of International Court of Justice also mentions this. It further provides that, subject to the provisions of Article 59 of the Court, judicial decisions are considered "as subsidiary means for the determination of the rules of law". Article 59 further states, "the decision of the Court has no binding force except between the parties and in respect of that particular case".

Despite the fact that the decisions of courts are not authoritative in all cases regarding the protection of children's rights, they have a significant function in interpreting international law, regional law and national legislations. For instance, the decisions of international criminal tribunals such as the ICTY, the ICTR, the Special Court for Sierra Leone, and the ICC have, impressively, increased the value of their statutes governing the protection of the rights of children in national or international armed conflicts.[79] The statements of the relevant tribunals have also been helpful in improving case law and the illumination of certain provisions relating to the interpretation of the law governing the protection of the rights of the child.[80]

However one should not confuse the decisions of national, regional, and international courts. Although all three have more or less similar functions for finding the truth and the implementation of certain provisions, their roles can, without doubt, broadly differ from one another. This is because the laws used and referred to in an international or regional court may be quite different from the laws referred to in a national court.[81] The reason is

---

[79] Valerie Oosterveld, *The Special Court for Sierra Leone, Child Soldiers and Forced Marriage: Providing Clarity or Confusion? 45* Canadian Yearbook of International Law (2007), pp.131-72.
[80] *Ibid.*
[81] For instance, although the provisions of the Convention on the Rights of the Child have achieved the level of *jus cogens international law*, its provisions are

that international courts are not necessarily bound by the provisions of national legislations while the reverse is not true.[82] This means that national courts *should*, within the process of justice, refer to regional and international legislations regarding the protection of the children's rights; however they do not.[83] That is why regional or international courts become responsible, owing to the principle of complementarity, for investigating serious cases regarding the violations of the rights of children, albeit that the process is very expensive. The complementarity principle establishes a legal duty over states to extradite and prosecute accused persons. Another of the reasons why national cases may be reinvestigated in regional courts is that a national court may firmly believe that the true application of the law has been fulfilled, and that it has not consequently made any incorrect interpretation or application of national, regional or international law. This is one of the essential reasons why the number of petitions is growing in regional courts. There may be a regular relationship and cooperation between several courts concerning the competence of juridical authorities dealing with the rights of children and the misinterpretation or misuse of their rights.

---

selectively entered into national legal systems which reduces the value of the Convention. Two of the most valuable and protective articles of the Convention are Articles 38 and 39. The articles have a core function for the protection of the rights of children in times of armed conflicts. Article 38 reads that "1. States Parties undertake to respect and to ensure respect for rules of international humanitarian law applicable to them in armed conflicts which are relevant to the child. 2. States Parties shall take all feasible measures to ensure that persons who have not attained the age of fifteen years do not take a direct part in hostilities. 3. States Parties shall refrain from recruiting any person who has not attained the age of fifteen years into their armed forces. In recruiting among those persons who have attained the age of fifteen years but who have not attained the age of eighteen years, States Parties shall endeavour to give priority to those who are oldest. 4. In accordance with their obligations under international humanitarian law to protect the civilian population in armed conflicts, States Parties shall take all feasible measures to ensure protection and care of children who are affected by an armed conflict ." Article 39 of the same Convention provides that "States Parties shall take all appropriate measures to promote physical and psychological recovery and social reintegration of a child victim of: any form of neglect, exploitation, or abuse; torture or any other form of cruel, inhuman or degrading treatment or punishment; or armed conflicts. Such recovery and reintegration shall take place in an environment which fosters the health, self-respect and dignity of the child".

[82] See the Statute of the International Criminal Court (ICC).

[83] For example, Sweden has been very slow about this matter.

In general, the decisions of national, regional or international courts are very valuable in determining the law and the protection of children's rights.[84] However, one has to exercise caution regarding the decisions of those national courts which have harsh laws and where the provisions of international law or international criminal law regarding the protection of children's rights are very poorly implemented within their systems.[85] This means that the decisions of those courts are not useful in the development of the law, and may even be harmful for the protection of the sovereignty of children in law. The laws referred to by these courts are most commonly known as one party, law such as the national legislation of Iran, which is based on religious 1 laws and a theological understanding of certain authorities in law.[86]

4.8. National Laws

Another source for determining the rights of children is national legislation, which can be of different kinds. The constitution of a state may thus directly refer to the protective rights of children and make their support and implementation one of the significant functions of the constitution. Similarly, national legislations may, in various ways, develop rights for children and make it clear that their violations are dealt with by the administration of justice. The legislations concerning the protection of the rights of children may be found under the provisions of criminal law,

[84] For instance see *Prosecutor v. Thomas Lubanga Dyilo*, International Criminal Court (ICC), Case No. ICC-01/04-01/06, Warrant of Arrest, February 10, 2006, http://www.icc-cpi.int/library/cases/ICC-01-04-01-06-2_English.pdf.
In fact, Lubanga is the first suspect to face charges against him under the jurisdiction of the permanent International Criminal Court. Serious violations of the system of international criminal law have been brought against him, in particular the use of children as soldiers which is the consequence of the atrocities in the Democratic Republic of the Congo during 2004. Lubanga was brought to the first public pre-trial hearing of the permanent Court on 20 March 2006. The Court lists among other acts of atrocities "enlisting and conscripting children under the age of fifteen and using them to participate actively in hostilities". The work of the Court has not, however, ended and the case will be one of the most valuable in consolidating the rights of children in a time of armed conflict.

[85] An illustrative example is the criminal legislation of the Islamic Republic of Iran.

[86] In particular, it is important to note that, juvenile courts completely ceased functioning after the revolution in Iran, in 1979. Ismail Sadri, Child Criminality in the City of Tehran and the Method of its Prevention (original language Persian, 1993), p. 63.

criminal procedure, family law, inheritance law, economic law, taxation law, social law, medical law, and environment law.

It is worth mentioning at this point that the provisions of the national legislation of a state are solely applicable within the territory of that state, and not any other territory. This is because all states have, in the international legal community, an independent international personality and their laws and legislations are accommodated for the purpose of implementation in the territories which are under their jurisdiction.[87] This means that the application of national legislation is restricted and cannot be enforceable over the nationals of other states. However, it is true that in certain cases, the laws of a state may be applicable to the children of other nationals if they have come under the jurisdiction of the relevant states. Good examples are children who have been granted asylum or been given refugee status. In this case, they are the protective subjects of the receiving state. [88] In any event, the provisions of the human rights law must give priority to the provisions of the national legislations if the latter do not offer higher security.

4.9. Publicists

Article 38 of the Statute of the ICJ refers to the teachings of the most highly qualified publicists/doctrines as a subsidiary source for the recognition of the rights of the child.[89] This source has been valuable for the progressive development of the law and its interpretation within

---

[87] Rochelle D. Jackson, *The War Over Children's Rights: And Justice for All? Equalizing the Rights of Children."* Buffalo Human Rights Law Review (1999) 223; David William Archard, Children, Family, and the State (2003); Michael J. Dale, *The Supreme Court and the Minimization of Children's Constitutional Rights: Implications for the Juvenile Justice System, Hamline Journal of Public Law and Policy* (summer, 1992); Katherine Hunt, Federle., *Constructing Rights for Children*, Family Law Quarterly (1993l); Sarah H. Ramsey., and E. Abrams Douglas. 2003. *Children and the Law in a Nutshell.* (2d ed., 2003); Susan Gluck Mezey., Constitutional Adjudication of Children's Rights Claims in the United States Supreme Court, 1953–92." *Family Law Quarterly* (1993); John E. Coons, Robert H. Mnookin, and Stephen D. Sugar-man. *Puzzling over Children's Rights*, Brigham Young University Law Review (1991); John, Mary. Children's Rights And Power: Charging Up for a New Century (2003).

[88] They are protected due to the provisions of refugee law and national law.

[89] In *North Sea Continental Shelf Case*, *opinio juris* was regarded as important evidence for the settlement of customary international law. *North Sea Continental Shelf* (1969), ICJ 42, 44.

different national legal systems. This means that the opinions of certain writers on the rights of children have a constructive effect for its improvement and implementation. Within the system of international law, an international court may refer to the opinions of a highly qualified publicist to illustrate certain matters or prove certain interpretations. Moreover, the views of a writer may be useful in the development of the idea of the protection of children's rights within the instruments of the United Nations, and clarify certain criteria. And the opinions of a writer who has been officially authorized by the United Nations to investigate a case may be presented in a report.[90]

---

[90] For instance see Human Rights in Palestine and Other Occupied Arab territories. Report of the United Nations Fact Finding Mission on the Gaza Conflict, A/HRC/12/48, 15 September 2009. The report by Justice Richard Goldstone is one of the best known, and is valuable in demonstrating the views of the United Nations, presenting the views of a publicist, and evaluating the huge suffering of children in the Gaza Strip. It surely demands the protection of the sovereignty of children in law and the prevention of national, regional and international crimes against their rights. Among many valuable examples of the violation children's rights, the report states that "The detention of members of the Palestinian Legislative Council by Israel insofar as it is based on political affiliation, [it] is unrelated to their individual behaviour and prevents those members from participating in the conduct of public affairs, is in violation of Articles 25 and 26 of ICCPR that provide for equal protection under the law and the right to take part in the conduct of public affairs. The detention also constitutes an instance of collective punishment prohibited under article 33 of the GC IV. The same can be said about the massive detention of adults and children. Detention of children in inhuman or degrading conditions and without the guarantees required by international law is also a violation of their rights under ICCPR and the Convention on the Rights of the Child". *Ibid.,* para.1740. According to the report for the protection of the rights of children, "The release of children should be an utmost priority". Para. 1769. The report has also emphasized the important function of the occupying power to provide equal protection for the children of the occupied nation. It states: "The Mission notes, with concern, that Israel has not provided the same level of protection from rockets and mortars to affected Palestinian citizens as it has to Jewish citizens. In particular, it has failed to provide public shelters or fortification of schools, for example, to the Palestinian community living in the unrecognized villages and some of the recognized communities. It ought to go without saying that the thousands of Palestinian Israelis– including a significant number of children – who live within the range of rocket fire, deserve the same protection as the Israeli Government provides to its Jewish citizens". Para. 1699.

Writers' opinions are also referred to in the presentation of cases brought before international courts by one group against another:[91] these opinions may be discussed from various points of view by the conflicting parties.[92] This also occurs in international cases of the protection of children's rights. In any event, great caution must be exercised when referencing writers' opinions, because there may be conflicting opinions about the legal reasoning and validity of the same case. Writers may even be bound by the official policy of their own states and thus not be impartial. Still, it is equally possible that their opinions will not be valued by national legal authorities, and thus be ignored at the time of application. For instance, the Iranian legal authorities have not taken into consideration opinion on the protection of children's rights, so the legal sovereignty of children has thus been violated by the authorities. Clear examples of these violations are the application of capital or corporal punishment to persons under 18.[93]

4.10. *Jus Cogens*

To some writers, *jus cogens* solely expresses the normative position of certain rules or provisions and thus does not constitute a source, but this argument has been correctly dismissed. According to some writers, "Although *jus cogens* 'compelling law' is not mentioned in the ICJ Statute's list of formal international law sources, it has become increasingly recognized as an international law source essential for recognizing the comparative authority of international legal norms".[94] "*Jus cogens*" therefore constitutes another source of the recognition of children's rights. The difference between this and other sources of law is that *jus cogens* cannot be modified by the rules or provisions of (eg) national or international law. Normally, *jus cogens* norms have priority to

---

[91] See case concerning the Application of the Convention on the Prevention and Punishment o f the Crime of Genocide (Bosnia and Herzegovina v. Yugoslavia (Serbia and Montenegro) (1996).

[92] Farhad Malekian, The Basic Principles for Recognition and Prevention of Crimes Against Humanity, No: 6, 7 Law and Political Science Quarterly, (Iran, 2009), pp.230-231.

[93] The Iranian legislation has, despite the ratification of the Convention on the Rights of the Child and International Covenant on Civil and Political Rights by the Iranian government, permitted executions of juvenile offenders. The administration of justice has, therefore, been deeply involved in serious violations of the rights of children. See_www.petitiononline.com/sce/.

[94] International Human Rights and Humanitarian Law (Francisco Forrest Martin, Stephen J. Schnably, Richard Wilson, Jonathan Simon, Mark Tushnet, editors, 2006), p.31.

all other systems of laws, and they have very high legal and moral value. In international law *jus cogens* norms are also recognized as peremptory norms. These are norms which are fundamental to the maintenance of international legal order, peace, justice, equality, and the safeguarding of human civilization as a whole. These norms are accepted by the international community of states as having a very effective function in the prevention of unjust treatments and the protection of mankind; they are to be respected by all states without any due consideration to their political, juridical, economic and military strength.

The 1980 Vienna Convention on the Law of Treaty is considered the basic source of the recognition of *jus cogens* norms. It states, "A treaty is void if, at the time of its conclusion, it conflicts with a peremptory norm of general international law". It further concludes that for the purposes of the Convention, "a peremptory norm of general international law is a norm accepted and recognized by the international community of states as a whole as a norm from which no derogation is permitted and which can be modified only by a subsequent norm of general international law having the same character". For this reason, a *jus cogens* norm generally refers to the position of certain provisions, rules, regulations or principles, the respect and application of which are obligatory for all states. Some of the recognized norms of *jus cogens* concerning the rights of the child are the right to life, to adequate food, to have a legal identity, the prohibition of torture, crimes against humanity, war crimes, various protections of children in time of armed conflict, the abolition of child slavery, the prohibition of the execution of juveniles and the criminalization of child exploitation or pornography.[95]

---

[95]The prohibition of child pornography is doubtlessly one of the consolidated norms of *jus cogens* law. This can be examined within provisions of national legislations, general principles of law, customary law, decisions of courts, and treaty laws. For instance, according to Article 8 of the Optional Protocol to the Convention on the Rights of the Child on the Sale of Children, Child prostitution and Child Pornography, "States Parties shall adopt appropriate measures to protect the rights and interests of child victims of the practices prohibited under the present Protocol at all stages of the criminal justice process…" These provisions are also strengthened by the provisions of Article 9, which states that "States Parties shall adopt or strengthen, implement and disseminate laws, administrative measures, social policies and programs to prevent the offences referred to in the present Protocol. Particular attention shall be given to protect children who are especially vulnerable to such practices…"

4.11. *Obligatio Erga Omnes*

One of the significant functions of a *jus cogens* norm is that it clarifies certain rights as being the absolute rights of children, and unchangeable, which means that they have the character of *obligatio erga omnes*, implying that they are obligatory and impossible to be denied by any state. In other words, "*obligatio erga omnes*" denotes the permanent character of certain protective rights of children and their non-changeability within national provisions. A state is therefore under a recognized international duty to combine all its relevant national rules with the sole function and spirit of *obligatio erga omnes*, such as rules regarding the protection of juveniles under the criminal justice system, the unchallengeable rights of children regarding *guardian ad item* for the purpose of their welfare, and the rules governing the prohibition of child soldiers.[96]The significance of the principle of *obligatio erga omnes* was emphasized in the *Barcelona Traction* case. The ICJ stated that:

> … an essential distinction should be drawn between the obligations of a State towards the international community as a whole, and those arising vis-à-vis another State in the field of diplomatic protection. By their very nature, the former are the concern of all States. In view of the importance of the rights involved, all States can be held to have a legal interest in their protection; they are obligations *erga omnes*…Such obligations derive, for example, in contemporary international law, from the outlawing of acts of aggression, and of genocide, as also from the principles and rules concerning the basic rights of the human person, including protection from slavery and racial discrimination. Some of the corresponding rights of protection have entered into the body of general international law … others are conferred by international instruments of a universal or quasi-universal character.[97]

It must be said that many international conventions or instruments concerning the protection of children should be regarded as an integral part of *jus cogens* law, and therefore obligatory for all states. These include the Convention on the Rights of the Child; the 2000 Optional Protocol to the Convention on the Rights of the Child on the Involvement of Children in Armed Conflict; the 2000 Optional Protocol to the

---

[96] See *Farhad Malekian, Prohibition Governing Child Soldiers Constituting an Integral Part of Jus Cogens and Obligatio Erga Omnes,* XVII World Congress of The International Association of Youth and Family Judges and Magistrates (2006).
[97] *Barcelona Traction*, Light and Power CO. Ltd. (Belg.v.Spain), 1970 I.C.J. 3, 32-33 (Feb. 5).

Convention on the Rights of the Child, on the Sale of Children, Child Prostitution and Child Pornography; the 1980 Hague Convention on the Civil Aspects of International Child Abduction; and the 1993 Hague Convention on Protection of Children and Cooperation in respect of Inter-Country. It could even be argued that certain provisions of the 1980 European Convention on Recognition and Enforcement of Decisions concerning Custody of Children and on the Restoration of Custody of Children raise it to the status of *jus cogens* law, and it should therefore be respected by all states given that its provisions are key to the protection of the rights of children as a whole.[98]

One of the great functions of *jus cogens* law is to invalidate a rule, provision, norm or practice which is inconsistent with any of the peremptory norms. Such practices or rules may be a part of a definite mutual and multilateral agreement or an integral part of national legislation. This means that the provisions of any treaty which are inconsistent with a norm of *jus cogens* are valid. A hypothetical example would be a treaty permitting child slavery. Since trafficking in children and slavery are prohibited, the provisions of such treaties would be invalid, and violate jus cogens norms. Other norms which have achieved *jus cogens* status are those abolishing capital punishment or those prohibiting corporal punishment.

However caution must be exercised in the case of rules, provisions or practices under national law, because whilst it is true that many of the provisions of national law may be against the peremptory norms of international law, they may still be valid; and this is because national legislation does not necessarily follow the inviolable characters of *jus cogens* norms. The reason is very controversial and mistreating the international validity of *jus cogens* norms. National legislation unfortunately follows the principle of international legal personality which is an integral part of the sovereignty of states and this inviolable principle can make the formulation and implementation of *jus cogens* norms rather irregular. The fact is that states are not necessarily under international compulsion to follow *jus cogens* norms because there is no international body with executive authority. Although most norms of *jus cogens* routinely follow the principle of *obligatio erga omnes*, they are practically

[98] The European Convention has similar structure to the Hague Convention on the Civil Aspects of International Child Abduction concluded in 1980 and entered into force in 1983. Both conventions deal with the return of the child abducted from one state to another.

powerless and have mostly been violated by states of the international legal community as a whole. Examples are Iraq, Rwanda, Darfur, Yugoslavia, China, Russia, Iran, the United States, the United Kingdom and even some Scandinavian countries. The principle of international legal personality does not permit legal or forceful integration of *jus cogens* norms into the national legislations of states. The result is that many consolidated international rights of children do not reach the judicial machinery of states and are virtually blocked by the principle of international legal personality of states. This looseness concerning *jus cogens* norms not only applies to such core crimes as genocide, crimes against humanity, aggression, slavery, apartheid, and discrimination, but also much more easily to the natural rights of children within domestic systems. These states have forgotten that "the protection of *jus cogens* norms is mostly a collective duty of the international legal community".[99] Nevertheless, the reality is somewhat different than it appears to be. The international community does not have any qualified enforcement apparatus for the protection of the rights of children on a national or international level, but, this does not decrease or invalidate the legal characteristic of *jus cogens* norms.

4.12. Reasons for *Jus Cogens* Norms

There are a number of reasons why the protection of children's rights is regarded as an integral part of *jus cogens* norms:

I) Children's rights are incorporated in the Universal Declaration of Human Rights constituting an integral part of *jus cogens* norms;[100]
II) There are a number of international conventions that imply the undeniable rights of children.[101]

---

[99] Farhad Malekian, *Emasculating the Philosophy of International Criminal Justice in the Iraqi Special Tribunal*, 38 CORNELL INT'L L.J. (2005), at 703. See also Farhad, Malekian: Documents on the Principles of International Human Rights (2007).

100 See Ian Brownlie, Principles of Public International Law 514-15 (3d ed. 1979). For the declaration consult Farhad Malekian Documents on the Principles of International Human Rights (2007).

[101] These are such as Geneva Declaration of the Rights of the Child, 1924; Declaration of the Rights of the Child, 1959; United Nations Standard Minimum Rules for the Administration of Juvenile Justice, 1985; Convention on the Rights of the Child, 1989; the United Nations Guidelines for the Prevention of Juvenile Delinquency (The Riyadh Guidelines), 1990; the United Nations Rules for the

III) There are a considerable number of international conventions that imply the prohibition of crimes against children during war and peacetime.[102]

IV) Various forms of sexual exploitation of children are nationally and internationally prohibited.[103]

V) The national legislations of a number of states protect the undeniable rights of children within social relations.[104]

VI) The international humanitarian law of armed conflict explicitly and implicitly recognizes the inviolability of the rights of children.[105]

VII) Child slavery has, for a long time, been absolutely prohibited within conventional international law.[106]

VIII) Trafficking in children is regarded as a transnational crime in a number of international agreements and treaties.[107]

Protection of Juveniles Deprived of their Liberty, 1990; Optional Protocol to the Convention on the Rights of the Child on the Sale of Children, Child Prostitution and Child Pornography, 2000; Optional Protocol to the Convention on the Rights of the Child on the Involvement of Children in Armed Conflict, 2000; Convention concerning the Prohibition and Immediate Action for the Elimination of the Worst Forms of Child Labour, 1999; European Convention on the Exercise of Children's Rights, 1996; African Charter on the Rights and Welfare of the Child, 1990.

[102] See *ibid.* See also conventions Declaration on the Protection of Women and Children in Emergency and Armed Conflict, 1974; Declaration on the Elimination of Violence against Women, 1993 and Beijing Declaration and Platform for Action, Fourth World Conference on Women: Action for Equality, Development and Peace, 1995.

[103] See the Statutes of the ICTY, the ICTR and the ICC. See also Convention on the Non-Applicability of Statutory Limitations to War Crimes and Crimes Against Humanity (New York, 26 November 1968).

104 See in this book articles by Kerstin Nordlöf., Sovereignty of Children Rights within the Legislations of the Nordic Countries. See also article by Kirsten Sandberg., Children's Rights in the Norwegian Constitution.

105 For instance see the 1948 Geneva Conventions and their 1977 Protocols; Declaration on the Protection of Women and Children in Emergency and Armed Conflict, proclaimed by General Assembly Res. 3318(XXIX) of 14 December 1974.

106 See the 1926 Convention of Slavery; Amendment of the 1926 Convention by 1953 Protocol; the 1956 Supplementary Convention on the Abolition of Slavery, the Slave trade, and Institutions and Practices Similar to Slavery.

107 See the1904 International Agreement for the Suppression of White Slave Traffic; the 1910 International Convention for the Suppression of the White Slave Traffic; the 1921 International Convention for the Suppression of the Traffic in Women and Children; the 1933 International Convention for the Suppression of the Traffic in Women of Full Age and a considerable number of conventions

IX) The provisions of general international law strenuously prohibit violence against females.[108]

X) The provisions of customary international law similarly prohibit violations of the rights of children in national or international relations.[109]

XI) The resolutions of the Security Council present a policy of *zero tolerance* for the violations of the rights of children.[110]

XII) Many of the resolutions of the General Assembly require the implementation of the rights of children.[111]

XIII)Constitutional requirements (eg in Norway) for the protection of the rights of children are growing.[112]

XIV) Regional courts are also firmly dealing with various violations of children's rights.[113]

XV) The Statutes of *ad hoc* international tribunals recognise certain violations of children's rights as constituting crimes.[114]

XVI) The Statute of the permanent International Criminal Court protects certain rights of children and recognizes their violations as international crimes.[115]

XVII) International criminal courts exercise jurisdiction over those who have violated the rights of children.[116]

XVIII) The judgments of international criminal tribunals/courts have seriously taken account of violations of children's rights.[117]

---

which have been adopted after the establishment of the United Nations Organization.

[108] www.whrnet.org/docs/issue-international_court.html - 69k (last visited Oct.27, 2006).

[109] *Ibid.*

[110] *Ibid.*

[111] See Res.58/185 (Dec.22, 2003); A/RES/48/104 (Feb.23,1994);A/RES/57/179 (Jan.30, 2003).

[112] See next footnote.

[113] See also article on this book by Kirsten Sandberg., Children's Rights in the Norwegian Constitution.

[114] See David S. Mitchell, *The Prohibition of Rape in International Humanitarian Law as a Norm of Jus Cogens: Clarifying Doctrine*15 Duke Journal of Comparative and International Law, 219-258 (2005).

[115] See the text of the Statute of the ICC.

[116] See the Prosecution against Thomas Lubanga Dyilo, who recruited children under 15. The charges presented by the Pre-Trial Chamber against the defendant are based on the violations of the provisions of national or international armed conflicts.

[117] *Ibid.*

XIX) The judges and judgments of national, regional and international courts reject any claim regarding the necessity of the commission of crimes against children in armed conflicts.[118]

XX) The Convention on the Rights of the Child and its Protocols demands that all states should prohibit all types of sexual violence against children.[119]

XXI) The Convention of the Labour Organization also recognises sexual exploitation as a crime against children.[120]

XXII) The Convention concerning the Prohibition and Immediate Action for the Elimination of the Worst Forms of Child Labour prohibits child labour.[121]

XXIII) The Recommendation Concerning the Prohibition and Immediate Action for the Elimination of the Worst Forms of Child Labour demands the implementation of children's rights.

5. Mobilization against Unjustified Actions

One of the core reasons for the recognition of the sovereignty of children in law is to give serious attention to the rights of the child, and put an end to any unjust action which goes against the fundamental rights of the child. Similarly, in international law, the power of sovereignty is interpreted as being the legitimate defence against the provisions and actions of an unjust world.[122] Thus, the recognition opens the door to the protection of the rights of the child and strengthens the rights of those who have, for one reason or another, been the victims of unjust actions or decisions. This means that the rights of the child will not be treated as being of secondary value, and this will create legal grounds for the recovery of the harm.

---

118 Articles 6, 7 and 8 of the Statute.

119 See for example the 1989 Convention on the Rights of the Child; the 1995 Amendment to article 43 (2) of the Convention on the Rights of the Child; the 2000 Optional Protocol to the Convention on the Rights of the Child on the Involvement of Children in Armed Conflict.

120 See the International Labour Organization Worst Forms of Child Labour Convention 182 (1992).

121 The International Labour Organization adopted the agreement on 17 June 1999. The Convention is known as the Worst Forms of Child Labour Convention as ILO Convention No 182. It came into force on 19 November 2000.

122 Shashi Tharoor and Sam Daws, *Humanitarian Intervention: Getting Past the Reefs, World Policy Journal* XVIII, no. 2 (Summer 2001), p. 25.

Contemporary evidence about the violation of children's rights at a national or international level also offers some of the strongest reasons for the recognition of their rights within a particular framework. Some of the clearest evidence of the sexual exploitation of children is the unjustified actions by certain organized national or international bodies.[123] According to United Nations' records, children are the most vulnerable victims of sex exploitation, sex slavery, sex pornography, and sex services.[124] In other

---

[123] International law struggles in various ways to protect children from unlawful and inhuman sexual exploitation. The protection of children has been confirmed by the Declaration on Social Progress and Development, 1969, Universal Declaration on the Eradication of Hunger and Malnutrition, 1974 , Declaration on the Elimination of All Forms of Intolerance and of Discrimination Based on Religion or Belief, 1981, Declaration on the Human Rights of Individuals Who are not Nationals of the Country in which They Live, 1985, Vienna Declaration and Program of Action: World Conference on Human Rights, 1993, Draft United Nations Declaration on the Rights of Indigenous Peoples, 1994, Cairo Declaration of Human Rights in Islam, 1990, American Convention on Human Rights, 1969,African Charter on Human and Peoples' Rights, 1981, Arab Charter on Human Rights, 2004, European Convention for the Protection of Human Rights and Fundamental Freedoms of 1950 as amended by Protocol No. 11 of 1998, Charter of Fundamental Rights of the European Union, 2000, Convention on the Reduction of Statelessness, 1961, Supplementary Convention on the Abolition of Slavery, the Slave Trade, and Institutions and Practices Similar to Slavery, 1956, Declaration on the Protection of Women and Children in Emergency and Armed Conflict, 1974, International Covenant on Civil and Political Rights, 1966, International Convention on the Protection of the Rights of All Migrant Workers and Members of Their Families, 1990.

[124] It is a most unfortunate fact that the rights of children in peace or wartime have also been violated by United Nations Organizations missions themselves. Peacekeeping missions and personnel of the UN have been engaged in the sexual exploitation and sex trafficking of children. The Security Council and the Secretary General of the United Nations have seriously condemned the violations of the sovereignty of law for the protection of children, but without any result. The zero tolerance policy of the UN for the prevention and prosecution of trafficking in persons by UN personnel has not been effective. The following are some of the regions in which sexual exploitation and sexual abuses have occurred: Cambodia, Mozambique, Somalia, Bosnia and Herzegovina, Mozambique, Sierra Leone, Haiti, Iberia, Guinea, East Timor, Eritrea, Ethiopia, the Democratic Republic of Congo, Burundi, Bosnia, Macedonia and Kosovo. The Security Council in one of its resolutions emphasises that "12. *Expresses its serious concern* at the violence, particularly sexual violence, suffered by women and children during the conflict in Sierra Leone, and emphasizes the importance of addressing these issues effectively; 14. *Expresses its serious concern* at allegations that some UN personnel may have been involved in sexual abuse of women and children in

words, the concept of the sovereignty of children in law empowers and

---

camps for refugees and internally displaced people in the region, supports the Secretary-General's policy of zero tolerance for such abuse, looks forward to the Secretary-General's report on the outcome of the investigation into these allegations, and requests him to make recommendations on how to prevent any such crimes in future, while calling on States concerned to take the necessary measures to bring to justice their own nationals responsible for such crimes". Resolution 1400 (2002), adopted by the Security Council at its 4500th meeting, on 28 March 2002. Another resolution *"Requests* the Secretary-General to take the necessary measures to achieve actual compliance in UNMEE with the United Nations zero-tolerance policy on sexual exploitation and abuse, including the development of strategies and appropriate mechanisms to prevent, identify and respond to all forms of misconduct, including sexual exploitation and abuse, and the enhancement of training for personnel to prevent misconduct and ensure full compliance with the United Nations code of conduct, *requests* the Secretary-General to take all necessary action in accordance with the Secretary-General's Bulletin on special measures for protection from sexual exploitation and sexual abuse (ST/SGB/2003/13) and to keep the Council informed, and *urges* troop-contributing countries to take appropriate preventive action, including the conduct of pre-deployment awareness training, and *take disciplinary action* and other action to ensure full accountability in cases of such conduct involving their personnel". Security Council Resolution 1622 (2005). See also Press Release, Secretary-General Kofi-Annan, Sexual Exploitation 'Utterly Immoral', Completely at Odds with United Nations Mission, says Secretary-General to New York Conference, U.N. Doc. SG/SM/10776 (Dec. 4, 2006),
http://www.un.org/News/Press/docs/ 2006/sgsm10776.doc.htm.; Elizabeth F. Defeis, *U.N. Peacekeepers and Sexual Abuse and Exploitation*: *An End to Impunity*, 7 Washington University Global Studies Law Review, 185-214 (2008); Anna Shotton, *A Strategy to Address Sexual Exploitation by U.N. Peacekeeping Personnel*, 39 Cornell Law Review 97 (2006), 103; AvRay Murphy, UN peacekeeping in Lebanon, Somalia and Kosovo: operational and legal issues in practice (2007). See *also* David W. Wainhouse , International Peacekeeping at the Crossroads: National Support—Experience and Prospects (1973); The Evolution of Un Peacekeeping: Case Studies and Comparative Analysis (William J. Durch, Ed., 1993); United Nations Department of Public Information, The Blue Helmets: A Review Of United Nations Peace-Keeping (3rd Ed. 1997); David W. Wainhouse, International Peace Observation: A History and Forecast, (1986); Paul F. Diehl , International Peacekeeping (1993); Peacekeeping, American Politics and the Uncivil Wars of the 1990s (William J. Durch, Ed., 1996); Barbara Benton , Soldiers for Peace: Fifty Years of United Nations Peacekeeping (1996); Peacekeepers and Their Wives: American Participation in the Multinational Force and Observers (David R. Segal And And Mady W. Segal, 1993); Avray Murphy, Un Peacekeeping in Lebanon, Somalia and Kosovo: Operational and Legal Issues in Practice (2007); Understanding Peacekeeping (Alex J. Bellamy, Paul D. Williams and Stuart Griffin, eds., 2004), 10-13.

encourages states to act more energetically regarding the rights of children and victims as a whole. More seriously, the huge income generated by the sexual use of children in the pornography industry calls for the mobilization of the rights of the children in law. Although we accept that the state remains the sole local guarantor for the implementation of children's rights and human rights, the human rights policies of states have not been as effective as was hoped. The international system has even failed to create, in the case of the application of children's rights, an appropriate collective ensuring force. A brief survey of international documents about the protection of children's rights under the legal supervision of a military mission of the United Nations confirms this,[125] as the mission heavily violated the concept of the protection of children's rights. The equal enforcement of their rights constitutes one of the chief arguments for the mobilization of the power of law against the perpetrators of crimes against children.

It is also because of this basic requirement that the Statute of the International Criminal Court (ICC) has openly mobilized its provisions against violations of children's rights. Although the Statute does not unfortunately contain any separate articles about the violations of children's rights, it clearly prohibits unjustified actions against them.[126] The Statute has strongly condemned war crimes,[127] crimes against

---

[125] See Anna Shotton, *A Strategy to Address Sexual Exploitation by U.N. Peacekeeping Personnel*, 39 Cornell Law Review 97 (2006), 103. Sally Baden, "Post-conflict Mozambique: Women's Special Situation, Population Issues and Gender Perspectives to be integrated into Skills Training and Employment Promotion" (Brighton: Institute of Development Studies, 1997). According to one writer, "A pilot study of child prostitution conducted by MULEIDE and UNICEF in 1993-1994, based on interviews with 50 girls in Maputo and Beira, found that 19 percent of the clients of girl prostitutes were UN soldiers. Social instability and desperate socio-economic conditions in the aftermath of war were identified as the underlying causes of child prostitution. Often girls were major contributors to household income, spending their money on food and clothing, and were selling their services with at least the tacit support, if not active encouragement, of parents". *Ibid.*, p.35.

[126] These prolonged unjustified actions against the rights of children can be seen in the preamble of the Statute. It reads that states parties to the Statute "mindful that during this century millions of children, women and men have been victims of unimaginable atrocities that deeply shock the conscience of humanity."

[127] Article 8 (2) (b) (xxvi) of the Statute states that "Conscripting or enlisting children under the age of fifteen years into the national armed forces or using them to participate actively in hostilities", constitutes war crimes.

humanity[128] and genocide[129] which may explicitly or implicitly be carried out against children.[130] These are recognized as core crimes, the perpetrators of which may be brought before the jurisdiction of states parties and, if necessary, under the provisions of the complementarity principle, before the jurisdiction of the Court. This means that the international criminal regulations effectively seek to organize and recognize all international crimes which may be committed against children. That is why these crimes are regulated by the Statute. The Court has, in fact, not only an international legal personality of its own, but is also the manifestation of the power of law over criminals. The Statute has even recommended the states parties when electing judges, to take into serious consideration those who have legal expertise in field of children in law.[131] In one of the recent cases concerning the violation of the rights of children in the Democratic Republic of the Congo by Thomas Lubanga Dyilo, the arrest warrant stated that there were reasonable grounds to believe that the accused was criminally responsible for the violations of the law of the ICC regarding the protection of children. According to the warrant, the war crime of enlisting children under 15, the war crime of conscription of children under 15, and the war crime of using children under 15 to actively participate in hostilities are all punishable under Article 8 (2) (b) (xxvi) or Article 8 (2) (e) (vii) of the Statute. These, and many other causes, are seen as fundamental reasons for bringing the accused to trial, which has also recently been under consideration by the Appeal Chamber.[132] The provisional release of Thomas Lubanga Dyilo, which was approved by Trial Chamber I, was therefore strongly rejected

---

[128] The Statute recognizes enslavement constituting crimes against humanity. According to it "“enslavement” means the exercise of any or all of the powers attached to the right of ownership over a person and includes the exercise of such power in the course of trafficking in persons, in particular women and children." Article 7 (2) (c).

[129]According to the Statute, for its purpose "genocide" means any of the following acts committed with intent to destroy, in whole or in part, a national, ethnical, racial or religious group, as such:... e) Forcibly transferring children of the group to another group." Article 6 of the Statute.

[130] Rhonda Copelon, *Gender Crimes as War Crimes: Integrating Crimes against Women into International Criminal Law*, 46 McGill Law Journal 217 (2000).

[131] Article 36 (8) (b). Article 42 (9) of the Statute has also strengthened the issue of legal expertise. It states that the "Prosecutor shall appoint advisers with legal expertise on specific issues, including, but not limited to, sexual and gender violence and violence against children".

[132] ICC: Appeals Chamber Says Lubanga Case Should Resume, www.iccnow.org/?mod=drctimeline Lubanga. See also ICC-01/04-01/06.

by the Appeals Chamber decision.[133] All these actions by the Court are based solely on the protection of the rights of children.

6. Conclusion

The theory of justice has gone through different stages of development. This is particularly evident within the system of criminal justice, which has a particular role in the evolution of the theory. Although the civil law system is jurisprudentially different from that of the common law system, the theme of both systems have recently been interlinked into one integral system in order to achieve their main goals, which are the prosecution and punishment of accused or convicted persons. A justification for this integration can be found in the Statute of the ICC. A similar conclusion can be drawn with regard to the contents of many international conventions which tend towards combining the different values of national legislation within one mechanism. Two clear examples are the Declaration on the Protection of Women and Children in Emergency and Armed Conflict, proclaimed by the General Assembly in 1974, and the 1989Conventions on the Rights of the Child. The contents of both instruments are definitely binding on all signatories, whether civil law, common law, or any other legal system.

The theory of the integration of different legal systems is not to simplify their rules or their essence, but to achieve better results by discovering the core principles of justice within various legal systems. An examination of various sources proves that a requirement for the implementation of social justice is not just the right of adults but also the established natural and legal right of children. The improvement of children's rights therefore requires improvements in practical jurisprudence, whether by collecting and recognizing their rights within one integral system for children, or by strengthening them in national legislation.

Nevertheless, it must be said that recognizing or not recognizing children as autonomous subjects of justice, does not help to resolve any relevant, fundamental issues, as long as the protection is being halted by different legislative measures and the conundrums of civilization, justice, reciprocity

[133] The decisions of trial Chamber I were taken on 8 and 15 July. They were both rejected by the Appeals Chamber decision on 8 October 2010. Cancelation of the stay of proceedings in the Lubanga case: victims are rejoicing and request celerity in the proceedings, www.iccnow.org/?mod=drctimelinelubanga. See also ICC-01/04-01/06.

and equality are not solved in practice. It is rather cynical to gather a number of significant provisions into treaties on children's rights, but simultaneously negate those rights by other interpretative measures. Justice is not the consequence of recognition and the collections of *status quo* norms, but the way in which it is done. It is personal existence which gives value to rights and not rights to the person.

THE SOVEREIGNTY OF CHILDREN IN LAW

KERSTIN NORDLÖF

Abstract

During the evolution of society the child has, from a legal point of view, been regarded in different ways under customary, religious, common, civil and other legal systems, most often under the legal responsibility of a grown-up. A child lacking such a guardian was, and still is in many cases, taken care of by other persons related to the child, by a voluntary organization or an authority. The motives—legalized or not—have been dressed up as love, or responsibility, but there may also be more selfish reasons such as labour or sexual services. In this paper we will research whether the international, regional and national legal structures—with a focus on Sweden—guarantee independent rules for children, that is to say, the sovereignty of children. Regarding the doctrine of theories as well as the practice of courts, improvements in many areas of jurisprudence have been requested, and although the autonomy of the child as a legal individual with self-determining rights of his or her own is still fragmentary in several legal areas, it is identified as being a solid legal structure.

1. Introduction

One of the most important subjects of national, regional and international society should be 'the child'. This is based on the reasoning that children constitute the most valuable subject of our social integration and development. Despite this, their legal personalities as individual subjects in different areas of each legal system are, contrary to the principle of the rule of law, not given proper attention by internal authorities. This has been proved in several cases, as can be seen in every society where children are in any case vulnerable, but particularly those very young or sick, or those with a physical or psychological handicap. Children as individual subjects, legal or not, are to be found in legal contexts in different areas of each legal system. But this does not mean that they exist as individual subjects in all areas of the law, and on equal footings. On the contrary, and which will be discussed further below, one can say that they are more or less absent—ignored, in other words—in several and different parts of the legal system of every country in the world. We have all observed how former areas of research are currently evolving within our national legal systems to deal with children in one way or another, for example, juvenile delinquency and juvenile victims to mention just two. Another illustrative paradigm is the legal approach to the Convention on the Rights of the Child, since most nations are reluctant to incorporate it. This raises a fundamental question: Why were, and are, children being essentially ignored in a legal context? In this article we will try to identify whether there is a need for improvement in the autonomy of the child as a legal individual with self-determining rights of his or her own, or in other words, *the sovereignty of the child.*

2. Inferiority of Children

As a *modus operandi* in nearly every legal system, the rights of children were, and still are in many areas of the law, inferior to the rights of adults. Traditionally, within most norms of national legal systems, the family, as an institution, as well as its parenting role, is often given superiority compared with the rights of the child. Simultaneously, due to the practice of authorities in communities, regions, and states etc., children are placed at the bottom of the hierarchy when supporting, discussing and solving questions, or imposing legislative measures relating to children. This can be regarded as a top-down perspective, where the legal structure has still not identified or implemented the rights of children in a satisfactory way.[1]

From the Swedish experience one might say that the child was for a long time classified as an integral part of the family, and therefore in the parents' custody. From this viewpoint, children were, not generally recognized as individuals with personal rights of their own.[2] Historically, if there were no relatives around willing or capable of taking care of them, children without one or both parents had to find their own way — or they

[1] The theories of bottom-up and top-down perspective are discussed within several disciplines. See e.g. Smith, Graham, Democratic Innovation Designing Institutions for Citizen Participation, Cambridge University press, 2009.

[2] According to the 1734 law, sexual relations outside marriage were a severe crime. See also e.g. 1917 års lag om barn utom äktenskap, 1920 års lag om barn i äktenskap and 1924 års förmynderskapslag.

might even have been sold at auction.[3] In particular situations, a charitable or community organization might have taken responsibility for looking after such children; this responsibility could also have been assumed by state authorities. These children were often kept together with sick, poor and elderly people, as well as criminals.[4] An illustration, and proof of the lack of coherent treatment of children, legally as well as in practice, and as a subject of individual rights, is the report of the Commission appointed by the Swedish government in 2010 to present a proposal for making restitution to those who had been subjected to molestation and abuse in the social child and youth care system from 1920 to 1980.[5]

3. Improvement in the Position of Children

As across the rest of the world, the situation of children in Sweden improved, from a legal and social perspective, when society was industrialized and the tendency towards a democratic relationship increased. This implies that, from a holistic point of view, improvements in the rights of children in a legal context may be achieved when society as a whole, but particularly in areas of fundamental importance for the development of the status of children, legally or socially, are improved, and there is direct or indirect interaction.[6] Areas which were primarily influenced by this social progress, and which resulted in alterations or new legislation, were a

---

[3] Selling children at auction, which was facilitated by the Committee for the Care of Poor people, was not made illegal until 1918.

[4] Fahlbeck, Erik, Förvaltningsrättsliga studier I (Stockholm, 1938, p. 92 f; Bramstång, Gunnar, Sociallagstiftningen (Stockholm, 1985), p. 188; Den offentliga barnavården, third ed. (Uppsala, 1978), p. 9; Holgersson, Leif, Socialvården (Jönköping, 1978) p. 21, 29, 38; Socialvården (Jönköping, 1988) p. 69, 71; Strömberg, Håkan, Speciell förvaltningsrätt, seventh ed (Lund, 1983) p. 153.

[5] Dir 2010:15; SOU 2011:9 Betänkande av Upprättelseutredningen, Barnen som samhället svek – åtgärder med anledning av övergrepp och allvarliga försummelser i samhällsvården. The investigation into the documentation and support of individuals who had been subject to molestation and abuse within social childcare should also be mentioned (Vanvårdsutredningen, S 2006:05).

[6] The general principle of holism may be traced back to Aristotle and his Metaphysics where he states: "The whole is different from the sum of its parts" (in Metaphysics by Aristotle, translated by W. D. Ross, at the Internet Classics Archive. Those eminent in the field of sociology that could be mentioned in connection with holism include Émile Durkheim, The Rules of the Sociological Method, (1895); Louis Dumant, Essais sur l'individualisme: Une perspective anthropologique sur l'idéologie moderne (1983); and David Bohm, *Wholeness and the Implicate Order* (1980) .

promotion of social care,[7] labour laws,[8] and the spread of education[9]. From originally peering at the integration of children in a legal context with a, so to speak, national monocle, we in Sweden, had — as in the rest of the world — to put on worldwide spectacles in the Twentieth Century. By international and regional agreements,[10] other areas had to be considered

---

[7] 1902 års lag om fosterbarns vård, 1902 års lag om uppfostran åt vanartade och i sedligt avseende försummade barn, Lag den 6 juni 1924 om samhällets barnavård och ungdomsskydd, Lag den 31 maj år 1934 om samhällets barnavård och ungdomsskydd, Lag den 29 april 1960 om samhällets vård av barn och ungdom, Socialtjänstlagen (1980:620) och Lag (1980:621) om vård av unga.

[8] In 1882, children under the age of 12 were forbidden to work in factories. Later, children were forbidden to work at night. But the law was not observed, as it was not adequately policed. In 1912, a labour law protection was implemented concerning children working in industry. In 1949, new legislation was enforced and is still in use, which states that children under the age of 14 are not allowed to work. The minimum age for factory work is 15, but a child under the age of 18 is not allowed to work more than 10 hours in a 24-hour period. Lars Olsson Då barn var lönsamma, Tidens förlag 1980.

[9]In 1842 Parliament free, four-year compulsory schooling. Landquist, Johan., Pedagogikens historia, Gleerup, Lund, (1963), p. 290 f. In 1882 schooling was extended by another two years. The education system was further improved in 1905, läroverksstadgan, with the purpose of providing the same education for all children and at the same time stated the condition for further education. Sandström, Carl Ivar., *Utbildningens idéhistoria: om samhällsförändringarnas inflytande på undervisningens mål och idéinnehåll genom tiderna i Sverige och utlandet*, Bonnier, Stockholm 1978, p. 173 f. In 1936 schooling was increased again by another year and yet again in the 1950s. Compulsory nine-year schooling, which is still in force, was introduced in 1972. Landquist, Johan., Pedagogikens historia, Gleerup, Lund, (1963), p. 295.

[10] Examples of such international documents include: The Universal Declaration of Human Rights, 1948; the Proclamation of Tehran, 1968; the Declaration on Social Progress and Development, 1969; the Universal Declaration on the Eradication of Hunger and Malnutrition, 1974; the Declaration on the Elimination of All Forms of Intolerance and of Discrimination Based on Religion or Belief, 1981; the Declaration on the Human Rights of Individuals Who are not Nationals of the Country in which They Live, 1985; the Declaration on the Protection of all Persons from Enforced Disappearance, 1992; the Draft United Nations Declaration on the Rights of Indigenous Peoples, 1994; Guiding Principles on Internal Displacement, 1997. Regional documents include: the African Charter on Human and Peoples' Rights, 1981; the American Declaration of the Rights and Duties of Man, 1948; the American Convention on Human Rights, 1969; the Additional Protocol to the American Convention on Human Rights in the Area of Economic, Social and Cultural Rights ("Protocol of San Salvador"), 1988; the Cairo Declaration of Human Rights in Islam, 1990; the European Convention for the Protection of

and added to a legal subject, *the sovereignty of the child,* where the interests of the child were virtually dominant. In practice, global developments have many similarities with national regulations, in the sense that international or regional agreements often only indirectly support various rights of the child. On the other hand it must be recognised that negotiations within international and regional legal and political communities have also resulted in treaties that deal exclusively with the rights of the child. Those are to be found *in the areas of juvenile delinquency* dealing with prevention, the deprivation of freedom—arrest, detention or imprisonment—or the administration of justice,[11] *in the areas of abuse of children* including the sale of children, prostitution and pornography; children in armed conflict; and child labour[12]—but also *in*

Human Rights and Fundamental Freedoms of 1950 as amended by Protocol No. 11 1998 (and 14 on 1 June 2010); the European Social Charter, 1961 and revised in 1996.

[11] Standard Minimum Rules for the Treatment of Prisoners, 1955; the United Nations Standards Minimum Rules for the Administration of Juvenile Justice, ("The Beijing Rules"), 1985; Body of Principles for the Protection of All Persons under Any Form of Detention or Imprisonment, 1988; The Convention on the Rights of the Child, 1989; The United Nations Guidelines for the Protection of Juvenile ("The Riyadh Guidelines") 1990; United Nations Rules for the Protection of Juveniles Deprived of their Liberty, 1990; Resolution of the Council and of the representatives of the governments of the Member States, meeting within the Council, of 14 December 2000 on the social inclusion of young people (OJ C 374 of 28.12.2000); Resolution of the Council and of the representatives of the governments of the Member States, meeting within the Council of 27 June 2002 regarding the framework of European cooperation in the youth field (OJ C 168 of 13.7.2002); European Commission White Paper on a new impetus for European youth (COM(2001) 681 final); Communication from the Commission to the Council on European policies concerning youth (COM(2005) 206 final); Recommendation No. R (87) 20 of the Committee of Ministers of the Council of Europe on Social reactions to juvenile delinquency, and, more recently, in Recommendation Rec (2003) 20 of the Committee of Ministers on New ways of dealing with juvenile delinquency and the role of juvenile justice; Resolution (66) 25 on the short-term treatment of young offenders of under 21 years; Resolution (78) 62 on juvenile delinquency and social change; Recommendation (88) 6 on social reactions to juvenile delinquency among young people coming from migrant families, and Recommendation (2000) 20 on role of early psychosocial intervention in the prevention of criminality.

[12] Vienna Declaration and Program of Action: World Conference on Human Rights, 1993; Optional Protocol to the Convention on the Rights of the Child on the Sale of Children, Child Prostitution and Child Pornography, 2000; Optional Protocol to the Convention on the Rights of the Child on the Involvement of

the areas of discrimination, for instance, regarding child marriage and ethnical background,[13] and furthermore *in the areas of disabled children* such as mental illness, health care, and commitments on HIV/AIDS[14].

4. The Agenda of Legislative Measures

Scrutinizing the legal context of children from a Scandinavian perspective, other legal areas, except those already mentioned, and which have been put on the legislative agenda, are questions of nationality, parental responsibility and the establishment of a national council or ombudsman for children. Because of the violations of the rights of children in peace as well as in wartime, in the latter part of the 20th century the global community was, after many serious discussions and negotiations, prepared to codify the rights of the child in an international treaty. The International Convention on the Rights of the Child, including its optional protocols on the involvement of children in armed conflict and on the sale of children, child prostitution and child pornography, are not yet juridically complete, although they do create, more or less, certain necessary international legal characterizations for *the sovereignty of the child*. It has been signed by 140 states, and ratified by 193 parties, excluding Somalia and the United States. It has been incorporated by South Africa, Ethiopia, Brazil,

---

Children in Armed Conflict, 2000; Convention concerning the Prohibition and Immediate Action for the Elimination of the Worst Forms of Child Labour, 1999; Declaration on the Elimination of Violence against Women, 1993; Inter-American Convention on the Prevention, Punishment and Eradication of Violence Against Women, 1994.

[13] Convention on Consent to Marriage, Minimum Age for Marriage and Registration of Marriages, 1962; Declaration on the Elimination of Discrimination against Women, 1967; Convention on the Elimination of All Forms of Discrimination against Women, 1979; Beijing Declaration and Platform for Action, Fourth World Conference on Women: Action for Equality, Development and Peace, 1995; Protocol to the African Charter on Human and Peoples' Rights on the Rights of Women in Africa, 2003; Protocol No. 12 on prohibition of discrimination (2000) to the Convention for the Protection of Human Rights and Fundamental Freedoms, EG- directive 2000/43/EG.

[14] European Social Charter, 1961; Declaration on the Rights of Disabled Persons, 1975; Principles for the Protection of Persons with Mental Illness and the Improvement of Mental Health Care, 1991; Standard Rules on the Equalization of Opportunities for Persons with Disabilities, 1993; Declaration of Commitment on HIV/AIDS, 2001; Convention on the Rights of Persons with Disabilities, 2006; Optional Protocol to the Convention on the Rights of Persons with Disabilities, 2006.

Ecuador, Venezuela and Norway among others; and in 2009, based on the provisions of the Convention, approximately 70 countries adopted children's codes into their national legislation.[15] Copying these particular legislative and prerogative movements, in 2010, in Malta, for instance, there was a call for the incorporation of the convention into Maltese law. Such a requirement has also been raised in the UK. The issue is also being discussed in Sweden where there is still reluctance to incorporate the Convention of the Rights of the Child: this view is based on the argument that implementing the rights of the child in Swedish legislation is preferable and sufficient. Sweden being one of the countries which actively took part in, and fully supported the establishment of, a convention on children's rights, its standpoint on this issue is surprising, and may even have an effect on other countries which are also reluctant to incorporate the Convention. The positive development of legal issues concerning the rights of children is thus being hampered.

5. Lack of Fundamental Remedy

As a legal instrument, incorporated or not, the Convention on the Rights of the Child lacks a fundamental remedy and may thereby not claim to have reached the basic level of a document securing the demands of the rule of law. This is not a new topic of discussion, as the question had already been raised at the drafting of the Convention on the Rights of the Child,[16] and it has been further discussed since then.[17] We do have regional institutions within which different legal issues of children may be tried, for example the European Court of Human Rights in Strasbourg. Some cases dealing with children, but in a limited way, have been successfully tried.[18] This is

---

[15] Ann M. Veneman, Executiv director, UNICEF, The State of the World's Children, Special edition, Celebrating 20 Years of the Convention on the Rights of the Child, 2009, p. ii.

[16] Geraldine Van Bueren, Children's Rights – Moving Forward http://www.gardencourtchambers.co.uk/imageUpload/File/speech%20to%20garden%20court%20website%2024%209%2009.pdf 6 Sept, 2010.

[17] Nordlöf, Kerstin, *The Legal Philosophy of Protecting a Suspect Child,* published by the XVII World Congress of the International Association of Youth and Family Judges and Magistrates, Belfast Northern Ireland, 27 August – 2 September, 2006, and in Årsboken för Juridicum, 2009, Örebro University, Sweden.

[18] E.g. Tyrer v. the United Kingdom (1978) on physical punishment; Campbell and Cosens v. the United Kingdom (1982) corporal punishment at school; A. v. The United Kingdom (1998), corporal punishment in the home; Okkali v. Turkey (2006) children in conflict with the law; Mubilanzila Mayeka and Kaniki Mitunga

because the European Convention for Human Rights and Fundamental Freedoms was not drafted with the aim of enforcing the rights of the child. Still, to this must be added The European Social Charter, under which collective complaints on behalf of children are referred to the European Committee of Social Rights. But by March 2010, only 14 of the 47 members of the Council of Europe had accepted a collective compliant procedure. In Africa the Charter of the Rights and Welfare of the Child is overseen by a Committee of Experts on the Rights and Welfare of the Child to which a child can petition for civil, political, economic, social and cultural rights, but given its working methods, it has yet to examine any complaints. On the continent of America, and in the Caribbean, a Special Rapporteur on Child Rights has been appointed by the Inter-American Commission on Human Rights, and this institution may receive communications from States, organisations and individuals. Asia and Australia are missing from this regional list. With the intention to create a global jurisdiction dealing with genocide, crimes against humanity and war crimes, the *ad-hoc* international criminal tribunals for the former Yugoslavia,[19] Rwanda,[20] the special court for Sierra Leone[21] and the permanent International Criminal Court[22] have to be mentioned where children are dealt with in their statutes and hereby appear in cases both as perpetrators, victims and witnesses.[23]

6. Petitioning Mechanism

In the international community, the current situation regarding this issue is that in June 2009 an Open-ended Working Group was established by the Council to investigate the possibilities of an optional protocol to the Conventions on the Rights of the Child, which would provide a communication procedure and complement the existing reporting procedure of each individual state which ratified it.[24] The importance of this step may

---

v. Belgium (2006) detention and deportation; Roda and Bonfatti v. Italy (2006) the right to be heard.

[19] Statute of the international tribunal for the former Yugoslavia, Resolution 827, 1166 and 1329.

[20]Statute of the International Criminal Tribunal for Rwanda, Resolution 955.

[21] Statute of the Special Court for Sierra Leone, Resolution 1315.

[22] The Rome Statute A/CONF.183/9.

[23] For discussions on individual criminal responsibility se e.g. Malekian, Farhad, International Criminal Law, The Legal and Critical Analysis of International Crimes, Vol I, (1991) p.40 ff.

[24] Resolution A/HRC/RES/11/1.

be exemplified by recalling the view of the Chairperson of the Committee on the Rights of the Child, who—in connection with "children's special and dependent status [which] creates real difficulties for them in pursuing remedies for breaches of their rights"—states that "the development of a communication procedure for the Convention on the Rights of the Child would significantly contribute to the overall protection of children's rights".[25] In March 2010 the mission of the Working Group was extended to prepare a proposal on a draft optional protocol.[26] And in September 2010 this draft optional protocol was, circulated in all the official languages of the United Nations to be employed as a fundamental document for forthcoming negotiations. It included a petitioning mechanism which means that a child will be able to bring complaints, individually or collectively, to an international level when their government has offended them by not properly implementing their rights in accordance with the Convention on the Rights of the Child and its two protocols, and all domestic legal remedies have been exhausted.[27] The outcome of those negotiations will have an impact on the child as a legal subject not only internationally, but also regionally and nationally, and hence on the *sovereignty of the child* as such. The child's status, special and dependent, may by the proposal concerning a right to complaint prove the child is to be recognized a legal subject. This will at least establish their equal rights with other individuals.

This mutual and multilateral achievement implies the fact that the child is more or less accepted as an individual legal subject with rights of his or her own. This progress development may be due to the jurisprudence of the country in question; it may also be the result of the explicit or implicit influence of the practice of other countries, which might be coordinated in the mechanism of co-operation relating to legal issues as in the EU, for example. Within this union a strategy for children has been developed,[28]

[25] 11/1 Open-ended Working Group on an optional protocol to the Convention on the Rights of the Child to provide a communications procedure www.biceinternational.org/.../un_hrc_open_ended_working__group_on_an_optional_protocol_to_the_convention_on_the_rights_of_the_child 19-05-2011.

[26] Resolution A/HRC/RES/13/3.

[27] A/HRC/WG.7/2/2.

[28] 15/02/2011 - COM(2011) 60 final - Communication from the Commission - An EU Agenda for the Rights of the Child , 2007/116/CE. Commission Decision 2007/116/EC of 15 February 2007 on reserving the national numbering range beginning with '116' for harmonised numbers for harmonised services of social

and the rights of the child have been implemented in its statutes.[29] However, the EU is still in the early stages of implementing its strategy whereby the European Court of Justice and the European Court of Human Rights play a vital role. The ECHR has in particular had an essential impact on the Charter of the Fundamental Rights of the European Union, with its cases based on the European Convention as well as on other instruments[30]. Many issues involving children are on the agenda, some of the more urgent ones being child trafficking, unaccompanied children entering the EU, and poverty.

7. Legislation

From a theoretical point of view, we might look upon children's rights in the light of the theory of legal positivism as examined from different viewpoints, and emphasised by Jeremy Bentham, a utilitarian with whom legal positivism begins; by John Austin, with his focus on the Sovereign; and by Hans Kelsen, with his very strict, scientific elaboration of legal regulations on different levels, further developed by H.L.A. Hart and the latter's pupil, Joseph Raz. Here, Ronald Dworkin should also be mentioned. He is critical of legal positivism, and advocates the theory of law as integrity. Like the former he has had, and still has, an impact on the development of jurisprudence and thus on legislation, international treaties, and cases based on the interpretation of such materials.

The starting point of this article was the *sovereignty of children*, with the purpose of discussing the position of children within a legal context, i.e. legislation and cases. My arguments are based on legal documents such as laws, travaux préparatories , cases and doctrine as well as international agreements. This does not necessarily mean that the statutes of the child, who may be regarded as a legal subject in different legal issues, have to be codified. Here we might find different standpoints due to legal traditions

---

value, 04/07/2006 - COM(2006) 367 final - Communication from the Commission - Towards an EU strategy on the rights of the child.

[29] The Treaty of Lisbon, 1 December, 2009, the Charter of Fundamental Rights of the European Union.

[30]European Convention on the Adoption of Children (1967); European Convention on the Repatriation of Minors (1970); European Convention on the Legal Status of Children born out of Wedlock (1975); European Convention on Recognition and Enforcement of Decisions concerning Custody of Children and on Restoration of Custody of Children (1980); European Convention on Nationality (1997); and the European Convention on the Exercise of Children's Rights (1996).

of common and civil law. Codification is consequently an issue in itself. We might, as an example, compare a codification on rhetorical speech, social equality and impartiality found in Egypt from about 3000BC, with modern day laws aimed at using the principle of legality to solve legal issues.

Legal rules, even being adopted for the sake and welfare of children, may be misinterpreted and open the door to degrading their rights and personal integrity. This has been proved in the proceedings of justice and within the domestic mentality of most legal systems. The absence of crucial and effective principles governing the rights of children, and sanctions against their violations within most constitutional regulations, has seriously hampered each aspect of law such as social, criminal, procedural, family, contract, financial, tort, insurance, medical and school law. Their issues are often considered to be marginal or secondary.

8. Theories

In the discussion of the child's sovereignty we may refer to legal theories of utilitarianism and realism, where utilitarianism stands for the moral value of an action being determined only by its overall contribution to the good of society, while realism stands for the value of an action being determined by its respect for fundamental, inherent rights.[31] This may be further extended in conjunction with the sovereignty of the child, which may theoretically be defended by referring to Immanuel Kant's doctrine of right, according to which individual rights have to be secured and protected for the well being of society, which Kant further developed as a necessity for peace.[32] In the discussion of the rights of the child the

[31] For further discussions on utilitarianism see e.g. John Stewart Mill www.utilitarianism.com/mill2.htm+utilitarianism 21.5.2011. American and Scandinavian legal realism could be mentioned as examples, and among them Karl Llewellyn as representative of the former and Axel Hägerström and Alf Ross, Karl Olivecrona and A. Wilhelm Lundstedt of the latter.

[32] Guyer, Paul editor, Kant and Modern Philosophy (Cambridge University Press, 2006), p. 439 ff; Byrd, B. Sharon and Hruschka, Joakim, Kant's Doctrine of Right, A commentary (Cambridge University Press, 2011), p.1 ff. As an example of children and rights in connection with wars see Malekian, Farhad, Prohibition Governing Child Soldiers Constituting an Integral Part of *Jus Cogens* and *Obligatio Erga Omnes*, XVII World Congress of the International Association of Youth and Family Judges and Magistrates, Belfast, Northern Ireland, 27 August –

question has also been raised whether the child is a right holder. Those taking part in this discussion may be divided into those who advocate the will or choice theory, amongst whom Hart, Steiner and Sumner should be mentioned.[33] According to them, a right is the protected exercise of choice. The alternative is the theory of welfare or interest. Adherents of this theory are MacCormick, Raz and Kramer.[34] According to them, a right is the protection of an interest of sufficient importance to impose duties on others, whose discharge allows the right-holder to enjoy the interest in question. The will or choice theory does not view children as right-holders, because they do not have the capacity to exercise choice. The welfare or interest theory, however, does see children as being right holders.

Discussions of theories are of fundamental importance when critically analysing legislation and its practice, but also in connection with the research of other sciences to find unifying concepts within a holistic view of children in a legal context investigating the boundaries of children's sovereignty. There are numerous ideologies of contemporary jurisprudence and they may therefore be categorized on different levels. There may, furthermore, be various attitudes according to which part of the legal system we are referring. The ideologies of contemporary jurisprudence are, owing to the complexity and interaction on national, regional and global levels, therefore much more broadminded, and may agree in some aspects and disagree in others in the exploration of the sovereignty of the child. What unifies theories of jurisprudence from the past with contemporary theories is that they both reflect their positions in

---

2 September, 2006. http://www.youthandfamily2006.com/welcome.htm, also published by the Institute of International Criminal Law (2007).

[33] For further discussions see Hart, H.L.A. Essays on Bentham: Studies in Jurisprudence and Political Theory (1982)

(1973). Bentham on Legal Rights in A.W.B. Simpson (ed.), Essays on Bentham: Jurisprudence and Political Theory, (Oxford: Clarendon Press, 1982); Steiner, H., An Essay on Rights, (Oxford: Blackwell. 1994); and Sumner, L.W., The Moral Foundation of Rights, (Oxford: Clarendon Press, 1987).

[34] MacCormick, N.,'Children's Rights: A Test-Case', in his Legal Right and Social Democracy, (Oxford: Clarendon Press, 1982) p. 154 ff; Raz, J., 'Legal Rights', Oxford Journal of Legal Studies, 1984, 4(1): p. 1–21; and Kramer, M.H., 'Rights Without Trimmings', in A Debate Over Rights, Philosophical Enquiries, M.H. Kramer, N. Simmonds and H. Steiner, (Oxford: Clarendon Press, 1998): p. 7 ff.

accordance with their time and place, and particularly their social structure.

9. Conclusion

We are aware of the fact that in philosophical terms, legislation may not be the only and final method but merely one of several methods within the legal system, such as continental and common law, and regional and international law, when identifying the need for improvements in consolidating the sovereignty of the child. Undoubtedly, a holistic view is to be applied in evaluating this very complex area, although it is simply referring to the rights of individuals on equal footings in implementing as well as exercising their rights. This jurisprudential exploration proves that the rights of children in a legal context must be evaluated and improved. Still, the search indicates fragments of an individual identity for children in a legal context, *the sovereignty of children in law*. A development of further research enhancements within the area of jurisprudence may be to consider a bottom-up approach, where the child's right has to be acknowledged equally with other individuals, and not only to be relevant to children's issues, but to society as a whole.

WHO IS A CHILD? THE INTERNATIONAL DEFINITION OF A CHILD

MARTA PRUCNAL*

Abstract

The answer to the question of who is "a child" plays the essential role in determining the catalogue of rights related to and reserved for the period of childhood. This article begins with the presentation of the concepts of childhood made on the grounds of historical and philosophical analysis. Further presentation focuses on the international legal definition of the term "child". The definition of "a child" appeared in international law with the entry into force of the UN Convention on the Rights of the Child on 2nd September 1990. According to Article 1 of the Convention "…a child means every human being below the age of eighteen years unless, under the law applicable to the child, majority is attained earlier."[1] The definition seems to have a universal character due to the number of ratifications of the Convention. The article illustrates the *travaux preparatoires* for the Convention that led to the adoption of the currently existing definition of "a child". The analysis is made on the provisions of the Convention which make up the modern definition in force. These are the provisions of Article 1 of the Convention and paragraph 9 of the Preamble. The article also discusses the age criterion designating the lower and upper limit of childhood. The author presents interpretative doubts that appear on the basis of the analysis of the definition of "a child" and suggests proposals for their removal.

---

* Doctor, Jagiellonian University, Cracow, Poland; Visiting Researcher, Max Planck Institute for Comparative Public Law and International Law, Heidelberg, Germany.

[1] United Nations Convention on the Rights of the Child, Nov. 20, 1989, 28 I.L.M. 1456, 1577 U.N.T.S. 3 [hereinafter the CRC].

1. Introduction

Why is it so important to have the definition of "a child" in international law? One of the responses to this question is that given by Geraldine van Bueren who stresses that the definition of "a child"/"childhood" in international law is crucial as children benefit from the special catalogue of additional rights related to, and reserved only for, the period of childhood. In order to determine which rights belong to this catalogue it is necessary to define who is considered to be "a child". This not only has a significant function under the provisions of domestic law but also under the system of international law which has, since the second half of the twentieth century, given special attention to children and the issue of child rights' protection.[2]

2. Concepts of Childhood

Children, as shown by studies of historians, have not always existed.[3] According to some, they have been invented; according to others, they have been discovered.[4] In his book, *Centuries of Childhood*, the French historian Philip Aries proves that "the child is a contemporary concept of modern society". He argues that it was not until the late seventeenth century that "the concept of childhood" began to emerge.[5] Most medieval languages did not even contain a word for "child": childhood wasn't seen as a distinct stage in life. At that time children were considered to be small adults. Medieval society distinguished only infants from adults.[6] According to Aries it was not until the late seventeenth century, in connection with changes in civilization (industrialization and the development of capitalism) and transformations within the family, that childhood began to

---

[2] Geraldine Van Bueren, The International Law on the Rights of the Child 32 (1998).

[3] The author refers only to concepts of childhood presented by chosen researchers. The question, however, requires further analysis.

[4] Maria Szczepska-Pustkowska, *Kategorie dzieciństwa - od Ellen Key do współczesności*, 90 Edukacja i Dialog (1997), http://www.eid.edu.pl/archiwum/1997,95/wrzesien,131/kategorie_dziecinstwa_-od_ellen_key_do_wspolczesnosci,617.html (last visited Sep. 30, 2010).

[5] Philip Aries, Centuries of Childhood (1973), *quoted in* Brocklehurst, *infra* note 6, at 2.

[6] Helen Brocklehurst, Who's Afraid of Children?: Children, Conflict and International Relations 2 (2006).

be seen as a distinct stage of human development and the child as a different person and thus requiring different treatment than an adult.

A similar position is taken by Jacques Le Goff, another French historian and essayist, who notes that during the Middle Ages, in conjunction with the significant involvement of children in agricultural work on the one hand, and in learning knightly crafts on the other, children became mature miniatures of adults too early. The distinction between a "child" and an "adult" appeared no earlier than the Renaissance. It was the result of "family nuclearization" and the spreading in an urban environment of the "home family" model, understood to be a small group of relatives living together. According to Le Goff, "childhood" is therefore a product of the town and townspeople.[7]

Aries' theory is denied by the British philosopher David Archard. He states that there is no evidence that "previous societies lacked a concept of childhood". In fact they did distinguish children from adults, but just did it in a different way. They had their own "concept of childhood".[8] Archard rejects the idea of "a child" being recognized as a person who is not yet "an adult",[9] and therefore, according to Anna Brzezinska, as a "non-adult", "pre-adult", or "another than adult".[10] Archard disagrees with the perception of "a child" as opposed to "an adult". He criticizes the vision of the ideal adult understood as being equipped with a range of cognitive abilities, rational thinking, physically independent, autonomy, having a sense of separateness, conscious of his beliefs and desires, and therefore able to make independent choices and bear the responsibility for them. In such a case "a child", as "a non-adult", is defined as being deprived of the capacities attributed to an adult. Archard believes that this approach favours adults and distorts the true picture of "a child" and "childhood".[11]

Archard criticizes the so-called "developmental model of childhood" presenting two conceptions of perceiving the direction of human development. The first conception assumes that "a child" has certain basic "children's abilities" and needs certain care and education so as to be able to convert them or replace them with "the abilities of an adult". The second conception perceives "a child" as "a partial or worse than an adult"

---

[7] Szczepska-Pustkowska, *supra* note 4.
[8] David Archard, Children: Rights and Childhood 24 (1st ed. 1993).
[9] Bueren, *supra* note 2, at 33.
[10] Szczepska-Pustkowska, *supra* note 4.
[11] Archard, *supra* note 8, at 30,36.

equipped with "the adult abilities" which still need to be developed. Both approaches assume that at a certain point the child finally reaches the state of adulthood. His childhood abilities either gradually turn into adult abilities, or the adulthood somehow outgrows the childhood. The author points out that none of these approaches allows a situation in which children's abilities could also exist in adulthood or co-exist in parallel to the capabilities of an adult. According to them, childhood is only "a stage on the way to adulthood".[12]

Archard proposes a new recognition of "childhood" understood as a maturation process that does not have a distinct point of complete separation from adulthood. He believes that an adult can be equipped with "the children's capacities", and that during childhood certain "adult characteristics" may also appear. This moment of a gradual transition from childhood to adulthood suggests the concept of "a child", recognized equally as a certain state of mind and a certain state of physical maturity. There is, therefore, no clear line between a child and an adult, and it thus seems that children's and adults' abilities coexist. Archard argues that "…childhood is construed not so much as an actual period in one's life, but more as a metaphorical immaturity which can be present to some extent throughout a lifetime."[13]

Archard distinguishes "the concept of childhood" from "a conception of childhood". He considers that "the concept of childhood" implies the distinction between children and adults in respect of some "unspecified set of attributes", while "a conception of childhood" is "a specification of those attributes".[14] According to Archard "a conception of childhood" can be deduced through examining the treatment of a child, and the legislative solutions regulating the legal situation of the child. Archard distinguishes three aspects of "a conception of childhood", useful in order to distinguish the forms and *content* of childhood. Among them he distinguishes "the boundaries of childhood", understood as the beginning and the end of childhood; "the dimensions of childhood", which include cultural, social and legal angles from which childhood can be understood; and "the divisions of childhood", understood as different stages of a child's life.[15]

---

[12] *Id.* at 32-36.
[13] *Id.* at 37.
[14] *Id.* at 22.
[15] *Id.* at 23-28.

2.1. The Boundaries of Childhood

There are many different criteria demarcating childhood. These include, among others age, the commencement of work, completion of education, onset of menarche, and the conclusion of marriage.[16] Children, depending on which social class they belong to and in which society they live, may reach adulthood at different periods of their life. It is connected with the socio-economic functions they perform within the societies in which they live.[17] In many countries, especially poorer ones, crossing the threshold of adulthood—or at least "a partial adulthood"[18]—may be equated with the moment of the acquisition of labour capacity by a child. This capacity may be achieved by children at different stages in their lives. For example, children living in societies which, owing to economic and social conditions involve them from an early age in a variety of household tasks, gain and develop their working skills significantly earlier than children living in industrial societies which consider "childhood" primarily as "a time of play and learning".[19]

Another criterion separating childhood from adulthood is the moment at which a child enters puberty, very often regarded as equivalent to the acquisition of the capacity to get married. In many cultures, a person's life up to the time he reaches sexual maturity, is equated with innocence, and regarded as being synonymous with childhood. Accepting such a criterion raises the question of whether a fifteen-year old girl who has given birth can still be considered to be "a child". There are many such situations in the world. A clear example is Nigeria, where more than half of the women (girls) give birth to their first child before they reach the age of eighteen.[20] However, in both national and international law, the most common criterion of the upper boundary of childhood is "the age of majority". This is not a uniform criterion. Children are treated differently within the machinery of justice. Those differences are connected with the issues of juvenile justice, the minimum employment age, the minimum age for marriage, and an entitlement to vote or to join the national armed forces. An illustration of such a variation is a situation reflected in United

---

[16] Jo Boyden & Deborah Levison, Expert Group on Development Issues, Ministry for Foreign Affairs, Children as Economic and Social Actors in the Development Issues (Working Paper) 28 (2000).

[17] *Id.*

[18] Brocklehurst, *supra* note 6, at 8.

[19] *Id.* at 8.

[20] *Youngest and oldest brides*, The Guardian, Feb. 28, 1996, at 22.

Kingdom national law. According to it, a sixteen-year-old cadet soldier can marry, with parental consent, at the age of seventeen can "make, risk and take life, but still cannot watch violent or pornographic movies until he reaches the age of eighteen".[21] In India, however, the law allows the employment of ten-year old children in industry.[22]

2.2. The Divisions of Childhood

A child goes through many phases of development. There is no single common approach for the sub-division and naming of the various stages of childhood. Within this sub-division we may, for instance, speak about "early childhood", "middle childhood" and "adolescence".[23] Another concept of sub-dividing childhood is based on the following terms: "neonate", "baby", "infant", "child", "juvenile", "adolescent", "teenager", "youth", "young person", "minor".[24] These terms are not, however, formulated consistently in international or national literature, and this inconsistency is the result of the lack of a satisfactory definition of these terms as well as the lack of awareness of the recognition of childhood as a distinct status in previous international instruments.[25] For example, the term "youth", defined in the 1985 International Year of Youth, includes persons between the age of fifteen and twenty-five. The term "juvenile" carries negative connotations and is most often associated with the concept of "juvenile justice". It is reflected in the international nomenclature of various international instruments such as The United Nations Rules for the Protection of Juveniles Deprived of their Liberty, and The United Nations Standard Minimum Rules for the Administration of Juvenile Justice, the so-called Beijing Rules. The term "minor" is often contrasted with the term "major". In this concept "minor" is very often described as *lesser* or *incomplete* being in principle incapable of taking care of his own best interests.[26]

In communities with a high rate of politically motivated violence whose victims are often children, it is in the interest of politicians to replace the term "child" with other terms. No politician wants to be accused of imprisoning, or even worse of killing, "a child". Thus, alternative terms

---

[21] Boyden & Levison, *supra* note 16, at 28.
[22] Brocklehurst, *supra* note 6, at 10.
[23] Brocklehurst, *supra* note 6, at 1.
[24] Bueren, *supra* note 2, at 32; Brocklehurst, *supra* note 6, at 1.
[25] Bueren, *supra* note 2, at 32.
[26] *Id.*

are used. For example, in South Africa the term "childhood" is associated with the period from birth until the age of ten, while the period between the age of ten and eighteen is commonly called "adolescence" and therefore children are called "young people".[27] The distinction between the concepts of "children" and "adolescents" may be broadly examined in the cultural or juridical literature of most countries of the world. Here, "a child" is understood as a young person who is about to complete his primary school, while with reference to secondary school pupils the term "youth" is used.[28]

Within the provisions of a considerable number of international treaties, we may find other concepts than "child" relating to a young person. The 1966 International Covenant on Civil and Political Rights, in its Articles 10 (2) (b), 14 (1) and 14 (4), uses the term "juvenile persons".[29] Article 24 (1) of the same instrument refers to the concept of "a minor".[30] The term "minor" is also reflected in the provision of Article 76 of the 1949 IV Geneva Convention Relative to the Protection of Civilian Persons in Time of War.[31] Article 10 (3) of the 1966 International Covenant on Economic, Social and Cultural Rights distinguishes between "children" and "young persons".[32] Similarly, "children" and "young people" can be found in Article 94 of the IV Geneva Convention. Article 6 (5) of the 1966 International Covenant on Civil and Political Rights speaks about "persons below eighteen years of age",[33] and Article 132 of the IV Geneva Convention uses the terms "children", "infants" and "young children".

In the provisions of international humanitarian law we can find many references to the so-called "ages of childhood" (or "stages of childhood") indicating the upper age limits which entitle special protection and preferential treatment. The IV Geneva Convention[34] and the 1977 Additional

---

[27] Ed Cairns, Children and Political Violence (Understanding Children's Worlds) 9 (1996).
[28] Marian Balcerek, Prawa dziecka 22 (1986).
[29] United Nations International Covenant on Civil and Political Rights, Dec. 16, 1966, 6 I.L.M. 368, 999 U.N.T.S. 171.
[30] *Id.*
[31] Geneva Convention Relative to the Protection of Civilian Persons in Time of War, Aug. 12, 1949, 75 U.N.T.S. 287 [hereinafter the IV Geneva Convention].
[32] United Nations International Covenant on Economic, Social and Cultural Rights, Dec. 16, 1966, 6 I.L.M. 360, 993 U.N.T.S. 3.
[33] United Nations International Covenant on Civil and Political Rights, *supra* note 29.
[34] The IV Geneva Convention, *supra* note 31.

Protocols relating to the Protection of Victims of International[35] and Non-International[36] Armed Conflicts refer to the following age intervals: "newborn babies", "infants" and respectively children under the age of seven, twelve, fifteen and eighteen. Though international law does not establish a separate status of "infants", the 1977 I Additional Protocol does extend them special protection emphasizing the physical dependence of "infants" on adults. Article 14 of the IV Geneva Convention provides special protection to "children under the age of fifteen years, expectant mothers, and mothers of children under seven", by placing them in special safety zones. Article 23 obliges each High Contracting Party to permit the free passage of all consignments of essential foodstuffs, clothing and tonics intended for "children under fifteen, expectant mothers and maternity cases". Another IV Geneva Convention provision protecting the rights of "children under fifteen, pregnant women and mothers of children under the age of seven" is Article 38 (5). It emphasizes the need to ensure preferential treatment for them when they stay, as aliens, in the territory of a Party to the conflict. In accordance with the provisions of Article 89 of the IV Geneva Convention "children under fifteen years of age, expectant and nursing mothers" are entitled to additional food, in proportion to their physiological needs.

Article 24 obliges Parties to the conflict to take the necessary measures to avoid leaving to their own resources orphaned, or separated from their families, "children under the age of fifteen". The states are also responsible for facilitating the maintenance, education and the exercise of religion of those children. Furthermore, they are obliged to facilitate the identification of "children under twelve". Persons under the age of eighteen years cannot be compelled to work for the Occupying Power (Article 51 of the IV Geneva Convention). "The death penalty may not be pronounced against a protected person who was under eighteen years of age at the time of the offence" (Article 68 of the IV Geneva Convention), and "the death penalty for an offence related to the armed conflict shall not be executed on persons who had not attained the age of eighteen years at the time the offence was committed" (Article 77 (5) of the I Protocol to the Geneva Conventions).

---

[35] Protocol Additional to the Geneva Conventions of 12 August 1949, and relating to the Protection of Victims of International Armed Conflicts, June 8, 1977, 1125 U.N.T.S. 3 [hereinafter the I Protocol to the Geneva Conventions].

[36] Protocol Additional to the Geneva Conventions of 12 August 1949, and relating to the Protection of Victims of Non-International Armed Conflicts, June 8, 1977, 1125 U.N.T.S. 609 [hereinafter the II Protocol to the Geneva Conventions].

In the presence of so many terms referring to "a child" the question which has often puzzled, and still seriously puzzles, is: Who is "a child"? The question of the definition of "a child" in international law therefore constitutes rather a serious issue. Is the term "child" defined in international law? And if so, is there a common universal definition of the term, or are there many definitions in contemporary international law?

3. The International Legal Definition of "a Child"

Analysis of international documents devoted to the protection of the rights of the child reveals the fact that some of them define the term "child" for their own purposes. The definition of "a child" can be found, for example, in the 1999 Convention 182 Concerning the Prohibition and Immediate Action for the Elimination of the Worst Forms of Child Labour,[37] the 1990 African Charter on the Rights and Welfare of the Child[38], and the 1989 Convention on the Rights of the Child.[39] At this point the question arises whether the definition of "a child" contained in any of the above mentioned documents can be recognized as a universal international legal definition of "a child"? Owing to the regionally limited scope of the binding force of the African Charter, its definition does not have a universal character. Does any of the definitions of "a child" contained either in the 182 ILO Convention or in the 1989 CRC have this character? One may argue that the very high number of states which have consented to be bound by the Convention on the Rights of the Child[40] is clear evidence for the universal definition of the "child" contained in the agreement. And although there is no doubt that the provisions of the convention are only applicable to the contracting parties, because of the well-known principle of *pacta sunt servanda*, the fact that there are 193 parties to the Convention suggests that an overwhelming majority of states concur with the definition. This may, however, require further analysis.

---

[37] International Labour Organization, Convention Concerning the Prohibition and Immediate Action for the Elimination of the Worst Forms of Child Labour, June 17, 1999, 38 I.L.M. 1207, 2133 U.N.T.S. 161 [hereinafter the Worst Forms of Child Labour Convention].

[38] Organization of African Unity, African Charter on the Rights and Welfare of the Child, July 11, 1990, O.A.U. Doc. CAB/LEG/24.9/49 (1990) [hereinafter the African Charter].

[39] The CRC, *supra* note 1.

[40] United Nations Treaty Collection, http://treaties.un.org/Pages/ViewDetails.aspx?src=TREATY&mtdsg_no=IV-11&chapter=4&lang=en (last visited Oct. 9, 2010).

According to Article 1 of the CRC "…a child means every human being below the age of eighteen years unless under the law applicable to the child, majority is attained earlier." Before I proceed to analyze the content of that provision, I will focus on the *travaux preparatoires* that led to the adoption of the current version of Article 1 and which have lasted since the first version of the provision was submitted in 2001.

3.1. Travaux Preparatoires – Towards the Elaboration of an International Legal Definition of "a Child"

When analyzing the term "child" we are forced to build our argument on one of the most recognized treaties in the system of international law, namely the United Nations Convention on the Rights of the Child. As a matter of fact, the term "child" incorporated in the Convention can be examined from two interrelated parts of the document. These include Article 1 of the Convention and its Preamble.[41]

3.1.1. First Proposals (Years 1978–1979)

The Draft Convention submitted by Poland in 1978 did not contain a definition of "a child". Article I of the Convention indicated that the rights contained in the Convention belong to "every child" without any explanation of who is considered to be "a child". It stated that "Every child, without any exception whatsoever, shall be entitled to the rights set forth in this Convention, without distinction or discrimination on account of race, colour, sex, language, religion, political or other opinion, national or social origin, property, birth or other status, whether of himself or of his family."[42]

Despite the lack of a definition of "a child" in the first version of Article I of the draft Convention, there was a brief reference, which might have served as a *nucleus* to this definition, in the 3rd preambular paragraph to the draft Convention. It stated that "Recognizing also that the child, by reason of his physical and mental immaturity, needs special safeguards and care, including appropriate legal protection, before as well as after birth.[43] This provision was taken from the 3rd paragraph of the Preamble

[41] More precisely 9th preambular paragraph.
[42] Sharon Detrick ET AL., The United Nations Convention on the Rights of the Child. A Guide to the "*Travaux Preparatoires*" 34 (1992).
[43] *Id.*

to the 1959 UN Declaration of the Rights of the Child.[44] Emphasizing the need for special safeguards and care before the child's birth, it pointed out the initial moment at which childhood begins which should be placed before birth. A similar commitment was reflected in the original Article IV of the draft Convention, which stated that the child shall be provided with adequate pre-natal and post-natal care. According to Article IV, the "child shall enjoy the benefits of social security. He shall be entitled to grow and develop in health; to this end, special care and protection shall be provided both to him and to his mother, including adequate pre-natal and post-natal care. The child shall have the right to adequate nutrition, housing, recreation and medical services."[45]

In 1979 the Commission on Human Rights established an informal Open-ended Working Group, entrusting it with the task of elaborating the Convention on the Rights of the Child. The Working Group began its work with the review of the revised text of the draft Convention submitted to it in the same year. This Working Group work resulted in the amendments of the provisions referring to the definition of "a child": the reference to the need to guarantee the legal protection of a child before its birth has been deleted from the Preamble. The Working Group has formulated a new reading of the new 5th paragraph which recognizes that "the child due to the needs of his physical and mental development requires particular care and assistance with regard to health, physical, mental, moral and social development as well as legal protection in conditions of freedom, dignity and security."[46]

In a similar convention, Article 1 of the draft has also been revised. According to it, "a child is every human being from the moment of his birth to the age of 18 years unless, under the law of his state, he has attained his age of majority earlier."[47] The new version of Article 1 clearly based the concept of "a child" on the age limit criterion indicating the beginning and the end of childhood. The new draft revision pointed out two significant facts. These were the initiation of childhood, and its termination. Accordingly, the moment of birth of a child constitutes its initiation, and the age of eighteen years implies its termination. Identifying the beginning of childhood with the moment of birth, the authors of the

---

[44] G.A. Res. 1386 (XIV), U.N. GAOR, 14th Sess., Supp. No. 16, U.N. Doc. A/4354, at 19, (Nov. 20, 1959).
[45] Detrick, *supra* note 42, at 34.
[46] *Id.* at 101.
[47] *Id.* at 115.

amendment excluded the foetus and the unborn from the concept of "a child". Confirmation of this approach has been reflected in the above mentioned amended preambular text.

3.1.2. Further Discussion (Years 1980–1988)

Further years of work on the adequate preambular provision and Article 1 of the draft Convention on the Rights of the Child, have focused on the issue of the lower and upper limit of childhood. Most of the differences arose around the initial point at which childhood begins. Some delegates spoke in favour of equating the initial point of childhood with the moment of conception; they[48] stated that such a regulation would be consistent with legislation in many countries.[49] Other delegates stressed that the Convention on the Rights of the Child is a document dealing only with the rights of a *born* child, and thus does not apply to an unborn one.[50] In the opinion of the Polish representative, "...the present formulation of the preambular paragraph did not exclude the protection of the child before birth, nor did it contradict a wider interpretation of the text or the application of other more comprehensive provisions".[51] The Italian delegate pointed out that owing to the common recognition by members of the international community of the need to protect life before birth (reflected in there being no manifest state opposition to the principles in the Declaration of the Rights of the Child emphasizing the need for pre-natal protection of a child), the rule regarding such a protection could be considered as "jus cogens".[52] The Moroccan representative proposed the cessation of attempts to determine the initial point of childhood, which in his opinion had caused the large number of differences among delegations. His proposal has finally been accepted.[53]

Some delegates also suggested a change to the point marking the termination of childhood. Many representatives opted for lowering the upper age limit from eighteen to either sixteen, fifteen, or even fourteen. They argued that that would be consistent with the national legislation of

---

[48] Such approach has been presented by Argentina, Austria, Colombia, Egypt, Federal Republic of Germany, the Holy See, Ireland, Italy, Kuwait, Malta, Philippines, Senegal, Venezuela.
[49] Detrick, *supra* note 42, at 108-109.
[50] *Id.* at 109.
[51] *Id.*
[52] *Id.*
[53] *Id.* at 115.

many countries where fourteen was the age at which compulsory education ended, and also the minimum legal age for marriage.[54] In the Nepalese delegate's opinion such a solution would satisfy the interests of poorer countries which might not have been able to shoulder the burdens imposed by the Convention concerning the guarantees of the rights for children up to eighteen years of age.[55] They also stressed that lowering the upper age limit for childhood would be consistent with the solution adopted by UN General Assembly in connection with the 1979 International Year of the Child that had set that limit at fifteen.[56] But this proposal met strong opposition from many other delegates, who expressed their conviction that the Convention on the Rights of the Child should be applicable to as many children as possible. Other delegates, however, stated that setting the upper age limit at a lower point would also establish a clear distinction between the concept of "the child" and "the minor". The observer for the International Union for Child Welfare suggested replacing the criterion of age as a terminal point of childhood by the criterion of majority age, in conformity with the law of the relevant state. His proposal stated that, "According to the present Convention, a child is every human being who has not attained the age of majority in conformity with the law of his state."[57] But the proposal was rejected. Its opponents argued that there were too many differences, among and within national legislations, determining the point at which majority is attained. [58]

3.1.3. Final Text (Year 1989)

On 25th of November 1989, the United Nations General Assembly in its 44/25 Resolution adopted the Convention on the Rights of the Child,[59] and it came into force on 2nd of September 1990. With the Convention's entry into force an explicit definition of "a child" appeared in international law. The Convention contains two provisions relevant to the analysis of the definition of "a child". These are the 9th preambular paragraph and Article 1, which were added to the content of the Convention after many discussions, conflicts and analysis among the delegations of various states or organizations. The relevant texts of the Convention provide that

---

[54] Sharon Detrick, A Commentary on the United Nations Convention on the Rights of the Child 58 (1999); Bueren, *supra* note 2, at 36.
[55] Detrick, *supra* note 42, at 118.
[56] Bueren, *supra* note 2, at 36.
[57] Detrick, *supra* note 42, at 116.
[58] Detrick, *supra* note 42, at 116; Detrick, *supra* note 54, at 58.
[59] The CRC, *supra* note 1.

> Bearing in mind that, as indicated in the Declaration of the Rights of the Child, "the child, by reason of his physical and mental immaturity, needs special safeguards and care, including appropriate legal protection, before as well as after birth", (9th preambular paragraph)

> For the purposes of the present Convention, a child means every human being below the age of eighteen years unless, under the law applicable to the child, majority is attained earlier. (Article 1)

3.2. The Convention on the Rights of the Child's Definition of "a Child"

3.2.1. The End of Childhood

In order to define who is to be considered "a child", the Convention's drafters decided to partly use the age limit criterion. They set only the upper age limit of childhood. In principle, childhood ends with the attainment of the age of eighteen years. The Convention on the Rights of the Child does not distinguish intermediate periods between childhood and adulthood, such as, for example, "infancy" and "adolescence".

Setting the upper age limit of childhood at eighteen is consistent with the legislation of most countries,[60] though the Convention allows for situations where majority is attained at lower than eighteen. In their national law, States party to the Convention can thus set a lower age for the end of childhood—this solution expresses respect for cultural and traditional diversities reflected in national regulations.[61] On the other hand, though, it leaves a gaping lacuna: if a child attains majority earlier, then those Convention rights which do not refer to a specific age will not apply to a person who, under national law applicable to him, is no longer regarded as "a child".[62] Permitting each State Party to decide at what age childhood ends has also a negative effect on the international uniformity of the

---

[60] Except for those countries in which majority is attained later, as in the case of Austria where majority is attained at 19 and Switzerland where majority is attained at 20.

[61] The principle of respect for cultural and traditional diversities of different societies was reflected in the 11th preambular paragraph to the CRC which reads "taking due account of the importance of the traditions and cultural values of each people", *see* CRC, *supra* note 1.

[62] Bueren, *supra* note 2, at 37.

Convention and "could even lead to the unequal treatment of children based solely on their national domicile".[63]

One solution to this could be that proposed by McGoldrick, which would be to include a minimum age limit for the national law declarations of majority in order to prevent states from setting the age of majority unreasonably low.[64] Another could be to set a strict eighteen-year limit for the end of childhood, without exception. Such an argument can be found, for example, in the definition of "a child" included in the African Charter on the Rights and Welfare of the Child, which in its Article 2 states "…a child means every human being below the age of 18 years".[65] A Similar definition has been used for the purposes of the Worst Forms of Child Labour Convention of 1999, Article 2 of which reads, "…the term "child" shall apply to all persons under the age of 18".[66]

3.2.2. The Beginning of Childhood

Drafters of the Convention have also not removed doubts concerning the initial moment at which childhood begins. Difficulties in obtaining consensus by representatives of countries working on the wording of Article 1 of the Convention led to a compromise determining, or rather, *non-determining*, the lower age limit of childhood. Thus, while interpreting Article 1 of the Convention we are confronted with two approaches referring to the adopted solution.

Some states believe that the concept of childhood includes the entire or partial period from the moment of conception. They find the support for their approach in the 9th preambular paragraph referring to the need to guarantee appropriate legal protection of a child before birth. They point out that this approach is also consistent with national legislation of many countries. Opponents believe that childhood begins only at the moment of birth: they state that although the Preamble forms part of the basis for the interpretation of a treaty, it has not got any binding international legal implications for determining the starting point of childhood.[67] According

---

[63] Detrick, *supra* note 54, at 59.

[64] Dominic McGoldrick D, *The United Nations Convention on the Rights of the Child*, 5 INT'L J. L. 132, 133 (1991), *quoted in* Detrick, *supra* note 54, at 59.

[65] The African Charter, *supra* note 38.

[66] The Worst Forms of Child Labour Convention, *supra* note 37.

[67] Bożena Gronowska, Tadeusz Jasudowicz, Cezary Mik, O prawach dziecka 12 (1994); Bueren, *supra* note 2, at 34; Detrick, *supra* note 54, at 56.

to Alston, suggesting that a provision in the Preamble “not reflected in the operative part of its [the CRC’s] text, can be relied upon, on its own,” “would be inconsistent with the general principles of treaty interpretation” and would “extend very considerably the natural and ordinary meaning of the actual terms used in the CRC itself”.[68] He also notes that “even if one were to accept for the sake of argument that paragraph 9 of the Preamble must be taken strictly into account when interpreting the CRC, or even that it imposes a binding obligation on States parties, the meaning of the paragraph could be described differently”. In his opinion, the obligation stemming from 9th Paragraph “to provide the child with ‘special safeguards and care, including appropriate legal protection, before .... birth’” could be seen “as endorsing the already widespread practice of taking whatever measures the State considers ‘appropriate’ with a view to protecting the unborn child”.[69]

Leaving aside doubts regarding the initial moment of childhood leaves many questions unanswered: From which point does a child have “the inherent right to life”?[70] Should it be protected from the moment of conception, from the moment at which the embryo becomes a foetus, from a specific period in the womb, or from the moment of birth? Going further, if we identify the beginning of childhood with the moment of conception, does it mean that we can speak about a general prohibition of abortion under the provisions of international law? Can the ban be extended to a variety of genetic experiments carried out with the use of, or on, the human embryo? Is the unborn child entitled to the rights relating to health and privacy protection? International law does not give an unequivocal answer to these questions.

The dominant doctrinal view combines the beginning of the international legal protection of the child with its birth.[71] Some authors speaking in favour of this view refer to the nature of the children’s rights. They state that some of them cannot be, by their nature, applicable to the unborn.[72] To them belong, for example, such rights as freedom of expression,

---

[68] Detrick, *supra* note 54, at 56.
[69] *Id.* at 56-57.
[70] “The inherent right to life” has been formulated in Article 6 (1) of the CRC, Article 2 of the European Convention on Human Rights, Article 6 (1) of the International Covenant on Civil and Political Rights and Article 4 of the American Convention on Human Rights.
[71] Detrick, *supra* note 54, at 57; Bueren, *supra* note 2, at 35.
[72] Detrick, *supra* note 42, at 109.

freedom of thought, conscience and religion.[73] Proponents of this position point out that in order to speak about the international legal guarantees of protection of the unborn an explicit norm ensuring such a protection is required.[74] As an example they refer to Article 4 (1) of the American Convention on Human Rights, under which every person's right to have respect for his life should be legally protected "in general, from the moment of conception".[75] Article 4 (1) of the Convention provides that "Every person has the right to have his life respected. This right shall be protected by law, and, in general, from the moment of conception. […]".[76]

In international law documents we can find examples of explicit, though indirect, protection of the unborn. Article 76 (3) of the I Protocol to the Geneva Conventions obliges the Parties to the conflict to avoid the pronouncement of the death penalty on pregnant women and forbids, without exception, the execution of such women; Article 6 (4) of the II Protocol to the Geneva Conventions does not allow sentence of death to be carried out on pregnant women; and the same ban is incorporated into Article 6 (5) of the International Covenant on Civil and Political Rights.[77]

Because of the lack of an explicit obligation for the protection of the unborn in the provisions of the Convention on the Rights of the Child, we have to conclude that the protection granted under the Convention's provision applies only to "a child" from the moment of birth.[78] The Convention does not, however, restrict the discretion of each state to extend, under their domestic law, the definition of "a child" to the unborn.[79]

---

[73] Article 13 and 14 of the CRC.

[74] Philip Alston, *The Unborn Child and Abortion under the Draft Convention on the Rights of the Child*, 12 HUM. RTS. Q. 156, 169-70 (1990), *quoted in* Detrick, *supra* note 54, at 53.

[75] Organization of American States, American Convention on Human Rights, Nov. 22, 1969, O.A.S.T.S. No. 36, 1144 U.N.T.S. 123.

[76] *Id.*

[77] United Nations International Covenant on Civil and Political Rights, *supra* note 29.

[78] Bueren, *supra* note 2, at 34-35.

[79] Alston notes that the use of the terms "child" and "human being" in Article 1, without the explicit determination of the initial moment of childhood, "was clearly intended to maintain maximum flexibility so as to enable potential signatories to the [CRC] to adopt whatever position they wished, for the purposes of their own domestic law, on the issue of the right to life of the foetus or unborn child". Philip Alston, *The Legal Framework of the Convention on the Rights of the Child*, 91/2 United Nations Bulletin of Human Rights: The Rights of the Child 3, 11-15

The exercise of this right has been reflected in states' reservations and declarations submitted in accordance with Article 1 of the Convention. For example, the Argentine Republic declared that Article 1 should be interpreted "to the effect that a child means every human being from the moment of conception up to the age of eighteen".[80] A similar position has been presented by the Government of Guatemala which referred in its declaration to Article 3 of its Constitution, establishing that: "The State guarantees and protects human life from the time of its conception, as well as the integrity and security of the individual".[81] This approach has been supported by the Holy See.[82]

4. Conclusion

In the lack of a clear interpretation of the term "child", it seems advisable to separate the concept of "a child" from the concept of conceived, but not yet born, human being. For example, one could use the term "the conceived human being", "the unborn", "human beings in the pre-natal period", "the human foetus", etc. Explicit legal protection under international law, either through exhaustive or exemplary catalogues of rights granted to the unborn, should be ensured. Such a standard could be incorporated into the 1989 Convention on the Rights of the Child, or into the regional international instruments, such as the International Covenant on Civil and Political Rights or the European Convention on Human Rights. Or maybe the best solution would be to elaborate a separate international document wholly devoted to the protection of the unborn.[83] The lack of a binding international legal norm, covering the moment of conception to the moment of birth, which can appropriately protect generations of human beings, leaves, in my view, a significant loophole that should be closed.

(1992), *quoted in* Detrick, *supra* note 54, at 57. A similar statement was presented by the International Committee of the Red Cross during the drafting process of *the Convention on the Rights of the Child.* In its opinion "the silence [not making it clear who is considered to be a child in Article 1] seems wise and will facilitate universal application of the Convention irrespective of local peculiarities." Detrick, *supra* note 54, at 58-59.

[80] *See supra* note 39.

[81] *Id.*

[82] Bueren, *supra* note 2, at 34.

[83] This question I would like to analyze in a separate article.

CHILDREN'S RIGHTS IN THE NORWEGIAN CONSTITUTION

KIRSTEN SANDBERG

A limited revision of the Norwegian Constitution is being prepared in order to strengthen the position of human rights. This article discusses the need to specifically include children's rights. There are at least three good reasons to do so: first, the visibility of children; secondly, as a response to adults' human rights; and thirdly, the need to strengthen children's participation in society. As to the contents of such a provision, the article discusses i.a. whether there should be a reference to all the three P's (Protection, Provision and Participation) and whether the general principles should be explicitly included. Provisions for children's rights in other countries' constitutions are used as examples.

1. Background

In preparing for the 200th anniversary of the Norwegian constitution in 2014, Parliament has set up a committee to consider and propose a limited revision of the Constitution with the purpose of strengthening the position of human rights in it. Apart from a few traditional rights, like the freedom of speech, the Norwegian constitution contains only a general reference to human rights. Thus, as opposed to the constitutions of a number of other countries, it has no provision regarding children's rights. This revision offers an opportunity to examine whether children's rights should be specifically included. The intention of this article is to discuss the need for that, and the possible contents of such a revision.

Some core human rights instruments which are incorporated into the Norwegian Human Rights Act of 1999 are the UN Covenants on Civil and Political Rights and on Economic, Social and Cultural Rights, the European Convention on Human Rights, the UN Convention on the Rights of the Child (of 2003) and most recently (2010) the UN Convention on the Elimination of All Forms of Discrimination against Women. Notably, the

Act empowers the conventions with a kind of semi-constitutional status by accepting that in case of conflict between an incorporated human right and provisions in other legislation, the convention is to have priority. However, since that priority is only contained in an ordinary Act and thus may be changed by an ordinary Act, the term "semi-constitutional" may not be entirely correct. But as long as the rule is in force, the reality is that the conventions are recognized above other Acts. Consequently, human rights carry great weight in the interpretation process, so that provisions in other Acts are interpreted in line with human rights provisions. If human rights are to a greater extent to be included in our constitution, the fate of the Human Rights Act and the priority rule must also be discussed.

The existing provision on human rights in the constitution states quite generally that the authorities of the State recognize the obligation to respect human rights (Section 110 c). According to the mandate of the Committee, the aim of the revision is to adapt the constitution to the present day conditions.[1] The Committee is responsible for preparing an appropriate consideration of the place of human rights within the constitution, and this should also include the relationship of the Human Rights Act to the priority rule, and the question of trying the rights before the courts. The purpose is to secure the formulation and implementation of the universal principles of human rights within the constitution. In other words, the ambition is not to present a list of rights, which in the Norwegian context would naturally belong in ordinary legislation.

2. Public Debate

Up till now, the revision has not been the subject of extensive media debate. However, a few lawyers have voiced their opinions. Frode Elgesem, a practising lawyer, has proposed a temptingly simple amendment in the form of an addition to the existing Section 110 c on the obligation to respect and secure human rights. He suggests that: "Provisions in international human rights instruments by which Norway is bound shall not be limited by legislation or other act of the authorities."[2] The grounds for his simple solution are to avoid Parliament's having to choose between human rights and favour some of them at the cost of

---

[1] Mandate of Parliament's Human Rights Committee (in Norwegian only): http://www.stortinget.no/no/Hva-skjer-pa-Stortinget/Nyhetsarkiv/Pressemeldinger/2008-2009/Menneskerettighetsutvalg/.

[2] Elgesem, Frode, *Grunnlovens garantier* (The guarantees of the Constitution), feature article, Aftenposten (newspaper) 29.08.2010

others, and to avoid juridical ambiguity by human rights being contained both in the constitution and in the conventions.

His suggestion has been opposed by others. Professor Graver (2010) responds that not all human rights are equally important, and that by giving priority to all human rights conventions the political bodies are deprived of the responsibility and authority to make the priorities that are necessary in practical politics.[3] In his response, Njål Høstmælingen, director of the International Law and Policy Institute, pointed out five problems with this simple solution.[4] These are: lack of clarity as to what should count as human rights conventions; the problem of treaty interpretation in practice; the possibility of Parliament indirectly reducing protection by withdrawing Norway from controversial conventions; the need to remove existing rights from the constitution because of changes and the lack of transparency, debate and priority-making.

Graver has indicated that some rights are more central than others.[5] With regard to that he addresses the fact that the UN Convention on the Rights of the Child (CRC)[6] is only about the concretization and implementation of the general human rights conventions. Consequently, children will be covered by the general human rights in the constitution, and there should be no need to include children's rights explicitly. The need to make explicit reference to the rights of children will be scrutinized more closely in the following sections.

3. The Need to Include Children's Rights

Children are in a special position as human beings since we are all, or have been, children. Childhood is a temporary, but long-lasting state, characterized i.a. by 'evolving capacities'. In the beginning, the child has a total dependence on others, which is gradually reduced in the course of childhood. The legal consequence is that children do not have full autonomy and that adults may, to a certain extent, legitimately control children and decide on their behalf. Over the last 20-25 years children have, to a growing extent, been seen as agents of their own life and

[3] Graver, Hans Petter, *Ikke hevet over politikken* (Not raised above politics), Aftenposten 06.09.2010

[4] Høstmælingen, Njål (2010), *Hokus pokus om menneskerettigheter?* (Hocus-pocus regarding human rights?) Aftenposten (newspaper) 07.09.2010

[5] Graver, Hans Petter, Ikke hevet over politikken.

[6] Hereinafter the Convention on the rights of the Child is presented as CRC.

development), and in line with this the CRC stipulates their position as rights holders.[7] However, there is a long way to go for children's rights to be taken as seriously as those of adults: adults still set the limits of children's autonomy and decide to what degree children may influence decisions, both in their own lives and in society. This particular dependency does not apply to other groups, and it needs to be met with rights; thus, when human rights are to be included in the constitution, it is basically essential to include children's rights.

It is actually a misrepresentation that the CRC is only about the concretization and implementation of general human rights. Some of the rights are actually not covered anywhere else. The right of the child under Article 12 to be heard in all matters affecting him or her, and the principle of the child's best interests as a primary consideration in all actions concerning children, are unique. Both rights are necessary, each in its own way, to meet with adults' right to decide for children. The coupling in Article 6 of the right to life with the right to development is also especially connected with children.[8] Other examples of rights that are not found in other human rights conventions are the right under Article 20 to care and protection when the child is deprived of his or her family, the right under Article 25 of children in placement for the purpose of care, protection or treatment to periodic review, and the right under Article 39 to rehabilitation if the child has been the victim of neglect, abuse, armed conflicts etc.

Indeed, many of the remaining rights may, to a certain extent, be viewed as concretizations of rights in the general UN conventions, but precisely by being specified and elaborated with children in mind, they are more adapted to the situations that children may be in, and thus far more useful to them . In particular, this holds true for social and economic rights (to health, Article 24; social security, Article 26; and living standard, Article 27) and many of the protective rights (Article 33, concerning drugs; and Article 34, on sexual exploitation). The CRC often imposes additional duties on the states; e.g. the right to health includes a provision

---

[7] Kjørholt, Anne Trine, *Barn som samfunnsborgere – til barns beste?* in Kjørholt, Anne Trine (ed.), Barn som samfunnsborgere – til barnets beste (Children as citizens – in the child's best interest?) 11-29 (2010) Universitetsforlaget.

[8] There is a right to development in certain other human rights instruments, but it is primarily concerned with the material conditions and circumstances, not with the personal development of the individual.

committing the states to work for the abolishment of traditional practices prejudicial to the health of children (Article 24 no. 3).

It is axiomatic that some of the rights in the CRC are virtually copies of general human rights law such as the freedom of speech and the freedom of assembly. However, it is still necessary to specifically mention that they apply to children. Children have to be made visible as rights holders, otherwise they may easily fall outside. This has the legal purpose of clarifying that children are actually covered by those rights, and the pedagogical purpose of reminding adults about that fact.

An additional argument for including children's rights in the constitution is that it may be necessary in response to the rights of adults. Experience from Ireland tells us that a constitutional right to family life is viewed as a strong right of parents, creating an imbalance between the rights of parents and child.[9] To counter that, children must be given explicit rights—in particular to protection, but also to be heard and to have their best interests taken into account as a primary consideration.

Strengthening children's participation in society should be paramount in most questions regarding children's rights. Children are not sufficiently included, either in democratic processes or in individual decisions affecting them. It is, indeed, important to recognize the diverse informal ways in which children actually do influence their own lives and participate in their communities.[10] This could be termed a bottom-up perspective on participation. Still, it is vital to include children in the formal processes where important decisions are made. Constitutional acknowledgement would mean recognizing children as citizens and make it more difficult to neglect children as participants in those processes. The Constitution has a strong symbolic value: if a solution were to be chosen where some human rights were included in the Constitution but children were not mentioned, it would be contrary to how children are viewed today.

The view that children's rights should be included explicitly is reinforced by the UN Committee on the Rights of the Child, which states that

---

[9] Conor O'Mahony, University College, Cork in lecture at the Law Faculty at the University of Oslo, 23/03/2010.

[10] Habashi, J., Driskill, Lang and DeFalco, *Constitutional Analysis: A Proclamation of Children's Right to Protection, Provision, and Participation*, 18 International Journal of Children's Rights 267 (2010), p.281.

guarantees of rights for "everyone" is not adequate to ensure respect for these rights for children.[11] The Committee welcomes the inclusion of sections on the rights of the child in national constitutions, reflecting key principles in the Convention.[12] Even if this does not create a formal obligation to do so, the statement demonstrates that children's rights are easily overlooked if they are not expressly mentioned. The Committee is the only body that can interpret the convention with some authority, and the arguments above show that there are a considerable number of good reasons for following the recommendation of the Committee.

4. What Rights to Include?

4.1 Introduction

Since it is not a question of including a catalogue of human rights in the constitution, but of securing the universal human rights principles, children's rights might not be listed. Depending on how comprehensive the chapter on human rights is, there may presumably be some room for a couple of provisions regarding children. One will probably have to settle for one provision which, at a general level, includes what is considered to be of the greatest importance in principle and at the same time, to the fullest extent possible, covers children's rights under the CRC.

A common classification of the rights is according to the three P's: protection, Provision and Participation. Most of the articles of the convention fall into one of those categories. I will begin in 4.2 by referring to the results of a study of the extent to which protection, provision and participation are covered in different states' constitutions. And, in 4.3 I shall discuss the need to cover each of the three P's in the Norwegian Constitution.

Finally, the four articles that have been appointed as general principles by the UN Committee on the Rights of the Child (Articles 2, 3, 6 and 12) are not to be neglected, and will be discussed separately in 4.4.

---

[11] UN Committee on the Rights of the Child, General Comment no. 5, *General measures of implementation* (2003), para. 21.

[12] Ibid.

4.2 The Three P's in Constitutions around the World

Some American scholars have made a study of the occurrence of children's rights in the constitutions of 179 countries around the world (Habashi et al. 2010). They are the countries listed in the Human Development Index (HDI) of 2008, and in line with the HDI, the researchers categorized the countries into three levels. These are high (level one, 75 countries), medium (level two, 78 countries) and low (level three, 26 countries). Interestingly, the researchers found that 64-68 per cent of the countries' constitutions covered protection of children, irrespective of level. The percentage of countries that endorsed provision—i.e. providing services pertaining to education, health, care or food—was 76 per cent at level one, 56 per cent at level two and 69 per cent at level three. The relatively high percentage at level three is explained as possibly being due to the fact that children in those countries are poor and suffer from health and food shortage. The countries covering both protection and provision in their constitutions are 64 per cent at level one, 53 per cent at level two and 54 per cent at level three. I was surprised at the relatively high numbers at all levels, particularly with regard to provision. One reason may be that many constitutions traditionally contain the right to education. Thus, they are counted in the category of constitutions covering provision, even if they do not cover the right to other services or subsistence as such.

When it comes to participation, the picture is dramatically different. Only 16 per cent of the countries at level one, 13 per cent at level two and 12 per cent at level three endorse participation of children in their constitutions. Even though one might think that the numbers ought to be higher at level one, where the countries are "more developed", the numbers are similar at all three levels. As the researchers suggest, the low numbers may reflect the controversial character of the participation domain of the CRC. They may also be due to the fact that the idea of children's participation at this more formal level—democratically and in decisions—is relatively new. Although states may not necessarily oppose the idea, it may take some time before it is included in the constitutions of the world.

4.3 Discussion of Participation, Protection and Provision

Among the three P's, children's right to participation is the most recent and most comprehensive right. Taking children's participation seriously implies including children in decision-making at all levels of society to a very different extent than today. Thus, it is also the most controversial of the three P's. The core of the right to participation is the right of the child to be heard in all matters affecting him or her, under Article 12. Other participatory rights are the rights to freedom of speech and freedom of assembly which put children on a par with adults. The human rights chapter of the Norwegian Constitution should contain a clear provision on children's right to participation. If only rights to protection and provision were included, it would maintain the image of the child as vulnerable and unable to act as an agent of its own life and of society. An explicit reference to the right of children under Article 12 to participate in decisions concerning their own lives is perhaps the most self-evident part of a constitutional provision on children's rights. The additional need to clarify that the general democratic freedoms apply to children follows from the arguments in paragraph 2 above.

The right of the child to protection under the CRC includes protection from a considerable number of harmful conditions. These are not only violence and degrading treatment (Articles 19 and 37), sexual abuse and neglect (Articles 19 and 34), but also trafficking in children (Article 35), recruitment as child soldiers (Article 38), the use, production and trafficking of drugs (Article 33) and all kinds of exploitation, whether economically, sexually or otherwise (Articles 32, 34 and 36 respectively). Since children are vulnerable, there is a need to include their right to protection in the constitution. The need is even greater if a right to family life is included, because such a right is often understood as a strong right of parents, which must be counterbalanced by the rights of children (see paragraph 3 above). The provision should probably be presented in a general way: listing the matters that the child should be protected against is not such a good idea because of the risk that some matters would fall outside, and it may also be contrary to the idea of the constitutional amendment.

Provision rights include rights to education, health services and social security. Those rights not only follow from the CRC, but also from the UN Convention on Economic, Social and Cultural Rights. A constitutional protection of human rights would not be complete without a reference to such rights, which are of fundamental importance to the right to life and, for children, to development. Even though children would be covered by general rights of this kind, an explicit reference would be necessary to secure that children's needs are actually taken into account. Economic and social rights for children are crucial, since they concern their well-being today as well as their opportunity to grow into tomorrow's well integrated citizens with a sense of community.

4.4 The General Principles

Another classification, introduced by the UN Committee on the Rights of the Child, is "general principles": the best interests principle in Article 3, the non-discrimination clause in Article 2, the right to life and development in Article 6, and the right to be heard in Article 12. I have already mentioned the latter as constituting the core of the participatory rights. The non-discrimination principle is the one out of the four which corresponds most closely to such a principle in general conventions. A general constitutional provision to that effect will presumably be included as one of the universal human rights principles, and will probably cover children's situation sufficiently. It might yet be considered whether either children should be mentioned specifically in the general clause, or the equality principle should be mentioned in a provision on children's rights. A special feature of the non-discrimination of children is the need to secure the principle not only with regard to the characteristics or status of the child itself, but also that of its parents or legal guardians. There may be a need to include that in a constitutional provision, whether one or the other solution is chosen.

One should also bear in mind that discrimination of children may either be of children as compared with adults, or between children. With regard to the former, but also relevant to the latter, age comes up as unlawful grounds for discrimination and should probably be mentioned if such grounds are included in the constitution at all. However, the meaning and extent of this and other grounds are not to be solved at the constitutional level.

The right to life may be regarded as the most fundamental of all human rights, for children as well as adults. Even if it is considered self-evident, there is reason to include it in the Constitution. As mentioned above, for children the right to life in CRC Article 6 no. 2 is linked with the right to development. The child has a right not only to survive, but also to be given sufficient life conditions, at present, to develop – physically, mentally, spiritually, morally and socially (see also Article 27). Indeed, children are to be recognized as individuals of equal worth here and now, but at the same time they are in a unique position because they are in an early phase of life where development is vital. A reference to that may be a natural part of a constitutional provision on the right to life.

The best interests principle under the CRC Article 3 applies to all actions concerning children, that is, decisions as well as counselling and other statements, and individual decisions as well as legislation, budgets, government directives and other general measures. The principle is well integrated into Norwegian legislation: for example, in the 2010 Children and Parents Act and the 1999 Child Protection Act it has a particularly strong and long-lasting standing, but it has also been included e.g. in the new 2008 Immigration Act. In the latter it has to be balanced against considerations of immigration control, which is a challenging task demonstrating what weight the best interests principle is given in a situation of strongly competing interests. However, since it is so central to all activity concerning children, it is hard to imagine human rights provisions in the Norwegian constitution without including the principle. The Constitution is supposed to safeguard against future changes in the legislation which may today seem unthinkable.

An almost inevitable feature of the best interests principle is paternalism, i.e. adults being the ones to determine what is the best for a child. This gives rise to continuous discussions about the principle. The only way to meet those doubts is to apply the general principle of participatory rights, giving the child the right to influence what is considered to be in his or her best interests. Thus, as argued above, the right of the child to be heard has to be included in a constitutional provision. It should be included not only as a procedural right, but as a right for children to have their views taken into consideration, as stated in Article 12.

4.5 Summing up

To sum up, all of the three P's ought to be covered by the constitution. Participation is self-evident in order to underline and reinforce children's position in contemporary society and their right to influence their own lives. However, one may not overlook the fact that children are still vulnerable and dependent on adults, the more so the younger they are. Accordingly, they still need some degree of protection in certain situations and from various perils, which the constitution should take account of. Furthermore, they cannot be expected to provide for themselves, and the economic, social and cultural rights that will hopefully be introduced in the Constitution should contain a reference to children.

The best interests principle cannot be omitted, being fundamental in all decisions concerning children, but which has to be balanced by the right to participation. A general right to life would also cover children, but the right to development might be added. Even if a non-discrimination clause covers children, it may be useful to add the equality principle for children specifically and— perhaps more importantly—to state that the child should not be discriminated against on grounds of his or her parents' or guardians' status or characteristics.

5. Contents and Formulation - Examples from Other Countries

In considering what the contents of a constitutional provision on children's rights should be, and how it could be formulated, we may look at other countries. I have examined the way in which children's rights are covered in several constitutions. Many contain long bills of rights, for everyone as well as for children. Since this is not the way it is supposed to be done in Norway, I have looked for provisions that express some principles rather than detailed rights. The Finnish and the Belgian constitutions are particularly relevant here.

The Finnish Constitution (1999) Section 6 on equality reads as follows:

> "*Section 6 - Equality*
> Everyone is equal before the law.
> No one shall, without an acceptable reason, be treated differently from other persons on the ground of sex, age, origin, language, religion, conviction, opinion, health, disability or other reason that concerns his or her person.
> Children shall be treated equally and as individuals and they shall be allowed to influence matters pertaining to them to a degree corresponding to their level of development.
> Equality of the sexes is promoted in societal activity and working life, especially in the determination of pay and the other terms of employment, as provided in more detail by an Act."

The third paragraph of the Finnish constitution on children not only deals with the principle of equality, it also stipulates children's right to participation. Since the right to be treated individually is a central aspect of the best interest principle, that principle is also covered to some extent. Children's need to be provided for is covered by Section 19, which gives everyone the right to basic subsistence and states that the public authorities shall support families and others responsible for providing for children so that they have the ability to ensure the wellbeing and personal development of the children. The protection of children is not generally mentioned in the Finnish Constitution, but a limited form of protection *is* expressed in Section 12 on freedom of expression, stating that restrictions on pictorial programmes which are composed of pictures that are necessary for the protection of children may be laid down by Act of Parliament.

The Belgian Constitution was amended in 2008 to contain a provision—Article 22 (b)—which reads:

> "Art. 22 (b)
> Every child has the right to respect for his or her moral, physical, mental and sexual integrity.
> Every child has the right to express his or her opinion in all matters affecting him or her; his or her opinion is to be taken into consideration in accordance with his or her power of judgment.
> Every child has the right to benefit from measures and services which further his or her development.
> In all decisions concerning the child, the interest of the child is the primary consideration.
> The law … guarantees these rights of the child."[13]

Protection of the child is covered by the first paragraph, since respect for the child's integrity implies protection against violence, abuse, harassment etc. It is formulated as a right, and it is comprehensive in that all aspects of a person's integrity are covered. Since integrity is a basic value, the formulation corresponds well with the committee's mandate to include universal principles in the Constitution. In my view this is a formulation well worth copying.

The second paragraph covers participation in the sense of Article 12, i.e. the right to influence decisions that affect the child or groups of children. The first part is quite similar to Article 12, but does not contain the explicit condition that the child should be capable of forming his or her own views. However, a child who does not have an opinion will not be able to express it, and so the condition may be implicit. As for the weight of the child's opinion, in the French version the article does not use the words "age and

[13] My translation from a combination of the French and Dutch versions which are found at http://www.senate.be/doc/const_nl.html#modif20081222, found by way of http://confinder.richmond.edu/.

maturity" but "discernment", which means something along the line of power of judgment. This actually seems to be more appropriate, since age is not really in itself an indication, and maturity is a wider term than it needs to be. "Power of judgment" goes directly to the core of what should be considered—as long as the child only has a right to influence the decision and not a right of self-determination.

Alternatively, the formulation in the Finnish constitution, giving children the right to "influence matters pertaining to them" might be a good solution at the constitutional level. However, in the subsequent expression "to a degree corresponding to their level of development" the latter should be substituted by "power of judgment" as mentioned.

The right to provision or social and economic rights is covered by the third paragraph in Article 22 b. It is a simple and straightforward reference to measures and services, and the confinement to those furthering the child's development seems necessary in order not to make the right too wide. The limitation should also be unproblematic from a child's perspective, provided it is understood in such a way as to secure acceptable life conditions for the child today. A question might be whether the formulation is too narrow when it comes to securing the child's basic subsistence (through its family), since the expression "measures and services" in Norway is not considered to include monetary support. Thus, the article might be supplemented by an addition like the one in the Finnish Constitution governing basic subsistence and support to families to secure the wellbeing and development of children, as mentioned above.
The fourth paragraph on the interest of the child does not include the word "best". This may be due to a national tradition, and it is hard to see that it makes any real difference, since "interest" must implicitly be understood as the result of considering different interests that a child may have, just as "best interest" would be. More interestingly, the article says that the interest shall be "the" primary consideration ("de eerste overweging", in the Flemish version), which is stronger than "a" in Article 3 of the CRC.[14] According to Norwegian legislation concerning children, the best interests of the child are to be the primary consideration (Children and Parents Act) or shall even be decisive (Child Protection Act). The new Immigration Act of 2008, however, only states that it shall be "a" primary consideration. The Constitution would need to take a position in this question, and the term "the primary consideration" would be the preferable solution to

[14] However, the weak formulation of the convention has been criticized.

taking care of the best interests of the child and will also mostly be in line with existing legislation.

6. Conclusion

From the discussion above it follows that there are several good reasons for specifically including children's rights in the Norwegian Constitution. These are legal arguments as well as pedagogical and symbolic ones. All the three P's ought to be included, participatory rights as well as rights to protection and provision. As for the formulation of such a provision, the Belgian Constitution seems to offer a good instance, with the addition of equal and individual treatment copied from the Finnish one.

The article on children's rights could thus be formulated like this:

> Every child has the right to respect for his or her moral, mental, physical, and sexual integrity.
>
> Every child has the right to influence matters affecting him or her to a degree corresponding to his or her power of judgment.
>
> Every child has the right to benefit from measures and services which further his or her development.
>
> Children shall be treated equally and individually. In all decisions concerning the child, the interest of the child shall be the primary consideration.

In addition, it ought to be clarified that the general articles on civil and political rights in the Constitution include children.

As I hope I have demonstrated in this article, in order to secure children's rights it is not sufficient to add general human rights principles to the Constitution. The revision of the constitution of Norway in 2014 is indeed a golden opportunity for the legislators of the country to join the number of states that already have constitutional provisions governing the rights of children and to reinforce those rights in our highest-ranking law.

SOME REFLECTIONS ON A DIALOGICAL APPROACH TO THE RECOGNITION OF CHILDREN IN THE DECISION-MAKING PROCESS

TITTI MATTSSON

Abstract

This article concerns the problem with the gap between principle and practice regarding child participation according to Article 12 of the Child Convention. Owing to the provisions of the article, the child should be able to participate in all decision-making that affects him or her, and be able to exert influence according to his age and maturity. However, international and national research indicates that it is, in practice, difficult to implement child participation rights. It would thus seem that granting children such rights in general does not necessarily create child participation. Advocating a dialogical approach to child participation, the author discusses the legislative need for specially adjusted procedural tools for children. Using Sweden as the framework for discussion, a so-called "participation veto" is put forth as an example.

1. Introduction

The international basis for child participation is the United Nations Child Convention (CRC) Article 12.[1] According to the article, the child should be able to participate in all decision-making that affects him or her, and be able to influence decisions according to age and maturity.

> State Parties shall assure to the child who is capable of forming his or her own views the right to express those views freely in all matters affecting the child being given due weight in accordance with the age and maturity of the child.

---

[1] For ease of reading, the term 'children' is used to refer to both children and young people.

The practical implications of this claim to the child's right to be able to participate in different decision-making processes have frequently been discussed in various fields.[2] According to Article 12, child participation includes the right to be heard prior to a decision relating to the child as well as the right to influence the decision in question, depending on the child's age and maturity.[3] The right to participate in the decision-making process is based on respect for, and recognition of, the child as an individual with human rights, and the potential of an autonomous individual. However, international and national research indicates that it is difficult to implement child participation rights in practice.[4] Though children themselves find it important to be viewed as individuals with feelings and opinions as well as subjects capable of participating in a decision, their voices and views are excluded from a variety of social activities and decisions.[5] This problem of realising Article 12 is a central issue in child law; the gap between theory and practice poses a dilemma in realising children's right to participation in matters relating specifically to their interests and welfare.

---

[2] One strong voice in this discussion is that of psychologist Roger A. Hart. He developed the so-called "participation ladder" and pronounced minimum standards for participation (see Hart 1997 and 1992). His participation ladder is considered uniquely influential and is referred to in a lot of research: see for example Shier 2001, Stern 2006, Dahlstrand 2004, Näsman 2004, Mattsson 2006. By formulating a ladder for participation, Hart wanted to demonstrate *how* participation may take different expressions. On the bottom of this eight-step ladder is "participation" by children acting as objects and in the interests of adults (described by Hart as manipulation, decoration and symbolism). These forms of behaviour, for example wearing a T-shirt with a political message formulated by adults, he disqualifies as child participation. The following five steps are different forms of child participation. These types of participation include the right to information, the right to be consulted, the right to initiate ideas, the right to influence decisions, and the right to decide (together with an adult).

[3] Although the right to influence a decision is an interesting and important part of Article 12, I consider that the first part, i.e. the right to be heard, has much significance for this article for several essential reasons. Firstly, research demonstrates that children themselves often view it to be of most importance to be listened to (see for example Tjelflaat & Ulset 2007). Secondly, the dialogical approach emphasises the dialogue as valuable in itself, irrespective of what autonomy it may bring to the individual. Thirdly, whereas the right to influence the decision is discretionary, the right to be listened to is not.

4 For example, see Hill et al. (2004); Davis and Hill (2006); Partridge (2005); James (2007); Stern (2006); Dahlstrand (2004).

[5] See for example Carol Smart (2002); A.B. Smith (2002); P.Parkinson, J. Cashmore and J. Single (2007).

My contribution to the discussion of this dilemma is to argue for a dialogical approach to child participation in administrative matters and in courts. In short, a dialogical approach demands legal procedural "tools" that emphasise the dialogue with the individual and the decision-maker in the process preceding a decision. The way in which child participation is regulated is a not unimportant issue. Indeed, it seems reasonable that different legal "tools" for allowing participation ought to make a significant contribution to the child's participation in practice, and the participation may, consequently, even result in a different final decision. The most common "tool" in Sweden is to allow the child's voice to be heard in the proceedings (either by the child or by an adult representative). Other examples of legal "tools" for child participation include the right to be a party to the proceedings, the right to initiate a case in court by filing a petition, and the right to have a say by consenting, or not consenting, to a decision. The aim of this paper is to discuss the standpoint for, and practical ways of, promoting child participation in different decision-making processes. Arguing for a dialogical approach, I propose the possibility of using a so-called "participation veto" as a legal tool for children to assure child participation in decision-making processes in relevant administrative matters and court cases.

By "participation veto" I mean the opportunity for a child to enter into the decision-making process under some form of rule demanding participation upon request of the child (or the child's representative). More precisely, I suggest that children, in some matters that concern them, should get *a procedural right to take part in the decision-making process*. My discussion is thus based on the idea that a participation veto may be used as a legal "tool" to begin or further participation by children who wish to be heard, thereby allowing the child the possibility of influencing the decision. In other words, the focus is on the demand for a dialogue in the process. Accordingly, in a scenario of a decision-making process concerning the child, the child should be able to claim and get attention in the decision-making process.[6] I use "veto" to describe such a legal "tool" because this term reflects the need for some kind of empowering procedural measure of involving children in the decision-making process.[7]

---

[6] It is assumed that the child has previously received information about the decision-making process.

[7] In many children's issue contexts, the "veto" term is not used, perhaps because it suggests the child having a degree of power that makes people uncomfortable. Also, the term veto may give the sense that participation implies hindering the decision-making process by stopping the process. Even the word "consent" is

The right to veto, as used in Swedish child law, also contains a "procedural participation ingredient". However, it ought to be emphasised that I am not addressing veto as a means of stopping a decision and thus hindering dialogue. As already mentioned, my principal interest in this article is in the right of the child to express his views and have a dialogue. My discussion is thus primarily a contribution arguing that child participation according to Article 12 must be taken seriously, and an argument for reasons for, and ways of, fulfilling this right.

2. Legal Proceedings and the Child

2.1 The Need for Procedural Tools for the Child

Legal proceedings fulfil legal protection in a two-fold way. Firstly, they are a means to reaching a correct and fair decision, a decision that often realises a right, such as the child's right to be protected by the state if molested in the home. Secondly, the process has a value in itself, giving the person the right to legal security, protection and the right to speak in court. In legal terms, this is often described as the right to a fair trial.[8]

As a consequence of the CRC demanding that children should be able to become involved in legal questions concerning them, procedural issues concerning children's participation and protection have become increasingly important within national legislation and legal practice. Traditionally, personal matters affecting children have often been defined and decided according to a need-based approach. Within this approach, adults (including custodians, judges, social welfare officers, etc.) defined and decided a child's needs in a considerable number of personal areas, without any participation by the child. However, the provisions governing the rights of the child legislated in the CRC necessarily focus on the child's rights, including the child's perspective and interests. As a consequence, present day decisions regarding children's personal matters are often supposed to be preceded by child participation of some kind. The result is the adoption and development of international legislation into national legal systems of different states.

---

typically not used for children under 18 years old in some countries, because it is believed that they are not capable of giving legal "consent." Instead, their parents "consent" on their behalf, and then there is a question of whether the child must "assent" as well.

[8] See for example ECHR Article 6.

This development has challenged national legal systems to adjust to the new demands for child participation in different ways. One way is to construct procedural tools for children that fulfil these needs, and that provide good conditions for reaching a correct decision in accordance with the best interests of the child. This may be a very difficult process. Legal proceedings have been formed across hundreds of years and are not always easily or automatically adjustable to structural changes in society. Also, as mentioned above, children comprise a vulnerable group, and often have problems claiming their rights. To attain a legal process compatible with the child's best interests, the procedure must optimise the child's legal security, protection of personal integrity, and successively increasing autonomy.[9] However, the next question is *how* such adjustments in the legal proceedings are made in practice.

As we have seen, a core problem seems to be that some regulations with the aim of harmonising with Article 12 in the CRC often fail to bring about these procedural rights in practice. One example is the type of regulation applied in many Swedish statutes, stating that the child's opinion should be taken into account in the legal matter according to the level of capacity of the child,[10] but such regulation is often not an efficient rule for allowing child participation in practice, as a study described below will demonstrate. Thus, in addition to questions as to when children may participate in administrative or court matters, issues arise as to what procedural tools should be applied to fulfil the goal of the CRC. An associated issue is how the child's participation should be secured by legislation. For instance, the question becomes highly relevant in issues where the parents' and the child's interests may overlap one another.

2.2 Swedish Court Practice Regarding Material Rights without Associated Procedural Rights

During the last decade, Swedish law has undergone a number of changes, moving towards a greater acceptance of the fact that the custodian's interest may sometimes collide with a child's material rights. One example is legislation allowing change of custody and guardianship to children in foster care to the foster family without the consent of the custodian, in

---

[9] Mattsson (2002)

[10] For example, see Chapter 3, Section 5 of the Social Services Act of 2001, and Chapter 6, Section 2a of the Children and Parents Code of 1949.

order to promote the child's right to a family.[11] Another example is allowing the Social Welfare Office to have a meeting with the child during a social investigation without the consent of one or both custodians, if necessary, in order to promote the child's right to state protection against violence or other social hardship.[12] The legislative changes in family decisions imply that the child's rights may not always be in accordance with the parents' rights and wishes. In such situations, the CRC emphasises the importance of considering the interests of the child as the guiding principle.

However, according to research into legal practice in decision-making concerning children's issues, the custodian's rights may still prevail over the child's material rights.[13] Or, to put it another way, the best interests of the child may be interpreted in a way that upholds the parents' rights and interests. The child seems to be especially vulnerable in cases where there are no clear procedural tools for child participation. As an example, I refer to an empirical study of Swedish District Court cases concerning the change of custody and guardianship during 2005-2009.[14] The purpose of the study was to examine the District Courts' arguments for their decisions in custody and guardianship cases in relation to the instructions in the Children and Parents Code of 1949, which focuses on the child's best interests and not on the custodian's fitness or willingness to have the child return home (alternatively to continue to have his or her child in foster care). The purpose was to investigate the practice of some new legislation concerning the increased responsibility of the Social Welfare Committee for initiating custody and guardianship cases for children in long-term foster care.

---

[11] Social Services Act Chapter 8 Section 6, Child and Parents Code Chapter 8 Section 6.

[12] Social Services Act Chapter 10 Section 11.

[13] Parental rights have a long tradition in Swedish legislative practice. Thanks to legislation, custodians have a strong influence on most kinds of decisions that concern their child, regardless of whether the custodian resides with the child. In addition, as a main rule, both custodians' consent is necessary for decisions concerning the child. This gives each custodian great opportunity to oppose changes or disagree on actions regarding the child, which the other custodian or authority may want to apply.

14 The study is published in Rätten till familj inom sociala barn- och ungdomsvården [The Right to Family in the Child Care System], Liber AB, 2010, pp. 133-170. The cases were collected from eight different courts from different parts of Sweden, and included a total of 77 cases from 2005-2009. Compare Schiratzki (2008) and Ponnert (2007) for other empirical studies.

One result of the study is that the opinions of the custodians dominated the cases, though according to the regulation the assessment should focus solely on the children.[15] The children's voices were often not audible in the documents preceding the judgements, or in the judgements themselves, making it difficult to trace the child's opinions and feelings in the relevant cases. In addition, the study proves that the occasions on which custody cases actually occur are often very late in childhood. Even in cases where the child's relation with the custodian would not run the risk of getting worse after a change of custody, the child remained in foster care for the same long time period.[16] The results display the difficulties of balancing child and parent interests without clear procedural tools for both parties, at least where there is a risk of imbalance in the assessment of the child's best interest.[17] The lack of procedural tools for the child may also be one explanation why children's voices and influences have not clearly emerged in the legal process. In other words, the imbalance of power between the adult and the child in the process is most probably not compensated procedurally.

3. The "Participation Veto" in Swedish Legislation

After admitting concern for the appropriate procedural "tools" for realising child participation, the next issue is to discuss how such tools could manifest themselves. The option for children to "veto" is used as a legal tool for consolidating child participation in several statutes in Sweden,

---

[15] Only in the group of cases where the custodians disagreed on a change of custody, was the petition for custody/guardianship turned down by the courts in half of the cases. In all the other cases in the study, the petition was approved. The reasoning in these cases focuses mainly on the custodians' fitness and willingness to remain as the child's custodians. Though these cases were not different from the other cases in the study (i.e. long-term foster placements; poor, non-existent or detrimental contact with the custodians; or children expressing that they wanted the change. The Court's cconclusion was that the custodians would get "one more chance" from the Court.

[16] As a matter of fact, in several cases in the study, the passivity of the Social Welfare Committee made the children finally act themselves. As a result, some custody cases were informally initiated by the children and young people themselves (informally, because the Social Welfare Office decided to act after the child had contacted the Office). The child has no right of formally initiating a case in court.

[17] Compare Ryrstedt & Mattsson (2008).

however in somewhat different constellations.[18] As mentioned abve, I use the term "participation veto" to include the opportunity for children to participate in the decision-making process more or less automatically, or without being denied entry in different ways during a decision-making process. This ingredient is found within several Swedish statutes under a number of terms, such as statutes regulating party status (*processbehörighet*), consent and veto.

In some statutes, the right to a participation veto exists as a general obligation for a custodian or an authority to involve the child in all decision-making based on the Act after the child has reached a certain age.[19] Thus, the participation veto affects situations where the authority is making an agreement with the custodians relating to the child. For example, according to the Social Services Act of 2001, a child 15 years or older must consent to all care or support proposed by the Social Welfare Committee (in addition to the custodian's consent).[20] This demand for consent includes a veto in the sense that it makes child participation mandatory in the whole decision-making process.[21] The option for the Social Welfare Committee in such situations is to have a dialogue with the youth, and perhaps persuade this youth to change his or her mind about the care or support, or to make another agreement to which the youth can give his or her consent.[22] Here, the main intention of the relevant regulation is to establish a dialogue between various parties and the child in order to improve the decision-making process.

---

[18] It is also used for giving the child a mandate to decide on the issue at stake because the child may hinder a decision by not accepting it. As already mentioned, my interest lies in the procedural perspective of the veto, i.e. the chance to participate in the decision-making process and not the chance to decide the material issue or hinder a decision.

[19] This type of regulation is not limited to the right to a participation veto; in other situations the same rule may also give the child the right to initiate or appeal a decision.

[20] Social Services Act Chapter 11, Section 10. Before that age, the custodians alone decide on such matters.

[21] In addition, if the Social Welfare Committee and the custodians should make a decision *without* involving the child, the child may claim its participation veto at another time, for example, by demanding a dialogue before agreeing to a plan for foster care or before continuing an earlier agreement for foster care.

[22] A last resort may be to apply to the Administrative Court for compulsory care according to the Care of Young Persons Act of 1990.

The right to a participation veto can also be regulated as a right to consent or veto in a specific decision-making situation. This kind of regulation regarding the child usually concerns the relationship between the child and the custodian, and is often directed towards crucial decisions having to do with the child's person, often in connection with issues of the child's body or integrity. Sometimes, the child has a right to participate irrespective of age. One such piece of legislation is the 2001 Act on Circumcision of Boys, according to which the child shall give his views before such bodily intervention. The child has the right to receive information if he is old enough to understand it. His attitude towards the intervention should be investigated, and he has the possibility to stop the procedure, irrespective of his age.[23] Thus, a decision-making process concerning a child that is old enough to understand the procedure must be preceded by the participation of the child in question.

Other legislation includes this right to a participation veto after a certain age. Another such legislation is The Act of Ethical Consideration with Regard to Research on Human Beings of 2003.[24] This Act deals with ethical issues and the consent given to certain types of research where human beings, or sensitive personal data about them, are involved.[25] According to Section 18, young persons 15 years and older must be informed about the research and consent to it, in the same way as the Act demands for research on adults. According to the same section, a younger child may also participate in a decision and leave his or her consent to let him or her take part in any research that the custodians have agreed upon, if the child seems to understand what the research implies for him or her. Another legislative approach is found in decisions concerning the child's freedom of religion. According to Section 4 of the Act on Religious Communities Signatures of 1998,[26] a child 12 years or older may not enter or leave a religious community without his or her own consent.[27] The

---

[23] 3 § i lag (2001:499) om omskärelse av pojkar.

[24] Lag (2003:460) om etikprövning av forskning som avser människor.

[25] The aim of the Act is to protect individuals and the respect for their dignity in research. Sometimes research involves children, such as interviewing children, studying their behaviour or using their personal data.

[26] Lag (1998:1593) om trossamfund.

[27] The Act on religious communities' signatures deals mostly with questions having to do with the registration procedures for other religious communities than the Church of Sweden. However, at the beginning of the Act, some legislation of principal importance is stated. Except for references to the right to freedom of

same age limit is used in the Names Act of 1982. A child's name may not be changed by the custodians without the consent of the child, if the child is 12 years or older.[28]

On adoptions, Sweden and many other countries have a provision that requires the court to have proof of the child's consent if the child is of a certain age. According to the Child and Parents Code of 1949, adoption must be preceded by the consent of the child if 12-years-old or more. Child participation thus becomes mandatory in the decision-making process. This 12-year-old limit is harmonised in the Nordic countries. The right to child participation in adoption cases is supported by the European Convention on the adoption of Children of 2008, stating in Article 5 that "an adoption shall not be granted unless the consent of the child is considered by law as having sufficient understanding, [and] a child shall be considered as having sufficient understanding on attaining an age which shall be prescribed by law and shall not be more than 14 years." Also, in the United States, participation rights for children in adoption cases are common. For example, in New York, children 14 and older must express their consent otherwise adoption cannot be granted.[29]

4. A dialogical Approach in the Decision-Making Process

The common arguments for child participation have, traditionally, been more or less based either on arguments resting on the human rights discourse, involving a claim for equal treatment with other humans, *or* a claim for the need for special treatment owing to a vulnerable childhood status.[30] Whilst valid arguments exist for both these justifications, a major problem with these types of justifying child rights is that both are, roughly, based on the idea of human beings as autonomous individuals with the possibility of claiming their rights. This is clearly the case in the equal-treatment argumentation model: in brief, the claim for participation or other rights demands the status of a subject with the legal capacity to claim his or her right. Children are seldom assigned this status of legal capacity themselves. Instead, their rights are bound to be taken care of by adults in

---

religion and the right not to have to belong to a religious community, the above-mentioned rule on children's autonomy in these questions is regulated.

[28] 48 § namnlagen (1982:679).

[29] For more reading on the abortion issue, see Parham v. J.R., 442 U.S. 584 (1979); State v. Perricone, 37 N.J. 463 (1962); In re A.M.B., 640 N.W.2d 262 (Mich.App. 2001).

[30] Compare Fitzgerald, Graham, Smith and Taylor (2010) pp. 298f.

different ways. On a daily basis, it is often the custodians in the home or the schoolteacher in the classroom who assists the child in fulfilling his or her rights. In some cases, other adults, such as judges, welfare officers, or health personnel take this role temporarily. Thus, child rights are most often fulfilled by adults, sometimes through the guidance of legal documents instructing the adults about a certain child right and its implementation, such as the right to education or health care. However, without legal guidance of children's rights and adults with the knowledge and willingness to implement these rights, it is very difficult to make them come true. In this sense, fulfilling a child's rights is dependent on the surroundings of the child.

The same sort of problem arises with the special-treatment argument. According to this way of arguing for children's rights, children are viewed as being vulnerable and dependent persons in need of special treatment. This attention to the special needs of children, legally and in practice, is supposed to compensate for their vulnerability. For instance, an expression of this is the principle that the best interests of child shall be the primary consideration in the individual case, which exists to compensate the child's inexperience, immaturity and inability to make decisions independently. However, here also the focus is basically on the individual's claim. The idea behind such an approach is ultimately that legal scrutiny of an individual's rights can take place without considering the environment in which the person lives and acts. Nevertheless, the focus on the subject, isolated from the setting, may have the consequence that certain problems in realising rights—such as child participation—are interpreted on an individual level and that structural explanations, such as social hardship in the family or linguistic barriers, are not made visible.[31] This certainly concerns administrative matters and legal proceedings with children, because—as already mentioned—they constitute a group with clear dependency on adults, both in a practical and a legal way. One practical example is the custody case study, which demonstrated that children's participation or children's interests may not always be given priority in the decision-making. A key to fulfilling children's rights and needs in practice thus seems to be the awareness of the contextual dimension of individual rights. In practical terms, children are excluded from participation because they are unable to assert and claim their rights. As a consequence, it is important to search for alternative foundations for child participation, which include a contextual and procedural perspective of participation.

---

[31] Andersson (2004); Nilsson (2007); Johansson (2009); Mattsson (2010).

An argument for another approach to child participation has been formulated in recent times. This approach for justifying children's participation as a struggle for recognition has been proposed in the field of child participation research by Fitzgerald et al.[32] The idea stems from the so-called recognition theory, which is, in short, based on the idea that the individual needs to be recognised by other individuals in a multidimensional way, to develop a personal identity or a positive relation to him or herself.[33] Some philosophers, such as Axel Honneth and Charles Taylor, propose that recognition is accomplished through dialogue with other people. This relationship, based on dialogue, is crucial for the development of the individual's identity and is created by a process of mutual recognition.[34]

This focus on the dialogue fits well with both societal developments in general and sociocultural theory in particular. The increasing emphasis on the dialogue between the individual/citizen/consumer and governmental administration/companies/private contacts is, for example, found as one goal in the rapid development and use of government development and other Internet-related forums.[35] A dialogical approach is also found in the sociocultural theory focusing on the study of childhood. Sociocultural theory emphasises the necessity for children to have the possibility to engage in a shared experience in order for them to understand and participate in a meaningful way.[36] According to the sociocultural theory, children need to be in dialogue with adults for many different reasons, such as to affirm, challenge and develop themselves. By not being listened to, or being unable to share the experiences, the child will feel unrecognised and socially invisible. This focus on dialogue in theory as well as in practice ought to bring increased attention to the practical and procedural issues of participation. The quality of the dialogue is also of relevance.

---

[32] Fizgerald, Graham, Smith and Taylor (2010) pp. 293-305.

[33] Honneth 2003, Heidegren (2009). The different forms of recognition originate from our near relations (love), our relations to other people (equal treatment in law) and our relations to those who have similar values (social esteem). These forms are interconnected, but are not always in harmony with each other: instead there are often tensions between them.

[34] Fizgerald, Graham, Smith and Taylor (2010), referring to Honneth 2004 and Taylor 1995.

[35] Mattsson (2010)

[36] Fizgerald, Graham, Smith and Taylor (2010), referring to Smith (2002).

The dialogical approach suggested by Fitzgerald *et al* fits well with legal child issues which almost always include several persons. These are, for example, the child, the custodian and the schoolteacher. It also focuses on relationships and interactions as a means of participation, which is especially crucial for child participation. Thus, instead of a traditional individualistic—or monological—approach to participation by claiming equal or special treatment, the claim for participation is based on claims of recognition by dialogue. By approaching the participation issue as a struggle over recognition, the emphasis is on the relational and mutual nature of participation.[37] In other words, recognition is based on a mutual experience, for example, by a dialogue, and therefore not an individualistic claim.

5. Conclusion

The main intention of this article has been to reflect upon the gap between theory and practice in child participation in general, and to discuss arguments and means for diminishing this gap. After having acknowledged the practical problems in implementing Article 12 with a traditional rights-perspective that demands a claim by the child (often without legal means of claiming the right), and also admitting the hesitation of some to allow child participation, the question is this: what should the strategy for furthering child participation in different situations be? While not intending to tackle this wide question in it entirety, I have examined some of the current discussions surrounding child participation doctrine. And taking into account the usefulness of the dialogical approach, I focussed on the practical and procedural issues of participation. Admitting that allowing child participation to be a part of the decision-making process necessarily relies on the individual decision-maker's subjectivity, the procedural tools for allowing child participation on equal terms with adults becomes a central issue. To illustrate how children in a few situations are given such procedural tools, I have proposed the term "the participation veto".

How, then, may the right to a participation veto be a dialogical approach? Veto may in one sense be viewed as a monological approach, in the sense of the having the right to stand up and make an individual claim. However, the purpose of this procedural "tool" is to make a dialogical approach *mandatory* in a decision-making process (on the condition that the child

[37] Fizgerald, Graham, Smith and Taylor (2010) p. 301.

wants to participate). In this way, someone with a crucial interest in the issue—the child—is obtaining the right to receive information, speak, and possibly influence the decision. It may even be an example of a procedural form of a dialectical approach in decision-making that could be a helpful tool in the struggle for children's recognition.

CHAPTER TWO:

GENDER LEGAL DILEMMAS

CONTRADICTIONS IN THE THEORY OF THE CHILD'S COMPETENCE

JULIA KÖHLER-OLSEN

Abstract

This Article discusses the question of when a child has the right to self-determination in relation to the civil right of freedom of religion. It is stipulated that proof of the child's being competent is not sufficient in order for him or her to be able to make an autonomous decision. The necessary condition which must be in place is the absence of the parental power of protection. This assumption is tested against the legal theory which reconstructs civil rights by detaching it from the capacity-principle.

1. Introduction

Whenever lawyers talk about the rights of the child, we are quick to point to the child's right to participate and influence the process of decision-making regarding matters concerning that child's life. This is without doubt an important tool for enhancing the implementation of the various rights of the child, and must play a significant role whenever adults are about to make a decision in a child's life. In this article, however, I will elaborate on the question of when a child has the right to make an autonomous decision in relation to religious norms, *cf.* Article 14 of the Convention on the Rights of the Child (CRC). The question is which preconditions or conditions must be in place in order for a child to have the right to self-determination in relation to religious norms as opposed to the parental right to raise a child according to their own beliefs and convictions, as found in the Convention on Civil and Political Rights (CCPR) Article 18(4) and the European Convention on Human Rights (ECHR) First Protocol, Article 2. There are two issues, here: one is about determining a child's capability to decide and the other is about the responsibility of parents to make sure that they have child's best interests at heart when raising it, as laid down in CRC Article 18. What I have in mind are children who have not yet reached a minimum legal age as set down in various national legislations when it comes to self-determination with regard to a specific civil right, especially the right to choose a different religious identity from that of its parents and family.

2. Method

When trying to answer the question of when a child has the right to self-determination in relation to various norms and different interests from its parents, it is almost impossible not to end up with arguments based mainly on personal opinions. Rules about the relationship between the child's rights and parental rights are worded generally, which creates the possibility of basing the argument as to whether the child or the parents should decide, on personal opinion on. Most case law is about the relationship between the child's right to religious freedom and the state, often brought before the court by the parents, relating to education or health care. The interests of the parents and the child in these cases are considered to be concurrent, while this Article seeks to discuss situations where the child has a different interest from its parents.

My own way of constructing the child's world and the relationship between a child and its parents can play a large part when assessing the question posed by this Article, since there are not that many legal sources to rely on. In order to make sure that my own method of construction will be valid I am trying to detach myself from the research question by basing my arguments on social constructivist methods. The scope of this Article is too narrow to permit a thorough discussion of this methodology, but in short one can state that it is about analyzing the way the language used in legal sources affects the child, the relationship between the child and its parents, the status of religion and belief, and the question of harm and protection of the child compared to the idea of the competent child.[1] I am thus relying on a legal dogmatic method, as well as on a social-constructivist one. The reason for taking the social-constructivist approach is the assumption that diverse prerequisites, conditions and circumstances must be in place before the child can decide on religious matters autonomously. Conditions which I hope to find in the legal construction of the child's world.

[1] In order to read more about social-constructivism, see for example Vivienne Burr, Social Constructivism (2nd ed. 2003).

Quite soon after I had started researching the question of a child's right to an autonomous decision in relation to religious norms, I saw that there was not much about the child's right to self-determination in legal precedents. For example, there were no obvious arguments on when a child can decide independently and autonomously about following a religious diet or not. Much depends on the construction of childhood, family ties, the view on religion, and so on. In order to find an answer to the main question on a child's right to self-determination, I had to take a closer look at the legal construction of the relationship between the parent and the child. In addition, elaborating on the child's right to make autonomous decisions in relation to religious norms might have some value when the question of decision-making is related to other civil rights norms.

3. The Construction of the Relationship between the Parents and the Child in the CRC

The CRC mainly defines the relationship between the parents and the child in Article 5, and Article 14(2), stating that parents have the right and duty to give direction to the child in accordance with the child's evolving capacities when the child is exercising its right, such as the child's right to freedom of thought, conscience and religion in Article 14(1). The wording is quite clear on this matter. It is the child who exercises this civil right, while the parents' role, which the state shall respect as part of parental freedom, is about guiding the child when it wants to exercise its right to freedom of religion. The concept of "exercising a right" is usually understood in terms of an individual claiming his right and acting in accordance with it. However, as we have learned from the field of legal theory, interest theory has given lawyers well-founded arguments about the child being a holder of rights, in the meaning of "exercising a right", even though the child might not be in a position to, or is considered to be incapable of, exercising its rights autonomously, claiming or waiving the respective right.[2] A child can thus exercise its right to freedom of religion using assistance from a proxy, and thus not exercise it by self-determination, but may still be considered a right holder.[3] Neither Article 14(2) of the CRC, nor Article 5, give any further insight which conditions must be fulfilled for a child to have the right to self-determination. A hint is, however, given by pointing to the child's evolving capacity when

---

[2] Neil MacCormick, *Children's Rights: A Test-Case for Theories of Rights, in* Rights 75 (Carlos Ninos ed., 1992).

[3] Id. at 83.

parents provide direction to it. Since the bulk of human experience is that children have become more and more competent in their lives over the years, this implicitly means that at some point parents might find that their guidance no longer even seems necessary. It is like a "sliding scale", where parental influence decreases as the child's capacity increases. Article 14 thus concerns the developing child, which under every circumstance is the right holder, though it is unclear what is implied in the child's right to "exercise" the freedom of religion. When does the child need a proxy with the right to take part in the decision-making process, and when does it have the right to self-determination?

My deduction from the provisions of Article 14(2) is that parents have a right, or a right not, to educate and teach the child in religious questions, in line with other international norms which provide the right for parents to decide on the child's religious or non-religious upbringing. However, the upbringing within either a religious belief system, or atheism, does not include the right of the parents to determine the religious identity or any other philosophy on life of the child. Within this framework, what then can parents do, when presented with the right and duty to guide a child in the exercise of its right to freedom of thought, conscience and religion? The upbringing according to the construction placed on Article 14(2) cannot involve any physical or mental violence, as also stated in Article 19 of the CRC. The parents' teaching has thus to follow the norm of non-violence, *cf.* Article 19 of the CRC, and in a form of dialogue, *cf.* Article 12 on the right to participation. The answer to when a child has a right to autonomous decision-making, however, cannot be found in the wording of the Convention. It is noteworthy that the CRC contains no provision that regulates a child's right to make decisions independently and autonomously.

The Committee on the Rights of the Child has not yet produced a thorough analysis on Article 14, or on the child's right to self-determination in relation to civil rights in general.[4] With regard to the right to freedom of thought, conscience and religion, analysis of the Committee's work must be based on Summary Records and Concluding Observations. Though being of little legal weight and relevance according to positivistic legal

---

[4] See for critical comments on the work of the Committee on the Rights of the Child: Ursula Kilkelly, *The Child's Right to Religious Freedom in International Law: The Search for Meaning, in* What is Right for Children 243 (Martha Albertson Fineman & Karen Worthington eds., 2009). Sylvie Langlaude, *Children and Religion under Article 14 UNCRC: A Critical Analysis*, 16 Int. J. of Children's Rights, 457 (2008).

dogmatic method, and though being few in number, there is to be found a coherent point of view by the Committee. The countries to which the Committee has spoken about the child's right in Article 14 have all heard that the provision includes the child's right to choose a religious identity, and it is the child's right to choose which type of religious or non-religious education the child wants to follow. As underlined by Sylvie Langlaude, the Committee is extremely straightforward, not only stressing the child's right to choose the religion of its choice, but that it must also be based on the child's free will.[5] One example is the Committee's comment on the state report of Morocco and its reservation about Article 14 excluding a child's right to choose another religion by saying that the: "*...freedom of religion included freedom to choose and change one's religion. No interpretation of such freedoms could restrict it to the possibility of holding one specific religion*".[6] In addition, when discussing the state report of Monaco, the Committee stresses that the CRC has a rights-based approach, and not an approach that shall secure the child's welfare or protect the child against harm.[7]

This rights-based approach shall be used when applying the child's right to freedom of religion.[8] The Committee's practice on the right to choose and change the religious identity seems to provide an argument that the child has a right to autonomously exercise its right to freedom of religion with regard to various other religious norms, such as religious dress codes, diets or hours of rest. The logic behind this is that if a child has the right to change its religious or atheistic identity, then it certainly must have the autonomous right to decide on less extensive questions in relation to its belief, for example whether or not to follow religiously-based dress codes. In other words, does the child have a right to self-determination in relation to religion, belief and philosophy of life? There are a number of reasons as to why there is not a straightforward answer to the above-mentioned question.

---

[5] Sylvie Langlaude, *Children and Religion under Article 14 UNCRC: A Critical Analysis*, 16 Int. J. of Children's Rights, 457, 484 (2008).
[6] U.N. Committee on the Rights of the Child, 13th Sess., Summary Record of the 317th Meeting, UN Doc. CRC/C/SR.317, para. 51 (Morocco, Sept. 26, 1996)).
[7] U.N. Committee on the Rights of the Child, 27th Sess., Summary Record of the 717th Meeting, UN Doc.CRC/C/SR.717, para. 62 (Monaco, Jun.13, 2001)
[8] U.N. Committee on the Rights of the Child, 27th Sess., Summary Record of the 717th Meeting, UN Doc.CRC/C/SR.717, para. 62 (Monaco, Jun.13, 2001)

Firstly, by pointing to the rights-based approach, the Committee indirectly, though maybe not consciously, links the rights of the child to the capacity-principle. In order to underline the importance of this in understanding the construction of civil rights, let me briefly explain its history. The feminist legal scholar Kathrine Hunt Federle and the philosopher John Wall have both discussed in depth the requirement of having achieved the full capacity to make autonomous choices by examining ideas like the Social Contract, as written about by Hobbes, Locke and Rousseau, and more recently by John Rawls, or Utilitarianism, propounded by Bentham and John Stuart Mill. Federle and Wall also analyze Kant's Moral Theory.[9] All these philosophies deny with the possibility of children being either right holders, or exercising their rights, because of their lack of capacity. Yet, more modern ideas—such as the will theory of H.L.A. Hart, the interest theory of Neil McCormick, and feminist legal theory—focus more on the relationship between human beings than on capacity, and all of them have, directly or indirectly, based the autonomous exercise of rights on the requirement of being competent.[10]

If a young child is considered to be incompetent, then interest theory dictates that others can exercise rights on the child's behalf, although that child is still considered as the right holder. An example of this theory being used in court is Zhu and Chen v Secretary of State for the Home Department, United Kingdom, at the European Court of Justice (ECJ), which raises the question (among others) of whether or not a child with the citizenship of an EU Member State has the right to free movement within the EU and can become a resident in a host EU Member State. The child, being only 8 months old, did not fulfill the requirements of free movement and residence, which demand self-sufficiency, as it depended on its parents resources.[11] An important fact in this case was that both parents were non-EU citizens and, as such, the child's right to free movement and residence in question was solely dependent on the child's legal status as being an EU citizen. The ECJ concluded that the child had a right to free movement and residence despite the fact that the child itself could not be

---

[9] Kathrine Hunt Federle, *Rights flow downhill*, 2 Int. J. of Children's Rights 343 (1994). John Wall, *Human Rights in the Light of Childhood*, 16 Int. J. of Children's Rights 523 (2008).

[10] H.L.A. Hart, *Definition and Theory in Jurisprudence, in* Rights 3 (Carlos Ninos ed., 1992) about the will-theory. Martha Minow, *Rights for the next Generation: A feminist approach for to Children's Rights,* 9 Harv. Women's L.J. 1 (1986).

[11] Case C-200/02, Kunqian Catherine Zhu, Man Lavette Chen v. Secretary of State for the Home Department, UK, 2004, E.C.R.

self-sufficient and was dependent on its parents economically (as well as emotionally, of course). In its ruling the ECJ stated:

> "Moreover, contrary to the Irish Government's contention, a young child can take advantage of the rights of free movement and residence guaranteed by Community law. The capacity of a national of a Member State to be the holder of rights guaranteed by the Treaty and by secondary law on the free movement of persons cannot be made conditioned upon the attainment by the person concerned of the age prescribed for the acquisition of legal capacity to exercise those rights personally... Moreover...it does not follow either from the terms of, or from the aims pursued by, Articles 18 EC and 49 EC and Directives 73/148 and 90/364 that the enjoyment of the rights with which those provisions are concerned should be made conditional upon the attainment of a minimum age."[12]

The civil right of free movement and residence within the EU is thus not conditional upon the EU citizen's acquisition of the legal capacity to exercise those rights personally. The judgment is in line with McCormick's theory, in that individuals are right holders even though they might not be able to exercise those rights personally either because they lack the actual capacity, or, as in this case, the legal capacity.

According to Martha Minow, feminist legal theory underscores children's dependencies, rather than rendering them irrelevant in connection with adults and children. Though adults are also interconnected to each other and to their children, according to Federle, Minow misses a crucial difference: children have no real choice in the creation or continuation of the relationship, precisely because they are thought to be incompetent and therefore "need" this relationship.[13] All the legal theories—some found in legal cases—have since the nineteenth century been establishing a construction of rights which requires that the right holder, in order to exercise his or her right autonomously, must be competent: in other words, that he or she fulfills the test of capacity. Children are often regarded as being incompetent and therefore unable to exercise their rights autonomously, as laid down in the CRC.

Secondly, the Committee itself very often refers to the right of the child to take part and influence a decision-making process in connection with Article 14 by pointing to the interconnectedness between the child's right

---

[12] Id at. para. 20.

[13] Kathrine Hunt Federle, *On the Road to Reconceiving Rights for Children,* 42 DePaul Law Review 983, 1018-19 (1992).

to freedom of religion and the right to participation as found in CRC Article 12.[14] Although the right to participate in a decision-making process must be greatly important to the child, its focus on Article 12 reveals that the Committee, and most adults, consider children to be too incompetent to make any final decision autonomously.

Thirdly, the Committee, perhaps to placate its critics, continually stresses the important role that parents have in guiding the child in its attempt to exercise its right to freedom of religion.[15] This underlines the assumption that the child is not capable of making an autonomous decision regarding religious norms. Some adults might misinterpret the "guidance-principle" in Article 14(2) and Article 5, repeatedly emphasized by the Committee, as being about the parents' right to make decisions on behalf of their child. Fourthly, the Committee is active in the work of reconstructing our conceptions of children both in its General Comment no. 7 on implementing child rights in early childhood, and General Comment no. 12 on the right of the child to be heard.[16] Based on newer research into developmental psychology, the Committee argues strongly in favour of the default point of view that children are competent until proved otherwise.[17] Furthermore, the Committee stresses research findings which show that children who are able to participate and play an active agent role in their own lives actually become more competent than other children of the same age who are not allowed to participate in the decision-making process.[18] The work on reconstructing our picture of children implicitly proves the Committee also considers that capacity is a precondition for autonomous choices.

---

[14] Sylvie Langlaude, *The Right of the Child to Religious Freedom in International Law* 112-13 (2007).

[15] Id. at 104-8.

[16] U.N. Committee on the Rights of the Child, 40th Sess., GC No. 7, Implementing child rights in early childhood, U.N. Doc. CRC/C/GC/7/Rev.1 (Sept. 20, 2006). U.N. Committee on the Rights of the Child, 51st Sess., GC No. 12, The child's right to be heard, U.N. Doc. CRC/C/GC/12 (July 20, 2009).

[17] U.N. Committee on the Rights of the Child, 51st Sess., GC No. 12, The child's right to be heard, U.N. Doc. CRC/C/GC/12 para. 20 (July 20, 2009). U.N. Committee on the Rights of the Child, 40th Sess., GC No. 7, Implementing child rights in early childhood, U.N. Doc. CRC/C/GC/7/Rev.1 para. 14 and 17 (Sept. 20, 2006).

[18] U.N. Committee on the Rights of the Child, 40th Sess., GC No. 7, Implementing child rights in early childhood, U.N. Doc. CRC/C/GC/7/Rev.1 para. 6 (d) (Sept. 20, 2006). U.N. Committee on the Rights of the Child, 51st Sess., GC No. 12, The child's right to be heard, U.N. Doc. CRC/C/GC/12 para. 29 (July 20, 2009).

Lastly, the Committee has been criticized for being positive about minimum legal age limits in national legislation. Some find it odd that the Committee is positive about age limits when it comes to ensuring civil freedoms for the child, or trying to convince member states to lower their age limits, while the Committee is often negative regarding age limits which actually confer a duty on the child, such as the lowest criminal age limit.[19] With regard to the last, the Committee often regards the age limit as being too low.[20] Others criticize the Committee for not taking a clear stand on which age limit is acceptable.[21] And yet others view the Committee's use of age limits as a principle in guiding its analysis of Article 14 in a negative light. However, rather than focusing on national minimum legal ages, the Committee should elaborate on the concept of the child's evolving capacities.[22] Furthermore, critics state that age limits, accepted by the Committee, are necessarily arbitrary.[23]

Though one can understand the broad criticism by legal scholars, one rather wants to make an assumption here. The Committee might just be positive on age limits, despite the fact that they do not seem to fit in with the concept of the evolving capacities of the child, because it has actually understood that the absence of parental power of protection provided for by a legal minimum age is, as of today's construction of childhood and family relations, the only guarantee of a child's actually being granted the right to self-determination in relation to religious norms. Thus, in order to ensure that the child does eventually achieve the right to autonomously decide in matters regarding religion and belief, national age limits below the ordinary age of maturity are considered positive. This positive consideration of minimum legal age limits reveals, at the same time, the Committee's understanding that rights are closely linked to the capacity-principle.

---

[19] Bruce C. Hafen & Jonathan O. Hafen, *Abandoning Children to Their Autonomy: The United Nations Convention on the Rights of the Child*, 37 Harvard Int. Law Journal 447, 466 (1996).
[20] U.N. Committee on the Rights of the Child, 44th Sess., GC No. 10, Children's rights in juvenile justice, U.N. Doc. CRC/C/GC/10 para. 30 (April 25, 2007).
[21] Sylvie Langlaude, *Children and Religion under Article 14 UNCRC: A Critical Analysis*, 16 Int. J. of Children's Rights, 457, 488 (2008)
[22] Sylvie Langlaude, *The Right of the Child to Religious Freedom in International Law* 126 (2007).
[23] Id. at 151.

4. Capacity and the Child's Best Interest in Various Legal Sources

According to what has been said up until now, the rational conclusion would be that the condition for a child to be able to make an autonomous decision regarding religious norms according to the CRC and the Committee's construction depends on a child's capacity, either considered individually, or based on a national minimum legal age. However, as already implied above, it seems as if capacity is a necessary precondition, yet not on its own sufficient, for a child to be granted the right to self-determination.

4. 1. Foreign Law

A well-known case, often referred to as a decision where English law had given legal recognition to a child's autonomy interest, is the 1985 case of Gillick v West Norfolk and Wisbech AHA and Department of Health and Social Security (hereinafter Gillick).[24] Rejecting the mother's argument, the House of Lords held that a girl under the age of 16 could provide a valid consent to contraceptive treatment, and a doctor could lawfully prescribe such treatment without her parents' knowledge and consent. Similarly, in the 2006 case of R Axon v Secretary of State for Health (hereinafter Axon), a mother argued that medical professionals were under no obligation to maintain confidentiality in relation to abortion advice and treatment unless disclosure might prejudice the child's physical or mental health.[25] The High Court rejected the mother's argument stating that the approach in Gillick was, and is, of general application to all forms of medical advice and treatment. Since both cases deal with the medical treatment of children who had not yet reached the legal minimum age for consenting autonomously to treatment in Great Britain, both cases stand for accepting a child's autonomous decision which is in conflict with the interests of the parents.

An very interesting analysis of these two cases, and supplemented by other cases from Great Britain, is given by the legal scholar Stephen Gilmore.[26]

[24] Gillick v. West Norfolk and Wisbeck AHA and Department of Health and Social Security, [1986] UKHL 7.

[25] Axon, R (on the application of) v Secretary of State for Health & Anor [2006] EWHC 37 [2006] EWHC 37 (Admin).

[26] Stephen Gilmore, *The Limits of Parental Responsibility, in* Responsible Parents & Parents Responsibility 63 (Rebecca Probert et al. eds., 2009).

Gilmore confirms that one part of the legal conditions for a child to be able to make an autonomous decision is that the child fulfils a stringent test for capacity, understanding all relevant matters. Yet that is only one part: apart from determining whether the child has a high enough level of understanding, English law considers whether or not the parents' function of protection for the child can safely be abandoned.[27] The Gillick case and its successors were essentially about children's welfare the judges were seeking to resolve the competing claims of adults to know what was in the child's best interests, for though recognizing a socially constructed and changing parent/child relationship, increasingly taking children's capacities into account, in the end it is still comes down to what is best for the child.[28]

The legal scholar Sinding Aasen argues that in a case where a child is denied medical treatment which would provide a reasonably good prospect of recovery and where the risk of death is fairly low, it must be legitimate to force the child to have treatment after repeatedly trying to convince the child to consent to it. She continues by pointing out that the use of force in such a case is more tolerable in the case of children than adults.[29] Her argument is in line with the assumption that a child's best interests will probably overrule a child's consent or veto to medical treatment. It is, however, important to point out here that Aasen's conclusion depends on what harm is inflicted on the child in relation to what can be achieved. Her conclusion is therefore different when the chances of recovery are fairly small.[30] Aasen thus considers what is in the best interests of the child in certain medical situations, the child's capacity being a necessary and relevant condition, in her view, but not a sufficient argument in itself.[31]

4.2. The European Court of Human Rights

As stated above, there are not many legal precedents relating to children considered to be capable of making a decision which is then contrary to their parents' understanding of the situation. Decisions by the European Court of Human Rights (ECHR) seem mainly to revolve around the construction of the child being an individual who must be protected. In

---

[27] Id. at 83.
[28] Id. at 83.
[29] Henriette Sinding Aasen, Pasientens rett til selvbestemmelse ved medisinsk behandling 565 (2000).
[30] Id. at 565.
[31] Id. at 567.

fact, cases dealing with the concept of the child's capacity have concluded with similar views to the parents. Those cases revolving around the question of a child's right to freedom of religion have, however, evolved from mainly considering the parental right to raise the child according to their own beliefs and convictions (as laid down in the second sentence of Article 2 of the First Protocol), to also considering the child's right to freedom of religion in its own right. The interests of the child and the parents are, in all of these cases, concurrent, but the right of the child, at least, is being separately considered, more and more.

When it comes to the construction of the child as an individual in these cases, we are of the opinion that the child is constructed as an individual who needs protection from the state either by law or by its parents in order to be able to exercise its right to freedom of religion. In the 2009 case of Lautsi v Italy, the question in particular was whether or not the display of the crucifix in public schools in Italy was an infringement of the right of the parents to ensure education in accordance with their own beliefs and convictions, and the parents' right to freedom of religion in general. The court clarified that:

> "The Court takes the view that these considerations entail an obligation on the State's part to refrain from imposing beliefs, even indirectly, in places where persons are dependent on it or in places where they are particularly vulnerable. The schooling of children is a particularly sensitive area in which the compelling power of the State is imposed on minds which still lack (depending on the child's level of maturity) the critical capacity which would enable them to keep their distance from the message derived from a preference manifested by the State in religious matters."[32]

The European Court on Human Rights talks about the child as a person put in a situation of dependency and where it is particularly vulnerable. Further, it stresses the relationship between the child and the state characterized by power and non-power. In addition, the court points to the lack of capacity—and not only capacity, but actually demanding a *critical* capacity, in the sense of being able to reflect independently on what the message, presented by a crucifix in a classroom, is. The threshold is moved from "capacity" to "critical capacity".

The construction of a child that needs to be protected in relation to its right to freedom of religion can be found in several other cases, with different reasons for why such protection is necessary, though there is often the

---

[32] Eur. Ct. H.R. Lautsi v. Italy, Application no. 3081/06, 48 (2009)

assumption that children are easily unduly influenced. In the case Dahlab v. Switzerland, the European Court of Human Rights was of the opinion that a teacher in a public elementary school should not be allowed to wear the hijab—the religious headscarf—since this might have a proselytizing effect on the children between the ages of four and eight.[33] This case is similar to Lautsi v. Italy, since it was the relationship between the child and the school which is the context for the court's consideration.

And in cases more related to pure family law, the court also bases its judgments on the construction of children being vulnerable and in need of protection. In the case of Hoffmann v. Austria, the ECHR followed the view of the Austrian Supreme Court with regard to the children's' situation.[34] The question was whether a mother's right to freedom of religion, CRC Article 9, and right to non-discrimination on the grounds of religion, CRC Article 14, were infringed by the Supreme Court of Austria when it ruled that her children should be living with their catholic father, because of the mother's religious beliefs and the impact that her membership of the Jehova's Witnesses might have on the children. Though ruling differently than the Austrian Supreme Court, the ECHR approved the judgment of the Austrian Supreme Court, saying that the protection of the health and rights of the children was a legitimate one.[35] The ECHR's wording demonstrates that it was first and foremost a question of protecting the rights of the children. Nothing in the Austrian Supreme Court's analysis of the facts, and likewise by the European Court, discussed the impact of the diverse beliefs by the parents on the child's right to exercise freedom of religion. The case in the lower courts of the Austrian legal system, in the Supreme Court, and later in the European Court all discuss the implication a ruling would have on the children's welfare. When highlighting the legitimate aim of protecting the rights of the children, it seems that the right being protected is the right of the child to its welfare—an important right, certainly, but nothing in the case considers the child as a right holder of the civil right of freedom of religion.

The ECHR had the opportunity to focus attention on the child's right to freedom of religion according to CRC Article 9, in the case of Valsamis v. Greece.[36] Here, the question was whether the suspension of two children

[33] Eur. Ct. H.R. Dahlab v. Switzerland, Application no. 42393/98, 10 (2001).
[34] Eur. Ct. H.R. Hoffmann v. Austria, Application no. 12875/87 (1993).
[35] Id. at para. 34.
[36] Eur. Ct. H.R. Valsamis v. Greece, Application no. 74/1995/580/666 (1996).

who refused to participate in a school procession, which they believed to be contrary to their religion, was compatible with, or an infringement of, Article 9. Having discussed the parental right in the second sentence of Article 2 of the First Protocol, the court concluded that the action by the school did not infringe the parental right. Further, the Court found that the obligation to take part in the school parade, *mutatis mutandis*, did not interfere with the school children's freedom of religion under Article 9.[37] Given that the scope of Article 9 is wider than that of the parental right related to education in the second sentence of Article 2 of the First Protocol, the Court, just on this basis, should have discussed whether mandatory attendance at the school parade infringed the children's right to freedom of religion. Instead of acknowledging the child as an autonomous and individual right holder by discussing this case under Article 9, the Court assumed that the child's right coincided with the right and interest of the parents. Even though the question of the child's welfare was not part of the discussion, the ECHR missed the possibility of actively using the child's right in court proceedings.

4.3. European Court of Justice

The ECJ has recently, in February 2010, decided two cases with rather similar facts. The case of Texeira v. London Borough of Lambeth, Secretary of State for the Home Department, and the case of London Borough of Harrow v. Nimco Hassan Ibrahim both regarded the question whether a child has a continuous right to residence based on its right to education in the host Member State even though the parent responsible for the care of the child is not an EU citizen and is not able to provide sufficiently for the child economically, meaning that the non-EU citizen parent was relying on the host Member State's welfare system.[38] The court has in both cases stated that Article 12 of EU Regulation No 1612/68, as well as EU Directive 2004/38 Articles 7 and 12, implied that the child could, in connection with his right of access to education, have an independent right of residence.[39] Even though the parent with the EU citizenship, who initially installed the child in the host Member State, had left the respective host Member State, the child had the right to undertake,

[37] Id. at para. 37.

[38] Case C-480/08, Maria Teixeira v. London Borough of Lambeth, Secretary of State for the Home Department, 2009. Case C-310/08, London Borough of Harrow v. Nimco Hassan Ibrahim, Secretary of State for the Home Department, 2009.

[39] Case C-480/08, Maria Teixeira v. London Borough of Lambeth, Secretary of State for the Home Department, 49, 2009.

continue and successfully complete its education and thus a right to residence.[40] The parent caring for the child, though not being an EU citizen, and therefore not satisfying the conditions laid down in Directive 2004/38, could claim a right of residence being the primary caretaker of the child.[41] These cases are examples of children who are descendants of EU citizens having independent rights in the host Member State, and moreover, of parents being able to claim rights depending on the status of the child being enrolled in the host Member State's school system. The ECJ stresses that the aim of the Regulation and Directive is, *inter alia* to simplify and strengthen the right of free movement and residence of all European Union citizens. Furthermore, the exercise of the child's right to education does not depend on the existence of a separate right of residence of the child[42]—in fact, it's the other way round. Once the child has acquired the right to access to education derived from Article 12 of EU regulation 1612/68, the right to residence can no longer be called into question.[43] Further, the overall aim of Regulation 1612/68 is to integrate the migrant worker's family into the host Member State, as stated in the fifth recital in the preamble to the respective regulation. According to settled case law, the ECJ states in the Ibrahim case, that for such integration to come about, the children of a worker who is a national of a Member State must have the prospect of undertaking and, where appropriate, successfully completing, their education in the host Member State.[44]

The Teixeira and Ibrahim cases are impressive decisions, since the ECJ stresses the *independent* right of the child to access to education, regardless of the current situation of its parents. Thus, one could argue that these cases are about the empowerment of the child within the EU market-system. However, I would like to underline that the right to access to education, upon which the right to residence is dependent, has the character of a welfare right. Adults do not usually object that the right to education is granted to a child since that is considered to be in the child's best interests, and nor are welfare rights linked to the right holder's having the capacity to claim the right. Furthermore, the right to education fits into the construction of childhood. Additionally, we construct education not

---

[40] Case C-310/08, London Borough of Harrow v. Nimco Hassan Ibrahim, Secretary of State for the Home Department, 38-41, 2009.
[41] Id. at 50.
[42] Id. at 37.
[43] Id. at 38.
[44] Id. at 43.

only as a good for the child, but also for society as a whole—and, as such, society would act contrary to its own best interests if it based the right to education on a child's capacity to claim the right.

Overall, all these cases and opinions by legal scholars read in conjunction construct a picture of the child as a right holder which not only must prove its capacity when it comes to civil rights in order to exercise them autonomously during decision-making, but where the adult world also wants to check that the decision is in the child's best interests. In cases where the child is actually granted an independent right, it is a right which is ordinarily considered to be good for society and in the child's best interests and where the adult world expects no harm to the child. Even in a world where we were able to exercise our civil rights without regard to maturity, age or competence, the *child* would still not be able to exercise *its* civil rights independently and autonomously.

5. The Capacity Principle and the Child's Welfare

If the proof of capacity were the only precondition for a child to act autonomously, then new legal theories which dismiss the capacity-principle would lead to full acceptance of a child's right to self-determination in relation to religious norms. Let me try to test this hypothesis by applying it to reconstructed legal theories. Kathrine Hunt Federle argued in a 1994 article, "Rights flow downhill", that a new rights theory offers some solutions to the inequality children find themselves in today in relation to civil and political rights.[45] She argues that rights should be premised upon powerlessness, rather than upon capacity which is the language of those with power. The right to assembly, the right to free speech, the right to freedom of religion should be granted to those who need to have the power to command respect and deference, who need to challenge hierarchy and to be treated non-paternalistically. These rights then should prohibit others from defining the nature and extent of those rights and deciding the limits of the rights holders. Having rights is thus not about the capacity to exercise or assert them: rather, these rights prevent those who already have power from exerting this power. Rights tied to power create zones of mutual respect for power that limits the kinds of things we may do to one another.[46]

---

[45] Kathrine Hunt Federle, *Rights flow downhill*, 2 Int. J. Children's Rights 343, 364 (1994).

[46] Id. at 365-367.

Applying this theory to the child's right to freedom of religion and the relationship between the child and the parents would change the hierarchy and power relation between both parties. When asking whether the child has a right to self-determination with regard to religious norms, we would no longer consider the capacity of the child. Federle's theory would mean that there would be no reason to distinguish the child's right to freedom of religion from those of adults, with all the implications attached to it. Children could not be prohibited or limited in their exercise of their rights, whether choosing or rejecting religious clothing, choosing or rejecting religious school attendance, or choosing or rejecting a religiously based diet.

Likewise, John Wall's theory, stated in his 2008 article "Human Rights in the Light of Childhood", may possibly alter the conception of rights.[47] His theory states that children's rights will sufficiently alter societies only when the body of "human rights" is re-imagined in the light of childhood. It is the responsibility of each one of us to construct ever more inclusive societies, especially the one we recognize as the "other" in the sense of being different. Children are constructed as being the "other", especially when we define human beings according to their capacities. Instead of concluding that the child does not have the freedom to decide in religious matters, since it does not have the necessary capacity, according to Wall's theory children should actually be incorporated into the right to freedom of religion since they are constructed as different. Human rights based on responsibility to otherness would find in children its clearest reason for being, since children, likely to be marginalized and unheard, need the greatest social response.[48]

But is it really enough to change the theory of right? It's doubtful. The question is thus not whether or not the child is competent enough to make its own choices, because it is not enough for a child to be able to make autonomous choices; the question is always whether or not the choice a child makes is in its best interests. If we imagine that every child, regardless of its level of development, can decide on religious matter, hen the adult world would still most probably look for the best possible outcome of that specific choice, and stop the child from choosing that path if they find it going against with the child's best interests. Reconstructing the legal rights theory may thus detach civil rights from the capacity-

---

[47] John Wall, *Human Rights in the Light of Childhood*, 16 Int. J. Children's Rights, 532 (2008).
[48] Id. at 539-541.

principle; yet at the same time this reconstruction might actually lessen the child's chances to make autonomous decisions. The child's capacity would no longer be relevant when assessing what is in its best interest. If one really supposes that children are not capable of making the right decisions, then one has to rethink all ideas about the relationship between the child and its parents, and also adults as a whole. The intention will then be to ease our anxiety governing the question of whether children can understand the scope of responsibility for their wrongful decisions.

6. Conclusion

In attempting to answer the question of when a child has the right to self-determination in relation to religious norms *versus* the parental right to raise the child according to their own beliefs and convictions, little help can be found in legal sources, although we can find there some patterns of how the child, and the child's right to exercise its rights, are constructed.

Generally, the child's right to autonomously exercise its rights is linked to an evaluation of the child's competence. Even though the child's capacity is a necessary condition for autonomous decision-making, legal precedents show that this is not a sufficient condition; and what seems to be additionally necessary is the absence of the parental power of protection. In order for the court to make sure that the parental power of protection can be dismissed, a test on what is in the child's best interests is made, thus following the principle of the child's welfare. In cases where the child, at first glance, seems to be granted an independent right, the right is not linked to the capacity-principle only, but also to the child's welfare. Reconstruction of the notion of civil rights by detaching them from the capacity-principle does not lead to the opportunity for the child to exercise its rights autonomously. The protection of the child will still be the principle guiding the consideration of a court. What might need to be in place is a reconstruction of childhood.

What Do We Mean When We Speak About Children's Right to Development?

Noam Peleg*

Abstract

Children's right to development has been a fundamental principle of international children's rights law since 1924 and is explicitly protected in Article 6(2) of the 1989 UN Convention on the Rights of the Child, but has thus far received limited scholarly attention. At the same time, though, the right to development in "general" international human rights law has gained extensive attention in the last four decades and is constantly debated. As children are absent from consideration in the latter, it is necessary to take the right to development of children seriously. This article attempts to make a scholarly distinction between children's right to development and the right to development in "general" international law, and argues that children's right to development and the right to development in "general" international law might share the same *title*, but not necessarily the same *meaning*.

1. Introduction

The right to development of children was first acknowledged in international children's rights law in 1924, when the League of Nations adopted the Declaration on the Rights of the Child.[1] Today, children's right to

---

* PhD candidate, University College London, Faculty of Laws. I would like to thank the participants of the 2010 International Conference on Children in Law, held in Örebro University in September 2010, for their comments. Thanks also to the staff of the UN library in Geneva, and especially to Cristina Giordano, for their kind help. Thanks to Matthew Nicholson for commenting. Many thanks to Prof. Michael Freeman for his comments, support and encouragement. Special thanks to Lana Tatour, who helped crystallize my thoughts. I would like to thank UCL

development is protected in article 6(2) of the UN Convention on the Rights of the Child (the Convention)[2], and defined as one of the Convention's four guiding principles.[3]The right to development has arguably become a fundamental principle of children's rights law.

A similarly named right, that is, 'the right to development', appeared in "general" international law as recently as the 1970s, as a corollary to the political-economic idea of "development". This article will address the parallel development of these two rights, and will suggest that their content is different, despite a shared title.

The first part reviews the three main instruments of international children's rights law and argues that the concepts of children as developing human beings and of the right to development are key concepts of children's rights law. However, as central as these concepts appear to be, a closer look at the drafting process of Article 6 of the Convention reveals that although the right is included in the Convention, the drafters did not put much stress on the term 'development'. This lack of clarity demands interpretation, and opens the window to further exploration. The second part will then discuss how the right to development in "general" international law emerged, and argues that its roots and objectives differ from the one pertaining to children's rights. The third part focuses on the main differences between the two rights, and argues that although these two rights share the same title, they have different meanings.[4]

Faculty of Laws for their generous support that enabled me to conduct this research. Additional support from UCL Graduate School allowed me to take part in the conference.

[1] League of Nations O.J. Spec. Supp. 21, at 43 (1924).

2 UN Convention on the Rights of the Child 1989 (Adopted by General Assembly Resolution 44/25 of 20 November 1989, entered into force on 2 September 1990).

[3] UNCRC 'General Comment No. 5 (2003) – General Measure of Implementation of the Convention on the Rights of the Child (27 November 2003) UN Doc CRC/GC/2003/5.

[4] This article does not address the relationship between the policy of the child's right to development and children, or the impact that development practices have on them. Nor does it address the ongoing lack of recognition of children as a distinct social group and as rights holders under the framework of both 'development' and the right to development in "general" international law. These important issues deserve separate attention.

2. Codifying the Right to Development of Children in International Law

An analytical approach to the structure of the three main international law instruments that recognize children as human rights holders—the 1924 Declaration on the Rights of the Child; the 1959 Declaration on the Rights of the Child; and the 1989 Convention on the Rights of the Child—indicates that the idea of children's development and of the right to development are fundamental to all three.[5] However, it is evident from the Convention's *travaux préparatoires*, and specifically from the drafting process of Article 6, that the drafters had only a vague understanding of the meaning of children's right to development, and that they did not take into serious consideration the meaning or scope that this right has in "general" international law.

2.1.The Beginning: 1924

The 1924 League of Nations Declaration on the Rights of the Child, also known as the "Geneva Declaration",[6] was the first instrument to identify children as human rights holders in international law.[7] Motivated by the aftermath of the First World War, the drafters of the Declaration believed that their ultimate goal was to protect children from the negative repercussions of wars.[8] The Declaration is a short document that includes a one-paragraph preamble, followed by five substantial sections.

The Declaration mandates that certain needs of children be met: the need of a hungry child to be fed, for sick children to be nursed, and to reclaim a

---

[5] Although all these three instruments constitute an integral part of international children's rights law, they have fundamentally different characteristics. The two declarations are not law-making treaties while the Convention does have the power of a law-making treaty and is therefore fully authoritative. Nevertheless, for the purposes of this article, the binding nature is of less importance, as my claims focus on the normative level concerning the centrality of the right to development and of the idea of children as developing human beings in international children's rights law.

[6] *Supra* 1.

[7] Philip Veerman, *The Right of the Child and the Changing Image of Childhood* 155-156 (1992).

[8] Dominique Marshall, *The Contraction of Children as an Object of International Relations: The Declaration of Children's Rights and the Child Welfare Committee of League of Nations 1900-1924*, 7 Int'l .J. Children Rts. 103, 108-110 (1999).

delinquent child (paragraph 2); the child should be the first to receive relief in times of distress (paragraph 3); the child's need to be in a position where he or she can earn a livelihood while at the same time being protected against every form of exploitation (paragraph 4); and the child's need to be brought up to be conscious that his or her talents must be devoted to the service of his fellow human beings (paragraph 5).

The child's development is formulated in the first paragraph, which states that: "The child must be given the means requisite for its normal development, both materially and spiritually." Here, protecting the child's 'normal' development includes two distinct elements: material development and spiritual development. The article creates the obligation to ensure that the necessary means for the facilitation of 'normal development' are available to the child. The Declaration does not, however, clarify what is meant by the term 'normal development', and what should be done in order to achieve this goal.

Despite its full name, the Geneva Declaration does not use the term 'rights' in any of the substantial paragraphs, instead emphasizing welfare over human rights.[9] As Janusz Korczak wisely described it, the Geneva Declaration is no more than 'an appeal to goodwill of adults'.[10] Regardless of these weaknesses, it is the first international law document to recognize children as human rights holders and to emphasize the idea of development before addressing other basic needs, or rights, such as the right to not be hungry. Since then, acknowledging and protecting the right to development has been a cornerstone of the provisions of the most significant international documents governing the rights of children.

2.2. The First UN Instrument to Acknowledge the Right to Development

Eleven years after the General Assembly adopted the Universal Declaration of Human Rights (UDHR), which included only limited and unsatisfactory protection for children and their rights,[11] the 1959 UN Declaration on the Rights of the Child was accepted, becoming the first

---

[9] Michael Freeman, *The Moral Status of Children*, 49 (1997).
[10] Janusz Korczak, *The Child's Right to Respect*, in Janusz Korczak's Legacy, 34 (2009. Originally published in 1929).
[11] Universal Declaration on Human Rights, General Assembly Resolution 217 A(III), 10 December 1948. Article 25 ties childhood and motherhood together as both require special protection and care. Article 26 protects the right to education.

UN instrument that specifically acknowledged children as rights holders.[12] Based on the Geneva Declaration, the 1959 Declaration includes ten principles, with the right to development as a key element. Principle 2 declares that the child is entitled to 'special protection', and ensures the child's 'opportunity and facilities, by law and by other means' so that the child can 'develop physically, mentally, morally and spiritually'. These are four different aspects of personal development that should be available for the child's enjoyment. In addition, the term 'development' constitutes a key concept of three other principles of the Declaration.

Principle 4 protects the child's right to social security, so 'he shall be entitled to grow and develop in health'. Principle 6 attaches the child's 'full and harmonious development' to the child's need for 'love and understanding', in protecting the child's right to grow up with his parents. And Principle 9 protects the child from being forced to work in a way that can 'prejudice his health or education, or interfere with his physical, mental or moral development'.

The 1959 Declaration takes a similar view of the child's development and children's human rights to the Geneva Declaration, but also makes further progress in this respect by attaching more dimensions of personal development to the rights of the child. Principle 2 should be particularly highlighted, since unlike the Geneva Declaration, the right to development is not attached to other rights, interests or external aspects (like social conditions), but rather acknowledged as an independent concept.

The centrality of development to children's rights in the context of this Declaration can be gleaned from two additional references. The first one is the UN Social Commission's resolution in 1950, which asked the Secretary General to draft a declaration on children's rights. The resolution asked that such a declaration should respect the child's *rights* to 'a name, nationality, security, health, education and protection against all forms of exploitation which might prejudice his development'.[13] In other words, the Commission asked that the child's development be protected from six potentially threatening elements. The second reference is to Cuevas Cancino, the drafting committee's rapporteur, while presenting the draft of

---

[12] Declaration on the Rights of the Child, General Assembly Resolution 1386 (XIV) 20 November 1959.

[13] *Legislative History of the Convention on the Rights of the Child* (Office of the United Nation Commissioner of Human Rights, New York and Geneva) Volume I, 5 (2007).

the final Declaration to the General Assembly. Cancino described the rationale behind the Declaration by saying that 'it is not surprising that the draft Declaration should attach such importance to the spiritual factors which determine the development of the child', adding that 'as being in a process of development, the child requires special protection in that process; his development must be neither impeded not forced into anti-social directions'.[14] The 1959 Declaration considers the child to be an 'immature being', said Cancino, and therefore 'sets forth those rights which it regards as essential to the child's full development'.[15]

When the Declaration was drafted and adopted there were no substantial discussions on development as a human right in "general" international law, and at the time it was only conceptualized as a policy issue. It is therefore notable that the 1959 Declaration is the first UN human rights declaration that conceptualizes development as an essential norm of international human rights law. As will be discussed in the next section, advocates for the right to development ignore children's rights instruments and to see the UDHR as their main normative source, though it does not name development as a human right.

2.3. Including the Right to Development in a Binding International Convention

The 1989 UN Convention on the Rights of the Child marks a turning point for children's rights in general, and for the conception of their right to development in particular. The Convention, unlike the two previous declarations, is a binding international law covenant: 193 states have signed and ratified the Convention,[16] making it the most ratified human rights convention of all.

The Convention on the Rights of the Child is central to the consolidation of children as human beings and as human rights holders, and it changed the image of the child under the law. This recognition is an important step but, at the same time, only a preliminary one. It is significant in its own right, since it gives children an agency in society and in law, and allows children, and those who advocate on their behalf, to demand protection of

[14] *Id*, 21.
[15] *Id*, 22.
[16] UN Treaties website [http://treaties.un.org/Pages/ViewDetails.aspx?src=TREATY&mtdsg_no=IV-11&chapter=4&lang=en] Last checked: 12.10.2010.

these rights. *Ubi jus, ibi remedium.*[17] The Convention constitutes a comprehensive document that recognizes various rights of the child—political and social rights alike. It also explicitly acknowledges the right to development in article 6, which is as follows:

> 1. State Parties recognize that every child has the inherent right to life.
> 2. State Parties shall ensure to the maximum extent possible the survival and development of the child.

In addition, the Convention's preamble and five articles refer to the right to development: the child's development is stated twice in the preamble. The first statement clarifies that the child should grow up 'in an atmosphere of happiness, love and understanding' for his or her 'full and harmonious development', and the second links the need to protect the child's 'harmonious development' to the need to recognize the importance of traditional and cultural values. In both instances, it is the undefined and romantic idea of 'harmonious development' of the child that must be fulfilled by either the family or society. It involves an emotional process of development that is motivated by abstract ideas such as love or culture.

Article 18 ensures parental responsibilities for the 'upbringing and development' of the child; Article 23 lists the special needs of children with disabilities and the need to provide them with education, training, health care services and rehabilitation services to facilitate their full integration within society and guarantee their 'individual development, including his or her cultural and spiritual development'; Article 27 protects the child's right to a standard of living which should be 'adequate for the child's physical, mental, spiritual, moral and social development'; Article 29 specifies what the aims of education should be, stating that its primary aim should be focused on 'the development of the child's personality, talent and mental and physical abilities to their fullest potential'; and Article 32 protects the child from economic exploitation and from work that may be harmful 'to the child's health or physical, mental, spiritual, moral or social development'.

The Convention protects and promotes the child's development in various ways, addressing the different constituent aspects of its life. More specifically, it aims to protect seven different components of the individual

[17] Michael Freeman, 'The Limits of Children's Rights' in The Ideologies of Children's Rights (Michael Freeman and Philip Veerman eds) 29, 29-32 (1992); Freeman, supra 9, 21-25.

child's development, including cultural, spiritual, physical, mental, moral and social matters, as well as personality and talent. In 2003, the UN Committee on the Rights of the Child endorsed this, and defined the right to life, survival and development as one of the Convention's four guiding principles, together with the right to non-discrimination, the right of participation and the 'best interests of the child' principle.[18]

Although children's right to development and the idea of children's development is clearly embedded within the Convention, the *meaning* of 'the right to development' remains unclear. In an attempt to understand the meaning or meanings of this right, the next sub-section will describe the way in which the right to development was incorporated into Article 6. I will study the Convention's *travaux préparatoires*, as they are the main source for understanding the 'original meaning' of the Convention, and as they provide insights into the question of how the Convention's drafters constructed the meaning of the right to development of children.[19]

Based on this analysis, two arguments can be made. First, it is evident that the drafters of the Convention were unable to give a substantial legal meaning to the idea of children as developing human beings, and that no concrete "ordinary meaning" can be assigned to the term.[20] Second, the drafters did not take into consideration the meaning assigned to the right to development in "general" international law.

2.4. It Is Only Natural, Isn't It?

In 1978, the government of Poland introduced a draft for an international convention on the rights of the child (the Draft), hoping that it would be adopted by the UN in 1979—which the UN had declared to be the International Year of the Child.[21]

---

[18] Supra 3.

[19] Antonio Cassese, *International Law* (2nd edition), 178 (2005).

[20] In the sense of article 31 of the Vienna Convention on the Law of Treaties 1969. Done in Vienna on 23 May 1969, Entered into force on 28 January 1980. UN Treaty series vol. 1155, p. 331.

[21] Draft Convention on the Rights of the Child, Annex to Commission on Human Rights resolution 20 (XXXIV) of 8 March 1978. United Nation Economic and Social Council (1978) Supplement no. 4 (UN Docs E/1978/34), Chap. XXVI, Sect A; Explanatory Memorandum submitted by the Polish government to the United Nations (18 January 1978) UN Docs E/CN.4/1284.

The Draft was based on the 1959 Declaration and, as with its precursors, the right to development is formulated into four articles—nos. 2, 4, 6 and 9—but not yet as a distinct right. It was only in 1988 that India suggested the following amendment:

> The State Parties to the present Convention undertake to create an environment, within their capacities and constitutional process, which ensure to the maximum extent possible, the survival and healthy development of children.[22]

This amendment was the first time that the right to (healthy) development was introduced. It constructed development as an independent right that required separate protection, but it should be noted that this suggestion does not employ the term 'right'. It also attaches the concept of 'survival' to that of 'development'.[23] Though the 1986 Declaration on the Right to Development had been adopted by the General Assembly just fourteen months earlier,[24] this proposal does not refer to it. This lack is particularly notable because the "general" right to development was subject to constant debates during the time the Convention was being drafted, and those debates could have been useful to the drafters in articulating their own understanding of the right to development of children.[25]

Since the idea of children as developing human beings was part of the first draft, it was already being debated during the first round of comments.[26] However, none of the comments made then touched upon the meaning of the right to development, although they all suggested protecting even more aspects of the child's personal development. The World Health Organization (WHO), for example, suggested including a reference to the child's healthy development, while the United Nation Educational, Scientific and Cultural Organization (UNESCO) requested additional references to 'cultural development', and the UN Food and Agricultural Organization (UNFAO) asked for 'emotional development' to be added to the list.

---

[22] Commission of Human Rights (28 January 1988) UN Docs E/CN.4/1988/WG.1/WP.13.

23 Manfred Nowak, *Article 6: The Right to Life, Survival and Development, in* A Commentary of the United Nations Convention on the Rights of the Child, 17-18 (Alen et al eds., 2005).

[24] The Declaration on the Right to Development, Adopted 4 December 1986. G.A. Res. 41/128.

[25] I will further elaborate on this point later on.

[26] UNECOSOC, 'Questions of a Convention on the Rights of the Child' (27 December 1978) E/CN.4/1324.

Some comments focused on the relationship between development and other rights within the draft. Sweden, for example, wanted to highlight the importance of medical attention and a healthy physical environment to the 'sound development' of the child, while UNFAO thought that the link between adequate nutrition and health should be stressed by including protection for the child's 'healthy growth and development'. Norway asked for protection the child's 'full opportunity of play, social activities and recreation, as a means to ensure their full mental and physical development'. According to the International Committee of the Red Cross, the child's 'harmonious background for his physical and mental development' ought to be protected under Article 8, which deals with the rights of children during armed conflict.

The most comprehensive suggestion was made by the Society for Comparative Legislation, suggesting amending the draft to include: 'the child shall enjoy special protection and shall be given opportunities and facilities, by law and other means, to enable him to develop physically, mentally, morally, spiritually and socially in a healthy and normal manner and in condition of freedom and dignity'. This suggestion encompasses a broad view of the individual child's development, and aimed to establish freedom and dignity as the platform on which five elements of the child's development—physical, mental, moral, spiritual and social—would be best fulfilled. The goal of the amendment was, however, very simple. It wished to enable the child to grow up maximizing his or her personal abilities.

The revised draft presented by Poland in 1980 gave the right to development a more significant place in the Convention.[27] Article 3(2) of the revised draft sought to ensure that the child would be protected and receive care 'taking due account of the various stages of his development…'; Article 13 protected the right to health, its aim being to support the 'physical, mental and moral development'; and article 15(1) introduced the right to a standard of living, determining that it should be 'adequate for his healthy and normal physical, mental and moral development in every phase of the child's development'. Debates over the meaning of the right to development ceased at this point, and were renewed only after India put forward its amendment in 1988.[28]

---

[27] Commission of Human Rights (17 January 1980) UN Docs E/CN.4/1349.

[28] See, for example, the working group session in 1982, in which family reunification, the question of citizenship, freedom of movement and the rights of disabled children were discussed (Commission on Human Rights, UN Docs

The official summary of the working group's meeting dedicated to India's proposal mentions that a discussion concerning the meaning of survival, development and the relations between these two concepts took place.[29] Nonetheless, a careful review of the *travaux préparatoires* does not shed much light on the content of these discussions, and it seems that most of them dealt only with the right to life and survival. These discussions provide more than a vague idea of the motives underlying the inclusion of the explicit right to development in the Convention.

India's proposal linked the concepts of survival and development together, arguing that 'many children died from preventable causes and that children could also survive in very poor conditions', and that 'the right to survival should be supplemented by the notion of healthy development'.[30] It thereby put the two concepts on one continuum, with survival closer to the right to life on one end, and development, representing the child's right to grow up and live a healthy life, at the other.

Few other amendments to this article were submitted, and all of them danced around the issue of protecting the life-survival-development continuum, but few definitive clarifications of the right to development were made in any of them. It is, however, worth investigating the comments made by the WHO and the representative of Italy during the last stage of discussions. The WHO representative explained that within the framework of the organization, 'survival includes growth monitoring, oral rehydration and disease control, breastfeeding, immunization, child spacing, food and female literacy',[31] and the representative of Italy argued that "survival" and "development" 'acquire [the] special meaning of ensuring the child's survival in order to realize the full development of his or her personality, both from the material and spiritual points of view'.[32]

E/CN.4/1983/62); The meeting held in 1985, which dealt with the right to health and the right to education (Commission on Human Rights, UN Docs E/CN.4/1985/L.1); the session of February 1987 was dedicated to different issues such as the contentment of children with their parents, traditional practices, access to information, the rights of indigenous children, exploitation of children, freedom of thought and freedom of movement (Commission on Human Rights, UN Docs E/CN.4/1987/WG.1/CRP.1).

[29] Commission on Human Rights (6 April 1988) UN Docs EC/CN.4/1988/28.

[30] Ibid.

[31] Sharon Detrick et al, *The United Nation Convention on the Rights of the Child: A Guide to the "Travaux Préparatories"*, 122 (1992); *Legislative History* (supra 13) 367.

[32] Detrick et al (n 31), 123.

While the WHO shed light on the substance of the right to survival, Italy developed the connection between survival and development, suggesting that survival constitutes a preliminary stage fundamental to assuring the child's 'full development of his or her personality'.

The final round of discussions on Article 6 was held in March 1989,[33] and two versions were presented: one by the chairman that changed little from India's original amendment; and one by Venezuela, which reads as follows:

> 1. For the purpose of the present Convention, 'child' means every human being up to the age of 18 years unless, under the law of his State he has attained the age of majority earlier.
> 2. The State Parties to the present Convention recognize that every child has the inherent right to life.
> 3. State Parties shall ensure to the maximum extent possible the healthy growth and development of the child.[34]

This version omits the right to survival, replacing it with the right to 'healthy growth', but keeps the right to development in place. Responding to this version, the observer from the WHO argued against replacing 'survival' with 'healthy development', claiming that the term 'survival' bore special meaning within the provisions of the UN. 'It will be a step backwards from standards already accepted', the observer concluded. The Italian representative agreed and stated that 'in the language of international organizations the two words 'survival' and 'development' had come to acquire the special conjoined meaning of ensuring the child's survival in order to realize the full development of his or her personality, both from the material and spiritual points of view'. At the end of the session, the article in its current form was adopted as Article 6 of the Convention.

Whether it is the 'natural' development, 'harmonious' development, or the development of the child's personality, the focus is on the individual child. These debates take the same line as the 1924 and 1959 Declarations, and

---

[33] Commission on Human Rights (2 March 1989) UN Docs E/CN.4/1989/28.

[34] Commission on Human Rights, Draft Convention on the Rights of the Child, Working paper submitted by the Chairman / pre sectional open ended working group / text as adopted at first reading with suggested revisions (24 November 1988) UN Docs E/CN.4/1989/WG.1/WP.2; Commission on Human Rights UN Docs E/CN.4/1989/WG.1/WP.10.

suggest that the drafters focused on protecting what they considered to be the organic process of growing up. This looks forward to the child's future, to when he or she becomes an adult, and stipulates the means required, both material and spiritual, to enable the process of growing up, and does not appreciate the time of childhood for the child him- or herself.

3. Incorporating the Right to Development in "General" International Human Rights Law

This section describes the way in which a right to development was formulated in "general" international human rights law, and argues that it has different roots and aims than the right to development in children's international human rights law. The term "general" is referred to in quotation marks, in order to highlight the illusions of generality and inclusion in international law, mainly in relation to children and their rights, and to differentiate it from international children's rights law.

The right to development in "general" international law is the legal expression of the political-economic agenda of development. The latter is traditionally attributed to US president Harry Truman, who introduced the concept of 'development' in his Inaugural Speech in January 1949. In his speech, Truman advocated that the 'developed' nations help the 'underdeveloped' ones to enjoy scientific advances and industrial progress, in order to facilitate better life conditions for all.[35] This concept of development is centred on economic development and is built upon the assumption that economic growth will trickle down to improve the material living conditions of all members of every society.[36]

Based on the belief that material living conditions should be improved, development and aid policies were, and still are, orientated and organized throughout 'underdeveloped' countries by governments, international non-governmental organizations and international bodies such as the World Bank. These trillion-dollar projects focus on alleviating poverty and increasing gross national product (GNP).[37] Although development

---

[35] G. Esteva, *Development*, in The development Dictionary, 6, 6-23 (Wolfgang Sachs ed., 1992).

[36] Two of the classic books which promote this view are W. Arthur Lewis, *The Theory of Economic Growth* (1955), and Paul A. Baran, *The Political Economy of Growth* (1957).

[37] Baran, id.

practices have changed during the years, and human rights principles such as participation and equality became part of development policy,[38] poverty reduction and rapid GNP growth are still the main objectives of development in practice.[39]

During the 1970's, legal scholars, mainly from 'underdeveloped' countries, began to advocate the formulization of development in legal terms, and to consider development as a human right—'the right to development'. This idea was first suggested by the Senegal jurist Kebe M'Baya in his 1972 Inaugural Lecture at the International Institute of Human Rights in Strasburg.[40] Five years later, it was M'Baya again, by then the chairman of the UN Commission on Human Rights, who led the commission to adopt a resolution calling on the Secretary General to conduct a study on the 'international dimensions of the right to development ...'.[41] This resolution is considered to be the moment that the 'right to development' snowball started rolling,[42] essentially creating the right.[43]

At that time, as discussed earlier, the idea of development and the right to development were already substantial elements of international children's rights law and part of the 1959 Declaration. Nevertheless, the discussions following the above-mentioned 1978 UN Commission on Human Rights resolution that suggested creating the 'right to development' made no reference to either the existence of the right in children's rights law, nor its meaning.

---

[38] Hans-Otto Sano, *Development and Human Rights: The Necessary, but Partial Integration of Human Rights and Development* 22 H.R.Q 734, 743-745 (2000); Peter Uvin, *From the Right to Development to the Rights-Based Approach: How 'Human Rights' Entered Development* 17 Development in Practice 597, 600-602 (2007).

[39] John Weiss, *The Aid Paradigm for Poverty Reduction: Does it Make Sense?*, 26(4) Development Policy Review 407, 408-410 (2008).

[40] Peter Uvin, *Human Rights and Development*, 40-41 (2004).

[41] Commission on Human Rights, Report on the Thirty-Third Session, 62 U.N. ESCOR Supp. (No. 6) U.N Doc E/5927 (1978).

[42] Uvin (supra 40), 40.

43 Jack Donnelly, *In Search of the Unicorn: The Jurisprudence and Politics of the Right to Development* 15 Cal. W. Int'l L.J. 473, 474-475, 477 (1985).

The overlooking of children and their rights continued. Take, for example, the famous 1985 debate between Jack Donnelly and Philip Alston.[44] Donnelly argued that the right to development is no more than an invention of human rights lawyers, that it has no legal or moral grounds, and that development is a policy objective rather than a human right.[45] In his response, Alston argued that origins of this right could be traced from Article 28 of the UDHR (although it does not explicitly name Development as a human right), ignoring the 1959 Declaration. Furthermore, Alston added three more reasons why development should be formulated as a human right. The first is the ability to use it as a rhetorical tool, which would force governments to speak about social and economic rights. The second is to enable the dissolving of the dichotomy between national and international obligations to protect human rights. And the third is the creation of a legal platform to discuss collective rights.[46] Alston did agree, however, that the legal grounds should be more solid, and expressed the hope that such grounds would eventually be created.[47]

This debate represents a standard for most, if not all, debates concerning the nature and meaning of the right to development in "general" international law. In these debates, children were not considered to be rights holders and were absent from these discussions. Moreover, when attempting to articulate what the right to development could mean in "general" international law, no attempt to use the formulation of the right to development in international children's rights law was made.

In December 1986, Alston's wish for a more solid foundation for the right to development was realized when the UN General Assembly adopted the Declaration on the Right to Development.[48] The Declaration acknowledges development as a human right, and defines it as follows:

---

44 Donnelly, Id; Philip Alston, *The Shortcomings of a "Garfield the Cat" Approach to the Right to Development*, 15 Cal. W. Int'l L.J. 510 (1985); Jack Donnelly, *The Theology of the Right to Development: A Reply to Alston* 15 Cal. W. Int'l L.J. 519 (1985). See also Dinah Shelton, *A Response to Donnelly and Alston* 15 Cal. W. Int'l L.J. 524 (1985) and Paul H. Brietzke, *Consorting with the Chamelon, or Realizing the Right to Development* 15 Cal. W. Int'l. L. J. 560 (1985).

45 Donnelly, (supra 43), 477-478, 482-483.

46 Alston (supra 44), 515-516.

47 Alston (supra 44), 514.

48 Supra 24.

> "The right to development is an inalienable human right by virtue of which every human person and all peoples are entitled to participate in, contribute to, and enjoy economic, social, cultural and political development, in which all human rights and fundamental freedoms can be fully realized."[49]

This version of the right to development protects four elements of development—economic, social, cultural and political—attaching them to the collective right to self-determination.[50] This version thus reflects the political-economic model of development, and serves as the legal expression of it. It refers to external aspects of the human being rather than to intrinsic aspects such as moral, physical or spiritual development. It aims to protect the entitlement of all people to enjoy all human rights and fundamental freedoms.

Critiques of development and of the right to development that emphasize the necessary consideration of disadvantaged groups in society and diversity between nations and societies, also do not address children and their rights. Take for instance the feminist critique: since 1970, when Ester Boserup published her pioneering work "Women's Role in Economic Development",[51] the feminist critique has stressed that women's role in the economy should be taken into account and that gender should be mainstreamed into development and into the meaning of the right to development.[52] The feminist critique has indeed made a significant impact on the way the right to development was articulated, and a direct reference to women and their rights was incorporated in article 8(1) of the 1986 Declaration.[53]

---

[49] Article 1(1).

[50] Article 1(2).

[51] Ester Boserup, *Women's Role in Economic Development* (1970).

[52] Janet Momsen, *Gender and Development*, 12-14 (2nd edition, 2010); Cecile Jackson, *Rescuing Gender from the Poverty Trap,* in Feminist Vision of Development – Gender Analysis and Policy, 39-64, 43-46 (Cecile Jackson and Ruth Pearson eds., 1998); Naila Kabeer, *Reversed Realities – Gender Hierarchies in Development Thought*, 42-50, 89-92 (1994).

[53] "States should undertake, at the national level, all necessary measures for the realization of the right to development and shall ensure, *inter alia*, equality of opportunity for all in their access to basic resources, education, health services, food, housing, employment and the fair distribution of income. Effective measures should be undertaken to ensure that women have an active role in the development process. Appropriate economic and social reforms should be carried out with a view to eradicating all social injustices."

Another influential critique, the radical critique, stresses the falsity of underlying assumptions of universality and unity among societies. It rejects the division between 'developed' and 'underdeveloped', and views development as a euphemism for colonialism. According to this line of thought, 'development' is blind to cultural differences, fails to recognize non-western economic and social models, and is connected to regimes of oppression and serves as a vehicle of exploitation.[54]

Even these two important critiques, which call for the recognition of marginalized groups in society and challenge culturally and politically biased social-political models, fail to recognize children and their rights in their critique. It is puzzling that these critiques, which try to undermine the assumption of neutrality, do not address children, as they, too, are part of each and every society, although they play different roles in different societies.[55]

4. Identical Titles, Different Meanings

Following the end of World War II and the establishment of the United Nations, the process of codifying human rights in international law began. In 1948 the General Assembly adopted the UDHR, and in 1966 it adopted two additional covenants—the International Convention on Economic, Social and Cultural Rights[56] and the International Convention on Civil and Political Rights.[57] These two instruments, as their names imply, aim to protect the first- and second-generation human rights, positive and negative rights alike, of 'all people'.[58] Although 'all people' were allegedly protected by them, and human rights were presumed to be universal, there

---

[54] Hassan Zaoual, *The Economy and Symbolic Sites of Africa*, *in* The Post Development Reader, 30-39 (Majid Rahnema and Victoria Bawtree eds, 1997; Arturo Escobar, *Encountering Development – The Making and Unmaking of the Third World* (1995). Some of these critiques can also be traced with feminist writing, as early as Boserup's book. See Lourdes Benería and Gita Sen, *Accumulation, Reproduction, and Women's Role in Economic Development: Bosreup Revisited*, 7 J. of Women in Culture and Society 279, 280-283 (1981);

[55] Heather Montgomery, *An Introduction to Childhood* 104-132, 201-231 (2009)

[56] Adopted and opened for signature, ratification and accession by General Assembly resolution 2200 A (XXI) of 16 December 1966. Entry into Force in 3 January 1976.

[57] Adopted and opened for signature, ratification and accession by General Assembly resolution 2200 A (XXI) of 16 December 1966. Entry into Force in 23 March 1976.

[58] Common article 1 of the two Conventions.

remained the necessity of addressing the needs of disadvantaged and weakened groups in societies, and tackling systematic human rights violations. Since 1966, the process of codifying international human rights law has advanced in these two area, and now covers the rights of groups such as women,[59] children,[60] and people with disabilities.[61] It has also created a unique covenant that prohibits the use of systematic human rights violations, such as torture and other cruel, inhuman or degrading treatment or punishment.[62] But while most of the rights protected in the covenants—for example the right to freedom of expression—are based on the same moral grounds and aim to enable the same freedoms, children's right to development represents a different case. The main differences are its philosophical and moral roots, its objectives, and the identity of the right holder.

4.1. Growing Up or a "Summing Up"?

The right to development was incorporated into the Convention relatively more quickly than were the other rights. This may have been due to the conception of 'childhood' that the drafter had in mind.

The Convention's right to development contains a presumption about what a child needs in order to develop and eventually become an adult. Article 6, as well Articles 18, 23, 27, 29 and 32, which also refer to children's development, are forward-looking and protect seven aspects of the child's well-being: physical, moral, mental, spiritual, social, health and normal development. Those Articles anticipate the facilitation of the child's process of maturation, allowing it safely to reach the age of 18.

Based on the view of childhood as 'the period of *growth*',[63] and since the child's main remedy for childhood is to grow up,[64] it was only natural to

---

[59] Convention on the Elimination of All Forms of Discrimination Against Women, General Assembly Res. 34/180 (1979).
[60] Supra 2.
[61] Convention on the Rights of People With Disabilities, UN Docs. A/61/611 (6 December 2006)
[62] Convention against Torture and Other Cruel, Inhuman or Degrading Treatment or Punishment, General Assembly Resolution 39/46 (10 December 1984), entered into force on 26 June 1987.
[63] Ěmile Durkhiem, *Essays on Moral and Education* (W.S.F Pickering ed.) 150 (1980, original 1911).
[64] Onora O'Neill, 'Children's Rights and Children's Lives' 98 *Ethics* 445 (1988).

follow the 'romantic developmentalism' approach[65] and to include a right that would protect what seems to be the organic and natural course of the child's life. The Convention creates and reflects a certain perception of children's lives, and conceptualizes them as humans 'becoming'.[66] Although the Convention can be read as seeing children as both 'being' and 'becoming',[67] the *travaux préparatoires* suggests that the drafters (like the drafters of the 1924 and 1959 Declarations), had only one perception of the child, as a human 'becoming'.

Unlike the case of children's right to development, there was nothing simple, self-explanatory or natural in the process of establishing the right to development in "general" international law, let alone in the process of formulating its meaning. The 1986 Declaration on the Right to Development did not solve the disputes about the potential meaning of the right, but only provided a new ground for interpretation.

Arjun Sengupta, previously a UN Human Rights Commission independent expert on the right to development, has suggested an understanding of the right as 'the right to a particular process of development in which all human rights and fundamental freedoms can be fully and progressively realized'.[68] A different definition was suggested by John O'Maniqu, who emphasized both the individual and the community, arguing that human development should be understood as a process of development that 'actualize[s the] human potential as defined by the individual and his or her community'.[69] This process of development should be 'the exercise of the full range of rights; as a goal it is the self-actualization of people through the exercise of their rights'.[70] Such a definition conceptualizes the right to development as a right that should lead to a concrete, external result once other human rights are fulfilled. This 'external result',

[65] Alison Diduck, *Law's Families*, 79 (2003).
[66] Allison James, 'Agency' in *The Palgrave Handbook of Childhood Studies* (Jens Qvortrup et al eds.) 34-45, 34-37 (2009).
[67] Michael Freeman, The Human Rights of Children, *Current Legal Problems* 2010 (forthcoming).
[68] Arjun Sengupta, The Right to Development, 32(2) *Oxford Development Studies* 179, 180 (2004).
[69] John O'Manique, Development, Human Rights and Law, 14 *H.R.Q* 383, 384 (1992).
[70] John O'Manique, Human Rights and Development, 14 *H.R.Q* 78, 101 (1992).

according to Hans-Otto Sano, is a space in which the dignity of the person is protected, and the process of development can move forward.[71]

Such interpretations are closer to the right to development in international children's rights law, in the sense that it potentially creates future benefit upon fulfilling of the right. However, while these suggestions try (with only limited success) to distinguish the meaning of this right from being a "summing up" of other human rights,[72] for children the first difference concerning the right to development is not about potential benefits that will arise once other human rights are fulfilled, but rather is an independent right with a meaning of its own.

4.2. An Individual or a Collective Right?

A second difference is the nature of the right as either an individual right or a collective right. This issue relates to broader questions of the content of the right, on one side, and of the nature of the different legal grounds protecting it, on the other.

The right to development in "general" international law is a third generation right, and, as such, one of its characteristics is being a collective right, for although the 1986 Declaration emphasizes that the right to development should be understood as an individual right,[73] it nevertheless includes the collective right of people to self-determination.[74] Moreover, it is argued that the right to development as a norm may only be fulfilled collectively.[75]

The Convention, however, does not recognize children's right to self-determination. Although some scholars from the child liberation movement have previously argued that children do have the right to self-determination,[76] they understood each child to have the *individual* ability

---

[71] Otto-Sano, supra 38, 751.

[72] Alan Rosas, 'the Right to Development' in A. Eida et al (eds.) *Economic, Social and Cultural Rights* (2nd ed.) 119, 123 (2001).

[73] Salomon, supra 80, 113-114.

[74] Article 1(2) of the 1986 Declaration.

[75] Brietzke, *supra 44*, 593.

[76] See, for example, Robert Ollendorf, *The Rights of Adolescents* in Children's Rights – Toward a Liberation of the Child (Paul Adams et al eds), 91-126, 120 (1971); Sharom Bishop, *Children, Autonomy and the Right to Self Determination, in* Whose Child 154, 161-169 (William Aiken and Hugh LaFollette eds., 1980); Howard Cohen, *Equal Rights for Children* 74-90 (1980).

to determine its future and to be free from adult domination, and not in the sense of defining their future as a *collective* social group. Furthermore, it seems that the Convention tends to protect the rights of the individual child and not of children collectively. Article 6(2) itself refers to the right of 'the child' to survival and development, and the *travaux préparatoires* also indicate that the drafters viewed it as an individual right. The Convention's name, preamble, and Articles 2, 3, 5, 6, and 7 identify the 'child' as the right holder. However, other articles which deal with institutional issues such as health care (Article 24), children with disabilities (Article 24), or education (Article 29) relate to children as rights holders. Nonetheless, article 3 establishes that when taking an action concerning '*children*', 'the best interests of the *child* shall be a primary consideration' and Michael Freeman argues that it grasps both the collective and the individual notion of the Convention,[77] which should not be mutually exclusive.

4.3. A Legally Binding Right or Lawyers' Aspiration?

The third difference is that the two different legal regimes i.e. the CRC and international human rights law, acknowledge and protect the two rights. For children, the right to development is protected in article 6(2) of the Convention, which is a binding international human rights convention that was universally ratified. In "general" international law, the right to development is acknowledged only in UN declarations, and has no formal legally binding force.

The 1993 Vienna Declaration and Programme of Action, adopted at the World Conference on Human Rights, reaffirmed development to be a human right.[78] Ironically, even the most authoritative advocates of the right to development in "general" international law—who for years were occupied with the attempt to establish legal grounds for the right, and who celebrated the recognition of the right in the 1986 and 1993 Declarations—failed to recognize that a right with the same name was acknowledged long before as a human right in children's rights instruments. But perhaps under the influence of the Convention and its wide universal ratification, the 1993 Declaration, unlike the 1986 Declaration, did acknowledge

[77] Michael Freeman, *Article 3 – The Best Interests of the Child*, *in* A Commentary on the United Nation Convention on the Rights of the Child, 46 (A. Alen et al eds., 2007).

[78] World Conference on Human Rights: Vienna Declaration and Programme of Action (12 July 1993) UN Docs A/Conf.157.23.

children as rights holders. It requires the promotion of respect for children's rights to 'survival, protection, development and participation'.[79] It echoes the words of articles 6(2) and 12 of the Convention, and although it does not change children's legal status, this recognition in "general" international law should not be overlooked.

In 2000, the United Nation Millennium Development Goals (MDGs)[80] were adopted as an expression for a universal commitment to human development. However, despite the progress made in the 1993 Declaration, children's right to development was ignored almost entirely in all ten development goals. The MDGs revived Truman's legacy and determined development to be an issue of poverty reduction (though it can be argued that human rights are essential elements of the MDGs)[81] and diminished children's moral status as rights holders. The only promises given to children by the MDGs are to achieve universal primary education (goal 2) and to reduce the child mortality rate (goal 4).These promises were, however, already declared as human rights of children in the Convention (Articles 29 and 24), so the MDGs did not create any new rights or obligations, but rather reaffirmed past promises.

5. Conclusion

A right with the name 'the right to development' exists in two streams of international human rights law. One is a "general" right, which presumably applies to "all people" and one is a particular right, that relates solely to children. The chronology from 1924 and 1959, when the Declarations on the Rights of the Child were adopted, to 1986 (Declaration on the Right to Development), 1989 (Convention on the Rights of the Child), 1993 (Vienna Declaration and Progress of Action) and 2000 (Millennium Development Goals) demonstrates the creation and evolution of two different and distinct legal regimes covered by the same title.

Children are too often not perceived as human rights holder, which is also implied in the case of the right to development in "general" international

---

[79] Id, articles 45-53.

[80] GA, United Nations Millennium Declaration (18 September 2000) UN Docs A/Res/55/2; Margot E. Salomon, *Global Responsibility for Human Rights*, 115 (2007).

[81] Philip Alston, *Ships Passing in the Night: The Current State of the Human Rights and Development Debate Seen Through the Lens of the Millennium Development Goals*, 27 H.R.Q. 755 (2005).

law. But what is most puzzling in this case is that advocates of the 'right to development' devoted much time and energy down the years to defining development as a human right, and subsequently making it gender- and class-sensitive, they paid no attention to children as a distinct social group; while at the same time, children already had their 'own' right to development protected in the Declarations and Conventions. Children's right to development is embedded in the Convention and considered to be one of its four guiding principles, with qualified reasons. Nevertheless, it requires further development and interpretation.

CHALLENGES AND DILEMMAS REGARDING NON-RESIDENT FATHERS IN PUBLIC LAW

JIM REID

Abstract

There are a significant number of family breakdowns in the UK that require the intervention of social welfare workers to ensure positive outcomes for the children who are at the centre of disagreement and animosity. Many of the situations will use the law to impose a solution when agreement between the adults is not otherwise forthcoming. There are frequent complaints from some fathers of inequity in social welfare practice and the law. These complaints are in part due to the contemporary nature of social welfare work and concomitant legal practice with families because, for example, of uncritical approaches to intervention. One negative outcome of this, particularly for children in contested contact proceedings, is denied familial and cultural experiences and lost identity as the possibilities offered by the non-resident parent's family, culture and community are denied and unavailable to the child. Practitioners worry about accountability both within and without the courtroom, and operate in an atmosphere of increased public hostility and scrutiny. Utility and professional agency are determined not just by statute but by working practices and culture, by knowledge and skills, and by the prevailing social and political priorities of the day, and this does not necessarily favour positive outcomes for children and non-resident fathers. This article is focussed on the legal aspects of such situations, and argues that those working for better outcomes for children should pay closer attention to, and take account of, the impact of agency.

1. Glossary of Terms

1.1 Framework for Assessment of Children in Need and Their Families[1]

Also known as the 'Assessment Framework' or the 'Framework' (both used throughout this article) this ecological model of assessment is mandated and is therefore the foundation for most statutory social work practice in England. Based on a triangle, the framework is implemented through a series of tools designed to take the practitioner through each of the identified areas before making a judgement about a child's needs. The framework is child-centred and interdisciplinary in approach.

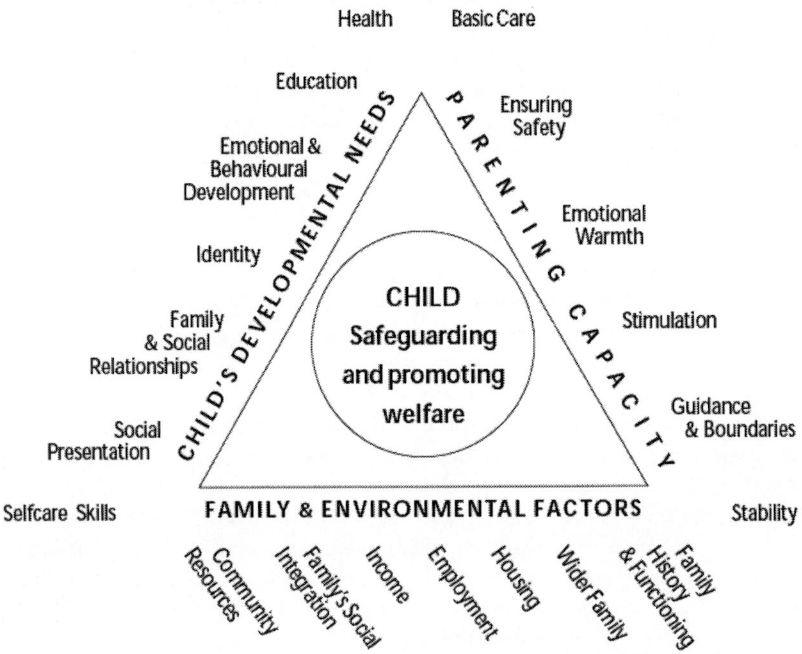

[1] Department of Health, *Framework for the Assessment of Children in Need and their Families*, London: The Stationery Office (2000, p.17)

Common Assessment Framework (CAF)[2]

CAF reinforces the inter-disciplinary nature of assessment in child welfare work and was introduced in the wake of concerns following the death of Victoria Climbié. It is a shared assessment and planning framework for use across all children's services, not just social welfare work, and is focused on children with additional needs with the aim of early identification of those needs. It is used to ensure effective inter-agency working and communication in assessment, and involves the use of a lead professional who may not be a social worker. Like the Assessment Framework CAF utilises standardised recording tools.

1.2 Integrated Children's System (ICS)[3]

ICS is based upon the dimensions of the Assessment Framework and as such is seen as 'an applied conceptual framework' for the assessment of children. It is, in effect, an electronic tool for recording and managing information from an assessment using the framework.

2. Introduction

The General Household Survey for 2007 undertaken by the UK Office for National Statistics shows that 23 per cent of families with dependent children in the UK were lone parent families, of these 20 per cent were lone mothers (10 per cent categorised as single, 6 per cent divorced, and 4 per cent separated) and 3 per cent lone fathers. This constitutes six per cent of the 24,700,000 households in the UK, or approximately 1,500,000 lone parent families with dependent children. In addition there are approximately 750,000 stepfamilies with dependent children, 86 per cent or 645,000 of which have one or more children from the woman's previous relationship(s).[4]

Although it isn't possible to extrapolate from the ONS data the numbers of children and families for whom contact is an issue, some insight into contact arrangements and patterns is provided by a significant survey

---

[2] Department for Education and Skills (DfES), *Parenting Support: Guidance for Local Authorities in England*. Nottingham: DCSF (2006)

[3] The development of the ICS was first signalled *in Learning the Lessons* (Department of Health, 2000) the Government's response to the Waterhouse report, *Lost in Care*.

[4] ONS, *General Household Survey 2007*. London: Office for National Statistics (2009)

undertaken by Peacey and Hunt[5] for Gingerbread, the UK charity for one parent families. Their research found that the majority of children whose parents have separated continue to live with their mother—conforming to the ONS data and previous findings,[6]—and that the majority of parents—71 per cent—reported face-to-face contact with the non-resident parent. However a significant minority of parents—29 per cent—reported no current contact, of which 63 per cent of respondents claimed no contact whatsoever with the non-resident parent since separation. A further 6 per cent said that the father was not aware of the child's existence.[7] There are, therefore, a considerable number of families for whom contact is an issue, and it is more usually the non-resident father in these situations who does not have contact with his child(ren).

It is important to note that this does not imply that mothers are preventing contact, since some fathers may choose not to exercise the contact available.[8] Nonetheless, many fathers continue to complain that their contact with the child, and the child's contact with the wider paternal family, are obstructed,[9] with the resident parent typically citing conflict with the non-resident parent or concern for their own and/or the child's safety or welfare as the reason.[10] Either of these contexts can lead to the involvement of social care workers with the family particularly if parental

[5] Peacey, V. Hunt, J. *I'm not saying it was easy: Contact problems in separated families.* London: Gingerbread (2009)

[6] for example: Trinder, L., Beek, M. and Connolly, J. *Making Contact*, York: Joseph Rowntree Foundation (2002); Trinder, L., Connolly, J., Keleet, J., Notley, C. and Swift, L. *Making Contact happen or making contact work?* DCA Research Series 3/06 (2005); Blackwell, A and Dawe, F. *Non-resident parent contact.* London: ONS (2003); ONS *The General Household Survey.* London: Office for National Statistics (2005); Cabinet Office and Department for Children, Schools and Families. *Families in Britain: an evidence paper.* London: Cabinet Office/DCSF (2008)

[7] Peacey, V. Hunt, J. *I'm not saying it was easy: Contact problems in separated families.* London: Gingerbread (2009, p.17)

[8] Smart, C., May, V., Wade, A and Furniss, C. *Residence and Contact Disputes in Court*, Volume 2. London, DCA Research Series 4/05 (2005) cited by Peacey, V. Hunt, J. *I'm not saying it was easy: Contact problems in separated families.* London: Gingerbread (2009, p.7)

[9] Bradshaw, J., Stimson, C., Skinner, C. and Williams, J. *Absent Fathers?* London: Routledge (1999); Wikeley, N. *National Survey of Child Support Agency Clients.* London: DWP (2001)

[10] Peacey, V. Hunt, J. *I'm not saying it was easy: Contact problems in separated families.* London: Gingerbread (2009)

conflict is considered to be affecting the emotional well-being of the child[11] or significant harm is a consideration either through violence, drug or alcohol misuse or child abuse.[12] Where there are concerns that a 'child is suffering or likely to suffer significant harm' [13] a social work assessment is inevitable.

Despite considerable research indicating the benefits to children of father contact,[14] and significant policy developments urging the involvement of fathers,[15] there are significant levels of non-resident father dissatisfaction

---

[11] Frosch, C.A., Manglesdorf, S.C., & McHale, J.L. 'Marital behaviour and the security of preschooler-parent attachment relationships'. *Journal of Family Psychology*, 14, 144-161(2000); Reynolds, J. (2001). *Not in Front of the Children?* London: One Plus One (2001); Cummings, E.M., Goeke-Morey, M.C., & Raymond, J. (2004). 'Fathers in family context: effects of marital quality and marital conflict.' In M.E. Lamb (ed.), *The Role of the Father in Child Development (3rd ed.).* New York: John Wiley & Sons(2004)

[12] Thoennes & Tjaden, 'The extent, nature, and validity of sexual abuse allegations in custody/visitation disputes', *Child Abuse and Neglect* 14:2. pp 151-163 (1990); Penfold, P.S. 'Mendacious mothers or devious dads? Some perplexing issues in child custody/ sexual abuse allegations disputes', *Canadian Journal of Psychiatry,* 40 (1995); Brown, T. Frederico, M. Hewitt, L. and Sheehan, R. 'Revealing the existence of child abuse in the context of marital breakdown and custody and access disputes', *Child Abuse and Neglect* 24:6 pp 849-859 (2000)

[13] HM Government, *Children Act 1989.* London: The Stationery Office (1989)

[14] see for example: Ryan, M. *Working with fathers.* Oxford: Department of Health, Radcliffe (2000); Lamb, M.E. (2002). 'Non-residential fathers and their children'. In C.S. Tamis-LeMonda & N. Cabrera (eds.), *Handbook of Father Involvement: multidisciplinary perspectives.* Mahwah, NJ: Lawrence Erlbaum Assoc. (2002); Flouri, E. 'Fathering & Child Outcomes'. Chichester, West Sussex: John Wiley & Sons (2005); Fortin, J., Ritchie, C., & Buchanan, A. 'Young adults' perceptions of court-ordered contact'. *Child and Family Law Quarterly*, 18(2), 211-229 (2006); Dunn, J. *Family Relationships: children's perspectives.* London: One Plus One (2008).

[15] HM Government, *Every Child Matters* (2004) Accessible online: www.dcsf.gov.uk/everychildmatters; Department for Education and Skills, *Parenting Support: Guidance for Local Authorities in England.* Nottingham: DCSF (2006); Department for Education and Skills, *Every Parent Matters.* Nottingham: DfES (2007); Department for Children, Schools and Families, *The Children's Plan; building brighter futures.* Norwich: TSO (2007); Department for Children, Schools and Families / Department of Health (2008) *Getting maternity services right for pregnant teenagers and young fathers.* Nottingham: DCSF/DH (2008)

with social work intervention.[16] Details of fathers and the wider paternal family are not always fully recorded by practitioners, or information may be minimal or not easily accessible; fathers are not consistently consulted during routine assessments or invited to meetings even though this improves child protection situations or when there is the prospect of the child's being looked after by the local authority.[17]

Several noteworthy barriers to engagement with fathers were raised by Page et al[18] in a report to the Department for Children, Schools and Families (DCSF),[19] which included;

- Worker gender—many men find it difficult to communicate with a predominately female workforce;
- Lack of time or resources to identify non-resident parents—if the resident mother refused to discuss the father's identity or whereabouts this would only be pursued by workers in the event of a safeguarding concern or the prospect of the child's being looked after by the local authority;
- Fear of aggression or violence and a lack of training in dealing with this;
- Stereotypes of fathers and mothers leading to negative views of fathers as carers.

For a number of practitioners, 'father engagement was unimportant and practice was orientated towards the most accessible parent, the mother'.[20]

---

[16] Daniel, B., and Taylor, J. 'The rhetoric versus the reality: A critical perspective on practice with fathers in child care and protection work'. *Child and Family Social Work* 4:209–20 (1999); Featherstone, B. 'Taking fathers seriously.' *British Journal of Social Work* 33: 239–54 (2003); Ashley, C. Featherstone, B. Roskill, C. Ryan, M and White, S. *Fathers Matter: Research findings on fathers and their involvement with social care services.* London: Family Rights Group (2006)

[17] Ashley, C. Featherstone, B. Roskill, C. Ryan, M and White, S.(2006), op cit; Roskill, C. Featherstone, B. Ashley, C. Haresnape, S *Fathers Matter Volume 2: Further findings on fathers and their involvement with social care services.* London: Family Rights Group (2008)

[18] Page, J. Whitting, G. Mclean, C. *A Review of How Fathers Can be Better Recognised and Supported Through DCSF Policy.* Research Report DCSF-RR040. Nottingham: DCSF (2008)

[19] In May 2010, the DCSF was renamed the Department for Education.

[20] Page, J. Whitting, G. Mclean, C. (2008) op cit, pp. 88-89

This correlates with Scourfield's[21] findings of negative practitioner attitudes about men, including men being seen as a threat, of no use, irrelevant, as absent and dead-beat. More recently Ashley[22] provides numerous instances where fathers have been treated less favourably than mothers, where their involvement has been minimised, where they have been excluded and their rights ignored. Professional agency favours utility and expediency over rights, as a result of which opportunities are being lost to consider the full range strengths and resources available to the child through the direct involvement of the father and, importantly, the father's wider family with the potential for loss of identity and cultural mores.

That practice with fathers can have such negative outcomes raises questions about the objectivity afforded by the law and the legally mandated 'Framework for the Assessment of Children in Need and their Families'[23]; about the nature of social welfare intervention, in particular of assessment practice; and ultimately about the efficacy of the Framework which, after all, requires practitioners to engage with 'each parent or caregiver' including 'fathers and father figures'.[24] Although there is some evidence that the Framework has achieved some of its aims, including greater partnership with parents and carers,[25] and that when used skilfully it can have (in the broadest sense of the term) a therapeutic impact,[26]

---

[21] Scourfield, J. *Gender and Child Protection*. Basingstoke: Palgrave MacMillan (2003)

[22] Ashley, C. (2008) 'Analysis of calls from fathers to Family Rights Group's advice service' in Roskill, C. Featherstone, B. Ashley, C. Haresnape, S. *Fathers Matter Volume 2: Further findings on fathers and their involvement with social care services*. London: Family Rights Group (2008)

[23] Macdonald, G. *Effective Interventions for Child Abuse and Neglect: An evidence-based approach to planning and evaluating interventions*. Chichester: John Wiley & Sons (2001); Horwath, J. 'The Missing Assessment Domain: Personal, Professional and Organizational Factors Influencing Professional Judgements when Identifying and Referring Child Neglect.' *British Journal of Social Work*, 37, 1285–1303 (2007)

[24] Department of Health, *Framework for the Assessment of Children in Need and their Families*, London: The Stationery Office, para 2.11, page 20; para. 2.12, page 20 (2000)

[25] Cleaver, H. and Walker, S., with Meadows, P. *Assessing Children's Needs and Circumstances: the Impact of the Assessment Framework*, London, Jessica Kingsley (2004)

[26] Millar, M. and Corby, B. 'The Framework for the Assessment of Children in Need and their Families—A Basis for a 'Therapeutic' Encounter?' *British Journal of Social Work*, 36,6, pp. 887–899 (2006)

questions remain whether the perceived benefits are as a result of routinised, behaviourist practice, or through a genuine development in the understanding, values, ethics and professionalism of practitioners in developing inclusive practice.[27] These questions also arise because the framework can be used subjectively by professionals with some groups of service users, with one aspect of the triangular arrangement being weighted either positively or negatively in certain circumstances, potentially favouring, for example, assessment of the parenting capacity afforded by a resident mother over that of the non resident father particularly if significant harm is a concern.

Assessment is much more than a cerebral process and it can be reactive to external demands.[28] Practitioner views of the framework of assessment and the accompanying Integrated Children's System include criticism of the temporal dimension of assessments, repetition, and information being gathered because the system requires it—a cut and paste approach to recording that prevents a holistic view of the child and family and creates a high-blame working environment.[29] Emotions and prejudices can affect assessments, fear of certain fathers,[30] for example, where practitioners have beliefs that mothers provide better care than fathers, or where the availability heuristic—the tendency of people to take into account (over

---

[27] Reid, J. 'Developing Inclusive Practice with Children and their Families' in Tovey, W. ed. *The PQ Handbook.* London: Jessica Kingsley (2007)

[28] Horwath, J. 'The Missing Assessment Domain: Personal, Professional and Organizational Factors Influencing Professional Judgements when Identifying and Referring Child Neglect.' *British Journal of Social Work,* 37, 1285–1303 (2007); Littlechild, B., Reid, J. 'Children and Families – Assessment and Planning' in Tovey, W. ed. *The PQ Handbook.* London: Jessica Kingsley (2007); Gilligan, P. Manby, M. 'The Common Assessment Framework: does the reality match the rhetoric?' *Child and Family Social Work,* 13, pp 177–187 (2008)

[29] Munro, E. 'Improving practice : child protection as a systems problem', *Children and youth services review,* 27 (4). pp. 375-391 (2005); Bell, M, Shaw, I, Sinclair, I, Sloper, P and Rafferty, (2007) 'The Integrated Children's System: An Evaluation of the Practice, Process and Consequences of the ICS in Councils with Social Services Responsibilities (Full Report)'. A Report to the Department for Education and Skills/Welsh Assembly Government. (May 2007); Broadhurst, K., Wastell, D., White., S., Hall., C., Peckover., S., Thompson., K., Pithouse, A and Dolores, D., (2009) 'Performing Initial Assessment: Identifying the latent conditions for error in local authority children's services.' *British Journal of Social Work* (2009)

[30] Smith, M. and Nursten, J. 'Social workers' experiences of distress – moving towards change?' *British Journal of Social Work,* 28, pp. 351-368 (1998)

other potentially relevant issues) those matters which are called to mind most readily within a situation—has influence.[31] Fear, and the prevailing culture of blame—both through the popular media and in the system of inspection and regulation of social welfare practice[32]—are also relevant, as is an approach to supervision that continues to focus on managerialist and bureaucratic requirements above others.[33]

Such external demands also have an impact on the social worker's interaction with the legal system and legal processes. It can therefore be argued that the current framework and accompanying structures are insufficient for taking into account the range of issues relevant to an assessment, and although the focus of this article is on non-resident fathers, the discussion is relevant to all service users.

3. Considerations of Approach

The incentive to consider social worker's assessments of inclusive practice with fathers came from teaching and interacting with students undertaking post qualification learning. Colleagues and I were increasingly aware of recurring messages in students' written and verbal reports about difficulties in engaging with, and involving, some fathers in assessment. Anecdotally, students were confirming previous findings in the literature of fathers being absent or marginalised and as a result the opportunities afforded by fathers and wider family networks were being minimised. A significant minority of practitioners had not considered the issue of paternal normalities and culture, particularly if the father was unknown, absent, difficult to work with or a risk to the child. It appeared that the rights of some fathers and children to contact were being negated despite

---

[31] Middleton, W., Clyne, A. and Harris, P. 'Risk Assessment and Decision Making', In Messer, D. and Jones, F., *Psychology and Social Care*, London: Jessica Kingsley Publishers (1999); O'Connor, I. Hughes, M. Turney, D. Wilson, J E & Setterlund, D S (2006),*Social Work and Social Care Practice* (5th Edition), London: Sage (2006)

[32] Sue White, pers. comm.

[33] Marsh, P. and Triseliotis, J. *Social Workers and Probation Officers: Their Training and First Year in Work.* Aldershot: Avebury (1996); Bradley, G. & Höjer, S. 'Supervision reviewed: reflections on two different social work models in England and Sweden -- Granskad handledning: reflektioner från två olika handledningsmodeller i England och Sverige'. *European Journal of Social Work, 12*(1), 71-85 (2009)

the 'ecological' construction of the Framework for Assessment and the inclusive intentions of the Common Assessment Framework.

Consideration was therefore given to exploring practitioners' approach to assessment involving situations where contact was an issue and to their understanding of fathers' rights to contact and what might impact upon realisation of those rights and subsequently the child's paternal identity and culture. A case study (appendix one), based on an actual situation, was used to develop discussion and insight. A group of 45 practitioners who were undertaking programmes of post qualification training or learning agreed to participate in a thematic analysis of social welfare practice centred on the case study and based on their own practice experience.

A narrative approach enables the social welfare practitioner to talk individually or in groups, to give voice to each participant and to the influences that shape practice, and to write about practice in the context of social, cultural and institutional influences[34]. This approach fits with the demands placed on practitioners undertaking post qualification learning to critically reflect upon, and discuss practice within, the narrative tradition of social welfare work. A thematic method is useful for seeking common themes across a number of participants and events. The idea of dialogical praxis[35] was also drawn upon. Dialogical praxis includes the notion that consciousness is developed through dialogue that illuminates both the personal and political, and thus the structures and discourses that perpetuate oppression. Dialogue is key and the researcher and participant are seen as having different but equivalent wisdom.[36]

The participants worked primarily within five unitary authorities, four of which had a shared history as part of a larger metropolitan body. Participants from these four took part in discussions as mixed groups. The fifth was geographically distant from the others, which allowed for more reliable data. The emerging themes chimed with the contemporary

---

[34] Gergen, KJ. Gergen, MM. *Narrative Psychology: the storied nature of human conduct.* Westport, CN: Preager (1986); Wertsch, J. V. *Voices of the mind: A sociocultural approach to mediated action.* Cambridge, MA: Harvard University Press (1991) cited in Moen, T. 'Reflections on the narrative research approach.' *International Journal of Qualitative Methodology*, 5(4), pp. 56-69 (2006), p.59

[35] based on Freire, P. *Pedagogy of the Oppressed.* London: Penguin; (1996)

[36] Ife, J. *Human Rights and Social Work: towards rights-based practice.* Cambridge: Cambridge University Press (2001), p.151.

literature on statutory social welfare practice with fathers. Those with a legal theme are discussed below.

4. Synopsis of Findings

The majority of the participants (over 70 per cent in each group) began by focusing on the concern for harm suggested in the case study, and indicated an approach to their assessment that concentrated solely on this. As such, many of the participants relied on the presenting information without seeking to enquire into the family's history, thus focusing on the child's needs as identified by the resident mother rather than on a broader needs assessment. The remaining participants did consider the maintenance of contact with dad to be a priority, but of these, only three believed that the potential for contact should involve the wider paternal family at this early stage. Utility and agency led the participants to use the law narrowly, and many were not conversant with the applicable duties and responsibilities to involve fathers. Reference to case law was also absent.

Analysis in assessment was also revealed as narrowly focused, since the participants relied on practice wisdom and intuitive reasoning to dictate the assessment strategy: only five participants developed a strategy that included a number of hypotheses, for example the impact of loss, in addition to that of the impact of harm. The participants did not explicitly identify the empirical evidence that they rely on in developing their analysis, thus highlighting their reliance on intuitive reasoning. Practice wisdom was also supported in the guise of advice from legal representatives and by their peers and managers—the latter of which are also assumed have gaps in their legal knowledge.

The main issues with a legal bearing arising from the case study are explored further below.

5. Qualified Rights – the 'Normal Chaos of Family Law'[37]

It is no surprise that legislation is identified as a theme, given its centrality to statutory practice and the ongoing struggle between partnership, rights,

[37] Dewar, J. 'The Normal Chaos of Family Law'. *Modern Law Review*, 61, 4, July 1998, pp. 467-471 (1998)

empowerment and accountability in practice.[38] The practitioners believe that they have good knowledge of the law, but acknowledge some anxiety in working with the law and legal processes.

This anxiety has partly developed out of perceived conflicts and contradictions within the law; for example, s1 of the Children Act 1989 asserts that the welfare of the child is paramount, but Article 3 of the UN Convention of the Rights of the Child expresses welfare as a 'primary' consideration. And whilst there is a duty to assess a child who is suffering, or likely to suffer, significant harm under s47 of the Children Act 1989, there is not similar statutory duty associated with children in need under s17 of that Act. A father has to do something to gain parental responsibility; a mother does not. Needs and the rights of fathers, including the need and right for contact between a child and father, therefore become weaker. These are further undermined because of the qualifications in other national statutes and international treaties. For example, the Human Rights Act 1998 confirms into UK law the European Convention of Human Rights and Fundamental Freedoms (ECHR). Article 8 of the convention declares that:

> (1) Everyone has the right to respect for his private and family life, his home and his correspondence.

However the conditions set out in Article 8(2) mean that the right is qualified and not absolute:

> (2) There shall be no interference by a public authority with the exercise of this right except such as is in accordance with the law and is necessary in a democratic society in the interests of national security, public safety or the economic well-being of the country, for the prevention of disorder or crime, for the protection of health or morals, or for the protection of the rights and freedoms of others.

Such qualification is also a feature of Article 9(3) of the UNCRC, which declares that:

> *States Parties shall respect the right of the child who is separated from one or both parents to maintain personal relations and direct contact with*

---

[38] Braye, S. and Preston-Shoot, M. *Practising Social Work Law*, Basingstoke, Macmillan (1997); Shardlow, S M (1998), 'Values, ethics and social work', in: In R. Adams, L. Dominelli, and M. Payne (Eds.), *Social Work: Themes, Issues and Critical Debates* (pp. 23-33). Houndmills, Basingstoke: Macmillan (1998)

both parents on a regular basis, except if it is contrary to the child's best interests.

Contact is therefore understood by practitioners as a qualified right, with such qualifications as are within their remit to define. However, whilst practitioners believed they had a good understanding of the law, and at a surface level they did, there is a significant decline in legal knowledge if it is not regularly used in practice.[39] Even when discussing the peculiarities of more often used statutes,[40] there was a consistent inability to cite these sections verbatim, and variations in understanding and interpretation of the relevant central concepts of 'significant harm'[41] and 'need'.[42] Whilst some of this is due to the policies and thresholds of particular agencies, and it can be agreed that these are not fixed concepts, it was significant that none of the practitioners regularly kept their legal knowledge up to date as an essential requirement of the social welfare role, and therefore do not, as a matter of course, refer to case law but instead relied on lawyers for guidance and direction.

This is in part a consequence of the supposed expertise of lawyers, but also of the prevailing environment of risk aversion, practice scrutiny and regulation. In the pursuit of error-free practice expertise, the practitioners do not believe themselves to be adequately informed to instruct or enter into a debate with legal representatives with authority subsequently vested in these representatives. This introduces an element of utility and agency into the decision-making process since local authority legal representatives have a dual, but contradictory, role—to advise the practitioner but also to protect the interests of the agency.[43] These lawyers are also informed by their own experience, values and stereotypes. The relationship between

---

[39] Preston-Shoot, M., Roberts, G. & Vernon, S. ' "We work in isolation often and in ignorance occasionally". On the experiences of practice teachers teaching and assessing social work law'. *Social Work Education*, 16, 4, pp. 4–34 (1997)
[40] Including sections of the Children Act 1989, op cit.
[41] S47 Children Act 1989
[42] S17 Children Act 1989, op cit.
[43] Dickens, J. 'Risks and responsibilities: the role of the local authority lawyer in child care cases', *Child and Family Law Quarterly*, 16, pp. 17–30 (2004); Dickens, J. 'Social Work, Law, Money and Trust: Paying for Lawyers in Child Protection Work', *Journal of Social Welfare and Family Law*, 28, 3, pp. 283-295 (2006)

practice and law, and the extent to which practice is shaped and determined by legal frameworks,[44] remains contentious.

When working with any family, social welfare workers have a responsibility to come to a balanced decision, taking into consideration the rights of the child, the rights of others—including parents—and the impact of agency due of their position and role, including their own powers to intervene and the broader welfare issues.[45] This is a difficult balance to achieve, as the factors facing the practitioner extend beyond the 'normal chaos of family law'.[46] Practitioners worry about accountability both within and without the courtroom, and practice in an atmosphere of increased public hostility and scrutiny. Agency is determined not just by statute, but by working practices and culture, by knowledge and skills, and by the prevailing social and political priorities of the day, and this does not necessarily favour positive outcomes for fathers. The tension between the Children Act 1989 and the wider rights legislation remains unresolved despite continued suggestions of the need for review.[47] Practitioners are conscious of public vilification and the view that they themselves are a risk to society, so they emphasise the knowledge, expertise and experience of lawyers and underemphasise their own. In this environment, agency is accentuated over rights, and this can be particularly illustrated by an examination of the concept of parental responsibility (PR).

---

[44] Braye, S. Preston-Shoot, M. Johns, R. 'Law in Social Work Education: Reviewing the Evidence on Teaching, Learning and Assessment', *Social Work Education*, 24, 5, 547-563 (2005)

[45] Parker, S 'Rights and Utility in Anglo-Australian Family Law', *Modern Law Review, 55,* 311 (1992); Eekelaar, J. (1994) 'Families and Children: from welfarism to rights', in McCrudden, C. Chambers, G. (eds). *Individual rights and the Law in Britain.* Oxford: Clarendon Press (1994); Henricson, C. Bainham, A (2005) *The child and family policy divide: tensions, convergence and rights.* York: Joseph Rowntree Foundation (2005)

[46] Dewar, J. 'The Normal Chaos of Family Law'. *Modern Law Review*, 61, 4, July 1998, pp. 467-471 (1998), p.467

[47] Reece, H. 'The paramountcy principle: Consensus or Construct?' *Current Legal Problems,* 49, pp. 267-304, (1996); Herring, J. (1999) 'The Human Rights Act and The Welfare Principle In Family Law – Conflicting Or Complementary?' *Child and Family Law Quarterly,* 223, (September, 1999); Eekelaar, J. 'Beyond the Welfare Principle' *Child and Family Law Quarterly,* 237, (September 2002), Ashley, C. Featherstone, B. Roskill, C. Ryan, M and White, S. *Fathers Matter: Research findings on fathers and their involvement with social care services.* London: Family Rights Group (2006)

6. Interpreting Rights - Parental Responsibility yes, but...

Parental Responsibility (PR) is

> *all the rights, duties, powers, responsibilities and authority which by law a parent of a child has in relation to the child and his property.*[48]

It is automatically attained by mothers but, since the introduction of the Act, by fathers only if married to the mother at the time of the child's birth. This was later amended in December 2003 to include unmarried fathers as long as their name appeared on the birth certificate at registration. PR can also be attained by a father if he obtains the agreement of those who already hold PR, or by court order. In effect, a father has to make an effort to attain PR: mothers always attain PR; unmarried fathers do not. This and other discrepancies, such as s52(9) of the Adoption and Children Act 2002 (ACA), which states that a father without PR is deemed to have consented to the placement even if he later obtains PR and objects, mean that PR is a contested, if not nebulous, concept, as Evans and Harris[49] point out:

> *...rules, even though we often think of them as unambiguous, can contribute to the uncertainty that creates discretion. He (Handler) noted the imprecision of statute law and the inability of policy makers to make clear rules stemming from statutes. Instead, law and policy are expressed in vague phrases, which are open to interpretation, and this creates wide discretion for the interpretation or generation of policy in the absence of guidance from managers.*

Knowledge and understanding of the law have a role in practitioners' decision-making in relation to PR, but the social welfare workers in this study again indicated that they did not systematically enter into debate or actively seek out case law. As a consequence, interpretation of the rights and rules pertaining to PR were influenced by practice wisdom and the prevailing working climate.

---

[48] s3(1) Children Act 1989

[49] Evans, T. And Harris, J. (2004) 'Street-Level Bureaucracy, Social Work and the (Exaggerated) death of Discretion.' *British Journal of Social Work,* 34, pp. 871-895 (2004) p. 885, when citing Handler, J. *The Coercive Social Worker.* Chicago: Rand and McNally (1973), p.138

Here we must consider the views of Lipsky[50] concerning 'street-level bureaucrats' and their willingness and ability to make ad hoc decisions based on their own needs rather than those of the client. According to Lipsky, more power afforded to the practitioner leads to broad interpretation of policy and objectives, and interpretation in turn emphasises utility. Evans and Harris[51] provide a useful critique of those who argue that discretion has been curtailed by the introduction of managerialism through the increased use of rules and regulations, but also point to Dworkin's[52] typology that includes the possibility of 'weaker' discretion or the ability of the practitioner to interpret within the rules. In discussion, the social welfare workers reported a primary concern to adhere to the laws, rules and regulations that define PR, but also the propensity to interpret within those rules in the light of the prevailing practice context—the outcome of which is that the 'rights, powers and authority' enshrined in the definition of PR are underemphasised in favour of the 'duties and responsibilities'. As such, PR may come to mean parenting capacity as enshrined by the Framework for Assessment.[53]

> *While the Children Act 1989 does make reference to parental responsibility, when more fully analysed it is described as capacity – perhaps reflecting the personal relationship and sometimes fluid and externally determined element of the parenting role. It also suggests a hint of something inherent, over which the parent does not have complete control.*[54]

Concerns about the quality of practitioner assessment of parenting capacity have been previously raised,[55] including questions about the focus and definitions used in such assessments. For example, Conley[56] considers parenting capacity to involve 'good enough' parenting over a sustained period. 'Parenting ability', however, is the capacity to meet a child's needs

---

[50] Lipsky, M. *Street-Level Bureaucracy: Dilemmas of the Individual in Public Services*. New York: Russell Sage Foundation (1980)

[51] Evan and Harris, 2004, op cit.

[52] Dworkin, R. *Taking Rights Seriously*. London: Butterworth (1978)

[53] Department of Health, *Framework for the Assessment of Children in Need and their Families*, London: The Stationery Office (2000)

[54] Henricson, C. *Government and parenting: Is there a case for a policy review and a parents' code?* York: Joseph Rowntree Foundation (2003), p.44.

[55] Budd, K.S., Poindexter, L.M. & Felix, E.D. 'Clinical assessment of parents in child protection cases: an empirical analysis.' *Law and Human Behaviour*. 25,1, pp.93-108 (2001); Conley, 2003

[56] Conley, C. 'A review of Parenting Capacity Assessment Reports'. *OACAS Journal*. 47, 3, pp.16-22 (2003), p.16

over a short period or in specific circumstances. Stewart and Bond[57] discuss the differences between parenting style and parenting practice, and question the cultural relativity of some parenting assessments. Cultural relativity is problematic in that all competing views of the world are deemed to be equal.[58]

Such definitions and variation in understanding of the concept of parenting are not systematically debated by the practitioners, nor is guidance always available from managers in supervision despite 'definitional clarity' being fundamental to effective parenting capacity assessments.[59] In addition, there is also inconsistent use of the parenting assessment tools accompanying the Framework for Assessment, and when they *are* used it appears that a tick-box approach is adopted, with little consideration for the relative nature of identified strengths or weaknesses.[60] One further concern, given social welfare workers reliance on legal opinion, is the lack of information about lawyers' understanding of parenting capacity and the impact of cultural relativity on their practice.

7. Summary

There are obvious limitations to this study. There were limited numbers of social welfare workers involved, and involving the practitioners was opportunistic insofar as they were undertaking programmes of study or professional development. A number of cautions should be exercised when generalising from such a sample: the exercise was exploratory, and based upon a single case study rather than actual practice; the case study was also focused on a particular situation at a particular time in the intervention.

Despite the obvious limitations of the discussions, the study does provide some useful insight into social welfare worker assessment and legal practice. There are some keenly held beliefs about the Framework for

[57] Stewart, S.M. & Bond, M.H. 'A critical look at parenting research from the mainstream: problems uncovered while adapting Western research to non-Western cultures.' *British Journal of Developmental Psychology.* 20, pp.379-392 (2002)
[58] Littlechild, B., Reid, J. 'Children and Families – Assessment and Planning' in Tovey, W. ed. *The PQ Handbook.* London: Jessica Kingsley (2007)
[59]White, A (2005) *Assessment of Parenting Capacity. Literature Review.* Ashfield, NSW: Centre for Parenting & Research, NSW Department of Community Services (2005), p.13
[60] Donald, T. & Jureidini, J. 'Parenting Capacity.' *Child Abuse Review.* 13, pp.5-17 (2004)

Assessment, the Integrated Children's System and some fathers. The majority of social welfare workers are exceptionally hard working and concerned to uphold the values and ethics of social welfare work in the face of unremitting public and political scrutiny and a system of regulation that values bureaucratic outcomes above the value of the relationship within their work. The fact that many fathers remain dissatisfied with the interventions of social welfare workers suggests inadequacies in current practices and approaches including those for assessment. Whilst there are contributing factors, such as contradictions within the law, that are beyond the immediate remit of individual practitioners to control, these factors are not being mediated by supervision and support of sufficient quality. It is notable that the Public Inquiries into tragic child deaths in England continue to highlight supervision as a concern. However, not all of the factors affecting assessment practice are external to the worker, and knowledge and understanding, practice wisdom, analytical capabilities and the self all impact upon practice. This applies to all professionals working with children and young people, including social welfare workers and legal representatives. These factors are not recognised within the current framework, suggesting the need for something different. Whilst social welfare workers appreciate the structure and ecological nature of the framework, they continue to confuse the collection of data with the analysis and critical enquiry necessary for assessment, which subsequently feeds into the legal context. There is error in assuming that following the guidance for the Framework for Assessment ensures a quality assessment.[61]

Since the introduction of the Framework for Assessment, the Integrated Children's System and the Common Assessment Framework, practitioners have become increasingly concerned about the issue of time limits for completing assessments. This temporal dimension does not easily lead to inclusive assessments, or create a foundation for robust partnership.[62]

---

[61] Crisp, B.R. Anderson, M.R. Orme, J. and Green Lister, P. 'Assessment Frameworks: A Critical Reflection.' *British Journal of Social Work,* 37, pp. 1059-1077 (2007)

[62] Bell, M, Shaw, I, Sinclair, I, Sloper, P and Rafferty, J. 'The Integrated Children's System: An Evaluation of the Practice, Process and Consequences of the ICS in Councils with Social Services Responsibilities (Full Report)'. A Report to the Department for Education and Skills/Welsh Assembly Government (May 2007); Broadhurst, K., Wastell, D., White., S., Hall., C., Peckover., S., Thompson., K., Pithouse, A and Dolores, D. 'Performing Initial Assessment: Identifying the latent conditions for error in local authority children's services.' *British Journal of Social Work* (2009)

Indeed, this situation is exacerbated as social welfare workers continue to carry child protection caseloads up to twice the limit recommended by the Laming Inquiry into the death of Victoria Climbie.[63]

The Assessment Framework emphasises the technical-rational approach of evidence-based practice,[64] but assumptions are made about the currency and relevance of the worker's evidence base and, indeed, of the worker's understanding of relevant theory and case law. The framework also assumes truthfulness on everyone's behalf, and a level playing field in terms of knowledge, skills and competence.[65] The question of balance between the autonomous professional and the mores and practices required as an employee or agent of the state is understated. Whilst the professional continues to exercise discretion within the rules, it is axiomatic that the professional autonomy of the social welfare worker has been affected by greater regulation and accountability. The argument is not that accountability is unwelcome, but that the elements used to measure outcomes should recognise the complexities of the social welfare task. This includes the nature of the relationship between the social welfare worker and the legal representative, and the currency of the worker's legal knowledge.

The outcome for the children described in the case study, and anecdotally for other children too, is that insufficient priority is given to the benefits to the children of father contact. As a consequence, the opportunities and benefits of the wider paternal family—and importantly the social and cultural dimensions of identity—are significantly diluted or lost. Simply because an outcome is legally possible does not mean that it is always in the best interests of the child. The utility and agency of the social welfare worker, and the legal representatives involved, impact upon outcomes. It is perhaps time to realise that, for many children involved in legal proceedings, the current Framework for Assessment for Children and Need and their Families needs redrawing:

---

[63] BBC *Child Protection 'Overstreched'*. BBC Online (Accessed online: 22/07/09) (2009)

[64] Taylor, C. and White, S. 'Knowledge, truth and reflexivity: The problem of judgement in social work', *Journal of Social Work*, 1(1), pp. 37–59 (2001); Horwath, J. (2007) 'The Missing Assessment Domain: Personal, Professional and Organizational Factors Influencing Professional Judgements when Identifying and Referring Child Neglect.' *British Journal of Social Work,* 37, 1285–1303 (2007)

[65] Littlechild, B., Reid, J. 'Children and Families – Assessment and Planning' in Tovey, W. ed. *The PQ Handbook.* London: Jessica Kingsley (2007)

Diagram 2: *A new framework for assessment*[66]

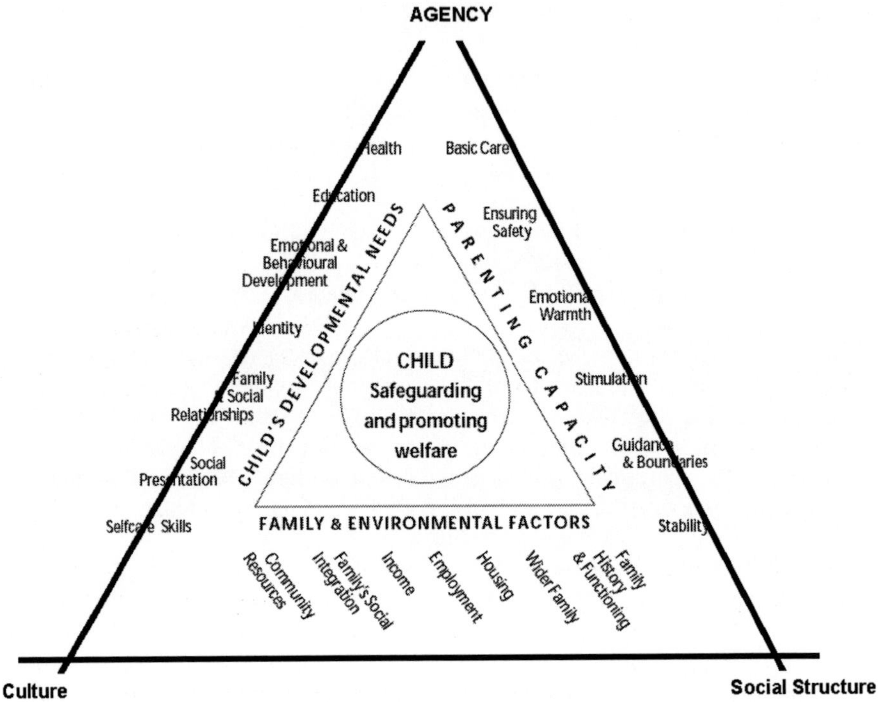

[66] Adapted from: Department of Health, 2000, p.17, op cit.

Appendix One

Case study

Peter and Sarah had been married for five years before their relationship failed; they separated, and subsequently divorced. There are two children, Sarah's 11-year-old child, Sally (Peter's stepchild), and Amy, 5-years-old. At the time of the separation there was agreement that the children would live with their mother on the understanding that Peter would have frequent and unhindered contact, and this worked well for over a year. However on the first contact, following an argument between them, Sarah informed Peter that the children were ill and would not be coming to stay. Over the next year the relationship between Peter and Sarah continued to deteriorate, with contact with the children being used as a weapon. Contact between the children and Peter was minimal or non-existent for months on end. Illness was a frequent reason cited, and the children also missed periods off school. Peter applied for a contact order and proceedings began. Sarah refused contact during the proceedings, alleging that the children were being adversely affected by the stressful situation. The court eventually agreed a contact order and Peter saw the children again, but only briefly as Sarah made a serious allegation against him and an investigation began.

The previous social worker, a female colleague of Peter, found Peter's presentation and behaviour challenging. He had a physical presence, and was also articulate and knowledgeable about child development. Indeed it would seem appropriate for her not to be involved but such was the constraint on resources that she, as an experienced social worker, was asked to take on this complex case.

THE INDIAN PERSPECTIVE OF GENDER DISCRIMINATION ON GIRL CHILDREN AND FŒTICIDE

NAVDEEP KOUR SASAN

Abstract

Female discrimination in the form of femicide, which includes female infanticide, sex-selective abortions, sex selection of embryos and other forms of forestalling the innate process of female fœtus (sperm separation) still persist in Indian society, indicating no change in the position of woman in this patriarchal society. It is inexcusable that about 50 million girls and women have gone "missing" from the demographic structure of India's population, as has been acknowledged by the United Nations Children's Fund,[1] which has, consequently resulted in a gender disproportion. These findings are further endorsed by the abnormal sex ratio figures in the Census 2001 Report of India, which indicates that more boys than girls are being registered. With the availability of new technology, the bias against by females from birth to the grave is being easily extended, although it has to some extent reduced the incidences of the earlier practice of infanticide involving barbarous techniques of sending the girl child to the grave, even though that was an offence under Indian penal laws. These distorted sex ratios are principally caused by the misuse of diagnostic techniques such as the widely available ultrasound tests or amniocentesis, which are conducted to determine the sex of the fœtus and subsequent fœticide, if female. However, the Pre-natal Diagnostic Techniques (Regulation and Prevention of Misuse) (PNDT) Act, 1994 as amended in 2003 to The Pre-conception and Pre-natal Diagnostic Techniques (Prohibition of Sex Selection) (PC PNDT) Act,

[1] Garg S, Nath A. Female fœeticide in India: Issues and concerns. J Postgrad Med [serial online] 2008 [cited 2010 Jan 07]; 54: 276-9. Available at: http://www.jpgmonline.com/text.asp?2008/54/4/276/43511 [cited on 2010 August 06].

curbs the revolting practice of sex-determination and sex-selection. It not only imposes a ban on sex selective abortions, but also an equal duty on the medical professionals and society at large. The intention of this research is to highlight that the non-resisting state of females in the patriarchal social order calls for attention to rising levels of felony committed against them at different stages of their lives, including the pre-conception phase.

1. Introduction

Indian Television, in its famous daily soap-opera *"Na Aana Is Des Meri Laddo"*, which depicts the plight of women and the disastrous destiny of female fœtuses or children before or after birth about which the main female character is totally ignorant, is trying to raise public awareness about the fact that female infanticide and fœticide are still practiced in some parts of India. It thereby stigmatizes the entire Indian community, who do not raise objections and thwart such inhuman acts. Although the Indian Parliament has approved a number of acts to avert such shocking acts of femicide or gender oppression, the skewed female population, especially among the 0-6 age range, demonstrates that they are not working. Many female children, without even attaining viability in the womb, never see the light of day, and die in darkness at the hands of killers who may even be their parents or grandparents. And even the medical fraternity is responsible to a greater or lesser extent, as they prompt the parents to abort unfortunate souls by disclosing the sex of the fœtus.

This article attempts to draw attention to all those involved in the unacceptable act of femicide, and show that the nation is not willing to tolerate such a demographic shift at the expense of the female child. The article therefore endeavours to analyze the factors responsible for such a shift, and also to evaluate the various laws that have been enacted to eradicate such actions that are seemingly continuing unabated. But before I enumerate various causes of femicide or analyze the protection mechanisms or safeguarding measures, there is a need to answer questions about the status of woman in general, and girl children in particular, in Indian society. What necessitates the protection of a fœtus? How do these protection mechanisms control infanticide or fœticide? These questions may be answered only after a thorough historical analysis of the status of women and of a number of censuses conducted in India, and an examination of protective measures laid down by the State in different stages of process of recognition of the status of women.

2. Status of Women vis-à-vis Girl Children in Patriarchal Society

It is correctly asserted that, *"Within the Indian subcontinent there have been infinite variations on the status of women diverging according to cultural milieu, family structure, class, caste, property rights and morals."*[2] A quick glance at history shows that women enjoyed equal status with men in Vedic society that can rightly be termed as period of feminine glory and masculine sagacity and liberalism;[3] there was no discrimination between a boy and a girl. All the same, the value of son could not be denied, on the grounds that they were useful to their parents as compared to daughters. The seeds of the uselessness of daughters were only sown in the later Vedic age (1700–1100 BCE), as is evident from the fact that sacrifices to family ancestors could only be made by sons, the daughters being incompetent to perform such acts. Additionally, a woman, by giving birth to a son, could save her marriage. A sonless woman, even if she had daughters, was of no value to the family.[4] Although the increasing dominance of males over females grew in post-Vedic society, women's right to property, *streedhan*[5] could still be found during this time. However, during the era of Epics, or Puranic period, Pind Daan[6] the ceremony of birth and rebirth, which was performed by sons or their male descendents alone, further increased Hindu women's subservience, where her function became mere production of sons. Daughters became unwelcome, and sons seen as a means to attain salvation or *moksha*, so as to free themselves from the cycle of birth and rebirth. Therefore, a woman who could not beget a son for her husband suffered from ignominy and

---

[2] Romila Thapar, "Looking Back in History", in Devika Jain (ed.), *"Indian Women"*, New Delhi: Ministry of Information and Broadcasting, Government of India (1975) at 6.

[3] Mamta Rao, *"Law Relating to Women and Children"* Second Edition, Lucknow: Eastern Book Company (2008) at 20.

[4] Anjani Kant, *"Women and the Law"*, New Delhi: A. P. H. Publishing Corporation (2008) at 5.

[5] Manu defined streedhan as that which was given to her before the nuptial fire, in bridal the procession, as a token of love, and she received it from her father, mother, brother or her husband. *Supra*, n 3 at 21.

[6] The ceremony of Pind Daan gave affiliation to the son, and for offering the Pind to the deceased the presence of a son was necessary.

hollowness. Conversely, life for woman in Buddhist society was not as deplorable as her life in Brahmanic, for the birth of son was not necessary for Buddhist rituals.

In the Mughal period, the position of women was generally subordinate to men; girls were seen as a liability from birth. The practice of female infanticide was exercised amongst some Rajput clans. According to James Tod, the author of *Annals and Antiques of Rajasthan*, "The Rajputs resorted to that practice due to the scarcity of suitable matches due to the same clan and continuous wars and feuds with the remote tribes together with the sentiment that unworthy match lowers the prestige of the bride's father."[7] Nonetheless, the position of women in the early British period did not improve, and they were subjected to exploitation and prejudice till certain reform movements to emancipate women were initiated. This period came to be known as the 'Renaissance' in India.[8] These movements were, to some extent, successful in bringing about an awakening among Indian women that their rights ought to be protected. The British period in India thus gave a further impetus to the cause of women by the enacting of various pieces of legislation affecting their lives. But the position did not change much, owing to the religious and social injunctions that proved to be more effective in blocking their emancipation. It can therefore be seen that social reform movements followed by social legislation proved to be of very little value, and that Hindu women gained little from it.

With Indian Independence in 1947, and the adoption of the Constitution of India in 1950, in order to prevent gender discrimination, the equality provisions were incorporated in Part III of the Constitution thereby prohibiting any discrimination against any person on the grounds of religion, race, caste, sex, place of birth, or any of them alone.[9] And the State has also been authorized to approve special provisions for the betterment of women and children.[10] Protection of life and personal liberty of every person of either sex is secured under Article 21 of the

---

[7] *Supra*, n. 4 at 52.

[8] Raja Ram Mohan Roy, a social reformer, also known as the father of Indian Renaissance, advocated that it was erroneous to consider women as weak in intellect and virtue and deficient in resolution, trustworthiness and control over passion. For further detail on the Indian Social Reform Movement, see *Supra*, n. 4 at 62.

[9] Article15, Constitution of India.

[10] Article 15(3), Constitution of India.

Constitution,[11] though the definition of 'person' in the Constitution does not include the unborn child. However, in the light of the term 'person' used in Hindu Law relating to partition of joint family property, a person in the womb is given equal status to that of a person in existence whereby a son in the womb at the time of partition gets a share equal to the share of a son in existence. But if a female is born, the sum equivalent to the marriage expenses is required to be reserved for her, and the surplus, if any, to be distributed among the coparceners. In case no share is reserved for the son in the womb, he may, after his birth demand a re-division.[12] From this, it is thus evident that the unborn child comes into existence at the time of its conception. In the case of *Tagore* v. *Tagore*, the Privy Council observed that, a general rule of jurisdiction the child in embryo, who afterwards comes into existence, should be considered as separate entity. A child in the mother's womb is considered to be a living entity.[13] The Indian Penal Code (IPC) 1860 also contains provisions pertaining to offences relating to 'Newly Born Child.'[14] It governs acts made with the intent to prevent a child being born alive, or to cause it to die after birth.[15] The offence of preventing child birth, that is fœticide or causing death

---

[11]Article 21 states: *"No person shall be deprived of his life or personal liberty except according to procedure established by law"*. Though the violation of the right to life by a private individual is not within the within the purview of Article 21, as held in case of *Bombay Dyeing & Mfg. Co.* v. *By. E.A. Group*, AIR 2007 SC 861, the state is also under a duty to take positive steps under the criminal laws of the country to prevent any act which tends to take away the life of a human being, and punish the culprits. See also. Narendra Kumar, *"Introduction to the Constitutional Law of India"*, Faridabad: Allahabad Law Agency (2009), p147.

[12] Paras Diwan, *"Modern Hindu Law"*, Fourteenth Edition, Faridabad: Allahabad Law Agency (2001) at 298.

[13] I.B.L.R.377 at 397 (P.C.). See. M.A.Alnasir, "Human Rights and Female Fœticide", in B.P.Singh Sehgal (ed.), *"Human Rights in India: Problems and Perspectives"*, New Delhi: Deep & Deep Publications Pvt. Ltd. (2004) at 157.

[14] See, Sections 315-318 of IPC.

[15]Section 315 of IPC states: *"Whoever before the birth of any child does any act with the intention of thereby preventing that child from being born alive or causing it to die after the birth, and does by such act prevent that child from being born alive, or causes it to die after birth, shall, if such act be not caused in good faith for the purpose of saving the life of the mother, be punished with imprisonment of either description for the term which may extend to ten years, or with fine , or with both"*. Under section 316 of IPC, even causing death of a quick unborn child by an act would amount to culpable homicide defined under Section 299 of IPC. All these provisions indicate in a very lucid manner that there is a strict prohibition of committing infanticide or fœticide.

after birth, that is, infanticide, has been made cognizable, non-bailable and non-compoundable.

Long before the 1990 UN Convention on the Rights of Child, the provisions for the protection and development of the children were contained in Article 24 of the Constitution of India that prohibits the employment of children in any factory, or mine or in any hazardous occupation. Articles 39(e) and (f) lay down that the State shall direct its policy in such a manner that the tender age of children is not abused. In addition, children are to be given opportunities and facilities to develop in a healthy manner, and childhood protected against moral and material abandonment.

In 1974, the Government of India adopted a National Policy for Children (NPC), declaring the nation's children as "supremely important assets". This policy imposes an obligation on the State to provide appropriate services to all children, both before and after birth and during the growing stages, for their full physical, mental and social development.[16] This policy mandates certain modifications regarding various developments so far as the social, political, economical and global fields are concerned. The Draft National Policy and Charter for Children 2001(NPC 2001) thus affirms that children's rights are fundamental human rights and must be protected through collective action by the State, civil society, communities and families through their obligations to fulfill children's rights by inculcating a sense of values directed towards the same end to the maximum extent of their available resources.[17]

Despite all the above provisions, the girl child in India does not yet have equal status. A very strong gender bias is entrenched in the cultural heritage of Indian society. It is a society that idolizes sons, an obsession

---

[16] Preeti Mishra, *"Domestic Violence Against Women: Legal Control and Judicial Response"*, New Delhi: Deep & Deep Publications Pvt. Ltd. (2007), p77.

[17] Asha Bajpai, "Child Rights in India: Law, Policy and Practice" New Delhi: Oxford University Press (2003), p444. Article 1 of the NPC further states that the State and community will undertake all appropriate measures to address the problems of infanticide and fœticide, especially of the female child and all other emerging manifestations which deprive the girl child of her right to survival. However, the widening sex ratio, to the disadvantage of the girl child, has not only created a challenge for socially conscious demographers, but also the policy makers.

that cuts across all social, religious, educational or economic differences.[18] Unfortunately, the spirit of patriarchy still retains a strong emotional hold over Indian families where sons continue to receive more favourable treatment than daughters. This often results in either the abortion of female babies or the sidelining of the girl-child in terms of such fundamental needs as nutrition, basic health, care and education, to which she is equally entitled. According to reports, genetic testing for sex-selection has become a flourishing business, especially in the country's northern regions, so the moment a woman discovers that she is expecting a girl, she chooses to end her pregnancy, but perseveres if expecting a boy.

3. Infanticide

Whilst infanticide amounts to murder under the Indian Penal Code, 1860, gender discrimination remains the principal cause of the humiliation of women.[19] The fear that it might be difficult to find husbands for daughters, or that they might subsequently become victims of domestic violence, as well as unfavorable inheritance laws, especially among the Hindus, led to the embracing of various traditional forms of female infanticide, such as killing the girl baby either at birth, or later in infancy by asphyxiation, poisoning the mother's milk during lactation, strangulation, choking by sand or salt, tearing the intestines with a meal of coarse grains, burying alive, or drowning in milk, etc. This social evil still prevails, as is evident from widening male-female ratio. One might expect that advances in technology have reduced the number of female infanticides, but the reported figures tell an entirely different story. There were 104 female infanticides in 2000, which was an increase of 19.5 per cent over 1999, although 87 cases were reported in 1999, which was actually a decrease in the number of infanticides compared with 1996-8, as shown in Table I.[20]

Table. I

Offence	Year 1996 1997 1998 1999 2000
Infanticide	113 107 114 87 104

Source: National Crime Record Bureau (NCRB)

[18] *Supra*, n. 14.

[19] Section 302 Of the Indian Penal Code 1860 stipulates punishment for murder as *"whoever commits murder shall be punished with death or imprisonment for life and shall also be liable to fine"*.

[20] *Supra*, n. 14 at 86, 465.

It seems that a family's weak economic condition might be a barrier to a baby girl's right to survival. However, this theory doesn't appear to be appropriate in the case of Punjab and Haryana, two rich Indian States experiencing economic growth, where despite this one cannot discern any gender-sensitive human development. Different census figures reveal a monotonous widening of the juvenile sex ratio in the 0-6 age group in these States.

4. Abortions and the Medical Profession

In medical terminology, abortion means termination of pregnancy before the fœtus has attained viability—is capable of independent intra-uterine life.[21] Sex determination and sex selective abortion are grave forms of discrimination against women in general, and girl children in particular. The misuse of medical technologies that have the potential to detect the fœtus's sex , or even select the sex at the pre-conception stage, have added a new dimension to the issue of sex selective abortions. The introduction of ultrasonography, and then amniocentesis in 1975, as a measure for detecting genetic disorders and abnormalities ironically 'quickened the pace of death of the female child from the born to the unborn stage'[22] and further added fuel to the fire.

Though the Indian Penal Code, 1860 provides for stringent penalties if a miscarriage is caused or carried to without the consent of the woman,[23] the menace of abortion and miscarriage remains. By the 1970s, the growth of

---

[21] *Supra*, Sehgal, n.13 at 159.

[22] Anand Grover, *Amniocentesis or Female Fœticide*, The Lawyers, March 1986, at 6.

[23] See Sections 312-314 of the IPC. Section 312 of IPC states: "*Whosoever voluntarily causes a woman with child to miscarry shall, if any such miscarriage be not caused in good faith for the purpose of saving life of the woman, be punished with imprisonment of either description for a term which may extend to three years or with fine, or with both and if the woman be quick with child, finally be punished with imprisonment of either description for a term which may extend to seven years, and shall also be liable to fine*". Explanation of this Section provides that the woman who causes herself to miscarry also falls within the ambit of this offence.

Section 313 deals with miscarriage without woman's consent. It provides: "*Whoever commits the offence defined in the last preceding section without the consent of the woman, whether the woman is quick with the child or not, shall be punished with imprisonment for life or with imprisonment of either description for a term which may extend to ten years, and shall also be liable to fine*".

quacks performing abortions had become a nuisance to the medical fraternity as they could not involve themselves legally, and openly conduct abortions since that was prohibited under the IPC, and these practices further increased gender disproportion. Consequently, the *Medical Termination of Pregnancy Act, 1971*(MTP Act)[24] legalized abortion as a health measure under certain conditions, on humanitarian and eugenic grounds, and with the genuine consent of the woman so as to prevent the further growth of unsafe abortions. However, permitting abortion up to twenty weeks, in cases where the pregnancy has resulted from the failure of contraception—e.g. by a couple trying to limit the size of their family, or to relieve the mother's anguish at such an unwanted pregnancy, which might cause grave injury to her mental health[25]—rather opened the gates to medical professionals and the killers of the female child.[26] As the Act provided a license to every registered medical practitioner to terminate pregnancy on certain grounds, under the guise of the legal umbrella they discovered a new way to increase their income by conducting illegal abortions under the pretext of legality.[27] This mainly occurred due to the lack of proper oversight.[28]

---

[24] On the recommendations of the UN mission to India in 1956, and also on the 1966 report of the Shantilal Shah Committee advocating strengthening population policy and reducing the number of illegal and unsafe abortions respectively, the 1971 MTP Act was passed. The Act also aimed at liberalizing abortions to some extent.

[25] See Section 3(2) of MTP Act, 1971. However this provision permits a registered medical practitioner without seeking the consent of the pregnant woman in case pregnancy is not more than twelve weeks, and where it is more than twelve weeks but does not exceed twenty weeks, opinion of two medical practitioners in good faith, to terminate the pregnancy with the consent of the pregnant woman who is eighteen years or above is required. In case she is under eighteen or is a lunatic, consent of her guardian in writing under section 3(4) is necessary.

[26] All other abortions continue to be punishable under Sections 312-316 of the Indian Penal Code. Abortion is thus still a crime, except as provided under the Medical Termination of Pregnancy Act, 1971.

[27] Though Section 4 of MTP Act provides that the pregnancy cannot be terminated except in a hospital established or maintained by the Government, or at a place approved by the Government.

[28] Vide Section 8 of the MTP Act; the State Government is competent to make regulations so as to control the working of the registered medical practitioners, thereby requiring them to certify the necessity of terminating pregnancy and also to give intimation of such termination of pregnancy to the Chief Medical Officer of the State. The number of fœticides increased, despite the fact that certain control measures have been provided under the Act.

It seems that the rights of the pregnant woman to abort under the MTP Act outweighs those of the fœtus. This is due to the psychological distress of her having an unwanted child, the pain and physical burdens of pregnancy, the stigma of unwanted procreation, and the burden of raising an unwanted child in the case of rape. So far as the right to abortion is concerned, it is a right given to the pregnant woman to decide privately between herself and her gynecologist whether she wishes to continue with the burden of unwanted pregnancy or wants to abort it.[29]

5. Pre-Natal Diagnostic Techniques (Regulation and Prevention of Misuse) Act, 1994

In the mid-80s, the problem of female fœticide became so acute that State intervention was demanded by various activist groups, media persons and intellectuals. Indian gender-detection clinics drew protests from women's groups after the appearance of advertisements suggesting that it was better to spend $38 now to terminate a female fœtus than $3,800 later on her dowry.[30] This led to the enactment of the *Pre-Natal Diagnostic Techniques (Regulation and Prevention of Misuse) Act, 1994* (PNDT Act). Nevertheless, this Act also had certain shortcomings. Although it banned abortions for the purpose of sex selection, it failed to keep track of the misuse of procedures like amniocentesis, CVS (Chorionic Villus Biopsy), etc, the methods devised to detect genetic abnormalities. In fact, the Act did try to regulate the centres offering these techniques for sex determination. Nonetheless, due to lack of social acceptability on account of its inconsistency with the MTP Act 1971, the Act of 1994 demanded a harmonization with the 1971 Act so as to achieve a common objective of having happy families based on the desirable sex ratio proportions, instead of showing a widening gap in juvenile sex-ratios.

The Census 2001 Report, not surprisingly, revealed a drastic increase in the sex ratio for the 0-6 age group, being dangerously masculine and signaling a demographic catastrophe on a nation-wide scale. The ratio in the 0-6 age group declined from 976 girls per 1000 males in 1961, to 945 in 1991, and then to 927 in the 2001 Census.[31] The juvenile sex ratio in

---

[29] Sarasu Esther Thomas, " Abortion: The Boundaries of Free Choice" *ILR*(1) 2009 at 169.
[30] M. R .Ansari, "*Protecting Human Rights*". New Delhi: Maxford Books (2006) at 279.
[31] *Supra*, n. 1.

different States of India is also of concern: the ratio as shown in the Census 2001 report has slipped alarmingly below 900 in the Union Territory of Chandigarh (773), New Delhi (821), Haryana (861), Punjab (874) and Uttar Pradesh (898). The lowest ratio of 845 has been recorded in the southwest district of Delhi. On the other hand, the North-Eastern States report sex ratio of above 950.[32] Even my own State of Jammu and Kashmir, despite having its own Act, *J&K Pre-Conception and Pre-Natal Diagnostic Techniques (Prohibition of Sex Selection) Act, 2002*, which relates to sex determination and the prohibition of female fœticide, has also failed to halt the decline in female births. In data compiled in 2009 by the Directorate of Economics and Statistics, the J & K State shows a constant increase in the juvenile sex ratio (0-6 years) compared to the Census 2001, where it was 937. In its Kathua district, there are 796 girls per 1000 boys in the urban area, and 847 in rural the part. Jammu and Udhampur districts have 820 and 873 females to 1000 males respectively, whereas various districts of Kashmir region like Kupwara show a better results, with 953 females.[33] The decline in numbers of female births from 976 per 1000 to 927 per 1000 between the 1961 and 2001 censuses, and took place at a much faster rate as compared with the overall decline across the country, of 941 to 933 from 1961 to 2001, as shown in the Table II below:

Table II[34]: Sex Ratio of Total Population and Child Population in Age Group 0-6: 1961-2001

Year	Sex Ratio in Age Group 0-6	Overall sex ratio
1961	976	941
1971	964	930
1981	962	934
1991	945	927
2001	927	933

---

32 *Ibid.*

33 Inderjeet Singh, 'Male- Female Ratio in Jammu and Kashmir' *Street Voice* Vol .XI, No. 10, Oct.2009 at 73.

34 *Censes of India*, Series 1, Paper 1 of 2001.

The skewed ratio of female to male births will have cascading effects on the population over a period of time, leading to a widening ratio over the country.[35] This imbalance is difficult to combat, and will take many generations to correct. At the very least, the sex ratio of 927 per 1000 in the 0-6 age group does not appear to augur well for India's future demographic prospects. People involved in female fœticide are ignoring the obvious fact that for the continuance of the human race, the correct balance of men and women is a *sine qua non.*[36]

6. Judicial Interference

The Supreme Court not only acts as the protector of the rights of human beings but has, at the same time, actively interfered in safeguarding the interests of the unborn child. Its pronouncement in the case of *Centre for Inquiry into Health and Allied Themes (CEHAT)* v. *Union of India*[37] was a landmark in Indian judicial history, as it was the first judicial measure to check the practice of killing female fœtuses: a stringent order in the form of warning was issued to all the concerned authorities created under the PNDT Act, 1994.

7. PC PNDT (Prohibition of Sex Selection) Act, 1994

The increasing gender bias has made the need to balance the sex ratio in the country practically and legally mandatory. This is because of the failure of the 1994 Act in that regard. As a result, the 1994 Act was amended in 2002, by the Amendment Act, 2002: that came into force in 2003, upon which the PNDT Act was renamed the Pre-Conception and Pre-natal Diagnostic Techniques (Prohibition of Sex selection) Act, 1994 (the PC PNDT Act).[38] An amendment to the PNDT Act was made with the

---

[35] Usha Tandon, "*Population Law: Instrument for Population Stabilization*". New Delhi :Deep & Deep Publications (2003) at 78.

[36] Dalbir Bharti, "Women and the Law" New Delhi: A. P. H. Publishing Corporation (2008) at 236.

[37] (2001) 5 SCC 577.

[38] The PNDT Act was enacted in 1994 and brought into force in 1996. However, there was no implementation of the law until the Supreme Court, in 2001, passed directives for its implementation in a public interest litigation filed by concerned health groups. Pursuant to Supreme Court directives, the law was amended in 2003 and renamed the PC PNDT Act, 1994.

dual objective of regulating pre-natal diagnostic techniques[39] which could be misused to determine the sex of the fœtus; and to prohibit the use of pre-conception methods for sex selection.[40] The PC PNDT Act allows the conduct of pre-natal diagnostic techniques only for the purposes of detection of any of the following abnormalities:[41]

1. Chromosomal abnormalities;
2. Genetic metabolic diseases;
3. haemoglobinopathies;
4. Sex-linked genetic diseases;
5. Congenital anomalies;
6. Any other abnormality or disease as may be specified by the Central Supervisory Board.

It also prohibits the disclosure of sex of the fœtus to the pregnant woman or any other person(s), to prevent sex selective abortions.[42] However, the prevention of disclosure is difficult to enforce as it takes place behind closed doors and can be done verbally. Hence the PC PNDT Act puts in place a system of registration and monitoring. Under the Act, a unit[43] can conduct pre-natal diagnostic techniques or provide genetic counselling

---

[39] Under Section 2(j) of PC PNDT Act, the term "pre-natal diagnostic techniques" includes both pre-natal diagnostic procedures and pre-natal diagnostic tests. 'Pre-natal diagnostic procedures' means all gynecological or obstetrical or medical procedures such as ultrasonography, fœtoscopy, taking or removing samples of amniotic fluid, chorionic villi, embryo, blood or any other tissue or fluid of a man, or of a woman before or after conception, for being sent to a Genetic Laboratory or Genetic Clinic for conducting any type of analysis or pre-natal diagnostic tests for selection of sex before or after conception [Section 2(i)]. The 'pre-natal diagnostic test' means ultrasonography or any test or analysis of amniotic fluid, chorionic villi, blood or any tissue or fluid of a pregnant woman or concepts conducted to detect genetic or metabolic disorders or chromosomal abnormalities or congenital anomalies or haemoglobinopathies or sex-linked diseases[Section 2(k)].

[40] Pre-conception techniques were brought within the ambit of the law under section 6(c) of the PC PNDT Act.

[41] Section 4(2) of the PC PNDT Act. The conduct of pre-natal diagnostic techniques is further subjected to the fulfillment of certain conditions under section 4(3) of the PC PNDT Act.

[42] Section 5(2) of the PC PNDT Act prohibits communication of the sex of the fœtus by words, signs, or in any other form.

[43] Depending upon the kind of services to be provided, the units can be registered as Genetic Counselling Centres (GCC), Genetic Clinics (GC), or Genetic Laboratories (GL)

only after it obtains registration. Once registered, the units are required to maintain records of all pregnancy related services provided by them.[44]

8. Conclusion

The question remains, despite a plethora of legislation, why is the girl child denied an adequate representation in the demographic set up of Indian society where many emancipation movements including judicial pronouncements[45] have been made for the betterment of women—including the girl child? After making an assessment of the laws passed by the Indian Parliament; especially the MTP Act, PNDT Act and the PC PNDT Act, and the sex ratio which is heavily weighted towards males, it is apparent that to a large extent the flaw lies in a weak implementation machinery that includes Central government, State governments, and the Appropriate Authorities constituted under these Acts. An emphasis on the strict maintenance and follow-up of the records of procedures carried out by the concerned persons[46] is imperative. Accountability has to be fixed for non- implementation or non-compliance with legislation. To remedy this, it is necessary that the medical professionals participate in the campaign against female fœticide by offering positive counselling, explaining the importance of girl children and the impact of female fœticide and the skewed sex ratio on society. In addition, they should also realize that the improper use of technology in the disclosure of the sex of the fœtus, and thus sex selective abortions, would escalate societal imbalance. Such unethical malpractice needs to be carefully monitored. There is also a need to change the socialization process, as the family is the cradle of violence that attaches a gender label to the girl child, not only

---

[44] Rule 9(2), (3) and (4) inserted by amendment in 2003, as well as PCPNDT Rules, 1996 mandate for maintaining record in Form D, if the unit happens to be GCC in respect of each women counseled, or on Form E , if the unit is GL in respect of each man or woman subjected to any pre-natal diagnostic procedure/technique /test, or in Form F, if GC in respect of each man or woman subjected to any pre-natal diagnostic procedure/technique /test respectively.

[45] Two writ petitions were filed under Article 32 of the Constitution of India where the Supreme Court of India issued directions to various authorities to implement the provisions of the PNDT Act and the subsequent petition led to the passing of the PC PNDT Act, 2002 which came into force in 2003. For directions of the court see, *CEHAT V. Union of India* (2001) 5 SCC 577: *CEHAT V. Union of India* (2003) 8 SCC 398. Also see *Supra,* n. 15 at 391-393.

[46] The word persons under Section 3(3) of PC PNDT, 1994 includes gynaecologist, pediatrician or registered medical practitioner.

before birth but also afterwards, thus making her position vulnerable. Further, the school curriculum should be amended to highlight sexual equality. Also the legal regime should be streamlined keeping in mind the advancing technology.

It is also true that acts of infanticide and fœticide are posing the biggest threat to women. It must be driven home that the termination of pregnancy after sex determination is a criminal act that casts an awful shadow over humanity. Though it appears to be a Herculean task, the efforts to create an Indian society with equal rights to life for males or females must continue in a positive direction so as to cope with the lopsided demographic setup.

CHAPTER THREE:

LEGAL PERCEPTION OF CULTURE

THE SOVEREIGNTY OF CHILDREN'S RIGHTS WITHIN THE LEGISLATION OF THE NORDIC COUNTRIES

KERSTIN NORDLÖF

Abstract

The Nordic countries—Denmark, Finland, Iceland, Norway, and Sweden—historically have certain undeniable comparable traditions and cultures within the continental legal tradition. Similar weight can be put on their jurisprudential notions of justification and the philosophy of law. Moreover, positivism and naturalism have had a very substantial effect on the development of Nordic laws, legislation, court decisions, and even the ratification of international agreements. All these countries have also been very cooperative in maintaining the principles of equality, justice, universality, and the principle of integrity of written agreements, i.e. the principle of *pacta sunt servanda*. Thus, based on the theories of naturalism and legalism affected by the principles of human rights, they have developed the idea of protection of the integrity of their individuals within and outside their territorial jurisdictions. This protection can be particularly studied with reference to children and juveniles who have occupied a very significant place in legislation and court practice. This article opens the door to a large number of rules and provisions applicable to the protection of the rights of children in civil or criminal procedures. The aim is to present and compare their effectiveness in the development of the integration of the rights of children within each country and whether there is any likelihood of establishing the idea of the legal sovereignty of children in Nordic countries.

1. Introduction

Despite the fact that many sources governing the rights of children can be examined within international and regional documents, national legislation have a definite role in the final and practical implementation of those rights. Within the Nordic countries, which in many ways have a concordant tradition in legislation within different areas of the rule of law, the protection of the child's interests is to be found in several laws of a constitutional character as well as legislation and instructions of superior authority. A study of existing legal documents shows that the European Convention for the Protection of Human Rights and Fundamental Freedoms has, because of the membership of the European Union by three of the Nordic countries, been incorporated into their legislation, and that Norway, in 1999, acted in the same way but not only with respect to the European convention alone, but also as the only Nordic country which incorporated the Convention on the Rights of the Child within its own laws. The reports of the United Nations Committee on the Rights of the Child are particularly important. Their commitment to scrutinizing the reports of the Nordic countries on their implementation of the Convention on the Rights of the Child, which are to be delivered every five years, may have an impact on improvements to the rights of children there.

In the Nordic countries, the fundamental rights of members, including children, are to be found in their respective constitutions, though the application of constitutional rights may most often be enforced by reference to particular legislation. In fact, the rights of children, or the protection of those rights, are mainly to be found within public legislation. Each relevant piece of legislation may instruct the authorities dealing with children to put emphasis on the opinion of the child and what is best for the child as well as limiting or forbidding the use of means of compulsion or other intrusions on the child's personal integrity. The legislation address the child's rights as a subject within legal procedures claiming rights to a special representative, rights to damages when violence is witnessed within the family and being considered as a part of legal procedures at the age of 15.

The rights of children are also protected within civil law, and particularly within the legal area of family law which indicates the duties of the custodian. In addition, labour law prevents children under a certain age from working, and in certain conditions. The limitations of a child's legal capacity appear in several other pieces of legislation in civil law where the ability to enter a contract, which is of fundamental importance, is fully developed and exercised at the age of 18.

Criminal law, constituting an integral part of public law, defines the actions which may be recognized as criminal and incur criminal liabilty, such as assault, trafficking or rape. Deciding upon the penal value of a crime can be complicated, though, because a crime affecting a growing child's confidence must be carefully considered. In cases where the offender is a juvenile, the criminal code limits the sanctions that can be imposed, since life imprisonment is not permitted. The legislation here prefers such measures as care or voluntary service. The legal system also encourages the non-prosecution of the accused because of the age of the person. Although the legislation of Nordic countries is supposed to fulfil regional and international measures with regard to protecting children's rights, they are still far from meeting all the demands of the Convention on the Rights of the Child. Some improvements have been made to the body of legislation, but there are still several gaps that need attention. Because children are vulnerable, the task of protecting their integrity not only belongs to their custodians, close relatives, teachers and others, but also to society as a whole.

2. Swedish Legislation

2.1. Nationality and Education

Children's rights within the Swedish system are contained in the constitution, legislation and instructions indirectly expressed or explicitly stated. The constitution declares the fundamental rights of citizens, including children as a whole. In constitutional law, the 2 sections of Chapter 2 of the Instrument of Government[1] explicitly contain the fundamental rights and freedoms with respect to children. The first section deals with nationality: it states that a child under 18 should have the same nationality as his or her parents, or one parent. The second is the right to free education at a state school.

The child`s right of nationality and to education is further developed by two acts. Regarding nationality, Swedish citizenship may be granted through birth, adoption, the marriage of the parents, or naturalization. In 2001, the 1950 Act on Swedish Citizenship[2], which is based on the principle of *Ius sanquinis*, was replaced by a new law[3]. The main change was the acceptance of dual citizenship was accepted. When considering the question of nationality, the Aliens Act[4] may be of interest. It includes

---

[1] SFS 1974:152 sec. 7 and 21.
[2] SFS 1950:382.
[3] SFS 2001:82.
[4] SFS 2005:716.

the rights of a child to receive a residence permit on the grounds of ties with Sweden, for instance his or her parent(s) are resident in Sweden.[5]

The child`s right to education has been further developed in several pieces of legislation; the oldest law dates from 1724. The current Education Act is from 1985 and contains common provisions for the national school system concerning education for children and young persons in a municipal school organization.[6] There have been several amendments since then, and on 1 July 2001 new education legislation was enacted.[7]

Compulsory education in Sweden also includes pre-school classes, from the age of 5. After nine years at Compulsory Comprehensive School, the child may study without charge for a further three years at Upper Secondary School, to qualify for university or to enter the labour market. The policy in general is to encourage access to education. In the 2001 Act of Education, school healthcare is also included.

Under the Act of Education, education is also a fundamental right for mentally disabled children and young persons: the Act also includes regulations for special schools for children and young persons with deafness or impaired hearing. There are also schools for the Sami population, a minority who mostly inhabit the north of Sweden.

Through knowledge, society will develop. Legislation therefore has an important function in the development of children's rights. The implementation of those rights at different levels of education has to be evident as well as visible, and at the same time protected. It is obvious that the acknowledgement of children's rights, whether by legal authorities or themselves alone, also has an important role in the education of children and young persons.

There is also an Ordinance relating to the education of those children who are not registered as being resident in Sweden.[8] According to the provisions of the Ordinance, they are entitled to the same education as other children and young persons living in Sweden.

---

[5] Chapter 5 sec. 3.
[6] SFS 1985:1100 and 2000:445.
[7] Ds 2009:25; prop 2009/10:165 Den n ya skollagen – för kunskap, valfrihet och trygghet.
[8] Ordinance concerning education and government grants for certain children and young people who are not registered residents of Sweden. SFS 2007:81.

2.2. Responsibility of the Custodian

The Children and Parent Code[9], originally from 1949 but with several amendments, is of particular interest when studying the legal effects of being a mother or a father. The Code is of fundamental importance in protecting the rights of children. It defines paternity, the name of the child, custody, guardianship, maintenance and adoption. It also prohibits beating one's child[10]. THE emphasis here is on the best interests of the child in compliance with Article 3 Section 1 of the CRC.[11]

The Swedish criminal code includes provisions for imposing criminal responsibility on parents or other persons responsible for raising the child, for example when the person has neglected to prevent a child under his or her care from committing a crime.[12] Although these provisions do exist, they have not yet been employed.

2.3. Responsibilities of Society

The Freedom of the Press Act,[13] representing a part of the Swedish constitution, especially protects children from being exposed to publications which "might have a brutalising effect, or otherwise seriously impair the moral tutelage of the young".[14] This safeguarding of the child's development is also covered by the Swedish criminal code, which contains the offence of *leading youth astray*.[15] The offence not only includes publications, but also technical recordings listed in the Fundamental Law on Freedom of Expression.[16] This third fundamental law also limits under 15s from accessing violent, or potentially violent, material: in furtherance of this, the criminal code lists the crime of crime *illicit purveyance of a technical recording*.[17]

---

[9] SFS 1949:381. The translation from 1995 is available as paper copy from Swedish statutes in translation.
[10] Chapter 6 sec. 1.
[11] Here may also the Marriage Code (SFS 1987:230), with subsequent amendments up to and including SFS 2000:1731 and Chapter 5. Divorce Section 1 be mentioned.
[12] Chapter 23 sec. 6.
[13] SFS 1949:105.
[14] Chapter 6 sec.2
[15] Chapter 16 sec. 12. SFS 1998:1444
[16] SFS 1991:1469. Chapter 3 sec. 12.
[17] Chapter 16 sec. 10c.

The social welfare committee, a compulsory committee in each municipality,[18] has several obligations under the Social Services Act[19] to enforce and protect the rights of children. Children and young persons are one of several groups included within their sphere of responsibility, and where their primary focus is the best interests of the child.[20] They are also responsible for the care in family homes and other care homes or residences.[21] The Act includes special provisions for the reception of children and, for example, compulsory reviews of care not taking place in the child´s own home, or provisions for intercountry adoptions. With respect to adoption, one may also mention the Act on International Legal Relations Concerning Adoption,[22] the Ordinance on Examination of Foreign Decisions on Adoption,[23] the Act Consequent on Sweden's Accession to The Hague Convention on the Protection of Children and Co-operation in respect of Intercountry Adoption[24], the Intercountry Adoption Intermediation Act[25] and the Ordinance containing instructions for the Swedish Intercountry Adoptions Authority.[26] An adoption which is not in accordance with the above mentioned relevant legislation may make the adopters guilty of the crime of *unauthorised procurement of consent or permission to adopt a child.*[27] Other crimes against the family are *tampering with family status,*[28]and *arbitrary conduct concerning a child.*[29] The rights of the child are also guaranteed by the Act Concerning Support and Service for Persons with Certain Functional Impairments.[30] It states that to guarantee good living conditions, and if the child is under fifteen years of age, "a person having custody, a personal representative, legal guardian or trustee"[31] may request necessary measures on the said child's behalf.

---

18 There are 290 municipalities in Sweden.
19 SFS 2001:453 and with amendments e.g. SFS 2004:851 .
20 Chapter 1 sec. 2 and chapter 5 sec. 1.
21 Chapter 6.
22 SFS 1971:796.
23 SFS 1976:834.
24 SFS 1997:191.
25 SFS 1997:192.
26 SFS 2007:1020.
27 The Swedish Penal Code (1962:700) Chapter 7 sec. 2 and 5.
28 Chapter 7 sec. 3.
29 Chapter 7 sec. 4.
30 SFS 1993:387
31 Sec. 8.

Compulsory care may be enforced under the terms of the Care of Young Persons Act.[32] The reason for an application of compulsory care submitted by the social welfare committee to the administrative court may be "due to physical or mental abuse, exploitation, neglect or some other circumstances in the home, [or] there is a palpable risk of detriment to the young person`s health or development".[33] In addition, the young person's own behaviour such as criminality, use of drugs, and "other socially degrading behaviour"[34] may also be sufficient reason(s) for a court to take a decision concerning compulsory care. As stated in the Act, such care should be reviewed every six months, and not last longer than when he or she reaches 18 if it was due to circumstances in the home, or 21 if it was due to the young person's own behaviour.[35] The best interests of the child have, however, a decisive role when the decision of care is taken by the court. At the age of fifteen, the child has the right to approve or to avoid compulsory care, [36] and at this age the child is also entitled to plead his or her own case in a lawsuit or a matter under the Care of Young Persons Act.[37]

As a victim of a crime, a child or a young person may for certain crimes receive a plaintiff council in accordance with the Act of Plaintiff Council and its Ordinance.[38] But if the young person is under 18, a special representative may be appointed by the court. Such victim's rights exist under the Act of the Special Representative of the Child, if the child's custodian is suspected of the crime; or the custodian, owing to his or her relationship to the suspect, is unable to take care of the rights of the child.[39] All these provisions of the Act are formulated in such a way as to protect the best interests of the child.

2.4. Criminalisation

The Swedish Criminal Code was adopted In 1962, and came into force on 1 January 1965 replacing the Penal Code of 1864. The general part of the

---

[32] SFS 1990:52 with amendments 2001:466, 2003:406, 2003:420, 2005:468, 2006:896, 2007:1312, 2009:804.
[33] Sec. 2 SFS 2003:406.
[34] Sec. 3 SFS 2003:406 and 2006:896
[35] Sec. 21.
[36] Sec. 1.
[37] Sec. 36.
[38] SFS 1988:609 and SFS 1997:408.
[39] SFS 1999:997

Criminal Code recognizes the age of criminal responsibility as 15.[40] Among those criminal laws particularly aimed at protecting the integrity of children are crimes against liberty and peace. The crimes of *kidnapping*[41] and *trafficking*[42] are to be found here. In the case of trafficking when the victim is a child, there are much serious provisions in the relevant legislation.

The law relating to sexual crimes was revised in 2005. To increase the integrity of the child under 15, the crime of *rape of a child* was introduced. This crime will also be regarded as having been committed if the child is older than 15 but under 18, and the perpetrator is a parent, custodian, or is responsible for the care of the child by an official decision of a legal authority. It may be regarded as *gross rape of a child* when, for example considering the age of the child.[43] If, due to circumstances the crime is considered less severe, the accused may be found guilty of the *sexual exploitation of a child.*[44] If another form of sexual act has taken place compared with those mentioned before, the perpetrator may be accused of the *sexual assault of a child.* The crime may be considered *gross sexual assault of a child* due, for example, to the age of the child.[45]

The crime of *exploitation of child for sexual posing* may occur when a perpetrator facilitates or exploits a child under 15 to perform or take part in sexual posing. This includes children between 15-18 if the posing is deemed to damage the child's health or development. The crime may be considered to be *gross* due to, for instance, ruthless exploitation of the child.[46] A person, who sexually touches a child under 15 or persuades the child to perform or take part in an act with a sexual meaning, may be accused of *sexual molestation.*[47] Even the person who contacts a child under 15 with the intent to commit acts that were mentioned in the above, and makes an agreement with the child to meet and thereafter take measures to facilitate meeting, will be considered.[48]

---

[40] Chapter 1 sec. 6.
[41] Chapter 4 sec. 1.
[42] Chapter 4 sec. 1a.
[43] Chapter 6 sec. 4.
[44] Chapter 6 sec. 5.
[45] Chapter 6 sec. 6.
[46] Chapter 6 sec. 8.
[47] Chapter 6 sec. 10.
[48] Chapter 6 sec. 10a. SFS 2009:343.

One of the crimes against public order, and which particularly aims to protect the integrity of a child who is under 18, or "whose pubertal development is not complete"[49] is *child pornography crime*. It may be considered as *gross*, for example if it has been part of systematic criminal activities. The period of limitation, which depends from case to case for prosecution, is different for sexual crimes where the victim is under 18. It does not start until he or she has reached 18, and includes the attempt to commit such a crime.[50] If a sexual crime is committed abroad against a child under 18, there is not any need to prove double criminality in order to prosecute the offender in Sweden. This is also true in the case of the attempt to commit such a crime against a child.[51]

2.5. Sanctions

When deciding upon the penal value of a crime, aggravating circumstances may be taken into particular account. Such circumstances are considered to exist if the accused has persuaded someone to take part in committing the crime by "misuse of that person's youthfulness".[52] Another aggravating circumstance was added in an amendment in 2003, and concerns crimes which damage the child's safety, and the child's trust in his or her relation to a close friend.[53]

Given the harm that a penalty, and particularly imprisonment, may cause a young person, the Swedish Criminal Code stipulates the options of imposing a more lenient punishment than is actually stated for a certain crime. This is the case for those who are under 21 when committing the crime. The most severe punishment to be imposed is imprisonment for 10 years; 14 years may be imposed if several crimes have been committed, or longer than 10 years, or life imprisonment, would be stipulated.[54]

As to the choice of sanction, there are limitations when considering imprisonment. When the accused is under 18, this penalty may only be chosen if there are extraordinary reasons. In such cases, closed juvenile care should be imposed. This sanction may vary from fourteen days to

---

[49] Chapter 16 sec. 10a.
[50] Chapter 35 sec. 1 and 4.
[51] Chapter 2 sec. 2.
[52] Chapter 29 sec. 2.
[53] Chapter 29 sec. 2.
[54] Chapter 29 sec. 7.

four years, and does not include conditional release.[55] The institution where this sanction should be enforced is also employed for those children who, due to their behaviour have been placed under compulsory care.[56] If the accused is older than 18, but not 21 when committing the crime, imprisonment may, in accordance with Swedish criminal policy, only be enforced if the penal value of the crime or other special reasons warrant it.[57]

Sanctions for juvenile offenders were altered in 2007. The purpose was to increase the predictability of sanctions imposed on persons under 21 when considering the penal value of the crime, the kind of crime and the juvenile's earlier criminality. *Youth care* could be imposed if the juvenile had a special need of it. It could mean voluntary care in accordance with a contract, or compulsory care as described in a plan of care, both being part of the judgement. If the juvenile agrees, *youth service* may also be imposed by the authorities: this includes carrying out unpaid work for between 20 – 150 hours, and is particularly aimed at juveniles under 18. *Youth service* or *fines* may be imposed, according to the penal value of the crime, or the juvenile's earlier criminality added to *youth care.*[58] Except for those sanctions particularly aimed at juveniles, other penalties may also be imposed, such as fines, suspended sentences, or probation.[59]

2.6. Criminal Procedure

With regard to compulsion, the Police Act[60] has to be taken into consideration here. If a child is found in such conditions as to suggest an imminent and serious risk to its health or development, the child may be taken care of by the police and handed over to the parents, other custodian or the social service committee.[61]

The Code of Procedure includes the provisions of employing means of compulsion in connection with a preliminary investigation. For example, a child suspected of a crime may not be kept for interrogation for more than

---

[55] Chapter 30 sec. 5, chapter 32 sec. 5, Act (1998:603) on enforcement of closed juvenile care.
[56] The Care of Young Persons Act sec. 12.
[57] Chapter 30 sec. 5.
[58] Chapter 32.
[59] Chapter 25, 27 and 28.
[60] SFS 1984:387.
[61] Sec. 12 SFS 1991:140.

six hours in total.[62] In general, remand in custody should be replaced with supervision.[63] The Ordinance of Preliminary Investigation clarifies how and by whom the interrogation should be performed. [64]

The Act with Certain Regulations on Juvenile Delinquents and its Ordinance is particularly important. It deals with children when, criminally responsible or not, or a young person under 21, is under suspicion of having committed a crime.[65] The option of mediation should be noted in this context. The juvenile's interest in taking part, regulated by the Act of Mediation Due to Crime[66] may have an effect on the prosecution's intention to prosecute or decide about *nolle prosequi*.[67] The social service committee is responsible for mediation for those under 18.[68]

Within the European Union a demand for cooperation in the area of criminal law and criminal procedural law resulted in the enforcement of the Ordinance on surrender to Sweden in accordance with the European Arrest Warrant.[69] The purpose of which is the execution of a custodial sentence or detention order.[70]

2.7. The Children`s Ombudsman

Each year a report on the situation of children and young people in Sweden is presented to the Swedish Government. Consequently, the Children's Ombudsman has a significant function in the implementing of the principle of the best interests of the child, although his legal authority is not actually that great. This official, created by the Children's Ombudsman Act, has a fundamental role in ensuring compliance with the intentions of the Convention on the Rights of the Child.[71] The first Ombudsman was appointed in 1993. In accordance with the CRC he or she takes action by enlightening the authorities and improving the rights of

---

[62] The Code of Procedure (1942:740) chapter 23 sec. 9.
[63] Chapter 24 sec. 4.
[64] The Notification of Preliminary Investigation (1947:948) sec. 15-19.
[65] SFS 1964:167 and SFS 1994:1763.
[66] SFS 2002:445.
[67] Act with Certain Regulations on Juvenile Delinquents sec 17.
[68] Social Service Act chapter 5 sec. 1c.
[69] SFS 2003:1178.
[70] Sec. 4 and 14.
[71] SFS 1993:335 and 2002:377.

children. The Ombudsman may suggest bills and amendments to the government, but is not authorized either to supervise other authorities or to interfere in an individual case except for reporting to the social services committee when, owing to the information the Ombudsman has received, there is a need to intervene to protect a child.

The importance of the Children's Ombudsman should not be underestimated. Even so, after long being an integral part of the Swedish criminal system, the Ombudsman has not become as effective as might have been hoped. Compared with other Ombudsmen, he is not equipped with any authority such as the right to start an investigation when the rights of a child have been ignored. Consequently, the Ombudsman may not press charges. And the lack of sufficient financial support makes the Ombudsman's situation more delicate. Nevertheless, it is the absence of effective means for enforcing children's rights that is the principal reason for the institution—not just to achieve a more convincing success within the national system. One might even add that it is surprising that the children's ombudsman is a body which is not only separated from the Swedish legal system, but also from the administrative authorities which could in many different ways benefit from the expertise that has been developed since of the Children's Ombudsman came into being in the early the 1990s.

3. Danish Legislation

3.1. Nationality and Education

As with the other Nordic countries, Danish nationality is based on the principle of *Ius sanquinis,* which is that "A child is a natural-born Danish national if born to a Danish father or a Danish mother".[72] Danish nationality may also be obtained upon notification and application.[73] In the Constitutional Act of Denmark the fundamental right of children to education has, like the other Nordic countries, been almost institutionalized. It includes all children of the age stipulated for compulsory education. Access to education is free, and carried out in municipal lower and

[72] Sec. 1.

[73] The Danish Nationality Act, cf. Consolidated Act No. 113 of 20 February 2003, with the amendments following from Act No. 311 of 5 May 2004.

secondary schools for nine years.[74] Details of the content and structure are to be found in the Primary Education Act.

3.2. Responsibility of Parent

The Constitution of Denmark recognizes the duty of parents to support their child until he or she reaches 18.[75] The details of the parents' responsibility are found in the Act on Parental Responsibility.[76] It states the provisions of custody including defining holders of custody, transfer of custody, for example in the event of the death of a parent. It also contains the provisions for the child's place of residence and advance notice of an impending move, contact with parents and other close persons, information about the child to the parent who does not have custody, contact with children in care, and decisions about foreign travel. Chapter 5 of the Act states the provisions for temporary decisions concerning custody and the child's place of residence and contact. The Act also includes procedural provisions for child welfare counselling and family mediation. The focus is on the child`s perspective, and states the child`s right to contact the regional state administration. The intention is to protect the integrity of the child when he or she is particularly considered an individual legal subject. And, as in the other Nordic countries, the child may not be exposed to corporal punishment.[77]

3.3. Responsibilities of the Society

In its first part, the Act of Social Services includes the responsibilities of municipalities and regions for providing different facilities like special daytime clubs and residential institutions for children and young persons whose physical or mental functions are substantially or permanently impaired.[78] The second part of the Act even guarantees the free counseling by municipal authorities to the child.[79] The rights of children and young persons are emphasized in Part IV of the Act of Social Services. Its first chapter promotes "the development, well-being and independence of children and young persons".[80] A cohesive child policy in writing should

[74] Sec. 76.
[75] Sec 75.
[76] Christiansborg Castle, this 6th day of June, 2007.
[77] Act on Parental Responsibility chapter 1 sec. 2(2).
[78] Chapter 2 sec. 5(1).
[79] Sec. 11.
[80] Chapter 6 sec. 19(1).

be prepared and adopted by the municipal council, which is also responsible for the implementation of suggested measures.[81] Moreover, the municipal council is directly involved with the situation of children and young persons. An incentive to putting the needs of those individuals at the top of the political agenda might be to stress that the future of the municipality itself is actually in the hands of the next generation. The provisions of day-care facilities, etc., are thoroughly described, and through financial subsidy provide an opportunity for parents to choose private day-care from the age of 24.[82] For older children and young persons there are facilities such as clubs and other socio-pedagogical leisure activities.[83]

Young persons between 16-18, whose mobility may be restricted by a permanent impairment of physical or mental functions, are entitled to 15 hours' supervision attendance each month. He or she, in this case, has the right to suggest a supervisor, but with the provision that a person with whom there exists close ties will not be employed or will not be considered for employment. It means, in other words, that the mother or father of a young person who would prefer to supervise the child and give up his or her work in part, will not be accepted. Despite such parents' obvious wish to take care of their own child by acting as supervisor, this must be contrasted with enabling the young person to get in contact with other persons, hopefully also suitable: any candidate has to be approved by the municipal council.[84] This part of the Act of Social Services also contains a chapter on special support for children and young persons.[85] The purpose is "to secure the best possible conditions for the upbringing of such children and young persons, thereby providing them with the same opportunities for self-expression, personal development, maturity and health as their contemporaries, despite their individual problems".[86] It also provides for the provision for taking care of a child even without the consent of the custodians or the child itself after he or she has reached 15. Such care may be decided upon:

> 58 (1) Where there is an obvious risk that the health or development of the child or young person will suffer major damage due to

[81] Sec 19(2-3).
[82] Chapter 7 and 9.
[83] Chapter 8.
[84] Chapter 10.
[85] Chapter 11.
[86] Sec. 46(1).

(i) inadequate care for or treatment of the child or young person;
(ii) violence or other serious ill-treatment; substance abuse, criminal conduct or other serious social difficulties on the part of the child or young person; or
(iv) other behavioural or adjustment problems in the child or young person.

As regards the principle of legality, one could argue that that court practice, and the application of the principle of proportionality, are highly important in child care matters.

As it is stated "(t)he municipal council shall at all times choose the least restrictive suitable measure(s) for the solution of the problems uncovered in the course of such an investigation".[87]

For young persons between18-22 the Act offers certain measures. It is thus of vital importance to take into account the young person's need for support although he or she has to consent for such a measure to be taken. This may consist of full-time accommodation, a welfare officer for the young person, and a permanent contact person for the young person.[88]The provisions for compulsory measures and other restrictions on self-determination are contained in Part VII of the Act on Social Services. In general, it is stated that such decisions may only be applied for a specific period of time.[89] Although the protection of the rights of children and young persons seem adequate at first glance, the actual imposition of compulsory care suffers, as in Sweden, from a fundamental error within the system. Child convicts under 15 may be found in those institutions providing full-time accommodation. One might thus state that the age of criminal responsibility has more or less been obviated by the provisions of compulsory care. The Act also provides penal provisions for a person who induces or assists a child or young person in care, to escape. A person who places or receives a child or a young person in care contrary to the provisions of the Act of Social Services is also criminally responsible.[90]

Complaints about decisions under to the Act of Social Service may be dealt with by a Social Complaints Board or a National Appeal Board

---

[87] Sec 52 (2). Se also chapter 24 sec. 123(1 and 3) and 124 (1).
[88] Chapter 12 sec. 76(1 och 3).
[89] Chapter 24 sec. 123 (2).
[90] Chapter 28.

before being handed over to the court. The provisions are to be found in the Act on Social Services and the Act on the Legal Protection and Administration in Social Matters.[91] This should be considered in the light of the European Convention for the Protection of Human Rights and Fundamental Freedoms, particularly Articles 5 and 6.

To ensure the safety of children in day-care or other similar facilities, a law was introduced in 2005 to investigate whether job applicants had any previous convictions for crimes against children. It applies to public administrative authorities and to private, physical and legal persons and where the person, if appointed, will come into direct contact with children under 15.[92]

3.4. Criminalisation

The Danish Criminal Code lists *child pornography* as a crime. In accordance with the framework adopted by the European Council Ministers in 2002, the minimum age of a person covered by the legislation was raised from 15-18. The maximum sentence for the *dissemination of abuse images of children* was raised from 2 to 6 years. A similar improvement took place with regard to the *possession of abuse images of children*, for which, the maximum sentence was raised from six months to a year.[93]

The child's sexual integrity is further protected by the provisions of the Danish Criminal Code. It states that sexual intercourse with a person under 15 is punishable by law and may incur imprisonment. It adds that if the child is under 12 length of the sentence may be increased.[94] Sexual intercourse with a person under 18 who is the perpetrator's "adopted child, step-child or foster child, or who has been entrusted to him for instruction or education"[95] is punishable. This is also the case for a person "gravely abusing superior age or experience"[96] and induces a person under 18 to have sexual intercourse.

---

[91] Chapter 30.
[92] No.520 of 21June 2005.
[93] Sec. 235.
[94] Sec. 222.
[95] Sec. 223.
[96] Sec. 223 (2).

Trade in human beings was criminalized in 2005.[97] A person may be found guilty "who, for the purpose of exploitation of the individual through sexual immorality, forced labour, slavery or slavery-like conditions, or the removal of organs, 1) recruits, transports, transfers, houses or subsequently receives a person under the age of 18 years".[98] To combat the crime, the Danish Government agreed on an Action Plan to Combat Trafficking in Human Beings 2007–2010, which includes children trafficked into prostitution, forced labour or otherwise exploited. There are various problems with this, especially with regards to finding those children who have already been trafficked. One of the measures mentioned in the plan is therefore to develop methods to identify those children. The Government Agency responsible is the Danish Ministry of Refugee, Immigration and Integration Affairs.

3.5. Sanctions

Under the Danish Criminal Code, and like the other Nordic countries, a person becomes criminally responsible at 14. It means that a young person may commit crimes, but not prosecuted, but a police investigation may still be carried out. The social authority may also, if necessary, enrol the juvenile delinquent in courses to learn about social relations. Furthermore, he or she may be placed in a closed 24-hour centre.

3.6. Criminal procedure

In Denmark, as in the other Nordic countries, criminal trials involving a juvenile delinquent take place in the same court as for adults, as there are no juvenile courts. During the trial the juvenile will be guaranteed certain rights, such as having the public cleared from the courtroom if the judge finds that it might have a negative impact on the juvenile on account of his or her age. This may often be the case when the trial has been the subject of much media attention.

3.7. The National Council for Children

The National Council for Children in Denmark, the first chairman of which was appointed in 1994, corresponds to the Children`s Ombudsman in Sweden and Finland. Apart from a chairman, it has six members. It is,

---

[97] Sec. 262 a No. 909 of 27 September 2005.
[98] Sec 262 a (2) 1).

as in the other Nordic countries, appointed to promote the interests and rights of children. This is carried out by supplying information about the conditions of children and giving advice to other authorities, as well as taking the views of children in matters concerning them. To get their opinion, the Council uses different methods, such as the Council´s website home page and the National Council`s Children`s Panel. The latter consists of about 1,200 children from 10-12. They voluntarily give their opinions on different issues involving children. The National Council for Children also evaluates conditions of children in Denmark as required by the Convention on the Rights of the Child. In recent years the Council has focused on the situation of children in divorces, bullying, physical punishment, sexual abuse, the physical school environment and inadequate parental care and control. And, like the corresponding institutions in the other Nordic countries, the Council pays serious attention to the Danish reports to the United Nations Committee on the Rights of the Child adding relevant materials, though it does not, regrettably, deal with specific complaints.[99]

4. Finnish Legislation

4.1. Nationality and Education

The Finnish Constitution contains basic individual rights,[100] implemented regardless of whether the person is a child or an adult. According to the constitution, equality means equality of treatment of treatment between children and grown-ups, but also between children. The right of equality is further developed in Chapter 2, Section 6, dealing with basic rights and liberties, and equality in particular, stating that the opinion of the child should also have an influence on matters affecting them, and in accordance with their development. The chapter provides that:

> Children shall be treated equally and as individuals and they shall be allowed to influence matters pertaining to themselves to a degree corresponding to their level of development.[101]

---

[99] Section 88 of Danish Act No. 453 of 10 June 1997 on the Rule of Law and Administration in Social Areas and the Ministry of Social Affairs' executive order no. 2 of 5 January 1998, nr. 847 of 8. September 2005, nr. 458 of 15. May 2006.
[100] 11 June 1999 (731/1999, amendments up to 802 / 2007)
[101] Chapter 2.

As in the other Nordic countries, nationality is based on the well-established principle of *Ius sanquinis*. Finnish nationality may also be obtained upon notification and application.[102]

The constitution strictly prohibits extradition and the transferring of a Finnish citizen to another country against his or her will, although an exception may be granted "in order to enforce a decision concerning the custody or care of a child",[103] though this is only acceptable when the receiving country guarantees human rights as well as legal protection.[104] On the one hand, regulations related to limiting extradition and transferral are welcomed within the provisions of the constitution. On the other hand, it raises fundamental questions when discussing the rights of children, namely, what precisely is meant by human rights and legal protection in this context? Can Finland consider herself capable of guaranteeing them? Finding a comprehensive answer to the first question will not be easy, but to the last question the answer, as in the other Nordic countries, is definitely *no*.

Section 12 of Chapter 2 contains the provisions of freedom of expression and the right of access to information. As in the other Nordic constitutions, limitats on accessing to pictorial programes are stipulated by reference to an Act: the Finnish Criminal Code states that *illegal exhibition or distribution of audiovisual programmes to a minor* is a criminal offence.[105]

Children`s access to free education in Finland is contained in the Finnish Basic Education Act,[106] which emphasizes bringing up pupils humanely and ethically, as well as developing them as responsible members of society.Local authorities are the providers of pre-primary and basic education:[107] basic education lasts nine years. The act also covers special-needs education. Chapter 7 of the Act contains the pupil's rights and duties, stipulating a "(r)ight to a safe learning environment".[108] Section 34 covers special provisions for health.[109] The Act also includes the regulation of before- and after-school activities, whose purpose is to

---

[102] Chapter 1 sec 5.
[103] Chapter two, sec 9.
[104] Chapter two, sec 9, 802/2007.
[105] Chapter 17 Sec. 18b (650/2004).
[106] Basic Education Act 628/1998, amendments up to 1136/2004.
[107] Chapter 2.
[108] Sec. 29.
[109] Sec. 34.

"promote children's welfare and equality in society and prevent exclusion and promote inclusion".[110]

4.2. Responsibility of Parents

The Decree on Child Custody and Rights of Access defines the relationship between children and parents in matters of custody and rights of access. The decree contains procedural provisions, provisions for the social welfare board and the provisions of private international law and the return of the child. According to the Act, and in accordance with the Child Welfare Act, the aim of child custody is to make sure that there is balanced development and welfare of the child, referring to his or her individual needs and wishes. The child should be guaranteed good treatment and upbringing, including adequate care and support to become an adult with the capacity for accepting full responsibility. And, as is stipulated in the Finnish constitution, the interests of the child should be taken into account in matters affecting the child; and that his or her opinions and wishes should be taken into account according to the child's age and development.[111]

The child`s rights to having access to his or her mother is regulated in the Finnish Criminal Code, which has regulated very many provisions regarding the protection of the status of the child. According to Chapter 18 it is a criminal offence to swap one child with another.[112] Criminalising the *unauthorized taking of the custody of a child* and *child abduction* further ensures a secure environment for children. If the *unauthorized taking of the custody of a child* is suspected, the prosecutor's options for bringing charges may be limited since he has, in this case, to analyse the interests of the child. this includes getting the opinion of the relevant social welfare board, and if the result is that it would be contrary to the interests of the child, the prosecutor may not bring charges. [113] This can also occur in the case of *child abduction*. Here, not only charges but also punishment may be waived if it is in the interests of the child. The provision in such cases is that the offender has voluntarily returned the child, or considering the reasons leading to abduction, the trial as well as the punishment seem unreasonable.[114]

---

[110] Chapter 8a, sc. 48a.
[111] Child Custody and Right of Access Decree (556/1994).
[112] Sec. 2.
[113] Chapter 25 sec 5-5a (1161/2005).
[114] Sec. 9a.

4.3. Society's Responsibilities

Interestingly enough, the Finnish constitution stipulates the responsibility of public authorities to offer support not only to families but also to others who are responsible for ensuring the wellbeing and development of a child, namely:

> the public authorities shall support families and others responsible for providing for children so that they have the ability to ensure the wellbeing and personal development of the children.[115]

The constitution further emphasizes the importance of an adequate social and health service and free basic education, which are particularly relevant to enforcing the rights of children.[116]

The Finnish social welfare legislation consists of several parts, some of which is very important to children's rights. One is the Act of Child Welfare, which came into force on 1 January 2008[117]. It replaced the earlier 1983 Act. The Act emphasises the right of the child to grow up in a safe, but stimulating environment, with a balanced and varied development. The welfare of the child and his or her interests should be of priority. The municipal social welfare board, including other relevant authorities, is responsible for following as well as developing the conditions under which a child or a young person grows up. If necessary, the board is responsible for removing or preventing obstacles to an adequate upbringing. This Act has taken serious account of the child's right to have his or her opinion heard under the CRC. Chapter 4, Section 21 of the Act states:

> *Exercising a child's right to be heard*
> In addition to the child's custodian or other legal representative, a child who is twelve years of age or more is entitled to be heard in a child welfare case concerning the said child.

Unfortunately, the reverse situation obtains regarding an emergency placement, which is stipulated in Chapter 8, Section 39 (2). Such a placement may last up to 30 days without an application being submitted to an administrative court.

---

[115] Chapter 2 sec. 19.
[116] Chapter 2 sec. 19.
[117] Child Welfare Act (417/2007 and amendments up to 1390/2007.

The Child Protection law has a particularly important place in the study of children's rights in Finland.[118] This legislation has several similarities with the corresponding Swedish Care of Young Persons Act.[119] It emphasises *inter alia* the child`s interest when restriction is enforced in parental contact. It includes provision for employing restrictive measures against a child in institutional care in order to protect the health or safety of the child or other persons, as well as provisions for isolating the child. When restrictive measures are employed it is compulsory to record them and evaluate their effect on plans of care.

In addition to the Child Protection Law, the 1973 Child Day Care Act is also worthy of mention.[120] Other legislation providing support to families is the Act on the Child Home Care Allowance and the Private Care Allowance.[121] Those two acts guarantee the parent the right to a place for day care, or financial support for the parent who stays at home with a child, who has not reached the compulsory schooling age. Like the other Nordic countries, since 1 January 2003 Finland has checked the criminal background of persons working with children.[122] Finnish legislation also includes special regulations for the health and welfare of children and young persons.[123]

In order to deal with the younger generation, Finland enacted a Youth Act in 1995, which was replaced by a new Act in March, 2006.[124] A youth is defined as a person under the age of 29. The legislation aims to consolidate activities involving bringing up young independent and active members of society, as well as improving their living conditions and to take note of their opinions. This is realized by a youth policy development programme which aims to implement national policy at a provincial and municipal level. It is administered at four-year intervals by the Ministry of Education. The school shooting in Finland, in 2007 and 2008, by young

---

[118] It was amended in Law No. 583 of 29 June 2006.

[119] SFS 1990:52 with amendments 2001:466, 2003:406, 2003:420, 2005:468, 2006:896, 2007:1312, 2009:804.

[120] 36/1973 1 April 1973.

[121] (1128/1996) 1 August 1997.

[122] Act on Checking the Criminal Background of Persons Working with Children (504/2002).

[123] Ordinance No. 734 of 21 June 2007, 29 June 2007, Nos. 733-739.

[124] YOUTH WORK ACT 235/1995, amendments up to 663/2002.

perpetrators, and with several victims, must have had a decisive effect on those programmes.[125]

The Law on Young Workers[126] and its Ordinance[127] stipulates the types of work considered to be particularly harmful and dangerous for young employees.

4.4. Criminalisation

The Finnish Criminal Code includes several sex offences to protect the child`s integrity. They are included in Chapter 20, and consist of the *sexual abuse of a child* and *pandering*. Both those crimes may also, in certain circumstances, be considered *aggravating*. Attempts at either of these crimes are also punishable.[128]

In accordance with the Finnish Criminal Code, the of crime *trafficking in human beings* may be considered *aggravating* if a child is involved. This is the case if "the offence has been committed against a child younger than 18 years of age".[129]

A person who is aware of the *aggravated sexual abuse of a child*, and *aggravating trafficking in persons* where a child is the victim, and does not report the criminal conduct to the authorities may consequently be held criminally liable. This is also the case if a person fails to warn a potential victim in time to prevent a crime from being committed.[130] But criminal liability is limited if it means that "he or she would have had to denounce a spouse, a sibling, a direct ascendant or descendant, a person living in the same household or a person who is close owing to another comparable personal relationship".[131] However, this restriction may have a negative effect on preventing criminality, as it is a well-known fact that it is more often than not committed within the family, or by close relatives or friends.

---

[125] rudar.ruc.dk/bitstream/1800/4078/1/Christian%20Norocel.pdf.
[126] 27 May 2004, Nos. 400-407.
[127] No. 475 of 15 June 2006 and 21 June 2006, Nos. 474-484 based on the Workers' Protection Law (No. 738) of 23 August 2002 and Council Directive 94/33/EC of 22 June 1994 on the protection of young people at work.
[128] Sec. 6-7, 9-9a.
[129] Chapter 25 sce. 3a.
[130] Chapter 15 (563/1998) sec. 10 (1) 212/2008.
[131] Sec. 10 (2).

Sexual abuse of a child, the aggravated sexual abuse of a child, rape, aggravated rape and *coercion into sexual intercourse directed at a child*—according to the Finnish Criminal Code—are treated differently to other crimes. The right to bring charges for those crimes may be exhausted at the earliest when the plaintiff reaches the age of 28.[132]

Distributing sexually obscene pictures of children is criminalised in Finland, to protect the integrity of the child in the case of the spread of child pornography.[133]To this can be added the crime of *aggravated distribution of sexually obscene pictures depicting children.*[134] As in the other Nordic countries, it is a criminal offence to possess obscene pictures of children.[135] A person may also be charged with the *unlawful marketing of obscene material.* This is the case when "(a) person who, for gain, markets an obscene picture, visual recording or object which is conducive to causing public offence, by (1) giving it to a person under 15 years of age…"[136]

4.5. Sanctions

According to the Finnish Criminal Code, there are also mitigating circumstances regarding the criminality of the accused. For instance, if the accused is between 15-18, his or her age may be a strong mitigating factor. The Code specifies that "when the said offence could have been punishable by life imprisonment, to imprisonment for at least two and at most twelve years. If the penalty in the provision in question is imprisonment for a fixed period or a fine, the sentence shall be at most three fourths of the most severe penalty provided and at least the minimum penalty provided in chapter 2".[137] Further evidence of society's abhorrence of offences against a child, such as the *aggravated sexual abuse of a child,* is in sentencing. In accordance with the Finnish Criminal Code, the court may, at the request of the prosecution, decide that the convicted person may not be released conditionally. It means that he or she will serve the

[132] Chapter 8 (297/2003) sec. 1 (5) (1161/2005).
[133] Law No. 1068 of 1 December 2006, 8 December 2006, Nos. 1066-1072 chapter 17 sec. 18.
[134] Chapter 17 sec. 18a.
[135] Chapter 17 sec. 19.
[136] Chapter 17 sec. 20.
[137] Chapter 3 sec. 2.

entire sentence that has been decided due to the provisions of the judgment of the court.[138]

4.6. Criminal Procedure

Under the Finnish Criminal Code, the age of criminal responsibility is 15. For measures concerning a child below this age, the Code refers to the Child Welfare Act. [139]

4.7. The Children`s Ombudsman

The office of the Children´s Ombudsman commenced work in 2005.[140] The Ombudsman's duties are to work for the implementation of children´s rights in Finland, and which are codified in the Convention on the Rights of the Child. It is also the duty of the Ombudsman to draft in public the relevant questions on the rights of the child. Regrettably, the Finnish Ombudsman for Children, like the corresponding Ombudsmen in the other Nordic countries, does not handle individual cases. This means that like the Convention on the Rights of the Child, and the other offices of Ombudsmen for Children in the Nordic countries, it lacks legal instruments for enforcing the rights of the child.

5. Icelandic Legislation

5.1. Nationality

As with the other four Nordic countries, Icelandic nationality is based on the principle of *jus sanguinis*. Icelandic citizenship may also, under the Nationality Act,[141] be obtained by naturalisation and by declaration. Like the other Nordic countries, adoption also results in receiving the nationality of the adoptive parents.

---

[138] Chapter 2c – Imprisonment (780/2005) sec. 11 (212/2008).

[139] 39/1889, amendments up to 940/2008, chapter 3, sec. 1.

[140] Law No. 1221 of 21 December 2004 on the children's ombudsman, 27 December 2004, Nos. 1215-1223. Act of Government Passed in Helsinki 21st day of April 2005.

[141] No. 100/1952 (23 December).

5.2. Education

The Constitution of the Republic of Iceland of 1994, which has been amended several times,[142] guarantees education in one of its sections. Furthermore it guarantees the protection and care necessary for the child's well-being.[143] The provisions of pre-school activities are to be found in the Pre-school Act of 2008. Such activities are aimed at children below the age of compulsory schooling.

The Compulsory School Act of 2008 provides the scope and rule of compulsory school and education. In general, children in Iceland attend school from 6-16, which means for 10 years. The municipalities are responsible for this, as well as for the cost of compulsory schooling. The Act includes the rights and responsibilities of pupils: one example of the former is the right of each pupil to have a supervisory teacher. As a responsibility of each pupil, the Act states that "Pupils shall obey instructions from teachers and school staff in every way regarding school related matters and shall follow general rules of conduct and orderliness in their communication with school staff as well as with their fellow pupils."[144] If the pupil fails in his or her responsibility, he or she may ultimately be temporarily or permanently suspended from school. The Act also provides provisions for pupils with special needs and a section on primary health care.

5.3. Responsibility of Custodian/Guardian/Parental

The Child Protection Act of 2002 contains the parents' obligations. It stipulates how the child should be treated, namely with care and consideration. The parents' obligation regarding their duties of guardianship and the upbringing of the child are also mentioned. Acceptable conditions should be also provided for the child as well as protecting their welfare.[145]

The 2003 Act in Respect of Children[146] deals with the rights of children in relation to his or her parents. Here, the legal effects of the maternity and paternity of a child are included as well as court action concerning the

---

[142] Constitution of the Republic of Iceland (No. 33, 17 June 1944, as amended 30 May 1984, 31 May 1991, 28 June 1995 and 24 June 1999).
[143] Sec. 76.
[144] Sec. 14.
[145] Sec. 1 art. 1.
[146] Act 76 and 115/2003.

paternity of children.[147] The Act also includes the provisions for the rebuttal of a child`s paternity and for the invalidation of the recognition of paternity and financial support in connection with childbirth and pregnancy.[148] Chapter 5 of the Act stipulates that the parents' duties are to care, consider, and bring up their child and to observe other duties of their custodianship in the best interests of the child. It also includes the provisions for custody in the case of the divorce or separation of parents; agreements between parents; and dispute resolution and court actions relating to the custody of children.[149] Chapter 7 contains details about implementing decisions relating to the custody of a child. The child's right of access to both parents is stipulated in Chapter 8. It states, among other things, that a parent who prevents the other parent who has due to a ruling, judgment, court settlement or agreement, access to a child, from this access, may be liable to pay daily penalties up to ISK 30,000.[150] The mutual obligation of parents to support their child financially is stated in Chapters 9 and 10.

5.4. Society's Responsibilities

The rights of children in Iceland are especially protected by the Child Protection Act of 2002.[151] The Act applies to children under 18, although measures based on the consent of the young person may remain in force until he or she reaches 20.[152] The focus is on children who live under unacceptable circumstances, or children whose health is placed at risk. These should be assisted by support to the family or other suitable measures.[153]

The Ministry of Social Affairs, the Government Agency for Child Protection, the Authority for Homes and Institutions, the Child Protection Appeals Board and Child Protection Committees are responsible for enforcing the applicable measures. The latter is obliged to report every year to the Government Agency for Child Protection the number of cases, issues and how they have been resolved. The chairman of the Appeal Board is a judge; the board's decision may not be appealed to a higher

---

[147] Chapter 1-2.
[148] Chapter 2-4.
[149] See also chapter 6.
[150] Chapter 8 art. 48.
[151]No. 80/2002.
[152] Sec. 1 art. 3.
[153] Sec. 1 art. 2.

authority. Each municipality is under obligation to provide an action plan for child protection.[154] In their work on child protection the following principle should be applicable: what is best for the child, the interests of the child considering his or her development, stability, respecting parents' views, good collaboration, consistency, equity, proportionality and legality.[155]

The need for protection may be considered by the Child Protection Committee when "a child's physical or mental health or development may be at risk due to neglect, incapacity or behaviour of a parent, harassment or violence by another person, or due to the child's own the behaviour".[156] If measures taken by the Committee, based on the consent of the parent or the child (if the said child has reached 15), are found inadequate, the following measures may be temporarily employed and reviewed every six months:

a. an order to monitor the home,
b. orders regarding the circumstances and care of the child, such as day-care, school attendance, medical service, tests, treatment or therapy,
c. a ruling that a child may not be taken out of the country.[157]

The Committee may also rule that the child has to:

a. remain resident for up to two months,
b. be removed from the home for up to two months, and on necessary arrangements, such as the placement of the child in foster care or in a home or institution, or seek other measures … to ensure the child's safety, or in order that suitable tests on the child may be carried out, and the necessary treatment and care may be provided.[158]

The Committee's decision may be appealed to by the district court judge. An appeal does not prevent the Committee's decision from being enforced. A decision to place the child outside the home has to be tried by a district court. Such an order by a judge means that the child placement outside the home is applicable for twelve months.[159] One might add here

---

[154] Sec. 1 art. 3; Sec 2 and 3.
[155] Sec 1 art. 4.
[156] Sec 5 art. 21.
[157] Sec 6 art. 26.
[158] Sec 6 art. 27.
[159] Sec 6 art. 28.

that the need for rapid action when dealing with such delicate matters as child protection, and which is emphasized in the Act, is neglected. There is, rather, too much emphasis on stability and consistency, which is not in accordance with Article 5 of the European Convention when dealing with measures of a compulsory nature.

To protect the integrity of the child, the Government Agency for Child Protection has a right to be informed by the State Penal Registry about persons being convicted of sexual offences where the victim was a child under 18. The Agency can use this information to inform the relevant Child Protection Committee when such a person "who is believed to constitute a considerable danger"[160] moves into its district. The Committee may then, if justified, warn other parties, after the Agency has given its consent. This infringement of the convicted person's private life must be considered in the light of the European Convention for the protection of human rights and fundamental freedoms. In such cases, only a search into the Agency's data can determine what degree of danger exists, and whether the infringement of that person's private life is in accordance with the European Convention Article 8.

A person with a criminal record, including sexual offences against a child under 18 may not be employed by entities operating on behalf of the Act of Child Protection. Information about the criminal records of an applicant for a job under their authority has to be given to the following: "Managers of schools, pre-schools, summer camps, sports and leisure centres and other similar institutions, or places where children gather or stay…"[161]

A person may also be forbidden to be in a certain place or area as well as follow, visit or otherwise contact a child. This is the case when "a child is at risk due to the behaviour or conduct of a person, such as violence, threats or menaces, or due to drug use or other actions, …[162]; a person may be excluded from the home under the same conditions. This point of law is very significant since the child will generally be removed from the home, which could negatively affect the child since he or she is being removed from his or her home without having done anything wrong.
In child protection matters, a 12-year-old child should always be given the opportunity to express his or her views, but the child is considered a party from the age of 15. A spokesman may also be appointed to guard the

[160] Sec 7 art. 36
[161] Sec 7 art. 36.
[162] Sec 7 art. 37.

rights of the child.[163] The Child Protection Act includes penalties for *violations of notifiability*. This will be the case:

> If a person neglects to notify a child protection committee of a child being subjected to such ill-treatment or poor conditions that his/her life or health is at risk, ... [164]

The penalty is a fine or imprisonment for up to two years. For a person "who removes a child who has been placed by a child protection committee under this Act, or is responsible for the violation of such an arrangement..."[165] the same penalties may be imposed. Any person who removes a child who has been placed by a child protection committee under this Act, or is responsible for the violation of such an arrangement, shall be subject to fines or imprisonment for up to two years. Offences against a child by a custodial party, including to "mistreat the child mentally or physically, abuse him/her sexually or otherwise, or neglect the child mentally or physically, so that the child's life or health is at risk"[166] are, under the Child Protection Act regarded as more serious crimes than the ones mentioned earlier. The penalty is imprisonment for up to five years, and can be more severe owing to the provisions of other legislation that might be employed.

The section on penalties in the Child Protection Act lists offenccs against children. To harm a child, as in the other Nordic countries, is a crime. The Icelandic legislation includes the act of "threats or menaces upon a child, that may be expected to harm the child physically or mentally, ...[167] In Iceland, the penalty may vary between fines and imprisonment for up to three years. Other behaviour considered criminal according to the Child Protection Act is:

> If a person incites a child to crime, promiscuity, the use of alcohol or drugs, or leads the child astray by other means, this entails fines or imprisonment for up to four years.

[163] Sec 8 art. 46 and sc. 10 art. 55.
[164] Sec 28 art. 96.
[165] Sec 18 art. 97.
[166] Sec 18 art. 98.
[167] Sec 18 art. 99.

> Any person who subjects a child to aggressive, abusive or indecent behaviour or hurts or insults him/her is liable to fines or imprisonment for up to two years.[168]

To improve the situation of the youth of Iceland a new Youth Act was adopted in 2007. It came into force the same year. It authorises a municipality to establish a special youth council. This council should supply the municipal authorities with advice about the young people within the community. [169] These councils are also found in Sweden, for example.

5.5. Criminalisation

In 1992 the Icelandic Penal Code lowered the age of consent for sexual intercourse to 14, which is the lowest among the Nordic countries.[170] Sexual intercourse, other types of sexual relations, as well as other types of sexual harassment with a person below this age are considered a sexual offence against a child. Criminal liability may also be imposed on a person who "by employing deception, gifts or other means, entices a young person aged 14-16 to participate in sexual intercourse or other sexual acts …"[171] Obviously, the protection of the child under 14 is stricter than for those between 14-18. On the one hand, the provisions still allow the impostion of criminal liability in certain cases where the child is older than fourteen. On the other hand, if the accused thought the child was old enough to give legal consent, it might be viewed as a mitigating circumstance.[172] And the punishment may even be waived if the accused and the victim of the offence were married or cohabiting at the time of the offence, or subsequently continued or entered into such a relationship.[173]

The penal code protects the child's integrity where a supervisor or employee of an entity in which the child may be an inmate, patient or pupil has intercourse or sexual relations with that child. A crime has also been committed when a person has sexual intercourse or other sexual relations "by grossly abusing the fact that the person is financially dependent on him or her, is in his or her employment, or is under his or her

[168] Sec 18 art. 99.
[169] No. 70/2007.
[170] No. 40/1992. Art. 202.
[171] Art 202.
[172] Art. 204.
[173] Art. 205. The legal age for marriage is 18 years old for both women and men.

protection in a relation of trust ... ".[174] If the victim is under 18, the penalty will be more severe.

As in the other Nordic countries, it is a crime to have sexual intercourse or other sexual relations with your own child; the Penal Code also includes other descendants in its provisions. The punishment will be more severe if the child is under 16.[175] This applies to the biological parents, as well as adopted or foster-parents, the cohabiting partner of the child`s father or mother, or the person who has been entrusted with the child's educational upbringing. Children up to 18 may be affected; if the child is under 16 a more severe penalty may be imposed.[176]

Prostitution is a criminal offence in Iceland. As regards children, a person may be criminally liable for "beguiling, encouraging or assisting a young person under the age of 18 to make his or her living from sexual promiscuity".[177] The same penalty, up to 4 years' imprisonment, may be imposed for "encouraging any person to leave or enter Iceland for the purpose of making his living from sexual promiscuity if the person concerned is under the age of 21 years or is unaware that this constitutes the purpose of the journey".[178] The protection of an individual's sexual integrity is in this case not limited to children, but also to a person who is under the age of 21. Iceland has taken a different approach to prostitution from Swden. Prostitution is, in itself, not criminalized, but those who buy or supply such acts are criminally liable. The reason for not criminalizing prostitution is so as not to criminalize the woman or man, or girl or boy, who may have entered into prostitution for various reasons such drug addiction, etc. The intention is thus to assist them away from prostitution. Child pornography is criminalised under with the Icelandic Penal Code. The provisions cover acts from producing, printing, importing, distributing and possessing such publications, pictures or other such items or films or other comparable representations of children.[179]

[174] Art. 198.
[175] Art. 200.
[176] Art 201.
[177] Art. 206.
[178] Art 206.
[179] Art. 210.

5.6. Sanctions

Under the Icelandic Penal Code, a child becomes criminally responsible at 15.The five Nordic countries, except Denmark, thus all impose the same of criminal responsibility. A difference when comparing with Sweden is the imposition of penalties on children between 15-18. In Iceland, the maximum term of imprisonment is 8 years, without taking into account provisions for conditional release. That is higher than in Sweden, where a sentence of imprisonment is generally commuted to closed care, which may not be longer than 4 years, but has no conditional release.

5.7. Criminal procedure

As in Sweden, the police force is authorized to take care of children under 16, although in Sweden it includes children of 16-18, in certain circumstances. This authorization exists when the child is found by the police in situations where his or her health or welfare is in serious danger. However, in such situations, the police are under a recognized obligation to take the child to his or her guardian or to the child welfare authorities if the police find it necessary, in Sweden.[180]

In accordance with the Icelandic Code of Criminal Procedure[181] the Child Welfare Committee has to be informed if there is a criminal investigation against a child under 16. The Committee may send a representative to be present during the questioning of the child. The trial may also be held *in camera* when the accused is under 18. Those children's rights are also guaranteed by the corresponding legislation in the other Nordic countries.

If a child has to appear as a witness, the judge must make a decision in each individual case, and the judge's decision should be based on the child's level of maturity in understanding the facts of the case. In addition, a child under 15should not take an oath, if he or she is giving evidence.

5.8. The Children`s Ombudsman

The first Ombudsman for Children in Iceland was appointed in 1995.[182] Like the corresponding Ombudsmen in the other Nordic countries, he or

[180] Police Act no. 90 13th June 1996 with amendments as made through to 14 April 2000. Chapter III sec. 18; the Swedish Police Act sec. 12.
[181] No. 19 of 1991.
[182] Act no. 83/1994.

she has to guard the rights and interests of the children in Iceland in both the public as well as the private sector. Furthermore, the Ombudsman should illuminate the interests of children in public discussions and present suggestions for improvements. The scope of the Icelandic Children's Ombudsman is similar to the other Nordic ones, although a study of the regulations upon which the office is established seems to show that the Icelandic Ombudsman may have the authority to go a bit further than his Nordic colleagues as he has free access to public or private entities where there might be children.

6. Norwegian Legislation

6.1. Nationality and Education

The provisions for Norwegian nationality are contained in the Act on Nationality from 2005. As in the other Nordic countries, Norwegian nationality is based on the principle of *Ius sanquinis*. It may also be obtained by application and notification.

The Act of Education of 1998 confirms the child's right to education. The Child's Ombudsman refers to the generally high standard of Norwegian schools in his 2009 report. Even so, the Ombudsman asks the UN Committee on Children's rights to make recommendations to the Norwegian state, with particular emphasis on four different topics concerning education. These are to assist and identify the problems and needs of pupils at an early stage; to improve the interaction of services for pupils with disabilities; to improve tuition in language for linguistic-minority pupils in order to achieve the requirements of the upper secondary school; and to impose effective measures to deter pupils from leaving school earlier than intended by the school..[183]

6.2. Parents' Responsibility

The custodian's responsibility is detailed in The Children and Parents Act, although society's responsibilities are also stipulated therein: the duty to rear the child in accordance with the Children Act and the Child Welfare

---

[183] The Child`s Ombudsman Supplementary Report to the UN Committee on the Rights of the Child 2009, p. 22.

Act, and the house in which the child should live.[184] Corporal punishment is forbidden: "The child must not be subjected to violence or in any other way be treated so as to harm or endanger his or her mental or physical health".[185] The child's right of access to the parents, even if they do not live together, is guaranteed.[186]

The question as to how to deal with the Act when any of the parties have connections to foreign countries, for instance, which legal system applies, is also dealt with.[187] The Act includes several of those rights of children which are to be found in the corresponding legislation of the other Nordic countries. For instance, there are provisions in cases where a parent with parental responsibility is accused of the manslaughter or murder of the other parent, in which case a provisional decision concerning parental responsibility may be taken by the court where the best interests of the child are the key issues.[188]

6.3. Responsibilities of Society

The rights of the child are also to be found in the Child Welfare Act. It deals in general with the welfare services of the child under 15. Measures based on the consent of the child may be maintained or replaced with other measures until he or she reaches the age of 23. The purposes of the Act are:

- to ensure that children and young persons who live in conditions that may be detrimental to their health and development receive the necessary assistance and care at the right time,
- to help ensure that children and young persons grow up in a secure environment.[189]

The municipal authorities are responsible for implementing the intentions of the Act.[190] The Act also provides the Board of Health Supervision and

---

[184] Chapter 5 and 8. Here may also be mentioned the Act relating to the recognition and enforcement of foreign decisions concerning custody of children etc. and on the return of children.
[185] Chapter 5 sec. 30.
[186] Chapter 6.
[187] Chapter 9.
[188] Chapter 7 sec. 60 a.
[189] Chapter 1 sec.1-1.
[190] Chapter 2-3.

an Expert Commission on Children, who act nationally[191]. The Commission's main task is to assess reports by experts that have been submitted in child welfare cases. The Act also includes two sections on unaccompanied minors who are refugees and asylum seekers.

When special measures are considered to be employed for a child, the Act for the best interest of the child specifies that a contact with an adult is of fundamental importance, and a care plan in which continuity is a priority:

> Decisive importance shall be attached to framing measures which are in the child's best interests. This includes attaching importance to giving the child a stable and good contact with adults and continuity in the care provided.[192]

The Act also includes provisions for placing the child in another home or institution with or without consent.[193] If circumstances warrant it, the child may be placed without the consent of either the parents or child if he or she has reached 15. The provisions for placement are:

(a) If there are serious deficiencies in the everyday care received by the child, or serious deficiencies in terms of the personal contact and security needed by a child of his or her age and development;
(b) If the parents fail to ensure that a child who is ill, disabled or in special need of assistance receives the treatment and training required;
(c) If the child is mistreated or subjected to other serious abuses at home;
(d) If it is highly probable that the child's health or development may be seriously harmed because the parents are unable to take adequate responsibility for the child.[194]

If the child's own behaviour warrants it, he or she may be placed in an institution without either the parents' consent or the child's consent if he or she has reached 15. This is if the child:

- has demonstrated serious behavioural problems
    - in the form of serious or repeated criminality

---

[191] Chapter 2 sec. 2-5.
[192] Chapter 4 sec. 4-1.
[193] Chapter 4.
[194] Chapter 4 sec. 4-12.

- in the form of persistent abuse of intoxicants or drugs, or
- in other ways.[195]

Like the corresponding legislation in the other Nordic countries, the content of the provisions may only be found by studying the cases of the courts. As mentioned above, this might contradict the principle of legality. It should be added that the provisions have to be tried in each individual case, and that the child's circumstances may vary from case to case. Still, in a decision about the care of a child, it is of fundamental importance that the principle of legality is applied, and that the child expresses his or her opinion concerning what constitutes his or her best interests. Although the scope of this right to an opinion is limited, this does not mean that it should be ignored. Consequently, as stated in Norwegian legislation, the authorities' primary intention should be care based on consent, with compulsory care the exception, and always with the emphasis on the best interests of the child. The social services do not deal with the enforcement of sanctions, and they are neither equipped nor authorized to do so. In those circumstances, compulsory care may only be enforced when there is a pronounced need for it.

To include voluntary care side by side with compulsory care in the same legislation, may have both advantages and disadvantages. In Sweden, they are presented in separate pieces of legislation in order to show that in one case we are dealing with care to which the parent(s) and young person over 15 had given their consent. The other legislation deals with compulsory care where careful attention has been paid very to not interfering with the child's integrity more than necessary (this legislative split did not come about in Sweden until 1985. In a suggestion presented by a government-appointed committee, those two, currently separate, bits of legislation should be combined. If such a bill were presented to parliament, one could note that the Swedish legislation would correspond to the Norwegian legislation in this area). The right of a child to be considered a party in a case is generally at 15. This may, however, be limited, for instance owing to the state of the child's development. The Acts states:

> A child may appear as a party in a case and exercise his or her rights as a party if he or she has reached the age of 15 and understands the subject matter of the case. The county social welfare board may grant a child under 15 years of age rights as a party in special cases. In a case

[195] Chapter 4 sec. 4-24.

concerning measures for children with behavioural problems, the child shall always be regarded as a party.[196]

Because of the incorporation of the Convention on the Rights of the Child into Norwegian law in 2003, the right of a child to express his or her views has been lowered from twelve to *7 years of age*. Even younger children must, on a case by case basis, be given an opportunity to state their opinion before decisions in cases that affect them.

In accordance with the Act of Child Welfare, legal counsel may be appointed.[197] The Act also provides a spokesperson for the child, in cases that are dealt with by the social welfare board.[198]

6.4. Criminalisation

In Norway, the age of consent for sexual intercourse is 16. This compares with 15 in Sweden and Denmark. According to the Norwegian Penal Code, a person who commits an act of indecency with a person under 16 is criminally responsible.[199] To this may be added criminal liability for acts of indecency with a person under 18 and "is subject to the offender's authority or supervision."[200]

With regard to child abuse, the Norwegian Penal Code states that "(a)ny person who commits or is accessory to another person's committing an act of indecency with a child under fourteen (14) years of age"[201] is criminally responsible, with a punishment not exceeding 10 years. If the offence was sexual intercourse, the punishment may not be less than a year's imprisonment. If the child is under 10 a sentence not exceeding 21 years may be imposed. If the accused was mistaken about the child's age, this would still not exclude criminal liability. With respect to acts of indecency, if the accused and the victim are approximately the same age and development it might in general be considered as a mitigating circumstance, and only incur a sentence below a stated minimum; and

[196] Chapter 6 sec. 6-4.
[197] Chapter 7 sec. 7-8.
[198] Chapter 7 sec. 7-9.
[199] Sec. 196.
[200] Sec. 197.
[201] Sec. 195.

there may not even be any penalty if "those who have committed the act of indecency marry each other".[202]

The Norwegian Penal Code includes provisions for when criminal liability may be enforced, for the protection of a child in an institution for which the child welfare authorities are responsible. Such is the case when a person commits an act of indecency with a person who is an inmate of such an institution.[203] Criminal liability is also imposed on a "person who commits or is accessory to another person's committing an act of indecency with a foster-child, child in his care, step-child, or any person under eighteen (18) years of age who is under his care or subject to his authority or supervision ...".[204] The criminal liability in those cases includes a "person who aids or abets another person to commit"[205] such an offence.

The Norwegian Penal Code also deals with the crimes of child prostitution and child pornography. The Code particularly protects children under 16 who are the victims of child pornography.[206]

6.5. Sanctions

As in the other Nordic Countries, a child becomes criminally responsible at 15. For those under 15, the Child Welfare Act includes measures that may be imposed with or without the consent of the parents in the case of serious or repeated criminality.

6.6. Criminal Procedure

The Norwegian Criminal Procedure Act provides the condition for a trial, its subjects and judges. Like the other Nordic countries Norway has not established any court specifically catering for juvenile delinquents.[207]

---

[202] Sec. 214.
[203] Sec. 199.
[204] Sec. 209.
[205] Sec. 209.
[206] Sec. 206 and 211- 212.
[207] See chapter on Children and Crime.

6.7. The Children's Ombudsman

Norway was the first country in the world to establish the Ombudsman of Children`s Rights. In 1981, the Norwegian parliament passed the Act on a Commissioner for Children on the provisions of which the institution has been based and developed. The Ombudsman has an Advisory Panel consisting of 8 members, and is, as in the other Nordic countries, an independent entity tasked with protecting the interests of children and young persons by taking part in public discussions, but also by informing the public and the private sector of the rights of the child. He takes an active part in the state`s obligation to report to the UN Committee on the Rights of the Child by adding a supplementary report. The Norwegian Ombudsman is not authorized to decide in individual cases, to change a decision taken by an administrative authority or to be involved in a court case.

7. Conclusion

The study of the legislation of the Nordic countries proves that they have quite a number of provisions which deal exclusively with the rights of children. Although the quality of the rules may vary from one Nordic country to another, the chief aim of Nordic countries is to protect the rights of children from any form of violation. The examination also reveals that the appropriate expression of the consent of the child in certain matters has a very significant function for the delivery of judgments. Different policies have been made regarding the participation of the view of the child. A child may express his or her views when he or she is only 7 in Norway, and the protection of the rights of the child may even be extended up to 23 in the same country. Whilst, it is true that the other Nordic countries do not have the same age policy with respect to children, it is a fact that they have, more or less, similar policies to protect children's rights.

Some of the problems of the Nordic countries stem from the implementation of the provisions of the Convention of the Rights of the Child, and others from the misinterpretation of the rules of law by the judicial and political authorities. Another serious problem has been the very late integration of the provisions of the Convention on the Rights of the Child into the legislation of some of the Nordic countries. This means that, in practice, development has been hindered or been rather slow, and consequently has not been modernized as it should have been owing to the provisions of a number of international conventions dealing, in one way or another, with the protection of the rights of children. A serious legal problem in the Nordic countries is that all three powers—the legislature, the executive and the judiciary—are obviously hampered by heavy bureaucracy, making the development and consolidation of the protection of the rights of children to a high international standard very difficult. For instance, the Nordic countries should realize that although education of children is one of the main keys to protecting of the rights of children and their future development and success, it is not a child's only need. They are to be protected not only by the philosophy of the law but also by the actual practice of domestic authorities, court procedures, and the decisions of the various supreme courts. This is because we can still practically see that a considerable number of children's rights have in practice been ignored or violated by the Finnish, Danish, Norwegian or Swedish courts. Some of these violations have been reported to the European Court, where the complaints take time and which makes, in turn, the reestablishment of those rights difficult, and sometimes completely impossible, when a child has possibly been suffering for a long time from unjustified acts by of organs of the state.

THE OTTOMAN STATE AND RELIGIOUS EDUCATION FOR A MAJORITY POPULATION: A SEARCH FOR THE BEST INTERESTS OF THE CHILD

FATIH ÖZTÜRK*

> "The West for its part has stubbornly refused to call the Ottoman Empire by its name instead labeling this multi- religious, multi-lingual, multi-ethnic polity as "Turkey" and its rulers "Turks." ...Even the republic of Turkey approaches its Ottoman past with ambivalence. The Turkey of Mustafa Kemal Ataturk and his successors were to be a nation-state in the European mold... It is, however, unacceptable to pass judgment on the Ottoman past and its possible influence on the present without a fair historical trial."[1]

Abstract

The Ottoman Empire conducted religious education in an inspiring manner with respect to Muslims, non-Muslims, or majority and minority populations. The Ottoman State and its pluralistic social decisions can therefore be remembered today with pride. The object here is to look at Ottoman society and the legal system within its territorial sovereignty with an analytical focus on the education system of the Empire for the Muslim majority and its enveloping populations. It is well known that the Ottoman rulers were principally religious believers, and that they adhered strictly to Islamic jurisprudence and its inspirations. However, the Ottoman state was

---

* I would like to express my sincere appreciations to Siobhan Mullally, professor of law at University College Cork in Ireland, for giving me the opportunity to do this study through her advice and encouragement.

[1] See L. Carl Brown, "The Setting: An Introduction" in *Imperial Legacy: The Ottoman Imprint on the Balkans and the Middle East*, ed. L. Carl Brown, (NY, CUP, 1996) at 5-6, a rare book in the academic world written in an objective manner. Quite frankly, I think objectivity here is impossible

one of the first secular states in terms of its modern style liberal democracy. In addition, the application of its method of religious-based education is still useful in contemporary liberal democracies. For this reason, the author believes that the requisite of a powerful civil society, a secular legal system and implementation of religious education should be encouraged within the social and scientific spheres. The aforementioned principles, pervading the period of Ottoman rule, seem indispensable in terms of the best interests of the child. This article will challenge conventional religious education and allusions as to what may be in the best interests of children in conjunction with concepts of the rights of minority groups (that is to say, non-Muslims).

1. Background Formation

1.1. Ottoman Society

1.1.1.The Dimensions of Religion

The Ottoman Empire was one of the world's longest lasting empires. Enduring for 622 years, from 1299 to 1923, it is arguably unrivalled in the modern era. The Ottoman State was predominantly governed by Islamic law, or the Hanefi school of thought.[2] Its dominion spread over three continents: Europe, Africa, and Asia. Following its collapse, the Turks established a Republic in 1923 based on a unitary nation state.

Islamic law does not segregate citizens based on their race, nationality, ethnicity or religious beliefs. There are, however, two distinctions in terms

[2] The western world must take Islamic law at face value and from scientific sources, not from CNN, BBC or Orientalists' perspectives. An original interpretation of Islam does not allow for the establishment of a religious autocratic state or group like Iran's Mullahs. An eminent religious scholar of Turkey stated in 2005 that 95 % of the Islamic commandments were related to individual duty, the remaining related to the state. For a comprehensive study of Islamic international law, international criminal law and human rights of citizens see Farhad Malekian, Principles of Islamic International Criminal Law (Brill, 2011). See also Farhad Malekian, The Homogeneity of International Criminal Court with Islamic Jurisprudence, 9 International Criminal Law Review (Martinus Nijhoff Publishers, 2009), pp.595-621.
See Interview with Mehmet Gündem, "Should the State Be an Objective for a Muslim?" online, http://www.fgulen.org/a.page/press/interview/interview.with.mehmet.gundem.of.milliyet.d... (accessed on January 30, 2005). A Turkish interview printed in Milliyet Newspaper in January of 2005.

of citizenship under Islamic law: rra'iyye and teb'a, or Muslim and non-Muslim. The distinction is not intended to establish any differences between Muslim and non-Muslim rights.[3] Everyone is still equal before the law. The Ottoman State crafted citizenship as nufus-i muslime (Muslim population) and nufus-i gayrimuslime (non-Muslim population) as a mere nominal distinction. This may be interpreted the way in which the Ottoman State could fully identify the traditional and legal integrity of the minority population.

As is commonly known among Turkish people, the original Turkish mainland was Middle Asia. The Ottoman Turks, as a state, first appeared in Anatolia. The first peoples of the Ottoman, such as villagers, came to Anatolia following their own traditions and settled in villages as farmers, while urbanites settled in the cities.[4] Classes of society in the Ottoman era were established according to an individual's occupation, religious background, and whether or not they lived in urban or rural areas. Many Ottoman historians have recorded that no group in society would enjoy distinction of any kind over another.[5] Moreover, there were no class barriers such as those existing in the western world.[6] People were appointed to their administrative positions because they had shown themselves worthy or capable of doing the particular job.[7] In other words, a fairly established meritocracy prevailed. None, except the Sultans, had a genealogical line of aristocracy[8], and it was easy to move from one class to another.[9] Thus, each individual in Ottoman society had equal opportunity to be treated with respect and become employed by the state.

Incidentally, during the Ottoman era social class was determined more or less by an individual's profession.[10] There were two main social classes in

---

[3] See Ahmet Akgündüz & Halil Cin, *Türk Hukuk Tarihi (Ozel Hukuk), Cilt II* (*Turkish Legal History* (*Private Law*), *Volume II* (Istanbul, Osmanli, 1996) at 332.
[4] See Fuat Köprülü, *Osmanli Devleti'nin Kuruluşu* (*Foundation of the Ottoman State*) (Istanbul, 1959) at 51.
[5] See Ziya Kazıcı, *Osmanli'da Toplum Yapisi* (*Structure of the Ottoman Society*) (Istanbul, Bilge, 2003) at 15. Professor Kazıcı, a theologian professor at Marmara University in Istanbul.
[6] *Id*, at 12.
[7] *Id*, at 16.
[8] *Id*.
[9] See Ogier Ghiselin de Busbecq, Turkiye'yi Boyle Gordum (I saw Turkey like this), translation of Aysel Kurutluoglu (Istanbul, Tercuman 1001 Temel Eser, undated) at 64.
[10] See Kazıcı, *supra note* 4, at 21.

a general sense: governors (*askeri*) and the governed or rural people (*reaya*). Anyone who worked for the state was integrated into the governor's class and was not required to pay any taxes. [11] In other words, they represented the state and were therefore exempt from income tax. There were also those who were known as "saray halki". These were palace members who lived with the Sultans; the "ilmiyye", or scientists, the seyfiyye, or military personnel, and the kalemiyye, administrative and civil personnel who worked under State authority.[12] The governed (ruled) classes were urban, rural, and nomadic people.[13]

1.1.2. Social Classes

In the Ottoman system, unlike in the west, there were no social class differences. A good illustration of this is how the Ottomans distributed land among its citizenry. Land was redistributed to the *reaya*, or rural people, almost as quickly as it was appropriated.[14] Moreover, the state had the task of distributing food and shelter to those living in poverty, and this practice tended to invoke voluntary submission to Ottoman rule - which in turn contributed to the legal and political stability of the Empire.[15]

The State also provided new lands to its military personnel to be cultivated on behalf of the State.[16] This was called the *timar system*. To have a *timar*

---

[11] *Id.*

[12] See Kazıcı, *supra note* 4, at 23.

[13] See Gül Akyılmaz, "Osmanlı Devleti'nde Reaya Kavramı ve Devlet Reaya İlişkileri" (The Concept of Reaya and State -Reaya Relationship in the Ottoman State), IV Osmanli (1999) at 41.

[14] The *Tımar System* was inherited and developed from pre-Ottoman Turkish and Muslim states. See footnote 22. Around the 14th century, with the establishment of the Ottoman state, the *Timar system* was crafted. The system broke down around the 18th century due to loss of power by central government and its inability to catch up with the industrial revolution. See Erol Özbilgen, *Bütün Yönleriyle Osmanlı: Adab-ı Osmaniyye* (All Aspects of Ottomans: Rules of Ottoman) (Istanbul, Iz, 2007) at 772-75.

[15] See Necdet Sevinç, *Osmanlı'nın Yükselişi ve Çöküşü* (The Rise and fall of the Ottoman) (Istanbul, Birharf, 2005) at 76. Sevinç claims that the first collective bargaining agreement was signed between an employer and 24 employees in 1776, according to court records (Kütahya Şer'i Mahkeme Sicilleri). The contract came into effect with the approval of the Kütahya Judge (Kadi), at 241-2. Moreover, the author argues that it was a social care action to establish and protect a society which had no special status privileges.

[16] *Id*, at 77.

meant that military personnel demonstrating extraordinary bravery during military campaigns were given land and property rights from the State (or Sultan).[17] The State did, however, retain ownership of the land. The *timar* owners gave the land to villagers for cultivation, and at the end of the year collected 10 per cent of their earnings. In return, timar owners helped to fund the state's military forces from their profits.[18]

Timar owners also oversaw the land for the State. Unlike a feudal system, the *timar system* was one where the government gave land to citizens, *reaya*, in return for compensatory employment, despite ownership remaining with the state. In the feudal system there existed the relationship between the lord and the serf, or owner and slave, in which land only belonged to lords.[19] Needless to say, the distinction clearly illustrates that the life of a common citizen under the Ottoman system was much more desirable for anyone who valued freedom. *Timar* owners did not have any rights over villagers, aside from their supervisory role with regards to the economics and management of the property. Any disputes between the timar and citizens employed therein would go directly before the courts. Timar owners even had to establish basic facilities and utilities for the property under their management.[20]

As a result, profits made by these *timar sahibi* (timar owners) could be used to eventually purchase the land - or the Sultan could donate it to the *timar sahibi*.[21] Moreover, if villagers cultivated the land for at least three years, they automatically obtained property rights over the cultivated areas.[22] Thus, the practice led to a productive cycle of timar owners operating new lands on behalf of the State, providing for military personnel expenditures, and consequently securing stability and responsibility in such territories.[23] Conversely, in a feudal system, the class of bourgeoisie was created by the state. The serf was never able to progress to anything beyond a peasant, while the lord was always the proprietor of

[17] *Id*, at 79.
[18] *Id*.
[19] See Ziya Kazıcı, *Islam Tarihi: Osmanlı Devleti ve Medeniyeti* (History of Islam: The Civilization and State of the Ottoman) (Istanbul, Bilge, 1995) at 408-16.
[20] See Sevinç, *supra note* 14, at 83.
[21] In doctrine, these lands were also called "military tax farms." See Mehmed Fuad Köprülü, *Some Observations on the Influence of Byzantine Institutions on Ottoman Institutions*, (Ankara, TTK, 1999) at
[22] See Sevinç, *supra note* 14, at 81.
[23] See Köprülü, *supra note* 20.

land or property. The analogy demonstrates that many fewer disputes occurred in the Ottoman system between common citizens and statesmen, when compared to a feudal system.

This is not to say that the timar did not have their fair share of disagreements with superiors of the state[24], though latter fact seems to be irrelevant within the Ottoman system since there were regulations to ensure against any abuse of power by the timar.[25]

1.2.3. Family Relationships

Understanding family relationships during the Ottoman era is imperative to fully graspig the social effects of the Ottoman brand of administration. Religious education and interests obviously derive primarily from the home environment, and have an influence on the social development of the child. The Qur'an constituting the main source of Islamic law, or *Shari'ah*, places great value on the mother and father, and is the main reason that Ottoman Turks developed a considerable number of social rules to provide stability to family relationships.[26] As Sura Isra (Sons of Israel), verse 23 states, for example:

> "Thy Lord hath decreed, that ye worship none save Him, and (that ye show) kindness to parents. If one of them or both of them attain old age with thee, say not "Fie" unto them nor repulse them, but speak unto them a gracious word."

---

[24] See general Kazıcı, *supra note* 4, at 9-18.
[25] See Sevinç, *supra note* 14, at 84-5.
[26] See Kazıcı, *supra note* 4, at 178. Professor Kazıcı notes that in the past there never existed any old age homes or retirement residences in a Muslim Turkish society; today's Turkish society does, however, have established old age homes. Moreover, seniors are highly respected, regarded among society members as tradition continuers, as such elder ladies or men, are referred to as aunt or uncle.
See Ilber Ortaylı, *Osmanlıyı Yeniden Kesfetmek* (Re-exploration of the Ottomans) (Istanbul, Timaş, 2006) at p. 44 Professor Ortayl currently works at Galatasaray University in Istanbul. Galatasaray High School language of instruction is French and is affiliated with France and has represented the French Ecole in Turkey.
-See more about Galatasaray High School and its influence on Turkish intelligence, Niyazi Berkes, *The Development of Secularism in Turkey*, (NY, Routledge, 1998). This book was originally published in Canada in 1963 by McGill University. Niyazi Berkes (1908-1988) was a leftist Turkish intellectual who escaped from Turkey after the 1960 military *coup d'état* and began to reside in Canada. He never returned to live in Turkey. His book is still considered the best in its field. See, Berkes, New Introduction by Feroz Ahmad, at XV-XXXIII.

Although men were the head of their household, women were to be deeply respected and protected at all times.[27] Unfortunately, however, not unlike today, women were not thought of as critical thinkers. [28] Most of countries in the world saw women as inferior, perhaps a consequence or outcome of social systems, cultural mistreatment, irrational judgment, or as a demonstration of power of male over female. To quote the Islamic Prophet, "your best (men) are those who take care of their wives in the best possible way."[29]

Interestingly, Professor Kazici notes that many Turkish historians found that during the Ottoman period polygamy was very rarely practiced because Ottoman society was opposed to this style of marriage, even though Islamic law permitted it occurrence.[30] Indeed, comparative analysis of contemporary Turkish society demonstrates that it is nearly impossible to find polygamous marriages. In former Turkish states, prior to the wide acceptance of Islam, many women held positions as governors and some even served as military officials.[31] Following the broader recognition of Islam during fourteenth century, women mostly obtained positions in civil society or became the lady of the house and the substantive part of household policy.[32] Even though religion was important to the Ottomans, many facets of Ottoman life did not involve religion in any noticeable fashion.[33] The reason was simply that the Ottomans were truly dedicated to secularism. In their private lives they were religious, but were quite

---

[27] See Kazıcı, *id*, at 179.
[28] See Ortaylı, *supra note* 25, at 37.
[29] See Kazıcı, *supra note* 4, at 179.
[30] *Id*, at 181.
[31] See Kazıcı, *supra note* 4, at 181-2. During the Ottoman era, after the 1839 Tanzimat Reforms, women began to appear in social life after taking on jobs as teachers in schools. Their roles began to change in the family as well. See Ortaylı, *supra note* 25, 42.
[32] See Kazıcı, *supra note* 4, at 181-2. The general rule was that guardianship of a child was under parental authority. If they were not available, a judge would appoint a guardian for the child. Sometimes, the courts handled this duty. Of course, there were children left on the streets, and the state appointed these children to woman from respectable families, who in turn were paid for this service. See Ortayli, *supra note* 25, at 43.
[33] See William Ochsenwald, "Islam and the Ottoman Legacy in the Modern Middle East" in *Imperial Legacy: The Ottoman Imprint on the Balkans and the Middle East*, ed. L. Carl Brown, (NY, CUP, 1996) at 267. If there was divorce, Ottoman Judges gave guardianship of daughters to their mothers.
See Ortaylı, *supra note* 25, 38.

averse to establishing public or political achievements based on the theory of religious experience.

2. The Ottoman Legal System

2.1. The Principle of Justice

In the Ottoman era, the primary relationship between the state and its people was based on principles of justice (adalet).[34] The Ottoman legal system was defined by hierarchies of codes and justice according to Sharia Law. [35] Everyone in the country, including the Sultans, was subject to the law.[36] Here, the Ottoman legal system "in practice…clearly, distinguished the state and religion, dealing with issues that concerned political power and administration independently from religion."[37] Even before the introduction of French secular practices (see below), the Ottomans clearly exercised the separation of mosque and state. During the Ottoman era, with a few exceptions of state suppression caused by the Shia movements, there were no sect uprisings in all the Turkish part of Europe. [38] Even in its early days, the Ottoman state believed one should "Render unto Caesar the things which are Caesar's; and unto God the things that are God's".

However, these hierarchies were not always adhered to in practice. The hierarchy in the Ottoman legal system was as follows: the Qur'an (God's Orders); Sunnah (the Prophet Mohammad's Orders and Practices); Ijma (Collective Decisions of Islamic Jurists and Scholars); Qiyas (jurisprudencial analogy); Orders of the Sultan that complied with Islamic law-Regulations of Islamic States; the Legal Codes of Newly Captured Lands that complied with Islamic law; Legal Customs that complied with Islamic law; Agreements with Foreign Governments, the Principle of Reciprocity in International law; Istihsan leaving a general rule and establishing an exceptional rule because of necessity); Istishab (if there is no absolute rule,

---

[34] See Özbilgen, *supra note* 13, at 117.

[35] Halil Cin & Ahmed Akgündüz, *Türk Hukuk Tarihi*, *Cilt I, Kamu Hukuku* (History of Turkish Law, Volume I, Public Law) (Istanbul, OAV, 1995) at 225.

[36] Id, at 226.

[37] See Halil Inalcık, "The Meaning of Legacy" in *Imperial Legacy: The Ottoman Imprint on the Balkans and the Middle East*, ed. L. Carl Brown, (NY, CUP, 1996) at 21.

[38] See Taha Akyol, *Osmanli'da ve Iran'da Mezhep ve Devlet* (Mezhep and State in the Ottoman and Iran) (Istanbul, Milliyet, 1999).

then it is permissible); and finally the Sharias of Prior Prophets.[39] Even with the myriad hierarchical structure of law, the Ottomans still introduced new and foreign laws into their society, often adopting the customs and values of other peoples while still maintaining Sunni philosophy.[40]

The Sunni jurisdiction of Islamic law makes no distinction regarding public and private law, as they are separated by rights bestowed by Allah (God) and basic human rights.[41] Current Islamic legal scholars claim that God's rights could pass for public law with basic human rights pertaining to private law.[42] When comparing the Islamic legal system with other systems of today, we see a similarity to Common law system of judge and jury. A Kadi (judge) describes and develops rules and cases and also looks over cases with a jury consisting of five or six trustworthy individuals from the local community.[43] Of the four main Sunni mezhebs (sects), the Hanefi school of thought was followed by the Ottoman Turks, as it was widely recognized at that time as the most rational and liberal.[44] This school greatly helped to rationalize the legal system, particularly in the field of criminal law where the state chose not to use capital punishment, and authorities preferred to compensate for damages or "blood money" (compensation to the victim's family). The Ottomans attempted to take on the role of a universal example of an infinitely diverse, yet harmonious, state.[45]

2.2. Customary Law

The Ottomans adopted customary law, which greatly influenced and shaped its legal system, adopting the practice largely from Ottomans living

---

[39]See Özbilgen, *supra note* 13, at 117. See more Cin & Akgündüz, *supra note* 35, at 159-64. See Mehmet Erdoğan, Fıkıh ve Hukuk Terimleri Sözlüğü (Dictionary of Terminology of Islamic Law and Law) (Istanbul, Ragbet, 1998).

[40] However, it should be stated here that Turkish is a secular state and no religion has priority over another.

[41] *Id*, at 118.

[42] *Id*.

[43] See Sevinç, *supra note* 14, at 93.

[44] See Özbilgen, *supra note* 13, at 122.

[45] See Ilber Ortaylı, *Üç Kıtada Osmanlılar* (Ottomans on Three Continents) (Istanbul, Timas, 2007) at 113. Professor Ortayli claims that the Ottoman was one of the three greatest empires in the region of the Mediterranean and the latest universal one. See general, Ilber Ortaylı, *Son İmparatorluk Osmanlı* (The Last Empire Ottoman) (Istanbul, Timaş, 2006).

in other Islamic societies or states.[46] This is another example of how the Ottoman state attempted to became more multi-ethnic, multi-lingual, and multi-religious: proving itself a state rather than an empire. If newly subsumed countries or land had no legal contradiction in their practices to Islamic law, the Ottoman rulers not only permitted but made these practices new codes of the entire state.[47] Again, this policy of the Ottoman state was one of the primary reasons why new citizens of the state acquiesced to the authority of their new rulers. Individuals who were subsumed by another society could hardly be disappointed by being able to keep up their traditions, whilst gaining some security and diversity. In practice, the orders of the Ottoman Sultan were limited by Sharia law or the customs of peoples.[48] There are even instances in which some customary laws were in opposition to Islamic law, but were still enacted by the Ottomans as the local rule.[49] The Ottoman authorities weren't religiously motivated.[50] Famous Ottoman historians Stanford Shaw, Ira Lapidus, and Professor Halil Inalcik have stated in a considerable number of writings that this concession to customary practices exhibits the genuinely secular nature of the Ottoman state.[51] In contrast, Akgunduz asserts that Sharia law permitted the Sultan (Ulul-Emr, head of the state) to adopt laws, and that all laws were indeed made to comply with the Sharia.[52]

This counterclaim, however, clearly overlooks the Devsirme system. This was a system that permitted many non-Muslims to access high bureaucratic and administrative positions, those beneath only the Sultans themselves. This is a clear evolution of classical Islamic law, where high

---

[46] During the Ottoman era, judges went through a three stage procedure to pass as candidate judge. After finishing medrese, their first duty was to be a consultant and answer people's questions, second, he had to teach at a medrese and finally if he was successful on these two duties he might be able to become a judge. See Ortayli, *supra note* 25, 128. A judge also had power over all officials within his own area. Moreover, judges were routinely supervised by higher judges. *Id*, 128-9.

[47] See Cin & Akgündüz, *supra note* 35, at 166-70.

[48] Id, at 197-8. See also Özbilgen, *supra note* 13, at 123.

[49] See Akyol, *supra note* 38, at 151.

[50] *Id.*

[51] See Stanford Shaw, *History of the Ottoman Empire and Modern Turkey,* Volume I, (Cambridge, CUP, 1987) at 134. Ira Lapidus, *A History of Islamic Societies*, (Cambridge, CUP, 1988) 319. Halil Inalcik, The Middle East and the Balkans under the Ottoman Emire, (Bloomington, 1987) at 86.

[52] See Ahmet Akgündüz, *Osmanlı Kanunnameleri ve Hukuk Tahlilleri* (Legal Rules of the Ottomans and Legal Analysis), Volume I (Istanbul, Fey, 1990) at 60.

state positions were granted only to Muslim citizens. This was also a demonstration of the fact that a liberal sense of diversity prevailed over all religious interpretation of governance under Ottoman rule.

Since its inception, the Ottoman state had all newly acquired customs and legislation registered by a state official (the Nisanci).[53] This person was the state's highest ranking legal adviser, to who even the Seyhul-Islam, or executive state clergy, came for interpretation.[54] Registrars wrote legal documents after discussions held between legal and religious scholars following the approval of the Sultan. And even decrees of the Sultan were overturned from time to time, so that this kind of amendment was deemed to attain greater societal trust in the legal system.[55] Even during the fourteenth century, the legal system was advancing far ahead of its time. It is worth noting, for instance, that Sultans did not overturn court verdicts.[56] Moreover, governors had no jurisdiction over judges appointed by the Sultan's ministry.[57] This made the Ottoman justice system independent of what are often intrusive elements, in any system, in the legislature and executive. The Ottoman political system, in actuality, closely resembled that of the modern United States. Also, much like today, judges, defendants and offenders were able to call expert witnesses.[58] One of the most important aspects of the Ottoman system was that sentences could not be passed down without the order of a judge[59], extremely rare at that time. In addition, if during trial one of the parties provided new evidence, the judge needed to review the case, any one party could apply to the Divan-i Human (the state's main council - located in the capital), where experienced higher court judges could examine the case.[60]

Also, in modern fashion, the Ottoman legal system permitted each party involved in a case to convene with a legal scholar prior to any decision to go to trial, which usually helped parties resolve their differences without

---

[53] See Özbilgen, *supra note* 13, at 108.
[54] See Akyol, *supra note* 38, at 150.
[55] See Özbilgen, *supra note* 13, at 127-8.
[56] See Halil Inalcık, *Turkey and Europe in History* (Istanbul, Eren, 2006) at 64.
[57] *Id.*
[58] See Sevinç, *supra note* 14, at 93-4.
[59] See Cin & Akgündüz, *supra note* 35, at 270-1. See Ozbilgen, *supra note* 13, at 219.
[60] See Özbilgen, *supra note* 13, at 183. See also Cin & Akgündüz, *supra note* 35, at 239-40.

going to court.[61] These particular intricacies could easily be seen to have developed from the diversity of custom integrated into the Ottoman legal system from the various different peoples subsumed therein.

2.3. Religious Education for a Majority Population: A Search for the Best Interests of the Child

In the Ottoman era, there was a clear relationship between the education system, religion, the majority population, and what was deemed to be in the best interests of children, all of which will be explored in this section. Ottoman Turks were not only provided with religious education for their children, but with an education system that integrated religion into studies of the natural and social sciences. This Ottoman practice could easily be a model for contemporary societies that struggle with competing interests in the education system.

2.3.1. The Education System of the Ottoman State

Throughout Ottoman society there was enough wealth to support extra schooling, or kindergarten education and medreses (institutions for private schooling from elementary school to university).[62] "Waqfs" (non-profit organizations), played an important role in society, and especially in education. So much so that pious Muslims were able to establish and maintain schools, mosques, hospitals, foundations, and other public institutions aimed at keeping societal standards at a high level.[63] Every school was equipped with resources for all course studies, ranging from science and technology, mathematics and logic, to arts and literature, philosophy and the social sciences.[64] Well-known medreses placed greater

---

[61] *Id*, at 223

[62] See Joseph S. Szyliowicz, "The Ottoman Educational Legacy: Myth or Reality" in *Imperial Legacy: The Ottoman Imprint on the Balkans and the Middle East*, ed. L. Carl Brown, (NY, CUP, 1996) at 289. See more for parallel info Ozbilgen, *supra note* 14, at 302. See Sevince, *supra note* 13, at 131-8. See Kazici, *supra note* 4, at 63-4.

[63] *Id*. Many Ottoman historians claim that the Ottoman was a waqf civilization. See Kazici, *supra note* 4, at 11-18.

[64] See Ziya Kazıcı, *Osmanli'da Eğitim Öğretim* (Education and Training in the Ottoman) (Istanbul, Bilge, 2004) at 79. Professor Kazıcı stresses that Ottoman schools (medreses) not only provided religious education but also science, social sciences, arts, mathematics, logic and philosophy.

emphasis on religion, but provided apt science, mathematics, logic, philosophy and literature courses.[65]

With very few exceptions, almost no schools provided a solely religious education.[66] Additionally, people were able to attend religious education courses and training in mosques, tekkes (large dervish (one who follows Sufi orders) lodges) and zaviyes (small dervish lodges) whenever they wanted.[67] There were different categories of schools within the Ottoman system: sibyan mektebi, kalem ögretimi, medreses, military schools, and enderun (see below). The Ottoman child had the chance to receive the best education under favourable conditions, starting at an early age.

Sibyan Mektebi (kindergartens): from an early age, children received the best education at these institutions. Most of these schools were established next to mosques, medreses, or almshouses opened by Sultans, governors or philanthropists.[68] Education offered an all year round resource, as schooling was continuous, holidays being distributed regularly throughout the year, with no long breaks as in modern school systems. Children were aged between four and seven, taught to read and write in the Ottoman language, memorized verses from the Qur'an, and were taught basic religious principles and theory, etiquette, and basic arithmetic.[69]

Kalem Öğretimi (technical schools): like today's institutions, these schools taught art, literature, occupational skills, and trades for specific vocations.[70] Moreover, there was the ahi teskilati (a trade guild), which required that those who were to proceed with a specific vocation be registered, trained and certified to carry out the job by professionals in the field.[71] Such individuals would first have to serve as apprentices, and then

---

[65] *Id.*

[66] *Id*, at 130-7.

[67] See İnalcık, *supra note* 37, at 51-2. Özbilgen, *supra note* 13, at 304-5. Kazıcı, *supra note* 4, 119-23.

[68] See Özbilgen, *supra note* 13, at 303.

[69] *Id.* Teachers of these schools had to complete many courses such as literature, logic, astronomy, theology formation and pedagogical courses due to orders of Sultan Fatih (Mehmed II) . See Sevince, *supra note* 14, at 139.

[70] See Özbilgen, *supra note* 13, at 306.

[71] See M. Hidayet Vahapoğlu, *Osmanlıdan Günümüze Azınlık ve Yabancı Okullar* (From the Ottoman Era to Today: Minority and Foreign Schools) (Istanbul, MEB, 2005) at 86.

foremen, until a final progression to shop foreman.[72] Thus, the developing child had an opportunity to use their educational skills in specific trades.

Medreses: the Ottoman focus on education extends to medreses. These were open to the public, just as all other educational institutions were.[73] There was one in almost every municipality, and they were usually constructed near mosques[74], emphasizing the bond, seen as being in the best interests of the child, between religion and education. A child could enroll in a medrese following kindergarten studies. Medreses had many different levels, and their education extended up to university level.[75] At that stage, students were able to choose their instructors or professors.[76] This is unknown even in modern universities and colleges, and it gave a great deal of freedom to students, allowing them not only educational freedom of course study, but even to shape the face of the faculty, in a sense.

One can see the natural advantages of this, as instructors would have to be more worried about complacency and their own efficacy. There were five types of medreses: 1) darulkurra (teaching Qur'anic sciences); 2) darulhadis (teaching the Prophet Mohammed's preaching and practices); 3) darultip (teaching medicine with practicum in a hospital); 4) darulkudat (teaching law and training judges); and 5) medresetul eimmei vel huteba (training imams for mosques).[77] Moreover, there were other kinds of special medreses such as those for literature, mathematics, and sciences.[78] The child was ensured of receiving only the best forms of education in his/her interests and future prosperity.

---

[72] *Id.*
[73] *Id*, at 307.
[74] *Id.*
[75] See Kazıcı, *supra note* 63, at 106-7. Kazıcı informs that medreses provided education from middle school to PhD level. Without the fulfillment of medrese orders no one could become a professor.
[76] See Özbilgen, *supra note* 13, at 309.
[77] See Kazıcı, *supra note* 63, at 130-49.See also Özbilgen, *supra note* 13, at 311-2. After the 16th century some medreses became places for students who wished to be exempt from tax payment, and did not want to enroll in the military. See Inalcik, supra note 37, at 52. This issue was a very serious social problem especially in the closing years of the Ottoman state.
[78] See Vahapoğlu, *supra note* 70, at 84.

Military Schools: the military schools educated and trained their own soldiers and officers.[79]

Enderun: this was established in the Sultan's palace, great attention being given to children, so they were kept close to special locations and institutions. The state chose its students from medreses or the public, and graduates became executive governors of the state. For many years only devsirme (children adopted from non-Muslim families) were taken into this school,[80] again showing the best interests for each and every child regardless of status. But it took longer than in the regular schools. This school produced many non-Muslim (mainly Christian) sadrazam (prime ministers) for the Sultans.[81]

Because Jews had always lived in cities and not in rural areas, the Ottomans never took any of them into the devsirme system. The Ottomans were not anti-Semites; this was just the rule of the time. Most urban children, because of their social position, acquired their identity at around ten to fourteen, but not village boys. The state wanted to give these children identities: they wanted to make them military administrators and rulers because it was very hard to give new identities to urban children. The idea was that they would actively participate and be employed in different state organs.

The devsirme system was enforced once every two or three years when state officials went to villages to enroll a few thousand voluntary members, usually from poor families who supplied their sons. But if a family had only one son, the State would not accept him. And this was done voluntarily; no coercion was applied. Examinations were generally held to find the most suitable and capable boys. Most of these boys were intelligent and physically healthy, though children who were Christian or non-Muslim needed to be circumcised. In other words, these young boys were from different ethnic backgrounds and were to be taken seriously by their peers. In the Palace, they were to study a variety of courses including Islam, the arts, literature, philosophy, math, science, and perhaps also undergo military training. With the devsirme system, the Ottoman Turks were able to establish a social contract among different ethnic and religious groups and the adults; however, children were converted to

---

[79] See Kazıcı, *supra note* 4, at 71-4.
[80] See Ortaylı, *supra note* 25, at 27.
[81] *Id.* 28-34.

Islam. They were usually between 8 - 10 , but they might sometimes be as old as 20.

This was a clear illustration of a meritocracy being created, and through which the system showed that it did not set any great store by genealogy.[82] In other words, it was evident that "high standards of scholarship characterized the religious educational system and Palace schools (Enderun)", …as "they were producing elites of ability and vision.

2.3.2. Religious Education for a Majority (Muslim) Population and the Best Interests of the Child

Unfortunately, in modern Turkey, there are only a handful of references remaining to religious education during the classical Ottoman era (before 1839) or the era of leniency of state over education (and perhaps religion). The reason for this came with the establishment of the national republic in 1923 or, in 1928, with the replacing of the Ottoman Turkish script by a Latin-based one.

Here we should note that in the Ottoman era education consisted of two distinct periods: first in the classical era, which began with the establishment of the Ottoman state, and second, in the period beginning with the secularization that started with the Tanzimat Reforms of 1839.[83] Since these two periods, and their effect on youth, are quite distinct, it is important to consider them.

2.3.3. The Theory of Limitation of Age

Islamic law - for the Ottomans – identified children individually as male or female. Additionally, when a girl reached the age of nine she became an autonomous, or adult, member of society while boys enjoyed this legal status of autonomy at twelve. Mecelle, Article 986 (1878, the Ottoman Civil Law), confirms these classifications[84], which are repeated in the

---

[82] *Id*, at 176.

[83] Tanzimat means that re-characterization of the Ottoman Empire between 1839 - 1876, which ended with the First Constitutional Era. This is in fact a period of social and legal reform with the aim of creating equality between Turkish populations.

[84] Mecelle was a codification of Islamic law, during the Ottoman era from 1868-1878, and was prepared by Ahmed Cevdet Pasha. It consisted of 1851 provisions

1917 Osmanli Hukuk-i Aile Kanunnamesi (Ottoman Family Law).[85] Also, most Islamic scholars claimed that even if there were no physical signs of adolescence displayed by girls by the time they reached fifteen, they were automatically classified as an adult; though some Islamic scholars posited that should no physical attributes of pubescence be evident by age 18 such individuals should, nonetheless, be accepted as young adults which included girls and boys.[86]

This is obviously controversial from a contemporary perspective, as children at rather tender ages could hardly be seen as being capable of complete autonomy. These regulations, however, had a more psychological purpose—it gave young determined students the right to choose their educational paths and to defend themselves in a court of law if such a right was violated. It also granted them legal recognition to work as apprentices. The only downside was that with all the legal freedom, they were also free to opt out of education at a young age—though exercising this option was generally frowned upon by cultural conventions.[87] As stated, the autonomy referred to here is not exactly like that intended for an adult, but is a no less considerable freedom to a child compared even with their modern day counterparts from around the world. And though these children—aged 9-12, and both male and female—even possessed the right to marry, the desire or tendency was largely subdued by Ottoman culture as it was generally considered much too premature.

2.3.4. Remedies for Offences of the Child

One thing to keep in mind is that standards for adolescence vary greatly depending on one's geographical location, climate, upbringing, and other factors.[88] This was kept very much in mind when dealing with criminal offences committed by children, who were tried in accordance with their age, and their families made to compensate for their actions, though no prison sentences were meted out to children. Offences committed by

---

of private law. Until 1926 it was used in the Ottoman Sharia Courts and Republic Courts. See "Mecelle-i Ahkam-i Adliye" available at http://tr.wikipedia.org/wiki/Mecelle (accessed on November 15, 2007).

[85] See Celal Erbay, *İslam Hukukunda Küçüklerin Himayesi* (Safeguarding of Minors in Islamic Law) (Istanbul, Ragbet, 1998) at 6.

[86] See Orhan Çeker, *İslam Hukunda Çocuk* (Child in Islamic Law) (Istanbul, Kayihan, 1990) at 54.

[87] See general Kazıcı, *supra note* 63.

[88] See Erbay, *supra note* 84, at 6.

children were mainly remedied through community service, as may be seen in current civilizations, such as assistance in the community or the reading or studying of certain books and subjects. Nowadays, the world generally regards an eighteen-year-old as an adult. Another thing to remember here is that it was important in Islam that classification as an adult occurred in order that children might be able to begin to pray five times a day. The crossroads of the western and the Islamic interpretations of adolescence, then, are merely at opposite ends of the spectrum of adolescence, with the western world generally placing adulthood at the end, roughly by age 18, and Islam locating its inception at the beginning.[89]

2.3.5. Education of the Child

In Islamic constitutional law, education and training is a constitutional right.[90] Islamic law places responsibility on the state to provide economic and social protection for the child.[91] Moreover, provision of elementary education is mandatory.[92] We have already stated that a child had the right to choose whether she or he did or did not attend school. In Ottoman practice, elementary schools were conventionally left in the hands of the public; and society did not force children to go to elementary school even though Islamic law dictated it. A child did not need to have the permission of her or his parents to enroll in an educational institution.[93] Parents were not able to limit their choices, and the child's wishes could be supported in a court of law.[94]

For instance, a child who chose to study mainly in music or arts still had to study some mathematics and sciences. It was actually quite common for parents to spend a great deal of effort in attempting to discern the child's aptitudes and interests prior to enlisting them in a school – which often even involved bringing their children to professional counsellors.[95] This was primarily because even the Qur'an, stresses that parents ensure a child

---

[89] See M. Siraj Sait, "Islamic Perspectives on the Rights of the Child" in *Revisiting Children's Right: 10 Years of the UN Convention on the Rights of the Child*, ed. Deirdre Fottre (The Hague, Kluwer, 2000) at 42.
[90] See Erbay, *supra note* 84, at 53.
[91] See Sait, *supra note* 88, at 41.
[92] See Erbay, *supra note* 84, at 53.
[93] See Erbay, *supra note* 84, at 55.
[94] *Id*. Professor Erbay claims that according to Islamic law even married women may continue with their education even against their husband wishes.
[95] *Id*, at 54-5. See general Kazıcı, *supra note* 63.

pursue their own interests rather than their own.[96] This emphasis on the importance of the rights of the child even reared its head in divorce suits, as Sait notes, with significant consideration given in assigning guardianship based on which parent displayed a greater tendency to promote the child's interests.[97]

As we have seen, there was no mandatory elementary education during the classic Ottoman era (1299-1839) [98]. However, with the help of the Waqf system and its members the country expanded education across the empire. The state took care not to impede the Waqf system, as they deemed its efforts necessary, and its charity provided for the general welfare – almost like a private non-profit extension of government.[99] Many types of Waqfs existed as social welfare organizations: ones that took care of the physically and mentally challenged, ones that cared for orphaned children, and some that even performed environmental efforts such as caring for birds that had lost their way during migration.[100]

In the period of "the Tanzimat reforms", "the public role of Islam in Ottoman life began to be limited by a secularizing trend in the education of the governing elite". [101] However, following the reforms (after 1839), a western style of secularism in education, imposed by the Ottoman state, became widespread.[102] The French education system became the curriculum of choice.[103] Unfortunately, the Ottomans didn't really grasp how different the French system was. "Broadly speaking, state education during the Tanzimat had been more about imitating the best attributes of western European education, the French in particular".[104] In the Ottoman era, there had been no physical confrontations between religious sects, whereas in France and most of Europe there were many confrontations among religious sects such as those of the Thirty Years' War. The

---

[96] See Sait, *supra note* 88, at 42. See Surah Bakarah, versus 220.
[97] *Id*, at 46-7.
[98] See Rıza Kardaş, "Sosyal Değişme Yönüyle Tanzimat Öncesinde Eğitim ve Yenileşme Hareketleri" (Before the Tanzimat Era Education and Movements of Regenerations in terms of Social Change) 114 Turk Kulturu Dergisi (1972) at 370.
[99] See Vahapoğlu, *supra note* 70, at 79.
[100] See Ziya Kazıcı, *Osmanlı Vakıf Medeniyeti* (Waqf Civilization of Ottoman) (Istanbul, Bilge, 2003) especially under the introductory section.
[101] See Ochsenwald, *supra note* 32, at 263.
[102] See general, Niyazi Berkes, *supra note* 25.
[103] See Benjamin C. Fortna, "Islamic Morality in Late Ottoman "Secular" Schools", 32 Int. J. Middle East Stud. (2000) at 372.
[104] *Id*, at 375.

Europeans had come to the conclusion that religion should be kept separate from state affairs, but perhaps with more distaste for its inclusion due to its persistent tendency to cause serious conflict. In the west, the Church had always had a say in state affairs during the Middle Ages. The Ottomans, however, kept religion and state affairs separate from the outset, never allowing the mosque to nurture ideas about interfering I, or exerting control over, state affairs.

With the adoption of the Tanzimat reforms, the Ottoman intellectuals—perhaps a fear of falling into the conflict that might arise from religious tensions permeating throughout Europe—believed they too needed to eliminate religion from all spheres of life. They did this despite never having suffered any of the turmoil that the west had, perhaps not truly understanding that they had succeeded where the west had failed, and that it was perhaps not even necessary to undertake such a transformation. It also seemed to be a good idea as the Empire was slipping into decline and this seemed to be a way to hold on.

2.3.6. Intervention in the Education of the Child

Abdulhamid the Second made provision of elementary education mandatory as a safeguard of the progress and modernity of the Ottoman state.[105] This was a grand effort in the promotion of modernization by religious and state institutions.[106] It was also the beginning of an "educating state", or indoctrinating state, for the Turks.[107] However, one could claim that this was also the beginning of the end of civil society, and the start of state intervention in religion and education in the land of the Turks. Thus, the best interests of the child, regarding religious education, now became an asset of the state and not of families and children. The state now determined what the best education was for its citizens. Ottoman society was now facing an interventionist state, where once they had been the masters of their own fate. Amit Bein stresses a misconception about the Hamidian regime—the regime of Abdulhamid the Second—which is that the Sultan did not touch on issues of the medreses or the project of reforms and modernity. In fact, as Bein argues in his essay, one of the aims of the

[105] See Amit Bein, "Politics, Military Conscription, and Religious Education in the Late Ottoman Empire", 38 Int. J. Middle East Stud. (2006) at 283.
[106] *Id*, at 298.
[107] *Id*, at 298.

education policy of the Hamidian regime was the reform of medreses and modernizing them.[108]

By the the 1890s the Ottoman capital had many medreses, but the great majority of them were academically outdated.[109] During the 1880s and 1890s, the state school curriculum was in line with the secularist policies of the Tanzimat era, but it added a more Islamic morality.[110] However, this addition was never fully realized, because the new crop of elites, indoctrinated with the new French version of secularism, became strangers in their native country, [111] being unfamiliar with their Islamic background. For instance, some of this elite were ignorant about the basic Islamic fundamentals such as the praying of *Cuma*, which is performed in a mosque, not at home. [112] We could maintain that students were at that time integrated into units that were both traditional and modern, just as happens today.[113] Most believe that the western style of living, or "the idea of secularism, tended to be accepted only by members of educated elites and technocrats, while the masses of the population remained devoted to various traditional forms of Islam and were susceptible to mobilization by political groups calling for the defense of Islam."[114]

Schooling was officially divided as follows: elementary (mekteb-i iptidai—three years, and mekteb-i rusdiye—another three years); middle school (mekteb-i idadi—five years, and mekteb-i sultani—three years).[115] Aside from institutes of higher education, school provided lessons in art, literature, mathematics, history, geography, and other relevant subjects of the time which were taught alongside courses in religion.[116] Institutions of higher education were specialized, with military studies, medicine, and teachers' college.[117] "Nationalistic and secular-minded Turks, including scholars, chose either pre-Ottoman Turkish societies or western European

---

[108] *Id*, at 284.
[109] *Id*, at 286.
[110] See Fortna, *supra note* 102, at 18.
[111] *Id*, at 388.
[112] See more examples D. Mehmet Doğan, *Batılılaşma İhaneti* (The Westernazation and Betrayal) (Istanbul, Iz, 2001). Praying of *Cuma* generally refers to the act of praying together in a common religious house.
[113] See Fortna, *supra note* 102, at 30.
[114] See Ann Elizabeth Mayer, "Law and Religion in the Muslim Middle East", 35 Am. J. Comp. L. (1987) at 128.
[115] See Vahapoğlu, *supra note* 70, at 87.
[116] *Id*.
[117] *Id*, at 88.

models for the reconstruction of Anatolia following the devastation of World War I and the struggle for independence in 1919-1922".[118] And it must be added that a "majority of both secularizing modernizers and fundamentalist Muslims have still tended to deprecate the legacy of the Sunni Islamic experience in the late Empire for today's Middle East".[119] In the end, even with the Tanzimat Reforms and their aspirations of achieving something better, the Ottomans were not able to satisfy their own people, still the case in contemporary political spheres. A misdirected reliance upon the French secularist model is still deeply entrenched, while the state continues to indoctrinate its citizens with distorted and confused ideological and religious influences. However, one cannot ignore the fact that under the current political climate, there are certain tendencies in the Turkish society towards consolidation of Islamic rules.

3. Conclusions

To reiterate, the main principles of the Ottoman period that pervade time, and what appear to comprise—in this writer's opinion—an ideal model of an educational system integrating religion: the sustaining of an integrated multi-dimensional society, and an independent education system. Without the detachment of education from the state, institutions will never truly evolve their own academic goals. The benefits of a secular legal system are inherently obvious, particularly in widely diverse societies, as religion—all things being considered equal—is one of the elements justice should be blind to, particularly with regard to the eligibility of individuals for academic study. This would help to draw institutions away from deeper ideological strains and focus on more contemporary practical aims.

The classical era of Ottoman religious education could be a model for today's liberal democracies with a strong sense of society. The flexibility permitted by secular states could easily achieve these goals. The Ottoman state had practiced this model from the fourteenth to the nineteenth centuries, demonstrating that systems of this sort can be successful. We should remind ourselves here that the Ottoman Empire was not exclusively Muslim, and Turkish. Stressing the importance of people's customs, the Ottoman Turks successfully distanced politics from religion where it mattered, and society was still successfully shaped by Islam. In the

---

[118] See Ochsenwald, *supra note* 32, at 264. The intention was to be independent from the power of the Allies.
[119] *Id*, at 265.

classical era, the best interests of the child, an autonomous person, were understood, since a choice was allowed children early in their lives in terms of their educational path. This successful and beneficial Ottoman system unfortunately went astray when they started to question this system under external pressure, by mistakenly attempting to make corrections where there really was no flaw, and to compensate for the errors of other societies or nations for which a deep sense of regret is still evident today.

LEGISLATION IN JAPAN RELATING TO THE CHARACTERISTICS AND ISSUES OF THE PREVENTION OF CHILD ABUSE

KIYOE TAKATA

Abstract

This article aims to identify the characteristics and legal issues in current Japanese legislation for child abuse prevention and the protection of the child through our comparative research on existing legislation in other countries. Firstly, this article outlines the general structure of that legislation in Japan, and secondly, it identifies the characteristics of the child abuse prevention legislation in Japan through studies based on international comparisons, which are based on the findings from our joint research "Comprehensive research on the Abuse Prevention Law—Approaches from International Comparison and Interdisciplinary Studies", conducted from 2009. Thirdly, the article points out several legal issues in Japan, based on those comparative studies. As to the subject of the review, this article focuses on the legal institutions with regard to the early phases of public intervention, including the prevention, discovery, reporting of child abuse, and temporary protection.

1. Introduction

Child abuse by parents or guardians[1] has become a serious social problem in present-day Japan. The increase in the number of child abuse cases where action has been taken or those that have been reported; the increase in the number of serious cases—those involving death, and the increasing frequency of child abuse occurring in homes that need social

---

[1] The term "guardian" means "a person who has actual custody of a child, that is, a person who has parental authority, a guardian of a minor, or any other person" (Child Welfare Act, Article 6).

aid, have been pointed out. Based on those findings, early action and prevention on the basis of the Child Abuse Prevention Law have been emphasized. However, the qualitative and quantitative insufficiency of the consultation and support system, which is essential for an early response, has been raised.

This article attempts to highlight several legal problems in Child Abuse Prevention legislation in Japan, based on the findings through our joint research project "Comprehensive Research on the Abuse Prevention Law—Approaches from International Comparison and Interdisciplinary Studies", conducted from 2009 to 2011.[2] This project was conducted by more than ten researchers from various fields, including social law, public law, criminal law and legal medicine, etc. The scope of this comprehensive research includes different types of domestic violence and abuse: child abuse, violence from a spouse, and abuse of elderly family members; but the focus of this article is on child abuse. Owing to space limitations, however, this article is limited to the "early phases" of legal measures regarding to child abuse; prevention, discovery, reporting of abuse, and temporary/emergency protection.

This article is structured as follows: firstly, it shows the reality of child abuse, and the general outlines of Child Abuse Prevention Legislation, in Japan. Secondly, it identifies the characteristics of Child Abuse Prevention Legislation, through studies based on the outcome of international comparative studies by our research project. Thirdly, the article points out several legal issues in Japan.

2. Outline of the child abuse prevention legislation in Japan

2.1. Current State of Child Abuse in Japan

In recent years, the problem of child abuse by parents or guardians has become a serious social problem in Japan. According to the statistics

---

[2] Scientific research (B), research No.21330014, supported by Grants-in-Aid for Scientific Research from JSPS (Japan Society for the Promotion of Science). This paper is based on this research's interim report, *The issues of the Legislation on Family Abuse and Violence in Japan—based on the comparative research among ten countries* (May 2010).

published by the Ministry of Health, Labour and Welfare, approximately 43,000 cases of child abuse were reported during 2008. This is roughly 40 times the number of cases reported for 1990. In addition, a higher number of serious incidents that involved death due to child abuse have also been noted, and we have not yet seen a decline[3].

As a characteristic of child abuse occurrences, a considerable number of issues are becoming increasingly conducive and foreseeable, for example, more homes with combined issues of poverty, social isolation, medical problems, childcare anxieties, and domestic violence.[4] As regards the childcare environment of homes in which abuse has resulted in death, the *Death Case Review Result Report* submitted by the Child and Youth Committee of the Social Security Council points out, *inter alia*, some of the essential grounds for child abuse. These are 1) the notably high number of low-income households, 2) the high number of households with little or no contact with the community, and 3) the high number of cases where the career has emotional or psychological problems, such as depression, child-rearing anxieties, or child-rearing inability.

Under such circumstances, legal amendments with an emphasis on the prevention of child abuse—and in cases where child abuse is already present, the early discovery and action before such abuse against the child becomes critical—have recently been passed in Japan.[5]

2.2. General outline of the Child Abuse Prevention Legislation in Japan—Focus on Discovery, Reporting, and Temporary Protection

In principle, two pieces of legislation in Japan constitute the fundamental

---

[3] The Ministry of Health, Labour and Welfare (2009), *the number of cases corresponded by Child Guidance Center.* The number of reports and consultations of spousal violence has increased by 1.5 during the five years from 2004 to 2009.

[4] The Child and Youth Committee of Social Security Council (2008), *Summary documentation of the first to fourth review reports on death cases caused by child abuse.* According to the Child and Youth Committee's statistics, 52 cases of death from abuse, excluding cases of murder-suicide, were reported in 2006, which amounts to one case every week. Including murder-suicide cases, 100 cases were reported for the year.

[5] Amendment of Child Abuse Prevention Law by Act No. 30 of April 14, 2004 and Act No.73 of June 1, 2007.

legal measures for the protection of the child in the case of child abuse. The basic law regarding child welfare in Japan is the 1947 *Child Welfare Act*[6], protective measures for "an aid-requiring child" (Article 25).[7] And in 1999, *the Act of the Prevention, etc. of Child Abuse*[8] was enacted as a special law concerning abuse inflicted by parents or guardians.

2.2.1. The Child Abuse Prevention Law

Article 1 of the *Child Abuse Prevention Law* acknowledges that "child abuse grossly infringes upon the human rights of the child as well as inflicts serious impact on the child's physical and psychological development, and the formation of its personality, resulting in a concern for the growth of future generations in Japan". The Act also provides the definitions of child abuse[9], which are defined as physical abuse, sexual abuse, neglect, and psychological abuse that fall under the description of the subordinate clauses 1-4 among the actions of parents or guardians.[10]

---

[6] Act No. 164 of December 12, 1947

[7] Article 25 regulates that "A person who discovers an aid-requiring child shall give notification directly to a welfare office or child guidance centre established by the municipal or prefectural government, or to said welfare office or child guidance centre through a commissioned child welfare volunteer; provided, however, that this does not apply to a child of 14 years of age or more who has committed a crime. In this case, notification shall be given to the family court" (Child Welfare Act, Article 25).

[8] Act No. 82 of May 24, 2000; commonly known as *Child Abuse Prevention Law*.

[9] Article 2 of the Child Abuse Prevention Law.

[10] Article 2 of the Child Abuse Prevention Law defines "child abuse" as following; 1) to inflict violence that causes or may cause injury to the child's body; 2) to commit an obscene act on a minor or force the child to perform an obscene act; 3) extreme underfeeding that prevents the proper physical and mental growth of the child; long hours of neglect; to neglect or an act similar to those specified in the above two clauses and the subsequent clause committed by a cohabiter besides the parent(s) or guardian(s); and to neglect to perform other childcare to be provided by the parent(s) or guardian(s); 4) gross verbal abuse or gross rejection of the child; violence against a spouse in a household cohabited by a child (unlawful attack on the body of a spouse (includes those who have not submitted a marriage notification, but in a *de facto* committed relationship equivalent to marriage) that endangers the spouse's life or harms the spouse's body, or other pursuant behaviour that grossly harms the spouse physically and/or mentally); and other behavior that inflicts gross psychological trauma on the child.

The Act prohibits not only child abuse by parents or guardians, but also stipulates a general prohibition of child abuse[11]. The act also stipulates the responsibilities of the state and local governments, taking measures concerning the prevention, early discovery and other prevention-related matters regarding child abuse, the measures for protecting abused children and for supporting their self-sustainability[12].

In particular, this Act regulates those legal provisions concerning the procedures for rapid and secure child protection in the case of child abuse such as: the early discovery obligation of child-related organizations and workers[13]; a reporting obligation for all people who recognize a suspect of child abuse[14]; procedures to check and ensure the safety of child for prefectural or municipal government,[15] etc.

Article 5, for example, provides the early discovery obligation of organizations involved with the welfare of children, including schools, child welfare institutions, hospitals and other bodies, as well as individual professionals involved with child welfare, including school personnel, child welfare institution officers, physicians, public health nurses, and attorneys, who should recognize that their position allows for the easier discovery of child abuse, and that they should strive for the early discovery of child abuse. A person who discovers a case of suspected child abuse is obliged, under Article 6, to promptly report to the welfare office or child guidance centre established by the prefecture, or to the municipality. The obligation to report is not inhibited by the criminal code of unlawful disclosure of confidential information or any other ordained confidentiality obligations[16]. The administrative body receiving the report has the duty to take measures to check the security of the child. Within forty-eight hours, the administrative body must conduct a visual check, such as an interview with the child in question.

The provision regarding checking the security of child when child abuse has been reported was one of the parts of this act which were expanded

---

[11] Article 3 of the Child Abuse Prevention Law.
[12] Article 4 of the Child Abuse Prevention Law.
[13] Article 5 of the Child Abuse Prevention Law.
[14] Article 6 of the Child Abuse Prevention Law.
[15] Article8- of the Child Abuse Prevention Law.
[16] Paragraph 3 of Article 4 of the Child Abuse Prevention Law.

under the amendments to it in 2004[17] and 2007.[18] A prefectural governor has the authority to order officers of a child guidance centre to conduct an onsite investigation or questioning when the governor suspects the risk of child abuse; and under the 2007amendment, the prefectural governor was granted the authority to summon parents or guardians with the child [19]when a risk of child abuse is recognized. If the parents or guardians reject, inhibit or avoid an onsite investigation, or won't comply with the summons, the prefectural governor can issue another summons to confirm the safety of the child[20], and, based on a prior permit issued by a judge of the district court in which the jurisdiction of the child's address or residential address lies, can order an onsite inspection at the child's address or residence, or a search for the child in question[21]. If deemed necessary, the assistance of the chief of police under jurisdiction may be requested when conducting an onsite investigation or check on the child's security[22].

2.2.2. The Child Welfare Act

On the other hand, the *Child Welfare Act* offers protective legal measures for a child, such as care by foster parent(s), infant home or foster home, and the temporary/emergency custody of a child, etc.[23]. Each prefectural government has the final responsibility for taking measures to protect the child, and each has the obligation to establish a *Child Guidance Centre*, which is a specialized administrative organization for child welfare, and the main organ for taking protective measures for

---

[17] Act No.30 of April 14, 2004.
[18] Act No.73 of June 1, 2007.
[19] Paragraph 2 of Article 8 of the Child Abuse Prevention Law.
[20] Summoning order: Paragraph 2 of Article 9 of the Child Abuse Prevention Law.
[21] Onsite inspection/investigation: Paragraph 3 of Article 9 of the Child Abuse Prevention Law.
[22] Article 10 of the Child Abuse Prevention Law.
[23] An infant home is a facility intended for admitting and fostering infants, as well as being intended for providing consultation and other assistance to those who have left (Article 37 of Child Welfare Act). A foster home is a facility intended for admitting, and providing foster care for children without a guardian, abused children, and other children in need of foster care in terms of their environment, as well as intended for providing consultation and other assistance for self-reliance to those who have left (Article 41 of Child Welfare Act).

children.[24]

Protective measures may be grouped into two types: those that do not separate the child from his/her parent or guardian; and others that require the child to be separated from his/her parent or guardian. The latter means mainly foster families, or care and admission to a child welfare institution, such as an infants' home or children's home.[25] In addition to this, the execution of a separation measure requires the consent of the custody holder.[26] Nevertheless, from the point of view of protecting the child, the legal system enables a separation measure upon the approval of the family court when such a separation is deemed necessary.[27] There has recently been growing emphasis on support to the offending parents, based on the philosophy of the reintegration of the child and parents.

On the other hand, the director of a child guidance centre has the authority to take *temporary custody* of the child as a provisional measure until formal child welfare measures (for instance, foster care, institutionalization, etc.) are decided.[28] Under such circumstances, the consent of the custodial parent or guardian and the child himself/herself is not required by the legislator—the head of the child guidance centre can execute the custody based on his own authority. The maximum duration of this custody is, however, two months.[29] The child guidance centre subsequently determines the necessary measures that have to be taken with regard to the child in question. This may include decisions concerning his/her home with regard to medical treatment, psychology,

---

[24] Article 12, Child Welfare Act. Article 2 provides that *"the national and local governments shall be responsible for bringing up children in good mental and physical health, along with their guardians"*. And a prefectural government shall, based on Article 27 (1), take a measure with regard to a child for whom a report pursuant to Article 25 has been issued.

[25] Paragraph 1-3 of Article 27, Child Welfare Act.

[26] Paragraph 4 of Article 27, Child Welfare Act.

[27] Article 28 of Child Welfare Act.

[28] Article 33 of Child Welfare Act. As temporary protection, a child guidance centre's director may, when he/she finds it necessary, take temporary custody of a child or entrust an appropriate person to do so until a measure, based on Article 26 of this act, is taken (Article 33 (1) of Child Welfare Act). The period for temporary custody shall not exceed 2 months (Article33 (3)), however, when it is necessary, a child guidance centre's director or a prefectural governor may continue the temporary custody pursuant to the provision of paragraph (1) or (2).

[29] Paragraphs 3 and 4 of Article 33 of Child Welfare Act.

education, sociology, or mental health, which are finalized by the prefectural governor.[30]

3. Characteristics of the Child Abuse Prevention Legislation in Japan—Based on the Comparative Study

In order to understand several core characteristics of the Japanese child abuse legislation, a comparative study between it and the legislation of other countries is useful here. The study is based on part of the results of our study project's comparative legal research regarding child abuse and domestic violence, which we carried out in Japan from 2009 onwards[31]. The countries we surveyed for comparison include the United States, The United Kingdom, Ireland, Germany, France, The Netherlands, South Korea, China, Sweden, and Finland.

3.1. Reporting System and the Prevention of Child Abuse—Prevention and Subsequent Responsive Actions

A comparative analysis between Japan's and other countries' legislation has resulted in a considerable number of useful outcomes regarding the way and the manner in which the rights of the child are abused and violated. This analysis is actually based on the interim report, *The Issues of the Legislation on Family Abuse and Violence in Japan—based on the comparative research among ten countries.* The report evaluates how each country regulates the "reporting obligation", which contributes to early finding *after* the child abuse problem has already occurred. It also indicates "the tendency of family support" which contributes, to some extent, to preventing child abuse problems from occurring in the first place. Accordingly, in most of the countries under exploration, the discovery of child abuse is expected to be made by a third party. In addition, all people, or related professionals, are strongly expected to report child abuse cases to a welfare administrative organization or similar entity. But the facts differ somewhat, as is illustrated in Figure 1 below.

---

[30] Article 27 of Child Welfare Act.

[31] Scientific research (B), research No.21330014, supported by Grants-in-Aid for Scientific Research from JSPS (Japan Society for the Promotion of Science). These analysis bases on this research's interim report, *The issues of the Legislation on Family Abuse and Violence in Japan — based on the comparative research among ten countries* (May 2010).

Figure 1. Form of family support and reporting obligation

A: Family support, No reporting obligation (Germany, the Netherlands) = Proactive support to families with an emphasis on family autonomy. Parents have primary childcare responsibilities. Public intervention is limited to when there is consent, or when there is judicial restriction on parental custody. B: Family support, rights of an individual (rights of the child, etc.), reporting obligation (Sweden, Finland) = Proactive family support with an emphasis on the rights and protection of an individual. = Active public intervention in cases of insufficient or inadequate childcare. C: Protection of the individual, with or without reporting obligation (United States, South Korea, (United Kingdom)) = Passive to family support, and centres on the post-incident protection of an individual. Infringements on the individual are dealt with as an offense under the criminal code.

Type A is where proactive support is offered to families and parents, but with no obligation to report, of which Germany represents a typical example. This approach takes the position of placing importance on the joint approach involving parents by reinforcing their childcare responsibilities through support and aid, rather than intensifying criminal sanctions, such as observed in Type C. Type A is based on the idea that it is not sufficient to resolve the child abuse issue solely with post-incident procedures and penalties.[32] The Netherlands also falls into this category.

Type B is similar to Type A in that in that society proactively supports the families, but it is a position that seeks active intervention, in particular by welfare administration, to protect the child in cases where the child is faced with infringement of his/her rights at home through

[12] Children's Rainbow Center, *Research Report on the Inspection of Child Abuse-related Systems in Germany and France 2003,* Vol. 1 Federal Republic of Germany, p. 2.

abuse or other offensive acts or is deprived of sufficient care. Thus, in type B, a reporting obligation is legally provided. Sweden and Finland belong in this category.

Type C places an emphasis on the post-incident protection of the child in the case of abuse. While the procedures are comparatively stringently defined in these countries, family policy undertakings are relatively passive, and the measures are centred on post-incident procedures. In type C, a trend that seeks to improve the effectiveness of reporting by criminalizing neglect of the reporting obligation can also be observed. Major governments falling under this type include the individual States of the United States, and South Korea. The United Kingdom was previously categorized under this type, based on the significant role of the police, but since cases of child abuse leading to death in the 2000s, family support has been reinforced, and recently he United Kingdom is closer in Type to A or B.[33]

In Japan, especially since the Child Abuse Prevention Law was enacted in 2000, the legal provisions for intervening in child abuse cases have become comparatively more developed, for example, the obligation to report child abuse, and investigate and ensure the safety of the child after abuse is reported. On the one hand, those procedures are stipulated in relatively more detail compared with other countries. But on the other hand, social measures for family support still remain limited compared with European countries. Considering the current situation in Japan where more child abuse cases occur in homes having social problems, there ought to be more proactive family-support measures in order to *prevent* child abuse at home beforehand. Japan has established the reporting obligation, which can contribute to detecting child abuse, but given the lack of penalties for failing to act on the obligation to report, it can be seen that the opportunities for discovering child abuse are limited compared with France and certain of the individual United States.[34]

---

[13] It is thought that the United States has basically adopted a separation and protection policy, but with the increase in funding and aid programmes, more support is being offered to families. (Children's Rainbow Center, *Research Report on the Inspection of Child Abuse-related Responses in the United States 2003,* p. 32, 84). However, compared with other countries, public funds for family policies remain low as in the case of Japan.

[14] Many of the states in the United States that set forth the reporting obligation establish penalties for the violation thereof.

3.2. Procedure for Temporary Protection

The report relating to *The issues of the Legislation on Family Abuse and Violence in Japan—based on the comparative research among ten countries* also compares the procedures for emergency or provisional temporary protection. All of the countries whose relevant legislation has been under examination, have some kind of temporary protection measures. However, there are differences in the method of the protection of the rights of the child and the procedure for providing protection, these differences particularly being in judicial and/or administrative intervention: these are demonstrated in Figure 2.

Figure 2. Form of Temporary Protection

A: Temporary protection based on administrative authority (South Korea, Japan) B: Temporary protection based on judicial decision (France, Germany, United Kingdom, United States) C: Temporary protection enforceable within a certain scope based on administrative authority, and the requirements being a post-incident judicial decision (Sweden)

Japan and South Korea are the countries that can enforce temporary protection based solely on the authority of the welfare administrative organization (type A). In other countries, as in the case of type B, the separation of the child from the parents against the will of the parents in principle requires a court decision, unless protecting the child with police authority. Sweden, as shown in type C, is similar to Japan and South Korea in that where temporary protection can be enforced by administrative authority, but it differs in the fact that such protection is limited to a considerably shorter term and also requires submitting a petition to the court within a week, with the court making the final decision.[35]

---

[35] In Sweden, based on Article 6 of LVU (Law of the special provisions for protection of Youth and Child),the municipality's social welfare office is allowed to separate a child from his/her parent immediately and take protective measures in emergency cases, and the case should be filed with the county administrative court within one week to demand a judgment of the court.

Even in Japan, some argue that it is desirable to leave the decision about separating the child from the parents up to the judicial body, even for temporary protection, in order to avoid antagonism between the child welfare administrative body and the custodial parents in cases of child abuse where family reunion is sought. This is also based on the Convention on the Rights of the Child adopted by the United Nations.[36] However, there is also a counterargument that a fundamental restructuring of judicial organizations and systems is required, to enable the judicial body to make the decision; otherwise, the function of temporary protection, which is to speedily ensure the safety of the child, will be at risk[37]. It is important that such concerns are given appropriate deliberation.

3.3. Temporary Protection Based on the Will of the Child

The temporary protection system in Japan not only bypasses parental consent, but also does not require the consent of the child himself/herself; it is to be executed by the authority of the administrative body. However, in view of the rights of the child as the "subject/actor" provided in the U.N. Convention on the Rights of the Child,[38] and from the principle of self-determination within the basic structural reform of social welfare in Japan, it should be presumed that there has to be a future revision in the temporary protection system.

Two trends can be observed from the international comparative study: one is the expanding scope of recognizing the child himself/herself as a legal actor who exerts petitions and claims for temporary protection; and the other is the granting to the child the right to receive information, and the opportunity to voice his/her opinion according to its age and maturity in order to protect it from incurring prejudice. For example, Germany provides the child's right to apply for temporary protection in Article 42 of the Child and Youth Welfare Law. This is in addition to the protection of the obligation of the administrative authority, namely the youth office. Sweden also recognizes in its social service law that 1) children of 15 years and above have, in principle, the right to apply for support through granting a legal status to the child to become the actor in the case; Sweden's Social Service law also prescribes 2) the child's right to voice

---

[36] The Convention on the Rights of the Child, Article 9.
[37] Noriko Mizuno, *parental-rights laws*, Jurist No.1384, 2009, p58-74.
[38] The Convention on the Rights of the Child, Article 12ff.

his/her opinion; and in 2008, it was amended to include 3) the child's right to receive information regarding its case.[39]

3.4. Personnel and Organization

As mentioned above, legal procedures for reporting child abuse or checking the security of the child have been comparatively thoroughly established and developed in Japan, although there is a serious problem of insufficiency in terms of the quality and quantity in the organization and their personnel framework in practice. It was documented in the *2006 Report from the Research Conference concerning the Future Structure of the Child guidance Centre*, which was directed by the Ministry of Health, Labour and Welfare, that the problem leads to a hindrance of the appropriate implementation of the legal measures regarding child abuse[40].

Specifically, the quantitative problem is the insufficient number of child guidance centres, which are at the centre of action against child abuse, and the shortage of child welfare caseworkers, who are assigned to child guidance centres as child welfare professionals. In addition, while municipalities became the primary contact point for child-family consultation from 2005, based on the amendment of the Child Welfare Act, the qualitative and quantitative insufficiency of specialized officers has been discussed. As at the end of 2008, it was identified that 60% of the officers in charge took on other jobs as well, and merely 12.3% of the

---

[20] In Socialtjänstlagen (2001:453, SoL) and Lag om särskilda bestämmelser om vård av unga(1990:52, LVU) in Sweden, minors over the age of 15 have his/her own right to apply for aid or support by SoL. In order to compensate for the "autonomous decision-making" of the child in the procedural process, a special system for selecting an attorney provided by law in Sweden, and to select a public defender for a minor in the procedure of enforced protection (Article 39, LVU), has been implemented by the Act for Special Attorney for Children (1999:997). Attorneys are also appointed to both the parent(s) and child, respectively, for court procedures regarding parent-child separation. The United Kingdom also enshrines in its law consideration of the demands and will of the child when the court makes the decision concerning the protection order.

[40] Ministry of Health, Labour and Welfare, *Situation of the Establishment of the Municipal Child and Family Consultation Operations and the Local Committees for Dealing with Children in Need of Protection (Local Child Protection Network) (As of April 2009)*, December 2009.

officers have the qualifications needed for a child welfare caseworker.[41]

The number of inhabitants per caseworker is shown in Figure 3. It is based on existing material, and not necessarily up-to-date investigations. However, it is evident that there is a shortage of qualified workers in Japan as compared with other countries.

Figure 3. International Comparison of the Number of Specialized Officers for Child Welfare[42]

	France	Germany[43]	U.K.	U.S.[44]	Japan
Specialized officer	Social worker in Health and Social Affairs Sector [45]	Youth office staff [46]	Child welfare caseworker	DCFS social worker	Child welfare caseworker
Inhabitants per specialized officer	3,000-5,000	Approx. 1,000	Approx. 5,000	2,486	50,000-80,000

[41] Ministry of Health, Labour and Welfare, ibid.

[42] Source: Children's Rainbow Center, *2003 Research Report on the Inspection of Child Abuse-related Systems in Germany and France,* Vol. 2 French Republic, pp. 63-64 and Vol. 1 Federal Republic of Germany, p. 19. *2003 Research Report on the Inspection of Child Abuse-related Responses in the United States,* p. 6. *2007 Research Report on the Inspection of Child Abuse-related Responses in the United Kingdom,* pp. 43-44.

[43] Number is from the youth office in Mitte Borough in Berlin.

[44] Number is from the Los Angeles County.

[45] State-certified. In-service training is mandatory by law (Children's Rainbow Center, *2003 Research Report on the Inspection of Child Abuse-related Systems in Germany and France,* Vol. 2 French Republic, p. 64.

[46] Ordered to employ personnel with specialized education or special experience in social work (Article 72 of the Child Protection Law).

The standard number of child guidance centres and child welfare workers per inhabitant are regulated in both the guidelines and orders of the Child Welfare Act. In the guideline for Child Guidance Centre Management before the amendment in 2009, at least one centre was to be established for each 500,000 people. The assignment standard for child welfare caseworkers is given in the Order for Enforcement of the Child Welfare Act. It was previously one worker for every 100,000-130,000 people, which in itself was considered problematically low. This was improved by an amendment to the Order for Enforcement of the Child Welfare Act in 2005, to having "one child welfare caseworker per a population of 50,000 to 80,000".[47] However, this could still be considered a problematically low level, requiring further development

4. Conclusion

From this comparative study, it can firstly be pointed out that Japanese laws, including the Child Abuse Prevention Law, Domestic Violence Prevention Law, and the Prevention of Elderly Abuse and Support for Attendants of Elderly Persons Act[48], provide well-developed reporting obligations and procedures for the safety checking system in comparison with the laws of other countries. On the other hand, however, these provisions are based on post-incident discovery and response, when abuse has been detected. To enhance the prevention of child abuse in the future, proactive support policies for families and parents, including general childcare support and financial support for low-income households, are required.

Secondly, as a procedural legal issue in response to child abuse, particularly in the case of child abuse accompanied by public intervention, the issue of whether to make decisions about temporary protection based solely on administrative authority or to mediate with a judicial decision must be examined. In addition, with regard to procedures, in consideration of the development and trend of the international protection of human rights, the status of victimized children as actors must be secured and the necessary conditions must be established in addition to their status as a

---

[47] Article 2, Order for Enforcement of the Child Welfare Act.

[48] Act on the Prevention of Spousal Violence and the Protection of Victims (Act No. 31 of April 13, 2001) and Act on Prevention of Elderly Abuse and Support for Attendants of Elderly Persons (Act No.124 of November 9, 2005).

subject of protection. From examples in other countries, there is an observable trend towards extending children's rights according to the child's age and maturity, especially the child's right to apply for temporary protection, the right to voice opinions, and the right to receive information about the case in question.

Thirdly, Japan is in need of a qualitative and quantitative expansion of the organizational framework to respond appropriately to the issues of child abuse. In order to enable an appropriate early discovery and response in comparison with other countries, it is imperative for Japan to first quantitatively expand the consultation access points and specialized officers. Appropriate responses will also require an increase in the quality of officers.

Finally, our research project is engaging in wider ranges of research on legislation regarding family violence, for example, the cooperation and collaboration of relevant organizations, care and support in foster families and child welfare institutions, support for the child's independent life in the future, or support measures for the reintegration of families. However, due to the limited space available, these must be left for future discussion

RULES GOVERNING CHILD CUSTODY IN IRANIAN LEGISLATION

HENGAMEH GHAZANFARI

Abstract

"Custody" may be broadly defined as any aspect of child protection covered by the legislation. It may cover various definitions of "care" including material, physical, intellectual, spiritual and various levels of the child's education. According to Article 1168 of the Iranian Civil Law, the term "care "consists of both the rights and duties of the parents. This means that parents have an established legislative responsibility relating to the custody and guardianship of the child and the law cannot, except in particular cases, deprive them of this juridical right. In addition, they are obliged to look after and educate their children while they are able and alive. In custody matters, the interests and well being of children are more crucial and have precedence over the rights of parents to keep children.

Under amendments governing the provisions of civil law, when parents divorce, the mother assumes custody of the child until it reaches seven. This is because it is thought that the mother can more appropriately offer emotional stability to the child and maintain its interests; and at seven, the father may legally be responsible for custody. However, matters such as legal affairs and administration of property are covered by separate provisions, and the rights of the mother there are restricted. Under the so-called "Velayat" principle, the father or paternal authority have domination over the child, until she/he comes of age. Much more surprising is when a mother remarries during the custody of a child, she will fully and absolutely lose the right to custody, whereas if the father of the child remarries he does not lose the right to custody. All these, and many other similar rules, imply the inequality between two sexes which finally affect the interest and well being of the child. This article thus attempts to present proposals for the reform of the current rules of the civil code. The intention is to defend the internationally recognized rights of the child and provide physical, material and mental protection of the child within Iranian society.

1. Introduction

"Custody" means the physical, spiritual, and material care of children and their education; and in the broad meaning of the word, any act which is necessary for child care.[1] According to this definition, child nutrition, health care, clothing etc., education, and the acceptance of the child into the warmth of a family provide the basis for personality development and growth in all areas physical and psychological, emotional and spiritual.

Yet it is impossible for legislators to identify all examples and requirements of care.[2] It therefore depends on the custom, conditions, and norms of society within civil or Common Law systems, and especially the interpretation of the word care. This means that with regard to practical circumstances governing the custody of the child, an act may seem necessary for the purpose of the protection of the rights of the child. Consequently, for the purpose of the appropriate protection of the rights of the child, parents must comply with statutory duties.[3] Otherwise, they have not fulfilled their legal obligations regarding custody of the child.[4]

For instance, in contemporary social construction, providing appropriate housing and the opportunity for the child's physical and personal development are among the aspects of care that the parent should be most sensible of. Parents should also provide care for a child in such a way that the child does not harm or cause damage to others. In this regard, although the child is exempt from criminal responsibility, the exemption is only applicable to the general aspects of criminal conduct.[5] Under the provisions of Iranian criminal law, if an injury caused by a minor results in personal damage, family relatives should, in accordance with the priorities assumed in the inheritance law, pay compensation for damages. Therefore, the situation definitely establishes parental responsibility.[6] The responsibility is irrespective of whether or not they have been negligent in the

[1] Jaafari Langeroodi Mohammad Jaafar, Law Terminology,1988, p216.
[2] Katoozian Nasser, Civil Law, Family Law Part,1992, p39.
[3] Article 1168, Civil Code.
[4] .Kar Mehrangiz,Structure of Family Law in Iran,1999, p52.
[5] Article 7, Civic Responsibility. See also Ismail Sadri, Child Criminality in the City of Tehran and the Method of its Prevention (original language Persian, 1993).
[6] Article 307,Islamic Criminal Law.

commission of the wrongful conduct.[7] This, and many other similar situations, such as the moral and physical protection of the child, engender a number of questions regarding custody and the boundaries of its interpretation and application. The intention of this article is to present proposals for reform in the current rules of the Iranian civil legislation regarding the protection of the rights of children; to defend the internationally recognized rights of the child; and to suggest ways of providing the physical, material and mental protection of the child within Iranian society.

2. The Dimensions of Custody

2.1. Damages

According to Article 1216 Civil Code, if children cause financial damage to someone else, they must assume civic responsibility; but under a law based on Article 6 of civic responsibility, if the damage caused by a child took place due to lack of parental care, the parents must compensate for this loss—otherwise, compensation should be made from the child's personal property.[8] Consequently, parents should provide adequate care for their children so as to prevent them from causing damage to others. Thus custody requires that the child be not only physically, but also emotionally and morally supported. This is stated within the provisions of Article 1117 Civil Code, which refers to the spiritual and moral aspects of custody. The Article stipulates that if, due to lack of care or the moral decadence of a parent who has the custody of a child, the child is at risk of immoral education or the like, the court shall take action accordingly.[9]

One of the most important issues which may be examined here is the powers and duties of parents during custody. In other words, the proper care of children custody requires the facilities and tools, as well as the authority for decision-making. How does legislation observe these aspects of the question of custody, and who has the responsibility? Although the questions may be easily answered within other legal systems, the position is quite different under Iranian legislation. The position has, generally, been tackled under a particular right called "*Velayat*", which is defined as "rule or paternal authority of the father and paternal grandfather over

---

[7] Article 306,Islamic Criminal Law.

[8] Article 6, Civic Responsibility.

[9] Seyyed Hossein Safaee and Asad Ullah Emami, Family Law, 2001, p119.

children", and continues until the child's coming of age (age of maturity). Article 1180 Civil Code states: "The minor child is under the father or paternal authority's rule", and also Article 1181, which provides further that "the father and paternal grandfather of a child are responsible and have the right over the children."

Under the above law, all decisions concerning financial affairs and important issues, and necessary living expenses and provision of child support (alimony) until the age of maturity are the established duty of the paternal grandfather and father. This means that the mother has no particular right under the provisions of *Velayat*.[10] In fact, even if we suppose, for legal reasons, that the custody of the child is given to the mother of the child, her responsibility is only for "care" and "education/ upbringing". On the one hand, this custody does not include child support, but on the other hand, the legal restrictions mentioned above hinder the mother from carrying out a number of affairs, even they are in the best interests of the child.[11] For example, a mother has no legal right to open a bank account or buy property for the child.[12] Neither does she have the right to take the child on any journey abroad without the official written consent of the father or paternal authority.[13]

2.2. Feeding

Whilst the parents naturally share the responsibilities of children, under Iranian law, providing the necessary facilities required for the realization of these affairs, child support is the sole responsibility of the father.[14] The mother, even if she has the ability to provide financial resources, has no legal responsibility. In other words, in the presence of a father or paternal authority, no responsibility is assumed for mothers, and this issue creates legal and practical conflict in the interest of the child.[15] Thus on the one hand, the law leaves one parent without any financial responsibility for the child's development, while on the other hand, it places a heavy duty on the shoulders of the other party.

[10] Ghorbannia Nasser and the others, Researches in Women Rights, 2005, p150.
[11] Kar Mehrangiz, ibid, p53.
[12] Kar Mehrangiz, ibid, p53.
[13] Kar Mehrangiz, ibid, p54.
[14] Article 1199, Civil Code.
[15] Moosavi Bojnoordi Mohammad, Law Family, 2007, p301.

An example of an issue governing the mother's custody is breast-feeding. The best food for a baby at birth is mother's milk. This means that the child's care and interest is promoted by a natural gift, i.e. the milk. Breast-feeding must be considered an example of child custody because the child is entitled to, and deserves, the best form of nutrition, nurturing, and spiritual and physical care. Nevertheless, according to Shiite jurisprudence, breast-feeding is not included in mother's custody of the child. In other words, the mother cannot be obliged to breast-feed children except under special conditions, and the relevant provisions of the law have accepted this spiritual interpretation.[16] Article 1167 Civil Code states: "The mother does not have to breast-feed the baby except if feeding other than breast-feeding is not possible". Although mothers usually withhold nothing legally from their child, and in fact the child owes his/her very own existence to the mother, it seems that the mother should provide her own milk.

2.3. Visitation Rights

In the Iranian law, one of the parents' rights is "visitation rights". If, due to divorce or any other reasons, parents do not live together, the parent who has not obtained custody has visitation rights. In case of disagreements between parents about the time and place and other details of the visits, the court will take a decision on the matter.[17]

2.4. A Lack of Proper Child Care

Regarding the limits of parents' rights, and the fact that parents have the right and duty to child custody and providing education, it seems parents can choose their own approach to the child's education and upbringing according to their judgment. However, the court has the right to prevent the rights of the parents if they abuse those rights. Obvious examples are the lack of proper childcare, moral decadence, or the lack of competence and suitability of parents for custody in such a way that the physical health or moral education of the child is at risk. In this case the court may intervene and decide what is necessary according to the interest of the child.[18] Typical examples of parental incompetence are addiction to drugs or alcohol, infamous behaviour or moral corruption, mental illness, and

[16] Katoozian Nasser, Civil Rights, 1992, p.141.
[17] Article 1174, Civil Code.
[18] Article 1173, Civil Code.

child abuse: we will discuss these below, under the cases that incur the denial or removal of the right to custody.[19]

In order to ensure the correct implementation of regulations related to custody, and in order to be able to exercise custody, Iranian legislators have decreed that anyone who does not comply with the decision of the court relating to child custody, or prevents, by one means or another, its implementation, or refuses to return the child, shall be detained by a Court order (if the other party requests it) until the court's decision is implemented by the violator's party. Whenever the court recognizes that agreements about meetings, custody, and care are contrary to the child's interest, or if the person responsible for custody refrains from performing assigned duties, or prevents the child from meeting with individuals entitled to the right, the court can take any appropriate decision about such matters. These may include transferring custody to another person or choosing a person to look after the child's interests.

3. Persons Responsible for Custody

3.1. Removal of Custody

Custody is the legal and natural right and duty of parents while they are alive.[20] However, there must not be any legal obstacle to the right. Consequently, as long as the parents are competent to provide care for their children, they will assume this, and no one can deny this right, and this situation continues until the child reaches puberty. The question that may be examined is whether in the course of daily life, parents have equal custody, or whether one or the other has priority. Some jurists, who are experts in Sharia Law, assert that according to traditions and religious narratives, the parents have equal rights and have therefore considered that parenting should be the common and shared task of couples.[21] However, the popular opinion of writers is that one parent has priority over the other based on the age of the child.[22]

Another relevant question in the implementation of the right of custody is whether it can be transferred to another person when the parents are alive.

---

[19] Kar Mehrangiz, ibid, p54.
[20] Article 1168, Civil Code.
[21] Seyed Ali Tabatabai, Riyadh Almsayl , 1997, p372.
[22] Moosavi Bojnoordi Mohammad, Law Family, ibid, p56.

In response to this question it should be stressed that under normal conditions, and where there is no legal obstacle, custody is the right of parents and others cannot claim any right in this regard. But this right is not absolute: for example, when the child's physical or educational well-being are at risk, and custody might militate against the child's best interests. The court can consequently take the appropriate decision regarding the custody of the child for the solid purpose of his/her protection.

Of course, the separation of children from the warmth and normal condition of the family is legally permitted if it seems vital for his/her well-being.[23] In such circumstances, the judgment of the court is purely based on expediency and the child's interests. To prevent possible abuse, Article 1175 of the Civil Code states that, "You cannot take away a child from parents who have custody or parents except in the case that there is legal cause".

3.2. Priority for Custody

Regarding the priority of each parent for custody, Shiite jurisprudential opinion is that the mother takes priority where the son is under two, or a daughter who is under seven, while others state that the mother has custody up to the age of nine if the child is female.[24] Yet some believe the mother also has absolute custody up to the age of seven, regardless of the gender of the child.[25] In civil law, before the 2003 reforms, the subordination of the famous jurists regarding custody, in accordance with Article 1169 of the civil law, was that the mother was given a priority for custody of a son who is under two years old and a daughter who is under seven years old, and then after that age the custody was given to the father. Since 2003, the Iranian Parliament has approved a law according to which the mother has custody up to the age of seven of the child, whether boy or girl. Up to the age of seven, the mother has legal priority, and after that age, the father has priority and takes responsibility for the rights of the child.

---

[23] Katoozian Nasser, ibid, p159.
[24] Moosavi Bojnoordi Mohammad, Law Family, ibid, p57-59.
[25] Najafi Sheikh Mohammad, Jawaher Al kalam, Bairut, p290.

3.3. The Scope of the New Law

The law approved by the legislators faced opposition from The Guardian Council of the Constitution.[26] Despite this, the Expediency Council,[27] regardless of the dispute between Parliament and the Guardian Council, adopted the above law with slight modifications. The law is currently enforceable. Article 1169 provided by amendment Act 2003 states: "For the custody of a child whose parents live apart from each other, until the age of seven years the mother has a priority and then the father after the age of seven". It is significant to say that if after seven years, a dispute occurs relating to the custody of the child; the court has to decide in accordance with the child's interest.

Some points about the civil law reforms are worth examining at this point. *Firstly*, the custody of the child, regardless of sex, is granted to the mother up to the age of seven. This has been seen as essential, because a two-year-old son continues to need his mother's support, training, and nurturing. It was obvious that entrusting custody to the father at the age of two could create multiple problems for the child's education and mental health.[28] The new law thus covered the the shortcomings of the law concerning the rights of the child, and brought a practical approach to the problem of the separation of parents and the custody of the child.

Secondly, while the family exists normally, and both husband and wife live together, child-care and education is their common right and duty: husband and wife must help each other, and the civil law amendment is in

---

[26] Negotiations of the Guardian Council, 2003. The Guardian Council of the Constitution is an organ consisting of twelve members that have a powerful influence in the Islamic Republic of Iran. According to the constitution, the Council has six Islamic fagihs who are expert in Islamic law and are selected by the Supreme Leader of Iran (a very high religious authority). The other six are jurists who have expertise in different questions of law and are elected by the Iranian Parliament from among a considerable number of Muslims who are themselves selected by the Head of the Judicial Power. But the interesting thing is that the Head is himself appointed to the post by the Supreme Leader. In other words, all twelve members of the Guardian Council of the Constitution are, directly or indirectly, selected and appointed by the Supreme Leader of Iran. This is a form of monopolization of power and politics.

[27] The Expert Council is an administrative assembly appointed by the Supreme Leader. Accordingly, the Leader delegates some of his own authority to the council in order to have political and juridical control over many governmental questions.

[28] Moosavi Bojnoordi Mohammad, Law Family, ibid, p58.

accordance with this norm.[29] However it should be noted that the question of priority of the parents does not arise as long as they live together. The question becomes important when they live apart.

If, for example, the parents live together, but they disagree about how the child should be raised, the mother's wishes take priority while the child is under seven. But the priority which exists for one of the parents does not mean that the other can disregard responsibility, because the child was jointly created by the mother and father, and they are therefore jointly responsible for its upbringing.[30] Both parents thus have the right to discipline the child with due regard to the child's interest. Apparently, the legislators assume that the mother is only able to provide care until the age of seven, after which responsibility for the children's needs and requirements is beyond her capacity, so that the father is recognized as being more competent to protect the child.

3.4. The Effects of the "*Velayat*" Law

According to the provisions of the new legislation, children only need the emotional and nurturing power of the mother up to the age of seven. Of course, this diagnosis cannot present a scientific fact and if the only basis for granting the right to custody is that of the child's interest, then it cannot either be justified or defended.[31]On the one hand the law ensures that parents each have a fair share of time with the children and of child custody. But on the other hand, the law is apparently under the effect of the "*Velayat*" right, which legalizes the ruling of a father and paternal authority over a child.

Undoubtedly, the "*Velayat*" right considerably limits the rights of the mother to custody before the age of seven, and reduces her powers over the child protection. The "*Velayat*" law also aims to deprive the mother of her rights when her child reaches seven years of age. These prevented rights of the mother include almost any right which is associated with the child. Obviously, in both situations—i.e. before seven years old and thereafter—the child's best interests and well-being may be overshadowed by the provisions of the "*Velayat*" law.

[29] Article 1168, Civil Code.
[30] Article 1178, Civil Code.
[31] Moosavi Bojnoordi Mohammad, Law Family, ibid, p58.

If one of the parents dies, the survivor will be legally responsible for custody. This ruling is prescribed in Article 1171 Civil Code. For example, if the mother dies, and the child is three, the father will have custody of the child. If the minor child is over seven when the father dies, the mother will have custody even if the minor child has a paternal grandfather. In any case, with the death of either parent, the remaining one will have custody. Moreover, if both parents die and the child has a paternal grandfather, he will assume custody. If the paternal grandfather is not alive, someone who is appointed by the father or paternal grandfather will assume custody of the child. According to Article 1188 Civil Code, both father and paternal grandfather, after the death of the other, can determine someone as executor for their children who is under his "*Velayat*". This means that after their death, the third person takes the child into his care and custody, and protects the property of the child in various respects. When a child has no kin to be determined as guardian, the court can appoint a guardian.

4. Positions Illegitimating Custody

4.1. Insanity

Insanity is one of the cases of interdiction, and one who is mad is not only incompetent to intervene in the affairs of others, but is not competent to decide for himself, either. He will need a guardian's involvement. It is therefore evident that children should not be left in the care of someone insane. Article 1170 Civil Code accordingly affirms: "If the mother, while having a child in her custody, happens to become mad ... the right to custody would be granted to the father". As noted, the legislature, in Article 1170 Civil Code, counts insanity as a case where custody could be denied.

There is, however, no mention of the case of the madness of a father. One could argue then, that the father's insanity would not lead to the loss of the right to custody since the law has not mentioned it. This argument is better avoided. Firstly, because a mother's madness is not in any way distinct from that of a father, and therefore there is no reason to exempt only a father. Secondly, an insane person is not competent to perform any legal act, and also having custody requires a clear ability of reasoning and capacity to act. An insane person cannot fulfill such requirements.[32]

[32] Katoozian Nasser, Civil Law in New Order Law, 2008, p706.

The madness of mother or father results in the denial of custody, and eventually transfers it to another. Thirdly, since the risk of mental illness can cause a parent to be denied the right to custody, insanity must also be treated likewise. If only one parent is alive and insane, custody is given to the paternal grandfather, and if he is not alive, then to the executor or guardian appointed by the father or the paternal grandfather. There is a debate in our law whether, if a parent loses custody due to insanity and later he or she recovers, they will get back the right to custody or not. In this regard, one can argue that when a right is taken from someone, restoring the right obviously requires legal approval by the authorities, given the circumstances. What seems to prevent the parent's right to custody is madness and insanity. If at any time it is eliminated, and the parent is restored to health, the right to custody should be re-established.[33]

4.2.Married Mothers

According to Article 1170 Civil Code if the mother remarries while the child is in her custody, the right to custody would be given to the father. This assumption has apparently been based on the reasoning that when a mother marries someone other than her former husband, a considerable number of obligations will result from the marriage to her new husband. She may fail to meet the requirements of custody to act appropriately and in accordance with the child's interests and well-being.

The question which has often arisen is whether the right to custody may be given to a mother whose capacity and suitability for custody is confirmed by the court? It seems that the inference from the Articles 12 and 13 of the Family Protection Law confirms the right of the mother. Accordingly, when the court recognizes that the mother, although married to a new husband, is more suitable for looking after the child than the father, custody of the child is given to the mother.[34]

4.2. Married Fathers

As a general rule of Iranian legislation, married fathers may not be deprived of the custody of their children. The question is why, in similar circumstances, if the father marries a woman other than the mother, his right to child custody is not taken away from him, and the legislators have

---

[33] Shahid Sani, Masalk Al Afham, vol 8, pp550-551.
[34] Safaee and Emami, *supera* p129.

not considered the rejection of the father's rights to custody? Similar reasoning to the case of the mother in the above paragraphs may be claimed regarding the remarriage of the father of the child and the question of his appropriate capability. This means that his new marriage may be an essential reason for the physical health or moral education of the child. In such a situation can the court deprive him of the right to custody?

4.3. Death of One Parent

Custody is a personal right, and like all personal rights, it disappears after death, unlike financial rights that are transferred to the rightful heirs. Custody depends on the existence of the mother or father: whenever a parent is dead, the right to custody will automatically terminate. In this regard, we must note that if a father has custody, but he dies, even if the child has a parental grandfather, that parental grandfather does not have the right to custody. Custody is the right of parents, and in this regard, Article 1171 Civil Code states that in the case of the death of one parent, custody is the other parent's right and duty, even though the deceased is the father and he had specified a guardian.

4.4. Physical Health of Child Being at Risk

Under the amendment to Article 1173 Civil Code, if at any time due to immorality or the lack of care of the parent who has custody, where the child's physical health is at risk the court can make any decision that may be necessary for the custody of the child.[35] For instance, the legislature has described cases of the lack of care or moral decadence, such as suffering from mental illness. However, this type of mental illness differs from the dementia that was examined elsewhere in this chapter. In any case, the current status of the child and his parents may not be easy to judge.[36] This means that the child may require more care than that for a normal one. Thus, the inability to provide care for a child, such as suffering from an incurable disease, long-term absence, prolonged detention, or the inability to make a living and supply child support and alimony, can be examples of a child's physical health being at risk.

[35] Kar Mehrangiz, ibid, p53.
[36] Article 1173, Civil Code.

4.5. Placed at Risk of Immoral Upbringing

According to the amendment to Article 1173 Civil Code, putting a child at risk, with some examples of cases, is one of the reasons for denial of the right to custody. Previously, matters of immoral upbringing were not mentioned in the reform act. However, the regulations stipulated that a harmful addiction to alcohol, drugs and gambling, reputed moral corruption and prostitution, child abuse, forcing children to enter immoral professions such prostitution and begging, or trafficking in drugs are cases of moral decline. One or several of these may cause immoral upbringing, so corruption of the parents should not be allowed to endanger the children; and society as a whole has a responsibility to them. In some cases, violent behaviour or unusual punishment, with the aim of disciplining a child may endanger the mental, and even the physical, health of the child. In this case, the court can remove the right to custody of the father or mother, and delegate this to someone else.

5. Conclusion

The issue of children's rights and responsibilities has long been debated within different legal systems. Therefore, the position of children constitutes one of the core issues within various national, regional and international societies. In particular, the international legal and political community has been involved in many serious discussions relating to the natural and positive rights of children. Attention to three points is therefore seen to be necessary: *i)* it is the primary responsibility of the family to offer protection and support to a child; *ii)* all children should enjoy fundamental human rights, but owing to the immaturity of children, we have to provide special protections, including moral or legal ones; *iii)* all efforts should benefit the child with the basic philosophy of guaranteeing the protection of the child's rights and care necessary for his/her welfare in a suitable environment and growth in the direction of his/her well-being.

In fact, in the face of each situation the child's interest, benefit, and well-being should be regarded with the highest priority, over any other matter. Iranian legislation has made good arrangements regarding the quantitative and qualitative aspects of custody, and the limits of the rights and responsibilities of parents for the custody of the child. But, as discussed above, certain problems exist, such as putting a duty on the father to provide facilities and financial costs, while exempting the mother from any responsibility if the father is alive, and depriving the mother from taking decisions like management of the child's financial affairs. These problems can be corrected by the implementation of particular measures in conjunction with the provisions of the Convention on the Rights of the Child and its Protocols, and the obvious presentation of equality between the parents of the child.

Under Iranian law, if one of the parents dies, the custody is given to the other one, and not to anyone else. The priority of parents shows the importance of families in the upbringing of children. That the legislature determines the cases conflicting with the proper education of children, and denies the right to custody of their parents if they are incompetent, is appreciable. Actions by parents that endanger the physical, mental and spiritual health of the child, such as corruption and drug abuse, are listed among these cases.

An important case that can lead to the termination of the right to custody is that, if the mother remarries, her right to custody automatically ends. The assumption is that there is a risk of jeopardizing the best interests of the child, but the merit of this theory is very pathetic and not justifiable due to the well-established principle of equality between genders. The better alternative may be that the mother's remarriage should not automatically remove the right to custody, but provide the opportunity to the court to investigate the father's request about eligibility for continuing the custody by the mother. Consequently, the mother and the father would be treated equally under the provisions of justice, and in both cases the objectivity of the judge and the appropriate interpretation of the legislation are to the genuine advantage of the children.

CHAPTER FOUR:

ECONOMIC LEGAL PROBLEMS

THE INDEBTEDNESS OF CHILDREN AND YOUNG ADULTS IN SWEDEN

ANNINA H. PERSSON

Abstract

There have been a number of legal modifications governing indebtedness within the Swedish legal system, all of which aim at solving the problems of indebted children and young adults. They are in conformity with the Swedish constitution, which provides that public institutions shall promote participation for all people, and equal treatment within different sections of society. This also includes children. The purpose of this article is to discuss the indebtedness of children and young adults in Sweden and it deals with two basic questions: a) what instruments exist for the prevention of over-indebtedness of children and young adults; and b) what measures may be employed for clearing the debts of persons who are already over-indebted? The economic vulnerability and indebtedness of children and young adults has lately been intensively debated by the Swedish legislature. This article will hopefully shed a little light on some of the legal modifications that have been introduced to avert this social problem.

1. Introduction

Indebtedness can be one of the core social problems for individuals, and indebtedness can sometimes be so great that it leads to insolvency proceedings. According to the Swedish Enforcement Authority, at the start of 2010 there were about 1100 Swedish children between 15-18 who were registered with the authority for debt (approximately €680/person),[1] and at

---

[1] See the homepage of the Enforcement Authority, www.kronofogden.se and their indicated reports. And see Rapport Överskuldsättning och ekonomiska problem bland ungdomar, 2008:3 samt Solidariskt skadeståndsansvar - en skuldfälla för unga, 2010-06-21, Dnr 9:2.0597/10, Cf. SOU 2004:112 p. 186.

the start of 2009, there were 38,196 persons between 18-25 who were registered with the authority for a debt of approximately €1,750/person. In the two Swedish counties of Skåne and Värmland, 5 per cent of the population between 18-25 were registered for an unpaid debt. How were these debts incurred? Closer examination reveals that they are connected with school pictures, mobile telephones, fines, damages, taxes for purchasing different materials and debts due to so-called SMS-loans.[2] Other common debts are unpaid loans to the Swedish Board of Study Support (CSN) or the County Council for health care services. The legislature, as well as several other authorities and organizations, have worked intensively in order to reduce the number of children and young adults who are in debt, which has, *inter alia*, led to several modifications to the law. The purpose of this article is to shed light on some of the legal instruments that have been introduced into Swedish legislation. The article deals with two basic questions: what instruments exist for the prevention of over-indebtedness of children and young adults, and what measures may be employed for clearing the debts of persons who are already over-indebted? Despite the efforts made, there have been disturbing reports that the number of young adults registered with the Enforcement Authority is continuously increasing. Given that, are those legislative modifications sufficient to decrease the indebtedness of children and young adults, or are other governmental measures still required to deal with this intricate aspect of the law?

2. Legislative Instruments for Preventing Indebtedness

2.1. The Code of Parenthood and Guardianship

In the Code of Parenthood and Guardianship (1949:381) (the FB) there are rules to prevent children from becoming over-indebted. These came into force on the 1January 2009. According to Chapter 13, Section 12 FB, the guardian may, acting on the minor's behalf, and with the consent of the chief guardian: 1) contract a loan or other instrument of debt; 2) enter into suretyship; or 3) furnish the minor's property as security for a contingent liability entered into by the minor or another party. A guardian who does not obtain the chief guardian's consent may only carry out cash transactions on the minor's behalf. It is stated in the *travaux*

[2] An SMS-loan means that the borrower can obtain credit between SEK 1,000 - 3, 000 by sending a text message from a mobile phone to the credit provider. The borrower's account can be credited within 15 minutes.

preparatoires[3] of the Code of Parenthood and Guardianship that it is of the utmost importance for the legislature to prevent children from becoming indebted. Debts give rise to many problems when the child becomes a young adult, thereby giving the child a bad start to adulthood. Consent by the chief guardian may be granted only if the measure is needed in order to secure the rest of the individual person's property, or is deemed necessary for his or her education or livelihood, or if there is otherwise special cause for it.

In the *travaux preparatoires*[4] there is a discussion about what constitutes a transaction that requires the chief guardian's consent. The transaction should mean an obligation to pay money. There must be a close link between the indebtedness of the minor and the transaction, such as when buying goods on credit. An agreement is also considered to be such a transaction, if it is clear in its words that a liability for the child will arise after some time. A typical example of such an agreement would be a subscription for a mobile telephone or Internet access. What determines whether such a contract requires the chief guardian's consent is if the minor under the contract is ordered to make payment at a later date. It does not count if the payment is fixed in amount or not. However, it does not matter if an agreement can give rise to a debt because of an act of the child that can lead to liability being incurred. Liability for the minor may arise because another contractual obligation is not met: for example, when borrowing a book from the library, the contract usually includes the condition that in case of the loss of the book it must be replaced. This agreement does not require the consent of the chief guardian.[5]

Chapter 12, Section 10 FB, governs the consequences of a transaction that has been concluded without the chief guardian's consent. Paragraph 1 states that if the guardian has signed an agreement on the minor's behalf without the consent of the chief guardian, even though the expression of consent is required, the counterparty to the contract may not withdraw from the contract if the guardian requests the chief guardian's consent within one month of the contract being concluded, and no other condition has been made. If the chief guardian does not consent, the counterparty has the right of withdrawal from the contract, unless otherwise agreed.

---

[3] See proposition Förmyndarskapsrättsliga frågor, 2007/08:150 p. 30.
[4] See proposition 2007/08:150 p. 66.
[5] See proposition 2007/08:150 p. 67.

Paragraph 2 states that if the guardian has signed an agreement for the minor, under which a debt occurs, without the consent of the chief guardian, the counterparty does not have the right to withdraw from the contract when completed. Thus, the agreement remains suspended until it is either approved by the chief guardian, or duly fulfilled, i.e. the payment of the money by the relevant minor. In the latter case, the agreement is valid, regardless of whether the chief guardian has given his consent. When the contract is signed, neither party can withdraw from it.[6]

The above-mentioned legislative alterations and modifications (which came into force in 2009) will reduce the risk of minors being in debt. However, the problem remains for those minors who are already in debt, because the law does not operate retroactively. The Consumer Ombudsman (KO) is thus now representing an adult girl who has been sued for an unpaid school photo. The girl was eleven when she ordered the photo, but her parents never paid the bill. The case has been handled by the Enforcement Authority, and now that the debtor is an adult, she is being sued by the creditor, a collection agency. She is required to pay SEK 809. However, the KO claims that even before the aforementioned changes were made in the FB, the law prevented parents from indebiting their children. Stockholm District Court, which is dealing with the case, has submitted the dispute under Chapter 56, Section 13 of the Code of Judicial Procedure[7] to the Supreme Court.[8]

2.2. The Health and Medical Services Act

The above-mentioned legislative changes in the Code of Parenthood and Guardianship do not cover liabilities that are based on provisions within the public law arena, because the alterations are aimed only at liabilities arising from transactions of private law matters. In view of this, further legislative modifications have been introduced in the Health and Medical Services Act (1982:763) and the Dental Services Act (1985:125), to the effect that liability for payment in respect of a child's health and dental care lies with the minor's legal guardian.

---

[6] See proposition 2007/08:150 p. 31.
[7] See SFS 1942:740.
[8] See Case of Stockholms Tingsrätt, T-6029-10, decided 2001-01-20.

The Swedish Data Inspection Board published a report on indebted children in the autumn of 2008.[9] The report stated that among debt collection agencies, there were just over 79,500 current cases against those who were minors when the debt was incurred. 63,000 of these cases involved persons who were still minors. Many cases concerned public claims where several state municipalities were the minors' creditors because of unpaid dental or health fees. In many cases, the minor was not even aware of the debt until they turned 18, and were informed of the debt by the collector.[10]

The Swedish Data Inspection Board also found that there were shortcomings among the debt collection agencies regarding the control of the debtor and the grounds for the claim. The agencies also lacked sufficient knowledge of how to administer these controls in an effective and accurate way.[11]

In the spring of 2009, the Swedish Ombudsman for Children made a similar investigation,[12] which reported that half of all state municipalities (there are 21 in Sweden) had indebted minors in their systems. Several of these municipalities had claimed the debt from the minor after he or she had turned 18.[13]

As the government stated in the *travaux préparatoires*[14] of the Code of Parenthood and Guardianship, it is of the utmost importance that children do not become indebted; amendments have now *inter alia* been introduced in Section 26 of the Health and Medical Act (1982:763).[15] This section stipulates that if the patient is under 18 when treatment is started, or if the patient fails to appear at the scheduled time, the fee should be paid by the patient's guardian. If more than one guardian is responsible, they will both

---

[9] See Datainspektionens rapport, 2008:2, Skuldsatta barn - hanteringen av underåriga gäldenärer hos inkassoombuden.

[10] See Ds 2009:41 (Betalningsansvaret för underårigas avgifter inom hälso- och sjukvården och tandvården) pp. 15.

[11] See Datainspektionens rapport, 2008:2, Skuldsatta barn - hanteringen av underåriga gäldenärer hos inkassoombuden, p. 5 and pp. 14.

[12] See Barnombudsmannen skrivelse till socialministern Göran Hägglund om landstingens och regionernas skuldsättning av barn, diarienr 9.2:0189/09.

[13] See Motion 2009/10:C276 av Egon Frid (v) med flera. Konsumentpolitik och överskuldsattas situation.

[14] See proposition 2007/08:150.

[15] See also Section 15a of the Dental Service Act (1985:125), Section 25 of the Medical Compensation Act (1993:1651) and Section 24a of the Physiotherapy Compensation Act (1993:1652).

be liable for the claim. In exceptional circumstances, the fee may be issued against the minor: the exception is to prevent the violation of the Swedish Secrecy Act (2009:400) when such a minor is seeking care without the guardian´s consent. A 17-year-old girl, for example can, without the guardian's consent, obtain a prescription for contraceptives.[16]

As I have shown above, the provisions of the new legislation will reduce the risk of minors becoming indebted, although the law cannot operate *ex post facto*. One suggestion is that Sweden's municipalities and counties waive public claims against those individuals.[17] Whether this idea will be accepted remains to be seen. It would be the right thing to do, especially with reference to what the Swedish Council of Legislation (Lagrådet) stated when responding to the amendments mentioned above. The Council of Legislation stated that compensation for expenses incurred due to a patient's failure to come to a pre-booked appointment should not be considered as a "hospital fee". There is, indeed, no specific provision of the Health and Medical Services Act that grants municipalities the right to charge such compensation.[18] It has, in other words, been illegal from the beginning for public authorities to impose such charges. Consequently, the only rational approach for local governments at present is to write off the debts of minors who do not come under the umbrella of the newly adopted legislation.

2.3. The Consumer Credit Act

The Consumer Credit Act (2010:1846) is another important instrument for the avoidance of over-indebtedness. Section 6 requires a businessman to adhere to accepted practices when in dealings with the consumer. The businessman must act in the consumer's interest, and give appropriate advice when necessary. And Section 12 requires the businessman, before granting credit, to investigate whether the consumer is financially capable of honouring his or her commitments under the credit agreement. The *travaux préparatoires* of the Act explain that the main purpose of this provision is to counteract over-indebtedness among consumers in general.[19] The requirement of the accepted credit-granting practice means that, both

---

[16] See Persson, Annina H, Vems är skulden? Festskrift till Lars Heuman, 2008, p. 377 and Ds 2009:41 p. 25, proposition 2009/10:88 p. 20.

[17] See Motion 2009/10:C276 by Egon Frid (Left Party) and others. "Konsumentpolitik och överskuldsattas situation".

[18] See Lagrådets yttrande, proposition 2009/10:88 p. 36, bilaga 4.

[19] See proposition 1991/92:83 pp 106, proposition 2002/03:139 pp. 252, 587.

prior to a credit agreement being entered into, and while it is in force, the credit provider must act judiciously and responsibly towards the consumer. The credit provider must act on the basis that a credit agreement can have important consequences for the consumer´s financial circumstances. The Consumer Credit Act of 2010 aims to control certain forms of credit that have proven to be a repayment trap, especially for young people.[20] The intention is to decrease the number of cases. These include SMS-loans, because credit assessments for SMS loans were not mandatory before the introduction of the Consumer Credit Act.

SMS loans have also turned into a repayment trap due to the very high rate of interest. For example, an SMS credit of SEK 3,000 is repayable within 30 days, and carries a charge of SEK 600, giving an effective annual interest rate of 792 per cent. Since many young adults have been registered by the Enforcement Authority after contracting such loans, the legislature has amended the Consumer Credit Act to prevent this problem. The number of applications for payment injunctions involving SMS loans among young people has now fallen.

3. Debt Restructuring—an Instrument that Aims to Clear the Debts of Persons Who are already Over-Indebted

Debt restructuring for natural persons as an instrument for aiding those who are heavily in debt has been under discussion in Swedish law since the end of the 1980s. The first Debt Restructuring Act (1994:334) came into law on 1 of July 1994 as a consequence of that debate. However, the Act has been subject to continuous monitoring and evaluation ever since. The main points have been that debt restructuring cases take too long to process, and the allocation of roles between the authorities involved has been unclear. Following a review, a new Restructuring Act (2006:548) was passed, effective from 1 January 2007. However, subsequent events have shown that the recent amendments to the 2006 Act are insufficient, as not many have been granted debt restructuring since the act entered into force. The act will be therefore be amended again on 1 July 2011.

According to the Enforcement Authority it is doubtful whether a child has ever been the subject of debt restructuring.[21] There are, however, cases of

[20] See Ds 2009:67 pp. 86, proposition 2009/10:242 pp. 53.
[21] Interview with Anders Cederberg, LLM, Östersund Debt Restructuring Team, Swedish Enforcement Service, 2006-10-02.

children, who have come of age, entering into suretyships for their parents or assuming joint and several liability with them for their debt.[22] In these cases, the suretyship has led to over-indebtedness, as precedents from the Enforcement Authority show. In a case tried by Trelleborg District Court[23] on 23rd February 2004, a 39-year-old man was granted debt restructuring. He had applied for it previously, but been refused. The facts of that case show, among other things, that he had entered into very great personal guarantee commitments with a high degree of risk, and that he should have known from the outset that he lacked the necessary financial capacity to honour them. The burden of debt amounted to approximately 25 million Swedish krone (25,972,270), and consisted mainly of suretyships relating to a business previously carried on by the debtor's father. The remainder of the debt, some 2.9 million Swedish krone, consisted of two loans—a property loan, and a relatively minor debt to an electricity company. All the loans, apart from a bank loan contracted in 1994, were contracted between 1989 and 1991, i.e. when the debtor was between 25-27. The indebtedness was accrued while the debtor was working for his father's motor company as a salesman. The business expanded and soon involved several different operations, with the debtor and his siblings as directors. What started as a small family business with an annual growth of MSEK 3.4, expanded into a conglomerate with an annual turnover of MSEK 150. After a time, however, the business went into decline, and at the end of the 1980s the debtor and his siblings were called upon by their father to furnish personal guarantees for loans needed to save the companies from bankruptcy. Given the debtor's trust in his father, and the father's assurance that the loans would be repaid in connection with an impending sale, the debtor did not hesitate in signing the guarantee commitment. No sale materialized, however. Instead, all the companies went bankrupt between 1991 and 1992. By then the businessman father's had moved abroad. Joint and several liability was applied to the greater part of the debts, mainly together with other members of the family. Furthermore, new debts had been accrued. When the debtor filed a new application for debt restructuring, the Enforcement Authority proposed that it be granted, partly on the grounds that all commitments had been entered into with reference to loans contracted for businesses carried on by the father. Other members of the family had also incurred extensive personal liability as a result: clearly, the debtor and the rest of the family had held a position of trust in relation to their father and, their directorships notwithstanding, had

[22] Interview with Anders Cederberg, LLM., Östersund Debt Restructuring Team, Swedish Enforcement Service, 2006-10-02.
[23] Trelleborg District Court is located in the South of Sweden.

not exercised any real management control of the businesses. The business had been successful for a considerable length of time, generating a high turnover; the debtor at the time of entering into the guarantee commitment must have realized that he would never have been able to honour it unaided, but confidence in the future of the business was evidently strong. This was witnessed by the fact that the credit providers had granted large credits, and accepted that the debtor, a young man at the time, act as a guarantor. Given the time which had elapsed since the debts arose and what had also emerged in the case, the Enforcement Authority saw no impediment to the debtor being granted debt restructuring. The District Court upheld this decision.[24]

4. Conclusion

There have been several legal amendments made in Swedish law aimed at solving the problems with indebted children and young adults. This is in line with the Swedish constitution[25] that states that public institutions shall promote the opportunity for all to attain participation and equality in society, including children. However, the question is whether the amendments are enough. There are several reasons to believe that children's economic vulnerability will again increase in Sweden given the financial crisis, persistent high unemployment and increased inequality between households.[26] Sweden has about 220,000 children living in so-called child poverty, i.e. living in families where the family has a low income or receives income support from the State. Child poverty among single parent families is more than three times higher than among families where the parents are cohabiting. Child poverty is also five times higher among children of immigrant families than among children of Swedish descent. Child poverty also varies widely between municipalities in Sweden, being highest in the country's metropolitan areas and lowest in the municipalities surrounding the big cities. The children who suffer from child poverty might not have the same opportunities as other Swedish children, such as being able to participate in fee-based recreational activities, having access to a computer at home, getting new glasses, etc. Studies show that children with poor economic conditions during childhood risk poorer health, and exposure to bullying and violence. It is

[24] See Trelleborg District Court, 2004-02-23, Ä 1686-03. Interview with Louise Pihl, LLM, Team Leader, Malmö Debt Restructuring Team 2006-10-02.

[25] See Chapter 1, Section 2 of the Instrument of Government, SFS 1974:152, amended SFS 2010:1408, 1.1. 2011.

[26] See Årsrapport 2010, Rädda barnen, Barns ekonomiska utsatthet.

therefore easy to understand that both the child and the parent will try to borrow themselves out of the situation. The above-mentioned legislative changes will reduce the risk of minors becoming indebted, although a parent in debt also impacts negatively on the child's future. How the equation can be solved is a subject for continuing debate.[27]

[27] According to recent studies by professor Tapio Salonen, it would cost about 15 billion SEK to solve the problem of child poverty (Sveriges television 2011-05-08).

THE SCALE OF SWEDISH TAX SYSTEM CONCERNING CHILDREN

ELEONOR KRISTOFFERSON

Abstract

Although a workable tax system within a country is vital to the fundamental structure of its society, it constitutes a very complex area of social, cultural, economic and legal factors. Highly developed countries thus have different tax scales within the tax system to accommodate taxpayers' differing circumstances. The legal philosophy is to establish, as far as possible, a fair and just social mechanism of tax and compliance. In particular, highly developed democracies like Sweden try not only to maintain social justice for all tax payers, but especially for all those who are, in one way or another, responsible for children. This article will, in a wider sense, focus on the legal aspects of effect of tax on children. It discusses expenditures by the state, such as contributions and services provided for children and their families under Swedish government programmes. Since the article deals with the pure theory of the relevant laws, it may be a useful basis for a comparative analysis with other legal systems. The political issues of how laws governing children should be taken into account in order to achieve the best interests of the child are not dealt here; nevertheless, there are some critical reflections on the current tax system.

1. Introduction

The aim of this article is to offer an overview of the Swedish tax system governing children. The article essentially deals with aspects of income tax, since every individual is a tax subject for income tax purposes. When income tax is assessed, the individual's personal circumstances are taken into account, and allowances made according to income. Deductions for child-related expenses may differ in different tax regimes. In some legislations, much of the child-related costs for parents are deductible—

clear examples are for education costs and child care. This typically occurs where such costs are primarily borne by the individual and not financed by public institutions. Indirect taxes, such as value-added tax (VAT), are not examined in this article, since the person of the consumer actually bearing the cost of the tax is of little interest; the amount of tax on a bar of chocolate or pizza is the same whether the purchaser is a child or an adult. Although there is neither a wealth tax nor a gift or inheritance tax in Sweden, how income tax affects gifts and inheritances is the main focus of the study here, which will be discussed as follows: first, the basics of the Swedish tax system, including children as taxable persons; then, I look at rules governing the taxation of parents, and income tax on gifts and inheritances; and finally, I examine some of the most important rules of taxation applicable to children.

2. The Basics of the Swedish Tax System

Sweden is well-known as a high tax country. The Swedish tax system is well organized, and includes direct and indirect taxes, and social security fees. Like many nations, the country's most significant direct tax is income tax, and it applies to individuals as well as entities that have obtained a legal personality, such as businesses and associations.

Again, like many countries, the general consumption tax in Sweden is VAT, which is a multi-level, indirect tax. The standard rate of VAT is 25 per cent, and is levied on an item's purchase price. Other indirect taxes are excise duties on alcohol, energy, tobacco etc.

The social security fees are made by individuals operating their own businesses, as well as by employers based on salaries paid. These fees are approximately 30 per cent of gross income, and may be divided into two separate parts. One part is, constitutionally, recognised as a tax.[1] The second part is a fee.

---

[1] The specific characteristic of a tax is that one has the obligation to pay it without getting something specific in return. However we cannot deny the fact that although a taxpayer does not get something particular in return, there are, in general, many social advantages for the taxpayer. Thus, one of the substantive characteristics of the tax system is to support directly and effectively government decisions relating to the maintenance of the legal personality of the state including its duties towards its population as a whole. These might include public works, public utilities, public services, education and health services, unemployment social benefits and any other governmental programmes, e.g. maintaining its

Different income tax rates are applied to individuals and legal persons. Partnerships[2] are transparent for income tax purposes even though they present legal persons.[3] Hence, when the owners are individuals, their income is taxed as income for individuals and as income for legal persons, when the owners are equally legal persons. The estates of the deceased are taxed as for individuals.[4]

Under current legislation, incomes of legal persons are taxed at a flat rate of 26.3 per cent.[5] However, income tax on individuals is progressive, on income from employment or from business. The tax owed is divided into a basic and a supplementary amount. The basic amount is paid on all income, and amounts to about 32 per cent (municipal tax).[6] The supplementary amount is paid above incomes of SEK 383,000 and SEK 548,000 respectively. Income above SEK 383,000 attracts a supplementary 20 per cent,[7] or approximately 52 per cent total. Income over SEK 548,000 attracts a further 5 per cent,[8] thus making approximately 57 per cent. Income from capital is taxed at a flat rate of 30 per cent.

The income tax rates in Sweden	
Legal persons	26.3 percent
Individuals	
Income from capital	30 percent
Income from employment	ca 32 % + 20 % +5 %
Income from business	ca 32 % + 20 % + 5 %

defence forces. Hence, when we assert that there is not any consideration for money paid, we are solely focusing on the direct tangible reflection of the tax and not necessarily on the indirect intangible consequences of the money for the taxpayer. Whilst the tax is an unavoidable transfer of resources from individuals or entities to the government, it is without doubt a corollary condition of social coexistence.

[2] *Handelsbolag* and *kommanditbolag*.

[3] Chapter 5 Section 1 Swedish income tax act (SITA), *Inkomstskattelagen* (1999:1229).

[4] Chapter 4 Section 1-3 SITA.

[5] Chapter 65 Section 10 SITA.

[6] Chapter 65 Section 3 SITA.

[7] Chapter 65 Section 5 SITA.

[8] Chapter 65 Section 5 SITA.

Tax rates affect how income is classified. In general, individuals prefer to have their income classified as income from capital rather than income from employment or. To avoid any inconsistency between the considerable number of special tax provisions, there are several different tax schemes preventing the reclassification of income in Sweden.[9] However, despite these tax schemes, the legal authorities do not have things all their own way, for in order to avoid incurring heavy taxes, individuals have resorted to different interpretations of the legislation and these interpretations have created numerous practical difficulties for the tax officials. Although the objective of the law is to hinder any conflict between taxpayers and the state authorities, it has been proved impossible to circumvent the divergence between the laws and personal interests of individuals.

3. Children as Tax Subjects

Under Swedish law, income tax is levied on individuals who are resident in Sweden.[10] Income tax is also levied on non-resident individuals, when the income is closely connected to a Swedish source.[11] This is, for example, the case with income related to real estate in Sweden.[12] The Swedish Income Tax Act[13] does not put any stress on the age of the taxable subject, which means that under the actual implementation of tax provisions the age of the taxpayer is not taken into account. In other words, the age of 18, referring to the legal position of a person as an adult, which is accepted as an integral part of the general principles of private law within most states, is not apparently in conformity with the Swedish legal system. From an international tax law perspective however, the recognition of children as tax subjects is common.

The fact that children are tax subjects, even though they are not able to enter into contracts themselves, means that they may have tax debts relating to contracts that they might not have had any financial interest in entering, and the debt enforcement service of the government agency may register the children if these debts are not paid. This is not only a potential, but also an actual, problem. One common situation is that parents with several different personal reasons transfer assets to their children. If, for

[9] See for example chapter 57 SITA regarding dividends and capital gains on so-called qualified shares in closely-held companies.
[10] Chapter 3 Section 3 SITA.
[11] Chapter 3 Section 17 SITA.
[12] Chapter 3 Section 18 SITA.
[13] This is called *Inkomstskattelagen* [1999÷1299].

example, the parents have sold shares in the names of their children, and not declared the income properly, a tax debt may occur. In 2008, the debt enforcement services registered the following children with the highest unpaid tax debts:

1. Boy born 1999: SEK 146,335
2. Boy born 1995: SEK 75,207
3. Girl born 1992: SEK 74,806
4. Boy born 1996: SEK 69,809
5. Boy born 1996: SEK 48,201
6. Girl born 1993: SEK 44,461[14]

The registrations by the debt enforcement services create serious problems for such children when they come of age, or later in life, for instance not being able to rent a flat, take up a loan, have a credit card, or have their own telephone or internet subscription. It is axiomatic that the issue of deliberately involving children in tax problems opens many questions regarding the infringement of "the best interest of the child" and raise the moral issues and legal policy governing the rights of children.

4. Taxation of Parents

4.1. General

The Swedish income tax system is based on individual assessment. There are no longer any traces of the joint assessment that was finally abolished in the mid 1970s. Everyone is consequently taxed on his or her own income. In calculating income tax, it is of no importance whether one is married, cohabiting, single, or has children. In other words, the dependency burden does not affect the tax burden.

4.2. Child Care Costs and Other Costs Related to Children

One effect of the individual assessment is that there is no income tax credit for dependent children (or spouses). Nor is there any tax-free amount in conjunction with the number of children. Instead, the government supplies

[14] See Grundberg, Sven, Tusentals barn hos fogden, E24 2008-02-27, www.e24.se, downloaded 2011-02-11.

a child allowance (a social security payment distributed to the parents and guardians of children) payable until the child attains 16.[15]

There is also an extended child allowance if the child is still in education over the age of 16; although most children over 16 are not still in education.[16]

Furthermore, parents that have two or more children receive a large family supplement,[17] and if parents live together with at least one common child and have children from previous relationships, all the children can be counted for large family supplement purposes.

Monthly child allowance and large family supplement[18]

Number of children	Child allowance, SEK	Large family supple-ment, SEK	Total, SEK
1	1,050	–	1,050
2	2,100	150	2,250
3	3,150	604	3,754
4	4,200	1,614	5,814
5	5,250	2,864	8,114

It should be pointed out that child allowance is not subject to income tax or any other taxes.[19]

The Swedish system also offers a study allowance comprising legal support for the education of a child. If the child is over 16, the same amount as in the table above is paid to him as study allowance. However, the allowance is solely paid to the child who is actively engaged in

[15] Chapter 15 Section 3-4 the Social Insurance Code (2010:110) (SIC) *social försärsäkringsbalken*.
[16] Chapter 15 Section 5-7 SIC.
[17] Chapter 15 Section 8 SIC.
[18] Försäkringskassan, Child allowance [*Barnbidrag*] and large family supplement [*flerbarnstillägg*], Information från försäkringskassan 01.07.2010, www.forsakringskassan.se, downloaded 2011-02-14.
[19] Chapter 8 Section 9 SITA.

education, and is provided by the National Board of Student Aid,[20] and is granted unconditionally.[21] In other words, the study allowance is granted automatically, with the core purpose of providing financial assistance to the student.

In Sweden, childcare is normally supported by the municipality, regardless of whether the childcare is private or public. By international standards, childcare costs for the parents are low in Sweden. Childcare costs depend on the parents' income. However, a maximum amount is applied by most municipalities, but varies from place to place. For instance, in Örebro, which is geographically in the middle of Sweden, and fairly close to the Stockholm, the capital, the maximum amount for childcare is 1,260 for the first child, 840 for the second child and 420 for the third child.[22] There is no any charge for the fourth child.

As a general childcare costs cannot be counted against parents' tax liability, as they are considered non-deductible personal life expenses.[23] However, since 2008 a tax credit for household services has come into force in Sweden, which applies to babysitting and other household services,[24] and amounts to 50 per cent of the costs of such services.[25] The tax credit is paid by the tax authorities to the person supplying the household services. The credit has functioned very positively and is workable for the persons acquiring the services, because they only have to pay half of the charges for the services and hence face the tax effect immediately, without having to wait until the tax assessment, which may take place several months later. This aspect of tax law has significantly encouraged the reporting of the relevant services to the tax offices and has, to some extent, decreased deliberate tax fraud constituting misrepresentation of information in order to reduce an employer's tax liability. In turn, an employee is also under legal obligation to report his/her income from the relevant services.

---

[20] CSN, *Centrala studiemedelsnämnden.*

[21] Försäkringskassan, Child allowance [*Barnbidrag*] and large family supplement [*flerbarnstillägg*], Information från försäkringskassan 01.07.2010, www.forsakringskassan.se, downloaded 2011-02-14.

[22] Örebro kommun, Riktlinjer för enskild förskola, fritidshem och pedagogisk omsorg i Örebro kommun, www.orebro.se, downloaded 2011-02-14, page 7.

[23] See Chapter 9 Section 2 SITA.

[24] Chapter 67 Section 13, 13 a and 13 b SITA.

[25] Chapter 67 Section 19 SITA.

The tax credit covers not only babysitting costs but also other household-related costs such as the washing and ironing of clothes, cooking, shovelling snow or mowing the lawn, renovations, extensions, and the conversion of buildings.[26] There are three core political elements for providing a tax credit for these costs:

1. To reduce, as far as feasible, the contradictions between working and family life;
2. To decrease underground economic incomes with the chief intention of brightening financial activities;
3. To support the building and construction sectors in times of economic recession

In general, the tax credit for household services has been more popular than expected. Thanks to it, employees who were formerly outside the social security system (and perhaps in the underground economy), are now within the social security system and thus entitled to sickness allowance as well as a pension.[27]

4.3. Family Owned Businesses

As mentioned above, Sweden applies an individual assessment of income, with progressive rates up to about 57 per cent.[28] For family owned businesses, it could therefore be tempting to divide the income among the family members in order to avoid incurring the highest tax rates. There is, therefore, a special tax scheme which applies to income from family owned businesses.[29]

Children below the age of 16 cannot be taxed separately for any income from family owned businesses. Instead, the parent with the highest income is taxed on the child's income.[30] Children between 16-18, as well as assisting spouses—that is, spouses that are not in a leading business

---

[26] Chapter 67 Section 13, 13 a and 13 b SITA.

[27] See Lodin, Sven-Olof, Lindencrona, Gustaf, Melz, Peter, Silfverberg, Christer, Simom-Almendahl, Theresa, Inkomstskatt – en läro- och handbok i skatterätt, 13 edition 2011 p. 49.

[28] Municipal tax ca 32 percent, depending of the tax rate of the municipality + 20 percent + 5 %.

[29] Chapter 60 SITA.

[30] Chapter 60 Section 2 and 12 SITA.

position—are only taxed on a fair market salary.[31] The business leading spouse/parent is taxed on the excess amount.[32] The provisions regarding spouses also apply to cohabitees who have been married before, or who have, or have had, children in common.[33] Homosexual cohabitees and spouses are treated the same as heterosexual cohabitees or spouses.

There is a certain concept of the *child* for Swedish income tax purposes. The definition includes not only a biological child, but also an adoptee, a stepson or stepdaughter, or foster child.[34]

The provisions regarding family owned businesses may apply to corporations, partnerships or one-man businesses. However, corporations are only included when more than 50 per cent of the votes for the shares are, explicitly, or implicitly controlled by four or fewer owners.[35] All related persons are, in this context, deemed as being the same person.[36] The following persons are deemed to be related for income tax purposes:

- Spouse
- Parent
- Grandparent
- Descendant
- Sister or brother, sister's or brother's spouse and descendant
- Estate in which the taxable person, or some of the above mentioned persons, owns a part[37]

5. Gifts and Inheritance

As mentioned above, there is no gift or inheritance tax in Sweden. The relevant tax objects for gifts and inheritance were terminated in December 2004. The gift and inheritance tax meant to formally end on 1 January 2005, but this was not accomplished, because of the tsunami disaster in Thailand, which occurred on 25 December 2004, in which many Swedes spending their Christmas vacation there lost their lives. The ethical aspects on levying inheritance tax on the many inheritances of persons dying a

[31] Chapter 60 Section 2, 7, 12 and 13 SITA.
[32] Chapter 60 Section 6, 12 and 13 SITA.
[33] Chapter 2 Section 20 SITA.
[34] Chapter 2 Section 21 SITA.
[35] Chapter 56 Section 2 SITA.
[36] Chapter 56 Section 5 SITA.
[37] Chapter 2 Section 22 SITA.

week before the planned termination of the tax resulted in this change. Before the gift and inheritance tax was abolished, transactions from parents to children in order to avoid a future inheritance tax were very common.[38] Nowadays, such transactions are seldom tax-driven, because gifts to children are not deductible for income tax purposes.[39] Gifts and inheritance are income tax free.[40]

The child is entitled to an orphan's pension (SV: *barnpension*) if one or both parents die before the child has reached the age of 18,[41] but this may be prolonged until the age of 20 if the child is still in full-time university education.[42] Unlike pensions in general, the orphan's pension is, partly subject to income tax provisions.[43] The orphan's pension shall merely be taxed when it exceeds 40 per cent x the basic amount for social security purposes[44] [2011: SEK 42,800), or when both parents are deceased 80 per cent x the basic amount for social security purposes on a yearly basis.[45] Consequently, an amount of SEK 1,426 per month when one parent is deceased, or SEK 2,854 when both parents are deceased, and is free of income tax.

6. Conclusion

This article has examined the different tax provisions affecting the income of various subjects of the tax system. This includes individuals and different types of entities. As a whole, the Swedish tax system does not contain many special tax schemes regarding the treatment of children. The system assesses individuals on a personal basis. There is no right to deduct childcare costs, or allowances to a child or spouse. Neither is there a tax-free amount based on family circumstances, such as the number of children.

---

[38] See Lodin, Sven-Olof, Lindencrona, Gustaf, Melz, Peter, Silfverberg, Christer, Simom-Almendahl, Theresa, Inkomstskatt – en läro- och handbok i skatterätt, 13 edition 2011 p. 606.
[39] Chapter 9 Section 2 SITA.
[40] Chapter 8 Section 2 SITA.
[41] Chapter 78 Section 2 and 4 SIC.
[42] Chapter 78 Section 5 SIC.
[43] Chapter 11 Section 1 SITA.
[44] SW: *prisbasbeloppet*.
[45] Chapter 11 Section 40 SITA.

The dependency of children is taken into account by the tax system—there is a definite, fixed child allowance, irrespective of income, for all, but a supplementary allowance is paid for the second child onwards.

Private as well as public childcare facilities are financed by public means in Sweden. It is the responsibility of the parents to pay a fee for the childcare, which is evaluated on the parents' income. However, most municipalities supply a maximum amount, which may seem rather low by comparison with other countries. In addition, costs for private babysitting are subject to a definite income tax credit.

Owing to the progressive tax rates on income from employment and business, a special scheme prevents family members from dividing their income between them with the aim of avoiding tax. Under this scheme, children below the age of 16 cannot be taxed on their own income. Instead, income tax is levied on the parent with the highest income within the family. Children between 16 and 18 can only be taxed on an income amounting to a fair market salary.

The gift and inheritance tax which had been in place for a long time, has been terminated in Sweden. Neither gifts nor inheritances are subject to income tax, and are thus tax-free in Sweden.

Under Swedish tax legislation, the individual, and not the family is the tax subject. The fact that a person has a family is of less significance in the assessment of tax. The technical solution of benefiting children—within the tax system or within the system of contributions and institutions financed by public bodies—is probably of little benefit to the child. If, however, the parents have no, or a very low, income, so that they cannot use tax deductions within the Swedish tax system effectively, contributions are more efficient than tax deductions or tax rebates. It is most important, however, that society endeavours to ensure the fulfilment of the basic needs of all children. But whether it has achieved this goal remains one of the most serious questions of the law and national debate. The reason is that social justice, social balance, and equality between children, cannot be solely regulated by law (especially by methods of taxation), but by the common understanding of different problems. This is because child allowance is not in itself a gift to the family members, but the way in which the social services are divided between families with children. Family needs naturally vary from family to family, not least depending on the income of a family as a whole. Thus, what is a major problem to one family may be no problem at all to another. In other words, the best interests of the child are not based solely on the equal division of child allowance, but also on the fundamental needs of each family. Fairness and social justice are thus not determined by the level of child allowance, but rather by how we understand the basic needs of a mother, father, or child; by how we understand that needs vary from one family to another.

'BRINGING UP BABY': USING PRE-PARENTING AGREEMENTS TO MANAGE THE CHILD-PARENT RELATIONSHIP THROUGH AND AFTER PARTNERSHIP BREAKDOWN

ANGELA BURNS

Abstract

Relationships begin and relationships end; unfortunately unresolved conflict abounds. Children of separated parents are caught in the crossfire. And it is not a minority. As the parents fight, the everyman-child suffers, "abuse, maltreatment and exploitation". It is well established that reducing negative parental conflict and promoting positive resolution is of benefit to children on parental separation. The government in England and Wales has introduced mechanisms to support this; yet the number of parents resorting to court in child matters is on the increase, and in-court conciliation demonstrates only short-term satisfaction. There must be more we can do. This paper considers whether introducing Pre-Parenting Agreements (PPA) into the mainstream family conflict resolution toolkit, in tandem with existing procedures, will reduce child harm on parental separation. It then investigates whether the PPA can be reconciled with the existing law, and finally contemplates drafting and practical considerations.

1. Introduction

Children are the centre of our world, the fulcrum upon which parents pivot and the family functions. At birth, proud parents beam, radiate love and vow to protect their child always and forever. Then, unexpectedly, the parents split up and the child, once so cherished, disintegrates at the centre of a 'tug of love', pulled between the parties as the relationship dissolves.

Let us make no bones about it: the breakdown of a relationship is traumatic for children. Research[1] demonstrates that parental divorce is more stressful for a child than the death of a close family member, and that damage suffered is directly related to the level of parental conflict experienced by the child[2]. Worse, parents admit deliberately extending court proceedings to make the process more painful for their spouses and, in doing so, of course increase the pain suffered by their children.[3] These children are not battling the extremes of existence: they are not enslaved or facing death on the front line of a war torn country and yet, all the same, the everyman-child is suffering "abuse, maltreatment or exploitation"[4] at the hands of their parents; their very lives are at risk. Children of conflict-based parental separation suffer an increased risk of suicide as a child (and adult), isolation, depression, anxiety, hostility, anger, negative parent-child relationships, increased alcohol or drug abuse, lower academic performance and future relationship issues[5]. And it is not a minority of children who are affected: in 2001 it was estimated that by the age of sixteen 28 per cent of all children in the United Kingdom will have survived their parents' divorce.[6] Taken in the context of a high divorce rate (currently estimated

---

[1] Gunda Herberth et al., *Relation between stressful life events, neuropeptides and cytokines: results from the LISA birth cohort study,* PEDIATRIC ALLERGY AND IMMUNOLOGY, VOL 19 ISSUE 8 722-729 (December 2008) cited in Mischon De Reya Solicitors, *The Policy Briefing Paper: Parental, Separation, Children and the Courts* (2009)
http://www.mishcon.com/assets/managed/docs/downloads/doc_2395/policy-briefing-paper-parental-separation-children-and-the-courts.pdf (last visited Nov. 3, 2010) at 1 and note 8.

[2] Paul Amato, *Children of Divorce in the 1990s: An update of the Amato and Keith (1991) Meta Analysis,* JOURNAL OF FAMILY PSYCHOLOGY 355 (2001).

[3] Mischon De Reya Solicitors, *supra* at 1.

[4] Convention on the Rights of the Child, Art 19 (Nov 20 1989) 1577 U.N.T.S. 3.

[5] Gordon Harold *et al.*, *Marital Conflict, Child Emotional Security about Family Relationships and Child Adjustment* SOCIAL DEVELOPMENT 350 at 376 (2004); Osnat Erel & Bonnie Burman, *'Interrelatedness of marital relations and parent–child relations: A meta analytic review* 118(1) PSYCHOLOGICAL BULLETIN 108 at 132 and see generally Gordon Harold *et al,* NOT IN FRONT OF THE CHILDREN? HOW CONFLICT BEWTEEN PARENTS AFFECTS CHILDREN (2001) and E. Mark Cummings & Patrick Davies, CHILDREN AND MARITAL CONFLICT: THE IMPACT OF FAMILY DISPUTE AND RESOLUTION (1994).

[6] JAN PROYOR & BRYAN RODGERS, CHILDREN IN CHANGING FAMILIES: LIFE AFTER PARENTAL SEPARATION, 4 (2001).

at 45 per cent[7]) the number of children suffering harm through divorce[8] is significant and likely, without action, to remain on the increase.

As lawyers we are not oblivious to this suffering and, when advising divorce clients, we adopt a child-focused[9] "welfare rights narrative",[10] doing our utmost, as outsiders, to minimise the pain. We suggest reconciliation where appropriate;[11] persuade parents that the children come first,[12] and that they should not be used as weapons of hate[13] or pawns in a financial fight;[14] suggest mediation[15] or round-table collaboration; and avoid contested hearings unless they really are the best (and often the only remaining) option. And it is not just us trying to redress the balance. The state and family law organisations regularly review family breakdown mechanisms and introduce new measures such as parenting workshops[16] to reduce conflict on family breakdown; and legislation purports to support the child.[17] But is it enough? Are we really fulfilling our obligations[18] and taking appropriate measures to protect our children, our future?

---

[7] Resolution, *Family Agreements Seeking Certainty to Reduce Disputes* (2010) http://www.resolution.org.uk/site_content_files/files/family_agreements.pdf (last visited Nov 3, 2010).

[8] A number which would be significantly increased if cohabitation breakdown was included in the statistics.

[9] Alison Diduck, *Solicitors and Legal Subjects, in* FEMINISTS PERSPECTIVES ON CHILD LAW 257, 251-270 (Jo Bridgeman & Daniel Monk eds. 2000).

[10] See Hilary Lim & Jeremy Roche, *Feminism and Children's Rights, in* FEMINISTS PERSPECTIVES ON CHILD LAW 233, 227-249 (Jo Bridgeman & Daniel Monk eds. 2000).

[11] The Law Society, FAMILY LAW PROTOCOL, 1.15-1.17, (2006) .

[12] Children Act, S1, 1989, c. 41 (Eng) and Resolution, *Guide to Good Practice,* 6 (2009) and The Law Society *id* at 1.1.21.

[13]The Law Society, *id* at 1.1.25.

[14] The Law Society, *id* at 1.1.24.

[15] The Law Society, *id* at 1.1.15 and Resolution *supra* note 9 at 6.

[16] On the recommendation of the Children and Family Court Advisory Support Service ('CAFCASS') courts can order parents to attend Separated Parents' Information Programmes; and Resolution has introduced Parenting after Parting workshops which can be booked voluntarily by one or both parents.

[17] For example, Children Act, *Supra*, note 14 at S: in matters concerning the upbringing of the child the welfare of the child is paramount or to put it another way, action or omission must be in the best interests of the child (the 'Paramountcy Principle').

[18] See generally, Convention of the Rights of the Child *supra,* note 4. As signatories to the Convention the government has agreed to be accountable ton the UN for failure to fulfilling the obligations under the Convention.

Both the state and lawyers react to problems with children, reasonably, empathically, objectively, but still reactionarily. The child is seen as the victim who must in the welfare narrative be protected through reaction. Little more than lip service[19] is given to the wishes and feelings of the child.[20] Addressing the problem with such passivity allows for intentional or unintentional harmful parental "exploitation, maltreatment or abuse"[21] of the child. In contrast, when it comes to finances, lawyers[22], the judiciary[23] and the state[24] are taking an increasingly proactive stance.

In 1998 the Supporting Families Consultation[25] recommended that, subject to six safeguards, voluntary pre-nuptial agreements should be enforceable. This area is currently being revisited by the Law Commission, with the final report due to be published in 2012.[26] In 2005 Resolution[27] published a paper proposing legislative reform to support pre-nuptial agreements.[28] This paper was updated and republished in 2010.[29] On 20 October 2010 the Supreme Court published the long-awaited *Radmacher*[30] judgment which clearly demonstrates the changing tide in favour of the pre-nuptial agreement. Although the court did not accept that the pre-nuptial agreement was a binding and enforceable contract, preferring to leave such major policy changes to the legislature, it did take account of the agreement within the confines of the existing ancillary relief legislation[31]

---

[19] See generally Hilary Lim and Jeremy Roche, *supra* 227-249.
[20] Children Act, S1, 1989, c. 41 (Eng).
[21] Convention on the Rights of the Child, *supra* note 4 at Art 19.
[22] Resolution, *supra,* note 7 generally.
[23] See *Crossley v Crossley* [2007][EWCA civ 1491 [2008] 1 FLR 1467, 1472 , *Macleod v Macleod* [2008] UKPC 64 [2010] 1 AC 298 and *Radmacher (formerly Granatino) (Respondent) v Granatino (Appellant)* [2010] UKSC 42.
[24] The Home Office, *Supporting Families: A Consultation Document* (1998). http://www.nationalarchives.gov.uk/ERORecords/HO/421/2/acu/sfpages.pdf (last visited 3 Nov. 2010) 31-33.
[25] The Home Office, *id* at 31-33
[26] The Law Commission, *Annual Report 2009-2010:The Forty-Forth Annual Report of the Law Commission* (29 June 2010) Law Com 323 http://www.lawcom.gov.uk/docs/lc323_web.pdf (last visited 3 Nov. 2010) 2.68-2.75.
[27] An organisation of 5,700 family lawyers committed to non-confrontation resolution of family disputes.
[28] And post-nuptial.
[29] Resolution, *supra,* note 7 generally.
[30] *Radmacher, Supra* note 25.
[31] Matrimonial Causes Act, S25, 1973, c. 18 (Eng.).

and provided guidance for lower courts on upholding pre-nuptial agreements.

The pre-nuptial agreement is arguably an unromantic but eminently practical arrangement addressing the financial fallout of relationship breakdown. Whilst there are jurisdictional differences in treatment, provided that safeguards are met the agreement is in general terms enforceable in law across most jurisdictions[32] or at the very least taken into account in court proceedings.[33] Arrangements made before the bleak winter of bitterness sets in,[34] when parties are amenable, agreeable and open to reasonable suggestion and negotiation, support personal autonomy[35] and offer some certainty, reduce animosity[36] and save costs, resources and time.[37] Why not so with arrangements pertaining to the children? If the finances can be considered at the beginning of (or during[38]) the relationship prior to the end-of-relationship animosity and such treatment reduces hostility; can something similar be introduced regarding arrangements for current or future children?

This paper, primarily addressing the position in England and Wales (although it has wider application), will consider whether the harm suffered by a child on relationship breakdown can be reduced if arrangements for children are mutually agreed in advance of relationship breakdown and recorded in a PPA. It will consider whether it is possible to address all conceptual and practical difficulties, and thereby produce a document which will be upheld by the court.

---

[32] The following countries accept the enforceability of pre-nuptial agreements: Austria, Australia, Belgium, China, Czech Republic, Denmark, Estonia, France, Germany, Greece, Netherlands, Norway, Portugal, Spain, Sweden and Switzerland. Pre-nuptial agreements are compulsory in Austria. In the United States 29 States have adopted the Uniform Premarital Agreement Act (9C UNIFORM LAWS ANNOTATED 35 (2007)).

[33] As in England and Wales.

[34] "Perhaps one reason that divorces are so ugly, marred by unkind acts of mutual deception, is that both parties perceive the 'last move' and a sharply truncated shadow of the future". DAVID BUSS, EVOLUTIONARY PSYCOLOGY, 258 (1999).

[35] The Home Office, *supra,* note 22 at 4.21 and *Radmacher*, *supra,* note 21 at 78.

[36] The Home Office, *supra,* note 22 at 4.20.

[37] Resolution, *supra*, note 7 at 4.

[38] The post-nuptial agreement. Note that a post-nuptial agreement differs from a separation agreement. A post-nuptial agreement is entered into before the couple consider separation, whereas a separation agreement is entered into on separation.

2. Conflict-Based Separation and Pre-Parenting Agreements

Parents will separate, and children will experience parental conflict. These experiences are part of a child's (and adult's) life. It is not the separation or conflict itself that harms the child, but the child's exposure to unresolved destructive parental conflict[39] including both overt direct hostility and parental emotional withdrawal from each other and the child[40] with conflict resulting in parental litigation being particularly destructive.[41]

Both emotional and cognitive research into child distress on parental separation[42] demonstrates a direct correlation between the negative effect on the child and the amount/type of conflict experienced. It is widely accepted that minimising negative conflict,[43] and in particular resolving the conflict positively, will reduce the harm suffered by a child on parental separation.[44] The government in England and Wales has, in recent years,[45] formulated its family policy on that basis. Emphasis is on reduced family conflict—and therefore child exposure to conflict—and diverting parents from contested court hearings. Litigation is the port of last rather than first call. Parents are encouraged to enter into parenting agreements[46] (PA) outside court or, if application to court is made, as part of the Private Law

---

[39] Gordon Harold & Mervyn Murch, *Inter-Parental Conflict and Children's Adaptation to Separation and Divorce; Theory, Research and Implications for Family Law, Practice and Policy,* CHILDREN AND FAMILY LAW QUARTERLY 185 at 191 (2005).

[40] Gordon Harold & Mervyn Murch, *supra,* note 41 at 190.

[41] HM Government, *Parental Separation: Children's Needs and Parents' responsibilities,* Cm 6273 (July 2004) http://nationalstrategies.standards.dcsf.gov.uk/node/84523 (last viewed 6 Nov. 2010) at 10.

[42] Mostly marital but equally applicable to partnerships.

[43] Secretary of State for Children and Families, *Green Paper: Support for All* 4.21 (January 2010).

[44] Mark Cummings *et al., Resolution and Children's Response to inter-adult Anger'* 27 Developmental Psychology 462 at 470 (1991).

[45] See generally Secretary of State for Children and Families, *supra*, note 44 and HM Government, *Supra* note 43.

[46] Also known as parenting plans.

Programme, attend in-court conciliation in an effort to reach agreement[47] rather than progress the case through the court.

On the face of it, such measures are very effective. Low levels of couples[48] attend court to resolve their child-based conflict, preferring instead to reach independent agreement; and research illustrates that in the selected samples there was a high degree of success in the use of the in-court conciliation programme.[49] Yet these advances do not show the whole picture. Since 2002 there has been an increase in the number of parents seeking resolution at the courts. In 2002 research[50] indicated that approximately 10 per cent[51] attended court, whereas in 2007 a comparative[52] study indicated that the number had increased to approximately 17 per cent.[53] Further, although high levels of agreements are reached at conciliation hearings, the levels of success appear to be not only reducing (from 76 per cent[54] in 2006[55] to 60 per cent in 2007[56]), but also offering

---

[47] See generally, President of the Family Division, *Practice Direction: The Revised Private Law Programme,* (01 April 2010).

[48] Alison Blackwell & Fiona Dawe, *Non-Residential Parental Contact* (October 2003) http://www.statistics.gov.uk/downloads/theme_social/parentalcontact2002.pdf (last viewed 5 Nov. 2010, 2003).http://www.statistics.gov.uk/downloads/theme_social/parentalcontact2002.pdf (last viewed 5 Nov. 2010) at 12 and Deborah Ladder, Non-Residential Parental Contact 2007-2008 (2008). http://www.statistics.gov.uk/downloads/theme_social/parentalcontact2007-08.pdf (last viewed 5 Nov. 2010) at 23.

[49] Joan Hunt, Parental Perspectives on the Family Law System in England and Wales, (May 2010) http://www.family-justice-council.org.uk/docs/Parental_Perspectives_final.pdf (last viewed 5 Nov. 2010) at 80.

[50] By sample.

[51] Alison Blackwell & Fiona Dawe, *Supra,* note 48 at 12.

[52] Comparing the 2002 and 2007 results.

[53] Deborah Ladder, *Supra* note 48 at 23.

[54] Based on sample, although an even and good-sized sample, this may include some inflation.

[55] Liz Trinder *et al. Making Contact happen or making contact work? The process and outcomes of in-court conciliation (2006)* DCA Research Series 3/06.

[56] Sir Mark Potter, *Speech: Report on the Private Law Programme,* (13 May 2008) http://www.judiciary.gov.uk/NR/rdonlyres/943A2883-6C1D-4FCF-8D74-D8B0183CD013/0/pfd_report_private_law_programme_130508.pdf (lasted viewed 5 Nov. 2010) at 3.

little in the way of long-term success. DCA research[57] prior to the adoption[58] of the Private Law Programme illustrated that of 300 cases just over half returned to court for further litigation. Of the returners, half required an update of the existing order.[59] Although the return to litigation rate following conciliation[60] is less (approximately 40 per cent) a hefty two thirds of the sample required legal intervention; in fact, two years after the original conciliation two thirds of the agreements[61] were no longer in place, and the reasons are telling. It would be expected for agreements to be updated on a regular basis to reflect change of circumstances, as is identified in the DCA[62] study; however, this is not the case with conciliation agreements where the majority of the amendments took place[63] because one party or the child did not assent to the contents of the agreement. Although the Programme does offer a short-term gain, the long battles that follow the implementation of the agreement result in children suffering sustained unresolved conflict.

There are a number of reasons for the high return rate under the original Private Law Programme. First, parties who attend the Programme are already firmly in ensconced in bitter battle, and the in-court conciliation offered does not attempt to address the root cause of the issues.[64] The agreements are a short-term, fix-it patch. Second, the Programme does not take account of the parties' individual autonomy: safety issues were often disregarded,[65] and many parties felt that the agreements were foisted upon

---

[57] The Department for Constitutional Affairs, HM Government, *supra* note 46 at 26.

[58] In Private Law Programme was under pilot in some areas but the relevant cases are excluded from this study.

[59] HM Government, *Supra* note 43 at 14.

[60] Liz Trinder & Joanne Kellet, *The Longer Term Outcomes of In-Court Conciliation* (November 2010) http://www.justice.gov.uk/docs/261107.pdf (last viewed 5 Nov. 2010) at 10-11.

[61] Liz Trinder & Joanne Kellet, *Id*, at 10.

[62] HM Government, *Supra* note 43 at 14. A further DCA study with a sample of 61 parents put this at 1 in 3 see Carol Smart *et al. Residence and Contact Disputes in Court Volume 2* (June 2005) http://www.dca.gov.uk/research/2005/4_2005_1.pdf (last viewed 7 Nov. 2010) at 76.

[63] H M Government, *Supra* at 14.

[64] Liz Trinder *et al. Making Contact Work, Making Contact Happen: The Process and Outcomes of In-Court Conciliation* (March 2006) http://www.dca.gov.uk/research/2006/03_2006.pdf (last viewed 7 Nov. 2010) at iv.

[65] Trinder *et al. Id* at iv.

them rather than a result of negotiated settlement.[66] Third, the Programme failed to consider the wishes of the children, preferring to follow the welfare narrative of third parties.[67]

The government has recognised that the Programme requires further improvement and in April 2010 issued a Practice Direction[68] amending the procedure in an effort to address the above issues. The new procedure requires CAFCASS[69] to undertake a safety analysis[70] before the in-court conciliation can take place, and in some cases to ascertain the views of the children prior to the in-court conciliation and, where appropriate, join them as parties to the action.[71] The new procedure still leaves the key relationship issues out in the cold and fails to give the parties the necessary individual autonomy to own the agreement, and therefore does not address the reasons for agreement breakdown and return to court. Although it is too soon to see what affect these amendments will have, they are unlikely to increase the effectiveness of the Private Law Programme overall because the Programme still fails to address the causes of agreement breakdown. This leaves the child at risk of suffering harm as a result of the prolonged unresolved conflict.

With a slow but steady increase in private child litigation, and the short-term nature of agreements reached under the Private Law Programme, it is clear that additional mechanisms are required to promote early resolution of parental conflict and consequently better safeguard children. Although it is accepted that there are a minority of a cases which will always require court intervention, there are additional methods which could be used to divert parents away from litigation or short circuit the litigation process, such as better parental education and increased access to reasonably priced and well-publicised mediation. It is important that additional mechanisms address the outstanding bitterness, increase personal autonomy and circumvent or address root causes of parental discord. The PPA could be a successful complementary mechanism.

---

[66] Liz Trinder *et al, Supra* note 65 at 47.

[67] Lord Chief Justice, *Practice Direction Revised Law Programme* (April 2010) http://www.judiciary.gov.uk/NR/rdonlyres/27290456-8E28-4E79-8C6A-D8B0AB9F286D/0/praticedirectionpfdprivatelawprogrammeapril2010.pdf (last viewed 7 Nov. 2010) at 2.

[68] Lord Chief Justice, *Id* generally.

[69] Children and Family Court Advisory Support Service.

[70] Lord Chief Justice, *Supra,* note 68 at 5.

[71] Lord Chief Justice, *Supra,* note 68 at 9.

PPAs are entered into at the beginning of, or during, a relationship. The PPA represents the parties' wishes before they are drowning in acrimony. It is likely that parents will find it easier to consider the best interests of the child before relationship breakdown. Like a pre-nuptial agreement, this will support personal autonomy;[72] the parents will own the agreement and therefore be more likely to follow it on subsequent relationship breakdown.

But life is not static, and the PPA needs to address this. It would be impossible to future-legislate for the whole of a child's life. Therefore a PPA must be reviewable. It should be reconsidered on each major life event, as well as annually. If drafted before the birth of a child, it must be reconsidered shortly after the birth. In this way, parents will become used to negotiating agreement and resolving conflict positively throughout their relationship. Thus, if the relationship breaks down, not only will the parties have an agreement on arrangements for the child, but even if the PPA does not quite reflect current circumstances parents will have a good starting point which can be used to address their child-conflict issues through reasoned negotiation. By enabling easier variation of the agreement between the parties—with the assistance of a third party (mediator, legal professional, etc.) if required—the root causes of parent conflict, and thus issues, are likely to be significantly narrower than if there was no agreement at all: conflict resolution is consequently more positive, and considerably shorter.

The PPA can also address the child's wishes; it therefore steps away from the constricting welfare rights narrative, and provides not only adult but child autonomy and ownership of the arrangements. Once the child is competent, the contents of the PPA can be discussed with the child, and the child's wishes and feelings incorporated. Including the wishes before relationship breakdown allows the child to state true wishes that have not been coloured by the parental separation. Competent children are used to being involved in such life discussions. For example, parents will often discuss guardianship with their children before drafting or amending a will. Allowing the child to be involved in the PPA will, in addition to involving the child in his/her own life, demonstrate positive conflict resolution.

Finally, the PPA can be used to reduce the effect of parental conflict on the child by offering child certainty. The arrangements can be used as an

---

[72] The Home Office, *Supra* note 37 at 78.

interim measure whilst amendments to the agreement are negotiated. As issues are likely to be narrow in most cases, the PPA post-separation negotiation process is likely to be truncated, and issues with maintaining the *status quo* reduced.

If the PPA offers solutions to outstanding parental conflict and child harm issues, why is it not being used? The simple answer is that it is difficult to accommodate the PPA within the existing legal structure. This paper will now consider whether the difficulties can be reconciled without the need for legislative change.

3. Reconciling the Existing Law

Supporting Families[73] proposed that, subject to six safeguards,[74] voluntary pre-nuptial agreements be recognised as legally binding. The first safeguard prevented any agreements where there were children of the family from being legally binding. Instead, these would fall to be considered by the judge under his or her discretion.[75] This approach was criticised by the Women's National Commission:

> If the value of the agreement is the reduction of conflict on break-up, this is most valuable where there are children of the marriage. But this is a circumstance where the agreement would not be binding."[76]

Although the justification for failing to include arrangements pertaining to children in the enforceable pre-nuptial agreement were not included in the consultation or the response document, the reasoning is nonetheless clear: the laws of contract would not permit the agreement to be enforceable, and in any event such an agreement is incompatible with the Paramountcy Principle[77].

---

[73] The Home Office, *Supra* at 31-33

[74] The Home Office, *Supra* at 33

[75] The Home Office, *Supra* at 38

[76] The Home Office, *Supporting Families Summary of Responses to the Consultation Document* http://www.nationalarchives.gov.uk/ERORecords/HO/421/2/cpd/fmpu/sfamr.pdf (last viewed 8 Nov. 2010) at 24

[77] Children Act, *Supra,* note 22 at S1

3.1. The Paramountcy Principle

The Paramountcy Principle, enshrined in the s1 Children Act 1989,[78] states that in matters of the upbringing of a child, the welfare of the child is paramount: in other words, all cases relating to the upbringing and maintenance of a child must be decided in the child's[79] best interests.[80]

PPAs could be considered incompatible with the Paramountcy Principle because the PPA attempts to future-legislate (prior to separation) what will amount to the best interests of the child at both the time of parental separation, and subsequently. Nevertheless, it is possible to reconcile the Paramountcy Principle and PPAs. This resolution will be demonstrated by analysis of the approach pertaining to prenuptial agreements taken in the recent Supreme Court case of *Radmacher*[81], the consideration of PPAs, and the court's approach to co-parenting agreements.

(a) The Pre-Nuptial Agreement Approach

In *Radmacher*[82] the Supreme Court examined the weighting given to pre-nuptial agreements. Under the ancillary relief regime[83] there is a similar limitation to the Paramountcy Principle in that on the distribution of family assets on divorce, property must be distributed not in the best interests of the child, but in accordance with the overarching umbrella of fairness measured by the yardstick of equality.[84] Fair distribution encompasses needs (including the needs of the children[85]), compensation, and sharing of matrimonial property. It was open to the court to suggest that parties were, prior to marriage, unable to determine what would amount to fair distribution on separation and, in particular—since "fairness like beauty lies in the eye of the beholder"[86]—reserve the analysis of fairness to itself under its unfettered discretion[87] to distribute family assets on divorce. But the court did not do this: instead, it stated that in some

---

78 Children Act, *Supra,* note 22 at S1

79 Child of the application

80 *See J v. C* [1970] A.C. 68 at 710, *Re M.B. (Medical Treatment)* [1997] 2 FLR 426 at 439 and *Re A (Male Sterilisation)* [2000] 1 FLR 549 at 555

81 *Radmacher, Supra* note 25

82 *Radmacher, Supra* note 25

83 See generally, Matrimonial Causes Act, 1973, c. 18 (Eng.)

84 *White v White* [2000] 2 FLR 981 at 605.

85 Matrimonial Causes Act 1973, *Supra* note 84 at ss25(1) , 25(2)(b) & s25(2)(c).

86 *White, Supra* note 85 at 599.

87 *Thomas v. Thomas* [1995] 2 FLR 668.

instances the agreement will reflect what the court would have ordered and it will be fair to uphold the agreement; and in other cases where the agreement does not reflect the approach the court would have taken, issued guidance on measuring the agreement against fairness[88] to determine whether the agreement should be upheld in entirety, partly, or not at all.

It is submitted that a similar course of action could be taken with regards to the Paramountcy Principle. On drafting, the best interests of the child must not only be the paramount consideration, but also be reflected in the agreement. Further, the agreement should demonstrate compliance with the Welfare Checklist[89] including, importantly, the wishes of the child. In *Radmacher*, the court commented that the older the pre-nuptial agreement, the less likely it was to be fair. The same is true of PPAs: the older the agreement, the less likely it is that PPA reflects the current best interests of the child. It is therefore imperative that the review regime outlined earlier in this paper is complied with, and that on each review the Paramountcy Principle takes centre stage. Where the court concurs with the agreement it can be upheld. If the court would have reached a different conclusion on application of the Paramountcy Principle there should be guidance for the court to follow to determine whether to up hold the agreement in full, part or not at all. This guidance should include ascertaining the wishes of the child at the time of the hearing.

(b) The Parenting Agreement Approach

PAs are an informal agreement between parents setting out arrangements pertaining to the children. They are actively encouraged by the government as a method of agreeing future arrangements for the children. The agreement is made on separation and, like PPAs, not enforceable in the courts. Just as suggested above with regards to the PPA, if the case goes to court, the court will take the PA into account and apply the Paramountcy Principle to determine the order which may or may not reflect the PA. Other than the fact that the PA may be closer in time than the PPA to the separation of the parties, and that the PA is drafted on, rather than prior to, separation, there is little to distinguish between the two agreements. Both agreements are required to future-legislate the application of the Paramountcy Principle, and both agreements offer flexibility to the parties. Arguably, if the parental separation disintegrates into a court hearing, the PPA, negotiated outsides times of stress and

[88] *Radmacher, Supra* note 25 at 30-33.
[89] Children Act 1989, *Supra* note 14 at S1(3)

acrimony, may be more use to the court and more likely to reflect the Paramountcy Principle than a PA. This is because, if the review procedure has been followed, the PPA will be a series of documents demonstrating family approach to child arrangements throughout the currency of the relationship and will, importantly, include the wishes of the child.

Further, if the PA is accepted as compatible with the Paramountcy Principle, it is difficult to appreciate how the PPA will fall at this hurdle. As demonstrated above, the two agreements are very similar, and it seems nonsense that the PA is an accepted approach to child arrangements, and the PPA is not. It is proposed that the similarities between the two agreements are so significant that the PPA should be acknowledged. Parallels can again be drawn with the pre-nuptial agreement case law.

In *Macleod*,[90] the Privy Council made a distinction between pre and post-nuptial agreements, finding that the post nuptial agreement was contractually enforceable, and the pre-nuptial was not. Yet the only substantive differences between the two agreements is that the pre-nuptial agreement is entered into before marriage, and the post-nuptial agreement is entered into after marriage, but prior to contemplation of separation, and is thus closer in time to the physical relationship breakdown. *Radmacher*[91] dismissed this distinction[92] and saw no reason that, "such an agreement, whether ante or post-nuptial…should not be enforced".[93] The same approach can be taken with the PA and PPA.

(c)The Co-Parenting Agreement Approach

Co-parenting agreements, entered into the on the birth or adoption of a child are, if not actually commonplace, readily used within same-sex communities. The agreements are particularly used to protect the position of all parties on adoption, or where one party to the relationship is the natural parent and the other is not. These agreements are successfully used to mitigate any conflict on future disagreement. Whilst not enforceable, they are treated in the same way as a pre-nuptial agreement in a matrimonial matter, but departure from the agreement relates to non-compliance with the Paramountcy Principle rather than fairness.

---

[90] *Macleod, Supra* at note 25.
[91] *Radmacher, Supra* note 25.
[92] *Radmacher, Supra* note 25 at 20.
[93] *Radmacher, Supra* note 25 at 29.

3.2. Contract

For a PPA to be binding under existing contract law, the elements of a valid contract—namely legality, agreement (offer and acceptance), intention and consideration—must be present. The PPA is both illegal and lacks consideration and therefore unenforceable.

(a) Consideration

The lack of consideration can be easily overcome. In the US, the Uniform Premarital Agreement Act,[94] which allows agreements to contain child upbringing clauses, addresses the omission of consideration by simply stating that the premarital agreement is one without consideration.[95] In England and Wales, there is no requirement to enact further legislation to recognise the contract; instead, the agreement[96] can be made by way of deed which does not require consideration.

(b) Illegality

The contention that PPAs would be unenforceable due to illegality is more troublesome. Contracts against public policy are illegal. PPAs are caught by two established and interlinked public policies. First, the PPA could be considered prejudicial to family life as it allows parents to contract away rights and duties pertaining to the child; and second, the agreements oust the inherent jurisdiction of the court to decide on matters relating to children.

This is not insurmountable, however: public policy is not inflexible, and is regularly moulded to reflect changes in societal and government viewpoint. For example, "it used to be against public policy for a married couple who were living together, or about to get married, to make an agreement that provided for the contingency that they might separate."[97] However, following the recent decisions of the Privy Council in *Macleod*,[98] and the Supreme Court in *Radmacher*,[99] it is clear that this public policy is "obsolete and should be swept away".[100] The courts could

---

[94] Premarital Agreement Act *Supra,* note 34.
[95] *Supra,* note 34 at s2.
[96] Pre-nuptial agreements are made by way of deed.
[97] *Radmacher, Supra,* note 25 at 11.
[98] *Macleod, Supra* note 25.
[99] *Radmacher, Supra,* note 25.
[100] *Radmacher, Supra,* note 25.

take the same approach to the objection that a PPA is prejudicial to family life.

PPAs are not about relinquishing rights and responsibilities, but are instead about responsibly sharing them. It would never be appropriate for a PPA to include an agreement to relinquish parental responsibility or contact. Moreover, if the review system outlined earlier, and the child's wishes and feelings, are included in the agreement, the changing needs of the child will be addressed and the child will be engaged in his or her own welfare narrative. In this way the PPA does not fight, but operates within, the framework of the Paramountcy Principle and is thus arguably not prejudicial to family life, but a part of supporting positive conflict resolution within family life.

The court has jurisdiction to decide matters pertaining to child arrangements; allowing parents to contract arrangements between themselves would oust the jurisdiction of the court. There are two mechanisms that could be implemented to prevent the PPA conflicting with this policy. First, the PPA, like the separation agreement (entered into by divorcing couples on break-up but prior to ancillary relief order) cannot include a clause prohibiting either party from recourse to court. Further, this could be strengthened by specifically including a clause which states that each party is entitled to seek recourse in the courts. Second, the approach in *Radmacher* could be taken.

A similar issue is apparent in the pre-nuptial agreement. The court has an unfettered discretion to make orders regarding ancillary relief. The pre-nuptial agreement, if it were an enforceable contract, ousts that discretion. The court in *Radmacher* offered a very simple solution to this problem. The court determined that it was a "red herring"[101] to examine whether the agreement was contractually enforceable, and deftly avoided the issue. Instead, the court considered the weight that should be given to the pre-nuptial agreement when the court exercised its discretion, and provided guidelines on determining weight allocation for future hearings. This simple approach allowed the court to determine that safeguards outlined in Supporting Families[102] were not required,[103] and sit within the current legislative framework.[104] It both allows the court to maintain jurisdiction

[101] *Radmacher, Supra* note 25 at 26.
[102] *Supporting Families, Supra* note 26.
[103] *Radmacher, Supra* note 25 at 28.
[104] *Radmacher, Supra* note 25 at 28.

and enables the parties to enter into an agreement that, if the guidance is followed, will in all likelihood be upheld by the court.

An equivalent approach could be adopted with regards to the PPA. Guidelines could be issued, and the court could determine whether the agreement will be upheld in accordance with the guidelines. Taking this stance will remove the relevance of the first safeguard outlined in supporting families, and simultaneously give parents and children greater certainty whilst ensuring the court maintains its jurisdiction. And such an approach is not alien to private child law; the PA and the co-parenting agreement are already formulated in this manner, and it is accepted that a court order can be amended between the parties if necessary.

4. Drafting and Practical Considerations

4.1. Drafting

Although it is not proposed that the PPA be a legally enforceable contract, as this would not be possible without legislative change, it remains important that the document is drafted in compliance with any guidelines that may be issued. A PPA that is drafted in consultation with the child, with the Paramountcy Principle at its heart, and regularly reviewed, is significantly more likely to be upheld. The following should be considered:

- Ideally, both parties should receive independent legal advice.
- If the child is competent, include the child in the arrangements (this may be something that is completed on review as the child increases in age).
- Explain the Paramountcy Principle and Welfare Checklist to all parties.
- Include in the background to the agreement:
    - The child's participation in reaching agreement
    - An explanation of Paramountcy Principle and Welfare checklist
    - Current arrangements
    - Intention to enter into an agreement
    - Intention not to oust the jurisdiction of the court.
- In the body of the agreement include:
    - A review position with a default provision. Reviews should be treated like codicils to a will. This will not

only save time and money, but the document as a whole will give a good history of the family relationship, and allow the agreement to be used as an issue-narrowing tool in any future legal, parent-to-parent or mediation based negotiations

- General terms, such as: definitions, childcare, contact, shared parenting, residence/shared residence, visits abroad, schooling, change of name, moving outside the area, name, contact with third parties, contact prohibited with third parties, national holidays, etc.

4.2. Practical Considerations

If the PPA is to reduce child harm caused by parental conflict on separation, and thus increase compliance with Article 19,[105] the public, legal professionals and mediators will need to be educated about the document and its potential uses. It is particularly important that the review procedure is adhered to, as this is designed to ensure that the PPA is flexible enough to address life-changes small and big, and assist parents in developing positive conflict resolution. Where appropriate, mediation can be used to reach agreement prior to relationship breakdown. Further, inclusion of the child's wishes will give the child a voice in an area where the child's voice is all too often lost (despite legislative requirement[106]).

On relationship breakdown, the parents will be better equipped to negotiate any appropriate amendments to the PPA (which will become a PA). If parents need to resort to court, the in-conciliation court will allow court review of the document. Agreement reached should offer longer-term satisfaction for the parents and children because it is likely to have some basis in the PPA, a document owned by both parties and thus prevent the child suffering long drawn-out, inadequately resolved, conflict.

5. Conclusion

Relationship breakdown will hurt everybody involved, but minimising the effect on the children must be a priority. Children are suffering "exploitation, maltreatment and abuse"[107] through conflict-based parental

---

[105] Convention on the Rights of the Child, *Supra* note 6.
[106] Children Act 1989, *Supra* note 14 at S1(3).
[107] Convention on the Rights of the Child, *Supra* note 6.

separation on a daily basis. Although it is recognised that a minority of cases will always require parties to attend court, the majority of cases will not. The mechanisms currently in place to support parents are reactionary, and despite the best endeavours of professionals involved are not giving the everyman-child sufficient protection from damage on parental separation. The PPA is a cost-effective, yet flexible, solution. It can be incorporated into the current legislative framework by the exercise of weight-based judicial discretion, and sits well alongside in-court conciliation, PAs and co-parenting agreements. The review process provides the agreement with flexibility, and assists parents in developing positive conflict resolution in a non-acrimonious context; and including the child not only exposes the child to the positive resolution, but allows the child to become the arbiter of his or her own welfare rights narrative. We must not ignore harm caused to our children because it is an everyday occurrence, but should instead review our procedures, and not be frightened or constrained from adopting mainstream change.

CHAPTER FIVE:

LEGAL PROCEDURE

THE DIMENSIONS OF A FAIR TRIAL WITH REFERENCE TO CHILDREN

LAURA ERVO AND HANNELE TOLONEN[1]

Abstract

The essence of Article 6 of the ECHR is to secure the active involvement of individuals in a trial. Participating and communicating helps parties to accept the decision—even if it is contrary to their claims—and engage in the outcome of the trial. From the sociological approach to law, participation is the most basic and productive element of experiential justice. The right to participate in a trial is also very vital for the framework of justice, if we regard the trial as an educational process. However, these views seem to cover only adults, while the attitudes to children's position in legal proceedings may be the opposite. In the name of protecting children, their direct participation is often avoided. It also seems that children may be more easily attend court and be heard when the outcome of the case does not personally affect them. The purpose of this article is to present arguments based on both normative and experiental justice, according to which it can be argued that participation is the essence of a fair trial, even for children.

1. Fair Trial

According to Article 6 of the European Convention on Human Rights (ECHR), in the determination of the individual's civil rights and obligations, or of any criminal charge against him, everyone is entitled to a *fair* and public *hearing* within a reasonable time, by an independent and impartial tribunal established by law. This right to a fair hearing is a basic norm and constitutes the core of Article 6, which contains some examples and details describing the substance of a fair hearing. For instance, the accused has to have the minimum rights mentioned in Article 6(3) in order for the hearing

[1] Both authors have contributed to sections 5 and 6. Sections 1, 2, 3 and 4 are written solely by Ervo.

to be classed as fair. Furthermore, the case-law of the European Court of Human Rights is a very significant, positive development of Article 6. But despite this, the only requirement in Article 6 is the demand for fairness. However, the question of what constitutes a fair hearing still remains.[2]

2. Fairness Means Communication, and Communication Means Participation

As we can see from studies of case law, Article 6 mainly concerns communication by the parties to a hearing. The right to communication is realized by the principle of adversariality, which nowadays covers much more than the traditional provision of a formal opportunity to answer the contentions of the other side. In its modern form, the adversarial principle (*audiatur et altera pars*) carries, as a human and fundamental right, the chance to be actively involved in a trial: the parties have to have an equal opportunity to present their case and to participate in the proceedings and be guaranteed sufficient practical means[3] to do this. Neither lack of resources nor ignorance should hinder the exercise of this right; nor should participation be prevented or restricted by the imposition of too strict a set of procedural limitations upon the hearing of the case. The trial is fair if the parties can participate in it and advocate in an active, factual and equal way.[4]

3. Experiential Justice

Justice can be divided into substantive and procedural fairness. Both concepts can further be divided into normative and experiential fairness. Fair hearing refers to procedural fairness in its normative meaning. Article 6 does not say anything about the substantive, that is material, fairness in the case: that part is based on the substantive legislation. Article 6 is a procedural rule. However, these concepts are—and they should be—often comparable and even identical. In a democratic society, legislation is based on the current values of the majority. It is also necessary for the legislation to be valid in a material sense. Otherwise, the law is not obeyed by citizens and the legislation is not valid in its substantive meaning if it is

---

[2] Ervo, Laura: Oikeudenmukainen oikeudenkäynti, (2005), p. 9.

[3] For instance, they have to be given knowledge of all trial documents and other trial material, and have equal opportunities to comment on that material and to present own.

[4] Ervo, Oikeudenmukainen oikeudenkäynti, pp. 421-422.

not consolidated in society.[5] Because of that, it is very necessary, and to some extent even essential, that normative fairness is close to experiential fairness, that is, what citizens feel is fair even if "sein und sollen" are in principle two absolutely separate worlds which may not be confused in jurisprudence.[6]

To sum up, experiential justice is a sociological phenomenon. In principle, it has nothing to do with procedural justice in its normative sense. However, in order to be acceptable, valid and democratic, legislation should respect society's moral values. If that is adhered to, a fair hearing, for instance, should be fair even in its experiential sense, which means that the parties should feel that the procedure was fair.

For example, Tim Tyler, has researched the trial as a sociological phenomenon. From his research, communication and participation seem to be the most important issues to the parties' accepting the decision, even if it was unfavourable to them. If they have had the opportunity to communicate and participate, that is, to advocate in its full meaning, they feel that the trial was fair, even if they lost the case.[7]

It seems that communication and participation are the most important elements in procedural fairness in its normative and experiential sense. A fair trial, based on the above-mentioned elements, therefore proves to be both healthy and legal.

4. The Trial as a Learning Process

The Finnish procedural reforms, and the implementation of reformed laws, has been researched as a learning process from the actor´s point of view. The research it is examined how the reformed procedures were actualized in everyday proceedings by judges, advocates and their clients. The findings of courtroom interaction suggested that although small and gradual, the courtroom changes have the potential for a deep-seated transformation.[8] We are almost talking about a new character of court culture in Scandinavia, and especially in Finland. The new court culture

---

[5] *Ibid*, pp. 73-81 and other sources referenced there.
[6] *Ibid*, p. 94.
[7] See Tyler, T.R.: Why People obey the law? (1990).
[8] Haavisto, Vaula: Court Work in Transition. An Activity-Theoretical Study of Changing Work Practices in a Finnish District Court (2002), pp. 302-305.

refers to the court service, where the focus is on the party as a client.[9]

A trial can itself also be seen as a learning process[10] for the actors, especially for the parties: an active, factual and equal participation is, again, a very important issue. The trial which is fair in its normative, and especially also in its sociological (that is, in its experiential) sense, has very important educational aspects[11] too. The question is not only to decide the case in a fair way, but also to improve the world, especially the parties´ current world and life, and to resolve the conflict in such a way that they continue their lives with some reasonable hope in their future. From this point of view, a fair trial should thus also contain therapeutic and restorative elements;[12] communication and participation are very important from that point of view.[13]

---

[9] Ervasti, Kaijus: Käräjäoikeuksien sovintomenettely. Empiirinen tutkimus sovinnon edistämisestä riitaprosessissa. Oikeuspoliittinen tutkimuslaitos (2004), p. 433 and Ervo, Oikeudenmukainen oikeudenkäynti, pp. 439.

[10] Nylund discusses the same problem in her current article,.and refers to Nils Christie´s idea of seeing conflicts as our property, our opportunities. They not only have negative aspects, which are necessarily a part of life, but can have positive sides, such as pointing the way to a better and wiser future. Conflicts are the building blocks of growth. Arg. based on Christie, Nils: Konflikt som eiendom. Tidsskrift for retsvitenskap (1977), pp. 113-132; Nylund, Anna: Lapsi riidan kohteena – lapsen asemaa koskevien asioiden haasteita (2010), pp. 1166-1182, at 1169. It seems to be obvious that behind these ideas of Christie and Nylund, is the conception of a procedure (covering both trial and mediation) as a learning process.

[11] In Finland it has been said that juveniles in particular should be present in a trial, thus a judgement should not be given in their absence.. Hallituksen esitys eduskunnalle rikosasioiden oikeudenkäyntimenettelyn uudistamista alioikeuksissa koskevaksi lainsäädännöksi, Government bill 82/1995 and Jokela, Antti: Rikosprosessi (2008), p. 428. However, this can also be seen as slightly problematic if we take the presumption of innocence into consideration. From that point of view, the criminal procedure especially should not contain any sanctions in itself, and the trial and its elements should not be seen as a punishment. Ervo, Laura: Ylimmät prosessiperiaatteet – oikeudenmukaisen oikeudenkäynnin osatekijät. Lakimiesliiton Kustannus (1996), pp. 156-166.The situation is different in civil cases, though.

[12] These aspects are mainly taken into consideration in mediation procedures of a special kind, where the approach is more therapeutic or educational by comparison with the traditional trial. Nylund, Anna: Lapsi riidan kohteena –lapsen asemaa koskevien asioiden haasteita, (2010), pp. 1166-1182, at p. 1171.

[13] More information on conflict resolution in Lindell, Bengt: Civilprocessen (2. Uppl, 2003), pp. 82-101; on therapeutic jurisprudence in Wexler, David. B: Therapeutic Jurisprudence. The Law as Therapeutic Agent. Carolina Academic

5. Is a Child an Exception?

Unlike the current view regarding participation by adults, attitudes about participation of children in trials may be described as somewhat ambiguous. It seems that the normative basis within legislation is often based on the idea that in the name of protecting children, their presence in a trial should preferably be avoided.[14] Even in special proceedings, such as mediation, the child may have the role of an outsider.[15] For instance, in the Finnish court-annexed mediation of custody cases, a child may only be heard under certain preconditions.[16]

It has to be asked whether the contents of a fair trial for children are entirely different from the demands of a just trial for adults.

In legal literature, the limits to children's autonomy[17] are seen to arise from their lack of capacity[18] and from their dependence on adults[19]. The

---

(1990) and on restorative justice in Iivari, Juhani: Rikosten ja riitojen vaihtoehtosovittelu refleksiivsen oikeuden konseptiossa (1991).

[14] The presumption is that the trial can cause so-called secondary victimisation to the child. Hirvelä, Päivi: Rikosprosessi lapsiin kohdistuvissa seksuaalirikoksissa (2006), p. 233.

[15] Nylund, Anna: Lapsi riidan kohteena –lapsen asemaa koskevien asioiden haasteita, p. 1173.

[16] In Government Bill 114/2004, it is stated that a child may be heard during mediation as decreed in Child Custody and Right of Access Act, Section 15, which states the following: "*The child may be heard in person before the court, if there is a substantial reason that makes this necessary in view of the decision in the case. He may only be heard if he consents to the same and if it is evident that the hearing cannot cause harm to the child.*" (Section 15 (2), Unofficial translation, Ministry of Justice, Finland). However, the Law Committee was of the opinion that a child could be heard more easily during mediation. Lakivaliokunnan mietintö hallituksen esityksestä riita-asioiden sovittelua ja sovinnon vahvistamista yleisissä tuomioistuimissa koskevaksi lainsäädännöksi, Law Committee's report 4/2005, p. 3. Parents and mediator may consider whether a hearing is necessary. Aaltonen, Anna-Kaisa – Auvinen, Maija: Lapsiriitojen sovittelusta yleisessä tuomioistuimessa (2010), pp. 1149-1165, at 1160.

[17] For a discussion of children's rights and autonomy, see for example Freeman 1984, pp. 32-60, Fortin 2009, pp. 3-32, Auvinen 2006, pp. 375-381, and the resources mentioned.

[18] For a discussion of competence and capacity, see Freeman, Michael: Why It Remains Important to Take Children's Rights Seriously, 15 International Journal of Children's Rights (2007), pp. 5-23, at 12-14. One way to evaluate a child's decision-making competence is to look at its goals: if they are not realistic, it is

capacity of individual children to take part in decision-making is also perceived to vary according to age[20] and maturity[21]. One of the main problems often pointed out is that the exercise of autonomy by children may be in conflict with their need for protection.[22] Children are seen to need protection against themselves: as they might make judgements that do not serve their best interests, restricting their autonomous decision-making is justifiable.[23]

A rough distinction between two kinds of perspective has been made when discussing the position of children and the weight given to their opinions. Where '*needs*' or '*welfare*' perspectives prevail, the therapeutic aspects of the hearing are emphasized, while it is left to adults to decide how much weight the opinions expressed by children carry. When '*rights*' or '*competence*' perspectives are stressed, children are seen as being capable of making their own judgement and their wishes may accordingly be decisive in characterizing the outcome of the decision.[24] However, the

---

possible that the decision is incompetent. Eekelaar, John: The Interests of the Child and the Child's Wishes: The Role of Dynamic Self-Determinism, International Journal of Law and the Family (Vol. 8, Issue 1, 1994), pp. 42-61, at pp. 55-56.

[19] See Fortin, Jane: Children's Rights and the Developing Law, (3rd edition, 2009) p. 5, and Auvinen, Maija: Huoltoriidat tuomioistuimissa. Sosiaalitoimi selvittäjänä, sovittelijana, asiantuntijana. Suomalainen Lakimiesyhdistys (2006), pp. 398-399. Dependence may be problematic in the proceedings, because the usual suppositions of parties acting independently of each other may not apply. Schiratzki Johanna: Mamma och pappa inför rätta (2008) p. 27.

[20] Dahlstrand, Lotta: Barns deltagande i familjerättsliga processer (2004), p. 163-166, and Auvinen, Maija: Huoltoriidat tuomioistuimissa. Sosiaalitoimi selvittäjänä, sovittelijana, asiantuntijana (2006), pp. 386 – 387.

[21] As children all develop at their own pace, it is risky to put too much stress on age. One should focus instead on their social, emotional and intellectual readiness. *Ibid.* pp. 163-164.

[22] For more on the problems of children making decisions, see, for example, Eekelaar, John: The Interests of the Child and the Child's Wishes, p. 53-54. In Finland, it has been pointed out that children's rights to participate and to be protected are difficult to combine in custody conflicts and even asked whether limits to the repeated, too-stressful hearings of children should be set by legislation. Auvinen, Maija: Huoltoriidat tuomioistuimissa, p. 534.

[23] On this discussion, op. cit. p. 18.

[24] On 'welfare' and 'rights' perspectives, see Fortin Jane: Children's Rights and the Developing Law (3rd edition, 2009), p. 25. Anna Singer discusses the division between 'kompetensorienterad' and 'behovsorienterad'. Singer, Anna: Föräldraskap i rättslig beslysning (2000), pp. 80-86 and 545. According to her, adopting a competence-related perspective may not necessarily mean that children are given

division between paternalistic and 'rights' approaches is not clear-cut, and it has been argued that the distinction is deceptive.[25] The differing perspectives may also be combined, for example by suggesting that the children's wishes may be overridden if following them would put the child's well-being at risk.[26]

In proceedings that concern children personally[27], a central reason for avoiding their participation in a trial seems to be to protect them from the dispute.[28] Preventing children from taking sides may strongly be preferred over their participation in the legal proceedings, especially when parents are in conflict.[29] Instead, adults take care of the cases, while children stay outside of the courtroom.[30]

---

full freedom to decide. On the discussion, see also Auvinen, Maija: Huoltoriidat tuomioistuimissa, p. 380.

[25] Freeman, M.D.A.: The Rights and Wrongs of Children (1983), p. 40.

[26] See op.cit., p. 18, especially Fortin, Jane: Children's Rights and the Developing Law, pp. 27-28. Well-known examples of approaches that combine children's autonomy and their protection are John Eekelaar's dynamic self-determinism (see Eekelaar, John: The Interests of the Child and the Child's Wishes, especially pp. 47-53) and Michael Freeman's 'liberal paternalism' (See Freeman,M.D.A.: The Rights and Wrongs of Children (1983), pp. 54-60 and Freeman, Michael: Why It Remains Important to Take Children's Rights Seriously. International Journal of Children's Rights 15 (2007), pp. 5-23, at 15.

[27] For example cases concerning custody and visiting rights. The role of the "child" as an accused will not be further discussed in this article.

[28] See Cashmore, Judy and Parkinson, Patrick: What Responsibility Do Courts Have to Hear Children's Voices? 15 International Journal of Children's Rights (2007), pp. 43-60, at 52.

[29] John Eekelaar concisely sets out the reasons for this: "Such children will be vulnerable to pressure from the disputing adults to decide in their favour, they risk being burdened with the guilt of an adverse outcome, and the hostility of the adult against whom they decide." Eekelaar, John: The Interests of the Child and the Child's Wishes, pp. 53-54. It has been suggested that if being heard in court during custody and access proceedings were to put a child in the position of a decision-maker, hearing his or her opinion should take place elsewhere. Haapasalo, Jaana – Kiesiläinen, Kari – Niemi-Kiesiläinen, Johanna: Todistajanpsykologia ja todistajankuulustelu (2000), p. 84.

[30] According to the Finnish Child Custody and Right of Access Act, Section 11 (1), the wishes and views of the child shall be ascertained, for example if the parents cannot reach an agreement. However, this shall not be detrimental to the relationships between the child and his parents (Section 11(2)). Hearing a child in court is restricted (Section 15, see op.cit. 17). Instead, a report by the social welfare board shall be obtained unless it is evident that one is required for a decision (Section 16(1), on translation, see op.cit. 17). According to an empirical

An interesting comparison can be made with criminal and civil cases where children are involved, but where the outcome does not personally concern them, for example a criminal case where a child is a victim or a witness. [31] It seems that in the latter cases there is a greater willingness to let a child participate in court proceedings and to amend the proceedings to better suit the needs of a child.[32] This gives rise to many serious questions:

---

study, Finnish children were seldom heard by judges in custody cases. In studied cases, the opinion of a child was taken into consideration as one criterion when looking for the best interests of a child. Auvinen, Maija: Huoltoriidat tuomioistuimissa. Sosiaalitoimi selvittäjänä, sovittelijana, asiantuntijana, pp. 533-534. However, attitudes towards hearing children personally in these cases have been seen to become more permissable, when compared with the discussion at the time of the legislation in the 1980s. Gottberg Eva: Lapsen subjektiudesta ja osallisuudesta huoltokysymyksissä ja lastensuojelussa (Defensor Legis N.o 3:/2008), pp. 319-333, at 320 and 323. At the start of 2011, a pilot project on mediation in custody and access cases was started in four court districts in Finland. The project was inspired by the Norwegian Follo model, according to which, children can be heard by expert counsel even in a trial when a judge and parents are present. The requirements are that parents give their permission, and that the age of the child as well as the situation are suitable for this procedure. The expert counsel can also talk to the child outside the court and arrange home visits. Asiantuntija-avustajan käyttö huoltoriitojen sovittelussa (Oikeusministeriön mietintöjä ja lausuntoja 61/2010), p. 17 and Aaltonen, Anna-Kaisa – Auvinen, Maija: Lapsiriitojen sovittelusta yleisessä tuomioistuimessa, pp. 1149-1150.

[31] See Cashmore, Judy and Parkinson, Patrick: What Responsibility Do Courts Have to Hear Children's Voices?, p. 44. It has to be noted that in a criminal case where children give their testimony, their best interests do not govern the substance of the decision, unlike, for example, in a custody case. For instance Päivi Hirvelä has pointed out that in the criminal case a child´s best interest means procedural rules instead of substantive matters. Hirvelä, Päivi: Lapsi rikosprosessissa (1997), p. 219 and 2006, p. 233. In a criminal case, even the child´s best interest does not exclude imposing negative sanctions on the accused.. Hirvelä stressed that it is possible to protect the child in the criminal proceedings with the help of procedural tools. Hirvelä, Päivi: Rikosprosessi lapsiin kohdistuvissa seksuaalirikoksissa, p. 235. In comparison, in family law mediation, the best interests of a child have to be taken into consideration, both in the proceedings and in the substantive sense, which means that the mediation in the family law cases should be organised in such a way that takes the child´s best interests into consideration. In addition, the result must follow the child´s best interests in the substantive meaning. Government Bill 114/2004, p. 117, see also Aaltonen, Anna-Kaisa – Auvinen, Maija: Lapsiriitojen sovittelusta yleisessä tuomioistuimessa, pp. 1159-1160.

[32] For similar observations in common law countries, see Cashmore, Judy and Parkinson, Patrick: What Responsibility Do Courts Have to Hear Children's

Do we want to appoint ourselves to act on behalf of those (ie the children) who are the main subjects of a case?[33] Or are we hindering their participation in trials, because we find it too difficult to tailor such procedures in which a child could be heard in a trustworthy and reasonable manner[34]? Do we more easily accept the hearing of a child in adults' interest than in the child´s own interest? We also have to ask whether this kind of system is fair in the normative and experiental sense. Is a child really an exception?

From a normative point of view, the legal dimension of a fair trial does not exclude children. The ECHR, and its Article 6, covers "everyone": in other words, individuals of all kinds—like minors—as well as juristic persons. According to the case law, the very essence of a fair trial is the opportunity to participate and communicate in a trial in an active, factual and equal way. This is a starting point even when a child is involved.[35]

During recent decades, progress in the field of international treaties has focused on children's participation.[36] It has been stressed in the *United*

Voices?, pp. 43-44. See also Singer, Anna: Föräldraskap i rättslig beslysning, p. 94. In Finland, those who have not yet reached the age of 15, may be heard as witnesses or for probative purposes "*if the court deems this appropriate and if(1) hearing him or her personally is of central significance to the clarification of the matter; and (2) hearing the person would probably not cause the said person suffering or other harm that can injure him or her or his or her development*". (The Code of Judicial Procedure, Chapter 17, Section 21 (360/2003)). Hearing these persons using technical means of communication with an audio and video link is at the court's discretion (Chapter 17, Section 34a (1.4)), and in a criminal case, a video recording of their statement may be admitted as evidence, provided that the defendant has an opportunity to present questions. (Chapter 17, Section 11 (3)). It is possible to appoint a support person for a young witness. (Chapter 17, Section 21). An unofficial English translation of Code of Judicial Procedure is accessible at www.finlex.fi. (Retrieved on May 6 2011).

[33] Based on the idea of professor Nils Christie, who sees conflict as a party´s own property. See Christie, Nils: Konflikt som eiendom, pp. 113-132.

[34] However, see op.cit p. 31.

[35] See also Nieminen, Liisa: Lasten perus- ja ihmisoikeussuojan ajankohtaisia ongelmia, p. 597.

[36] See for example Nieminen, Lisa: Lasten perus- ja ihmisoikeussuojan ajankohtaisia ongelmia (Lakimies 4/2004), pp. 591-621, at 594-595 and p. 597, describing the development in children's position with a phrase "from an object to a subject". Because of the effective control mechanisms, Nieminen sees the ECHR as having an even more important role in the development of children's rights than the CRC has. The risks that the more active position may pose for children have

Nations Convention on the Rights of the Child that the child should have a right to participate in her/his case.[37] In the *European Convention on the Exercise of Children's Rights,* the same right has been expressed in a more detailed way, as a procedural right of a child.[38] According to Article 3 of the European Convention, a child has the right to be informed and to express his/her views in proceedings. The Article states that "a child considered by internal law as having sufficient understanding in the case of proceedings before a judicial authority affecting him or her, shall be granted, and shall be entitled to request, the following rights: to receive all relevant information; to be consulted and express his or her views; and to be informed of the possible consequences of compliance with these views and the possible consequences of any decision".

When children from 47 member states of the European Council were recently consulted on their experience of 'justice',[39] the importance of being listened to was emphasized. When the children were asked whether they thought it was important that a person making a decision affecting them hears their views, over 80 per cent of the respondents answered affirmitavely. Most of them wished to speak directly to the decision-

---

also been pointed out. Gottberg Eva: Lapsen subjektiudesta ja osallisuudesta huoltokysymyksissä ja lastensuojelussa, p. 321.

[37] According to article 12 of the Convention on the Child's Rights, "*States Parties shall assure to the child who is capable of forming his or her own views the right to express those views freely in all matters affecting the child. The views of the child are given due weight in accordance with the age and maturity of the child. For this purpose, the child shall in particular be provided the opportunity to be heard in any judicial and administrative proceedings affecting the child, either directly, or through a representative or an appropriate body, in a manner consistent with the procedural rules of national law*".

[38] At http://conventions.coe.int/Treaty/Commun/ListeDeclarations.asp?NT=160&CM=&DF=&CL=ENG&VL=1, a list of declarations can be found. (Retrieved on 2 May 2011.)

[39] The data was collected from the questionnaires of 3,721 children, from over 25 countries. Most of these children had had some direct contact with the justice system. In addition, reports and transcripts of various group discussions—principally with children in conflict with the law—were submitted to the Council. European Council, child-friendly justice. Listening to children about justice: Report of the Council of Europe Consultation with Children on Child-Friendly Justice. Report prepared by Dr Ursula Kilkelly. Available on the web: http://www.coe.int/t/dghl/standardsetting/childjustice/CJ-S-CH%20_2010_%2014%20rev.%20E%205%20oct.%202010.pdf. (Retrieved April 25 2011), p. 6 and p. 19-20.

maker.[40] Children's positive views on direct involvement in contested custody cases have been reported in an Australian study: even though most of the children participating in the study, who were involved in contested cases, had access to indirect means of participation—such as being interviewed for a family report or having a children's representative appointed to them—many of them stated that they would have preferred a more direct manner of hearing. The primary reasons for this were wanting to have their views heard and to be acknowledged by the decision-maker. Concerns were voiced by children on possible misinterpretation of their views, if transmitted to the court by 'second-hand' means. Giving the judge a better understanding of the matter was also perceived to improve the quality of the decision. [41]

In the survey conducted by the European Council, the importance of families was expressed in the answers. Many children would confide in their parents or carers, and they most often identified their parents or

[40] Ibid., p. 29 and p. 51. The children who wanted the decision-maker to hear their views were then asked in the questionnaire how they would like to be heard. There were four different options to select from. The first option suggested speaking directly to the person making the decision, and the other three options suggested having the parents or a lawyer speak for children or having the help of another person of their choice. To each of these options, it was possible to provide a "yes" or "no" or "don't know" answer. Being heard directly was—overwhelmingly—the most popular alternative (2408 "yes" – 198 "no"). The reactions towards being heard via parents or via a lawyer were more often negative than positive (in both cases, over 1300 "no"), while in the last option (other) "yes" and "no" were distributed almost evenly.

[41] Cashmore, Judy and Parkinson, Patrick: What Responsibility Do Courts Have to Hear Children's Voices?, p. 52, see also pp. 49-51. In the study, 47 children (mean age 11.8 years) were interviewed about participation in residence and contact issues following their parents' separation. 25 of them were involved in contested cases. The largest group of children (*n*=12), most of whom were from incontested proceedings, preferred talking with one or both parents. The second largest group (*n*=8) preferred talking directly to the judge, and two other children preferred to talk to 'the court'. All of the children indicating 'judge' or 'court' were involved in contested proceedings. The authors refer to a conference paper by Parkinson, Cashmore and Single. See also Cashmore, Judy and Parkinson, Patrick: Children's and Parent's Perceptions on Children's Participation in Decision Making after Parental Separation and Divorce Family Court Review, 46: p. 91-104. doi: 10.1111/j.1744-1617.2007.00185.x. Available on the web: http://onlinelibrary.wiley.com/doi/10.1111/j.1744-1617.2007.00185.x/full. (Retrieved May 5 2011)..

families as a preferred source of information and explanations.[42] When children's participation is discussed, worries have sometimes been voiced about loyalties and dependencies affecting the proceedings.[43] In the light of the results of the survey, where family and friends were identified as a priority by children,[44] these issues merit serious consideration. Interestingly, many children participating in the consultation process expressed mistrust towards authorities.[45] Officials were criticized for lack of respect and empathy, and the majority of children who took part in the survey did not feel listened to.[46] These results illustrate that meeting children's expectations in proceedings and taking into account their integrity pose a challenge to the public authorities.

Trials can be complicated from a child's point of view[47], but being heard by the court may not necessarily be traumatising, even when the matter is very serious. According to a psychological study of child victims of sexual abuse, those children who were waiting for their hearing were more distressed in comparison with the children who had already given evidence in their cases. Interestingly, anxiety levels were most likely to improve among the children who had personally given evidence at juvenile court.[48]

---

[42] Kilkelly European Council, Child-Friendly Justice, pp. 21-23, p. 31 and p. 39. Most children (77 per cent) would have wanted to be given more information about their rights.
[43] Op. cit. 20.
[44] Kilkelly European Council, Child-Friendly Justice, p. 39.
[45] Ibid., pp. 23-23 and p. 39. When children were asked who they would tell if they were unhappy with how they were being treated, official or public persons did not fare well.
[46] Ibid., pp. 35-39.
[47] See Cashmore, Judy and Parkinson, Patrick: What Responsibility Do Courts Have to Hear Children's Voices?, pp. 44-48. Many of the difficulties described relate to the conventional strategies of cross-examination.
[48] Runyan, Desmond K., Everson, Mark D., Edelsohn, Gail A., Hunter, Wanda M., and Coulter, Martha L.: Impact of Legal Intervention on Sexually Abused Children. 4 Journal of Pediatrics (1988), pp. 647-653. The research focused on 75 children, who were 6-17 years old. Although seeing their data as supporting the hypothesis that 'juvenile court testimony is not harmful and may actually be therapeutic for child victims,' the researchers urge for caution in interpreting the results as definitive. Ibid., p. 652. Also see Haapasalo, Jaana, Kiesiläinen, Kari, and Niemi-Kiesiläinen, Johanna, p. 84.

6. Conclusion

From the experiental point of view, the opportunity to participate and communicate in the proceedings seems to be valuable. This is undisputed in the literature relating to adults, but opinions vary in the case of a child. However, when children are asked about their views on participation, many of them prefer to be heard and to contribute directly to the legal proceedings affecting them, and wish to be supported in their participation. Perceiving "my case" as important, children are not unresponsive to experiental justice. Obviously, hearing children is also an important tool for realising their autonomy and integrity. The right to be present, participate actively and communicate all contribute to autonomy. The concept of integrity can be interpreted to comprise respect for someone´s opinions and taking them into recognition.[49]

Even if one accepts that for the protection of children, there may be some limitations to their decision-making and even to their participation in proceedings, it has to be taken into account that even if there are risks involved, the children may also benefit from communicating and participating.[50] If we want to keep a child in the centre[51] of the case presented in the court room - and avoid essentially focusing on adults' needs and interests - these aspects should not be ignored. In this sense, children's participation can be perceived as a central issue not only from the perspective of 'rights', but also in light of the 'needs' perspectives.[52]

When making decisions on a child's participation in a trial, both safety and respect have to be taken into account in the best interests of the child.[53] In order to realise this, we have to take a critical look at court proceedings and examine how they should be modified to better

---

[49] Mattsson, Titti: Barnet och rättsprocessen. Rättssäkerhet, integitetsskydd och autonomi i samband med beslut om tvångsvård (2002), p. 159.
[50] See also Cashmore, Judy and Parkinson, Patrick: What Responsibility Do Courts Have to Hear Children's Voices?, p. 55.
[51] Nylund, writing about custody and access rights cases, has recently stressed that the child should be in the center and suggested that processes be modified. Nylund, Anna: Lapsi riidan kohteena –lapsen asemaa koskevien asioiden haasteita, p. 1168 and pp. 1181-1182.
[52] For more on these perspectives, see op.cit. p. 25.
[53] Mattsson, Titti: Barnet och rättsprocessen. Rättssäkerhet, integitetsskydd och autonomi i samband med beslut om tvångsvård (2002), p. 455.

accommodate the requirements of children, taking into recognition the aspects of *their* experience of justice.

THE NEPALESE EXPERIENCE OF THE JUDICIAL ENFORCEMENT OF CHILDREN'S RIGHTS[1]

RAJU PRASAD CHAPAGAI*

Abstract

The article offers an overview of the national and international legal framework on child rights applicable in Nepal and provides an analysis of select decisions of the Supreme Court in the light of the CRC provisions. The analysis reveals that the Supreme Court has positively benefited from the CRC provisions especially in terms of invalidating legislative and executive actions inconsistent with international human rights standards as well as the Constitution. And the exercise of Supreme Court's constitutional review power, combined with Public Interest Litigation jurisdiction has been instrumental in shaping and developing the domestic legal regime regarding children. The article finally argues for the continued use of PIL in order to enhance the judicial enforcement of children's rights, including invalidating legislative and executive actions, and requiring the government to take measures giving effect to constitutional and treaty obligations.

1. Introduction

Nepalese Children, in the sense of a formal guarantee, have no fewer human rights than children in other parts of the world: but the practical application of those rights is quite a different matter. For most Nepalese children, human rights are limited to articles in the Constitution, and

---

* Legal Adviser, Office of the High Commissioner for Human Rights, Nepal (OHCHR-Nepal). This article reflects the views of the author and not necessarily those of the OHCHR-Nepal.

[1] This is an extended version of a presentation delivered by the author at the 2010 International Conference on Children in Law, 16-17 September, Orebro University, Sweden.

human rights treaties and legislation, since little of it is actually implemented by the authorities.

Children endure a considerable number of problems including acute poverty, malnutrition, corporal punishment, harmful tradition and customary practices, labour exploitation, human trafficking, sexual abuses, and widespread violations of other economic, social and cultural rights. Female children across the community, children from poor households and marginalized communities, children with disabilities and children affected by armed conflict are especially vulnerable to discrimination, exclusion and violence. Turning paper guarantees of rights into reality still remains a big challenge.[2]

However, growing judicial activism appears to have been a positive force for translating these paper guarantees into reality. Over the past 20 years the role that the Supreme Court of Nepal ("Supreme Court")[3] has been exercising is commendable. Through its extraordinary jurisdiction,[4] it has made a valuable contribution to holding authorities accountable for non-compliance of rights and freedoms guaranteed under the national and international legal framework applicable to Nepal. This accountability is based on the well-established principle of *pacta sunt servanda*, which literally means the legal duties upon states to fulfill their obligations. A wide range of children's rights issues relating to juvenile justice, corporal punishment, exploitation of labour and harmful traditions and customary practices have been the subject of judicial intervention through Public Interest Litigation ("PIL").[5] There has also been growing judicial application of the Convention on the Rights of the Child ("CRC") in adjudicating children's rights issues. For instance, upholding children's

---

[2] See, U.N. Comm. on the Child Rights Convention, Thirty-ninth Session., Consideration of Reports Submitted by States Parties under Article 44 of the Convention: Concluding Observations of the Committee on Child Rights Convention: Nepal, CRC/C/SR.1032 and 1033 (June 2005). U.N. Comm. on the Child Rights Convention, Twelfth Session., Consideration of Reports Submitted by States Parties under Article 44 of the Convention: Concluding Observations of the Committee on Child Rights Convention: Nepal, CRC/C/SR.301-303 (May 1996).

[3] Nepal has a three-tire court system (Supreme Court, Appellate Courts and District Courts). The Supreme Court is at the apex, which remains as a highest judicial authority of Nepal.

[4] See, NEP. INTERIM CONST (2007), art. 107.

[5] Id, art 107. cl. 2

right to form an organization guaranteed under Article 15 of the CRC,[6] the Supreme Court invalidated a decision of the Ministry of Home Affairs that denied the registration of a children's club under the Institution Registration Act on grounds that minors were not eligible to form such clubs.[7]

Against that backdrop, this article offers an overview of the national and international legal framework on child rights applicable in Nepal and their interface, and provides an analysis of selected decisions of the Supreme Court which illustrate growing judicial application of the CRC with the intention of shaping and developing domestic legal regime for the promotion of child rights.

2. Legal Protection of Children's Rights

2.1. National Legal Framework

The Interim Constitution of Nepal, 2007 (Interim Constitution),[8] which is the supreme law of the land,[9] provides a fundamental legal basis for the protection and promotion of human rights for all, including Nepalese children. Nepal has a tradition of constitutional protection of basic rights and freedoms as "fundamental rights".[10] Following this tradition, the Interim Constitution lists a comprehensive catalogue of fundamental rights particularly emanating from international Bills of Rights. These rights, in

---

[6] CRC Article 15(1) reads, " States Parties recognize the rights of the child to freedom of association and to freedom of peaceful assembly." Article 15(2) reads, " No restrictions may be placed on the exercise of these rights other than those imposed in conformity with the law and which are necessary in a democratic society in the interests of national security or public safety, public order (ordre public), the protection of public health or morals or the protection of the rights and freedoms of others".

[7] *Tilotam Paudel v. Ministry of Home Affairs and others*, NKP. 423 (SC. 2001). Note: NKP stands for 'Nepal Kanoon Patrika', ("Nepal Law Journal"). It is the Supreme Court's publication of its decisions.

[8] The Interim Constitution came in force from 15 January 2007 replacing the 1990 Constitution. The Interim Constitution is in force until a new Constitution is adopted by the Constituent Assembly of Nepal.

[9] NEP. INTERIM CONST. (2007). art.1. cl.1: This Constitution is the fundamental law of Nepal. All laws inconsistent with the constitution shall, to the extent of such inconsistency, be void.

[10] Previous written constitutions of 1951, 1959, 1962 and 1990 had also guaranteed a number of rights and freedoms as "fundamental rights".

particular, include the right to live with dignity,[11] the right to liberty and fundamental freedoms,[12] the right to equality and non-discrimination,[13] the right to privacy,[14] the right against torture,[15] the right against exploitation,[16] the right to a fair trail[17] and a number of economic, social and cultural rights protecting the rights of children.[18] Paying special attention to children, the Interim Constitution also contains a set of rights that include the right to identity and name; the right to be nurtured, and to basic health and social security; the right against physical, mental or other form of exploitation; the right of the helpless, orphans, the mentally retarded, conflict victims, the displaced and vulnerable and street children to special facilities from the State; the right of minors against their employment, engagement or use in a factory, mine or similar other hazardous work or in

---

[11] NEP. INTERIM CONST. (2007). art. 12, cl. 1: Every person shall have the right to live with dignity, and no law which provides for capital punishment shall be made.

[12] Id, cl. 2 & 3.

[13] Id, art, 13 reads, " (1) All citizens shall be equal before the law. No person shall be denied the equal protection of the laws. (2) There shall be no discrimination against any citizen in the application of general laws on grounds of religion, race, gender, caste, tribe, origin, language or ideological conviction or any of these. (3) The State shall not discriminate among citizens on grounds of religion, race, caste, tribe, gender, origin, language or ideological conviction or any of these. Provided that nothing shall be deemed to prevent the making of special provisions by law for the protection, empowerment or advancement of women, Dalits, indigenous ethnic tribes [Adivasi Janajati], Madhesi or farmers, labourers or those who belong to a class which is economically, socially or culturally backward, or children, the aged, disabled or those who are physically or mentally incapacitated."

[14] Id, art. 28 reads, "Except in circumstances provided by law, privacy in relation to the person, and to their residence, property, documents, records, statistics and correspondence, and their reputation are inviolable."

[15] Id, art. 26 (1) reads, " No person who is detained during investigation, or for trial or for any other reason, shall be subjected to physical or mental torture, or be treated in a cruel, inhuman or degrading manner. (2) Any such an act pursuant to clause (1) shall be punishable by law, and any person so treated shall be compensated in a manner determined by law."

[16] Id, art. 29 (1) reads, " Every person shall have the right against exploitation. (2) No person shall be exploited in the name of custom, tradition and practice, or in any other way. (3) No person shall be subjected to human trafficking, slavery or bonded labour. (4) No person shall be subject to forced labour. Provided that nothing in this clause shall prevent the enactment of a law requiring citizens to be engaged in compulsory service for public purposes."

[17] See, Id, art. 24

[18] See, Id, art. 16, 17, 18 & 21.

army, police or conflict.[19] The Constitution, under the Chapters on State Responsibilities, and Directive Principles of State Policies, also obliges the government to take special measures in the interest of children.[20]

Using the ongoing constitution-making process[21] as an opportunity to revisit constitutional protections of human rights, the Constituent Assembly's preliminary draft on Fundamental Rights and Directive Principles has proposed additional rights specific to children for the new Constitution.[22]

Apart from the Constitution, Nepal has several laws dealing with children's rights issues. The Act Relating to Children, 1992 ("Children Act"), which was adopted following the promulgation of the 1990 Constitution and ratification of the CRC, is the key piece of legislation dealing with children. The Act incorporates a significant number of provisions protecting the rights and interests of Nepalese children which include ensuring their physical, mental, and intellectual development. The Act

---

[19] Id, art. 22 (1) reads, "Every child shall have the right to his or her own identity and name. (2) Every child shall have the right to be nurtured, to basic health and social security. (3) Every child shall have the right not to be subjected to physical, mental or any other form of exploitation. Any such act of exploitation shall be punishable by law and any child so treated shall be compensated as determined by law. (4) Helpless, orphaned or mentally retarded children, children who are victims of conflict or displaced and street children at risk shall have the right to receive special privileges from the State to ensure their secure future. (5) No minor shall be employed in factories, mines or in any other hazardous work nor shall be used in army, police or in conflicts."

[20] E.g., Id, art. 35, cl. 9 reads, "The State shall pursue a policy of making special provision for social security
for the protection and welfare of single women, orphans, children, the helpless, the aged, disabled, incapacitated persons and tribes on the verge of extinction."

[21] The Constitution drafting process was started with the first sitting of the Constituent Assembly on 28 May 2008 with a mandate to complete the drafting within 2 years, which was extended to May 2011.

[22] Additional rights proposed in the Preliminary Draft Text of the Constituent Assembly Committee on Fundamental Rights and Directive Principles include : "No child shall be subjected to physical, mental or any other kinds of torture at home, schools or any other places under any conditions.; Every child shall have the right to child-friendly justice; No child shall be subjected to child marriage, illegal trafficking, kidnapping or be held hostage; No child shall be recruited or used in army, police or armed conflict or groups, or be subjected to abuse, neglect through any means or way or to physical, mental, sexual or any other kind of exploitation, or be used in an improper way in the name of cultural and religious practice."

defines a child as a person below the age of 16,[23] and states that a child who has not attained the age of 14 shall not be employed in any work as a labourer. It also contains a significant number of provisions on parental duties, juvenile justice, child welfare, and sexual and other abuses against children.

There are several other laws protecting the rights and interests of children, including the Labour Act, 1992;[24] the Child Labour (Prohibition and Regulation) Act, 1999;[25] and the *Kamaiya* Labour Prohibition Act, 2001.[26] Other relevant laws include: the Civic Rights Act, 1955; the Prison Act, 1962; the Country Code, 1963; the Human Trafficking Control Act, 1986; the Drug Trafficking (Control) Act; the Local Self-Governance Act, 1997; and the Breast-Milk Substitutes (Control of Sale and Distribution) Act 1991.

2.2. International Legal Framework

Nepal has a very good track record in terms of ratifying international human rights instruments. It is noteworthy that Nepal has taken the positive step of ratifying the CRC[27] and its optional protocols relatiing to the involvement of children in armed conflict[28] and the sale of children, child prostitution and child pornography.[29] Nepal is also a party to most of the other core international human rights instruments, including the International Covenant on Civil and Political Rights (ICCPR),[30] the International Covenant on Economic, Social and Cultural Rights

[23] Children Act, 1992, S. 2(a).

[24] This legislation basically contain specific provisions for the prohibition of employment of children below the age of 14 years and prohibits admission to hazardous work for minors (aged between 14 and 18 years);

[25] This legislation followed Nepal's ratification of the ILO Minimum Age Convention (No. 138), and has made important amendments to itslabour laws. The Child Labour Act enlists specific occupations as hazardous work and prohibits the use of children below 16 in such activities. It also prohibits the engagement of children below 14 in any kind of employment.

[26] Prohibits bonded labour; declares emancipation of bonded labourers and extinguishes debt flowing from such arrangements. As a result of the Kamaiya Act, many Kamalaries (bonded girls in domestic servitude) have been withdrawn and reintegrated into their families.

[27] Acceded on 14 September 1990.

[28] Acceded on 3 January 2007.

[29] Acceded on 6 January 2006.

[30] Acceded on 14 May 1991.

(ICESCR),[31] the Convention Against Torture, and other Cruel, Inhuman or Degrading Treatment or Punishment (CAT),[32] the International Convention on the Elimination of all Forms of Racial Discrimination (CERD),[33] the Convention on the Elimination of all Forms of Discrimination Against Women (CEDAW);[34] and the Convention on the Rights of Persons with Disabilities (CRPD).[35] In addition, Nepal is a party to a number of ILO conventions protecting the interest and rights of children including the Worst Forms of Child Labour Convention (no. 182); the Minimum Age Convention (no. 138) and the ILO Forced Labour Convention (no. 29).

By virtue of the above-mentioned instruments, together with those under customary international law (as embodied for instance in the Universal Declaration of Human Rights), Nepal is under international legal obligations to respect, protect and fulfil a wide range of human rights of children within the territory of Nepal or subject to the control of Nepalese authorities.

2.3. Interface between National and International Law

The Interim Constitution does not include provisions relating to how international law (either treaty or customary law) should be treated under the Nepalese legal system. The Constitution remains silent on the question of whether international law is deemed to be part of the law of the land. However, the Interim Constitution, in its Chapter on Responsibilities of the State, does refer to the State obligation to implement effectively the international treaties and agreements to which Nepal is a party.[36] This provision is yet to be interpreted, especially with respect to how this responsibility should be carried out. It is also notable that the Constitution empowers the courts[37] to deliver justice not only in accordance with the constitutional provisions and other laws, but also in accordance with

[31] Id.
[32] Id.
[33] Acceded on 13 January 1971.
[34] Acceded on 22 April 1991.
[35] Acceded on 7 May 2010.
[36] NEP. INTERIM CONST., art 33. cl. m.
[37] Under article 100(1) of the Interim Constitution, the "courts" are defined to include the Supreme Court, Appellate Court and District Court, as well as special types of courts, judicial institutions or tribunals established and constituted by law for the purpose of hearing special types of cases.

"recognized principles of justice",[38] which offers an opportunity for the courts to read into this phrase the legal principles and standards that are incorporated under the international treaties to which Nepal is a party.

The Nepal Treaty Act 1990[39] remains the key piece of legislation dealing with the subject of treaties. This Act sets out norms governing the ratification process of treaties as well as describing their effect in Nepal. A key provision is Article 9(1), which provides that, "In case the provision of a treaty to which the Kingdom of Nepal or HMG[40] has become a party following its ratification, acceptance or approval by the Parliament conflict with the provisions of current laws, the latter shall be invalid to the extent of such conflict for the purpose of that treaty, and the provisions of the treaty shall be applicable in that connection as Nepal law." Thus the effect of the provision is that in the case of *conflict* between provisions under ratified treaties and those under Nepalese laws,[41] the provision(s) of Nepalese law is invalid to the extent of such conflict. In these circumstances, the provisions of the human rights treaties including the CRC are applied as Nepalese law. Thus, these constitutional and Treaty Act provisions provide a strong basis for the judiciary to benefit from the CRC in order to shape and develop Nepalese law.

In the context of the ongoing constitution-making process, there has also been a discussion on what should be the status of international human rights law within the framework of the new Constitution. One of the suggestions made by the human rights communities is that the status of international human rights treaties be upgraded either by including an explicit provision in the new Constitution giving core human rights treaties including the CRC a constitutional status,[42] or stipulating that the

---

[38] NEP. INTERIM CONST. art. 100, cl. 1.

[39] Under the authority of article 126(1) of the 1990 Constitution (identical to article 156(2) of the Interim Constitution), the Nepal Treaty Act was enacted by the then parliament.

[40] The monarchy was abolished in 2008.

[41] As defined by the Section 2(M) of the Interpretation of Statute Act, Nepalese law does not include constitutional provisions.

[42] E.g. KOSOVO CONST (2008), art 22: This article provides for direct application of certain international human rights instruments including the CRC providing them with "constitutional hierarchy".

courts interpret the Constitution and law in harmony with international human rights law.[43]

3. Judicial Powers to Enforce Rights

The Interim Constitution not only provides a wide scope of rights, but also paves the way for judicial remedy in case of their violation. The right to Constitutional remedy is guaranteed as a separate fundamental right,[44] which can be invoked to directly access the Supreme Court. As the key judicial institution designed to safeguard rights and freedoms guaranteed under the Constitution, the Supreme Court is empowered to exercise its independent check against legislative and executive excesses infringing on the exercise of fundamental rights and freedoms.

Most importantly, the Interim Constitution empowers the Supreme Court "to declare any law void, either *ab initio* or from the date of its decision if it appears that the law in question is inconsistent with the Constitution".[45] Besides, the Supreme Court has original jurisdiction over "any constitutional and legal question involved in any dispute of public interest and concern".[46] In order to settle any such dispute of public interest and concern, the Supreme Court has extraordinary power to issue any

---

[43] E.g. SOUTH AFRICA CONST. (1996), art. 39: Under this article, South African courts, and other legal bodies are obligated to consider international law when interpreting the Bill of Rights under the South African Constitution.
[44] NEP. INTERIM CONST. (2007), art. 32.
[45] Id. art 107. cl. 1 reads, " Any Nepali citizen may file a petition in the Supreme Court to have any law or any part thereof declared void on the ground of inconsistency with this Constitution because it imposes an unreasonable restriction on the enjoyment of the fundamental rights conferred by this Constitution or on any other ground, and extra-ordinary power shall rest with the Supreme Court to declare that law void either ab initio or from the date of its decision if it appears that the law in question is inconsistent with the Constitution."
[46] Id. art. 107, cl. 2 reads, "The Supreme Court shall, for the enforcement of the fundamental rights conferred by this Constitution, for the enforcement of any other legal right for which no other remedy has been provided or for which the remedy even though provided appears to be inadequate or ineffective, or for the settlement of any constitutional or legal question involved in any dispute of public interest or concern, have the extraordinary power to issue necessary and appropriate orders to enforce such rights or settle the dispute. For these purposes, the Supreme Court may, with a view to imparting full justice and providing the appropriate remedy, issue appropriate orders and writs including the writs of habeas corpus, mandamus, certiorari, prohibition and quo warranto."

appropriate order and writs including writs of habeas corpus, mandamus, certiorari and any other appropriate orders.[47] By virtue of the PIL jurisdiction, disadvantaged and marginalized groups, including women, children and other poor and vulnerable groups can be represented by any public-spirited organizations and individuals before the court.[48] For the past 20 years, the Supreme Court has been able to scrutinize a significant number of children's rights issues through utilizing its constitutional review and public interest litigation jurisdiction. With that in mind, the Constituent Assembly has proposed extending the PIL jurisdiction to provincial High Courts under the future Constitution,[49] which could be instrumental in terms of enhancing access to justice for poor and marginalized communities.

In addition, the Supreme Court of Nepal has an important role in developing the common law, as the Interim Constitution entrusts the Supreme Court with the final authority to interpret this Constitution.[50] Similarly, the Interim Constitution states that 'any interpretation given to a law or any legal principle laid down by the Supreme Court in the course of the hearing of a law suit shall be binding on the Government of Nepal and all offices and courts.'[51] By virtue of these provisions, the Supreme Court is in a better position to play a vital role to shape and develop a domestic legal regime for children through interpretation of the law in harmony with international human rights documents.

---

[47] Id.

[48] In several cases, the Supreme Court has frequently accepted the locus standee of non-governmental organizations (e.g. Pro Public, FWLD) to file PIL petitions.

[49] The Constituent Assembly Committee on Judiciary's Preliminary Draft Text recommends empowering future provincial High Courts with PIL jurisdiction. Under the Interim Constitution, this jurisdiction is limited to the Supreme Court only.

[50] NEP. INTERIM CONST. art. 102, cl. 4: Except on the matters which fall under the jurisdiction of the Constituent Assembly Court, the Supreme Court shall have the final power to interpret this Constitution and other prevailing laws.

[51] NEP. INTERIM CONST. art. 116, cl. 2: Any interpretation given to a law or any legal principle laid down by the Supreme Court in the course of the hearing of a suit shall be binding on the Government of Nepal and all offices and courts.

4. Review of Selected Supreme Court Judgments Enforcing Child Rights

4.1. Enforcing Right to Freedom of Association

Nepalese Children were formally denied the right to freedom of association until the Supreme Court of Nepal's decision in *Tilotam Paudel v. Ministry of Home Affairs et al*[52] which invalidated the Ministry of Home Affairs ("MOHA")' denial to register the *Jagriti* Child Club. The Club had approached the District Administration Office for its registration as a non-government organization. The registration was denied on the grounds that, in MOHA's view, minors were not eligible to form such clubs under the Institution Registration Act that provides a legal framework for establishment of non-government social organizations. When invalidating the MOHA decision, the Supreme Court relied on the children's right to form an organization guaranteed under Article 15 of the CRC, and reasoning that the Children Act did not impose any restriction upon children forming an organization. The Court also issued an order of mandamus for registration of the club with a view to enable children to exercise their right to form an organization. As a result, the *Jagriti* Child Club was registered as an NGO to undertake social welfare works. This intervention subsequently lead to the establishment of a significant number of child clubs/organizations. As of 2004, it was estimated that there were more than 1,500 children's clubs/groups active in promoting child rights in the country.[53]

4.2. Combating Corporal Punishment

Corporal punishment and ill treatment of children is still prevalent in the family, in schools, and in other institutions. The problem was basically aggravated by a number of faulty laws legitimizing corporal punishment. The UN Committee on Child Rights Convention, in its Concluding Observations,[54] was also seriously concerned about the provisions in the

[52] Supra note 7.

[53] Nepal's Second Periodic Report (2004) on the CRC submitted to the CRC Committee (See CRC/C/SR.301-303 and CRC/C/15/Add.57), Para 221.

[54] The Committee, in its Concluding Observations (CRC/C/SR.1032 and 1033, June 2005), makes a set of comprehensive recommendations, "(a) Expressly

Children Act and the Muluki Ain (Country Code), 1963, which provided for corporal punishment, inconsistent with Article 19 of the CRC.

Such provisions have been scrutinised by the Supreme Court in a couple of cases invoking its PIL jurisdiction. In *Devendra Ale et al*[55] the Supreme Court invalidated a proviso of Section 7 of the Children Act, which exempted from criminal liability 'an act by the mother, father, family member, guardian or teacher to scold the child or give him/her minor beating for the sake of his or her interests'. The law was basically responsible for the persistence of traditional practices and attitudes that were seriously hampering the enjoyment of the rights of the child. Taking into account the government's Constitutional and CRC obligations, a directive was also issued requiring the authorities to pursue appropriate measures to prevent corporal punishment as well as other cruel, inhuman or degrading treatment or punishment or abuse inflicted on children.

Similarly in another case, *Raju Prasad Chapagai et al*[56], the Supreme Court made an important intervention in terms of combating corporal punishment. Filing a public interest petition under the Constitution of the Kingdom of Nepal, 1990 (1990 Constitution),[57] the Supreme Court was called upon by the petitioners to invalidate Section 6(3) of the Chapter on Homicide of the Country Code[58] and to order the authorities to adopt

---

prohibit corporal punishment and ill-treatment of children by law in the family, schools and other institutions; (b) Expedite the process of amending the relevant provision of the Children's Act and the 1963 Muluki Ain to ensure compliance with article 19 of the Convention; (c) Strengthen awareness-raising campaigns to inform parents, teachers and professionals working with children, particularly in institutions, as well as the public at large about the negative impact of corporal punishment and ill-treatment on children and actively involve children and the media in the process; (d) Ensure that positive, participatory, non-violent forms of discipline are administrated in a manner consistent with the child's human dignity and in conformity with the Convention, in particular article 28 (2) as an alternative to corporal punishment at all levels of society".

[55] *Devendra Ale et al v. Office of the Prime Minister & Council of Ministers et al*, SC decision dated, 6 January 2005.

[56] *Raju Prasad Chapagai et al v. Office of the Prime Minister and Council of Ministers et al*, NKP 34 (SC 2008).

[57] The Supreme Court under the 1990 Constitution had also judicial powers identical to the Interim Constitution. See, Supra note 44, 45 & 46.

[58] The challenged provision reads, "In cases where a person engaged in taking care of or educating another person beats that other person or does any other act for the

appropriate legislative, administrative and institutional measures dealing with prevailing practice of corporal punishment and violence against children.

The petitioners' main contention was that the Section in question virtually protected the perpetrators of violence against children from criminal responsibility, and promoted acts of corporal punishment inconsistent with the right against torture, right of the child against violence and the right to life guaranteed under the Interim Constitution and the CRC. In this case, the Supreme Court observed that those providing education and protection could not be allowed to create terror, giving physical and mental torture, and in the name of education could not be allowed to spank or beat the child, which might even have fatal consequences.

The Supreme Court further observed that "Such a questioned provision does not seem to respect autonomy of the person. The person to be educated is entitled no less right than those providing education. Such a person is also entitled to live a dignified life and enjoy all other rights on equal footing to the person giving care and education….for the reasons including that a person is physically weak, uneducated, poor or disabled, it does not restrict to or create any disability in the exercise of rights." According to the court, the very legal thinking that the person engaged in taking care of or educating another person can use physical force against the person receiving education and care results in gross violation of inherent right to freedom, dignity and equality.

Finally, the Court invalidated Section 6(3) of the Country Code, referring to the rights to live with dignity, to equality, against exploitation, guaranteed under the Interim Constitution, as well as the rights guaranteed under Articles 19(1) 28(2), 37(a) of the CRC[59]. Stressing the need for a

---

benefit of the deceased and an accidental homicide occurs as a result of such act, the person shall be liable to a fine of up to Fifty Rupees".

[59] CRC art. 19(1) reads, " States Parties shall take all appropriate legislative, administrative, social and educational measures to protect the child from all forms of physical or mental violence, injury or abuse, neglect or negligent treatment, maltreatment or exploitation, including sexual abuse, while in the care of parent(s), legal guardian(s) or any other person who has the care of the child. CRC art 28(2) reads: States Parties shall take all appropriate measures to ensure that school discipline is administered in a manner consistent with the child's human dignity and in conformity with the present Convention. CRC art. 37(a) reads: No child shall be subjected to torture or other cruel, inhuman or degrading treatment or

legal as well as institutional arrangement to discourage the practice of physical and mental torture and abuses against children, the Supreme Court also ordered the respondents to enact a law offering an appropriate remedy to children, as well as disciplining those teachers and other persons who are engaged in torturing and harassing children and to construct mechanisms to ensure effective implementation of such a law.

4.3. Promoting Infant and Maternal Health

The Supreme Court's activism is also noticeable in relation to promoting the health rights of infants and mothers. The Supreme Court, through its Public Interest Litigation jurisdiction, has addressed several issues including promoting breastfeeding, maternity leave, and child care facility in the workplace.

For example, in *Prakash Mani Sharma et al*[60], a number of unfair and discriminatory maternity leave provisions were brought to the scrutiny of the Supreme Court, invoking the 1990 Constitution, the CRC and the CEDAW. [61] The Supreme Court was called upon to order the Government to adopt a uniform national standard on maternity leave, taking into account international standards and best practices.[62] As required, the Supreme Court directed the Government to formulate the national standard on maternity leave to be applicable to all working women, and make essential arrangement for maternity protection in compliance with Nepal's national and international commitments.[63] The Supreme Court held that it is a State obligation to make proper arrangements concerning nutrition of infant and health care of a working woman during her pregnancy and post-

---

punishment. Neither capital punishment nor life imprisonment without possibility of release shall be imposed for offences committed by persons below eighteen years of age".

[60] *Prakash Mani Sharma et al v. HMG, Ministry of Women, Children and Social Welfare et al*, NKP 726 (SC. 2003).

[61] Nepal lacks a comprehensive legal framework dealing with maternity protection. There exist inadequacy as well as lack of uniformity in terms of providing maternity leave for workingwomen (e.g. 60- days for public service employees , 52- days for employees regulated under Labor Act, and 45- day for employees regulated under Tea Estates Regulations).

[62] ILO Convention on Maternity Protection, 2000 (to which Nepal is not a party) sets 98 days as a minimum standard.

[63] The ILO Convention, special protection clause of the Constitution, Breast milk Substitute (control of sale and distribution Act) 1992, Labor Act 1991 and Child Act 1992 .

delivery period. In terms of the importance of maternity leave for maternal and child health, the Court observed:

> Maternity benefits including maternity leave are provided in order to enable working women to have a complete rest before and after pregnancy and facilitate them to provide proper care for their newly born baby. Weak health status of those who are pregnant and mother of newly born baby may result in miscarriage and premature birth and it may also cause a risk to fetus or newly born baby. Taking into account the role of women to care and breastfeed baby as well as the baby's right to be breastfed, working women can't be denied the rest period or maternity leave in such a situations.

In response to another PIL case, *Prakash Mani Sharma et al*,[64] the Supreme Court drew the attention of the government towards implementing a provision of the Labour Act requiring all enterprises that employ at least 50 women to provide child care and breastfeeding facilities at the workplace,[65] Though the provision was made in order to make sure that women do not face difficulties in pursuing their employment, and that the health of children is not jeopardized because of their reproductive role, many of the enterprises didn't comply with this legal requirement. The case was, therefore, brought to the Supreme Court with a view to getting the law effectively implemented.

The Court expressed serious concerns about the health of the children in *Raju Chapagai et al.*[66] The petitioners drew the attention of the Court on the long standing non-compliance of the Mother's Milk Substitutes (Control of Sale and Distribution) Act.[67] Even 10 years after the promulgation of the Act, the government had failed to comply with the statutory obligations in relation to supervising and monitoring the production, sale and distribution of mother's milk substitutes. The government had not even appointed the inspectors that were required by the Act. In this case, the government was ordered to implement the Act by appointing inspectors responsible for compliance monitoring.

---

[64] *Prakash Mani Sharma et al v. HMG, Ministry of Labour et al* , WPN 34 of the year 2059 BS, , SC decision dated 2 May 2005.

[65] Labour Act 1998, S. 42.

[66] *Raju Prasad Chapagai and Others representing Pro-Public v HMG, Ministry of Health et al*, WPN 2621 of the year 2059 BS, SC decision dated, 5 Nov. 2004.

[67] The Act came into operation on 27 Feb. 1995.

The Supreme Court also noted the importance of breastfeeding, stating that children are indisputably entitled to exclusive breastfeeding for six months, since there is nothing as nutritious as breast-milk. It also observed that the State and the respective companies are under a legal and moral obligation to comply with the national and international standards aimed at promoting the health of the children and mother. It is also relevant to emphasize that the Supreme Court, linking the right to breastfeeding with the right to a dignified life, held that the government has prime responsibility to keep children healthy by preventing them from being victim of malnutrition.

Giving effect to the principles incorporated into the 1990 Constitution which required the State to take care of maternal and child health,[68] the Supreme Court held that the government must not defer enforcing legal and Constitutional provisions aimed at promoting children's health. It was also observed that as a matter of public policy, the judiciary should not refrain from intervening in such a sensitive issue. Through its decision, the Court thus made an important contribution to protecting the right of children to healthy food and safety condition and the fulfilling of the State's obligation to safeguard the rights and interest of its citizens under the Constitution and the CRC.

4.4. Combating Harmful Traditions and Customary Practices

Several harmful traditional practices causing extreme insecurity, health hazards and cruelty to girls continue to prevail in Nepal. Most notably, such practices include *Kumari,*[69] *Kamlari,*[70] *Chaupadi*[71] and early marriage.

[68] A number of relevant directive principles enshrined under Art. 26 of the 1990 Constitution include: The State shall pursue a policy of making the female population participate, to a greater extent, in the task of national development by making special provisions for their education, health and employment (Clause 7). The State shall make necessary arrangements to safeguard the rights and interests of children and shall ensure that they are not exploited, and shall make gradual arrangements for free education (Clause 8). The State shall pursue such policies in matters of education, health and social security of orphans, helpless women, the aged, the disabled and incapacitated persons, as well as ensure their protection and welfare (Clause 9).

[69] There is a customary practice of appointing girls from the Newar community to serve as human goddesses in some Hindu temples, especially in some parts of the Country including the capital, Kathmandu.

[70] Kamalari is one of the forms of bonded labour system which existed in the far west and mid-west parts of Nepal. In this system, girls from the Tharu community

The CRC Committee has regretted the absence of any legal sanction against these traditional practices which harm the enjoyment of rights by children affected by the practices.[72] Invoking constitutional guarantees and provisions of international human rights treaties, including the CRC, a number of concerns about these practices were raised before the Supreme Court through filing PIL petitions. In response, the Supreme Court has had an effective role in holding the Government accountable for not taking necessary steps to eliminate or reform these practices.

For instance, in *Som Prasad Paneru V. Office of the Prime Minister at al,*[73] the Supreme Court was called upon to order the Government to take steps to eliminate the practice of *Kamalari.* Responding to the case, the Court made an interesting ruling requiring the Ministry of Education and Sports to incorporate key human rights treaties (including the CRC, ICCPR and ICESCR) into the school curriculum, so that the rights of the Child could be protected and the legal framework on child labour implemented effectively. The Supreme Court also directed the Government to enact a comprehensive law dealing with domestic workers, not only abolishing the practice of *Kamalari*, but also preventing the exploitation of children on any other grounds; and for the the rights of the child under the CRC to be protected, the Court also ordered the government to frame plans and policies to protect the interests and social security of children emancipated from *Kamalari* and other forms of exploitation.

In *Pundevi Maharjan v. Office of the Prime Minister et al,*[74] the Court held that *Kumaries* are equally entitled to rights under the Interim Constitution and the CRC. The government was ordered to constitute a committee

---

are employed as domestic workers by landlords. Such bonded girls in domestic servitude are called Kamalaris.

[71] Chaupadi is a traditional practice prevalent in some parts of the far west and mid-west regions, which treats girls/women as untouchable/impure and keeps them in isolation, especially while they are menstruatinge.

[72] The Committee recommends that the State party, as a matter of urgency, take all necessary measures to eradicate all traditional practices harmful to the physical and psychological well-being of children, by strengthening awareness-raising programmes. The Committee further recommends the State party to adopt legislation prohibiting such practices.

[73] *Som Prasad Peneru et al v. HMG, Office of the Prime Minister and Council of Ministers et a*l, WPN 3295 of the year 2061BS, SC decision dated 10th September, 2006.

[74] *Pun Devi Maharjan v. Office of Prime Minister and Council of Ministers and Others*, WPN 3581 of the year 2062 B.S, SC decision dated, 16 August 2008AD.

under the terms of reference it stipulated, to conduct an extensive study of this practice from the perspective of children's rights. It was especially ordered to investigate how the rights and interests and social security of *Kumaris* could be promoted by adopting suitable legal and administrative measures. The Supreme Court also issued a writ of mandamus requiring the government to implement the committee's report once it had been submitted.

With regard to *Chaupadi*, in *Dil Bahadur Bishwokarma et al*[75] *the* Supreme Court ordered the Government to make a pro-active intervention, including raising awareness, to eliminate this tradition. Expressing serious concern over governmental reluctance to abolish such an inhuman tradition, the Supreme Court directed the government to bring in a comprehensive law to deal with the customary practices like *chaupadi* that are detrimental to the health of girls and women. The case was brought to the Court by a dozen lawyers representing different social organizations working for human rights and gender justice. In response to this decision, the government subsequently developed and issued guidelines on *Chaupadi* aimed at raising awareness about the practice.

Widespread practice of early marriage within certain ethnic and religious communities has also been a matter of serious concern from the perspective of children's rights. The CRC Committee also recommended strengthening the enforcement of the existing legislation on preventing early marriage, and to develop sensitization programmes, involving community and religious leaders and society at large, as well as children themselves, to curb the practice of early marriage. The State was required to take measures to ensure that when underage girls are married, they continue to enjoy their full rights, as set out in the Convention, including the right to education.[76] In view of these recommendations, a public

[75] *Dil Bahadur Bishwakarma et al v. HMG, Cabinet Secretariat et al*, WPN 44 of the year 2062 B.S., SC decision dated 5 April 2005 AD.

[76] See UN Committee on CRC, Concluding Observations in response to Nepal's Second Periodic Report (see CRC/C/SR.1032 and 1033, held on 20 May 2005): The Committee recommends that the State party strengthen its enforcement of the existing legislation to prevent early marriage and that the State party develop sensitization programmes, involving community and religious leaders and society at large, including children themselves, to curb the practice of early marriage. It also recommends to the State party that it take measures to ensure that when underage girls are married, they continue to fully enjoy their rights as set out in the Convention, including the right to education (Para 66).

interest case, *Sapana Malla et al v. Office of the Prime Minister et al,*[77] was brought to the Supreme Court demanding its intervention in combating the practice of early marriage. In this case, the Supreme Court directed the government to amend marriage laws and create a uniform legal standard on marriageable ages for men and women[78] and ensure effective implementation of anti child-marriage laws, especially under the Country Code.

Acting upon another PIL case, *Prakash Mani Sharma et al for Pro Public,* the Supreme Court directed the government to strictly implement the penal provisions under the Country Code to control the widespread practice of child marriage. The Court nullified a discriminatory part of Section 9 (2) of the Country Code's Chapter on Marriage, which provided that the victim of a child marriage can approach the court only after attaining 18 years of age if he or she wants to get the marriage annulled. Also, the Government was ordered to launch preventative measures, including awareness programmes, against the practice of child marriage across the country.

4. 5. Outlawing Recruitment of Minors in Security Forces

The recruitment of young boys into the security forces was protected under Nepalese law. The Army Boys Recruitment Regulation permitted the then Royal Nepalese Army (currently the Nepalese Army) to recruit boys between 15–18; and the Police Boys Recruitment Regulation allowed the Nepal Police to recruit boys between 13-18. Upon reaching 18, they were converted into full members of the forces. By filing public interest litigation, both regulations were challenged before the Supreme Court in order to get them invalidated.[79] The petitioners basically relied on the arguments that the regulations were contrary to the CRC and the Option Protocol Regarding Involvement of Children in Armed Conflict, to which Nepal is a party. The Supreme Court found both regulations in contravention

---

[77] *Sapana Malla et al v. Office of the Prime Minister et al,* WPN 98 of the Year 2062 BS, SC decision dated, 13 July 2006.

[78] Conflicting provisions on marriageable age in the laws relating to marriage include: Section 4 (3) of the Marriage Registration Act, which states that the marriageable age for men is 22 and 18 for girls, while Article 2 under the Matrimonial Section of the Country Code states that the marriageable age for men is 20 and 18 for girls.

[79] *Sabin Shrestha et al v. Office of the Prime Minister and Council of Ministers et al,* WPN 71 of the Year 2062, SC decision dated, 15 Sept. 2005.

with provisions under the CRC and the respective Optional Protocol, and struck them out, using its judicial review power. In doing so, the Court applied the CRC,[80] and Optional Protocol regarding the Involvement of Children in Armed Conflict 2000 that imposes an obligation upon the State to refrain from recruiting minors in the armed forces.

4.6. Protection of Right to Privacy of Children Involved in Court Proceedings

Taking into account the fact that the identity of women, children and persons infected with HIV and AIDs involved in court proceedings continue to be disclosed in the media,[81] in contravention with the right to privacy, a PIL was brought to the Supreme Court calling for an order of mandamus compelling the authorities to adopt adequate legislative measures on the protection of anonymity and confidentiality.[82]

In this case, the Supreme Court directed the government to formulate law protecting anonymity and privacy of information about the special category of persons (i.e. female victims of violence, abuse and exploitation; and children and persons infected or affected by HIV and AIDS) involved in court proceedings, consistent with Nepal's treaty

---

[80] CRC Art. 38 provides, "(1) States Parties undertake to respect and to ensure respect for rules of international humanitarian law applicable to them in armed conflicts which are relevant to the child; 2) States Parties shall take all feasible measures to ensure that persons who have not attained the age of 15 do not take a direct part in hostilities; 3) States Parties shall refrain from recruiting any person who has not attained the age of 15 into their armed forces. In recruiting among those persons who have attained the age of 15 but who have not attained the age of 18, States Parties shall endeavour to give priority to those who are oldest; 4. In accordance with their obligations under international humanitarian law to protect the civilian population in armed conflicts, States Parties shall take all feasible measures to ensure protection and care of children who are affected by an armed conflict".

[81] See UN Committee on CRC, Concluding Observations in response to Nepal's Second Periodic Report (CRC/C/SR.1032 and 1033, held on 20 May 2005): The CRC Committee urges the State party to establish mechanisms to ensure that all materials broadcast in Nepal respect the child's right to privacy such as a code of conduct and/or self-regulation, and to ensure that appropriate human rights training is given to media professionals, paying particular attention to children's rights to privacy (Para 46).

[82] *Sapana Pradhan Malla and others Vs. Office of the Prime Minister and others*, WPN 3561 of the Year 2006, SC decision dated, 25 Dec. 2007.

obligations. Addressing the interim period till such law is made, the Supreme Court also issued 'A Procedural Guideline for the Protection of Privacy of Parties in the Entire Prosecution and Court Process in Regard to the Cases of Special Nature 2007'. In doing so the Supreme Court has followed its own precedents,[83] as well as the precedent that the Supreme Court of India had set in term of designing judicial guidelines to fill a gap in the law.[84] The Court found this indispensable in promoting people's enjoyment of the rights guaranteed under the Constitution[85] and the CRC.[86] The procedural guideline provides a catalogue of the cases in which privacy must be maintained as well as defining the term 'personal details', the conditions in which privacy is required to be maintained, details of the procedures to be applied in protecting confidentiality. The

---

[83] *Gopal Siwakoti v Ministry of Finance et al*, NKP 255 (SC 1994): The Supreme Court of Nepal, for the first time, issued a set of judicial guidelines prescribing a procedure on how to seek, receive and impart information of public importance. The guidelines was issued in view of the absence of enacted law to give effect to the right to information guaranteed under article 16 of the 1990 Constitution.

[84] *Vishaka v. State of Rajasthan* AIR 1997 SUPREME COURT 3011: In issuing a set of judicial guidelines to regulate practice of sexual harassments in the workplace, the Supreme Court of India observes, "In view of the above, and the absence of enacted law to provide for the effective enforcement of the basic human right of gender equality and guarantee against sexual harassment and abuse, more particularly against sexual harassment at work places, we lay down the guidelines and norms specified hereinafter for due observance at all work places or other institutions, until legislation is enacted for the purpose. This is done in exercise of the power available under Article 32 of the Constitution for enforcement of fundamental rights and it is further emphasized that this would be treated as the law declared by this Court under Article 141 of the Constitution."

[85] NEP. INTERIM CONST. (2007), art. 28.

[86] Article 16 of the Convention of Rights of Child, 1989 has also provided that: "No child shall be subjected to arbitrary or unlawful interference with his/her privacy, family, home or correspondence, nor to unlawful attack on his/her honour and reputation". And, by further providing that "The child has the right to the protection of the law against such interference or attacks", it seems to have recognized children's right to privacy. Article 8(4) of the Optional Protocol to the Convention of Rights of Child on the Sale of the Children, Child Prostitution and Child Pornography, 2000 seems to have included the matter of taking appropriate steps, in accordance with the national law, to remove undue flow of information regarding introductory matters relating to a child in order to protect his/her identity and privacy. ("Protection as appropriate to the privacy and identity of child victim and taking measures in accordance with the national law to avoid the inappropriate dissemination of information that lead to the identification of child victim." - Art. 8(6)," observed the Court in a confidentiality decision.)

guideline prohibits publication of information where privacy must be protected, and makes punishable a breach of privacy.

4.7. Promoting Juvenile Justice System

Although Nepal was under national as well as international legal obligations requiring special treatment of the child engaged in conflict with law, for a long time the procedures for children in criminal proceeding remained similar to those of adults. However, the Supreme Court's affirmative intervention in a number of cases has extensively contributed in shaping and developing the Juvenile Justice System in Nepal.

In Santosh Mahato v. Office of the Prime Minister et al,[87] the Supreme Court ordered the government to establish juvenile courts to hear cases where children are implicated either as perpetrators or victims. In doing so, the Supreme Court applied Article 40 of the CRC that guarantees rights of the child in conflict with law. The Supreme Court noted that as it is a binding obligation to establish separate juvenile courts, the Government cannot be relieved from the respective obligations merely on the ground that it has created juvenile benches within the ordinary court system. A positive outcome of this judicial intervention has been that the government has adopted a separate Juvenile Justice (Procedure) Rules 2006, which prescribes child-friendly procedures to be followed for trying cases involving children. The Rules lay down the processes and provisions for effective implementation of the Juvenile Justice System and functioning of Juvenile Courts or Juvenile Bench.[88] The current juvenile benches within

---

[87] *Santosh Mahato v. Office of the Prime Minister et al*, WPN 60 of the Year 2061 B.S., SC decision dated, 24 Nov. 2005.

[88] Major highlights of The Juvenile Justice (Procedures) Rules 2006 include: (i) assigning a separate unit with specialized police personnel in a police office to investigate juvenile cases (where the accused is a child); (ii) defining investigation and prosecution procedures; (iii) defining procedures for the formation of the Juvenile Bench; (iv) informing the child through his or her parents or guardians; (v) defining the qualification and selection criteria of social workers and child psychologists to work in a panel with the Judge while hearing and deciding juvenile cases; (vi) procedures for hearing juvenile cases in court; (vii) the process of collecting and verification of proofs, (viii) the process of verifying the age of the child, and (ix) the preparation of a roster of service-providing organizations. The Rules also provide for the formation of a Juvenile Justice Coordination Committee at the central level for giving advice and making recommendations to the government on laws and policies to strengthen the Juvenile Justice System in Nepal.

the district courts are required to follow the procedure prescribed in the Rules. However, stand-alone juvenile courts have yet to be created. Instead of courts, juvenile benches have so far been created in 28 out of 75 district courts.

Similarly, in several cases involving juvenile justice issues, the Supreme Court has ordered the government to make necessary arrangements towards the establishment and operation of juvenile welfare and reform homes as mandated under the CRC and the Children Act;[89] to put children in conflict with the law in reform homes instead of prisons;[90] and to release the juvenile from arbitrary imprisonment and detention.[91] These interventions illustrate a proactive attitude b the Supreme Court towards developing the juvenile justice system in Nepal, consistent with international standards.

4.8. Recognition of Children as Persons before Law

In contrast, citizenship has been the area where the Supreme Court remained conservative. In a number of cases, the Supreme Court has upheld the primacy of discriminatory constitutional provisions on citizenship over treaty provisions. For example, in *Benjamin Peter*,[92] the Supreme Court declined to apply treaty provisions that conflicted with citizenship provisions under the 1990 Constitution, which disallowed Nepalese women's rights to transfer citizenship to their children. In upholding the constitutional provisions, the Supreme Court stated that the provisions under any treaty that the government has entered into do not apply if they are inconsistent with special provisions of the Constitution. More explicitly, in *Chandrakanta Gaynwali* [93] the Supreme Court upheld the supremacy of constitutional provisions on citizenship that conflicted with provisions of the Convention on the Elimination of All Forms of

---

[89] *Ashish Adhikari vs. His Majesty's Government et al*, WPN 3391 of the Year 2000 AD, SC decision dated, April 15 2002. In

[90] *Pode Tamang v. Sindhupalchowk District Court et a*l, WPN 4022 of the Year 2001AD, SC decision dated, (July 25, 2001 A.D).

[91] *Sarita Tamang v. Illam District Court et al*, WPN 21 of the Year 2001.

[92] *Benjamin Peter v. Ministry of Home Affairs et al,* SC decision dated, 17 July 1991.

[93] *Chandrakanta Gaynwali v.HMG, The Secretariat of Council of Ministries et al*, SC decision dated, 7 February 2002: The Court was called upon by the petitioner to strike down the citizenship provisions which discriminated on the basis of gender under the 1990 Constitution and the Citizenship Act, 1964.

Discrimination against Women (CEDAW) that guarantees equal rights for men and women in terms of citizenship of their children. The Court stated that the treaty provisions cannot be read as being superior to the constitutional provisions. If the constitutional provisions were interpreted in harmony with the CEDAW and CRC, the child's right to citizenship through its mother could have been protected.
However, in *Tek Tamrakar et al*[94] the Supreme Court nullified a discriminatory provision of Section 4(1) of the 'Birth, Death and Other Private Incidence Registration Act 1976' that deprived women from enjoying the right to get the birth of their children registered. The nullified provision had allowed a 'senior member among male family members' to register the birth. Similarly, the Supreme Court issued an order of mandamus requiring the government to ensure effective implementation of Article 9(2) of the Constitution; which provides that every child found within the Kingdom of Nepal, the whereabouts of whose parents are not known shall, until the father of the child is traced, be deemed to be a citizen of Nepal by descent.

5. Conclusion

While the Nepalese legal system essentially remains dualist, there has been an increasing judicial trend to utilize international rights standards in adjudicating children's rights. With the exception of access to citizenship,[95] the Supreme Court has positively utilized CRC provisions, especially in terms of invalidating legislative[96] and executive actions[97] inconsistent with the international human rights standards and the Constitution. The Supreme Court has also had recourse to the CRC in ordering the Government to adopt legislative measures in line with international legal obligations regarding children.[98] It is important to underscore that the Supreme Court's constitutional review power, combined with PIL jurisdiction, appears to have been instrumental in shaping and the developing domestic legal regime regarding children. The issues that the Supreme Court scrutinized by virtue of its PIL jurisdiction contain a wide range of children's rights issues including corporal punishment, maternity protection,

94 *Tek Tamrakar et al V HMG Cabinet Secretariat et al* , Writ No. 121 of the Year 2060, SC decision dated, 15 Sept 2005.
95 See, Supra note 54, 55, 78 & 93.
96 See, Supra note 7.
97 See, Supra note, 91 & 92.
98 See, Supra note, 62, 72, 73, 74, 76, 81 & 86.

breast-feeding, juvenile justice, confidentiality and harmful and traditional practice.

Nevertheless, there remain a number of challenges. Many of the Supreme Court verdicts are still awaiting implementation; harmonization of national laws and practice with the CRC has not yet been achieved. In view of this, continued judicial activism through PIL in creative and innovative ways makes a lot of sense in terms of turning children's rights guarantees under the CRC and the Constitution into reality. Capacity building initiatives aimed at enhancing sensitization of judicial officials and human rights lawyers on international child rights standards and comparative jurisprudence would also be an advantage in furthering the judicial role.

The importance of ongoing constitution-making processes in this regard should not be underrated, as this could be an opportunity to secure constitutional superiority of ratified human rights instruments such as the CRC, which will put an end to disharmony between the CRC and the Constitution. This purpose may be achieved through formulating or adopting explicit provisions within the structure of the new Constitution. This may be reached either a) by accepting automatic incorporation of core international agreements including the CRC into the legal body of the Constitution; or b) through authorizing and obliging the courts to interpret the existing fundamental rights provisions under the Nepalese Constitution, consistent with the international human rights treaties to which Nepal is a party.

COERCIVE LEGISLATION: CHILDREN'S INVISIBILITY IN THE LEGAL PROCESS

HJÖRDIS FLODSTRÖM ENQUIST

Abstract

Social welfare law is administered by elected local authorities in municipalities in Sweden, the municipal social welfare committee, but most of the decisions in client cases are delegated decisions taken by the employed social workers. When children need to be taken into care by the welfare service, and the parents do not agree and coercion is necessary, the case is then referred to the county administrative court. Within the legal process the child, regardless of age, has the right to have a Child's Representative (CR) on their own, when using the Care of Young People Act, (LVU 1990:52). The CR's task in the case of children younger than 15 is to both interpret and convey the child's wishes, and furthermore make their own independent assessment of what is in the child's best interests in each case.

This research particularly examines the knowledge of child welfare of the 'Child's Representative' (CR) appointed by the 23 county administrative courts in Sweden in the Care of Young People Act (LVU) Cases. The research model incorporated all 23 county administrative courts in Sweden in 2007, and 22 of them responded to the questionnaire. The findings of this study are that (a) the skills requirements of the CRs is too broad and therefore not focused enough on children and young people's welfare; (b) the county administrative courts do not require that the CRs have specialist knowledge and experience relating to children and young people's welfare; (c) in the case of very young children (under 3) the CR is not expected to meet either the child or its respective carers before the LVU-hearing.

1. Introduction

In order for a society to protect its children appropriately, one of the fundamental principles is that those who have been commissioned to investigate and help children in need become aware of the child's situation and experience.[1] Information relating to the child should be as accurate as possible and reflect the child's actual conditions. Of course, the child itself is the one who can give the best picture. The position of children and their invisibility in the legal process has been discussed and confirmed in a considerable number of research programmes which have been conducted by Swedish or international researchers. In Sweden, coercive legislation relating to children and young people is available, such as the Social Services Act[2] and Care of Young People Act. Most of the aid and relief efforts for children and young people are carried out in collaboration with children and parents through the Social Services Act. The Care of Young People Act protects children and young people in very complicated situations, and when cooperation does not really function properly.

Despite many years of debate and research, and evidence that the child's voice is weak, and does not clearly emerge in the legal process, the judicial system has not been significantly improved in this area. Although many of the provisions of the Convention on the Rights of the Child (CRC) have been implemented within Swedish legislation in order to strengthen the child's perspective and its visibility before the national authorities and services, it may be argued that there has been no really significant change.

Children in need of community support and help—usually when intervention under the Care of Young People Act (LVU) becomes necessary—may have lived in a precarious situation for a long time. They are in a very fragile condition, and it is therefore reasonable and necessary that special competence and skills are required by the CR. It is essential that this person is capable of understanding the child's situation, and has the training and skills to listen, observe and talk to it, and will thus be able to clarify to the child what is happening, and why. In Swedish legislation there is no specific requirement for the CR to be a lawyer or have legal training. Despite this, though, county administrative courts invariably assign the CR's role and function to lawyers, who have often been proved

---

[1] Schiratzki, J. *Barnrättens grunder.* (2006) p.30-43.

[2] SoL 2001:453. Norström, C & Thunved, A (2010) *Nya sociallagarna med kommentarer…*

not to have adequate knowledge, training or experience of children's expressions, needs, and development.

The aim of this article is to discuss the effects of the provisions of Articles 3 and 12 of the CRC within the Swedish social system. The articles constitute two pillars of the development of the protection of the rights of children from a national and international perspective. Article 3 emphasises that in all actions concerning children, whether undertaken by public or private social welfare institutions, courts of law, administrative authorities or legislative bodies, the best interests of the child shall be a primary consideration. Article 12 endorses the provisions of Article 3. It stresses that the child has a legal right to be heard in matters concerning it. Our purpose is thus to discuss the content of these articles and their effects in our national legal system. The final ambition is to evaluate our legal system and children's invisibility in the legal process. The results are also seen in the light of the Swedish legislature's attempt to strengthen the rights of children based on the CRC.

2. Dimensions of Legal System

The dimensions of legal systems have been analysed from various aspects and different conclusions have been reached. As early as 1992, researchers in the field of children's rights examined several serious questions of criminal justice. For instance, two writers from the UK examined the paradox in determining children's welfare in court. They evaluated the protection of children's rights from various points of views and sharply criticised the systems of the Anglo-Saxon countries. According to them:

> The more the legal system takes on itself the burden of protecting children and promoting their interests, therefore, the less able it is to act swiftly to resolve conflicts and provide certainty. If courts were actually able to offer the environment for long-term problem solving and resources to help children and families in difficulties, there would be less of a problem. Unfortunately, in Anglo-Saxon countries which operate upon an adversarial system of justice, this is not possible. Courts are there to make decisions on specific, isolated issues. Furthermore, despite all the trappings of welfarism—the specialist lawyers, the social workers, the mental health experts and the guardians ad item—when it comes to the crucial decision-making, the courts often revert to type and concentrate on issues of "proved" and "not proved". As we shall see from some of the cases discussed, complex issues concerning disturbed and damaged children may, once they enter the legal arena, so easily be transformed into the simple question of whether the abuse did or did not take place. And the

> outcome for the child depends much more upon the answer to that question than upon a careful analysis of that child´s needs.[3]

Another writer has a similar view. According to her, there is a clear risk that child welfare investigations can be "infiltrated" by legal thinking and requirements. Her research has shown how social workers try to work from the position of children and their families in order to avoid, as far as possible, any unfair enforcement; this is because there is uncertainty about the adequacy of evidence and its practical effects. Gathering evidence is accordingly difficult. Social workers do not want to expose children and their families to legal processes until they are sure that that is the only option. This is because there is a risk that in the process of waiting for evidence, the children are exposed to hard conditions and situations.[4]

A Norwegian writer, who has spent many years researching the child's voice in the legal process, has also dealt with the question of using coercive legislation in Norway. According to her, the question of a child's rights to be heard is still dominant in Norwegian law. In a comparative Nordic study, she highlights a similar experience to that in the above paragraph. She examines how social services hesitate in child cases and how social workers sometimes wait for a long time before submitting an application to the county administrative court regarding a care order of the child, until they feel confident that the application will be granted. The reason is that the process is indeed very long and is therefore very stressful for the parents. As she expresses, "*fylkesnemndssak* is doing something with parents".[5]

A relevant question about social work which was raised in Norway, dealt with the position of various actors and their competency and capacity relating to the needs of the child. It raised the question of who is the best "expert", and how legal competence is valued more highly than other skills and how the hearings are carried out on a legal premise and are sharply criticised. According to one writer:

> I am tired of social workers being so easily placed at the bottom of the hierarchy, while they bear greatest responsibility, are the worst paid and

---

[3] M King & J Trowell, *Children´s welfare and the law* (1992) p.6.

[4] Ponnert, L (2007) *Mellan klient och rättssystem –tvångsvård av barn och unga*...p.81-87.

[5] Vogt Grinde, T. Rapport 18/04. *Nordisk barnevern, Terskelen for barneverntiltak og beslutningsprocessen ved bruk av tvang*. Nordisk institutt for forskning om oppvekst, velferd og aldring. (2004)

> are often those who will be hanged if something goes wrong. I feel not only morally outraged but also concerned that child protection service action goes from help, support and problem solving, in a skewed rule of law with emphasis on respect for parents.[6]

Another writer describes a similar question concerning another early issue. He writes about how social law is a part of public law and basic principles have been taken from court procedure and private law. In his opinion, the legal system has only a limited application to problems in the welfare society. He stresses that the variations in practice between court procedure and activities at street level are "formidable", and in addition, that many problems and situations in social practice which are regulated by social welfare legislation hardly fit into the traditional legal pattern. He highlights the importance of bridging the traditional gap between legal and professional thinking and practice. One of the conclusions in his article is that, "We are not talking about different worlds, but participants in the same world who need to be enabled to cooperate. As a starting point, there is no doubt that we find common values and interests in the legal and the social policy system".[7] He means that it is also a challenge to the professionals in welfare services themselves to participate in the creation of functional legislation. As he finally says, "After all, to grasp and understand the complexities of a system makes it easier to do a decent job within it."[8]

Another writer has studied the child's legal status and how the Care of Young People Act (LVU) meets the requirements of legal certainty, protection of privacy and a gradual increase in autonomy for children in Sweden. She also compares Swedish legislation with that of Norway and England. Part of her book is based on 390 judgments from four county courts, and one of the conclusions is that the requirement of legal certainty may clash with the need for the child's privacy and right to autonomy. She recalls in particular the built-in dilemma for the 'Child's Representative' when the child is under 15 years (and not *processbehörigt - procedural capacity)* to represent and interpret the child's needs and its own interests and desires. She fears that the child´s voice will not be presented or

---

[6] Vogt Grinde, T Artikel 01/97, Norges Barnevern. *Fylkesnemndene og barnevernets kompetanse.* (1997)

[7] Andenaes, *The Law and the Nonlegal Professionals On Decision-Making by Medical Doctors and Social Workers*, International Journal of Law and Psychistry. Vol.12.263 -274, (1989)

[8] Andenaes, ibid (1989)

considered adequate in the legal process. From a legislator's view, she describes how important it is that a CR should be a person with special aptitude for child welfare, and not just a legally qualified person with procedural experience.[9]

In 2008 the National Board of Health and Welfare in Sweden (Socialstyrelsen) made a follow-up study on "the Child in Care of Young People Act (LVU)-process" from 1993. The results showed a "weak" commitment by the CR, with a very low level of engagement from a child welfare point of view. It demonstrates that there had been no detectable change during the previous 15 years in terms of the CR's governing behaviour and skills. They found that the courts, nowadays, very rarely use experts in LVU hearings, although they are permitted. In addition, it was clear that the witnesses who appeared at the hearing were the parents' witnesses. These conditions reduce the child's visibility and further empowered the parents.

The investigator also noted that the CR's expenses were substantially lower than the parents' representative. Both children's and parents' representatives, and lawyers, provide costs at each hearing, which is reported in the final Judgement. The investigator also noted that in all 35 cases examined, all the CRs were lawyers. Young people who are competent in the process were well supported, but when it came to younger children, the picture was more mixed. In addition, the study shows, from the cost study aspect, that some children had not met their representative at all, especially not the youngest. Overall the study shows how the "child's voice" is still as weak as it was in 1993.[10]

3. Attempts to Strengthen Children's Visibility in Coercive Legislation: the Child in Care of Young People Act (LVU)

A strengthening of the position of children in the legal process was proposed by the investigator (2000) from the Ministry of Health and Social Affairs in Sweden, to be effected by the county administrative courts hearing appropriate child experts at the LVU hearing. She also suggested that a fixed number of child experts should be appointed to assist the courts. The investigator raised several issues regarding the

[9] Mattsson, T *Barnet och rättsprocessen.* (2002) p. 167-172.

[10] National Board of Health and Welfare (Socialstyrelsen), 2009-126-182 p.40.

strengthening of the child's visibility, including demands for the CR to have special child skills. These interesting suggestions for the strengthening of children's visibility in LVU hearings were never acted upon. Her comments about the reasons for the child's invisibility are relevant here: "I have, during the investigation, found that the conditions for intervention to be made under the Act are too narrow, and would need to be extended." She goes further and emphasises that although the legal conditions for intervention are being changed, the child is not still being given necessary recognition within investigations or in judicial decisions. It is rather a question of changing the viewpoint of those applying the law."[11] The investigator's radical proposals also included greater demands for education and special skills for both social workers and CRs. The final enactment of the Care of Young People Act (LVU) in 2002 was an amendment, the opening paragraph of which stipulates that "The decision reached under this Act, what is best for the young person, is to be decisive".

3.1. Problem

To ensure the child's legal rights, the CR has the job of interpreting and conveying the child's desire, and making their own independent assessment of the young child, and what is in its best interests. What chance is there of being able to interpret and understand a small child in a vulnerable position if you lack the necessary knowledge about its needs and ways of expressing itself and, moreover, without meeting the child or its carers?

In the legislation there is neither a specific requirement for the CR to be a lawyer, nor even to be legally trained, which means not only lawyers, but also social workers, could be a CR if the latter have specific competence in children's welfare. Despite this, all county administrative courts in Sweden give those mandates to lawyers: they all require legal and procedural skills as being the core competencies in the LVU-hearing. The child's right to be heard should mean that the CR must understand the child and be able to convey to the court its experience, situation and conduct. The CR should also possess the skills and ability to converse with children. If the best interests of the child are to be of primary consideration in these difficult

[11] LVU investigation "Omhändertagen" SOU 2000:77,p. 94.

decisions, it is necessary for CR to meet the child or its respective carers in order to provide a fair and just view.

3.2. Methodology

After establishing personal contact with two judges with long experience of LVU Cases, a survey was designed, to be answered by the judges, highlighting the judicial procedures in the appointment of CRs. Questions about CRs meetings with children were also formulated. Cooperation with the two judges was important to eliminate any risk that the questions could be misinterpreted. The sample was made up of all 23 county administrative courts in Sweden in 2007, 22 of whom responded to the questionnaire. The research participants were the judges, who are managers of the county administrative courts. The answers were thematically analyzed; the themes for were based on important aspects relating to the child's voice within the judicial system, as identified and discussed above. This study considered the ethical implications; for instance, the summaries of survey responses are anonymous, and the materials have been handled confidentially.

3.3. Findings

This article details three core facts emerging from this study. The first is the prevailing opinion among judges showing why they do not require any special competence in the relevant cases. No legal skills were required from social workers or other professionals. 18 county administrative courts do not demand any specific knowledge and competence and one court did not respond to the question. There is plenty of evidence to show that the lawyers who are interested accept those missions (in charge) and are therefore considered appropriate. There is also a consensus that the main issue is about how to handle the legal procedures. The choice of CRs was mainly based on legal competence and not on earlier Court experience.

The second issue is the CR's experience when using the Care of Young People Act. Only two judges describe the specific criteria for making a conscious choice that deals with children's special needs. One judge considered that a locally-based CR was important, because it facilitated meeting the child. In addition, the significant vital function of CRs was only considered by one judge. Only one judge answered that a social worker had been commissioned. None of the judges from the other 21 county administrative courts talked about other professions, such as social workers, etc.

Another issue was the question of how often the CR met a very young child or its respective carers before an LVU-hearing. (Table 1.) These questions were answered by all the 22 judges, and five of them answered that they did not know whether there had been meetings or not. In the case of children between 0-2, 10 judges answered that the CRs seldom, if ever, meet the child. For children between 3–5, 8 judges said that there were no meetings with the child. Conversely, 7 judges said that the CRs often met with children in the 0-2 age group, and 9 judges stated that the CRs often met with children in the 3-5 age group. Interestingly, with children in the 6-8 group, meetings between CRs and children became more frequent: 15 judges responded that meetings often took place at this age. And with children and young people aged 9-14 in the LVU cases, 20 judges answered that there were meetings with the CR. Still, 2 judges indicated that they did not know if meetings took place. Where judges did not know about meetings, it could mean that no one had asked during the hearing whether there had been meetings with the children or not.

Table 1. How often the 'Child's Representative' meet the child

	Child 0-2 y	Child 3 –5 y	Child 6-8 y	Child 9-11 y	Child 12–14 y
Not known	5	5	4	2	2
Never	2	1	-	-	-
Rare	8	7	3	-	-
Often	7	9	15	20	20
Total	22	22	22	22	22

The third issue was how important the judges thought it was for the CR to meet the children or their respective carers before LVU hearings (Table 2). As in the previous issue, a dividing line is shown at age 6. 7 judges thought that it was less important, or not important at all, for CRs to meet children younger than 6, which conversely means that 14 judges believe it *is* important. At 6-8 years, 19 judges thought that meetings were important for children, and between 9-14, all shared the view that it is important to meet and listen to the child.

Table 2. The importance of the 'Child's Representative' meeting the children

	Child 0-2 y	Child 3 –5 y	Child 6-8 y	Child 9-11 y	Child 12–14 y
Not important at all	1	1	-	-	-
Less important	8	6	3	-	-
Important	12	14	19	22	22
No answer	1	1	-	-	-
Total	22	22	22	22	22

3.4. Discussion and findings

The very youngest children living in difficult circumstances are most vulnerable and therefore most in need of representatives who are engaged in their cases. This research shows how CRs have been, and still are, exclusively lawyers by profession. This is in spite of the fact that there is no specific legal requirement that the CR be a lawyer or be legally trained. The fact that judges from 21 county administrative courts did not comment about other professions such as social workers or other equivalent professions can be understood in different ways. It may also depend on the fact that there is no need of anyone other than lawyers when there are a sufficient number of interested lawyers. Or perhaps, most likely, there are no other professionals who have expressed an interest in working in the 21 county administrative courts.

Why do the judges not ask the CR for their experience and knowledge of children? Are they just being tactful in not asking lawyers about their relevant experience and knowledge of children in these cases? Is it offensive to ask for experience and knowledge of children's needs from the one who interprets and assesses the child's situation? Social workers are not aware of the possibilities of becoming a CR; nor does the court require social workers for those tasks. But that is particularly important to younger children who have no opportunity of influencing the choice of their representatives. Children have no real impact on the selection of public counsel, even when they are over 15 and have their own standing.[12]

---

[12] Mattsson, T *Barnet och rättsprocessen.* (2002) p. 173-183.

This research also shows how the very youngest children in cases of coercive actually lack a representative who is prepared to engage in meetings with them. As a consequence, the very young child's voice is not heard, and their best interests are not the primary consideration.[13] One interesting point is that the judges in the county administrative courts think it is more important to meet and talk to the very young children, though in practice this happens less often than they think. But judges do not ask whether the CR has met the child or not: it seems that most judges avoid doing this. It is not requested, and never especially noted in court summaries or the final judgement. What is not required or requested may not have any significance.

This is revealed by expense accounts, which show that CRs have more difficulty getting travel expenses for meetings with children approved and paid for by the court. This is something that could further deteriorate due to the organizational merger carried out in 2010 in Sweden, when 23 county administrative courts were merged into 12 administrative tribunals in larger regions. This administrative change is likely to impair the ability of the CR to meet the children unless the courts have a change of attitude. The judges should ask whether a meeting with very young children has occurred, and of course reimburse the CR for any costs. It should even be possible to apply cost reductions for the CR who fails to fulfil his/her task properly—a positive example I received from a judge in charge of a county administrative court where children's participation in the process was taken seriously.

The paradox in determining children's welfare in court, which King & Trowell (1992) describe, is an experience that social workers recognize in LVU hearings in Sweden. The hearing may take on the semblance of a trial, ending up in a discussion of evidence of what did or did not occur, overlooking the central question of the child's problematic behaviour, what caused it and what in the child's needs is missing.

Social workers sometimes wait until they feel confident about the application going through the court, with an obvious risk that the child will continue living in difficult and vulnerable circumstances.[14] Current research has also analyzed the problem, basing its discussions on the Norwegian

---

[13] This is a fact that Titti Mattsson (2002) and the investigator of the coercive law in Ministry of Health and Social Affairs (2000) have highlighted.

[14] Ponnert, L. (2007) *Mellan klient och rättssystem –tvångsvård av barn och unga*...p.81-87.

Child Welfare Service (CWS) workers, and how they explain why children need to be placed out-of-home at a given time. They often refer to a long-term back-and-forth process that ends when a trigger factor appears, which determines that an out-of-home placement finally takes place. The findings emphasize the difficulty for street-level bureaucrats in these cases and the importance of acknowledging the contradictory position of the CWS workers.[15]

The MUNICIPAL social services in Sweden have in recent years worked for the development of child investigations and for the development of skills in talking with children. The BBIC (Children's Needs at the Centre) investigative tool includes a better structure of the investigations based on the child's view, and also hopefully contributes to a clearer picture of children in need of the social services, and also in court. The expansion of Children's Houses in Sweden has also contributed to an improvement in the protection of children suspected of being abused. In addition, cooperation has developed between the social services, police, and medical professionals. Talks and the interrogation of children take place in a calm environment with regard to the vulnerability of children.

But how does it look in the legal arena, is it possible for the lawyers and judges in this process to be more welfare orientated? By tradition, lawyers are said to be norm-orientated and therapeutic professionals goal-orientated. Is it therefore an impossible challenge? How can courts and other actors in the legal arena reach a greater understanding of the importance of increasing knowledge about children, how to talk to children, and especially understand the youngest child's right to be heard? As the LVU investigator put it, "There is nothing wrong in law. It does not help to change the legal texts; it is rather a question of changing the viewpoint of those applying the law".[16]

The change must come at an early stage, during law school. Prospective lawyers not only need elective courses in child protection law as it exists today, but those who will be working within the Family and Social Justice also need a knowledge of child development and needs and how to converse with children. There is no good rule governing a CR of a small who does not believe it is possible to "interrogate" the very young child

---

[15] Christiansen and Anderssen, (2010), Child & Family Social Work, 15: p.31–40.

[16] LVU investigation "Omhändertagen" SOU 2000:77,p.94

who is unable to speak, and therefore believes it is not necessary to meet, see or hear them where they are.

Another option for change is to encourage social welfare professionals themselves to participate in the creation of functional legislation. By this, I mean the importance of social workers taking responsibility for change and daring to enter the legal arena by offering their services as CRs. One could see it as an opportunity or even an obligation for social workers to be involved in the mission within the legal sphere in which they are entitled to participate. As a CR, you can work to ensure that children are made more visible in the judicial process and thereby promote a change in the mindset of all those who would use coercive legislation concerning children.

The Ministry of Health and Social Affairs has proposed a comprehensive new law on children and young people in Sweden. The Act on the Support and Protection for Children and Youth (SOU 2009:68) Care of Young People Act (LVU) should be incorporated unchanged into the combined new law. The proposal includes increased skill requirements for social workers working with children and young people. However, there is no demand for change with regard to the CR's knowledge about children's needs.

In particular, Article 12 of the CRC, which is one of the pillars of the convention, states that the child has the right to be heard in matters concerning them. From this perspective, the result of this research leads to further questions and debates related to Children and Young People's welfare within the judicial systems and procedures. Would the possibility of change increase the opportunity for the child's voice to be heard, if "players in the judicial arena" opened up and offered other professionals the assignment they ought to have access to as the law allows them?

Other actors such as CRs with different skills could contribute to a change in the "dialogue" within the hearings, and to a better and more obvious way of bringing up children's needs and making them more visible in the process. To make this into a reality requires interested social workers and/or other appropriate professionals being made aware that these positions are available to them. Judges and lawyers in the legal arena will also have to accept that the hearings will not be as "clean and legally due and proper, as you are used to", as a judge put it.

EMPOWERING CHILDREN AS VICTIMS OF CRIME IN THE CRIMINAL JUSTICE PROCESS

ANNA WERGENS

Abstract

A point of departure in the Child victims in the Union - Rights and Empowerment (CURE) project and in the recommendations directed at the member states and the European Commission has been that all child victims of crime should be considered as particularly vulnerable, so that they can benefit from the specific treatment best suited to their circumstances. The background to the recommendations is the limited support currently given to certain groups of child victims in the judicial system: the aim of this article is mainly to evaluate, from different angles, the cornerstones of the project and its objectives for the protection of the rights of the child victims.

1. Introduction

The CURE project has been about children as victims of crime in the criminal justice system. It has been run by the Crime Victim Compensation and Support Authority in Sweden, together with partners in eight member states of the European Union, and the Republic of Croatia. Apart from the Portuguese Association for Victim Support and the Public Defender of Rights in the Slovak Republic, all partners have been ministries of justice.

CURE has been co-funded by the Prevention of and Fight against Crime (ISEC) programme of the European Commission. The project was set up by two lawyers who had served as the project leaders in the Crime Victim Compensation and Support Authority. They have been assisted in the development of questionnaires and recommendations by an international group of experts representing such different areas as law, psychology and the police.

2. Background, Objectives and Ideas

The name CURE stems from the belief that it is possible to avoid secondary victimisation of child victims by means of granting them rights and support throughout the process, and that this should be the overarching aim of the legislature and the criminal justice professionals. The CURE project underlines the importance of doing this, not only because it will support effective procedures and just outcomes, but also for the child victim's own sake and for the appropriate treatment of child victims. CURE's fundamental objective of has been to strengthen the position of child victims in the criminal justice process.

An important feature of the CURE project and its recommendations is their universality with regard to various categories of crimes and various groups of children. In plain language, this means that the project has been carried out without limitations pertaining to specific categories of crimes. It is also intended to reflect a mindset aimed at bringing attention to children as a group of victims of crime, and not merely to certain groups of child victims. It must, however, be stressed that the project has applied first and foremost to crimes directed by one individual against another individual, or to violations of criminal laws in the member states. The CURE recommendations are consequently not developed for situations involving abuse of power and international crimes.

Since governments are ultimately responsible for the protection of children, the primary target group of the project has been the decision makers, with the emphasis on ministries of justice, but the project is also directed at professionals in the criminal justice system. There are very many obvious reasons as to why a project dealing with the situation of children as victims in the criminal justice system is needed. Children have special needs by virtue of their age and their dependency on adults; and as crime victims they are in a particularly vulnerable position. In the European Union, a Framework Decision regulates the standing of crime victims in criminal proceedings.[1] Research has been found that the implementation of this piece of legislation is rather poor, and it is easy to conclude that it is even worse when it comes to child victims. In the ongoing overview and revision of this legislation, the vulnerability of certain groups of crime victims has been brewing as a topic of great

[1] Council Framework Decision 2001/220/JHA of 15 March 2001 on the standing of victims in criminal proceedings.

concern. In addition, the balance between respecting the victims of crime and the demands for due process must always be kept in mind, and in cases that involve child victims maintaining this balance is very often particularly pertinent and complex.

2.1. Themes

Like many other projects, CURE aims to raise awareness and to educate. Some principles regarding the protection of child victims have been established, and one of the project's aims is to raise awareness about them. One way of doing so is to highlight both the problems of child victims, and the progress made in the member states regarding the position of child victims in the criminal judicial process. This has been done by directing a number of questions to various stakeholders and by reporting on the state of affairs in the member states. Drawing on what was learned about this matter, a number of recommendations have been put forward.

To limit the scope of the project, four central themes were established:

- Giving information to child victims;
- The interview with the child victim during the investigation stage;
- Legal representation for the child victim;
- The child victim's appearance in court

In the CURE report, surveys are divided according to the project's themes. Under various headings, examples of different forms of legislation, and of measures taken in the member states to facilitate the situation of the child victims are provided. The project's title suggests a twofold perspective, implying that CURE embraces theory as well as practice. In other words, the CURE project is about implementing rights by means of mechanisms targeting the child victim in the criminal justice process. During the course of the project, studies have been conducted reflecting its two perspectives. The report does not aim to compare the various member states, nor to "name and shame", but to identify some tendencies with regard to legislation and possible gaps in the protection provided to child victims across the EU.

CURE is characterised by a rights-based approach, a basic assumption of which is that particularly vulnerable victims should be able to benefit from specific treatment best suited to their circumstances (a statement which is quoted from Article 2 of the Framework Decision on the standing of victims in criminal proceedings). An obvious point of departure in the project has been the UN Guidelines on Justice Involving Child Victims and Witnesses of Crime, which is the main document in this area. It has served as a basis for the studies and the conclusions and it reflects a number of principles that should apply when child victims are involved in the criminal proceedings.[2] In accordance with this, the use of UN guidelines in training and the translation of the guidelines into the languages of the European Union are promoted in CURE's recommendations.

One objective of the project (with respect to the empowerment perspective) has been to show how hardship can be avoided by means of child-friendly mechanisms in the criminal justice process. From the perspective of the CURE project, this refers to the empowerment of child victims as well as the empowerment of justice professionals.

Some core questions that were raised in the CURE project concerned (a) how child victims can be empowered to go through the criminal justice system; (b) how the needs of child victims may be taken into consideration given the general principles of criminal procedural law; (c) how secondary victimisation caused by ignorance among justice professionals can be avoided; and (d) how the rights of child victims can be furthered at the European Union level. The major study dealt with the legal position of the child victim, and it was based on a questionnaire sent to the ministries of justices in the 27 member states. Replies were received from almost all member states, a total 26 replies being provided. The response rate must therefore be regarded as satisfactory.

3. The Findings

With regard to the findings of the studies, it seems appropriate to start with a wide-ranging reflection related on certain kind of answer provided by many respondents. Most of the member states claim that child victims have the same rights as other victims. Although this might be correct in theory, it is easy to see that it is a qualified truth, because of the limited opportunities for child victims to access their existing rights.

Thus, the right to information has very little relevance if there is none adapted to children, and no policies on how to provide children with

[2] UN Guidelines on Justice in Matters Involving Child Victims and Witnesses of Crime, Economic and Social Council Resolution 2005/20 of 22 July 2005.

information. As to the right to be heard, from the information received in the CURE project, only a few member states reported on legislation or policies that have the aim of ensuring account is taken of the views of the child with regard to the choice of assistance with testifying, or their personal appearance in court.

It becomes clear from the CURE studies that all the member states have taken legislative measures to facilitate the position of the child victim in the criminal justice system. Most member states have also adopted special procedures for the hearing of children in criminal proceedings. These are mainly characterised by taking steps to prevent the child victim from having to testify repeatedly, and by the provision of psychological expertise when child victims are giving evidence. One promising sign is that many member states have quite recently adopted legislation concerning child victims in the criminal justice process. These legal provisions may apply to vulnerable witnesses in general, and child victims may either fall into this category, or there may be specific legislation applying only to children, justified by their need for special protection. Three kinds of provisions pertaining to child victims have been identified as more common than others in the member states:

- *Facilitation of the child victim's testimony;*
- *Avoiding a confrontation between the child victim and the alleged offender;*
- *Child-sensitive provisions aimed at securing respect for the vulnerable position of the child victim in the process and to avoid intrusive questioning.*

3.1. Information

Most of the member states have legal stipulations governing the provision of information to crime victims, although these provisions are often qualified, and do not apply to all crime victims in all situations. In member states where the right to information is established in the legislation, most respondents claim that the information given to child victims is similar to that for all victims. However it becomes clear from the studies that very few member states have enacted child-specific provisions on information, and almost none referred to policies regarding supplying information to child victims.

Many of the member states refer to Non-Governmental Organisations (NGOs) and other services outside the judicial system for the provision of information to child victims. Fewer than half of the respondents—or about ten of the responding states—have developed information directed at child victims that emanates from their Ministry of Justice or a similar body within the judicial system. Although a need for information about the criminal justice system adapted to children has been recognised in some parts of the EU, only a few member states have addressed the issue of how information is actually provided to a child victim entering the criminal justice system. Telephone help-lines set up for children at risk and for crime victims exist in most of the member states, and they are considered as important sources of information for child victims.

All in all, the measures that have been taken seem ad-hoc and scattered. The conclusion is hat there is much room for improvement in this area, with regard to both oral and written information.

3.2. The Investigative Interview

With regard to the investigative interview, a central issue turned out to be the audio-visual recording of the interview with the child victim. The majority of member states claim that measures have been taken to restrict the number of interviews conducted with minor victims. Still, most of the respondents refer to repeat examination as one of the major problems concerning child victims in the criminal justice system. All member states make it possible to use audio-visual recording when the child victim testifies, this forms part of the legislation in most member states. It has, however, been proven that this situation does not necessarily restrict the number of interviews with the child.

It can be shown that the options for recording an interview with the child victim apply only to certain groups of child victims, and only under certain conditions. To clarify; in the Scandinavian countries and Luxembourg, the option exists for all minors, whereas in France, recording of interviews is only available to child victims of sexual crimes, and in Belgium an audiovisual recording is only made for a specific list of offences detailed in the Code of Criminal Procedure, though in exceptional circumstances it may also be used for other offences.

We therefore feel that the main reason why repeat questioning is still such a big problem is because the use of audio-visual recording of child victim statements is not unconditional, and the law is not applied in a child-friendly way. However, this is an area where more research is needed; the application of law and policies in this respect is one of the issues that should therefore be considered more deeply. A related issue is the existence of guidelines and/or codes of conduct which facilitate the interviewing of child victims. About half of the respondents refer to such guidelines, although their form differs considerably across the Union.

Almost no governments make reference to child-friendly mechanisms for reporting crimes; the most frequent reply here is that specialised police officers and units exist. Several of the member states report a legal obligation to notify the social services about crimes against children. Legislative measures have also been taken to regulate the balance between the confidentiality imposed on certain groups of professionals and the need to protect a child in danger. The impression is however, that opinions on the mandatory reporting of crimes against children vary considerably in the member states.

The need for child-friendly interview rooms appears to be accepted in the majority of the responding states, although most have not given priority to modifying their premises to accommodate this. From this follows that child-friendly interview rooms are available throughout the Union, but in a patchy manner. Very little information has been supplied by member states about the persons present when the child victim is interviewed, or the timing of the interview.

The majority of the member states claim to have requirements about the persons conducting the forensic interview with the child victim, but this claim is seldom supported by legislation or named policies. The specialisation of forensic interviewers is consequently seen as good practice rather than a requirement. Training activities related to the situation of the child victim, which target different groups of criminal justice professionals and which are conducted in a consistent manner, do not seem to be common.

3.3. The Child Victim's Appearance in Court

A minority of the member states report on age limits with regard to the issue of a personal appearance in court. It seems, though, as if a number of the member states have set up informal age limits or rules of thumb with respect to the hearing of child victims/witnesses in criminal proceedings. It is a common feature in most of the member states that the issue of whether the child victim should appear in person in court is subject to individual assessment by the judge or by the prosecutor on a case-by-case basis. In CURE's view, age should not be the determining factor as to whether or not the child victim appears in court.

The differences with regard to appearances range from countries like Romania, where it is mandatory for child victims above the age of 10 to appear in court, to member states where summoning child victims under 18 is restricted to a minimum. About a quarter of the responding states belong to the former group. On a more general basis, information from member states seems to indicate that it is a recognised principle on paper in most of them that young child victims should not appear in person in court—options exist in all the member states to allow pre-trial evidence (i.e. recorded statements) in the court. However, the legislation covering this depends on a number of circumstances, and is curbed in different ways.

As far as the child victim being obliged to appear in person in court goes, apart from the provision of support persons often provided by NGOS, very few member states referred to any machinery aimed at preparing the child for a court appearance.

3.4. The Major Problems of Child Victims in the Criminal Justice Process

In the CURE project, ministries of justice, as well as the members of the European Network of Ombudspeople for Children, were asked about what they conceived as the major problems of child victims in the criminal justice process. It is possible to distinguish three issues which stand out in the information provided to this question:

- repeat questioning of child victims;
- lack of professionals trained to deal with child victims;
- the length of the proceedings.

Taking into account other information from the member states during the course of the project, lack of co-operation among bodies in the judicial system, and lack of cooperation between these actors and the NGOs, should also be included in this list.

3.5. Practical Measures to Empower the Child Victim

When analysing the information and achievements in member states with respect to the twofold approach of the project, one may distinguish between what has been done by means of legislation, and what is done on a practical and concrete level by means of practices, services, development of information, etc.

The last ten years reveal proof of legislative activity in the area of child victims, although predominantly with the emphasis on child victims subjected to sexual crimes and human trafficking. The results of the request for best practices made to a great number of actors in the project proved to be disappointing. Whatever the reasons, we consider that the poor response is an indication that the practice is not comparable with the provisions of legislation in the member states.

A critical matter is whether specialised services are available for child victims. "Specialised services" alludes here to measures taken to inform the child victim, to prepare the child victim for the proceedings, and to provide the child victim with legal advice as well as with emotional and practical support. From what has been understood in this project, and based on a number of contacts with experts and NGOs, there are few specialised services targeting child victims in the Union. This is obviously not in accordance with the view expressed in the Framework Decision that the most vulnerable victims should be given special attention. Nor does it accord with what the EU member states agreed on in the Council conclusions on support to persons who fall victim to crime in the European Union. This means that specialised services and NGOs offering appropriate service to persons who fall victim to crime, acting at national, regional or local levels throughout the European Union, should be made available.[3]

A striking feature to emerge from the questionnaire is that only a minority of the member states mention legislation for the provision of emotional support to crime victims in the course of the criminal justice process—the majority of member states talk instead about various NGOs when reporting on how support to child victims in the criminal justice process is addressed. There are primarily two kinds of NGOs that may be involved

[3] Council Conclusions on a strategy to ensure fulfilment of the rights of and improve support to persons who fall victim to crime in the European Union, 2969th Justice and Home Affairs Council meeting, Luxembourg, 23 October 2009.

when a child becomes a victim of crime; organisations working for children at risk, or children who are victims of abuse on a more general basis; and NGOs working with victims of crime, i.e. victim support organisations. The help-lines for children and for crime victims are also seen as important providers of assistance and information.

In CURE's view, it is obvious that if member states want to claim that they comply with the Framework Decision, they must then ensure that there are specialised services directed at child victims. To this end, they must either provide continuous support to existing NGOs working for crime victims or to children's rights organisations; or they must support the establishment of new services. Today, many of these organisations do not have the resources to assist this particular category of victim.

One major impression from the studies is that when reporting about child victims, the member states often report that child victims are dealt with within the framework of another issue, for example juvenile delinquency or domestic violence. One example is the strategies which are established in several of the member states aimed at promoting the rights of the child or preventing violence among juveniles. Another example is the units set up within the national police authorities, and which are mainly targeted at victims of domestic violence or juveniles in general.

In view of this brief summary, the backdrop of the CURE recommendations is, above all, the lack of child-specific legal provisions, the lack of specialised support to child victims, and the exclusion of support to certain groups of child victims.

CURE's view on empowering the child victim in the criminal justice process is that one must broaden the protection to other groups of children than those who are subjected to sexual crimes and human trafficking. It suggests that the focus should be shifted from specific crimes, and from the age of the child in a given situation, to the common needs of victimised children as well as to the needs of the individual child victim. This approach makes use of the child's perspective while at the same time emphasising the need for flexibilty.

4. CURE's Recommendations

In accordance with the objectives and the project plan, two sets of recommendations were developed in the CURE project. To begin with, recommendations have been directed to the member states of the European Union. Given the fact that these recommendations cover most of its 27 member states, they are not intended to conform with the legislation in all of them, but to strike a balance between being visionary and complying with the general standard. The recommendations are intended to be used by the legislature, in policy making, awareness-raising activites, and training.

The recommendations cover a wide range of contexts and situations. They are divided up into 12 headings, which include the themes of the project and topics such as training and the prevention of repeat victimisation. In this respect, CURE's recommendations could be described, not as detailed but rather as inclusive and extensive. Given these preconditions, making these recommendations user-friendly in language and format has been made a priority. The recommendations could serve as a kind of shopping list and the different sections could very well be read separately.

In addition, 13 recommendations were directed at the European Commission. They concern matters in which the EU institutions could be instrumental in improving support to child victims. They are primarily connected with the Commission's work on strengthening the rights of crime victims and protecting the rights of the child, and they consequently refer to some recently adopted documents establishing policy objectives relating to the position of children and crime victims in the Union. An example of particular importance is the future strategy on the rights of the child which aims to identify priorities for future action in the European Union.[4] CURE's recommendation relating to this objective seeks to direct the attention of the Commission to the issue of child victims in the work on future strategy. The two sets of recommendations begin with a statement of principles which encapsulate some basic assumptions of a general character that are applicable to all the recommendations, and a number of conclusions sum up their essence.

Below are some of the recommendations directed at the member states that have been singled out in order to highlight some of the project's critical issues. Regarding General Matters, the object is to establish a holistic approach towards the child victim, and to children who are potential victims of crime, by means of legal procedural safeguards and policies. To

---

[4] Communication from the Commission, Towards an EU strategy on the rights of the child Brussels, 4 July 2006, COM (2006) 367 final, {SEC(2006) 888} {SEC(2006) 889}

this end, it is recommended that member states should increase eligibility for special measures and procedural safeguards for children under 18, and promote the expansion of offences for which the child victim can qualify for assistance with testifying, and special measures. These two recommendations really summarise the project in a nutshell, and they represent the essence of the recommendations. They should be contrasted with the general aim of highlighting children as crime victims and the exclusion of certain groups of child victims from special protection.

Regarding Reporting and Access to Justice, the aim is to ensure that most of the crimes against children are reported and that, to this end, they can be reported by the children themselves; and the intention is also to ensure that crimes against children are investigated with full respect for the child victim. In view of this, it is recommended that the member states should establish specialised units within the police which are authorised to deal with child victimisation; are trained to manage these cases in an effective and child-sensitive way; and are accessible throughout the country. This recommendation should be contrasted with the fact that specialised units, competent to deal with child victims and available on a nationwide basis, are not very common, and unevenly spread across the Union.

Under the heading Investigative Interviewing, the objective is to make sure that interviews with the child victim are conducted by trained professionals in a way that reduces secondary victimisation, while at the same time maximising the value of the testimony. In furtherance with this goal, it is recommended that member states should develop national guidelines for interviewing child victims in accordance with applied research, including basic criteria and guidance for a structural and consistent use. It is also recommended that the member states should put in place legal provisions with the aim of avoiding unnecessary repeat examination of child victims, and, for this, purpose encourage the systematic use of audio-visual recording of any interview with the child victim. This recommendation should be read together with the similar recommendation which urges the European Commission to further the development of European guidelines on the investigative interviewing of child victims.

As far as the appearance of the child victim in court is concerned, a starting point is that the member states should safeguard the right of the child to be heard, while, when appropriate, allowing the child victim to testify outside the court. Along these lines, it is recommended that the member states should establish procedures which allow sufficient flexibility regarding the individual needs of the child victim, his/her specific age and maturity and in accordance with the principle of the best interests of the child.

Specialised Services deals with the support provided to victimised children throughout the criminal justice process. Services may be instrumental in providing information, legal advice and counselling to the child victim, and empower the child to testify and participate in the proceedings. CURE's opinion is that whether such support is provided by NGOs or through governmental services, the State should bear the ultimate responsibility for the provision of services. In view of this, the State should either establish or provide continuous support to specialised services which are directed to children and/or to crime victims, and which act at national, regional or local levels throughout the European Union.

5. Conclusion

The conclusions of the project apply to all recommendations and have been grouped in to four themes. The first is about children as vulnerable victims of crime. It consists of three statements which have been considered essential to improve the protection of child victims in legislation as well as in practice:

- In setting out legislative provisions and designing protective measures, the legislature should consider the common needs of children who are victims of crime in the criminal justice process, irrespective of the crime to which they have been subjected;
- Legislation should consider that all children subjected to crime are particularly vulnerable, so that they can benefit from the specific treatment best suited to their circumstances;
- Child victims should be defined and considered as being children in the context of the criminal justice process up to the age of 18.

CURE's perspective on child victims embraces the prevention of repeat victimisation of children as well as secondary victimisation. The second theme is meant to further expand this by emphasising that meeting the needs of child victims necessitates a response based on a multidisciplinary approach, and collaboration between agencies in the judicial system as well as with NGOs and agencies outside the judicial system. This theme furthermore concludes that policy responses, as well as the individual responses to child victims in the criminal justice process, should always consider the need for flexibility, taking into account the individual circumstances as presented in each case, including the seriousness of the crime.

The third theme deals with the need for a child-specific response. It deals with the age aspect, and underlines the need for a developmental perspective by the criminal justice system, recognising that the needs of children change as they grow. A principal finding is that many of the member states claim that child victims have the same rights as other victims. From this statement it might be inferred that they are sufficiently protected. In consideration of this assertion, CURE recommends that child-specific provisions are needed to better meet the specific needs of child victims in the legal process. It is furthermore claimed that age should not be the only factor governing the legal protection and provision of support to child victims, but the variable levels of maturity and evolving capacities of the individual child should also be considered. Likewise, child-specific legal provisions and supportive measures should be developed in order to improve access to justice and support to child victims.

With regard to how the needs of child victims should be met on a practical level, these conclusions are gathered under the heading Empowering the Child Victim. Here, some of the most important measures identified in the CURE project are summarised, such as the development of national strategies protecting the child victim in the criminal justice system, and the availability of information targeting child victims developed in child-friendly language and design. It is also stressed that information given to child victims in the course of the criminal justice process should be adapted to the child needs and provided in accordance with a system of control and a detailed set of policies. Furthermore, these conclusions state that all criminal justice professionals who come into contact with victimised children must be trained to deal with child victims, and that all investigative interviewers must have specialised training in interviewing techniques and issues related to child victimisation. Special attention should be given to the training of judges who try cases involving child victims. This latter conclusion is an example of how some of the CURE recommendations are more far-reaching than, for example, the Framework Decision on the standing of crime victims in criminal proceedings and the UN Guidelines on Justice involving Victims and Witnesses of Crime.

In accordance with the recommendations, the CURE report ends with an invitation to the European Commission and to the member states of the Union to draw on, and elaborate on, the recommendations with a view to establishing a minimum standard of legal protection and support of child victims in the criminal justice process. This could be done by bringing forward and exchanging research and best practices related to the situation of the child victim in the European Union.

Two other topics are also pinpointed in the conclusions. The first one stresses that issues related to the situation of the child victim in the criminal justice process should be included in common training for criminal justice professionals at the level of the European Union. The second calls attention to the importance of developing child-friendly information directed to children who are crime victims in the Union.

The research conducted within the framework of the CURE project proves that a correct and appropriate understanding of the philosophy of the protection of the rights of the child, in particular the child victim, is not solely about the application and implementation of the provisions of national or international legislation, but the way in which the criminal justice process and the legal and professional authorities face and solve the problems of child victims. Consequently, one may assert that the chief question has not exclusively been to reduce the contradictions between different criminal justice systems regarding the treatment of child victims, but just as much to reach to the centre of justice and recognize the need for a victim-centered perspective within the legislative mechanism for the best interest of the child. Thus, this research demonstrates that, in relation to issues pertaining to child victims, the concept of "the best interests of the child" extracted from the International Convention on the Rights of the Child, is particularly difficult to apply. The report clearly points out, however, that the methods by which the child victim is treated in Member States of the EU are not at all adequate.

WAR CHILDREN'S PROCEDURAL CAPACITIES IN INTERNATIONAL PROCEEDINGS

HELEN HAMZEI[1]

Abstract

War children participate in international justice, truth and reconciliation proceedings. While the presence of the child was anticipated and subsequently specifically addressed in the statutory rules and regulations of international truth and reconciliation commissions, such as in Sierra Leone and Liberia, the very first case before the International Criminal Court against Thomas Lubanga Dyilo, who is charged with the war crime of recruiting children under 15 and using them in hostilities, proves that participation by children in international mechanisms gives rise to procedural particularities which have not been anticipated. The protection of the substantive rights of the child during armed conflicts, received broad recognition in international law. Surprisingly, the procedural legal status of children as claimants, witnesses or perpetrators has not been subject to extensive legal research, and thus constitutes a challenge for the existing international mechanisms that involve children. The intention of this article is therefore to provide an overview of the procedural capacities in which children of war may participate in international proceedings.

1. Introduction

War children participate in international justice, truth and reconciliation proceedings. While the presence of the child was anticipated and subsequently specifically addressed in the statutory rules and regulations of in-

[1] The author would like to thank Emma Davies, Anna Gouwenberg and Michelle Grossman for their fruitful comments. She would also like to thank the Gieskes Fund which created the chair that is held by Prof. Dr. Liesbeth Zegveld at Leiden University. All errors remain, of course, my own.

ternational truth and reconciliation commissions (the TRC), such as in Sierra Leone and Liberia, the very first case before the International Criminal Court (the ICC) proves that children participate in various capacities despite the lack of an extensive regulation in the procedural law. Furthermore, the current drafting of a complaint procedure under the UN Convention on the Rights of the Child (the CRC) provides another incentive to the growing attention to the procedural capacities of the child in international proceedings.[2]

Children's particular vulnerability is reflected in the existence of a broad range of substantive legal protection under international law—especially in the legal protection of children during armed conflict.[3] The present contribution's source, however, deals with international procedural law. It particularly examines four core procedural capacities of children of war. It thereby intends to establish the international legal subjectivity of children in international procedural law—a subjectivity which is not limited to the substantive protection of children, but a subjectivity which includes war children's procedural legal status.[4]

The term *child*, within this procedural context, is (at least) for four reasons less clear cut than under substantive law. Firstly, international procedural law does not provide a definition for the term *child*. Secondly, the various institutions sometimes use *child* in the context of the concept of childhood without meaning to refer to specific age categories. Thirdly, in other instances, children are distinguished on the basis of specific age categories, in particular, children under 15, and children between 15-18. Finally, in combination with the above, and depending on the mandate of the relevant international mechanism, the term *child* is used with regard to various

---

[2] Resolution adopted by the Human Rights Council, 13/3 Open-ended Working Group on an optional protocol to the Convention on the Rights of the Child to provide a communications procedure, 1-2, 13th Sess., U.N. Doc. A/HRC/RES/13/3 (Apr. 14, 2010).

[3] INTERNATIONAL COMMITTEE OF THE RED CROSS, *Summary Table of IHL Provisions Specifically Applicable to Children* (2003), http://www.icrc.org/eng/assets/files/other/ang03_03_juridique_newlogo.pdf, Visited on 2010-11-23.

[4] See generally Perumpidy. K. Menon, *International Personality of Individuals in International Law: A Broadening of the Traditional Doctrine*, 1 J. TRANSNAT'L POL'Y, 1992, at 151.

procedural capacities, such as children as claimants, witnesses or perpetrators of international crimes. Consequently, international procedural law lacks a common definition for the term *child*. Instead, international procedural law mirrors a fragmentation of this term and thereby also splits the procedural status of the child actor. Accordingly, it is necessary to explicitly examine the understanding of the term *child* and the specific age-categories of children under each international mechanism as referred to within the various procedural capacities.

In the light of the above, this article addresses the procedural capacity of the child as a claimant, witness, perpetrator and perpetrator's child.

2. Various Procedural Capacities of the War Child

Armed conflict and large scale violence result in numbers of child victims.[5] The Preamble to the Rome Statute stipulates, in this regard, 'that during this century millions of children, women and men have been victims of unimaginable atrocities that deeply shock the conscience of humanity'. The particular risks for children of armed conflict and large-scale violence, such as immediate threats to their lives, being recruited or becoming a victim of sexual slavery are broadly recognized.[6] The recognition of these risks is furthermore reflected in children's substantive protection under human rights law, international humanitarian law and international criminal law.[7]

Before the core procedural capacities of children of war can be addressed, there are three preliminary points with regard to the term *child victim*. Firstly, international procedural law does not define the term *child victim*.

---

[5] Karin Arts, *General Introduction: A Child-Rights-Based Approach to International Criminal Accountability in* INTERNATIONAL CRIMINAL ACCOUNTABILITY AND THE RIGHTS OF CHILDREN 3 (Karin Arts & Vesselin Popovski eds., 2006).

[6] Impact of Armed Conflict on Children, Report of the expert of the Secretary-General, Ms. Grac'a Machel, G.A. A/51/306, 18, U.N. Doc. A/51/306 (Aug. 26, 1996), INTERNATIONAL COMMITTEE OF THE RED CROSS, *Children in war* (2009),
http://www.icrc.org/eng/resources/documents/publication/p1015.htm.
Visited on 2010-11-23.

[7] *See* INTERNATIONAL COMMITTEE OF THE RED CROSS, *supra* note 2.

Instead, human rights law, in particular the CRC, defines children as '*every human being below the age of eighteen years [...].*'[8] The Statute of the ICC provides a recent definition of the term *victim.*[9] Rule 85 of the Rules of Procedure and Evidence (the RPE) of the ICC defines victims as 'natural persons who have suffered harm as result of the commission of any crime within the jurisdiction of the Court [...].'[10] According to this definition, children are not excluded since age is not a decisive factor. Instead, *all natural persons* may qualify as a victim.[11] The drafters of the ICC RPE gathered their inspiration for this definition from the General Assembly Declaration of Basic Principles of Justice of Victims of Crime and Abuse of Power, and the later adopted Basic Principles and Guidelines on the Rights to a Remedy and Reparation for Victims of Gross Violations of International Human Rights Law and Serious Violations of International Humanitarian Law.[12] Principle no. 8 defines victims as:

> Persons who individually or collectively suffered harm, including physical or mental injury, emotional suffering, economic loss or substantial impairment of their fundamental rights, through acts or omissions that constitute gross violations of international human rights law, or serious viola-

---

[8] United Nations Convention on the Rights of the Child, Nov. 20, 1989, 1577 U.N.T.S. 3, art. 1.

[9] Similarly Rule 2 of the Rules of Procedure and Evidence of the International Criminal Tribunal for the Former Yugoslavia and International Criminal Tribunal for Rwanda defines the term *victim*, *available at*
http://www.icty.org/x/file/Legal%20Library/Rules_procedure_evidence/IT032_rev44_en.pdf and http://www.unictr.org/Portals/0/English/Legal/ROP/100209.pdf. Visited on 2010-11-23.
See also Rule 2 SCSL of the Rules of Procedure and Evidence of the Special Court for Sierra Leone, *available at*
http://www.sc-sl.org/LinkClick.aspx?fileticket=yNjqn5TIYKs%3d&tabid=176. Visited on 2010-11-23.

[10] Rules of Procedure and Evidence, adopted by the Assembly of States Parties, first session, New York, 3-10 September 2002, Official Records ICC-ASP/1/3.

[11] For further explanation on the victim criteria see generally Situation in the Democratic Republic of the Congo, Decision on the Applications for Participation in the Proceedings VPRS 1, VPRS 2, VPRS 3, VPRS 5 and VPRS 6, 79 (Jan. 17, 2006), ICC-01/04-101.

[12] Theo van Boven, *The Position of the Victim in the Statute of the International Criminal Court in* REFLECTIONS ON THE INTERNATIONAL CRIMINAL COURT – ESSAYS IN HONOUR OF ADRIAAN BOS, 77, 78-79, (Herman A.M. van Hebel, Johan G. Lammers & Jolien Schukking eds., 1999).

tions of international humanitarian law. Where appropriate, and in accordance with domestic law, the term "victim" also includes the immediate family or dependants of the direct victim and persons who have suffered harm in intervening to assist victims in distress or to prevent victimization.[13]

Secondly, being a child victim in does not itself constitute a procedural capacity. Instead, child victims' procedural role must be read together with the following four core procedural capacities. These are a) child claimant, b) child witness, c) child perpetrator, and d) perpetrator's child.

Thirdly, not all child victims under 18 may qualify as a child claimant, witness, or perpetrator. Instead, a child victim's qualification for these procedural capacities may be dependent on the age of the child. While under substantive law a sharp distinction is made, with regard to children under 15, and children under 18, the following assessment therefore also examines to what extent procedural law distinguishes between different age categories in a procedural context.

2.1. Child Claimant

Victimized children of armed conflict and large-scale violence may participate in international proceedings as child claimants when submitting a complaint about alleged violations of their rights. This capacity extends to proceedings of various natures. Yet not all international mechanisms allow war victims, including children, to participate as claimants.[14] With regard to the permissive mechanisms, a distinction is necessary between proceedings under international criminal law (the ICC), human rights law (regional courts) and the quasi-judicial proceedings before a UN Treaty body. While these mechanisms pursue different aims, the proceedings have in common that children, like all individuals, only have direct access to the

[13] Basic Principles and Guidelines on the Rights to a Remedy and Reparation for Victims of Gross Violations of International Human Rights Law and Serious Violations of International Humanitarian Law. G.A. Res. 60/147, U.N. Doc. A/RES/60/147 (Mar. 21, 2006).

[14] To date, international humanitarian law does not provide for a complaint procedure for victims. For further information, see generally Jann K. Kleffner & Liesbeth Zegveld, *Establishing an Individual Complaint Procedure for Violations of International Humanitarian Law*, 3 YINTLHL, 2000, at 384.

proceedings if the existence of an interest with regard to the case at issue which establishes their legal standing (*locus standi*) is successfully ascertained.[15] Frequently, international documents do not provide for a definition of *locus standi*, but instead establish the procedural capacities of a person. The extent of this procedural capacity is legally regulated, and primarily determines whether children are included or excluded from claimant status. For that reason, this procedural capacity is not dependent on the procedural strategy of a party involved, such as the prosecution or defence strategy to call certain witnesses, but on the factual decision that the child claimant fulfills the *victim requirement*. For the first time in the history of international criminal law, the Statute of the International Criminal Court provides for the participation of war victims. Article 68(3) of the ICC Statute provides for *locus standi* by requesting the existence of a 'personal interest'. It states that '[w]here the personal interests of the victims are affected, the Court shall permit their views and concerns to be presented and considered at stages of the proceedings determined to be appropriate by he Court […].'[16]

Similarly, human rights law, as for instance the European Convention on Human Rights, entails a victim requirement.[17] Likewise, Article 2 of the Optional Protocol to the International Covenant on Civil and Political Rights necessitates a victim requirement.[18] These provisions underline that the qualification of the *claimant status* does not, in principle, depend on the age of the individual. Children are not therefore excluded from this procedural capacity.

[15] Gioia Greco, *Victims' Rights Overview under the ICC Legal Framework: A Jurisprudential Analysis*, 7 INTLCLR 531, 539 (2007).
[16] *See also,* Situation in the Democratic Republic of the Congo, Decision on the Application for Participation in the Proceedings of VPRS 1, VPRS 2, VPRS 3, VPRS 4, VPRS 5 and VPRS 6, *supra* note 10, at 61.
[17] European Convention for the Protection of Human Rights and Fundamental Freedoms as amended by Protocol No. 11, Art. 34 Nov. 4, 1950, 213 U.N.T.S. 221 (hereinafter ECHR); American Convention on Human Rights, art. 23 Jul. 18, 1978, 1144 U.N.T.S. 123 in conjunction with Rule 27 of the Rules of Procedure of the Inter-American Commission on Human Rights *available at* http://www.oas.org/xxxivga/english/reference_docs/Reglamento_CIDH.pdf. Visited on 2010-11-23.
[18] Optional Protocol to the International Covenant on Civil and Political Rights, Mar. 23, 1976, 999 U.N.T.S. 302.

The particular age of the child claimant may, however, prevent children from being recognized as a child claimant in two instances: firstly, while the statutory *victim requirements* do not limit the concept of child claimant to a specific age category, various Chambers of the ICC established that applications for participation of children under 18 may be rejected if not having been submitted by a parent or legal guardian of the minor.[19] This practice recognizes the international standard of the CRC for restricting purposes. By contrast, such a practice has not been applied by regional courts or the UN Treaty bodies. The Commission of the European Court of Human Rights (ECHR) explicitly recognized that children may submit an application of their own accord. In *X. v. Austria* the respondent government raised the argument that an applicant lacks the capacity to bring a legal action without the representation of a legal guardian under Austrian law. The Commission, however, held that that Article 25 (now, Article 34)

> Makes no distinction between adults and minors or persons deemed to be minors; whereas it follows that the Applicant, who, being under a participant incapacity, has the status of a responsible minor, shall, nevertheless, be held to be a "person" within the meaning of Article 25, whereas, consequently, the Applicant has the right, of his own accord and without being represented by his guardian, to refer an application to the Commission; and [...] the Applicant therefore had the right under Article 25 of the Convention, [...] to correspond freely with the Commission [...].[20]

Secondly, conditions may link certain crimes to a specific age of the victim. This is the case with regard to the crime of recruitment, as enshrined in Article 8 of the Rome Statute.[21] This particular crime stipulates that children may only qualify as victims if they were below 15 when conscripted, enlisted or used to actively participate in hostilities. Children

---

[19] Situation in the Democratic Republic of Congo, Decision on the Applications for Participation Filed in Connection with the Investigation in the Democratic Republic of Congo by Applicants a/0189/06 to a/0198/06, a/0200/06 to a/0202/06, a/0204/06 to a/0208/06, a/0210/06 to a/0213/06, a/0215/06 to a/0218/06, a/0219/06, a/0223/06, a/0332/07, a/0334/07 to a/0337/07, a/0001/08, a/0030/08 and a/0031/08, 33 (Nov. 4, 2008), ICC-01/04-545; Situation in Uganda, Decision on victims' applications for participation a/0014/07 to a/0020/07 and a/0076/07 to a/0125/07, 20 (Nov. 21, 2008), ICC-02/04-172.

[20] X. v. Austria, Application no. 1527/62, decision of 4 October 1962, Y.B. Eur. Conv. H.R., Volume 5 (1962), 246.

[21] Rome Statute of the International Criminal Court, Jul. 1, 2002, 2187 U.N.T.S. 90, art. 8(2)(b)(xxiv) and 8(2)(e) (vii).

above this age are excluded from being qualified as direct victims of this crime, and consequently do not meet the victim requirement.

Compared with the overall number of complaints brought by individuals, the actual number of child claimants in international proceedings remains rather low, with the exception of the percentage of child claimants before the ICC. Various Chambers of the ICC recognized the status of child victims, and authorized their participation as claimants (participants).[22] The percentage of child claimants in the proceedings in the first case before the ICC is remarkable. A total of 103 victims successfully applied for participation, among them 48 victims who still are or were children when the application was submitted (app. 46 per cent). The majority of the remaining victims that successfully applied for participation were former child soldiers that have since attained their majority.[23]

In contrast, fewer numbers of child claimants have appeared before the other international bodies. The ECHR ruled on alleged violations filed by child applicants.[24] From 1968 to March 2010, 255 cases were relevant to

---

[22] *See* among other decisions concerning child victims of the crime of recruitment, Situation in the Democratic Republic of Congo, Decision on the applications for participation filed in connection with the investigation in the Democratic Republic of Congo by Applicants a/0047/06 to a/0052/06, a/0163/06 to a/0187/06, a/0221/06, a/0226/06, a/0231/06 to a/0233/06, a/0237/06 to a/0239/06, and a/0241/06 to a/0250/06, 91, 93, 95, 97, 99 (Jul. 3, 2008), ICC-01/04-505. Children as indirect victims –, *see* Situation in the Central African Republic, Case of the Prosecutor v. Jean-Pierre Bemba Gombo, Fourth Decision on Victims' Participation, 41-51 (Dec. 12, 2008), ICC-01/05-01/08-320.

[23] See generally Reports on the activities of the Court (Oct. 29, 2008), ICC-ASP/7/25. *See* particularly on child applications, ICC-01/04-01/06-1556; Decision on the applications by 3 victims to participate in the proceedings (Dec. 18, 2008), ICC-01/04-01/06-1562, Order issuing public redacted annexes to the Decisions on the applications by victims to participate in the proceedings of 15 and 18 December 2008, ICC-01/04-01/06-1861-AnxA1 (May 8, 2009), ICC-01/04-01/06-1861-AnxA2.

[24] Application submitted by parents, *see* amongst others: Mrs. X and Miss X. v. the United Kingdom, App. No. 9471/81, 49 Eur. Comm'n H.R. Dec. & Rep. 36, 49 (1984); Eriksson v. Sweden, App. No. 11373/85, 156 Eur. Ct. H.R. (ser. A) 1 (1989). Only a few cases in which children *applied in personam* to the Commission and the European Court of Human Rights: *See* amongst others: Commission: X. and Y. v. The Netherlands, App. No. 6753/74, 1-3 Eur. Comm'n H.R. Dec. &

children.[25] Considering that, to date, the Court delivered more than 12.000 judgments, the number of child cases is just a small percentage.[26] Moreover, the majority of cases dealt with the substantive protection of children under the ECHR, such as the protection under article 8 ECHR (right to respect for private and family live).[27]In these cases, parents regularly argued that their conventional rights as regards, for example children's separation from parents, or the medical treatment of their children had been violated.[28]Children were thus rather the objects of the dispute before the Court instead of taking a more active role as applicants. To date, approximately 18 cases have been brought by children themselves to the ECHR (app 8 per cent). About 40 were submitted by parents on their own behalf, or on behalf of their children.[29] Even fewer cases were brought by children before the Inter-American Court of Human Rights. To date, the Court has delivered 176 judgments. A very small selection dealt with child-related issues. However, not a single case has been brought to the Commission by a child. Instead, the few cases that concerned children were brought by the parents, relatives or national or regional NGOs.[30]

Rep (1975-76), 118; Tyrer v. United Kingdom, App. No. 5856/72, 26 Eur. Ct. H.R. (ser. A) (1978); V. v. United Kingdom, App. No. 24888/94, Eur. Ct. H.R. 1999- IX; T. v. United Kingdom, App. No. 24724/94 (1999); S.C. v. United Kingdom, App. No. 60958/00, 2004-IV Eur. Ct. H.R..

[25] Council of Europe, http://www.coe.int/t/transversalprojects/children/caselaw/CaseLawChild_en.asp. Visited on 2010-11-23.

[26] EUROPEAN COURT OF HUMAN RIGHTS, *50 Years of Activity, The European Court of Human Rights – Some Facts and Figures* (2010), http://www.echr.coe.int/NR/rdonlyres/ACD46A0F-615A-48B9-89D6-8480AFCC29FD/0/FactsAndFiguresENAvril2010.pdf. Visited on 2010-11-23.

[27] *See* amongst others Tyrer v. the United Kingdom, *supra* note 23; Marckx v Belgium, App. No. 6833/74, 31 Eur. Ct. H.R. (ser. A) (1979).

[28] European Convention for the Protection of Human Rights and Fundamental Freedoms as amended by Protocol No. 11, art. 8. *See* amongst others, K and T v. Finland, App. No. 25702/94, 2001- VII Eur. Ct. H.R.; Haase v. Germany, App. No. 11057/02, 2004- III Eur. Ct. H.R..

[29] A. v. The United Kingdom, Application no. 25599/94, 7, 1998- VI Eur. Ct. H.R.; X and Y v. The Netherlands, Application no. 6753/74, Eur. Comm'n H.R. Dec. & Rep (1974), 118-119; P., D.P., and A.T. v. the United Kingdom, 20 May 1996, unpublished, Commission report (Apr. 11, 1997), Eur. Comm'n H.R. Dec. & Rep 89-A, 31; A. and B. v. The United Kingdom, App. No. 25599/94, 31 Eur. Ct. H.R., 9.

[30] "Street Children" (Villagrán-Morales et al.) v. Guatemala, Inter-Am. Ct. H. R.

Finally, the quasi-judicial mechanisms of various UN Treaty mechanisms, in particular the Human Rights Committee, also ruled on individual complaints brought by child complainants. Since 1977, the Human Rights Committee has registered 1613 communications with respect to 81 countries.[31] 283 cases were pending before the Committee at time of writing,[32] just one having been submitted by a 16-year-old boy, while the others were submitted by parents or close family members of the child victims. [33]

It can thus be concluded that compared to the following capacities of the child, the child claimant capacity enables the child to join international proceedings on his or her 'own' motion and pursue his or her personal interest, instead of being a tool for the prosecution or defence strategy. Comparing the actual numbers of child claimants in international proceedings, the ICC has actively allowed the most extensive participation by war children. Despite the lack of a specific complaint procedure under international humanitarian law, child claimants do participate in most international proceedings, and are therefore recognized as subjects under international procedural law as claimants.

2.2. Child Witness

Children witness numerous atrocities and crimes during armed conflicts and large-scale violence, which constitute traumatic experiences.[34] Strug-

---

Rights (Nov. 19, 1999), Ser. C No. 77 (2001); Yean and Bosico Children v. The Dominican Republic, Inter-Am. Ct. H. R. Rights (Sept. 8. 2005), Ser. C No. 130 (2005); Vargas-Areco v. Paraguay, Inter-Am. Ct. H. R. Rights (Sept. 26, 2006), Ser. C No. 155 (2006).

[31] Statistical survey of individual complaints under the Optional Protocol to the International Covenant on Civil and Political Rights (Jan. 23, 2008), http://www2.ohchr.org/english/bodies/hrc/stat2.htm. Visited on 2010-11-23.

[32] *Id.*

[33] *See* amongst others, S.H.B. v. Canada Communication No. 192/1985, U.N. Doc. CCPR/C/29/D/192/1985 (Mar. 24, 1987); A. and S.N. v. Norway , Communication No. 224/1987, U.N. Doc. CCPR/C/33/D/224/1987 (Jul. 12, 1988); Darwinia Rosa Mónaco de Gallicchio v. Argentina Communication No. 400/1990, U.N. Doc. CCPR/C/53/D/400/1990 (Apr. 27, 1995).

[34] Promotion and Protection of the Rights of Children – Impact of armed conflict on children, note by the Secretary-General, addendum, G.A. 51st Sess., 4, U.N. Doc. A/51/306 /Add.1 (Sept. 9, 1996); Children and armed conflict, Report of the Secretary-General, G.A. 58/546 - S.C. 2003-1053 U.N. Doc. A/58/546-S/2003/1053

gles such as the Palestinian conflict prove that children may be unable to escape from witnessing violent acts.[35] They witness acts such as torture, killing, shelling and shooting.[36] Children become witnesses as by-standers, or by being victims or perpetrators of violent acts.[37] If children are witnesses they give evidence with regard to particular crimes through examination and cross-examination.[38]

Before examining the institutions that call child witnesses, two preliminary notes need to be made with regard to the definition of the term *child witness*.[39] Firstly, not a single international court or tribunal defines the term *child witness* in its statutory rules when specific reference is made to the term.[40] Secondly, due to the lack of a definition, there is uncertainty as to

---

(Nov. 10, 2003).

[35] Ahmad Baker & Nadera Shalhoub-Kevorkian, *Effects of political and military traumas on children: The Palestinian case*, 19 CLIN PSYCHOL REV 935, 940 (1999).

[36] *See, e.g.*, of Lebanon, Mona S. Macksoud & J. Lawrence Aber, *The War Experiences and Psychosocial Development of Children in Lebanon*, 1 CHILD DEVELOPMENT 70, 75-76 (1996).

[37] *Id*, 75. *See also* KYRA SANIN & ANNA STIRNEMANN, CHILD WITNESSES AT THE SPECIAL COURT FOR SIERRA LEONE' WAR CRIMES STUDIES CENTER UNIVERSITY OF CALIFORNIA, Berkeley (Mar. 2008), 7, http://ist-socrates.berkeley.edu/~warcrime/documents/ChildWitnessReport.pdf. Visited on 2010-11-23.

[38] Stuart Beresford, Child Witnesses and the International Criminal Justice System. Does the ICC Protect the most Vulnerable, 3 JICJ 721, 722 (2005).

[39] To date, there is no definition of the term *witness* in international law, *see, e.g.*, Felföldi Enikö, *The rising importance on the protection of witnesses in the European Union*, 77 LE DROIT PÉNAL DE L'UNION EUROPÉENNE 313, 317 (2006). Pre-Trial Chamber I of the ICC provides a general witness definition, Situation in the Democratic Republic of the Congo in the Case of the Prosecutor v. Thomas Lubanga Dyilo, Decision on the Prosecution Request for Extension of Time, Clarification and Provision of Information, 5 (Sept. 1, 2006), ICC-01/04-01/06-376-Corr.

[40] *See, e.g.*, Situation in the Democratic Republic of the Congo in the Case of The Prosecutor v. Thomas Lubanga Dyilo, Decision Regarding the Practices Used to Prepare and Familiarise Witnesses for Giving Testimony at Trial, 22-24, 32 (Nov. 30, 2007), ICC-01/04-01/06-1049; Situation in the Democratic Republic of the Congo in the Case of the Prosecutor v. Thomas Lubanga Dyilo, Decision on certain practicalities regarding individuals who have the dual status of witness and victim, 72 (Jun. 5, 2008), ICC-01/04-01/06-1379.

the age that young witnesses qualify as a child witness. This uncertainty is, however, only legally relevant and needs to be taken into account if, for instance, protective measures are solely applied to child witnesses below a certain age.

Whilst information on the exact numbers of child witnesses called by the prosecution or defence fence to testify in court is not made publicly available by the courts and tribunals for reasons of protection, it is submitted that before the *ad hoc* Tribunals and the Special Court for Sierra Leone (the SCSL) only a small number of children had been invited to testify. This is based on a careful reading of court practice. The ICC has a different approach to child witnesses and has, to date, called proportionally more children to the witness stand.

Thus far, only three witnesses 21 or younger have testified before the International Tribunal for the Former Yugoslavia (the ICTY).[41] Considering the overall number of witnesses that gave testimony before the ICTY—more than 6000—the number of child and young witnesses remains very low (0.5 per cent).[42] Irrespective of the lack of a definition *child witness*, the ICTY does recognize children as particularly vulnerable witnesses that need to be protected by specific measures.[43] Since neither the VWU nor the Chambers of the ICTY implemented a particular policy with regard to child witnesses, the application of protective measures is left to the discretion of the particular bench in each case. In practice, protective measures have, indeed, been applied to witnesses of the age of 21 or under.

---

[41] The Witness Unit of the ICTY produced statistics since 1996 until 2007 which list how many witnesses have testified at the ICTY who are 21 years or younger. Statistics received from ICTY by e-mail. *See, e.g.*, Galic case (2002) and Haradinaj case (2007), 8274,
http://www.icty.org/x/cases/haradinaj/trans/en/070911ED.htm,
Visited on 2010-11-23.
4028-4080, http://www.icty.org/x/cases/galic/trans/en/020219ed.htm.
Visited on 2010-11-23.

[42] *See* Witness Statistics as of 1 January 2010, http://www.icty.org/sid/10175.
Visited on 2010-11-23.

[43] The Prosecutor v. Dusko Tadic A/K/A "Dule", Case No. IT-94-1-T, Decision on the Prosecutor's Motion Requesting Protective Measures for Victims and Witnesses, 45-48 (Aug. 10, 1995).

More extensive participation of child witnesses occurred before the Special Court for Sierra Leone.[44] By June 2009, 20 former child soldiers had testified before the SCSL.[45] Comparing these 20 former child soldiers with the overall number of witnesses called,[46] a rather small number of young witnesses were called to give testimony (app. 4 per cent). Interestingly, the SCSL did not limit protection of child witnesses to persons under 18. Instead, it also applied a broader concept of a child witness. The prosecution's decisive criterion for categorizing a witness as a child witness in case of uncertainty with regard to the person's age is their belief that the witness was a former child soldier.[47] In practice, Trial Chamber II followed the prosecutions categorization and applied protective measures for the listed witnesses in the child category, even if they were over 18.[48] On the one hand, a deeper inquiry into the young witness's age was thus not deemed necessary with regard to the application of protective measures.[49] On the other hand, Trial Chamber I applied a stricter approach, by requiring a vulnerability assessment of persons over 18 before applying

---

[44] *See* amongst others, Case No. SCSL-04-15-PT, Trial Chamber I, The Prosecutor of the Special Court v. Issa Hassan Sesay, Morris Kallon, Augustine Gbao, transcript of 19 July 2004, witness TFI-199: first witness of the prosecution of Category B. Witnesses of this category are child witnesses, 38, 15-17. Same case, transcript of 20 July 2004, p. 9, 16-21; p. 13, 25. *See* also transcript of 27 July 2004, p. 2-3, 34-35. Case No. SCSL-2004-16-T, Trial Chamber II, The Prosecutor of the Special Court v. Alex Tamba Brima, Brima Bazzy Kamara, Santigie Borbor Kanu, transcript of 8 July 2005, witness TF-180: 2, 21.

[45] *See* SANIN & STIRNEMANN, *supra* note 36, at 13-14, approximately 13 until March 2006. Information received by e-mail from SCSL Press and Outreach Office SCSL (Jun. 23, 2009): 5 in the AFRC case; 5 in the CDF case; 4 in the RUF case; 6 in the Taylor case. Information about the overall number of witnesses http://www.sc-sl.org/CASES/tabid/71/Default.aspx. Visited on 2010-11-23.

[46] In total 516 witnesses gave testimony, to date (4 August 2010). This number is comprised of the witnesses called in the 3 closed cases and the prosecution witnesses of the still ongoing Taylor case.

[47] The Prosecutor of the Special Court v. Sam Hinga Norman Moinina Fofana Allieu Kondewa, Case No. SCSL-2004-14-T, Trial Chamber I, 9 March 2005, http://www.sc-sl.org/LinkClick.aspx?fileticket=7n9jeKdWUpQ%3D&tabid=154. Visited on 2010-11-23. The Prosecution distinguishes between different categories of witnesses. Child witnesses fall within category B, *see* The Prosecutor of the Special Court v. Charles Ghankay Taylor, Case No. SCSL-2003-01-AR73; SANIN & STIRNEMANN, *supra* note 36, at 12.

[48] SANIN & STIRNEMANN, *supra* note 36, at 12.

[49] *Id*, at 4.

child-specific protection measures.[50] Granting (even if not principally) to over-18s indicates that the Court felt (in some instances) a need to treat these young witnesses as children as far as their procedural protection was concerned. At the same time, one cannot conclude from this practice whether an upper age limit exists for the application of child specific protective measures.

As regards the participation of child witnesses before the ICC it is submitted that, to date, not a single case has been concluded. The following assessment therefore only presents the practice of the ICC, in particular the practice of the Office of the Prosecutor in the first two cases against Thomas Lubanga Dyilo, and the combined case against Germain Katanga and Mathieu Ngudjolo Chui.[51] Both cases establish a different approach towards child witnesses, and a remarkably higher percentage of child witnesses who gave in-court testimony (app 23 per cent) compared to the previous international institutions.[52] The importance of child witnesses is already reflected in the decision confirming the charges. Pre-Trial Chamber I repeatedly relied on the statements provided by former child soldiers,

---

[50] The Prosecutor of the Special Court v. Sam Hinga Norman Moinina Fofana Allieu Kondewa, Case No. SCSL-2004-14-T, Trial Chamber I (Mar. 9, 2005), http://www.sc-sl.org/LinkClick.aspx?fileticket=7n9jeKdWUpQ%3D&tabid=154.SANIN & STIRNEMANN, *supra* note 36, at 12-13.

[51] For an overview of the situation and cases, *see* http://www.icc-cpi.int/Menus/ICC/Situations+and+Cases/.

[52] It should be noted that the following calculation is only preliminary, owing to the ongoing proceedings: nine young witnesses below the age of 21 in the Lubanga proceedings, and four children in the proceedings against Katanga and Ngudjolo Chui. A total of 56 witnesses have been listed to give testimony in court, to date: 30 witnesses Lubanga case (28 prosecution witnesses, 2 expert witnesses called by Trial Chamber I, official defence witness numbers are not yet published, *see* Case Information Sheet The Prosecutor v. Thomas Lubanga Dyilo (Jun. 24, 2010), ICC-PIDS-CIS-DRC-01/004/10); therefore the alleged number of 18 witnesses is not included in the calculation, *see* http://allafrica.com/stories/201006161029.html. Visited on 2010-11-23. In the Kantaga Ngudjolo Chui case the prosecution stated that it intends to call 26 witnesses, Situation in the Democratic Republic of the Congo, In the Case of the Prosecutor v. Germain Katanga and Mathieu Ngudjolo Chui, Directions for the conduct of the proceedings and testimony in accordance with rule 140, 7 (Nov. 20, 2009), ICC-01/04-01/07-1665.

including children under 18.[53] The prosecution case against Thomas Lubanga Dyilo was concluded on 14 July 2010. In total, 28 prosecution witnesses appeared before Trial Chamber I. The prosecution called nine former child soldiers.[54] In its opening statement, it underlined the need to recognize these former child soldiers as vulnerable witnesses. Particular reference was made to their *short lives* which indicate that witnesses are still young human beings. Explicit reference to a child witness—without providing a definition of the term *child*, however—is only made once, namely with regard to witness 157.[55] It seems that the ICC prosecution recognizes former child soldiers (irrespective of their age) as particularly vulnerable witnesses in terms of protection. Again, due to the application of protective measures, in particular in the form of redactions and closed session hearings, it is not possible to determine the exact age of the young witnesses at the moment of testimony. It can nevertheless be established that at least nine young witnesses were called by the prosecution in the Lubanga case. [56] The Court classified these witnesses as vulner-

---

53 Situation in the Democratic Republic of the Congo in the Case of The Prosecutor v. Thomas Lubanga Dyilo, Decision on the confirmation of charges, 329, 385-390 (Jan. 29, 2007), ICC-01/04-01/06-803-tEN; Situation in the Democratic Republic of the Congo in the Case of the Prosecutor v. Germain Katanga and Mathieu Ngudjolo Chui, Decision on the confirmation of charges, 144, 260 (Sept. 30, 2008), ICC-01/04-01/07-717.

54 *See*, *supra* note 52.

55 Witness 157, Situation in the Democratic Republic of the Congo in the Case of the Prosecutor v. Thomas Lubanga Dyilo, Prosecution's Clarifications to the 'Prosecution's Request for Non-Disclosure of the Identity of Twenty-Five Individuals providing Tu Quoque Information' filed on 19 December 2008, 9, (Jan. 26, 2009), ICC-01/04-01/06-1650-Anx.

56 Child witness 157: Situation in the Democratic Republic of the Congo in the Case of the Prosecutor v. Thomas Lubanga Dyilo, Prosecution's Clarifications to the 'Prosecution's Request for Non-Disclosure of the Identity of Twenty-Five Individuals providing Tu Quoque Information' filed on 19 December 2008, 9 (Jan. 26, 2009), ICC-01/04-01/06-1650-Anx. Child witnesses: 7, 8, 10, 11, 293, 294, 298. See generally, Witness 7: http://www.icc-cpi.int/iccdocs/doc/doc694162.pdf, ICC-01/04-01/06-T-148-ENG, 13 March 2009. Visited on 2010-11-23. Witness 8: http://www.aegistrust.org/images/reports_briefings_2009/lc02.pdf, http://www.icc-cpi.int/iccdocs/doc/doc808985.pdf. Visited on 2010-11-23. Witness 11: http://www.icc-cpi.int/iccdocs/doc/doc649086.pdf, ICC-01/04-01/06-T-138-ENG, 22 February 2009. Visited on 2010-11-23. Witness 7 and 294: http://www.icc-cpi.int/iccdocs/doc/doc801424.pdf, 28; http://www.icc-cpi.int/iccdocs/doc/doc728408.pdf. Visited on 2010-11-23. Witness

able—irrespective of being a child or being over 18.[57] In the ongoing proceedings against Katanga and Ngudjolo Chui, at least four children have been called by the prosecution to give testimony regarding the charge of using child soldiers under 15.[58] While the ICC does not draw a sharp distinction based on age when assessing the vulnerability of a witness and his or her need for specific protection, the international standard of 18, as enshrined in Article 1 of the CRC is applied in so far as the consent of children's parents is asked before calling children to the witness stand.[59] Thus, while in terms of protection it is not decisive whether the young witness is older or younger than 18, requesting the consent of a parent (or legal guar-

---

298:
http://www.lubangatrial.org/2010/04/02/lubanga-trial-goes-on-recess-after-witness-testifies-via-video-link/. Visited on 2010-11-23. To date, Lubanga defence called 18 witnesses, http://allafrica.com/stories/201006161029.html.
Visited on 2010-11-23.

[57] 25 prosecution witnesses gave testimony under protective measures, case Information Sheet – The Prosecutor v. Thomas Lubanga Dyilo (Jun. 24, 2010), ICC-PIDS-CIS-DRC-01-004/10. In addition, Trial Chamber I called 2 expert witnesses, Report of the International Criminal Court, U.N. Doc. A/64/356 (Sep. 17., 2009, 10). *See also*
http://www.icc-cpi.int/NR/exeres/3AD78C1A-3D71-4FA7-B38F-05DF735EC38A.htm. Visited on 2010-11-23.

[58] The Prosecution intends to call a total of 26 witnesses in the Katanga case, Situation in the Democratic Republic of the Congo, In the Case of the Prosecutor v. Germain Katanga and Mathieu Ngudjolo Chui, Directions for the conduct of the proceedings and testimony in accordance with rule 140, 7 (Nov. 20, 2009), ICC-01/04-01/07-1665. The following witnesses are children: witness 157 and 280, Situation in the Democratic Republic of the Congo, In the Case of the Prosecutor v. Germain Katanga and Mathieu Ngudjolo Chui, Prosecution's Observations Addressing Matters that Were Discussed at the Confirmation Hearing, 16, 18 (Jul. 22, 2008), ICC-01/04-01/07-692; witness 28 and 279, Situation in the Democratic Republic of the Congo, In the Case of the Prosecutor v. Germain Katanga and Mathieu Ngudjolo Chui, Submissions of the Defence of Mr. Mathieu Ngudjolo in the Context of the Confirmation Hearing, 51, 53 (Jul. 28, 2008), ICC-01/04-01/07-699-tENG. Witness 28, 157, 279 and 280 are all former child soldiers (witness 28 also called in Lubanga), Confirmation of Charges Hearing, 42 (Jul. 3, 2008), ICC-01/04-01/07-T-42-ENG.

[59] In the Case of the Prosecutor v. Germain Katanga and Mathieu Ngudjolo Chui, Prosecution's Observations Addressing Matters that Were Discussed at the Confirmation Hearing, 16-18 (Jul. 22, 2008), ICC-01/04-01/07-692, 22 July 2008.

dian) establishes that in this regard, child witnesses are strictly seen as children under 18, with limited legal capacity.

Having examined the practice of the various institutions with respect to child witnesses, it can be concluded that all recognize children within this procedural capacity. Moreover, each institution recognizes children's *and* young human beings' particular vulnerability and need for specific protection—a conclusion that is significant in the sense that within human rights law, humanitarian law and international criminal law, the particular substantive protection of children is not extended towards persons over 18. Accordingly, in international criminal procedural law, it is rather the experience of children during their childhood—in particular as a child soldier—that determines their classification as a child witness or a vulnerable witness. Such practice departs from the sharp distinction between children below 18 and young human beings over that age, as far as their substantive protection under international law is concerned. In light of the above, it is submitted that the term *child witness* is mostly understood and referred to as a general term covering *young* human beings. Additionally, the practice of the SCSL and the ICC establish that children are predominantly witnesses in cases against alleged perpetrators who are responsible for the war crime of recruiting children below the age of fifteen years.[60] Common to all institutions is that they only called *young* adolescents into the witness stand. Infants have not been called to testify—a practice that, by contrast, is applied in national proceedings as for instance in cases of child sexual abuse where young children are the only witnesses. While it is too early to draw definite conclusions, the practice of both the SCSL and the ICC establish that the prosecution teams tend to call other witnesses than children for crimes that do not particularly address children.[61]

---

[60] With regard to the SCSL, *see* SANIN & STIRNEMANN, *supra* note 36, at 3.

[61] Children are particular used as insider witnesses due to their experience as child soldiers and/or as commander's wives, *see* BERESFORD, *supra* note 37, at 722.

2.3. Child Perpetrator

Children participate as soldiers in hostilities.[62] The phenomenon of child soldiers and their involvement in conflict situations is a well-established practice, and a continuing reality. Today's estimated number of child soldiers amounts to more than 300,000 children.[63] Within this capacity, children committed and continue to commit the most atrocious crimes.[64] The term *child perpetrator* does not include all children under 18 in a procedural context. Instead, the international procedural capacity of child perpetrators is limited to a certain age category of children.

While children as (alleged) perpetrators of crimes under international law have never been charged with such crimes in international (judicial) proceedings, the first and only international mechanism that explicitly entailed the jurisdictional mandate for the prosecution of alleged child perpetrators is the Special Court for Sierra Leone. Article 7 of the Statute stipulates that the Court has jurisdiction over minors that were between 15-18 when the alleged crime was committed.[65] Consequently, the SCSL admits that children may be perpetrators but lacks jurisdiction over child perpetrators under 15. Because of the jurisdictional mandate over minors of this particular age category, extensive discussion was held whether children should be held criminally responsible under international law.[66]

---

[62] See generally REDRESS, STUDY ON CHILD SOLDERING IN NORTHERN UGANDA AND THE DEMOCRATIC REPUBLIC OF THE CONGO, VICTIMS, PERPETRATORS OR HEROES? CHILD SOLDIERS BEFORE THE INTERNATIONAL CRIMINAL COURT (2006), 5-22, http://www.redress.org/downloads/publications/childsoldiers.pdf. Visited on 2010-11-23.

[63] UNICEF, Factsheet: Child Soldiers, http://www.unicef.org/emerg/files/childsoldiers.pdf. Visited on 2010-11-23.

[64] COALITION TO STOP THE USE OF CHILD SOLDIERS, CHILD SOLDIERS GLOBAL REPORT 2008, 36, http://www.childsoldiersglobalreport.org/files/country_pdfs/FINAL_2008_Global_Report.pdf. Visited on 2010-11-23.

[65] Statute of the Special Court for Sierra Leone, art. 7, available at http://www.sc-sl.org/LinkClick.aspx?fileticket=uClnd1MJeEw%3d&tabid=176. Visited on 2010-11-23.

[66] See generally, Matthew Happold, *The Age of Criminal Responsibility for International Crimes under International Law in* INTERNATIONAL CRIMINAL ACCOUNTABILITY AND THE RIGHTS OF CHILDREN 69-84 (Karin Arts &

Numerous arguments were raised for and against the criminal prosecution of minors.[67] The Prosecutor of the SCSL stated in this context that he did not intend to start proceedings against minors, regardless of his jurisdictional mandate, but would instead focus on the ones who bear the greatest responsibility.[68] As children, in principle, did not bear command responsibility in the Sierra Leonean conflict, he underlined that children who committed crimes are instead to be recognized as victims.[69] At the time of writing, the last case before the Special Court for Sierra Leone—the trial of the former Liberian president Charles Taylor—reached the defence stage.[70] None of the cases had involved children in the capacity of a child perpetrator being charged with crimes within the Special Court's jurisdiction. The subsequent inclusion of Article 26 in the Rome Statute of the International Criminal Court brought the discussion concerning the international criminal responsibility of children to an end by excluding persons under 18 from its jurisdiction.[71] Compared with the existing (though very limited) practice of prosecuting minors under national law, international

Vesselin Popovski eds., 2006). *See* in particular Report of the Secretary-General on the establishment of a SCSL, S.C. 2000/915, U.N. Doc. S/2009/915, (Oct. 4, 2000).

[67] ICTY Prosecutor v. Naser Orić, Judgment, case no. IT-03-068-T, 400 (Jun. 30, 2006) 30 June 2006. Critical assessment of the exclusion of minors from the Court's jurisdiction, *see* Micaela Frulli, Jurisdiction ratione personae *in* THE ROME STATUTE OF THE INTERNATIONAL CRIMINAL COURT: A COMMENTARY 527-541 (Antonio Cassese & Albin Eser eds., 2002),. Christine Bakker, *Prosecuting International Crimes Against Children: The Legal Framework*, Innocenti Working Paper 2010-13 (2010).

[68] Press release SCSL, http://www.sc-sl.org/LinkClick.aspx?fileticket=XRwCUe%2BaVhw%3D&tabid=196 (Nov. 2, 2002). Visited on 2010-11-23. SARA KENDALL & MICHELLE STAGGS, *Interim Report on the SCSL*, , Berkeley War Crimes Studies Center, (Apr. 2005), 7, http://warcrimescenter.berkeley.edu. Visited on 2010-11-23.

[69] Press release SCSL, http://www.sc-sl.org/LinkClick.aspx?fileticket=TazwrTR%2bT7Q%3d&tabid=196 (Jun. 24, 2004). Visited on 2010-11-23.

[70] Top Officers of Special Court for Sierra Leone describe trial of Charles Taylor as critical for fragile peace, stability in West Africa, Security Council 6163rd Meeting, SC/9707 (Jul. 16, 2009).

[71] *See also* SHARANJEET PARMAR ET AL., CHILDREN AND TRANSATIONAL JUSTICE xxv (Harvard University Press 2010).

justice mechanisms have not been used and recognized as a forum to fight the impunity of child perpetrators.[72]

Notwithstanding the non-existence of international judicial proceedings against children in the capacity of child perpetrators, children were recognized as perpetrators of the most heinous crimes of concern to the international community, and participated in such a capacity in non-judicial procedures of Truth and Reconciliation Commissions as, for instance, in the TRCs of Sierra Leone and Liberia.[73] For the first time in the history of TRCs, the Sierra Leonean TRC explicitly referred to child perpetrators in its regulation and final report.[74] The TRC Act of 2000 addressed not only the needs of child victims, but also introduced special procedures and measures of protection for child perpetrators.[75] In its final report of 2004, the Commission pointed out that most child perpetrators are also child victims.[76] In addition to the general findings on child perpetrators, the TRC's final report includes an entire chapter on children in armed conflict in which the particularities as regards child perpetrators are addressed.[77] The Commission emphasised that while it does not aim to determine the guilt of former child soldiers, it does attempt to assess children's roles as

---

[72] For a brief historical overview, *see* Roger S. Clark & Otto Triffterer, *Article 26 Exclusion of jurisdiction over persons under eighteen in* COMMENTARY ON THE ROME STATUTE OF THE INTERNATIONAL CRIMIINAL COURT—OBSERVERS' NOTES, ARTICLE BY ARTICLE 771-775 (Otto Triffterer ed., 2008).

[73] SIERRA LEONE TRUTH & RECONCILIATION COMMISSION, WITNESS TO TRUTH: REPORT OF THE SIERRA LEONE TRUTH & RECONCILIATION COMMISSION, Vol. 3B, Chapter 4,
http://www.sierra-leone.org/Other-Conflict/TRCVolume3B.pdf. With regard to the TRC of Liberia, *see* Volume III, Title II, Children, the Conflict and the TRC Children Agenda, 65,
http://www.trcofliberia.org/memorials/videos/video_search?page=4&location=None&date=0-0&speaker=b. Visited on 2010-11-23.

[74] *See* PARMAR, *supra* note 70, at 164.

[75] *See* for example section 6(2), 7 (2) and 7(4) The Truth and Reconciliation Act (2000).

[76] SIERRA LEONE TRUTH & RECONCILIATION COMMISSION, WITNESS TO TRUTH: REPORT OF THE SIERRA LEONE TRUTH & RECONCILIATION COMMISSION, Vol. 1, Chapter Five,
http://www.sierra-leone.org/Other-Conflict/TRCVolume1.pdf, 190.

[77] *Id.* at 286.

"victim-perpetrators".[78] In this regard, the TRC published statistical information on children who committed crimes during the Sierra Leonean conflict.[79] The capacity of the child actor as a perpetrator is thereby not only consolidated in the TRC's regulation, but also reflected in its findings.

2.4. Perpetrator's Child

Being the child of a perpetrator who is brought before an international criminal court or tribunal bears numerous and far reaching consequences for children. Children are likely to be confronted with the often lengthy separation from their parent(s), considering that institutions such as the *ad hoc* tribunals or the ICC in the Hague, can be situated far from their homes, and proceedings (including detention) tend to last for several years. Being a perpetrator's child may also lead to the stigmatization and exclusion of the child in his or her community. These consequences are not legally regulated by the institutions, since they fall outside their mandate.

In contrast, legally regulated consequences that may indirectly victimize children are the result of an act or omission by the institutions against the parent perpetrator. Such victimization of children requires distinction from the previous understanding of the term *child victim*. Firstly, the victimization of perpetrators' children is not caused by a commission of an international crime against children, but the result of judicial proceedings and detention of the parent perpetrator. Secondly, child victims are, in this context, indirect victims, since the parent perpetrator is the direct 'addressee' of an act or omission by the institution. Thirdly, the term *child victim* is understood as referring to the biological (or 'legally' recognized) child of the perpetrator. As regards the age of the child, the CRC standard of 18 years constitutes the benchmark. Finally, this procedural capacity of children varies from the foregoing capacities (claimant, witness and perpetrator capacity) in the sense that it does not enable children to participate

---

[78] *See* SIERRA LEONE TRUTH & RECONCILIATION COMMISSION, *supra* note 72, at 439.

[79] Statistical Appendix to the Report of the Truth and Reconciliation Commission of Sierra Leone, *A Report by the Benetech Human Rights Data Analysis Group of the Truth and Reconciliation Commission*, Appendix 1 (2004), 19, http://www.sierra-leone.org/Other-Conflict/APPENDICES/Appendix%201%20-%20Statistical%20Report.pdf. Visited on 2010-11-23.

in the proceedings, but rather constitutes a capacity that exists due to their parent's procedural capacity as a perpetrator or detainee. It is nevertheless recognized as a procedural capacity since this capacity only functions within the ambit of judicial proceedings.

The procedural capacity of perpetrators' children is of particular relevance with regard to two issues. Firstly, being the child of an alleged perpetrator has procedurally-caused consequences for the child and family life at home. Enforcement measures, such as the freezing of assets, have implications for the family of the accused. If applied without sufficiently taking into account the particular needs of children of the accused in their daily lives (such as the payment of school fees or other family allowances), children of the accused are at risk of being victimized due to freezing of their parent's assets.

Secondly, the various institutions grant the accused and convicted parent the right to family visits. [80] This right not only aims to serve the well-being of the detainee, but also to enable children to grow up in a family environment despite the detention of a parent. The CRC stipulates in this regard that, '[n]o child shall be subjected to arbitrary or unlawful interference with his or her privacy, family, home or correspondence […].'[81] In practice, the organization of family visits gives rise to various difficulties that might constrain children's ability to visit their parent—as illustrated by the various decisions concerning family visits of the accused Thomas Lubanga Dyilo, Germain Katanga and Mathieu Ngudjolo Chui before the ICC.[82]

---

[80] Rule 58-64bis ICTY Rules Governing the Detention of Persons awaiting Trial or Appeal before the Tribunal or otherwise Detained on the Authority of the Tribunal, UN doc. IT/38Rev. 9 (Jul. 21, 2005). Rule 41 Rules Governing the Detention of Persons Awaiting Trial or Appeal before the SCSL or Otherwise Detained on the Authority of the SCSL as amended on 14 May 2005, http://www.scsl.org/LinkClick.aspx?fileticket=sSNS1UL5T3w%3d&tabid=176. Visited on 2010-11-23.

[81] U.N. Convention on the Rights of the Child, art. 16 in conjunction with art. 9(4).

[82] Report of the Court on the financial aspects of enforcing the Court's obligation to fund family visits to indigent detained persons (May 6, 2009), ICC-ASP/8/9. Situation in the Democratic Republic of the Congo in the Case of The Prosecutor v. Germain Katanga, Request to the Democratic Republic of the Congo for the Arrest and Surrender of Germain Katanga (Jul. 6, 2007), ICC-01/04-01/07-6-tENG; Situ-

Some difficulties have been anticipated, and are therefore reflected in the applicable rules of the various institutions, while others are not. Questions that have not been addressed relate to the concept of a family, and whether children of all spouses are eligible for family visits. There are other questions about the need for children traveling on such visits to have a visa, as well as the frequency and costs of family visits, particularly when the prisoner is indigent. What these questions have in common is that they all demand procedural awareness and regulation in order to guarantee that children's indirect victimization is not made worse by procedural decisions against their parent.

Keeping the above in mind, it is crucial that international criminal courts and tribunals recognize children as indirect victims of the proceedings against a parent perpetrator. On the one side, the freezing of assets and restrictions to family life may be justified within the context of criminal proceedings. But, on the other side, a lack of understanding of the peculiarities of the child limits, or even prevents, children from visiting their parent or living in child adequate circumstances.

3. Conclusion

Despite the broad silence of the statutory rules of the various institutions—the foregoing procedural capacities of war children are recognized in international practice. The international procedural legal subjectivity of children is therefore established and not solely limited to the substantive protection of the fundamental rights of the child. Despite this recognition,

---

ation En Republique Democratique Du Congo Affaire Le Procureur c/Germain Katanga & Mathieu Ngudjolo, Troicième rapport du Greffe sur l'état d'avancement des demandes de visas pour les familles des personnes détenues dans la cadre des visites familiales (Nov. 3, 2008), ICC-01/04-01/07-733. Report of the Court on family visits to indigent detained persons (Nov. 5, 2008), ICC-ASP/7/24. Situation in the Central African Republic in the Case of The Prosecutor v. Jean-Pierre Bemba Gombo, Redacted version of "Decision on legal assistance for the accused" (Nov. 26, 2009), ICC-01/05-01/08-567-Red, 18. Situation in the Democratic Republic of the Congo in the Case of The Prosecutor v. Germain Katanga and Mathieu Ngudjolo Chui, Confidential, *ex parte* only available to the Defence of Mr Ngudjolo Chui and the Registrar, Decision on "Mr Mathieu Ngudjolo's Complaint Under Regulation 221(1) of the Regulations of the Registry Against the Registrar's Decision of 18 November 2008", 16, 35 (Mar. 10, 2009), ICC-RoR217/02/08-8.

war children's procedural capacities are not founded on a common understanding of the definition of who is considered to be a child. Instead, international procedural law distinguishes between various age categories of children and young adolescents that might even include young human beings over 18—which is, from a protectionist point of view, a welcoming and child-friendly international practice. This fragmented recognition and practice as regards the war child as a procedural actor makes it, however, indispensable in taking sufficient account of the war child's peculiarities in the various procedural capacities.

CHAPTER SIX:

JURISDICTION OF CRIMINAL COURTS

CHILDREN AND CRIME

KNUT SVERI

Abstract

The questions about children's age, criminality, and criminal responsibility constitute some of the most problematic issues of criminal justice and procedure within most domestic legal systems. Although these issues have been dealt with in different ways, they have not been solved, and are regarded as the core subjects of discussion in the writing of legal scholars. The intention of this article is to re-examine these issues of criminal procedure and justice, and to simultaneously present some philosophical and practical solutions to the relevant issues. The article therefore looks at the effect of cultural dependency, the variation of the age of criminal responsibility, and the level as well as the degree of seriousness of crimes with a reference to the figures from the criminal statistics.

1. Introduction

In common usage the words "child" and "children" have a very wide range of meanings. Everyone seems to agree that the concepts have to do with life span, but we are not in agreement about when this begins or when it ends. Does it start with the fertilized egg, or with birth—and does it end with the end of obligatory schooling, or the end of college? Do we include all teenagers, or do we refer to those who do not yet have the right to vote or are forbidden to visit a pub, to buy alcohol or get a driving licence? The most extreme use of the word "child" is in the UN's Convention on the Rights of the Child, which in Article 1 includes human beings "below the age of eighteen years".

Our sentiments towards children also have a wide range—from the pure innocence of the child in the Madonna's lap, to the obstinate teenager. Between these two images is to be found a huge development of which we have some, but far from complete, knowledge. For a criminologist one particular part of this development is of fundamental interest, namely, the process of *internalization of norms*. I will come back to this later, but first a few words on children and the law.

2. Cultural Dependency

In most cultures there has been some sort of rite-of-passage, when a person leaves childhood and becomes an adult. I believe that this is a custom as old as human culture itself, and has simply to do with the onset of puberty. In our cultures this seems to have taken place around 14-15 for boys and sometimes a little earlier for girls. This is what we found in Roman law and in all Christian societies. The ritual—still in existence even in our time—is called in Christian societies the "confirmation"; it has different names in other cultures. At the same time, it meant the end of compulsory schooling. After going through this ritual, life changed for most ordinary youngsters in terms of the responsibilities placed upon them, such as finding work and—if still living within his or her family—to hand over most of his wages in support of the family. In recent years one great change has taken place in the industrialized part of the world: we now expect that youngsters will continue going to school until they are about 18, which gives rise to a completely new situation—social, psychological and economical—for this age group.

3. The Age of Criminal Responsibility

At what point has a child developed both psychologically and socially, to the extent that it can be considered responsible for the crimes he or she commits? In most European countries we have placed this "age of responsibility" at 14 or 15. However, there are important exceptions. In England it is 8, in Switzerland **7**, and in the Netherlands 18. But this should not be taken too seriously because these countries obviously have special systems for handling juveniles. But sometimes these special juvenile court laws fail—a strange example is the trial of the killers of the 2-year-old-James Bulger in England, in 1993. The two boys who committed the terrible crime were only 10 at the time, but were tried not according to English juvenile law, but according to criminal law and procedures created for adults.[1] As I see it, the German and Scandinavian laws have their advantages. They state that a person who, at the time of the offence, was under 14 (15 in the Scandinavian countries, except Denmark)

---

[1] This was, incidentally, condemned by the European Court of Human Rights in 1999.

is not criminally responsible, which means that it is not a matter for the criminal legal system, but for the social services.

This may seem fair enough, but there certainly are many practical problems involved: let me mention one. The legal rights of anyone above the age of criminal responsibility include, for example, the right to have a defence lawyer, to have a court trial, and the duty of the prosecutor to be objective. None of these safeguards exists in a child welfare board. Who decides whether a boy or a girl at the age of ten actually was the perpetrator of the crime? In practice it is—in the majority of cases—the police. We know very little about how the police handle such cases. It is not necessarily so that all cases are routinely sent to the child welfare board—it may be so that some police forces decide to inform the guardian of the child if the crime is considered to be "a trifling" matter, and subsequently close the case. Or it may be it stops with an informal reprimand from the police officer on the spot. Whether the incident is registered or not is also a matter for different police authorities.

What I have said above may be seen as critical to the work of the police and the child welfare boards, but since we lack knowledge of how these authorities actually handle children suspected of crimes it should be considered more as a vague suspicion of possible injustices.

4. The Degree of Seriousness of Crimes

How serious are the crimes committed by children? In recent years there seems to have been a tendency to consider it as a "no problem" for criminal policy. An example of this is that the Swedish criminal statistics no longer specify the under 15 age group. I do not know the reason for this, but there can only be one of two explanations. Either it is part of a policy which wants us to disregard the problem, or it is because the information from the police is considered unreliable—and it is outside the statistical authority to adjust this.

However, we do have such statistics from Norway—in the following, I am using figures from the criminal statistics for 2009.

In that year, 82,809 persons above the age of 4 were charged with criminal offences (both crimes and misdemeanours). Of these, 4.6 per cent were in the 5-14 age group. It is interesting to note that girls had a higher rate than boys (8 per cent, in comparison to 3.9 per cent for boys). If we leave out the misdemeanours and look at crimes alone, we find that of the 34,304 charged, 6 per cent were under 15.

The number of children charged is understandably not equally distributed in each age category—there are very few aged 5 and 6, but a steady increase up to 14. Taking into account the number of individuals in each age group in the population, 13 and 14-year-olds have crime rates per 1,000 inhabitants of 17 and 27 respectively. The corresponding figures for 15 to 30 are about twice as high. The explanation for this is to be found in the fact that older persons commit a whole range of crimes which we do not find among children. Mostly this has to do with (e.g.) traffic violations, violence, burglaries, and narcotic offences, but also with more (or less) sophisticated crimes such as fraud and forgery. However, it may be of some interest to see what kind of offences children commit.

Of 262 persons charged with breaking and entering, 46 (18 per cent) were in the 5-14 age group. For arson 18 (37 per cent) of 49 (in some cases the property destroyed may have been very valuable). Of 1,166 persons charged with sexual offences the figure was 102 (8 per cent) of which 40 was for rape. For physical violence, 340 (10 per cent) of 3,370 were charged with something we might call minor violence. As may be expected, children often destroy property, and this is confirmed by the fact that of the 2,131 persons charged, 731 (34 per cent) were children. Simple theft is, however, most common. Of 8,520 persons charged for such offences (probably mostly shop-lifting) 1,717 (20 per cent) were under 15. This is also the only type of offence where girls are almost as active as boys.

There are a couple of other pieces of information in the Norwegian statistics which are worth noting. The statistical unit (charge) may contain more than one offence, and we can see from the tables that children are less often caught for more than one offence as compared with older age groups. Furthermore, they have committed their offences together with others significantly more frequently—they have a much higher degree of group activity.

Lastly, a word about recidivism is also necessary here. In the Norwegian statistics we have figures showing whether the persons charged in 2004 have been charged again within a period of 5 years. They do not reveal what kind these new offences are, or how often the persons have been caught again. However, the figures give us a hint as to whether the fact that a registration for an offence indicates continued criminality. The general recidivism rate for all offenses is 48 per cent, but excluding misdemeanours it is no less than 62 the highest being for the age group 15-17 (70 per cent). Children have fewer recidivists (58 per cent), but these figures refute the idea that children's offenses are just play which have no implication for their development. We see that 63 per cent of those charged with crimes of violence were recidivists, similar figures being 67 per cent for burglary, 82 per cent for robbery, 51 per cent for destroying property, 35 per cent for simple theft (mostly shop-lifting), and 52 per cent for sex-crimes.

The aim of this short statement has been to draw attention to the delinquency of children—persons under the age of 15 years. These years are of the utmost importance in the development of an individual as a human being. One fundamental part of this is the internalization of the norms of the surrounding culture. One might say that our criminal law represents the minimum standard of what any citizen must internalize in order to make society functional.

5. Conclusion

When a norm is internalized it becomes a part of ourselves, and is a greater deterrent against law-breaking than anything else. Just the thought of doing something contrary to the norm may be painful because it triggers our conscience and feelings of guilt. Studies by child psychologists have given us an insight into how this strange process takes place. Today there seems to be an agreement that love and care lead to a more easy adoption than the old rule in the Book of Proverbs stating that the more you love your son the more you thrash him.

However, as the child grows older it must try to spread its own wings and get away from the total dependence of its parents. Perhaps the most important way this is done is in contact with other children. Below the age of 13-14 these groups have a loose structure; it is in the famous "gang age" between 15-18 that we find that they are more structured and bound together.

As a part of these "training" processes children confront the norms in order to test them and to challenge grown-up society. Most of it is done for fun, although sometimes it may have important consequences for the community—such as serious fires or schools that have been destroyed.

When we look at the low clear-up rates for "simple, daily, ordinary crimes" it is not impossible that many of them are committed by children. Perhaps this is not that bad after all, since we know that most delinquent children stop this kind of behaviour without any interference from the authorities. But as we have seen, some are caught, and of these quite a few are recidivists. These are probably the "hard core" of future professional criminals. Looking more closely at them, we find that they may have had all kinds of problems in their short lives—psychological as well as social. During the last 150 years many efforts have been made to turn them into decent, law-abiding citizens. This is a tragic story with a lot of suffering—and nothing seems to work.

WHAT HAS THE AMERICAN JUVENILE JUSTICE SYSTEM DONE TO THE CHILDREN?

LYDIA WANG

Abstract

This article reviews the transformation of American judicial treatment of juvenile delinquents in procedure and substance. In international criminal practice, children are recognized as different from adults and accorded special treatment. In the early 19th century, some big American cities established separate institutions for the committal of delinquent children. The Chicago Juvenile Court introduced in 1899, was a pioneer institution tasked with rehabilitation rather than punishment. The success of the American juvenile court's reformative enterprise attracted much attention and the model spread across the nation, and the world, during the first half of the twentieth century. However, in the mid-twentieth century, the lines began to be blurred between juvenile and adult criminal justice. The American judiciary doubted the constitutional and theoretical basis of the juvenile court system, and suggested that the essentials of due process could be attributed to a therapeutic attitude as far as the juvenile was concerned. Most states revised their statutes to treat children as adults when severe crimes were committed, meaning that the courts could only extend the general constitutional protections of procedure rights and fair treatment to which adults were entitled. Thus, at the turn of twenty-first century, the United States was the only country retaining the death penalty and life imprisonment for children, and lagged far behind international human rights standards. In 2005 and 2010, the U.S. Supreme Court abolished the juvenile death penalty and life sentence respectively, but public opinion remains divided over these issues.

1. Introduction

Children are generally recognized as different from adults in criminal codes and accorded special treatment as such. For example, in Taiwan, the criminal code of 1935 proscribed convictions for children under the age of 14, and life imprisonment and the death penalty for those under the age of 18. Likewise, in Sweden, the age of criminal responsibility is 15, and more lenient punishments are the standard for young persons, with prosecutors able to waive prosecution when the offender is under the age of 18. For those between 18 and 21, special requirements must be met before the court may impose a sentence of imprisonment, and no one may be sentenced to life imprisonment for a crime committed below the age of 21. Similar norms have developed over time in some international treaties on human rights, such as the International Covenant on Civil and Political Rights,[1] or the Convention on the Rights of the Child.[2]

In contrast, in the United States, a child as young as 12 or 13 may receive a multi-decade sentence in adult prison, may have been sentenced to life without parole for an offense other than homicide before May 2011, and before 2005 could have been put to death. Such treatment of young children was forbidden even under the ancient Roman law, and we are unable to find other instances anywhere else in the modern world. We note that the United States of America resorts to penal sanctions against adults and children more than any other country in the world, having 5 per cent of the world's population, but 25 per cent of the world's prisoners. An Amnesty International report in 1998 noted that 200,000 children were being prosecuted in adult courts every year, and that over 11,000 children were incarcerated in adult prisons. Before 2005, the United States had executed the largest number of juveniles in the world. In 2007, the Los Angeles Times reported that 2,327 young people were serving life without parole sentences for crimes committed while they were under the age of 18; the highest such figure in the world. Israel came in a distant second, with 7 young people serving life sentences.

At the turn of the millennium, it seemed an embarrassment to the United States that it remained the only country still to sign the United Nations Convention on the Rights of the Child. Yet the United States continued

---

1 (1976) 999 U. N. T. S. 171.
2 G. A. Res. 44/25, 28 ILM 1448.

executing juveniles and sentencing juveniles to life imprisonment without the possibility of parole until in a series of cases from 2002, and later, the U.S. Supreme Court seemed ready to alleviate the harshness of American judicial punishment. Generally, in democratic countries, in keeping with the principles of the separation of power, the legislature makes criminal law: it is within the scope of its power to decide whether or not to retain the death penalty, and to determine the severity of punishments for children. However, riding a wave of international opinion in favor of abolishing the death penalty, at least six countries abolished the death penalty by judicial means since 1990. In these countries, which include South Africa and several Eastern European countries, the judicial branches presumed some degree of responsibility for criminal policy-making power, and announced that the death penalty was unconstitutional as it violated either the right of life or prohibitions against cruel punishment in national constitutions.

Two decades earlier, the U.S. Supreme Court had attempted to use its judicial power to correct the exceptional harshness of American punishments, finding, in 1972, that death penalty statutes in all states and in federal courts were cruel and unusual, and in violation of the Eighth Amendment of the American Constitution. At the time, some Americans had expected that the death penalty would be eliminated altogether. However, led by President Nixon, thirty-five states and the federal government rewrote their death penalty laws so as to satisfy the new standards set by the Supreme Court and were successful in reinstituting the death penalty in 1976. Thereafter, U.S. states have deviated from the standard practices of other Western countries in their approach to the death penalty. In the protection of children's rights, the U.S. also lags behind much of the world community. Corresponding with popular opinion favouring harsh punishments of children offenders within American society, the Supreme Court has remoulded the juvenile punishment slowly and cautiously.

This article will explore what the American judiciary has done for justice for the nation's children. Firstly, it briefly reviews some key trends in the early history of the juvenile court, beginning with social reformers' founding of houses of refuge and reform schools for children in the 1820s, then focusing on the formal beginnings in the Illinois Juvenile Court Act of 1899. The Juvenile Court—a pioneer movement, the idea of which was to establish a separate court to administer justice as a kind and just parent might treat his children—attracted the attention of much of the world. However, after several decades of experimentation, the outcomes were quite disappointing in the United States. I will try to analyze at least some of the reasons for this failure. This paper will then review some U.S. Supreme Court cases which addressed juvenile justice, and probe the evolution of the Court's interpretation of the cruel and unusual punishments clause of the Eighth Amendment to the Constitution, and how to use it as a legal basis to reduce the harshness of the punishment of children.

2. The Early History of American Juvenile Justice

In the British Common Law tradition, children were relieved of criminal culpability if they were under the age of seven. This was based on the established principle of substantive infancy defence.[3] But above that age, they were considered as having attained the age of reason and were subjected to arrest, trial and to punishment like adult offenders, though there was a rebuttable presumption of incapacity to commit a capital felony until the age of 14. Under this theory, a 7-year-old child could be subject to capital punishment. American colonialists brought this tradition to the new continent. In American history, at least two ten-year-old boys were sentenced to death.[4] As part of the post-revolutionary movement to differentiate the new country from the old, early American reformers sought to discard the widespread use of capital punishment, which they saw as one of the worst aspects of their British inheritance. At the beginning of the nineteenth century, in Pennsylvania and New York, Quaker reformers succeeded in sharply reducing the number of offences punishable by death, and introduced alternative periods of long-term incarceration in newly established penitentiaries. The reformers hoped that stays in these institutions would also provide opportunities for inmates to be rehabilitated through religious penitence. At that time, from the view of European visitors, America had the most lenient criminal justice system in

[3] It called "irrebuttable presumption" in Blackstone's Commentaries. *See* 4, W. BLACKSTONE, COMMENTARIES ON THE LAW OF ENGLAND, 23-24 (1792); BLACK'S LAW DICTIONARY 777 (6th ed. 1990) (defining infancy).

[4] In 1855, an unnamed black boy was put to death in Alexandria, Louisiana. *See* QUINBY, THE GALLOWS, THE PRISON AND THE POOR HOUSE, 49-50 (1856). A Cherokee Indian boy named James Arcene was put to death in Fort Smith, Arkansas. *See* G. SHIRLEY, LAW WEST OF FORT SMITH 218 (1968).

the world.[5] It was even expected that the United States would abolish the death penalty in the near future.[6]

New York reformers also developed the idea of establishing a separate institution for juvenile offenders in which rehabilitation could proceed without the perceived contamination of incorrigible adults. Thus New York opened a House Of Refuge in 1824, and the Philadelphia House Of Refuge opened in 1828, and by 1850, eight more cities had houses of refuge, with many more founded in other cities throughout the 1850s. The houses of refuge emerged in eastern cities during the first half of the nineteenth century in conjunction with the first burst of industrialization, immigration and urbanization. They provided the first specialized institutions for the formal social control of youth, and juveniles' segregation preceded their judicial separation. The New York House Of Refuge was intended as an asylum, in which boys below a certain age, who became subject to the notice of the police, either as vagrants, or indigents, or after being charged with petty crimes, might be received. The typical practice of this era was to treat poor and neglected children and young criminals as a homogeneous group. It was believed that all such children needed to be controlled and reformed to prevent them from further eroding the social order as adult criminals. Poor and neglected children who were not yet criminalized by harmful influences of their depraved home environments were committed to the Houses of Refuge so that they would not become criminals.[7]

The legislation authorizing the commitment of children to institutions was thoroughly reflective of this belief that delinquent juveniles, minor offenders, and abused and neglected children could benefit from similar institutional placements: youths were segregated from adult offenders, the centrality of the rehabilitative goal, and the application of this system only to children deemed amenable to treatment. As of 1875, the Wisconsin

---

[5] *See, e.g.,* ALEXIS DE TOCQUEVILLE, DEMOCRACY IN AMERICA, (1835), reprinted (N.Y.: Vintage,1945)

[6] *See* HARRIET MARTINEAU , SOCIETY IN AMERICA (N.Y.: Saunders & Otley, 1837). In a sense this expectation is correct. The state of Michigan abolished the death penalty in 1846—the first territory to abolish capital punishment in the English-speaking world, and in few years Wisconsin and Rhode Island followed suit.

[7] R.PICKETT, HOUSE OF REFUGE: ORIGIN OF JUVENILE REFORM IN NEW YORK STATE, 1815-157, at 191 (Syracuse U. Pr., 1969).

legislature authorized the commitment of children who begged or received alms, wandered the streets without a home or proper guardianship, frequented the company of thieves, resided in a poor house, had one or both parents in prison, were orphaned, , , , or were abandoned by their parents. An important case upholding the involuntary commitment of these children to institutions, without the formal proceedings of criminal trial was *ex parte Crouse* decided in Pennsylvania in 1838.[8] The court relied on the doctrine of *parens patriae*—a Latin term for "parent of the country", which allowed the state to intervene when deemed necessary to fill the role of a parent of a minor.[9] This case set a precedent for twentieth century cases, holding that the juvenile court could similarly commit children without the traditional legal formalities.[10]

But by the 1850s, as the number of incarcerated children swelled and the seriousness of their offenses escalated, these institutions were replaced by larger ones in the form of industrial schools or reform schools. By then, such children were seen as needing not only kindness and care to be rehabilitated, but also stern discipline to remind them of the importance and authority of the law. In 1856, the Chicago Reform School was established, and legislation in 1857 and 1863 restricted placements in this school to those who—in the opinion of the court—would be a fit and proper subject for commitment. That court considered what was best for the welfare of the delinquent children, often with no formal charges laid against them, and without due regard for the severity of the crimes for which they had been arrested[11]. By the late 1860s, this system was proving unworkable. In 1870, the Illinois Supreme Court held it to be unconstitutional to confine to the Chicago Reform School a child who had not been charged with criminal conduct and not accorded due process at

[8] 4 Whart. 9 (PA 1838).

[9] "In the exercise of the state's *parens patriae* power, the courts of justice may, in their sound discretion, and when the moral, or safety, or interests of the children strongly require it, withdraw the infants from the custody of the father or mother, and place the care and custody of them elsewhere." J. KENT, COMMENTARIES ON AMERICAN LAW 203-205, (11th ed. Boston: Little Brown, 1867). *See also* Neil Cogan, *Juvenile Law before and after the Entrance of 'Parens Patriae'*, 22 S.C. L. REV. 147-151; Douglas Rendleman, *Parens Patriae: From Chancery to the Juvenile Court*, 23 S.C.L.REV. 205-259 (1971).

[10] *See* Commonwealth v. Fisher, 213 Pa.48, 62 Atl.198 (1905).

[11] Laws of Mar. 5, 1867, Sec. 4.3, Ill.Private Laws 32.

trial.[12] In 1872, the Chicago Reform School closed. Juveniles convicted of criminal offenses were committed to the prisons once again. Thus, for the last quarter of the nineteenth century, Illinois had almost no juvenile justice system whatsoever.

The Chicago Juvenile Court was established in 1899 by the "Act to Regulate the Treatment and Control of Dependent, Neglected and Delinquent Children".[13] Substantially, the Act did not create a new court, but articulated rules to be followed by the county court when it was considering children's cases, at which time, the court may be called the "Juvenile Court." The reform efforts behind the passage of the Illinois statute were intended to improve institutions that intervened on the behalf of children. Reformers showed little concern for the procedures used in these interventions, and the resulting statutory language provides few procedural guidelines. The only part of the law that addressed judicial procedures stated: "The court shall proceed to hear and dispose the case in a summary manner." The Act settled some of the placement issues raised by the reform campaign; validated the role of private agencies in the care of children; accepted the brokerage function of private organizations like the Visitation and Aid Society and religious institutional segregation; and proscribed detention of children in local jails or police stations, but provided for no alternative facilities. During the first year of the Court, the presiding judge sent 37 boys to the Grand Jury as not fit subjects for juvenile court treatment.[14] In so far as the Juvenile Court Act was intended to effect significant changes in the institutions to which Illinois children were subject, it was a failure.

In interpreting their mandate to act in a summary manner, juvenile court judges engaged in a kind of interpersonal exchange with the children who came before them. The cultivation of intimacy and trust between judge and child was a new phenomenon. This aspect of court practice may have originated with the Illinois court, or it may have been the result of the influence of the court of Judge Ben B. Lindsey in Denver, Colorado. In 1901, Lindsey was appointed to the county court bench in Denver, a position he was to hold until 1927. Within a year of his appointment,

---

[12] People *ex re.* O'Connell v. Turner, 55 Ill. 280 (1870).

[13] Illinois Juvenile Court Act, sec.5 (1899) Ill.Laws 133.

[14] *See* Sanford J. Fox, *The Reform of Juvenile Justice: An Historical Perspective*, 22 STAN. L. REV., 1187, at 1191(1970).

Lindsey came across an 1899 Colorado compulsory school statute designed to deal with children who had become school disciplinary problems. His attention soon focused on the plight of the young offenders. He convinced the district attorney to proceed against all children under this law. In 1903, after examining the laws in Illinois and Massachusetts, he successfully advocated the passage of "An Act Concerning Delinquent Children." In several respects, the Colorado juvenile court statute was broader than the 1899 Illinois act. It included jurisdiction over adults who contributed to the delinquency of minors, and it permitted county courts to place convicted youths between the ages of 16 and 21 on the same probation terms as those applied to younger children. Such developments promoted by the Denver juvenile court began informally and anonymously, but proved effective.[15]

Under Judge Lindsey's ægis, the Denver court uniquely embodied a deeply personal judicial involvement in the lives of the juvenile court children. Judge Lindsey was in reality a muckraking champion of the poor and the working class throughout the period he served as a kind of super salesman for the children's court. He preached the virtues of community treatment, probation, and a juvenile court fueled by optimistic compassion.[16] These methods were irregular, but they were practical, and in hundreds of episodes greatly aided the popularity of the juvenile court movement.

By 1905, 10 states had enacted some sort of juvenile court law; and by 1915, a total of 46 states, three territories, and the District of Columbia had done so.[17] However, the enthusiasm for enacting juvenile court statutes far outstripped changes in actual adjudication of cases. Most juvenile court judges could not follow Judge Lindsey's standard of employing personal charisma to engage and reform youths. They could rely only on existing programs to reform the children who came before the court. In addition to the institutions already in place, community-based intervention began through the use of probation. Even Lindsey relied to some extent on his

---

[15] C. Larsen, THE GOOD FIGHT: THE LIFE AND TIMES OF BEN B. LINDSEY, 29 (Chicago, Ill: Quadrangle Books, 1972).

[16] Early in the 20th century, Denver's Judge Ben Lindsey became the eighth most-admired man in America—a distinction as yet unequalled by any other member of the juvenile judiciary. *See id.*, at 7.

[17] K. LENROOT & E. LUNDBERG, JUVENILE COURTS AT WORK, United States Children's Bureau Publication No. 141 (Washington, D.C.: U.S. Government Printing Office, 1967).

probation staff to carry on his work of shepherding the court's children along the right path. In the other juvenile courts, probation officers were seen from the outset as critical to the success of the juvenile court's reforming enterprise.[18]

However, expanding caseloads and the increasing severity of the offences committed by the juveniles made clear the limitation of relying on untrained probation officers. It was becoming apparent that many of these children were psychopathic, and that they needed more skilled care and individual scientific investigation. In 1908, a Juvenile Psychopathic Institute was established in Chicago to support the reform responsibilities taken on by the initial cohort of juvenile judges. New scientific skills could considerably raise the efficiency of juvenile courts in their rehabilitation efforts. These had been generally adopted and recognized, and thus the core of the reform of delinquents moved gradually away from the judges into the hands of other professionals. Volunteer probation officers evolved into college-trained personnel and graduate social workers. Over time, professional psychologists and psychiatric consultants were added to the effort. Some child guidance clinics were attached to the juvenile courts. Individualized dispositions based on a scientific understanding of each child became the key after Judge Lindsey's tenure of the Denver juvenile court bench concluded.

3. American Juvenile Justice Policy was Changing after the Mid-20th Century

In the early twentieth century, with the development of new scientific knowledge, responsibility for rehabilitating juvenile offenders passed from the judiciary into the hands of professional psychologists, psychiatric consultants and social workers. The emphasis on the individual psychological lives of children was popularly recognized, and gave a rise to a child guidance movement that promised to raise considerably the efficiency of juvenile courts in their rehabilitation efforts. However, faith in the help offered by child guidance clinics was not to last. In 1934, criminologists published the results of a follow-up study of delinquents from Boston juvenile court who had the benefit of clinic procedures. This

[18] J. L. Schulz, *The Cycle of Juvenile Court History*, 19 CRIME & DELINQUENCY 457-76 (October 1973).

study revealed a recidivism rate of nearly 90 per cent.[19] Court clinics continued to exist following the disclosures, but belief in the ability of the clinics to rehabilitate diminished. The juvenile delinquent reform problem had presented society with a tough task since the industrialization and urbanization in American history, but law cannot by itself solve social problems. Many experiments have sought help from other different disciplines, but these have proven unable to stand the tests of time and change. Inevitably, later statutes and case law demanded that juvenile courts function as courts of law. As juvenile violent crime dramatically increased in the later half of the twentieth century, whenever a minor committed a heinous crime, people called for harsh punishment. Thereafter, the (Republican) President Nixon's "tough on crime" policy became popular in American society.

The 1960s brought great change to juvenile justice, beginning a trend toward blurring the lines between juvenile and adult criminal justice. With *Kent v. United States*, the Supreme Court heard the first of many cases that would profoundly change proceedings in the juvenile court.[20] In *Kent*, the Court held that juveniles are constitutionally entitled to the essentials of due process and fair treatment, and therefore ruled that Kent was entitled to a waiver hearing and explanation of the juvenile court's waiver decision. One year later, the Supreme Court continued its extension of constitutional due process rights to juveniles in *In re Gault.*[21] The Court explicitly rejected the concept of *parens patriae* and replaced individualized assessment and discretion with the juvenile's right to notice of the charges against the child, to legal counsel, to protections against self-incrimination, and to confront and cross-examine witnesses.[22] The Court stated that the early conception of the juvenile court proceeding was one in which a fatherly judge touched the heart and conscience of the erring youth by paternal advice and admonition, and benevolent and wise institutions of the State provided guidance and help to save him from a downward career. The Court concluded that the constitutional and theoretical basis for this

[19] S. GLUECK & E. GLUECK, ONE THOUSAND JUVENILE DELINQUENTS, 151 (Cambridge, MA: Harvard U. Pr., 1934).

[20] Kent v. United States, 383 U.S. 541 (1966).

[21] *In re* Gault, 387 U.S. 1 (1967).

[22] These kinds of protections and rights, as right to due process, right to fair trial, all are prescribed in the Fifth, Sixth and Seventh Amendments, known as procedural due process to protect a person accused of a crime.

peculiar system was debatable, citing the evidence provided by recent studies which sharply dissented on the validity of this gentler conception of the law, and suggested that the essentials of due process might present a more impressive and more therapeutic aspect of the law, so far as the juvenile was concerned; whereas Justice Stewart warned in his dissent that by requiring such due process guarantees, the Court's ruling served to convert a juvenile proceeding into a criminal prosecution.[23]

In the following years the Court continued to erode the difference between juvenile courts and adult criminal courts, in requiring the application of the proof beyond a reasonable doubt standard, and applying the double jeopardy protections of the Fifth Amendment. However, it expressly denied juveniles the constitutional protection of the right to trial by jury enshrined in the Fifth and Seventh Amendments.[24] In 1974, Congress passed a law designed to persuaded the states that 14- and 15-year-old boys and girls should not be detained in secure institutions resembling prisons, just because they disobey their parents or absent themselves from school, but the implementation of this legislation proved controversial.[25] From 1980 on, additional evidence that the juvenile justice pendulum had continued to swing from rehabilitative goals toward prosecution and retributive goals can be seen in the increased transfer of juveniles to the criminal court.[26] The 1980s and 1990s ushered in an era of substantial misperception regarding increases in juvenile crime. Professor John Dilulio, Jr. of Princeton University coined the term "juvenile super-predators" in describing this minor group. He warned the public that "on the horizon…are tens of thousands of severely morally impoverished juvenile super-predators."[27] Many states reacted by passing laws intended to

---

[23] *See supra* note 18, at 79 (Stewart, J., dissenting) ("A juvenile proceeding's whole purpose and mission is the very opposite of the mission and purpose of a prosecution in a criminal court. The object of the one is correction of a condition. The object of the other is conviction and punishment for a criminal act").

[24] *See, e.g., In re* Winship, 397 U.S. 358, 376 (1970); McKeiver v. Pennsylvania, 403 U.S. 528, 545 (1971); Breed v. Jones, 421 U.S. 519, 541 (1975).

[25] Juvenile Justice and Delinquency Prevention Act of 1974, 42 U.S.C. § 3723 (10) (H) (1974).

[26] *See* Bree Langemo, *Serious Consequences for Serious Juvenile Offenders: Do Juveniles Belong in Adult Court?* 30 OHIO N.U. L. REV.141 (2004).

[27] John J. Dilulio, Jr., *The Coming of the Super-Predators*, WEEKLY STANDARD, Nov. 27, 1995, at 23.

increase the incidence of dealing with juveniles as adults.[28] From 1992 to 1997, forty-four states, and the District of Columbia, modified transfer provisions in order to streamline the transfer process and facilitate easier prosecution of juveniles in criminal courts.[29] As at the end of the 2007, all states allowed adult criminal prosecution and sentencing of juveniles under some circumstances.[30]

Transfer laws vary by state, but generally fall into three categories: (1) Judicial waiver—certification, remand, or binding over; (2) concurrent jurisdiction—prosecutorial waiver, prosecutor discretion, or direct file; (3) statutory exclusion or legislative exclusion.[31] The mechanisms differ regarding where the decision responsibility for transfer exists. Under the third category (statutory exclusion), criminal courts are granted jurisdiction over a whole class of cases involving juveniles. A state legislature is essentially predetermining the question of criminal prosecution and taking the decision out of the hands of both the court and prosecutor. For example, in Illinois there are five specific crimes that automatically transfer a minor offender from juvenile to adult for adjudication purposes. These include first-degree murder, aggravated sexual assault, aggravated battery committed with a firearm, armed robbery committed with a firearm, and aggravated car hijacking committed with a firearm.[32] The severity of the crime, not the age of the accused, is what mandates trial and punishment as an adult. Like Illinois, twenty-seven states have made a sentence of life without parole mandatory if the juvenile is convicted of certain crimes. Additionally, forty-two states permit juveniles to be sentenced to life without parole.

It must be noted that without state transfer mechanisms, juveniles would never be subjected to such harsh punishments. In some states, certain adjudicated juvenile offenders face mandatory sentences of thirty years' imprisonment. A judge who sentenced a 15-year-old to life imprisonment without parole lamented the injustice resulting from his inability to use

---

[28] *See* HOWARD N. SNYDER & MELISSA SICKMUND, JUVENILE OFFENDERS AND VICTIMS: 2006 NATIONAL REPORT 96 (2006).

[29] *See* Donna M. Bishop, *Juvenile Offenders in the Adult Criminal Justice System*, 27 CRIME & JUST. 81, 84 (2000).

[30] Patrick Griffin, National Center of Juvenile Justice, NATIONAL OVERVIEWS: STATE JUVENILE JUSTICE PROFILES (2008).

[31] *See* SNYDER & SICKMUND, *supra* note 24, at 110.

[32] 705 Ill. Comp. Stst. 405/5-130 (2006).

discretion in the individualized case.[33] Another judge in South Carolina had extremely limited options under state law and was forced to sentence a 12-year-old child to imprisonment for thirty years without possibility of parole.[34] Approximately 73 children are serving life sentences for offences committed when 13 or 14,[35]and hundreds more are incarcerated due to a sentence imposed by judges whose hands were tied by mandatory sentencing schemes for adult offenders.[36] There is also a disturbing racial aspect that may catch the eye of public. Almost all of those children are African-American: ateast 70 per cent of the 73 13- or 14-year-old defendants are members of a racial minority. The tragedy of the situation should call attention to the core values of American society concerning the treatment of juveniles and punishment. Unfortunately, the zeal for retribution, which has replaced the desire to reform the individual child, ignores both the interests of the child and ultimately the interests of society.[37] It simultaneously loses sight of the innate developmental differences between adult and child, and fails to accommodate those distinctions.

4. The Evolution of the Interpretation of Cruel and Unusual Punishment

Are the proceeding protections of due process of law really in accord with the interest of juveniles? It would be better if children were recognized as belonging to a different category than adults, and received special treatment. But how can state statutes hostile to special treatment of children be challenged? Under a federal system, how can federal courts interfere with state legislatures? America's founding fathers had no prior concern with the fundamental rights or protections for people in drafting their Constitution. Only in the later ten Amendments of 1791, known as the Bill of Rights, which were strongly influenced by the 1689 English

---

[33] *See, e.g.* , ALISON PARKER, THE REST OF THEIR LIVES: LIFE WITHOUT PAROLE FOR CHILD OFFENDERS IN THE UNITED STATES, 90- 92 (2005).
[34] S.C. Code Ann. Sec.16-3-20(A)(2007) ("A person who is convicted of or pleads guilty to murder must punished by death, by imprisonment for life, or by a mandatory minimum tern of imprisonment for thirty years").
[35] EQUAL JUSTICE INITIATIVE, CRUEL AND UNUSUAL: SENTENCING 13- AND 14-YEARS-OLD CHILDREN TO DIE IN PRISON 20 (2007).
[36] *See supra* note 29.
[37] *See supra* note 25.

Bill of Rights,[38] are there any provisions concerning criminal proceedings and punishments. Among the Ten Amendments, the aforementioned Fifth, Sixth and Seventh Amendments concern due process of law. The Eighth Amendment is the only article of the constitution that mentions punishment, in which an anti-cruelty norm had accidentally developed as a substantive due process protection to criminal defenders, either of adults or children. This Amendment—the shortest article of the constitution—quoting directly from the English Bill of Rights, concisely prescribes that: "Excessive bail shall not be required, nor excessive fines imposed, nor cruel and unusual punishments inflicted".[39] In all English colonies, similar provisions were widespread. In the United States, this was initially presented in the charters of American colonies, and later in American state and federal constitutions. Much later, the same appeared in South Africa's constitution of 1993, and thus afforded a legal basis for its constitutional court to abolish the death penalty there in 1995.[40]

What does "cruel and unusual punishments" mean? Following the English Glorious Revolution of 1688, the Bill of Rights was introduced to outlaw certain gruesome methods of punishment—such as torture, bodily mutilation, burning at the stake, disemboweling, quartering or crucifixion, in order to prevent the ruler from making use of such cruel and unusual punishments to suppress political dissent.[41] In 1833, a Harvard law professor commented that this clause is superfluous in America's modern, civilized society, and is only retained for admonition.[42] Indeed, it was effectively dormant for nearly a century, never cited or mentioned in legal field. One of the reasons for its relative desuetude is that prior to the

---

[38] For example, the right to due process of law provided in the Fifth Amendment has been recognized since 1215, when the English Magna Carta was issued.

[39] "That excessive bail ought not to be required, nor excessive fines imposed, nor cruel and unusual punishments inflicted." R. PERRY, SOURCES OF OUR LIBERTIES 247 (1959).

[40] State v. T. Makwanyane and Mchunu, Case No. CCT/3/94 (1995), in the Constitutional Court of the Republic of South Africa. *See* WILLIAIM A. SCHABAS, "South Africa's Constitutional Court Outlaws the Death Penalty," in WAR CRIMES AND HUMAN RIGHTS : ESSAYS ON THE DEATH PENALTY, JUSTICE, AND ACCOUNTABILITY (2008).

[41] *See* Anthony F. Granucci, *"Nor Cruel and Unusual Punishments Inflicted": The Original Meaning*, 57 CAL. L. REV. 856-60 (1969).

[42] *See* JOSEPH STORY, COMMENTARIES ON THE CONSTITUTION OF THE UNITED STATES 710-11 (1833).

adoption of the Fouteenth Amendment, the protections in the first Ten Amendments limited only the actions of the federal government. But beginning in 1925,[43] the Supreme Court, in what is called "the doctrine of incorporation" interpreted the Fourteenth Amendment to apply most provisions of the Bill of Rights to state and local governments as well. The cruel and unusual punishments clause was incorporated in *Robinson v. California* in 1962,[44] and thereafter applied to the states.

At the end of Nineteenth century, the Supreme Court had, for the first time, to consider whether newly invented execution methods were cruel and unusual in two cases. In *Wilkerson v. Utah,*[45] the Court held that in Utah territory, which was under federal jurisdiction, using a firing squad to replace hanging was not cruel and unusual. In *In re Kemmler,*[46] the Court held that New York State's use of the electric chair to replace hanging was unusual, but not cruel. At the time, the Eighth Amendment had not yet been applied to the states, and the federal court had no jurisdiction over state sanctions, so the Court deferred its decision to New York. In the past, the death penalty was imposed in jurisdictions around the world. In the United States, although few states had abolished the death penalty, nobody doubted its constitutionality until the mid-twentieth century.

The cruel and unusual punishments clause prohibits the imposition of inherently brutal punishments under all circumstances. If strictly confined to its original meaning—prohibiting ancient, gruesome methods of punishment that withered away long ago—the clause would have become a dead letter. But in a 1908 lecture, Chief Justice Hughes said: "We are under a Constitution, but the Constitution is what the judges say it is,"[47] thereby asserting that the institution with the absolute authority to interpret the legal document is the lawgiver.[48] In 1910, in *Weems v. United States*,[49]

---

[43] Gitlow v. New York, 268 U.S. 652 (1925).
[44] 370 U.S. 660 (1962)(holding that sentencing narcotics addiction imprisonment for 90 days is cruel punishment). The first two clauses concerning excessive bail and excessive fines have not incorporated by the Supreme Court, therefore cannot be applied to states yet.
[45] 99 .U.S. 130 (1878).
[46] 136 U.S. 436 (1890).
[47] CHARLES EVENS HUGHES, ADDRESSES, 139 (N.Y.: G.P. Putman & Sons, 1908)
[48] *See* Thayer, *The Origin and Scope of the American Doctrine of Constitutional Law*, 7 HARVARD. L. REV. 129, 152 (1893); A. MASON & W. BEANEY, THE SUPREME COURT IN A FREE SOCIETY 1 (1968).

the Court expanded the meaning of cruel and unusual punishments, when the Court considered punishments challenged not as inherently brutal but disproportionate to the crime. The Court emphasized that the concept of proportionality is central to the Eighth Amendment. Embodied in the constitution's ban on cruel and unusual punishments is the precept of justice that punishment for crime should be graduated and proportioned to the offence. The Court further pointed out that the meaning of cruel punishments "is not fastened to the obsolete, but may acquire meanings as public opinion becomes enlightened by a humane justice". In this case, the Court held that disproportionate punishment was cruel and unusual.

In the mid-twentieth century, the Court stepped in, further expanding the meaning of cruel punishments. In *Trop v. Dulles*, the Court said: "The prohibition against cruel and unusual punishments…must be interpreted according to its text, by considering history, tradition, and precedent, and with due regard for its purpose and function in the constitution design. To implement this framework we have established the propriety and affirmed the necessity of referring to the evolving standards of decency that make the progress of a maturing society to determine which punishments are so disproportionate as to be cruel and unusual".[50] The *Trop* plurality is most well known for invoking "the evolving standards of decency" which infers that determinations of what constitutes cruelty should change with time. The four-Justice dissent (Frankfurter, J., dissenting, joined by Justice Harlan) pointed out that objective evidence of decency standards, including nearly a century of federal practice as well as the laws of other countries, belied the majority's conclusion. The "objective evidence of decency standards" argument in dissent also prefigures the "national consensus" rationale in later cases like *Atkins, Roper,* and *Kennedy*.[51] This was a groundbreaking decision which afforded the development of cruel and unusual punishments application, and expanded the legal basis for later courts to strike down many harsh and grossly disproportionate

[49] 217 U.S. 349 (1910).

[50] 356 U.S. 86 (1958) (holding unconstitutional, as beyond Congress's war power, a statute authorizing expatriation of a soldier convicted by military court martial if deserting the United States army, because in a civilized country expatriation could not be allowed).

[51] Atkins v. Virginia, 536 U.S. 304 (2002); Roper v. Simmons, 543 U.S. 551 (2005); Kennedy v. Louisiana, 554 U.S.__; 128 S.Ct.2641 (2008).

punishments, including the juvenile death penalty and life imprisonment without parole.

The U.S. Supreme Court revived the cruel punishments clause, in an episode worthy of note. The first person who had the idea of using the cruel punishments clause as a defence for his client was Gerald H. Gottlieb, of the American Civil Liberties Union (ACLU) in Los Angeles. During the days of the civil rights movement, lawyers had used various means—the due process of law, equal protection clause, a series of statistical data as evidence of race discrimination—to attack the death penalty, but without success.[52] In a 1961 case, Gottlieb prepared a new argument, citing the cruel punishments clause to defend his client should he be sentenced to death. Instead, he was sentenced to life imprisonment, but Gottlieb let the argument be published.[53] In 1962, the newly appointed Justice Arthur Goldberg was so much annoyed by a flow of death penalty cases being appealed to the Supreme Court that he assigned his law clerk, Alan Dershowitz, to collect all possible arguments to attack the death penalty and prepare a memorandum for future decisions. When this memorandum first appeared in the courtroom, it shocked the Justices. The argument that, according to the evolving standards of decency, the death penalty cannot be accepted in a civilized society as it violated the Eighth Amendment, had never before been heard. It was considered so shocking that the Chief Justice Earl Warren—known for his most liberal court—held onto this document lest it undermine the reputation of the Court, should it be released to the public.[54]

In that Court only two Justices, William O. Douglas and William J. Brennan, agreed with Goldberg, and thereafter the three Justices joined together in writing a dissenting opinion supporting this argument.[55] Building on that publicized minority opinion, civil rights lawyers successfully used the moratorium strategy by large-scale appealing death

---

[52] J. Greenberg & J. Himmelstein, *Varieties of Attack on the Death Penalty*, 15 CRIME & DELINQUENCY 114-15 (1969).

[53] Gerald H. Gottlieb, *Testing the Death Penalty*, 34 S. CAL. L. REV. 268-81 (1961).

[54] This document was published 25 years later. Arthur J. Goldberg, *Memorandum to the Conference Re: Capital Punishment*, October Term,1963, 27 S. TEX.L.REV.493-506 (1986).

[55] Rudolph v. Alabama, 375 U.S. 889 (1963) (Goldberg, J. dissenting from the denial of *certiorari*) (joined by Douglas and Brennan, JJ.).

sentences to the Supreme Court, which culminated in almost ten years without a single execution from 1967, and then the landmark *Furman* decision in 1972.[56] The innovative ideas of these three persons, Gerald Gottlieb, Arthur Goldberg and Alan Dershowitz, and the five concurring Justices, civil rights lawyers, individuals and associations may be collectively credited with the *Furman* victory.[57] From its first use in 1878, to *Furman*, the cruel and unusual punishments clause had been cited only ten times.[58] After *Furman*, the clause became one of the most-cited constitutional rights in the U.S.

Furman was an epoch-making decision: the first case to invalidate all state statutes on the death penalty in American history. Just a year before, in *McGautha v. California*,[59] the Supreme Court had upheld the constitutionality of the death sentence, and the public was shocked by this reversal. The case presented no majority opinion, only a short *per curiam* stating: "This Court holds that the imposition and carrying out of the death penalty in these cases constitutes cruel and unusual punishment in violation of the Eighth and Fourteenth Amendments". Of the five concurring Justices, only two justices, William Brennan and Thurgood Marshall, held that the death penalty sentence by itself was cruel and unusual; the other Justices recognized the death trial process was unfair: full of racial discrimination, lacking consistency, and (in Justice Stewart's words) so wanton and freakish. It seemed that if the death sentence could be administered fairly, free from arbitrariness, caprice and discrimination,

---

[56] Furman v. Georgia, 408 U.S. 238 (19 72). One of the significant decisions of the United States Supreme Court is Furman v. Georgia, 408 U.S. 238 (1972). The case ruled on the condition for a degree of consistency in the implementation of the death penalty. The case became a cause of a *de facto* suspension of capital punishment in the United States, coming to an end when Gregg v. Georgia was decided in 1976.

[57] Although Justice Goldberg left the Supreme Court before the *Furman* case was decided, he still cared, and supported abolishing the death penalty. *See* Goldberg & Dershowitz, *Declaring the Death Penalty Unconstitutional*, 83 HARV. L. REV. 1773 (1970).

[58] Wilkerson v. Utah, 99 U.S. 130 (1878); *In re* Kemmler, 136 U.S. 436 (1890); O'Neil v. Vermont, 144 U.S. 323 (1892) (dissenting opinions); Howard v. Fleming, 191 U.S. 126 (1903); Weems v. United States, 217 U.S. 349 (1910); Badders v. United States, 240 U.S. 391 (1916); Louisiana *ex rel.* Francis v. Resweber, 329 U.S. 459 (1947); Trop v. Dulles, 356 U.S. 86 (1958); Robinson v. California, 370 U.S. 660 (1962); Powell v. Texas, 392 U.S. 514 (1968).

[59] 402 U.S. 183 (1971).

they could support it. Hence, four years later, in *Gregg v. Georgia*,[60] only Brennan and Marshall remained in the minority, resisting the reinstitution of the death penalty in the United States.

5. What has the Supreme Court done for American Juvenile Justice?

The British Parliament announced a moratorium on the death penalty in United Kingdom in 1965, around the same time the United States delayed executions for some death cases pending in the courts. The British Parliament formally abolished the death penalty in 1969, and thereafter initiatives to reinstitute the death penalty came to Parliament every year for 14 successive years, but none ever passed. The last, unsuccessful, attempt to reinstitute the death penalty was made in 1994. After the *Furman* decision, some Americans might have expected that the United States would abolish the death penalty forever, as is the case in the UK. But that is a quite different case. In an integrated society with substantial racial minorities and immigrants, the United States had extremely high rates of violent crime, compared with any other western country. Voters demanded harsh treatment of criminals, and politicians responded with tougher sentences and more criminal prohibitions. This dynamic was particularly powerful during the late 1960s and 1970s. Presidential candidate Richard Nixon's election theme "tough on crime" was very popular, and he won the election. The *Furman* decision attracted public attention and prodded more people to support the death penalty, and the decision became a target of scorn for the public. A large scale nation-wide backlash was unavoidable. President Nixon appointed Robert Bork, a famous death penalty supporter, as his Solicitor-General, and instructed him to seek to overturn the case. Thirty-five states and the federal government subsequently revised their death penalty laws to remedy the unfairness deficit of the trial that *Furman* court had pointed out. Four years later, in *Gregg*, the Court held that, in some strictly defined circumstances, the death penalty did not violate the Eighth Amendment.

As powerful as the American judiciary is, the Supreme Court cannot necessarily resist popular pressure. President Nixon, and successive Republican Presidents, had opportunities to appoint more conservative

[60] 428 U.S. 153 (1976).

Justices to the Court, and thus brought about the very conservative court of Rehnquist. After *Gregg*, all the states had to improve the trial process, by adopting a bifurcated procedure. This includes the guilt stage and penalty stage, and instructing juries to consider all relevant aggravating and mitigating circumstances: some states even required a pre-sentence hearing during the penalty stage. The trial process may even consider the establishment of a specified set of aggravating circumstances before imposing a death sentence. The Court would defer to the states if the sentences were not grossly disproportionate to the severity of the crime. Thereafter, although the Court had apparently shifted in a conservative direction, it acted cautiously to restrain the application of the death penalty, for example, invalidating mandatory death penalty statutes, [61] and removing some categories from the list of capital offences.[62] The Court has done much more than for adults in the area of juvenile justice. As for abolishing the death penalty for all offences, it failed in 1976. However, it did succeed in abolishing the juvenile death penalty and life imprisonment without parole, and that relatively limited was more or less in concert with American public opinion, and thus continues to lag far behind the standards of the world community.

In a 1982 juvenile death penalty case, *Eddings v. Oklahoma,*[63] the Court eschewed the issue of the constitutionality of putting a 16-year-old boy to death, noting only that the age of the condemned was a mitigating factor in considering the sentence. In 1988, the Court was involved with the juvenile death penalty issue when it heard *Thompson v. Oklahoma.*[64] The defendant, Thompson, committed murder when he was 15 years old. A plurality of the Court determined that American standards of decency did not permit the execution of any offender under the age of 16 because no death penalty state that had conducted any examination of the issue had chosen an age lower than 16. The Court observed that it would offend civilized standards of decency to execute a person who was under 16 at the time of his offence, and made reference to the English Common Law

[61] Woodson v. North Carolina, 428 U.S. 280 (1976); Robert v. Louisiana, 428 U.S. 325 (1976).

[62] Rape without killing, such as adult woman rape, Coker v. Georgia, 423 U.S. 584 (1977); child rape, Kennedy v. Louisiana, 128 S.Ct. 2641 (2008); No intent to kill and not the person who actually kill, Enmund v. Florida, 458 U.S. 572 (1982).

[63] 455 U.S. 104 (1982).

[64] 487 U.S. 815 (1988).

tradition, and to the views of the leading members of the western European community. The opinion further underlined that the imposition of the death penalty on under 16-year-olds by juries is rather rare, the last such execution being carried out in 1948. Also, the Court stressed the that lesser culpability of offenders under 16 made the death penalty inappropriate as a form of retribution. And it furthermore declared that it was unlikely that offenders engaged in the kind of cost-benefit analysis that attached any weight to the possibility of execution, which made the death penalty ineffective as means of deterrence. With Justice O'Connor concurring in the judgment, the Court set aside the death sentence imposed on the 15-year-old offender.

However, the next year, in *Stanford v. Kentucky*,[65] the Court referred to the prevailing public mood and concluded the Eighth and Fourteenth Amendments did not proscribe the execution of juvenile offenders over 15 but under 18. The Court noted that 22 of the 37 death penalty states permitted the death penalty for 16-year-old offenders, and 25 states permitted it for 17-year-old offenders. These numbers indicated there was no national consensus sufficient to label a particular punishment cruel and unusual. Justice Scalia, writing for the opinion, emphatically rejected the suggestion that the Court should bring its own judgment to bear on the acceptability of the juvenile death penalty. The same day that the Court decided *Stanford*, it delivered its decision in *Penry v. Lynaugh*,[66] holding that the Eighth Amendment did not mandate a categorical exemption from the death penalty for the mentally retarded. The Court stressed that only two states had enacted laws banning the imposition of the death penalty on a mentally retarded person convicted of a capital offence, which, even added to the 14 states that have completely rejected capital punishment, did not provide sufficient evidence of a national consensus. After these two cases, the Court regularly used a state-counting method to determine whether or not a national consensus existed.

In 2002, sentencing the mentally retarded death was reconsidered in *Atkins v. Virginia,*[67] and the Court held that standards of decency had evolved since *Penry*, and now demonstrate that the execution of the mentally retarded was cruel and unusual punishment, based on objective indicia of

---

[65] 492 U.S. 361 (1989).
[66] 492 U.S. 302 (1989).
[67] 536 U.S. 206 (2002).

society's standards, as expressed in legislative enactments and state practices with respect to executions of the mentally retarded. When *Atkins* was decided, 30 states prohibited the death penalty for the mentally retarded, including states that had abandoned the death penalty altogether. In 2005, when the Court reexamined the juvenile death penalty in *Roper v. Simmons,*[68] a similar state-number calculation had applied to demonstrate national consensus. There were 30 states prohibiting the juvenile death penalty, and even in the 20 states without formal prohibition, the practice is infrequent. In the previous 10 years, only three states, Texas, Virginia and Oklahoma, had executed juvenile prisoners. In December 2003, the Governor of Kentucky commuted Kevin Stanford's[69] death sentence to life imprisonment without parole, and ensured that Kentucky would not be added to the list of states executing minors. The consistency in the trend towards abolition of the practice provided sufficient evidence that contemporary society viewed juveniles as categorically less culpable than the average criminal. Basing its decision on a majority of states having rejected the imposition of the death penalty on juvenile offenders under 18, the Court held that this standard was required by the Eighth Amendment.

The Supreme Court also exercised its own independent judgment. As the death penalty is the most severe punishment, it must be limited to those offenders who commit the most serious crimes and whose extreme culpability makes them the most deserving of execution. Three general differences between juveniles and adults demonstrate that juvenile offenders cannot reliably be classified among the worst offenders: a) juveniles' susceptibility to immature and irresponsible behaviour means that their conduct is not as morally reprehensible as that of adults; b) their vulnerability to peer pressure means they have a greater claim than adults to be forgiven for failing to escape negative influences in their whole environment; c) the reality that juveniles still struggle to define their identity means it is less supportable to conclude that even a heinous crime committed by a juvenile is evidence of irretrievably depraved character. This judgment found confirmation in the stark reality that the United States was the only country in the world that continues to give official sanction to the juvenile death penalty.[70] Acknowledging that Article 37 of the United Nations Convention on the Rights of the child, Article 6(5) of

---

[68] 543 U.S. 551 (2005).
[69] Stanford v Kentucky: see above
[70] Iran is also notoriously known for imposing the death penalty on juveniles.

the International Covenant of Civil and Political Rights (ICCPR), and other parallel significant international treaties expressly prohibit capital punishment for crimes committed by juveniles under 18, the Court concluded that although the overwhelming weight of international opinion against the juvenile death penalty did not determine the court's outcome, it did provide respectable and significant confirmation of the court's conclusions.

This decision nonetheless met with four dissents. Evidenced by 20 states' enactments, the dissenters argued that there was no national consensus. The dissenting opinions are even longer than that of the majority. Justice Scalia argued that the state-counting method should not include states that had abolished the death penalty altogether, because 18 of 38 states—or 47 per cent of the states that permit capital punishment—now have legislation prohibiting the execution of offenders under the age of 18, and the views of less than 50 per cent cannot by itself be sufficient to constitute a national consensus. Scalia also protested the referencing of the views of other countries and the so-called international community that took centre stage in the Court's opinion. He noted that the United States made a reservation to the ICCPR in 1992 of the right to impose capital punishment on persons below 18, and that that reservation was still in place. He also reminded Court watchers that, in addition to barring the execution of offenders under 18, the United Nations Convention on the Rights of the Child prohibited their punishment with life in prison without the possibility of release. If the Court were truly going to get in line with the international community, then its reassurance that the death penalty is not needed since "the punishment of life imprisonment without the possibility of parole is itself a severe sanction", must be read as ironic. This reminder may have foreshadowed the recent case of *Graham v. Florida*,[71] which was decided in May 2010.

In *Sullivan v. Florida* and *Graham v. Florida*, Florida sentenced juvenile defendants to life in prison without the possibility of parole for non-homicide offenses. These are two "companion" cases which the U.S. Supreme Court agreed to review in 2009. On May 17, 2010, the Court decided on *Graham* but dismissed *Sullivan* as improvidently granted. In *Graham*, the Supreme Court follows its 2005 *Roper v. Simmons* decision, expanding its finding that young offenders must treated differently than

[71] 130 S.Ct. 2011 (2010).

adults. The Court ruled 6-3 that juveniles may not be sentenced to life in prison without parole for any crime short of homicide. Chief Justice Roberts joined the majority in agreeing that Graham's sentence was unconstitutionally harsh, but then broke with the rest of the majority in arguing that sometimes even non-homicidal crimes by juveniles are so reprehensible that they deserve life without parole. The ruling marked the first time that the Court excluded an entire class of offenders from a given form of punishment outside the context of the death penalty. No longer was it true that only "death is different"; children were also different. Following *Graham*, life without parole for non-homicide crime is disallowed. This falls short of the international standard, which rejects that punishment for any crime, but it is a small step in that direction. This is what the Supreme Court can do now under the public pressure in American society.[72]

6. Conclusion

The institutions and mission of the child-saving movement of early attempts to reform American juvenile justice were based on the doctrine of *parens patriate* – that the state steps in as a substitute parent to act in the best interests of delinquent and troublesome youth. The juvenile court was founded in 1899 in Illinois, and charged with employing the concepts of diminished responsibility and room-to-reform to explore what principles of punishment were most appropriate for adolescent delinquents. This new court was granted jurisdiction over cases in which minors were found to be neglected, dependent, or delinquent. The objective of the court was to provide assistance to all children who came under its authority. Informal proceedings were preferred to formal ones, so that the degree of state intervention lay within the discretion of the judge. There is compelling evidence demonstrating that key early twentieth century romantic and authoritarian figures of juvenile courts were sincerely dedicated to the welfare of youth. Writing in 1909, Judge Julian Mack declared that the purpose of the juvenile court was not so much to punish as to reform; not to degrade but to uplift; not to crush but develop; not to make him a criminal but a worthy citizen.[73] The rule of this rehabilitative ideal went unchallenged for more than a half-century.

---

[72] See the Appendix for facts regarding these two cases.

[73] Judge Julian Mack, *The Juvenile Court*, 23 HARV. L. REV., 104-122, at 107 (1909).

It was not until the final third of the twentieth century that the U.S. Supreme Court considered the question of procedural protections required under due process in cases in which the accused delinquents were in jeopardy of being sentenced to secure confinement in state institutions.[74] The important issue in *In re Gault*, decided in 1967, was the need for informality if the court was to achieve its child-saving mission. In *Gault*, the Court held that due process requires recognition of a privilege against self-incrimination, the right to confront witnesses and the right to cross-examination. Justice John Harlan, dissenting from the *Gault* majority, thought that rigid due process might do a disservice to the cause of juvenile justice, and would create an atmosphere akin to an ordinary criminal trial, thereby frustrating a central purpose of these specialized courts. Since then, the original theory of governmental beneficence and childhood dependence that *Gault* rejected has not been replaced with any substantial framework of basic legal principles. Nevertheless, the core concern of the juvenile court—preventing children from being treated as criminals—although differing in its procedures, remained as sharply in focus in 1999 as in 1899.

In the late twentieth century, the modern juvenile court came under sustained attack. At the federal level, the legislative majorities attempted to use federal financial incentives to push a series of standards designed to push for more punitive sanctions within the delinquency jurisdiction of the juvenile court, and easier transfers of serious juvenile offenders to criminal courts.[75] A century after its creation, the major premises supporting the creation of the juvenile court have been uniformly adopted and enshrined in policy in every advanced legal system. Transferring defendants still young enough for juvenile court to criminal court has become the universal exception, rather than a universal rule. In almost every American state, while particular procedures and the circumstances that justify the recourse to exceptions vary, provisions for the transfer of some cases are just as universal as the general policies they modify.

By the time *In re Gault* was decided, the punitive content of juvenile court sanctions for delinquency had become the central factual premise on which modern procedural protections were based. A typical worst case

---

[74] Francis Allen, *The Juvenile Court and Limits on Juvenile Justice*, in THE BORDERLAND OF CRIMINAL JUSTICE 42, 50-54 (Chicago: U. of Chi. Pr. 1964).
[75] *See, e.g.*, S.10, 105th Cong. (1997); H.R. 3 105th Cong. (1997).

facing a metropolitan juvenile court with a maximum jurisdiction age of 18 would be intentional homicide committed by a 16- or 17-year-old. In some such cases, it seems apparent that the range of punishments available to a juvenile court would fall far short of community expectations. Some accommodation to public pressure for greater punishment in serious cases became universal across the United States. All manner of older, recidivist, and recalcitrant juveniles thus found themselves pushed into criminal courts once the channel between the two institutions was opened. American juvenile offenders constitute the largest number of youths, worldwide, still sentenced to death or life imprisonment. With the United States' reservations to the International Covenant on Civil and Political Rights, and with the country having not yet signed the Convention on the Rights of the Child, this situation will not likely be changed by American legislative power in the near future. The next-best hope for rapid action to redress the plight of American delinquent children comes from the judiciary branch. The Supreme Court has gone some distance down that path at the start of the twenty-first century, but the system still falls short of world community standards.

Appendix: Facts of Two Cases

Case I

In 1989, Joe Sullivan, 13, and two older accomplices robbed an elderly woman. Sullivan and one accomplice returned later that day and Sullivan allegedly beat and raped the 72-year-old woman. Pursuant to an automatic transfer for this serious felony, Sullivan faced trial in adult criminal court and was sentenced to life in prison without the possibility of parole. He appealed his conviction, but his court-appointed lawyer filed an *Anders* brief, which means that he wishes to withdraw from a case believing an appeal to be frivolous. The state intermediate appellate court affirmed the conviction without an opinion in 1991. The Florida Supreme Court dismissed review without an opinion later that year. In 1992, Sullivan filed a petition for post-conviction review without an attorney, which was denied in 1996. He did not appeal the denial of this petition for post-conviction relief. In 2005 The U.S. Supreme Court struck down the death penalty for juvenile murderers in *Roper v. Simmons*. He in turn filed a motion for post-conviction relief under Florida's Rule of Criminal Procedure. In October 2007, a Florida trial court dismissed the motion, finding that *Roper* only applied to death-penalty cases and should not be extended. He appealed to the State Intermediate Appellate Court, which affirmed without an opinion in 2008. Because the Florida Supreme Court cannot hear a case from a *per curiam* affirmed decision of the lower court, Sullivan petitioned the U.S. Supreme Court for review. The Court granted his petition on May 4, 2009.

Case II

In 2003, 16-year-old Terrance Jamar Graham attempted to rob a restaurant with two other individuals. One of the other perpetrators hit the restaurant manager over the head with a steel bar. Prosecutors charged Graham as an adult with armed burglary, assault and battery, and attempted armed robbery. Graham pleaded guilty to the crimes in December 2003. Under his guilty plea, he spent 12 months in a pretrial detention facility and was to be on probation for three years. In December 2004, six months after his release from the detention facility, he was arrested after participating in a home-invasion robbery. His probation officer filed an affidavit alleging that Graham has violated terms of his probation. The court revoked Graham's probation and sentenced him to life imprisonment. Graham filed a post-sentencing motion with the trial court challenging the legality of his sentence on Eighth Amendment grounds. That motion was denied. He appealed to the Florida District Court of Appeal. The appeals court denied the claims and refused to follow the *Roper* line of reasoning because "death is different." The Florida Supreme Court declined to exercise its discretionary jurisdiction. Graham then petitioned the U.S. Supreme Court, which granted review on May 4, 2009.

List of Cases

1.	People *ex re.* O'Connell v. Turner,	55 Ill. 280	(1870).
2.	Wilkerson v. Utah,	99 .U.S. 130	(1878).
3.	*In re* Kemmler,	136 U.S. 436	(1890).
4.	Commonwealth v. Fisher,	213 Pa.48, 62 Atl.198	(1905).
5.	Weems v. United States,	217 U.S. 349	(1910).
6.	Gitlow v. New York,	268 U.S. 652	(1925).
7.	Trop v. Dulles,	356 U.S. 86	(1958).
8.	Robinson v. California,	370 U.S. 660	(1962).
9.	Rudolph v. Alabama,	375 U.S. 889	(1963).
10.	Kent v. United States,	383 U.S. 541	(1966).
11.	*In re* Gault,	387 U.S. 1	(1967).
12.	*In re* Winship,	397 U.S. 358, 376	(1970).
13.	McKeiver v. Pennsylvania,	403 U.S. 528, 545	(1971).
14.	McGautha v. California,	402 U.S. 183	(1971).
15.	Furman v. Georgia,	408 U.S. 238	(1972).
16.	Breed v. Jones,	421 U.S. 519, 541	(1975).
17.	Gregg v. Georgia,	428 U.S. 153	(1976).
18.	Woodson v. North Carolina,	428 U.S. 280	(1976).
19.	Robert v. Louisiana,	428 U.S. 325	(1976).
20.	Coker v. Georgia,	423 U.S. 584	(1977).
21.	Enmund v. Florida,	458 U.S. 572	(1982).
22.	Eddings v. Oklahoma,	455 U.S. 104	(1982).
23.	Thompson v. Oklahoma,	487 U.S. 815	(1988).
24.	Stanford v. Kentucky,	492 U.S. 361	(1989).
25.	Penry v. Lynaugh,	492 U.S. 302	(1989).
26.	State v. T. Makwanyane and Mchunu,	Case No. CCT/3/94	(1995).
27.	Atkins v. Virginia,	536 U.S. 304	(2002).
28.	Roper v. Simmons,	543 U.S. 551	(2005).
29.	Kennedy v. Louisiana,	554 U.S.; 128 S.Ct.2641	(2008).
30.	Graham v. Florida,	130 S.Ct. 2011	(2010).

THE SWEDISH ENFORCEMENT OF CLOSED JUVENILE CARE

LISA RAGNESTEN

Abstract

This article describes the application of the criminal sanction of closed juvenile care in Sweden. It is meant to try to answer the questions why the criminal sanction was introduced into the Swedish Penal Code, how the courts are assessing it and in what way the court's sentence is enforced. The first section contains a brief introduction to the topic, describing some of the related problems. This is followed by three sections, each trying to answer the questions *why?*, *how?*, or *in what way?* with respect to closed juvenile care. The article ends with a discussion about some of the conclusions that are drawn.

1. Introduction

According to The Swedish Penal Code (19762:700)[1] (SPC) Chapter 1, Section 3, there are only two types of punishment—fines and imprisonment. Criminal sanctions are, besides the two types of punishment, conditional sentence, probation, and committal for special care. The SPC also lays down that a person cannot be sentenced at all until the age of 15 (Ch. 1, Sec. 6). If the juvenile commits a crime on which imprisonment can follow before the age of 18, the SPC declares that 'the court may impose imprisonment only if there are extraordinary reasons for doing so'. If the juvenile was 18, but not 21, when the crime was committed, the court may instead 'impose imprisonment only if, in view of the penal value of the crime or other special reasons, this course of action is justified' (Ch. 30, Sec. 5). To clarify, the maximum difference between the two of them lies in extraordinary reasons compared to special reasons. For the former of

[1] Brottsbalk (1962:700). The translation is in accordance with Ds 1999:36, http://www.sweden.gov.se /content/1 /c6/02/77/77/cb79a8a3.pdf , 2010-10-08.

these two categories of young offenders, the law declares that they should, as a principal rule, be sentenced to closed juvenile care instead of imprisonment (Ch. 32, Sec. 5). The arguments are that it is not reasonable that young perpetrators should be sentenced as severely as adults, and also that imprisonment leads to particular risks for juveniles.[2]

Closed juvenile care is a fixed term custodial penalty: the term can be set from 14 days at the least to 4 years at the most (Ch. 32, Sec. 5 of the SPC). The enforcement takes part in a specially approved home, often also known in Sweden as a 'Section 12-home', so-called because the confinement takes place at the same location as youths who are being involuntarily cared for according to Section 3 of The Care of Young Persons Act (1990:52)[3] (CYPA). If a person under 20 who exposes his or her health or development to a palpable risk of injury through the abuse of addictive substances, criminal activity or some other socially degrading behaviour, needs to be kept under particularly close surveillance, he is sent to the same specially approved home as those who are sentenced to closed juvenile care (Sec. 3 and 12). Juveniles who have committed serious crimes may consequently serve their time in the same place as children who are in need of care and are cared for without consent (Sec. 1 and 3).

The discussion in this article is concentrates on both the 15-18 and 18-21 age groups, but with a particular focus on the former group. Both of these groups are the ones referred to when using terms such as 'the young', 'young offender' or similar. In the second section, *The Background of Closed Juvenile Care*, there is a brief report about why closed juvenile care was introduced into the Swedish legislation mechanism. The chapter is meant to answer the question 'why?' The next section deals with *Closed Juvenile Care – the Court's Assessment*, which examines what the exceptional and special sentencing reasons mean, together with the circumstances which militate against closed juvenile care being imposed. The main intention is hence to answer 'how?' In *The Enforcement of Closed Juvenile Care*, a discussion is held about how closed juvenile care is enforced, and the correlations between closed juvenile care and care without consent according to Section 3 CYPA.The chapter thus attempts to answer the question '*in what way*?' The final section is the *Conclusion*,

---

[2] Prop. 1997/98:96 Vissa reformer av påföljdssystemet, p. 156 f.

[3] Lag (1990:52) med särskilda bestämmelser om vård av unga. The translation is in accordance with www.swed en.gov.se/content/1/c6/04/34/03/0aed5a2b. pdf, 2010-10-08.

in which there is a discussion about some of the conclusions drawn in the article.

2. The Background of Closed Juvenile Care

Predictability, proportionality and consistency were previously considered to have not enough impact or clarity amongst the criminal sanctions for young offenders.[4] To give them greater weight, a new sanction was introduced on 1 January 1999—closed juvenile care.[5] Through closed juvenile care it became possible for the courts to pass a sentence that was considered to be sufficient intervention with regard to the current crime.[6] If the crime would have merited imprisonment, the court should, as a principal rule, sentence the youth to closed juvenile care instead. When making this assessment, the juvenile's need of care should not be taken into consideration. The intention was not to change the possibility according to court practice of depriving juveniles of their freedom.[7]

The purpose of the sanction, as explained above, was to replace imprisonment with closed juvenile care as a principal rule. It was seen as an increased risk that the young considered him- or herself as a criminal if he or she was in care of the Swedish Prison and Probation Service.[8] For this reason, the main responsibility for confinement continued to be laid on the social services.[9] Another reason was that the Swedish Prison and Probation Service had a lack of experience with imprisoned juveniles, since only a small number were sentenced to prison.[10]

Sweden has ratified the United Nations Convention on the Rights of the Child (CRC). Section 37 (c) CRC declares that 'every child deprived of liberty shall be separated from adults'. One exception is made and that is if it is considered in the best interests of the child not to be separated. That section is considered one of the main reasons why closed juvenile care was introduced.[11]

---

[4] Prop. 1997/98:96, p. 144.
[5] Prop. 1997/98:96, p. 156 ff.
[6] Prop. 197/98:96, p. 160.
[7] Prop. 1997/98:96, p. 160.
[8] Kriminalvården.
[9] Prop. 1997/98:96, p. 143 f.
[10] Prop. 1997/98:96, p. 157.
[11] SPC Ch. 29, Sec. 1. Jareborg, Nils and Zila, Josef, Straffrättens påföljdslära, third edition, Norstedts Juridik AB, Mölnlycke, 2010, p. 51.

One can question why closed juvenile care is placed in the SPC's Chapter 32, when the determination of the fixed term for closed juvenile care is based on the same grounds as those for imprisonment. It is not the juvenile's need of care that determines the length of the criminal sanction, but the assessment of the penal value.[12] According to some writers, it is for 'distinctly political reasons' that the criminal sanction is applied in Chapter 32.[13] The Government bill of SPC claims that closed juvenile care is systematically correlated with the care of social services, and that is why they should be in the same Chapter. The intention was to make the sanctions easier to survey.[14] According to another opinion, the introduction of a new type of enforcement for imprisonment would have been better than closed juvenile care.[15]

3. Closed Juvenile Care – the Court's Assessments

According to Chapter 1, Section 6 in SPC, '[n]o sanction shall be imposed upon a person for a crime committed before attaining the age of fifteen'. To clarify: a person under the age of 15 is considered able to commit a crime, but no sanction can be imposed for the deed. A person must take full responsibility for crimes committed after the age of 21 (Ch. 29, Sec. 7). The court's assessment in the case when a person has committed a crime before turning 21 is a rather complex procedure. The following briefly describes the method and some of the problems that come with it. It should be pointed out that a remanding sanction is strictly the last alternative.[16] However, when describing the court's assessment below, no regard will be taken of other sanctions than imprisonment and closed juvenile care.

2.1. Assessing the Penal Value

To determine which criminal sanction the juvenile will be sentenced to and the length of the punishment for a crime that has been committed, the

---

[12] Prop. 1997/98: 96, p. 160.
[13] Borgeke, Martin, Månsson, Catharina, Den nya lagstiftningen om påföljder för unga lagöverträdare, SvJT 2007 s. 181, p. 183 f.
[14] Prop. 2005/06:165 Ingripanden mot unga lagöverträdare, p. 94 f. In English referred to as Government bill on Interventions with young offenders, http://www.sweden.gov.se/content/1/c6/07/16/92/68d81cee.pdf, 2010-10-08.
[15] Sitte Durling, Catharina, Påföljder för unga lagöverträdare, JT nr 1 2000/01 s. 236, p. 245.
[16] Prop. 1997/98:96, p. 160.

court applies Part Three, On Sanctions in the SPC. First, the court must assess the concrete penal value of the crime within the crime's scale of punishment, or its abstract penal value (Ch. 29, Sec. 1).[17] The concrete penal value shows how severe the crime committed is considered to be. The assessment of the penal value is the starting point for the entire determination of the appropriate punishment.[18]

When carrying out the assessment, the court shall give special consideration to aggravating and mitigating circumstances in accordance with Chapter 29, Section 2-3. For persons under 21, one of the mitigating circumstances is of interest: if the actions of the accused were connected with his manifestly deficient development, experience or capacity for judgment, this should be taken into account when assessing the penal value (Ch. 29, Sec. 3 (3)). It is asserted that these grounds should be taken into consideration when the juvenile is exceptionally immature, but according to court practice, it is not.[19]

2.2. Choosing the Criminal Sanction

After assessing the penal value, the court must then choose a sanction (SPC Ch. 30, Sec. 1).[20] In Chapter 30 there are two Sections that are of special interest—Section 4 and 5. Under the provisions of subsection 1 in Section 4, the court 'shall pay special attention to any circumstance or circumstances that argue for the imposition of a less severe punishment than imprisonment'. This means that there is a presumption against imprisonment. When doing so the court shall give reasonable consideration to extenuating circumstances, such as whether the accused suffered severe bodily harm as a result of the crime, or whether the accused would suffer harm through expulsion from the Realm by reason of the crime (Ch. 30, Sec. 4 and Ch. 29, Sec. 5).

The second subsection of Chapter 30, Section 4 declares that the presumption in subsection one can be disregarded when regarding the penal value, the nature of the crime and whether the accused has previously been guilty of committing a crime or crimes. For the latter of these three, the amount of time since the last conviction, if it was a serious

[17] Jareborg, N., Zila, J., cit., p. 103 ff.
[18] Prop. 1987/88:120 om ändring i brottsbalken (straffmätning och påföljdsval), p. 36 f.
[19] Jareborg, N., Zila, J., cit., p. 152
[20] Jareborg, N., Zila, J., cit., p. 104 f.

crime and if the crimes were similar, is of great matter.[21] Not only can the presumption be disregarded according to subsection 2, but these grounds can also be taken into consideration as a reason for imprisonment.[22]

According to Section 5 'the court may impose imprisonment only if there are extraordinary reasons for doing so', when the accused was 15 but not 18 when the crime was committed. If the juvenile was 18 but not 21 when committing the crime, the court may instead 'impose imprisonment only if, in view of the penal value of the crime or other special reasons, this course of action is justified'. As explained above, the principal difference between the two of them lies in *extraordinary reasons* compared to *special reasons*. In the Government bill it is declared that the penal value of the crime is the main extraordinary reason. Special reasons can be the penal value, the nature of the crime and that the accused has previously been guilty of committing a crime—which are the same reasons that can cause the presumption to be disregarded according to Section 4.[23]

In a case in the Supreme Court, a boy had committed gross theft at the age of 17, but had turned 18 by the time of the trial (SPC Ch. 8, Sec. 4). The Court regarded the penal value, the nature of the crime, previous convictions and the character and extent of the actions of the social services when arguing whether extraordinary reasons were at hand. Those grounds are not discussed in the Government bill.[24] In another Supreme Court case there were no extraordinary reasons for imprisonment. That case involved an 18-year-old boy who was convicted for gross assault and theft, which he had committed at the age of 17 (SPC Ch. 3, Sec. 5 and Ch. 8, Sec. 1). The gross assault was an unprovoked street fight, which relates to 'the nature of the crime'. The Supreme Court ruled that the penal value was not high enough to be an extraordinary reason to sentence the youth to

[21] Prop. 1987/88:120, p. 53 ff.

[22] There is an ongoing debate in Sweden whether 'the nature of the crime' should be a reason for imprisonment and, if so, how it should be applied by the court. The main argument why it should not be applied is that the Government bills do not give the courts any guidelines how the nature of the crime should be used. The courts apply the nature of the crime to an extent that some argue was not the Government's original intention. Read e.g. Jareborg, Nils (ed.), Påföljdsbestämning, Straffrättsliga studier utgivna till hundraårsminnet av Ivar Strahls födelse, SvJT 1999 s. 107 and von Hirsch, Andrew, Wersäll, Fredrik, Victor, Dag (ed.), Korta fängelsestraff och alternativa påföljder – en seminarieserie om påföljdssystemets grunder och struktur, SvJT 2003 s. 109 for more information.

[23] Prop. 1987/88:120, p. 103.

[24] NJA 2001 s. 225.

imprisonment and the nature of the crime was not sufficient in itself. The youth also had no previous convictions.[25]

When the court has decided upon imprisonment, and if the accused was younger than 18 when the crime was committed, the court should, as a principal rule, sentence the accused to closed juvenile care. This should not be applied if, regarding the age of the accused at the time of prosecution or other circumstances, *special reasons* argue against the criminal sanction. Closed juvenile care is imposed for a fixed term of 14 days to 4 years. (Ch. 32, Sec. 5). The offender should not be older than 21 when serving closed juvenile care.[26] How old the juvenile is during the enforcement of the criminal sanctions relates to special reasons. If the accused has committed extensive and serious crimes both before and after 18, that is also considered a special reason.[27]

Another reason that is apparently a special reason against closed juvenile care is if the accused would be sentenced to a short imprisonment. A girl of 17 had been sentenced to closed juvenile care in the District Court and the Court Of Appeals, when she had committed perjury at the age of 16 (SPC Ch. 15, Sec. 1). In the Supreme Court, her counsel argued that she should be sentenced to imprisonment instead—imprisonment for not longer than six months can be enforced by electronic monitoring (Sec. 1, Act on Intensive Supervision with Electronic Monitoring (1994:451)[28]). Even though imprisonment is regarded as a more interfering and serious sanction than closed juvenile care, the Court ruled in favour of the girl. This is controversial, because it is not the courts that decide how the imprisonment should be implemented, but the Swedish Prison and Probation Service (Sec. 1 The Prison Treatment Act (1974:203)[29]). It should be said here that the Court did not take the electronic monitoring into examination in the verdict, though it seems that the Court judged with the Act in mind.[30]

---

[25] NJA 2005 s. 690.

[26] The youths who are cared for according to Section 12 CYPA are not older than 21 years old.

[27] Prop. 1997/98:96, p. 162.

[28] Lag (1994:451) om intensivövervakning med elektronisk kontroll. Referred to in Section 1 the Prison Treatment Act (1974:203), www.kriminalvarden.se/upload/Informationsmaterial/The_Prison_Treatment_Act.pdf, 2010-10-08.

[29] Lag (1974:203) om kriminalvård i anstalt.

[30] NJA 2001 s. 913. It is arguable whether it is the nature of the crime or how the sanction is enforced that is determining. General prevention which has an impact

2.3. Determining the Appropriate Punishment

When the court has assessed the penal value and chosen closed juvenile care as being the correct criminal sanction, it must determine the appropriate punishment. This is the last step for the court. In this last step, the court must first remove one third of the term from the penal value. This is because according to SPC Chapter 26, Section 6, a person who is sentenced to imprisonment for a fixed term shall be conditionally released after serving two thirds, but not less than a month, of the term. There is no similar Section for closed juvenile care, but a juvenile should not serve a longer part of the term than those who are imprisoned. Removing one third of the term makes them more equal.

If the court could not give sufficient consideration to circumstances through the choice of criminal sanction, it 'shall, besides the penal value of the crime, take reasonable account of whether the accused has previously been guilty of committing a crime'. In that context, special consideration should be given to the extent of the crimes, the elapsed time since the last conviction and whether the new and the previous criminality are similar in nature or if they are both of especially serious character (Ch. 29, Sec. 4). As written, the Section describes aggravating circumstances when the offender has relapsed.

The court should also act according to the provisions of Section 5 in Chapter 29, if not done when choosing the sanction.[31] These grounds are sometimes mentioned as grounds for fairness. According to the second subsection, the court can impose a less severe punishment than prescribed for the crime if there are *special grounds* covered by the first subsection for doing so. The reference to special grounds means that this should be used restrictively. If it is manifestly unreasonable to impose a sanction when regarding Section 5, the court shall, according to Section 6, grant exemption from sanction. This Section should be used very rarely.[32]
If the accused was younger than 21 when committing the crime, the court should take the age into special consideration. In such cases, a punishment that is milder than the prescribed can be imposed (Ch. 29, Sec. 7). This is often referred to as a 'juvenile discount'. It is the age itself that the court

---

through 'the nature of the crime' should not have the same impact for young perpetrators as for adults. Overall, the general prevention does not belong at the court level, but at the legislative level.

[31] Read *Choosing the Criminal Sanction* above.

[32] Prop. 1987/88:120, p. 60.

takes into examination, not whether the age actually had any impact on the youth's conduct.[33]

In a case in the Supreme Court, the Prosecutor-General argued for a determined percentage when applying SPC Chapter 30, Section 7. The case in the Supreme Court was about two juveniles who at the age of 18 had together committed two cases of robbery and two cases of preparation to commit robbery (Ch. 8, Sec. 5, Ch. 8, Sec. 12 and Ch. 23, Sec. 1). In the district court and the court of appeals they had been sentenced to imprisonment for one year and nine months each. In the Supreme Court, the Prosecutor-General argued for a more severe punishment with reference to a determined percentage and meant that a determined percentage would promote consistency, predictability and a consistent application of the Section. The Supreme Court did not rule in favour of the Prosecutor-General, though it agreed that a younger offender would have a bigger reduction than a criminal that was closer to 21 years old.[34]

Determining the appropriate punishment is quite a complex procedure, even though it may seem like the court can go step by step. In short, the court must take Chapter 29 Section 4-7 into consideration at the same time as it applies Chapter 30 and 32. In Chapter 30, the court chooses a sanction and in Chapter 29 Sections 4-7 it determines the appropriate punishment. All in all, there is an assessment of the entity.

---

[33] Jareborg, N., Zila, J., cit., p. 152. There is more than one theory how the juvenile discount should be calculated. Writers argue that their recommended guidelines should be used since they are a result of Swedish court practice and it is also good for principled reasons. The following is a chart of their theory, cit. p. 153.

Age	**Reduction of term**	**Approximate term**
15 years	75-85 per cent	1/5
16 years	65-75 per cent	1/4
17 years	55-65 per cent	1/3
18 years	45-55 per cent	1/2
19 years	30-40 per cent	2/3
20 years	20-30 per cent	3/4

[34] NJA 2000 s. 421.

4. The Enforcement of Closed Juvenile Care

When the juvenile has been sentenced to closed juvenile care, the enforcement is carried out in a specially approved home (Sec. 1, Act (1198:603) on Enforcement of Closed Juvenile Care[35] (ECJC)). It is the National Board of Institutional Care that is responsible for the enforcement. It should be planned and carried out in close cooperation with the social welfare committee in the juvenile's municipality (Sec. 3). In the Government bill it is stated that 'most of those detained should be in need of care and treatment'[36]. It is questionable whether young offenders really have a greater need of care than adults. It seems that *parens patriae* is still of relevance in Swedish Criminal Law.

According to Section 1 of The Social Services Act (2001:453)[37] (SSA) and Section 3 in CYPA, measures are first to be undertaken on the basis of an agreement with the young person and his or her guardians. The activities shall first and foremost be based on respect for the youth's self-determination and privacy. The best interests of the child shall be specially observed when measures affect children: a child is any person under the age of 18 (Sec. 2 SSA).[38] Only if the necessary care presumably cannot be given with the consent of the 15-18 year-old and his guardian, can measures pursuant to ECJC be provided. If the youth is 18 but not 20 years-old, care pursuant to Section 3 may also be given, if it is more appropriate than any other care in view of the young person's needs and general personal circumstances. For 18-20 year-olds, it is also a vital element that necessary care presumably cannot be given with consent (Sec. 1 CYPA).

There are two types of care without consent—one based on the environment (Sec. 2), and one based on the young person's own behaviour (Sec. 3).[39] The latter Section declares in its first subsection that, if the young offender exposes his 'health or development to a palpable risk of injury through the abuse of addictive substances, criminal activity or some other socially

[35] Lag (1998:603) om verkställighet av sluten ungdomsvård. Referred to in Chapter 31, Section 2 of Ds 1996:36 The Swedish Penal Code.
[36] Prop. 1997/98:96, p. 158. The translation is mine.
[37] Socialtjänstlag (2001:453). The translation is in accordance with www.sweden.gov.se/content/1/c6/04/34/02/9 d488738.pdf, 2010-10-08.
[38] This is consistent with Section 1 CRC.
[39] These are often referred to as the environment situation and the behaviour situation.

degrading behaviour', measures without consent can be taken. The second subsection stipulates that if the young person has been sentenced to closed juvenile care in accordance with SPC Chapter 32, Section 5, a care order is to be made if the youth, 'in connection with completion of the sentence, is considered to be in manifest need of continued care so as not to run the risks referred to in paragraph one'. If the young offender is in need of particularly close surveillance on these referred grounds, he / she is to be maintained for care in a specially approved home (Sec. 12 CYPA).

If read altogether, the young offender can be in the same specially approved home before, during and after the enforcement of closed juvenile care. Before the young offender is sentenced, he or she may be in need of particularly close surveillance because of his or her criminal activity (Sec. 3 subsection one, Sec. 12). The enforcement of close juvenile care itself is carried out in a specially approved home (Sec. 1 ECJC). Afterwards, the young offender may perhaps be in manifest need of continued care, in particular close surveillance (Sec. 3 subsection two, Sec. 12 CYPA). All in all, there is a possibility that the young offender is cared for in the same specially approved home for a longer time than the actual enforcement of the criminal sanction.

Young offenders under 18 should only be held in custody as a last resort.[40] If it is feared that the detention may cause serious harm by reason of the suspect's 'age, health status or similar factor, detention *may only take place if adequate supervision* of the suspect cannot be arranged'[41] (The Swedish Code of Judicial Procedure (1942:740)[42] (SCJP) Ch. 24, Sec. 4, first subsection). The second subsection in SCJP Chapter 24, Section 4 declares that there are special provisions with additional restrictions for detaining those who are under the age of 18. According to Section 23 of The Act with Special Provisions for Young Offenders (1964:167)[43], a person who is under 18 can only be held in custody if there are *extraordinary reasons* for doing so. If there is reason to believe that a suspect cannot be detained under SCJP Chapter 24, Section 4, the prosecutor must attempt to

[40] Prop. 1964:10 Kunglig Maj:ts proposition till riksdagen med förslag om införande av brottsbalken m.m., p. 164.
[41] Emphasis added.
[42] Rättegångsbalk (1942:740). The translation is in accordance with Ds 1998:000 The Swedish Code of Judicial Procedure, www.sweden.gov.se/content/1/c6/02/77/78/30607300.pdf, 2010-10-08.
[43] Lag (1964:167) med särskilda bestämmelser om unga lagöverträdare. The translation is mine.

arrange necessary supervision as soon as possible (Sec. 26 Decree on Preliminary Investigation (1947:948)[44]). In a case in the Supreme Court, the Court ruled that an immediate care order by the social welfare committee is adequate supervision (Sec. 6 CYPA).[45] Instead of being held in custody, an immediate care order should be issued for the young. There is a possibility that the young may be in need of especially close surveillance. In that case, the care is maintained in a specially approved home (Sec. 3, 12 CYPA).

When regarding the principle of proportionality, it is a problem that the enforcement cannot be reduced by the period for which the young offender has been cared for in a specially approved home.[46] The underlying cause is that a care order and a criminal sanction have different purposes. This can also be considered as a problem when regarding the principle of equality. The sentence can be reduced by the time they are under arrest and in custody. However, it cannot be reduced by the amount of time that they are cared for in accordance with Sec. 3 and 12 CYPA (SPC Ch. 33, Sec. 6 and Sec. 19 Act on Determining the Sentence Term (1974:202)[47]). This can be seen as a withdrawal from the affirmative action, according to which young offender should be treated more positively.[48]

Another problem when regarding the principle of proportionality is the fact that a care order can be issued even after the enforcement of close juvenile care. That requires that there is a need of care which presumably cannot be given with consent (Sec. 1 and 3 CYPA). As written above, if the young offender is in care for any of the grounds in Section 3 CYPA, and particularly close surveillance is needed, the care is maintained in a specially approved home (Sec. 12). It ought to be very difficult for the young offender to know the difference when being cared for according to CYPA or serving a sentence. It is possible that the young offender sees the entire time he or she is in care as a criminal sanction.

An essential difference between close juvenile care and a care order is that the care order is indefinite. Because of this, the young offender is in

---

[44] Förundersökningskungörelsen (1947:948). The translation is mine.
[45] NJA 2008 s. 81.
[46] Read *Determining the Appropriate Punishment* above.
[47] Lag (1974:202) om beräkning av strafftid m.m. The translation is mine.
[48] Nordlöf, Kerstin, Unga lagöverträdare i social-, straff- och processrätt, Studentlitteratur, Lund, 2007, p. 182. Compare with the so called juvenile discount (Ch. 29, Sec. 7 SPC).

danger of first being sentenced for a fixed term, for which the young offender's need of care should not be taken into consideration.[49] Afterwards, the young offender may be cared for in the same specially approved home, but then it is because he or she is in need of care. It is not reasonable that a young offender should be sentenced to what he or she may perceive as an indefinite term. The Government bill declares that '[c]losed juvenile care must [...] be designed in a way that it is clear that it represents the Society's reaction to the offender's crime and that it meets the principles on predictability and proportionality. Closed juvenile care must therefore be a criminal sanction on a fixed term'[50]. These statements ought not to be in conformity with how it is perceived in practice.

5. Conclusion

Previously in this article I have tried to describe some of the problems related to close juvenile care. Clearly, there are some issues with the regulations.

My first reflection is why the young offender's need of care should not be regarded when assessing the penal value, but when enforcing the criminal sanction? Of course, the penal values in themselves and the enforcement have different purposes. But why closed juvenile care? Why care for someone who is not in need of care? The criminal sanction is a reaction for committing a crime, not because the young offender is in need of care. The court does not even examine whether care is needed. Even though the need for care for a young offender is greater than it is for an adult, it is not obvious that closed juvenile care is the right way to go.

Perhaps Sweden is in need of an additional criminal sanction. Closed juvenile care should then be used only if the court can determine that the young offender really is in need of care. The other criminal sanction can be imposed when the need for care cannot be determined by the court. One cannot have a definite view regarding how the additional sentence should be chosen or imposed. However, the intention is not that the young offender should be treated more severely than at present. But obviously, even young offenders should have a proper understanding of their crimes. If they are not in need of care, then closed juvenile care is not the correct sanction.

---

[49] Prop. 1997/98: 96, p. 160.

[50] Prop. 1997/98: 96, p. 161. The translation is mine.

If closed juvenile care is to continue to be the only criminal sanction imposed instead of imprisonment, it should certainly not be enforced in a specially approved home together with young who are in need of care with particularly close supervision (Sec. 1, 3 and 12 CYPA). Even if they are in separate wards, it is inevitable that they meet each other (Sec. 14 ECJC). The young offender who really is in need of care because of his or her criminal activity could be taught by the young offender who has been convicted of committing a serious crime. Practically, it is not always about the young offender, criminal behaviour, criminal conduct or irrational violations, but it can also be about the impact the young offender has on other young individuals. Those who are in need of care should be cared for and not put together with those who do not need to be cared for. It cannot be in the best interests of the child to care for them together (Sec. 1 CYPA, Sec. 3 CRC).

Another problem is that a care order can be issued before and after the enforcement of closed juvenile care. I consider it very serious that the young offender does not know for how long he or she is to be cared for. The care order is indefinite, and the young offender should be cared for as long as it is needed. Closed juvenile care is a criminal sanction on fixed terms, but there is a possibility that the young offender experiences it as indefinite. The young offender does not know if he or she is considered to be in need of care with particularly close supervision at the end of the term. If that should be the case, the young offender does not know how long the care should continue. Even though the purposes are different, it is not certain that the young offender understands that. The young offender may consider it all as one, indefinite sanction as a reaction to the crime. If all the time spent in the specially approved home is considered, the reaction is much stronger than it should be when regarding the juvenile discount. To make matters worse, if the young offender is cared for in a specially approved home instead of being held in custody, the term seems even longer. There should be the possibility of reducing the sentence by the amount of the time spent in such a home instead of custody.

It may seem that that the conclusion goes against closed juvenile care as a criminal sanction, but such a deduction is certainly incorrect. There is no criticism against such a criminal sanction; rather the criticism is against the method in which it is applied. If the young offender is indeed in need of care, then closed juvenile care is appropriate. If the young is not, another criminal sanction should be applied instead. No matter whether a new criminal sanction is introduced or not, the rules and regulations governing closed juvenile care are in need of a review.

I have based all these arguments on the basic philosophy of justice, the principle of equality and the principle of proportionality. Obviously, those who have violated the system of criminal jurisdiction are to be brought before the proceedings of a court, but not solely for the application of punishment, but also to achieve the goals of rehabilitation. This is particularly significant in the case of juvenile justice and the implementation of their natural or legal rights, due to the provisions of a considerable number of international documents on human rights law. In other words, criminal justice is not solely the implementation of criminal sanction, but the very sense of understanding the offender's nature in conjunction with the harm inflicted on the victims.

THE INTERNATIONAL CRIMINAL COURT'S PERSPECTIVE ON CHILD SOLDIERS

SHAMILA BATOHI

1. Introduction

No child should ever fight the wars of their countries, nor should they ever have to live in such fear. But the truth is that millions of children are doing just that every day: their lives and innocence are lost—children who never had a doll or a video game, but know how to load an AK 47 and shoot to kill and are killed. "It is estimated that 43 per cent of all armed organizations in the world use child soldiers, 90 per cent of whom see battle. And, in the last decade, more than 2 million children have been killed in combat": [1] UNICEF estimates that approximately 300,000 children are involved in conflicts throughout the world. [2] Precise documentation of the prevalence of child soldiers is often hampered by, *inter alia*, the fact that the use of child soldiers is denied by military commanders and inaccessibility to areas of conflict by observers.

Child soldiers, some younger than 10, are used in every region of the world. Africa has the largest number of child soldiers. They are being used in armed conflict in Burundi, the Central African Republic, Chad, the Democratic Republic of Congo, Rwanda, Somalia, Sudan and Uganda[3], and we know that one of the charges faced by Charles Taylor in the Special Court for Sierra Leone was the conscription of children under 15.

---

[1] Teach Kids Peace.
[2] UNICEF, Factsheet: Child Soldiers http://www.unicef.org/emerg/files/childsoldiers.pdf.
[3] Coalition to Stop the Use of Child Soldiers, FAQs.

2. Rome Statute

On 17 July 1998, the 120 states which adopted the Rome Statute decided that, in the context of armed conflict over which the International Criminal Court (ICC) has jurisdiction, conscripting or enlisting children under 15, or using them to participate actively in hostilities, is a war crime.[4] As of 1 April 2010, there were 113 State Parties to the Rome Statute.[5] The ICC does not have jurisdiction over any person who was under the age of 18 at the time of the alleged commission of a crime.[6]

2.1. Situations and Cases before the ICC

It is rightly stated that "It is the duty of the Prosecutor and of his Office to ensure that the Statute's provisions are implemented in practice, and that perpetrators of the crime of recruiting children and using them to participate actively in armed conflicts are prosecuted for their actions."[7] The ICC is presently focusing its judicial activities on defending those most vulnerable, children among them, and prosecuting those most responsible. In all the cases currently before the Court,[8] serious crimes have been perpetrated against children. For example:

a) Five arrest warrants have been issued against the leaders of the Lord's Resistance Army in Uganda, including charges of recruiting and using child soldiers.[9]
b) The first case before the Court, *The Prosecutor versus Thomas Lubanga Dyilo* (see below), focuses on children. The Prosecution evidence shows that children, sometimes no older than seven, eight or nine years of age, were victims. Most of the children were abducted: abducted on the road, with other children, in very large numbers; abducted from schools; abducted from their parents'

---

[4] RS article 8(2)(b)(xxvi) (international armed conflict); RS article 8(2)(e)(vii) (non-international armed conflict).
[5] The most recent State Party being Bangladesh, which ratified the Statute on 23.3.2010. There are currently 192 Member States of the United Nations (October 2011).
[6] RS article 26.
[7] Speech by Mrs. Fatou Bensouda, page 2, 25 March 2009, at OTP-NGO Roundtable.
[8] Including the Republic of Kenya.
[9] One of the five leaders (Raska Lukwiya) is deceased.

home, in front of their families. Very often, families were helpless to do anything for fear of being killed themselves.

c) Other children joined armed groups voluntarily. They did so for a variety of reasons: out of a desire for revenge felt by orphans whose families had been killed by militias, or even out of a desire to acquire a certain social standing. Others just felt a need for protection and shelter or simply wanted to survive, in particular by having something to eat.

Children were taught to kill 'enemies', with no distinction between combatants and civilians. The children—girls and boys alike—were compelled by their commanders to fight at the front. Compelled by threats of execution.

Many child soldiers were killed. Others seriously wounded.

2.2. Lubanga

Mr. Lubanga is the alleged founder of the *Union des patriotes congolais* [Union of Congolese Patriots] (UPC); president of the group since it was founded in September 2000; and was the alleged former Commander-in-Chief of its military wing (Patriotic Forces for the Liberation of Congo] (FPLC)), from September 2002 until at least late 2003. Lubanga is charged with enlisting and conscripting children under the age of 15 into the FPLC and using them to actively participate in hostilities. The *Lubanga* trial commenced on 26 January 2009. In his opening statement in *Lubanga*, the Prosecutor said:

> It is a responsibility of the Office of the Prosecutor of the International Criminal Court to prove the crimes committed against the most vulnerable and during the course of this trial, my office will make it its mission to ensure that Thomas Lubanga Dyilo is held criminally responsible for the atrocities committed against those little girl soldiers, when he enlisted and conscripted them to be used as sexual prey, when he used them in combat.
>
> Under the Rome Statute, crimes related with children involved in armed groups can be committed in three ways without making any distinction as to gravity: by conscripting children, by enlisting them, or by using them to participate actively in hostilities.
>
> The Rome Statute renders irrelevant that children joined 'voluntarily', or that parents entrusted them 'voluntarily' to the Lubanga's militia.

> Accepting for military service so-called volunteers under the age of 15 constitutes criminal conduct.

The prosecution concluded the presentation of its case on 14 July 2009, and the defence opened its case on 27 January 2010. During 74 days of hearings over 22 weeks, the Court heard 28 witnesses called by the Office of the Prosecutor. By 5 January 2010, the judges had granted 103 persons the status of victim authorized to participate in the case.[10] These victims had the right to express their position on matters heard before the Court and, subject to the judge's authorisation, they may examine witnesses on specific issues. The reader may be aware that the Rome Statute establishes a framework for victim participation, and represents a key innovative feature of this Court and is, in the prosecution's view, a milestone in international criminal justice. 25 witnesses who testified were granted procedural protective measures.[11] These measures included voice and facial distortion and the use of pseudonyms. Exceptionally, a support assistant or psychologist was allowed to sit in the courtroom to support and monitor the witness. Thomas Lubanga and his defence team were able to see all witnesses during their testimony, even though some of them required further special measures in the courtroom to avoid direct eye contact with the accused.[12]

2.3. Developments in *Lubanga*

During the investigation and trial, former child soldiers provided information and testified on their abduction by UPC soldiers, their military training, including marching and shooting exercises, and their participation in attacks on villages in the Ituri district in north-eastern DRC, stating "*Yes, I shot at people [...]; I fired and people fell*". A witness spoke of feelings of extreme fear and panic. Being an adult in such circumstances in such situations is difficult enough. One can only imagine sheer horror of the atrocities committed on children.

One witness testified that he was held two weeks in an underground hole as punishment for escaping military training. Another testified that children were regularly beaten or whipped in the military camps, by UPC/FPLC officers and also children younger than the witness. Young

---

[10] ICC Press Release, 05.01.2010.
[11] Case Information Sheet, *Lubanga*.
[12] ICC Press Release, 14.07.2009.

girls were regularly raped. Others have told us their shame at having being forced to rape young girls.

Political insiders and former high level officials of the UPC provided evidence on the context of the conflict, the creation and structure of UPC and its armed wing the FPLC, the presence and use of child soldiers under the age of 15 in the UPC/FPLC, recruitment methods and the specific role of Thomas Lubanga.

Political insiders also testified that Lubanga used children as bodyguards: according to one witness, all UPC commanders had children as bodyguards, some appearing to be as young as 13. A witness also testified that Lubanga did read out a demobilization order to the UPC leadership regarding children in his militia, in order to appease NGOs that were then addressing the issue of child recruitment in Ituri.

On 7 January 2010, Radhika Coomaraswamy, United Nations Special Representative of the Secretary-General on Children and Armed Conflict, gave expert testimony to the Court. Among the many valuable contributions made by Ms Coomaraswamy, apparent from her written submissions and expert testimony, and very significant with respect to the work of the ICC, was her testimony regarding the deterrent effect of the *Lubanga* case:[13]

> The deterrent effect of these proceedings [i.e., the *Lubanga* case] is already being felt with regard to a large number of armed groups engaging with the United Nations to release children from their ranks and to cease all new recruitment.
>
> The willingness on the part of the Court to prosecute these cases [of alleged recruitment and use of child soldiers] has sent many armed groups to us - the United Nations—willing to negotiate action plans for the release of children; most recently yesterday [6 January 2010] in Nepal where the release of 3,000 children is about to begin today [7 January 2010].
>
> I was recently in southern Sudan. We entered into [an] action plan with the SPLA [Sudan People's Liberation Army] for the release of children . . . [14]
>
> And we have now negotiated quite a few [action plans] around the world, helped a lot by some of the fear of the ICC Prosecutions, etcetera. A lot of these action plans have been agreed to. And in that, now we are seeing the

[13] Excerpts taken from ICC-01/04-01/06-T-223 (7 January 2010).
[14] South Sudan is now an independent State.

> post-action plan, where children are going to these groups, and we are seeing how these groups have responded by handing the children over to UNICEF or to child protection actors, and telling them take them from us.
>
> And one of the things our child protection partners try to do on the ground is to negotiate with all the parties to make schools into safe zones. That is one of the preventive things we try to do in different conflicts to say, "You can have the conflict, but let the schools be safe zones." So, that's one of the negotiations we have with armed groups. Secondly, when groups take children from the schools, we do try to get them back through negotiations of action plans for their release, and this is done, they are made aware of the international rules and regulations of Security Council Resolution 1612 and the kind of procedures, and we try to negotiate the release of these children through action plans. We have been fortunate in some cases to be able to do so.

The above shows that, regardless of the outcome of this case, it will send—has, in fact, already sent—a signal to the DRC and around the world that using children as soldiers is a serious crime that will be prosecuted.

2.4. OTP and the Protection of Children

We have a Gender and Children Unit that is "responsible for providing advice to the Prosecutor . . . in all areas related to [inter alia] violence against children. The unit contribute[s] to evaluation during the preliminary examinations, investigations and prosecutions in those areas."[15]

In the determination of a provisional case hypothesis, the joint investigation team aims to select incidents reflective of the most serious crimes and the main types of victimisation—including [*inter alia*] violence against children—and which are the most representative of the scale and impact of the crimes (OTP Regulation 34(2)).[16]

In planning investigative activities, the joint team endeavours, in particular through consultation with the Gender and Children Unit, to ensure the well-being of victims and witnesses and to avoid their re-traumatisation (OTP Regulation 35(3)).

---

[15] OTP Regulations (23 April 2009), Regulations 6, 12.

[16] Office of the Prosecutor.

The physical and psychological well-being of persons who are questioned by the Office and are considered vulnerable (in particular children, persons with disabilities and victims of gender and sexual crimes) shall be assessed by a psychologist, a psycho-social or other expert during a face-to-face interview prior to questioning. This assessment determines whether the person's condition at that particular time allows him or her to be questioned without risk of re-traumatisation (OTP Regulation 36(3)).

Interviews with children must take into account, and be sensitive to, the child's developmental stage and level of traumatisation. Investigators must introduce themselves and the ICC in a child-friendly, simple manner, and inform the child that information will be kept confidential. Moreover, children should be informed that they will not be prosecuted or punished by the court. Investigators should try to reduce anxiety and fear in the child.[17]

The OTP has recently adopted a draft Operational Manual codifying the best practices of the Office's operations. The following are some provisions indicating the Office's commitment to the protection of children:

> With respect to witness interviews, "Whenever possible, victims of sexual violence, traumatised witnesses, children or elderly persons should initially be approached through an intermediary who has already developed a relationship of trust with the person".[18]
>
> The screening and initial phase of the interview of a sexual violence victim, a child witness or an otherwise vulnerable individual should focus on understanding the individual's personal circumstances and establishing a relationship of trust and respect. Where necessary for establishing trust, additional time or built-in flexibility may be budgeted in the planning of interview missions.[19]
>
> Prior to an interview, based on the profile of the witness and information compiled in the preparatory process, the interview team shall assess whether a psycho-social pre-interview assessment is needed. However in the case of children and adolescents, this assessment is mandatory.[20]

[17] OTP/ICC Guidelines on Psycho-Social Aspects of Interviewing Children.
[18] OTP Operational Manual (version 17.2.2010), Chapter 8, para. 1.1.9.
[19] OTP Operational Manual (version 17.2.2010), Chapter 8, para. 2.1.
[20] OTP Operational Manual (version 17.2.2010), Chapter 8, para. 3.1.1.

Where a witness is unable to attend an interview because of the needs of dependant(s), the Office shall make efforts to provide the logistical or financial means to secure domestic assistance for the care of children or other dependants.[21]

2.5. Recent Developments within the OTP/ICC for the Protection of Children

The Office is in the process of drafting a policy paper on gender. Pursuant to this draft policy paper, "All Office staff shall have cognizance of the law and lived realities of . . . crimes against children, including the consequences of trauma".[22]

The Office has also drafted a policy paper on the Preliminary Examination which leads to the selection of situations and cases for investigation and prosecution. In terms of this draft policy paper:

> The Office's assessment of gravity includes both quantitative and qualitative considerations based on the prevailing facts and circumstances. As stipulated in Regulation 29(2) of the Regulations of the Office, the non-exhaustive factors that guide the Office's assessment include the scale, nature, manner of commission of the crimes, and their impact:[23]
> (a) The scale of the crimes may be assessed in light of, *inter alia*, the number of direct and indirect victims, the extent of the damage caused by the crimes, in particular the bodily or psychological harm caused to the victims and their families, and their geographical or temporal spread (intensity of the crimes over a brief period or low intensity violence over an extended period);
> (b) The nature of the crimes refers to the specific elements of each offence such as killings, rapes and other crimes involving sexual or gender violence and crimes committed against children, or the imposition of conditions of life on a community calculated to bring about its destruction;

---

[21] OTP Operational Manual (version 17.2.2010), Chapter 8, para. 20.11.1.
[22] OTP Operational Manual (version 17.2.2010), Chapter 4, para. 3.1.1.(e).
[23] *See*, in concurrence with the Prosecution's submissions, *Prosecutor v. Abu Garda,* Decision on the Confirmation of Charges, ICC-02/05-02/09-243-Red, 8 February 2010, paras. 31; *Situation in the Republic of Kenya*, Decision Pursuant to Article 15 of the Rome Statute on the Authorization of an Investigation into the Situation in the Republic of Kenya, ICC-01/09-19-Corr, 31 March 2010, para 188.

(c) The manner of commission of the crimes may be assessed in light of, *inter alia*, the means employed to execute the crime, the degree of participation and intent in its commission, the extent to which the crimes were systematic or result from a plan or organized policy or otherwise resulted from the abuse of power or official capacity, and elements of particular cruelty, including the vulnerability of the victims, any motives involving discrimination, or the use of rape and sexual violence as a means of destroying communities;
(d) The impact of crimes may be assessed in light of, *inter alia*, their consequence on the local or international community, including the long-term social, economic and environmental damage; crimes committed with the aim or consequence of increasing the vulnerability of civilians; or other acts the primary purpose of which is to spread terror among the civilian population.

3. Conclusion

The OTP's undertaking is judicial in nature and must not be confused with the essential work of monitoring and condemning human rights violations being done by international organisations and associations, and in particular by Ms. Radhika Coomaraswamy. The Prosecutor's activities are limited to the courtroom. Yet how can the OTP play a preventive role, in compliance with the preamble to the Rome Statute?[24] Prevention is a priority for any judicial system. The Office of the Prosecutor must garner extensive support from other actors in the international community in order to maximise the impact of judicial proceedings. States, international organisations, and NGOs can amplify the impact of our judicial activities by carrying the message not only to the countries directly involved—but also to all other countries on all continents: the use of child soldiers constitutes a serious war crime which will be prosecuted. We have already seen some initial progress being made as armed forces take the precaution of revising their operational procedures; we must further exploit this response.

The campaign to end the recruitment of children is far from over. We must continue to explain that recruiting children is not a lesser crime. We must not fail to recognise the manifold consequences and enduring impact the crime has—we cannot disregard the fact that children are being used to

[24] "Determined to put an end to impunity for the perpetrators of these crimes and thus to contribute to the prevention of such crimes." (Preamble, paragraph 5)

commit the worst of atrocities; that child victims are being turned into executioners, thereby isolating them from the support of their communities; that these children are becoming lost, wasted generations on continents and in countries where the young people should be the primary asset; and that by recruiting children today the cycle of violence will inevitably continue into the future. The advocacy activities carried out in this area by UNICEF and the Special Representative of the Secretary-General are fundamental. Within the limits of our respective mandates, we are all actors in this campaign, and the OTP stands ready to work with other organisations, whilst preserving its independence and its strictly judicial role.

The Court's judicial work cannot, of course, stand in as a substitute for the domestic judicial activities of States, which retain primary responsibility for preventing and punishing crime. Each State must still bring the perpetrators of such crimes before their own criminal courts. The ICC is an instrument of last resort, complementing domestic courts.

We are pleased to note that not only has the United Nations system in its entirety been mobilised in implementing all-inclusive strategies, but also regional organisations, including the European Union and the African Union. In this regard we support the envisaged aim of the "Paris Commitments to Protect Children from Unlawful Recruitment or Use by Armed Forces or Armed Groups", adopted in February 2007, to find solutions that are both all-inclusive and mindful of the fundamental principle of justice and the over-riding need to fight against impunity. Archbishop Desmond M. Tutu asserts that: "It is immoral that adults should want children to fight their wars for them… There is simply no excuse, no acceptable argument for arming children."

However, the campaign to end the recruitment of children is far from over.[25] We must continue to explain that recruiting children is not a lesser crime. We are the first to recognise that there is no single, individual solution. With no hope of social reintegration or economic advancement, children will rejoin armed groups; this is evident from Uganda. Unless concerted action is taken to end the funding of such groups and to expose all of the weapons trafficking networks, this scourge will never be eradicated.

[25] See also Farhad Malekian, Prohibition Governing Child Soldiers Constituting an Integral Part of *Jus Cogens* and *Obligatio Erga Omnes*: Belfast Declaration (Institute of International Criminal Law, 2007).

CONCLUSION

FARHAD MALEKIAN

The classical philosophers of law, ethics and sociology like Plato, Socrates, Aristotle,[1] Confucius, Avicenna, Bentham, Hegel, Kant and many others attempted to present a correct concept of philosophy of justice. They emphasised the concept of morality, social relationships, and personal duties in various forms. Socrates launched a different analysis of justice.[2] Plato compared democratic equality with proportional equality in the laws. The former applies solely to an effortless equality, but due to the latter the reasonableness varies quantitatively because of a given claimant's value. This theory was already being taught within the political discourse of the ancient world and was considered the ruling principle of antiquity. Nevertheless, the apparent democracy that was relentlessly proclaimed, still viewed an equality that allocated an appropriate degree of honour, or the right of entry to privilege in relation to a *ratio* expressing the recipient's worth.[3] Plato consequently teaches us to collect all that we have to understand about the reality of things, rights and justice and also avoid all things that become the cause of our misunderstanding.[4]

Avicenna, a Persian polymath, the father of classical medicine and the author of two internationally well-known books—the Canon of Medicine and The Book of Healing—did not believe in just the actual effect of medicine on our physical body but also in the therapeutic curing of our natural body. Thus his second book does not actually deal with the

---

[1] J.P. Anton, Aristotle's Theory of Contrariety (1957); Ursula Coope, Time for Aristotle (2005); Norman Melchert, The Great Conversation (2011). Pp.157-198.

[2] Roslyn Weiss, The Socratic Paradox and its Enemies (2006), pp.135-136. See *also* Sara Ahbel—Rappe and Rachana Akamekar, A Companion to Socrates (2006).

[3] Hayden W. Ausland, The Mathematics of Justice in Reading Plato in Antiquity (Harold Tarrant and Dirk Baltzly, 2006), p.107. See *also* Daniel Russell, Plato Pleasure and the Good Life (2005).

[4] Harold Tarrant, Platonic Interpretation and Eclectic Theory in Reading Plato in Antiquity, *ibid*, pp.9-16.

theories of real medicine but how to treat the essence of our spirit and understand the dignity of mankind. He therefore tried to heal the ignorance of the soul or our vision regarding different social matters, through our cognition. He, or others like Kant, did not speak specifically about the rights of children and the way to get them recognised, but endeavoured to get beyond the problems of metaphysics by stating that objects should obey the rules of our cognition. The metaphysics constitutes, in fact, the philosophy of the nature of existence and beings, although it is without consolidated definition and is not purely scientific. It is also the ultimate fundamental principle that forms the basis of our specific sovereignty of knowledge that needs to be identified in a national or international context. Metaphysics is, however, a conceptual discussion: it denotes the existence. Thus rights, even though of a hypothetical nature, are the proof of our existence and wisdom. In other words, the proof of rights and the existence of individuals, adults or minors are the primary basis of all thought. Whilst one may not deny the fact that Bentham objected to the idea of natural law, he launched the idea of equality between men and women, the condemnation of slavery, the abolition of the death penalty, the abolition of corporal punishment, and the protection of children from any type of penalties.

Similarly, Mill who was one of the leading thinkers of his day, on politics as well as political economy, struggled for a theory of working for human good and happiness. According to him morality-intoxication and liberticide are interrelated. He propounded the idea that if the good of others is the sole duty of everyone, then the question is: why should we not have a statute under which this duty is enforced?[5] This is one of the ways to ensure the rights of others in a social context.[6] Mill had also long

---

[5] Johan Skorupski, Why Read Mill Today (2006), pp.15-16.

[6] According to him, "There is a standard of altruism to which all should be required to come up, and a degree beyond which it is not obligatory, but meritorious. It is incumbent on every one to restrain the pursuit of his personal objects within the limits consistent with the essential interests of others. What those limits are, it is the province of ethical science to determine; and to keep all individuals and aggregates of individuals within them, is the proper office of punishment and of moral blame. If in addition to fulfilling this obligation, persons make the good of others a direct object of disinterested exertions, postponing or sacrificing to it even innocent personal indulgences, they deserve gratitude and honour, and are fit objects of moral praise. So long as they are in no way compelled to his conduct by any external pressure, there cannot be too much of it; but a necessary condition is its spontaneity; since the notion of a happiness for all,

realised that the individual is sovereign in his thought, mind, nature and his/her existence. Therefore, the rights deriving from this sovereignty should not be ignored by the state or others. Mill goes further and states that:

> That the only purpose for which power can be rightfully exercised over any member of a civilised community, against his will, is to prevent harm to others. His own good, either physical or moral, is not a sufficient warrant. He cannot rightfully be compelled to do or forbear because it will be better for him to do so, because it will make him happier, because, in the opinion of others, to do so would be wise, or even right. These are good reasons for remonstrating with him, or reasoning with him, or persuading him, or entreating him, but not for compelling him, or visiting him with any evil in case he does otherwise. To justify that, the conduct from which it is desired to deter him must be calculated to produce evil to someone else. The only part of the conduct of any one, for which he is amenable to society, is that which concerns others. In that part which merely concerns himself, his independence is, of right, absolute. Over himself, over his own body and mind, the individual is sovereign.[7]

Kant's theory about the notion of justice, the ethics of judgment and humanity without doubt created a revolutionary idea in the philosophy of man's thoughts and attitudes towards the personality of the individual. According to him, it is wholly impossible to write a law or legislation the intention of which is to preclude all future enlightenment, progress and the understandings of human beings. Such an agreement would be considered null and void, regardless of the fact that it had been ratified by the supreme power of the state or made law by the legislature. He explains by saying that it "would be a crime against human nature, whose essential destiny lies precisely in such progress; subsequent generations are thus completely justified in dismissing such agreements as unauthorized and criminal".[8] Thus rights, justice and knowledge are an integral part of one another and the very important concepts for the development of social relations. In other words, the provisions of the law cannot be the same at all times.

---

procured by self-sacrifice of each, if the abnegation is really felt to be sacrifice, is a contradiction." X Collected Works, pp.337-8. Quoted in *ibid.*, p.17.

[7] XVIII: Collected Works, pp.223-4; L1:9. Quoted in *ibid.*, pp.41-2.

[8] IMMANUEL KANT. An Answer to the Question: What is Enlightenment? (1784) in www.english.upenn.edu/~mgamer/Etexts/kant.html; see *also Karl Ameriks,* Interpreting Kant's Critiques (2005); Paul Guyer, The Cambridge Companion to Kant and Modern Philosophy (2006); H. Allison, Kant's Theory of Freedom (1990); M. Baron, Kantian Ethics Almost without Apology (1995); Richard Dean, The Value of Humanity in Kant's Moral Theory (2006).

The question is, therefore, how can we prove or deny our existence or the existence of our children and their rights. In other words, rights are an integral part of our existence and these rights, whether natural or legislative, cannot be separated from the actual facts of the existence of things. They should be constantly modified in order to adapt themselves to the needs of the time. More obviously, all things in our environment have natural, legal and even physical rights, and they should not therefore be treated without rights, or with quasi-existent rights. Similarly, existence implies identity and the latter is concurrent with the concept of existence. With all these we mean that all things have their own sovereignty of rights, such as the sovereignty of rights for animals, sovereignty of rights for birds, sovereignty of rights for flora and plants, sovereignty of rights for states, organizations, individuals and equally, the sovereignty of rights for children.

At the present time, all states claim to fulfil the provisions of the Convention on the Rights of the Child, and their laws and legislations coincide with the core principles of international human rights law regarding the protection of children. But all these claims are obviously not true, and the rights of children are not fully protected. Violations of the rights of children in war and peacetime continuously occur. Examples include sexual trafficking and the pornographic abuse of the rights of children in America, Africa, Asia, Europe, Latin America and many parts of the world; the use of children for various industrial economic gains e.g. in China, India and Pakistan; the very narrow protection of children in criminal and procedural intercourse in most countries of the world; the capital punishment of very young children, e.g. in Iran[9]; sexual slavery and rape imposed on children during armed conflicts, e.g. in Rwanda, Yugoslavia and Sierra Leone; targeting children in armed conflicts, e.g. in Gaza, Saudi Arabia, Afghanistan and Pakistan; the ignoring of the social rights of sick children, e.g. in Russia; the poor implementation of the social rights of children in even some democratic countries such as Sweden, Denmark and Finland; and exploitation of children through cybercrime all across the world.

The legal term regarding children that has now been generally accepted is the 'rights of the child' and it is employed in most relevant regional or

---

[9] In addition, the Iranian Criminal Court recently carried out the death penalty on a boy of 17 who stabbed a well-known Iranian weightlifter in self-defence in 2011. The Court representative ruled that he had reached the legal age according to the Islamic calendar, while ignoring his solar age.

international legal documents and the legislation of a considerable number of states. The rights of the child are even incorporated into the constitutions of a number of states. Other terms employed to denote the same concept include 'children's rights', 'protection of children', 'protection of juveniles', and 'protection of the young'. The language employed seems to assume that each child in the world necessarily has a territory of rights, which may be called the sovereignty of children in law.

The position generally accepted by the majority of writers, and which has been expressed in the legislation of a number of states is that children have rights amounting to sovereignty over civil and criminal law. This means that in national, regional or international proceedings, their rights must be fully respected by civil or criminal authorities. This can also be seen within the provisions of European Union legislation and particular regulations granted for the protection of children. The European Court of Human Rights has even participated in the protection of the rights of its minor citizens and been active in ruling against those member states that have not been cooperative or whose internal rules do not conform to various regional or international conventions.

Generally speaking, increased sophistication in preventing risks to the future of children and their protection from various forms of violations of their rights, has created an international movement for better protection for these young inhabitants of the globe. It is for this reason that, throughout this work, the term the "sovereignty of children" is used to describe the legal competence which already exists within various national, regional and international documents for the protection of the rights of our children. The relativity of the concept of the sovereignty of children is underlined by the principle that a state should not plead the regulations of its own law in response to the claim against it for an alleged violation of the rights of the child integrated into international conventions. The state obviously has legal responsibility for the violations of the rights of children under its territorial jurisdiction. The primary purpose of state responsibility is to increase compliance in its international obligations. This is clearly expressed within the provisions of the law of state responsibility which was enacted by the International Law Commission of the United Nations. The state therefore bears responsibility for its national or international violations of public international law. The Commission has vividly stated in its draft that "every internationally wrongful act of a State entails the international responsibility of that State".[10] This responsibility may be the result of an action or omission which is, according to the provisions of international law, attributable to the state in question. This means that the realm of children's rights has to be given serious superiority within the law of all nations in the world. Nevertheless, we are aware that the enforcement of the concept of international responsibility of states for the violations of the rights of children is not an easy task, and creates many juridical problems. One may therefore suggest that the creation of an international court which can deal specifically with the rights of children is a necessary condition for the future development and consolidation of this particular region of national, regional and international law. This task thus has to be carried out, whether by a new court or by the creation of complete sections within existing international courts. The result will be that the rights of children will be debated and judged with similar parameters for all the children in the world.

[10] Article 1.